Andrew Braid

Ontario history

vol. 22

Andrew Braid

Ontario history
vol. 22

ISBN/EAN: 9783741135354

Manufactured in Europe, USA, Canada, Australia, Japa

Cover: Foto ©ninafisch / pixelio.de

Manufactured and distributed by brebook publishing software (www.brebook.com)

Andrew Braid

Ontario history

Ontario Historical Society

PAPERS AND RECORDS

VOL. XXII

TORONTO
PUBLISHED BY THE SOCIETY
1925

CONTENTS.

(Alphabetically arranged under authors' names)

I. John Galt—Canadian Pioneer. ANDREW BRAID............................ 5

II. The Settlement of Waterloo County. W. H. BREITHAUPT, C.E................. 14

III. Notes on the Galt Churches. A. J. CLARK................................. 18

IV. A Memoir of Lieutenant-Colonel John Macdonell of Glengarry House, the first Speaker of the Legislative Assembly of Upper Canada. BRIG.-GEN. E. A. CRUIKSHANK, LL.D., F.R.S.C., etc.. 20

V. The Inception of the Welland Canal (1824). BRIG.-GEN. E. A. CRUIKSHANK, LL.D., F.R.S.C., etc.. 60

VI. An Address on Turning the First Sod of the Pioneer Monument—Waterloo County Pioneers' Memorial, Schoerg Farm, near Kitchener, June 24, 1924. BRIG.-GEN. E. A. CRUIKSHANK, LL.D., F.R.S.C., etc................................. 89

VII. John DeCou, Pioneer. ERNEST GREEN....................................... 92

VIII. Construction of the Rideau Canal, 1826-1832. HAMNETT P. HILL, K.C.......... 117

IX. Historical Notes on Finance in the Great War and Afterward. A. F. HUNTER, M.A. 125

X. Social Conditions Among the Negroes in Upper Canada before 1865. FRED LANDON, M.A... 144

XI. Anthony Burns in Canada. FRED LANDON, M.A............................ 162

XII. Commodore Alexander Grant (1734-1813). GEO. F. MACDONALD............... 167

XIII. Address of the President, Waterloo County Pioneers' Association, Turning-the-Sod Exercises, June 24, 1924. D. N. PANABAKER............................ 182

XIV. The Legislature of Upper Canada and Contempt.—Drastic Methods of Early Provincial Parliaments with Critics. HON. WM. RENWICK RIDDELL, LL.D., F.R. S.C., etc... 186

XV. When a Few Claimed Monopoly of Spiritual Functions—Canadian State Trials—The King against Clark Bentom. HON. WM. RENWICK RIDDELL, LL.D., F.R.S.C., etc... 202

XVI. Criminal Courts and Law in Early (Upper) Canada. HON. WM. RENWICK RIDDELL, LL.D., F.R.S.C., etc.. 210

XVII. The "Ordinary" Court of Chancery in Upper Canada—An Attempt by the Lieutenant-Governor to Act as Chancellor. HON. WM. RENWICK RIDDELL, LL.D., F.R.S.C., etc... 222

XVIII. Pierre du Calvet; a Huguenot Refugee in Early Montreal: His Treason and Fate. HON. WM. RENWICK RIDDELL, LL.D., F.R.S.C., etc...................... 239

XIX. "His Honour" the Lieutenant-Governor and "His Lordship" the Justice. HON. WM. RENWICK RIDDELL, LL.D., F.R.S.C., etc............................ 255

XX. The Place and Stream Names of Oxford County. W. J. WINTEMBERG.......... 259

XXI. The Rev. John Ogilvie, D.D., An Army Chaplain at Fort Niagara and Montreal, 1759-1760. PROFESSOR A. H. YOUNG, M.A., D.C.L......................... 296

I.

JOHN GALT—CANADIAN PIONEER.*

By Andrew Braid.

John Galt, the son of a captain of a West India vessel, was born in the town of Irvine, County of Ayr, Scotland, on the 2nd of May, 1779, and died 11th April, 1839, at the comparatively early age of sixty, paying the penalty of over-taxed powers in working hard at literature to compensate for ill-success in commercial ventures.

As an author, his work is very unequal, parts of it being of the first quality and parts of it very indifferent. In depicting the life of small Scottish towns and villages, however, he stands almost equal to Scott.

In 1790, when he was eleven years old, his family moved to Greenock; and, destined to follow the occupation of a merchant, in due course he became a clerk in the custom house there, and afterwards in a mercantile house; but his heart even then was already given to literary pursuits, and he early began writing verses and plays. In 1803 he resigned his situation in Greenock and went to London, where he entered into partnership with another young Scot named McLachlan in a business which, for reasons unknown, is mentioned only under the vague name of a "commercial enterprise," but the business failed after two years. He re-established himself in a business along with a brother, but this attempt also proved abortive. Resolving to devote himself to the profession of law he entered himself at Lincoln's Inn, but was soon over-taken by a nervous disposition which unfitted him for dry legal study, and he again turned to literature. The question of bread and cheese, however, becoming urgent, he was obliged to accept employment in promoting various commercial ventures on the continent of Europe. In August, 1809, he betook himself in the first instance to Gibraltar, where, in the Garrison library, he made the acquaintance of Lord Byron (whose biography he wrote in after years) and Sir John Hobhouse. The three journeyed eastwards to Sardinia and Malta. Galt met Byron again at Athens. This was at the time of Napoleon's endeavour to enforce his decree which he had designed with the object of annihilating British commerce. Galt conceived the idea that these plans might be evaded by introducing British goods into the Continent through Turkey, and he selected an island in the Aegean archipelago which possessed an excellent harbour as a

---

*The portrait of John Galt given with this article was the frontispiece to his "Annals of the Parish," published by W. Blackwood & Sons, Edinburgh and London. It was painted by W. J. Thomson and engraved by G. B. Shaw.

distributing point; after which he returned to Malta to make known and develop his scheme; and whilst awaiting the result of communications with London he filled up the time with further travels in Turkey, amassing notes on which were subsequently based two of his books.

All these commercial schemes failed, however, and he returned to London in 1811, with the necessity of still looking to literature as a means of existence. His industry in that direction already had been extraordinary—history, biography, epic and dramatic poetry, romance—he had tried them all, and during his residence abroad and frequent movements from place to place he had found time to write accounts of his travels, with statistics of foreign trade. He seemed doomed to taste every bitter experience of the bookseller's hack before the chance came to him of showing that a genuine humour and a gift of keen observation of character and manners had been concealed and unsuspected amid the dreary waste of compilation of statistics and the making of books. He was forty years of age when his opportunity came by the famous Edinburgh publishing house of Blackwood accepting, in 1820, "The Ayrshire Legatees" for the magazine. Though now first published this book was not the earliest written, the success of the Blackwood story having encouraged Galt to search for and complete an earlier venture which he had abandoned in consequence of the unfavourable opinion of Constable, another Edinburgh publisher, to whom he had submitted it; and in the following year (1821) appeared his masterpiece, "The Annals of the Parish," which Blackwood also published.

It is not the purpose of this paper to detail Galt's literary career, and we will therefore pass on to his work as a pioneer in our province, then called Upper Canada.

During the War of 1812, the British troops in the Province had provided a good market for products of all kinds; and, actual warfare having been confined practically to the borders, the main centres of trade and industry had been spared. The peace of 1815, however, put an end to the British government's abnormal expenditures, and left some financial questions to be solved, among these being the claims for compensation for those who had suffered during the war from contributions levied by the American invaders; and a commission was appointed in London to examine such claims and decide the compensation. At first, no specific funds were decided upon from which to pay these awards; but later, the proceeds of estates confiscated because of the treachery of their proprietors were ordered to be used. That source, however, did not produce any great sum. The commissioners reported to the British government the amount required to meet awards they had passed upon, but this sum appeared excessive to the government; and before payments were made a commission of revision was appointed, the award of this new commission to be considered final. But five or six years passed in which no payments were made, and thus matters stood when, in 1820, Galt was appointed London agent for the Canadian claimants; how he came to be selected does not appear, but his reputation stood high as one well acquainted with the principle and practice of commerce. Then began a correspondence in which Galt was to be engaged for several years. He set to work zealously to get the claims allowed by the Treasury, and at length gained his point, subject to conditions, it being agreed by the government that the claims should be satisfied from the proceeds of the sale of certain Crown Reserve lands in Upper Canada. To find purchasers for these lands now became Galt's object, and, mainly through his efforts, the "Canada Company" was formed, and arrangements with the government were finally agreed upon whereby the proposed company should purchase and settle all the Crown Reserves and half the Clergy Reserves in certain townships and that the value of the lands should be determined by commissioners to be sent to Canada.

Galt was one of these commissioners. The party landed at New York on the 25th of February, 1825, and journeyed via the Hudson River and Albany to Upper Canada, gathering en route information about the development of the country and the value of lands. On the way he viewed Niagara Falls by deputy. He tells the story in these words:

> I was exceedingly unwell with the variolid when we reached Manchester [now Niagara Falls in New York State], and as the fire in the hotel was very inviting my disposition did not incline at the time to go abroad, so I sent my servant to look at the Falls, with orders to come back and tell me what they were like and if it were worth while to go and look at them. No doubt the lad's downright character had some influence in making me give this ludicrous order, but his answer when he returned was beyond expectation. "It is a very cold night," he said, "and there is nothing to be seen but a great tumbling of waters," advising me at the same time not to go out that night. Thus it came to pass that although within a hundred yards of the Falls of Niagara, I was induced not to visit them, nor did I during my first journey to America.

The commissioners met at York (now Toronto) and began work on the 16th of March, planning to hold meetings at least every two weeks; and on the 2nd of May their report was signed and they returned to London, where the report was handed to the Colonial Office. But months of delay, discussion and dispute lay ahead. The Colonial Office deemed the report unsatisfactory in many ways, and the Church of England clergy in Upper Canada protested against the granting of the Clergy Reserves. Not until May of 1826 was the matter adjusted by the company accepting in place of the Clergy Reserves one million one hundred thousand acres in the Huron Tract, and being allowed sixteen years for fulfilling their contract; and a charter incorporating the company was finally granted on the 19th of August, 1826. The policy adopted by the company later on was to sell their lands to colonists in detached lots or separate farms, of all sizes from fifty acres upwards, and take the payment in the course of five years by annual instalments of one-fifth part of the purchase price each year, with the colonial interest at six per cent., the first fifth being payable down on getting what was called a location ticket for taking immediate possession. Under certain circumstances, for a time at least, the company engaged to convey the immigrant from Quebec or Montreal to York in the Upper Province free of expense.

In passing, it might be here stated that in a pamphlet issued by the Canada Company for the information of intending emigrants, whiskey was described as "a cheap and wholesome beverage" in Canada. Its cheapness and abundance caused it to be used in somewhat the same way as the "small beer" of England, and it was a common practice to order a jug from the grocer along with the food supply of the family.

A few days after the incorporation of the company it was settled that Galt should go to Canada as soon as possible to select the part of the Huron

Tract substituted for the Clergy Reserves, and he sailed early in October, arriving in New York about the middle of November and in York on the 12th of December. At once began troubles with the Lieutenant-Governor, Sir Peregrine Maitland, who suspected him of unfriendliness to the Provincial Government, a suspicion which was given colour by Galt, during his first visit, having corresponded with William Lyon Mackenzie and accepting from him the gift of a complete file of his anti-government paper, *The Colonial Advocate*, and which he (Galt) had acknowledged in a rather indiscreet letter. Prior to Galt's second visit to Canada, Mackenzie's office had been raided and his printing press wrecked, and he had used Galt's letter in a suit for damages he had instituted. On landing at New York Galt had heard of this, and from Niagara had written a hot protest to Mackenzie.

Having registered the Company's charter at York, Galt made a winter's visit to Montreal and Quebec, where he went for the purpose of also registering the charter, and returned early in March, to take up his duties seriously. In York (a town, by the way, of which he had a very poor opinion, branding it as "one of the vilest blue-devil haunts on the face of the earth") he obtained a room for an office about ten feet square, for which he paid a dollar per month.

For the purpose of finding in a block or tract of upwards of forty thousand acres of the Company's purchase an eligible situation for a town, Galt had an inspection made, and all reports made to him agreed in recommending the spot where Guelph now stands, and it was fixed upon; but as the year was still too young for outdoor operations and the immigrant season had not commenced, he went to New York to make arrangements and to appoint an agent for the company in that city; and upon his return to Upper Canada started operations for the founding of Guelph, which was set for St. George's Day, 1827.

The previous day he met his old schoolboy friend, Dr. William Dunlop, in former years a fellow-contributor to Blackwood's Magazine and who now held the position of Warden of Forests. This meeting took place at a settlement eighteen miles, half of the distance in the forest, from the proposed site of Guelph, called Shade's Mills. In 1816 the Hon. William Dickson, a Scot from Dumfries, purchased Block No. 1 (afterwards known as the Township of Dumfries) of the Six Nation Indian lands, originally conveyed by Joseph Brant to Philip Stedman. He at once took active steps to establish a village on the Grand River and place his lands on the market, and he engaged the services of a young man, a carpenter by trade, named Absolom Shade, to look after his affairs. By midsummer they reached the future site of Galt, which was covered by a thick growth of forest trees, at the junction of Mill Creek and the Grand River. Mr. Shade secured the services of a number of workmen in Buffalo and returned, and they set to work and erected some log buildings, the name Shade's Mills being given to the place. Mr. Dickson lost no time in putting the land on the market for sale, and immediately had a survey made, to which the name of Dumfries was given in honour of his native shire in Scotland. When Shade's Mills obtained a post-office Mr. Dickson christened it Galt, in honour of his former schoolmate. Galt himself in his Autobiography says, "On the 22nd of April (1827) I went to Galt, which my friend the Honourable William Dickson named after me long before the Canada Company was imagined; it was arrived at the maturity of having a post-office before I heard of its existence."

On the morning of St. George's Day, April 23rd, 1827, Galt and Dunlop set out for the proposed site of Guelph, but soon lost their way in the woods, and wandered about until they chanced on the hut of a shoemaker, who set them on the right path. It was not until about sunset, in a downpour of rain and dripping wet, that the pair arrived at the place where it had been arranged they should meet the workmen, and Galt lost no time in going to the spot chosen for the site of the town. Let us take from his Autobiography Galt's own account of this auspicious occasion:—

> "It was consistent with my plan to invest our ceremony with a little mystery, the better to make it be remembered. So, intimating that the main body of the men were not to come, we walked to the brow of the neighbouring ground, and Mr. Prior having shown the site selected for the town, a large maple tree was chosen, on which, taking an axe from one of the woodmen, I struck the first stroke. To me at least, the moment was impressive—and the silence of the woods, that echoed to the sound, was as the sigh of the solemn genius of the wilderness departing forever. The doctor followed me, then, if I recollect correctly, Mr. Prior, and the woodmen finished the work. The tree fell with a crash of accumulating thunder, as if ancient Nature were alarmed at the entrance of social man into her innocent solitudes with his sorrows, his follies, and his crimes. I do not suppose that the sublimity of the occasion was unfelt by the others, for I noticed that after the tree fell there was a funereal pause, as when the coffin is lowered into the grave; it was, however, of short duration, for the doctor pulled a flask of whiskey from his bosom, and we drank prosperity to the City of Guelph. The name was chosen in compliment to the Royal Family, both because I thought it auspicious in itself and because I could not recollect that it had ever been before used in all the King's dominions. After the ceremony we returned to the shanty, and the rain which had been suspended during the performance began again to pour."

In his novel "Lawrie Todd," written three years after the founding of Guelph, describing the founding of the Town of Judiville, Galt details almost the same procedure:

> "All being ready, and the important day being arrived, we were summoned to the ceremony at sunrise,—When we reached what was destined to be the centre of the town, the axemen or choppers cleared the brush or underwood from around a large tree, and, the cannon being properly placed, the old gentleman took an axe and struck the first stroke, upon which the seven cannon were fired three times. I struck the second, and so it went round, until the tree fell with a sound like thunder, banishing the loneliness and silence of the woods forever. Then we gave three cheers, the cannon were fired again, and the drink being poured out into the tin jugs which the settlers had brought with them, Mr. Hoskins gave for a toast, "Prosperity to Judiville," which was re-echoed by all around, all the tin horns and trumpets sending forth a great shout."

Galt's ill-fortune pursued him even in this most striking episode of his Canadian career, for, as he says in his Autobiography, "from the day that I announced the birth of this metropolis to the directors of the Canada Company my troubles and vexations began, and were accumulated on my unsheltered head till they could be no longer endured." It was not long before the directors notified him of their disapproval of his choice of the name of the new town, and he was ordered to change it from Guelph to Goderich. Galt's first consultations on Canadian affairs were held personally with Viscount Goderich when he was still a commoner with the common name of Robinson and holding the portfolio of Secretary of the Treasury, but his was a great name with the company and the directors had decided to immortalize him by founding a city in his honour. Galt, however, stuck to his choice of the name, more especially, as he pointed out to the directors, that it would be necessary to get an act of the Provincial Legislature before the change would be made. As the name could not easily be altered he called the other town on Lake Huron founded about this time by the name of his Lordship.

During the work of chopping, clearing and building, Galt journeyed to York; and, the only road between York and Guelph at the time being a circuitous one passing through Dundas and Galt, he conceived the idea that a storehouse at the head of Lake Ontario would be of advantage, and therefore resolved to apply for a grant of land on the shores of Burlington Bay. But his application was couched in unfortunate language by referring to the opposition conceived as having been shown to the company by influential persons, and it was not until June that the grant was made to him. The wording of this application apparently rankled in the memories of Lieutenant-Governor Maitland and some officials at York, and gave Galt a load of trouble later on.

To make himself familiar with the Huron Tract, which by this time had been explored and surveyed by Doctor Dunlop, Chief Brant, and others, Galt departed from York early in June, travelling by Yonge Street and Newmarket. Descending the Holland River and crossing Lake Simcoe and then overland, he reached Penetanguishene, where a government boat had been placed at his disposal, and at length reached the place which had been chosen by Dunlop as the site of the future town of Goderich, named as already stated in honour of the British Secretary of State. A day was spent exploring the River Minnesetung, which was renamed the Maitland, and then Galt paid a visit to Detroit, returning to York via Niagara Falls.

About this time Galt settled himself at Burlington, in order to be nearer Guelph, the scene of the company's chief activities. Here he was visited by 135 immigrants from Venezuela, for which country they had left England in 1825, but had been disappointed in the climate, the soil and political conditions, and their appeal for help had brought out a British frigate to transport them to New York, from whence they had been sent on to Galt's headquarters.[1] Galt decided to settle them at Guelph, and, having no funds, and taking the view that these immigrants, although thoughtlessly sent on to him, were in fact under the protection of Government, took upon himself to withhold £1,000 from a payment due to the government by the company. His action displeased every official in the Provincial Government, the Colonial Office, and the Canada Company. Other causes of friction brought matters to a crisis, and Galt seriously considered handing in his resignation. He also received a reprimand from the directors of the company in regard to the application for the Burlington Beach grant of land, and became involved in correspondence with various officials. He decided to resign from the Company, and sent his letter to the chairman, who, however, after consulting some of Galt's friends, withheld it from the directors, and wrote Galt of his action. Amid all this worry, pleased with a little courtesy from Sir Peregrine Maitland in the form of a hint that His Excellency had some thoughts of appointing him to the command of a regiment—an inten-

---

[1]For an account of this migration, see "The Last of the La Guayarians," by C. C. James, C.M.G., LL.D., Papers and Records, Ont. Hist. Society, XV, 40.

tion which was not carried out, however—he had decided to give a fancy-dress ball to the inhabitants of York, and the event took place on New Year's Eve and was a great occasion in York society circles, although even in this social function he fell foul of some of the Provincial politicians.

A road from Guelph to Goderich, cut through nearly one hundred miles of bush, at length established communication for the first time between Lake Ontario and Lake Huron, the townships bordering the road being named after the Company directors—Easthope, Ellice, Logan, McKillop and Hullett. Galt's policy at all times was to open roads to render remote lands accessible and of course more valuable, and to give employment to poor immigrants. Describing the operations followed on the road thus opened through the forest of the Huron Tract, nearly a hundred miles in length, he says in his Autobiography:—

"All the woodmen that could be assembled from the settlers were directed to be employed, an explorer of the line to go at their head, then two surveyors with compasses, after them a band of blazers, or men to mark the trees in the line,—then went the woodmen with their hatchets to fell the trees, and the rear was brought up by waggons with provisions and other necessities. In this order they proceeded simultaneously cutting their way through the forest, till they reached their spot of destination on the lonely shores of Lake Huron, where they turned back to clear off the fallen timber from the opening behind."

About this time Galt went to New York to meet his family, and on their arrival his wife and sons were temporarily installed in the house at Burlington Bay; and a little later, when the boys had been put to school in Lower Canada, Mrs. Galt accompanied her husband to Guelph, where the Priory was fitted up for her reception, although it was Galt's intention to have his residence near Burlington Bay and had purchased a small farm for the purpose.

The Company's accountant, Thomas Smith, arrived from London in July, 1828, and was welcomed by Galt, he having been hampered all along by an inadequate staff. A general business depression in England made shareholders and directors of the Canada Company determined to cut down expenses, and Smith had been sent out, nominally as accountant and cashier, but also as a check on Galt, the superintendent. It was not very long before friction was felt between the two, and grew to such a height that Galt determined to go to London and come to some understanding with the directors, and he sent word of his purpose; but he was forestalled by Smith, who hastened across the Atlantic to lay his version of the case before the directors, and Galt felt that there was nothing to do but that he remain at his post if the Company's interests in Canada were not to be abandoned. But, convinced from various circumstances that he had been condemned by the directors, he began collecting material for his defence, and secured from the agent of another land company in New York State an endorsement of the work he had accomplished and a recommendation that he be given the most ample discretionary powers. He made a farewell visit to Goderich, where a large clearing had been made and several houses built, and in his Autobiography he says, "My adieu to Lake Huron was a final farewell; for, from the moment I lost sight of its waters, I considered my connection with the company closed." On his return to Guelph he prepared for his departure, although he had as yet received no official recall. In New York, however, he was informed that a successor had been appointed in the superintendency, though he was still reluctant to admit that his dismissal was final and had left his family in Canada in the hope that he might return, but continued on his voyage to London, after two and a half years in Canada.

With the remaining ten years of Galt's life it is not my purpose to deal, excepting to state that, following his dismissal and before he could turn elsewhere for a livelihood, and almost penniless, his creditors became urgent, and one of them caused his being committed to the King's Bench Prison, where he suffered a long confinement, during which he wrote "Lawrie Todd" (1830), the best of his later novels, with a long rambling plot describing the career of a Scottish immigrant to the State of New York, the story said to be based on the life of Grant Thorburn, a thrifty Scot who made his fortune as a seedsman in New York City, which seed business is still doing business at this very day. After gaining his freedom from prison he fell back on literature, and also attempted to form another land company—The British American Land Company—but this was not successful. The scene of the earliest operations of this company was to be in Lower Canada, and particularly that part of it lying on the south side of the St. Lawrence, but the company intended, according to the direction which the stream of immigration might take, to carry its operations into all the British American provinces.

It is always interesting to know the opinion of a man's contemporaries; and I quote the following from Major Samuel Strickland's book, "Twenty-seven Years in Upper Canada." The Major, a brother of Susanna Moodie and Catherine Parr Traill (all three being well known in Canadian literature), and of Agnes Strickland, the historian of the Queens of England, entered the service of the Canada Company under Galt in February of 1828.

"In person, Mr. Galt was, I should think, considerably above six feet in height, and rather of a heavy build; his aspect grave and dignified, and his appearance prepossessing. His disposition was kind and considerate; but at the same time he commanded respect; and I can say with sincerity, I always found him an upright and honourable gentleman.

"Of Mr. Galt's fitness for the office of superintendent of the Canada Company, it would perhaps be considered presumptuous in me to give an opinion. His position was an unfortunate one, and from his first residence in the country till his resignation, there appears to have been a serious misunderstanding between him, the Governor, and the Executive-council, in consequence of which, Galt's character was misrepresented at home as that of a meddling politician and troublesome person. Other charges regarding the wasteful expenditure of money in forming the new settlements were laid before the Directors, and these repeated complaints against him left him no other alternative than to resign his situation.

"My own opinion is, that Galt was ill-used by the Canadian Government. He said in his 'Autobiography' that his whole and sole offence consisted in having accepted a file of the 'Colonial Advocate' and shaken hands with the editor, the notorious William Lyon Mackenzie. In those days of ultra-toryism, such an instance of liberality and freedom from party-prejudice was sufficient to excite the displeasure of the Governor and his council. There is no doubt that Galt acted imprudently in this matter, though I fully believe without any intention of opposing the Government.

"In regard to the Company's affairs, more might be said to his prejudice—not in respect of his integrity, for I believe him to have been a most honourable man, and incapable of any meanness—but in regard to his management. Although, as the original projector of the Canada Company, he evinced much cleverness, and afterwards displayed considerable judgment in the choice of the best situations for building towns and villages, yet he committed some grievous mistakes. His ideas were generally good; but often not well carried out in detail."

It cannot be asserted that Galt on all occasions acted wisely during his days in Canada. His activity, unfortunately, was not always balanced by an equal amount of prudence; he often was tactless when he could easily have adapted himself to the petty policies of the province without sacrificing any of his independence. But he was energetic; he had perseverance and foresight; he could glimpse the future; he was a colonizer who advocated the theory that roads should precede settlement, and that the settler should not be compelled to bear the labour and the cost of their construction; he had confidence in himself both as an author and a man of business affairs. In organizing the whole business management of the Canada Company he showed genius, and brought to the province a good type of settler, for, as he himself says, he was not unqualified for the business of colonizing, as the settlement of colonies had been with him long an object of study. But, to quote his words:

> "In the administration of nearly a million (pounds) of money I was hampered with the most inconsistent restrictions. I was not allowed to take with me any clerk, far less a person in whom I could confide. I was left destitute of advice and information, which the nature of my mission so greatly required."

Had the policy of the Canada Company been different perhaps its fame nowadays would be as great as that of the Hudson's Bay Company.

Books Consulted.

Galt's Autobiography, 2 vols. London: Cochrane and McCrone, 1833.
In the Days of the Canada Company, 1825-1850. By Robina and Kathleen M. Lizars. Toronto: William Briggs, 1896.
John Galt. By R. K. Gordon. University of Toronto Studies Series. University Library, 1920.
Historical Reminiscences of Galt and Other Writings. By Hugh Cant.
John Galt. Lives of Eminent Scotsmen. Glasgow: Blackie & Sons, 1855.
John Galt. By Sir George Douglas. Famous Scots Series, "The Blackwood Group" volume. Edinburgh: Oliphant, Anderson and Ferrier, 1897.
Makers of Canada. Various volumes. Toronto: Morang and Company, 1906-1911.

II.

THE SETTLEMENT OF WATERLOO COUNTY.

By W. H. Breithaupt, C.E.

The first settlers from Pennsylvania to arrive in Upper Canada located in Lincoln County in 1786. About 1794 a party of German Protestants from the Pulteney Domain in New York State, and shortly before from Germany, was granted 64,000 acres near Yonge Street, about twenty miles from Toronto. This is known as the Markham Colony. The grant was not all taken up by them and part of it reverted later to the Government. Settlers from Pennsylvania also went to Markham, from 1804 on. By far the largest number of settlers from Pennsylvania came to Waterloo Township.

There are several accepted authorities on the history of Waterloo County. Among them, Ezra Eby, a descendant of early settlers, ranks as having done the most. He published in 1896, in Berlin, now Kitchener, two large volumes, his main work, entitled, "A Biographical History of Waterloo Township and Other Townships of the County," containing a general history of the townships and brief biographies of nearly 8,500 individuals, Pennsylvania settlers and their descendants. Rev. A. B. Sherk, a grand nephew of the two first settlers, published several good papers on Waterloo history. Hon. James Young published, in 1880, a comprehensive history of Galt and the township of North Dumfries.

In general Canadian histories there is little mention of the settlement of Waterloo County. In Shortt and Doughty's "Canada and its Provinces," published ten years ago, there is, however, by A. C. Casselman, a very good detail of Waterloo County history.

In the year 1800 three townships of the later County of Waterloo, not so organized until 1852, were part of the Grand River Indian Lands, a territory twelve miles in width, with the river approximately its centre line, extending from Lake Erie to the falls of the river, now Elora. This territory had been granted, along with other lands, to the Six Nation Indians, allies of the British in the Revolutionary War, by Governor Haldimand, in 1782. Upwards from the forks of the river, now Paris, the territory had been divided into blocks 1, 2, 3 and 4, and sold. Block 1 comprised the townships of North and South Dumfries in Waterloo and Brant Counties, respectively. Block 2, Waterloo township, was sold to Richard Beasley, John Wilson and John B. Rousseau; and Block 3, approximately, formed Woolwich township.

Block 2 was the first on the Grand River to be taken up for settlement. Hither came, early in the spring of 1800, prospecting and exploring, two sturdy, adventurous farmers from near Chambersburg, Franklin County, Pennsylvania, who, with their families, had left their native country in the fall of 1799, crossed the Niagara River at Black Rock ferry and had stayed over winter with compatriots who had preceded them to Canada. These two pioneers were Joseph Schoerg and Samuel D. Betzner, brothers-in-law. Joseph Schoerg, whose grandfather emigrated from Switzerland to Pennsylvania in 1727, was born in Franklin County, February 3rd, 1769. He married his deceased brother's wife, Elizabeth, daughter of Samuel Betzner, sister of Samuel D. Betzner. She had a son, Samuel, by her first husband, John Schoerg, who died in 1792. When they came to Canada the family comprised five children. Samuel D. Betzner was born probably in 1770, married Elizabeth Brech, and had apparently two children when coming to Canada. His father, Samuel Betzner, was born in Wurtemberg in 1738 and came over to Pennsylvania in 1755. Schoerg and Betzner were the forerunners, the vanguard of a large party of their countrymen who came in the next following years, and constituted the first larger settlement in the then far interior of Upper Canada.

With the keen judgment of these people for good farming lands, the explorers found what they sought in the heavy timbered lands along the river, selected sites, Schoerg on the high ground on the east bank of the river and Betzner about two miles farther down, on the flats of the west bank, below the mouth of a river, the Speed, coming from the east, and at once brought in their families and began the work of building houses.

The Waterloo township settlers were of the Mennonite faith, as are mostly their descendants. For the previous hundred and more years, their ancestors had been coming to Pennsylvania, first on the invitation of William Penn, mostly from Switzerland, largely from Germany, from the Rhine Palatinate whence originated their peculiar dialect, and partly from Holland and elsewhere, to find relief from religious persecution. Their choice of Canada as a land of settlement was without doubt, shortly after the Revolutionary War, to large extent determined by their desire to return to stable British government, and in this sense they were United Empire Loyalists.

Later in 1800 three more families came from Pennsylvania, from Lancaster County: Samuel Betzner, the father of John D., John Reichert and Christian Reichert. Samuel Betzner located alongside his daughter, later lot 12, German Company Tract, containing the site of the little cemetery on the river bluff. Joseph Schoerg's location was later lot 11, German Company Tract.

During 1801 seven more families came: Gingerich, Bechtels, Kinsey, Rosenberger, Brickers, Baer—from Lancaster, Montgomery and York Counties. During 1802 further settlers came from Cumberland, Montgomery, and other Pennsylvania counties. All located near the first comers.

The journey from Pennsylvania to the new settlement on the Grand River was a difficult one, of about 500 miles, over mountains and through forests and swamps, and took from four to eight weeks. The last stretch from above Dundas to the Grand River through the treacherous Beverley swamps was the worst. It is now a provincial highway over which the automobile rolls in less than an hour over a distance which then took days. The standard transporter was the well-known Conestoga waggon, drawn by four or five horses. The Waterloo Historical Society Museum has one of these waggons which brought Abraham Weber and family to the site of the present city of Kitchener in 1807.

In 1803 came what threatened to be disaster to the settlers in the accidental discovery, such was the uncertain state of land tenure in those days, of a large mortgage, covering all their lands, which had been bought from Richard Beasley. This peremptorily put a stop to further emigration from Pennsylvania. Beasley finally proposed that the settlers buy a large block of the land and pay off the mortgage. For this purpose Joseph Schoerg and Samuel Bricker were sent to Pennsylvania. They at first found no sympathy and Schoerg in despair returned to Canada, while Bricker persevered. At a meeting at his house in Lancaster County, old Hannes Eby put the appeal in a new light, as a Christian duty to brethren in distress. This found response and eventually, influenced no doubt also by the glowing accounts as to the quality of the new lands, a strong company was formed which bought 60,000 acres outright, paying off the mortgage thereon.

Samuel Bricker and Daniel Erb were entrusted with the purchase money and carried it, twenty thousand dollars in silver coin, packed in a strong box, in what is described as a "leicht plaisir waeggele"—a light pleasure waggon, the arduous journey to Canada. What a light pleasure waggon meant in those days can be judged from the two front wheels of this historic waggon, now in the museum of the Waterloo Historical Society.

This purchase, the greater part of Waterloo township, became known as the German Company Tract, and is so called in deeds. It was surveyed by Augustus Jones into lots of 448 acres, which were distributed by lot among the shareholders. The deed, drawn by the Hon. Wm. Dickson of Niagara, was to Daniel Erb, described as "of Block Number Two on the Grand River in the County of York and Home District of the Province of Upper Canada," Yeoman, and Jacob Erb, of the same place, Yeoman, in trust. Separate titles for individual holdings were derived from Daniel and Jacob Erb. The colony grew apace and a few years later, in 1807, another company of Pennsylvanians bought 47,000 acres in the adjoining Block three, later Woolwich township.

Settlement was interrupted by and during the war of 1812. In this some of the settlers took part, not as combatants but as teamsters. It is on record that Christian Schneider, Jr., was paid five dollars per day for time he served with a two-horse team and eight dollars per day for time with a four-horse team. Some of them lost their horses and waggons. All such losses were made good by the British Government. None of the Waterloo settlers lost their lives in this campaign.

By 1823 most of the lands in Waterloo and Woolwich townships had been taken up by Mennonites from Pennsylvania, who, however, continued to come until about 1835 and some stragglers later, up to the beginning of the American Civil War. Common names among their descendants to this day are Betzner, Brubacher, Baumann (Bowman), Bechtel, Bean, Bergey, Bingeman, Burkholder, Cressman, Detweiler, Eby, Erb, Gingerich, Groff, Hallman, Hagey, Honsberger, Hoffman, Kinsey, Kolb, Martin, Moyer, Musselman, Reichert, Schneider (Snyder, Snider), Stauffer, Shantz, Weber (Weaver), Witmer and others.

At first Waterloo, then Berlin, now Kitchener, became the trading centre in this district. Preston and Bridgeport, on account of their mills and water power, were also active villages. John Erb, who came with his family from

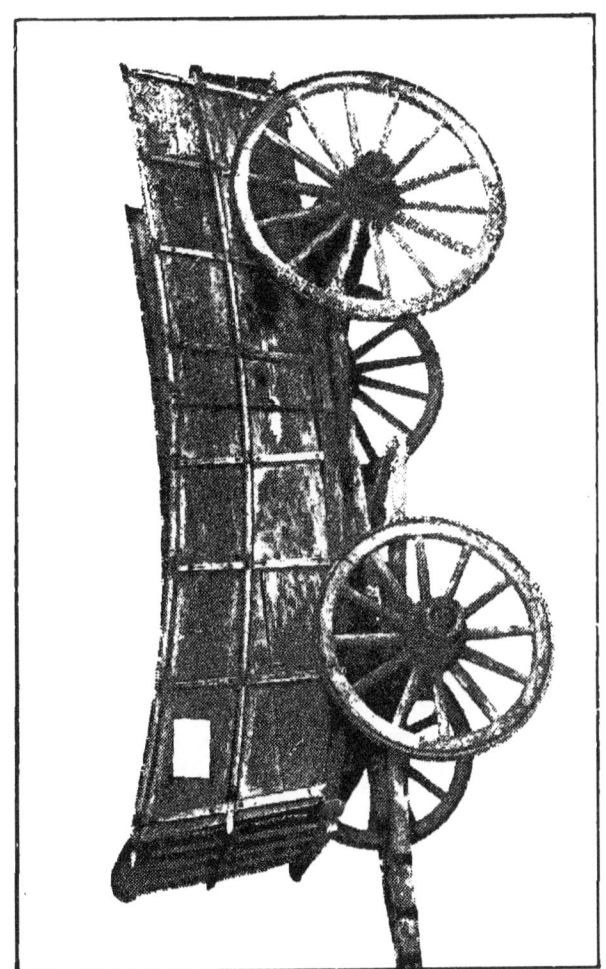

Four-horse Settlers' Wagon driven by Abraham Weber, 1807, from Lancaster Co., Pa., to the site of Kitchener, Ont.—Waterloo Historical Society's Museum, Kitchener, Ont.

Lancaster County in 1805, built a grist mill in Preston in 1807, and his brother built one in Waterloo in 1816. Both of these industries continue to flourish to this day. From about 1820, Germans and others directly from Europe began to come to Waterloo township, mostly to Berlin and Waterloo, also to Preston.

The settlement of Galt and North Dumfries township proceeded according to a different method. It was proprietary, controlled by an individual owner, a method which has its advantages. In 1816 the Hon. William Dickson, of Niagara, a member of the Legislative Council of Upper Canada, bought the whole of Block 1, Grand River Indian lands, 92,160 acres, later North and South Dumfries. Mr. Dickson had no doubt watched with interest the progress of the Pennsylvania settlers, whose legal adviser he was, and now decided to invest in Grand River lands himself. He at once engaged Absalom Shade, an enterprising young contractor from Buffalo, whom he had known before, as his agent and representative, and together they set out to explore the purchase and to select a suitable site for a trading centre for the future colony. This latter they did at a well adapted location on the river, the picturesque present city of Galt, so named in 1827 after John Galt, the author, and at that time commissioner for the Canada Company at Guelph, a friend of Dickson. The colony soon attracted settlers, many of them brought directly from Scotland. Shade had built a small grist mill at first, and operated a store. His engagement with Mr. Dickson was no doubt on liberal terms. He was the enterprising local head of the colony, full of resources and expedients. One of his exploits was the rafting of timber down the river to Lake Erie, in the spring, which he did several times. He became Member of the Provincial Parliament, and one of the principal men of the county. By systematic attention, Galt soon grew to be the principal trading centre for the whole district, as far as Goderich on Lake Huron. Up to 1890 it was the largest town in the County of Waterloo.

The Township of Wilmot was taken up by settlers from Europe, among them a large party of Amish, an early offshoot of the Mennonites. This was in 1822. Their leader, Jacob Nachtsinger, obtained from Governor Maitland a grant of fifty acres for each family and the right of buying more land at a liberal price. Nachtsinger applied in person to the Government in London for confirmation of this grant, which he obtained.

Wellesley Township was in greater part settled by Scotchmen, and partly by a colony of German Catholics.

III.

NOTES ON THE GALT CHURCHES.

By A. J. Clark.

It is ever pleasing, in connection with historical research, to be able to confirm already chronicled events from the memory of one who was an actual participant in or an observer of the events themselves. It is perhaps still more gratifying to be able, from such a source, to amplify the record in even minor details.

In several of the histories relating to the early settlement of Galt, Ontario,[1] extended reference has been made to the justly esteemed Rev. Dr. John Bayne. As a missionary under the Colonial Committee of the Church of Scotland, he came to Canada in 1834. In 1835 he accepted a call to St. Andrew's Presbyterial Church, in the little Scottish community on the Grand; a pastorate in which he was destined to labour for nearly a quarter of a century.

The writer's mother, just prior to the time of her death in 1922, in her 89th year,[2] was in all probability one of the few survivors who could recall his ministry before and immediately after the disruption of the Presbyterian Church in Canada, a denominational struggle in which he was by no means a lesser participant. Receiving baptism at his hands and being one of the scholars in his Sunday school, she was one of a band of little girls who were assembled to fold the sheets for his pamphlet address to those who had remained in the Established Church.[3] A copy of this pamphlet was among her treasured papers at the time of her decease. Going through its eighty-three pages of well-marshalled facts and cogent arguments there can be little doubt but that its author, had he been alive in 1924, would have opposed the passage of the Federal Church Union Bill as one embodying in substance at least a form of the Erastianism to which he contended the Established Church of his day had bowed. While the faded pages served to recall the far-off days filled with a controversy too profound for childish comprehension, it was to more familiar personal memories of the man to which she preferred to refer.

One little incident, often mentioned, served to illustrate that he who could be so forcibly eloquent in the pulpit, forcible in gesture as well as word, for he pounded the bindings from more than one pulpit Bible, and so facile in argument with his pen, was in truth one of the humblest of men.

---

[1]"Early History of Galt and Dumfries." By Hon. James Young.
"History of Central Presbyterian Church, Galt. Memorial Volume, 1856-1904." By Rev. J. A. R. Dickson, B.D., Ph.D.

[2]Mrs. Mary Clark (née Allen), relict of William Clark. Born in Beverley Tp., Wentworth, 1834. Died at Maple, Ont., 1922.

[3]The title page of the pamphlet reads: "Was the Recent Disruption of the Synod of Canada in connection with The Church of Scotland Called For? An address to the Presbyterians of Canada who still support the Synod in connection with the Church of Scotland. Published at the Request of the Commission of the Synod of the Presbyterian Church of Canada. Galt. Printed by James Ainslie, Main Street, 1846."

REV. DR. JOHN BAYNE.

Old St. Andrew's Church, Galt, during the Rev. Dr. John Bayne's ministry.

It was his custom to go from class to class in the Sunday school, and coming to her class one morning he said: "Now I suppose, my little girls, that you think that because I am the minister I never do anything wrong or bad. That is not so, for I do, but I want to tell you that whenever I do anything that is wrong I always feel something just like a pin-prick right here," indicating his heart.

How many of his little auditors of that Sunday morning carried a transfer of that sensation into mature life can never be known, but one of them often confessed that she did so.

Another memory of the days of Dr. Bayne's ministry was of a Sunday morning when she and her parents arrived to find only the stringers of a new bridge in position. Excuses for non-appearance at church were not sought in those days. Holding tightly to her father's hand they together made the trip across, followed by her mother. Those familiar with the location will know that the feat was one involving considerable danger. The reward was one of Dr. Bayne's sermons.

Those clinging to the Establishment were of course left in possession of St. Andrew's Church. This little frame structure, with its spire surmounted by a gilded metallic fish as a weather-vane, stood near the site of the present memorial pergola erected some years ago from the gravestones of the once surrounding churchyard. To carry on the work a call was extended in the fall of 1846 to Rev. John Dyer, and it was in connection with his brief pastorate that one other memory was associated. On a visit to an aunt whose home was located just at the base of the hill below the church, she clearly remembered what was to her the strangest event connected with that little holiday. The incoming minister found his new charge in none too prosperous a condition, incident to the loss of so many of its members in the recent disruption. Nothing daunted, he took up his duties with great vigour and when the repainting of the church was undertaken, and no one could be found who was willing to paint the steeple, he promptly volunteered. Rigging a "boson's" chair and tackle he had himself pulled to position and his loud calls of "Ye hoy" to those in charge of the ropes could be clearly heard by the children playing below. Perhaps this offhand acceptance of so non-ministerial a task was one of the clues which eventually led to the discovery that he was not a minister at all, but an ex-sailor, whose real name was Wevil. Anyway the discovery was made. He was proved to be an impostor and as such was summarily dismissed by an outraged and indignant board of trustees. Other historians make record of the painting of the church, but fail to give due credit to the painter of the steeple. Whether the trustees in their final settlement with their erstwhile minister were equally forgetful, there seems no way of proving.[1]

---

[1] James Croil, in his history of the Presbyterian Church, in connection with the Church of Scotland, describes Dyer—alias Wevil—as: "the sailor, an orator of high degree, an enthusiast, a sensationalist; altogether a very extraordinary man."

IV.

A MEMOIR OF LIEUTENANT-COLONEL JOHN MACDONELL, OF
GLENGARRY HOUSE, THE FIRST SPEAKER OF THE
LEGISLATIVE ASSEMBLY OF UPPER CANADA.

By Brigadier-General E. A. Cruikshank, LL.D., F.R.S.C., F.R.H.S.

The subject of this memoir was the eldest son of Alexander Macdonell, of Aberchalder, in the County of Inverness, in Scotland, who was a relative and "tacksman" (or a feudal tenant) of the chief of Glengarry. In 1745 the "Laird of Glengarry" was described by Lord President Forbes of Culloden, in an official memorandum, as having "a pretty good estate, all holden of the Crown, which lies in Countreys of Glengarry and Knoidart, both on the continent, and can bring out 500 men."[1]

He and all his clansmen still adhered to the Church of Rome and the cause of the Stewarts as rightful sovereigns of the country. On July 29th, 1745, Donald Macdonell, of Scothouse, came to welcome Prince Charles Edward on board the ship which brought him from France, as the delegate of his chief, and soon after with other gentlemen of the clans of Cameron, Macdonell, and Stewart, promised to have their people in arms in his support at Glenfinnan, a small hamlet at the head of Lochiel, two weeks later.

On August 16th, the Macdonells of Glengarry attacked two companies of the Royal Scots near Loch Lochie, while on the march, and compelled the whole to surrender. A few days later, the whole of the Macdonells of Glengarry, "being 600 good men," including, however, the men of Knoidart, Glencoe, and Glenmoriston, under the leadership of Macdonell of Lochgarry, arrived at Glenfinnan. On August 27th, Prince Charles began his march southward from Aberchalder, with all the fighting men of Glengarry at his command.

At the battle of Gladsmuir, or Preston Pans, on September 21st, the regiments of Clanranald, Glencoe, Glengarry, and Keppoch, mostly Macdonells or Macdonalds, under their respective chiefs, composed the right wing of the Jacobite army. They all wore the Highland garb. The front ranks were composed of persons styling themselves gentlemen, who were better armed than those in the ranks behind, all of them having targets or shields, which many of the others had not. They were paid one shilling per day. In the march into England, the regiment of Glengarry, numbering five hundred men, formed the escort for the artillery. In the retreat it formed part of the rearguard and

---

[1] Memorandum from Culloden Papers, quoted in "The Rising of 1745," by C. S. Terry, pp. 5-11.

The Glengarry estate was about 100,000 acres of "mountains, lochs and glens." Part of it was sold after the death of Alastair Ronaldson Macdonell, the fifteenth chief, to Lord Ward, afterward Earl Dudley. The vast property is now owned by Major Ellice, formerly of the Coldstream Guards, and of a family which was intimately associated with this province in its earliest days.

at Clifton House was briskly attacked by the Duke of Cumberland's pursuing cavalry, whom the Macdonells repulsed in a hand-to-hand fight with their broadswords only, and "stood their charge as firm as a wall, behaving like lions." Not less than fourteen broadswords were broken on the steel skull-caps of the dragoons in this encounter. Having at one time to pass by a stone dyke, which was lined by men of the Glengarry regiment, the dragoons received such an effective fire "from that brave corps that such as outlived it were fain to make the best of their way back."

The last victorious battle at Falkirk was fought in a fierce storm of wind and driving rain, when darkness was already falling, as it began at four o'clock in the afternoon. The Macdonells were again engaged in the successful charge made by the right of the Prince's army, defeating and pursuing the regular foot regiments opposed to them and taking their artillery.

Next day an event occurred which was followed by serious results. Colonel Æneas Macdonell, second son of the chief of Glengarry, "a brave and good-natured youth," who commanded the Glengarry regiment, was mortally wounded by the accidental discharge of a musket in the hands of a man who was cleaning it. "Nothing could restrain the grief and fury of his people, and good luck it was that he (who shot him) was a McDonald, (tho' not of his own tribe, but that of Keppoch's)," says an eyewitness, "and after all they began to desert daily upon this accident, which had a bad effect upon others also, and lessened our numbers considerably."[1]

The letter to Prince Charles, advising a retreat to the Highlands, dated on January 29th, 1746, was signed by Lochgarry and Scothouse as well as by Clanranald, Keppoch, and other chiefs.

In the fatal battle of Culloden, the Macdonells of Glengarry, to their great mortification, were assigned the extreme left of the line of battle. When the clan regiments on the right made a fierce but wholly unsuccessful attack, the regiments on the left, being the Farquharsons and the three regiments of Macdonells, who saw it, did not advance nor attack in the same manner. They, indeed, approached so near the royal forces as to draw their fire, which they returned with a general volley and the Macdonells had "drawn their swords to attack in the usual manner; but seeing those regiments that had attacked sword in hand repulsed and put to flight, they also went." Keppoch was killed, and in their retreat on the main road towards Inverness, they were hotly pursued by cavalry and suffered much loss. The lands of Glengarry were mercilessly harried as a punishment for the part his clansmen had taken in the rising, his tenants were disarmed, and Invergarry, the chief's castle, was burnt.

John Macdonell, the subject of this sketch, was born at Aberchalder in 1750, when the memory of these events was still fresh and bitter. The glen had not yet recovered from its losses and humiliation. Many of the chiefs had sought safety in exile and were exempted from the act of indemnity passed in 1747. A still greater number were so impoverished that they were unable to continue their former mode of life. The feudal system of the Highlands was rapidly passing away. Wearing the Highland costume and weapons was strictly

---

[1]C. S. Terry, "The last Jacobite Rising," p. 130.

proscribed by an act of parliament. Sheep farming was being extensively introduced by the Laird of Glengarry, and many of his tenants were notified that their holdings must be vacated to permit their conversion into sheep-walks.

Alexander Macdonell was still able to send his sons to a good school at Fochabers, in the county of Elgin, where they remained for several years, but his income was so much diminished that he determined to emigrate to America with many of his clansmen who had suffered in the same manner. They entered into correspondence with Sir William Johnson, who, although born in Ireland and bearing an Anglicized name, traced his descent in the direct line from the MacIan branch of the Macdonells of Glencoe, and was thus a distant kinsman. His offers of lands and assistance in settling upon them were satisfactory and in 1773 the families of Macdonell of Aberchalder, Collachie, Leek, and Scothouse, in Glengarry, with many of their relatives and dependents, forming a body of more than six hundred persons, emigrated to the province of New York in His Majesty's ship "Pearl." A few of the leaders purchased lands; the others were established as tenants on lands belonging to Johnson, on easy terms, and were even supplied with food, cattle, and provisions valued at two thousand pounds. Sir William died very suddenly next summer, but was succeeded by his son, Sir John, who continued to take a kindly interest in their welfare.

As John Macdonell had been educated for a commercial life, he was sent to Montreal and obtained employment in the office of an accountant.

The arrival of the Highlanders had not been welcomed by the majority of the Dutch and German settlers in the Mohawk Valley, who were the descendants of sturdy Protestants, whose sufferings for conscience sake had not been forgotten, and to whom the very name of Papist was hateful. To them the newcomers seemed a rude, fierce, and quarrelsome race, constantly wearing dirk and broadsword and enslaved by superstitious and idolatrous doctrines. The revolutionary leaders took advantage of this prejudice to draw them into their way of thinking. So far the inhabitants in general had given every sign of loyalty and content. In June, 1774, the supervisors of the county of Tryon, embracing all the settled parts of western New York, bluntly refused to assent to the complaint against the British Ministry formulated by the Congress. "It did not appear," they declared, "to tend to the violation of their civil or religious rights, but merely regarded a single article of commerce (tea) which no person was compelled to purchase, and which persons of real virtue and resolution might easily have avoided or dispensed with." Nine months later at the quarter sessions held in the month of March, 1775, the judges, sheriff, clerk, magistrates, and grand jury reaffirmed this opinion in a written document, adding that they "abhorred and do still abhor measures tending through partial representation to alienate the affections of subjects from the Crown, or by wresting the interest and meaning of a particular act to draw in the inhabitants of a wide and extensive territory to a dangerous and rebellious opposition to the parent state, when exerting itself to preserve that obedience without which no state can exist. They do therefore resolve to bear faithful and true allegiance to their lawful sovereign, King George the Third, and that in the true and plain sense of the words, as they are, or ought to be understood, without prevarication, which has often accompanied the same expressions from his warmest opponents."

No organized revolutionary effort seems to have occurred in that part of the province of New York until May, 1775, when it was forcibly suppressed by the loyalists. A Whig committee was afterwards formed at Cherry Valley, but were evidently aware that as yet they represented an insignificant and uninfluential minority. On May 18th, they addressed a written appeal for assistance to the Committee of Safety at Albany, stating that "this county has for a series of years been ruled by one family, the several branches of which are still strenuous in dissuading the people from coming into Congressional measures, and have even last week, at a numerous meeting of the Mohawk district, appeared with all their dependents armed to oppose the people considering of their grievances; their number being so great, and the people unarmed, they struck terror into most of them and they dispersed." About the same time a liberty pole which had been set up was cut down by the sheriff. Guy Johnson described this meeting as having been called by "an itinerant New England leather-dresser, and conducted by others, if possible, more contemptible." Both he and Sir John Johnson were soon after warned that a body of New Englanders were on their way to attack them. In consequence, they fortified their houses and assembled their friends and tenants for their defence. A body of Mohawks collected for that purpose, and without Guy Johnson's knowledge, as he afterwards asserted, summoned the Oneidas to their aid. This message was intercepted and used to prejudice the people against him and his friends. Their movements were closely watched; their letters were opened and read; the supplies ordered for the Indians were detained at Albany as well as articles for their' ordinary household use. Threats of an attack upon them were openly made; seditious toasts were proposed on public occasions, and loyalists were forced to sign articles of association against the government. Guy Johnson told the committees that he had persuaded the Indians to remain quiet during the preceding winter in spite of great provocation, and warned them that if they now learned that their supplies were stopped, their council-fire disturbed, and their superintendent insulted, they might take a dire revenge. His office was of the greatest importance to the safety of the frontier and the interests of trade and it was his duty to maintain peace. "I desire," he added, "to enjoy liberty of conscience and the exercise of my own judgment, and that all others should have the same privilege."

About this time a new actor unexpectedly appeared upon the scene, who was destined to play a considerable part in future events. This was Lieutenant-Colonel Allan Maclean, who had already served with distinction for many years in Highland regiments and possessed considerable influence among his countrymen. He had informed the Ministry that as a great many emigrants from the Highlands were settled in communities in the various British provinces in North America, he believed that "the Associations then beginning to be formed by the Rebels might receive a very Effectual check by engaging proper persons who had influence among the aforesaid Emigrants to form Counter-Associations which, with the assistance of the Loyal part of the Natives, and both being properly supported by His Majesty's Governors and Commanders might, if adopted in time, have produced very salutary Effects without having recourse to arms."

After some delay, he was furnished with instructions to the Governors and the Commander-in-Chief to co-operate with him in carrying out this plan, and directed to sail for Boston. On his arrival, he found that hostilities had begun and General Gage authorized him to recruit a regiment of two battalions of six hundred men each, to be known as the "Royal Highland Emigrants." His beating warrant is dated June 12th, 1775, and the commissions of John Macdonell and Ranald Macdonald as ensigns in it are dated only two days later.

Maclean related that he made "many journeys from Philadelphia to New York, thence to Boston, back to New York, and from thence to Canada, in disguise and often without a Servant or Baggage, with great Expence, imminent danger, and incredible fatigue."[1]

On July 20th, 1775, the *Quebec Gazette* announced that Colonel Maclean had been authorized to raise two battalions of Highlanders to consist of twenty companies of fifty men each, and that their uniform would be the same as that of the 42nd Regiment. On August 19th, that newspaper published the conditions of enlistment in the new regiment over the name of its commanding officer as an advertisement. On September 14th, it announced that he had marched for Montreal with his recruits on the 9th.

General Gage, writing from Boston, informed the Secretary of State that Maclean had posted officers in many of the provinces to enlist men, but added that "the great difficulty is to transport them to Canada, where the Colonel has established his Head Quarters. He writes from there that he has recruited 100 at Quebec and had engaged 400 more on the Mohock River, who waited opportunity to get to Canada, which will not be easy as the Rebels have possessed themselves of Lake Champlain."

Maclean had evidently returned almost immediately to Quebec, for on September 30th, Lieut.-Governor Cramahé reported that "with the Assistance of Lieut.-Colonel MacLean, who is very zealous and extremely diligent on the occasion, we have got the Town in a little better Posture of Defence."

At that time a small detachment of his regiment, consisting of a captain and nineteen other ranks, formed part of the garrison besieged at St. Jean. Another detachment was at Montreal and, about the middle of October, Ensign John Macdonell was sent with a small party to arrest the noted agitator, Thomas Walker, whose house at L'Assomption had become a centre of sedition. He was successful in this mission but received a very severe wound.

The Governor gave the following account of the manner in which this service was performed:

"On information that Mr. Walker still continued to preach up Disobedience & Rebellion, a party of Troops with some Canadians were sent to apprehend & bring him Prisoner, he had prepared his House for defence & fired several Shots at those who surrounded it. Ensign Macdonell was wounded in the arm, & a soldier received a bad wound in the thigh, occasioned by their Humanity; the House was then sett on fire, & Mr. Walker, his Wife & Servants surrendered."[2]

Another writer gives some further particulars:

"A Mr. Walker, a gentleman of Lower Canada, had the temerity to bid defiance to Government and to fortify his house against an attack, Ensign M'Donell was sent with a party to take

---
[1]Memorial of Colonel Allan Maclean to Haldimand, undated.
[2]Carleton to the Earl of Dartmouth, October 25, 1775.

him, a service of more danger than could have been supposed. Here his humanity was no less conspicuous than his courage, for although he might have set fire to the house, in which he would have been justified from the rashness of the defence, he chose rather to try every expedient to induce the culprit to surrender. Having in vain exhorted Mr. Walker to give himself up and pointed out the folly of unavailing resistance, he commanded his party to break open the door, which was accordingly done, but aware of the desperation of the person whom they were attacking, the soldiers refused to enter. Mr. M'Donell, snatching the lantern from one of them, for the attack was made in the night, stepped into the house, but the moment that he crossed the threshold, the arm holding the lantern was shattered by a shot from above. It was not till this desperate act was committed that he threatened to set fire to the house, unless Mr. Walker instantly surrendered, with which that gentleman thought proper at length to comply."[1]

It seems probable that Macdonell served with his regiment as part of the garrison of Quebec during the siege in the winter of 1775-6, but I have not been able to find any record of the fact.

In January, 1776, a large force under General Philip Schuyler marched into the Mohawk Valley and compelled Sir John Johnson and Allan Macdonell of Collachie to accept terms of capitulation. The fourth article of this agreement, when presented for their signature, read as follows:

"That the Scotch inhabitants of the said County (Tryon) shall, without any kind of exception, immediately deliver all arms in their possession, of what kind soever they may be; and that they shall each solemnly promise that they will not at any time hereafter, during the continuance of this unhappy contest, take up arms without the permission of the Continental Congress or of their General Officers; and for the more faithful performance of this article, the General insists that they shall immediately deliver up to him six hostages of his own nomination."

These were felt to be unreasonable demands and the Highlanders positively refused to give hostages, saying that no one man among them had command over another or power to deliver up any as such. Schuyler at length consented to the addition of a supplementary article which read:

"Fifth: Neither Sir John Johnson nor the Scotch gentlemen can make engagements for any other persons than those over whom they have influence. They give their word of honour that, so far as depends on them, the inhabitants shall give up their arms and enter into the like engagement as the Scotch inhabitants."

Between two and three hundred Highlanders were accordingly assembled for the purpose of delivering up their arms and six of the principal gentlemen were sent away as prisoners to Lancaster in Pennsylvania.

About the end of May, Schuyler became alarmed by a report that Johnson was instigating the Indians to begin hostilities, and he ordered a regiment, then on its way to Canada, to march to Johnstown with instructions to denounce the recent treaty, and bring off as prisoners of war all the leading loyalists. Johnson received timely warning of this sinister plan, and accompanied by two hundred of his friends and tenants, mostly Scotsmen, made his way by an Indian trail through the woods to Lake Champlain and thence to Montreal, where he arrived on June 20, the day after its reoccupation by Carleton, having marched steadily for nineteen days, during which he "encountered all the sufferings it seemed possible for man to endure."

The Royal Highland Emigrants received many recruits and during the following winter were quartered in Montreal and the regiment was retained in

---

[1] *The Canadian Courant and Montreal Advertiser*, 28th January, 1811.

Canada for its defence when General Burgoyne began his ill-fated expedition to the Hudson River. In June, 1777, one company was stationed at Sorel and detachments were employed at other points along the Richelieu River, to assist the militia officers in the execution of their orders and the enforcement of corvées.

Recruits continued to come in considerable numbers from the Mohawk and other parts of the province of New York. A good many of these bore the name of Macdonell. A letter from Major James Gray of the Royal Regiment of New York to Governor Haldimand, gives a glimpse of the arrival of one of these parties:

"There is a number of men come from the Mohawk & country under the Command of Three Gentlemen of the name of McDonald, one of them a Captain in Colonel Maclean's Regt.,[1] the other Two his Brother and Nephew, command a party of Highlanders which is ordered under my care until your Excellency's Pleasure is Known; these Gentlemen were under Arms with Sir John Johnson since the beginning of the Troubles until January, 1776, when by Capitulation they were obliged to lay down Their Arms, at which time these three with Three other Gentlemen of their People were Kept Prisoners until this Spring which was the reason they were not Appointed In Our Regiment, the oldest of the Two as a Captain & the other a Lieutenant[2] of which Rank they were when taken Prisoners. Forty-five of these men Choose to serve during the War, but are so attached to their Chiefs that they can't think of parting with them, those that have joined the Regiment I shall give the cloathing of the Regiment. I shall wait for Directions concerning the Rest. I shall administer the Oath of Allegiance to the whole of them and I shall send a list of their Names according to former Directions. I should be happy these Two McDonalds were taken notice of by your Excellency as they are destitute of cash and every necessary, being obliged to quit the Country in the manner they did."

In the course of the summer, Colonel Allan Maclean was appointed a brigadier-general, and in October he was ordered to occupy a post at Chimney Point near Crown Point, with his own regiment and the 31st Foot, to keep up communication with Ticonderoga. After the convention of Saratoga became known, these garrisons were withdrawn to the frontier posts at the northern end of Lake Champlain and on the Richelieu river.

A return of the officers of the first battalion of the Royal Highland Emigrants, dated at Isle aux Noix on the 15th of April, 1778, shows that John Macdonell had been promoted to the rank of lieutenant, being ninth in order of seniority. He had evidently grown tired of the monotony of constant garrison duty and applied for leave to serve with a regiment in the field. He had made the acquaintance of Walter Butler, who had escaped from a long and trying period of captivity under sentence of death, and had come from Niagara to Montreal in the hope of recovering strength. This chance meeting induced him to ask permission to join the corps of rangers lately raised by Butler's father to act in conjunction with the Indians, in which he would be likely to find active employment and meet a full share of hardship and adventure.

His application was, perhaps unexpectedly, successful, as under date of 31st July, 1778, General Haldimand wrote to Lieut.-Colonel Mason Bolton, commanding at Fort Niagara:

"Lieut. McDonell of Lieut. Col. Maclean's Corps, an officer, who is well spoken of for his gallantry and activity, has desired leave to serve with the Rangers, which I have granted him and intend, provided Major Butler approves of and recommends Mr. McDonell, to place him in that Corps as seems to be his wish."

---

[1]Allan Macdonell.
[2]Angus Macdonell and Archibald Macdonell.

This transfer gave him a step in rank, as on August 29th, Bolton replied from Niagara:

"I have filled up the blank Commissions sent by Capn. Butler agreeable to the Major's desire & Mr. MacDonell has received his commission as Captain in the Rangers."

Up to this time the officers of the Rangers had not received commissions and feared that they might suffer ill-treatment or perhaps be put to death in consequence, by the rebels, if they were taken prisoners.

Walter Butler, as senior captain, was sent at once to Aughquaga to take command of the Rangers and Indians "assembled there in order to cut off the German Flatts."[1] This force was expected to amount to five or six hundred whites and Indians. Macdonell accompanied him. Before their arrival, however, the expedition had been carried out successfully under the command of Captain William Caldwell.

Soon afterwards a large hostile force advanced from Wyoming as far as Tioga, apparently with the intention of invading the country of the Six Nations, and every effort was made to assemble as many Rangers and Indians as possible to attack it, assisted by a few volunteers from the 8th (King's) Regiment, in the garrison of Fort Niagara. The Indians were greatly alarmed and the danger of a successful invasion of their territory seemed so serious that Bolton wrote to Haldimand on October 12th:

"I believe Your Excellency will agree with me that whenever the Six Nations are forced to a neutrality these posts must be in danger, notwithstanding everything a handful of men can do to defend them; last year when we had an army in Philadelphia & another in New York I am convinced the enemy wou'd have sent a strong body of Troops here if it had not been for the determined resolution of the Indians to oppose them."

He reported that the main body of the Rangers was then assembled at Aughquaga and neighbourhood, "ready when joined by the Indians for an Incursion into the Enemies' Frontiers or to assist in defending the Indian Country in case of any attempts of the Rebels." They were soon after forced to retire from that place and the Indian village there was burnt by the invaders with equal severity, as those of the Mohawks had been destroyed some time before. They then swiftly retired, leaving a garrison of five hundred men in a fort at Wyoming.

Finding his force increased to eight hundred men, of whom one-half were Seneca warriors, Walter Butler promptly determined to retaliate by attacking Cherry Valley, where the enemy was reported to have a garrison of Continental troops and a large stock of cattle and grain.

After his return to "Onondella" on November 17th, he wrote a careful and lucid account of the expedition, which met with partial success, but was disgraced by much unnecessary bloodshed on the part of the Indians, who were enraged by the destruction of their villages.

"After a tedious and fatiguing march our Party, composed of the Rangers and 321 Indian Warriors, encamped on the evening of the 10th inst., within about six miles of the settlement, having the day before taken a Rebel Scout consisting of a Sergeant & 8 privates from whom we learned that a Colonel Alden with 300 Continental Troops occupied a Piquetted Fort erected for the defence of the Settlement and that the Militia of the place were computed at 150; that

---

[1]John Butler to Haldimand, Niagara, 17 September, 1778.

the Enemy had notice of our approach two days before by means of an Oneida Indian and also that the Colonel with his Principal Officers usually lodged at an house about 400 yards from the Fort. I here convened the Indian Chiefs and proposed to them that as in all probability the Enemy, tho' informed of our coming, were not apprised of our being so near them, we should as soon as the moon rose, march directly into the Settlement and with a party surround the house and take the officers while the main Body of Rangers & Indians endeavored to surprise the Fort; to this they unanimously agreed, but in the meantime a heavy rain falling and continuing all night so much discouraged the Indians that I could not get them to move till daylight when it was resolved that Capt. McDonald, with two subalterns and fifty chosen Rangers, should march with the Body of the Indians, and with one part surround the house & cut off communication between the Fort and inhabitants while the other began the attack upon the Fort which I was to support with the main Body of Rangers. We came unperceived till within about a mile of the Fort, when the Indians made a halt and two of them unknown to the rest, advanced & fired upon two men cutting wood, one of whom tho' wounded made his escape and allarmed the Officers at the house, of whom the Major and a few others had time to get safe into the Fort, many more attempting to do the same were killed and the rest taken Prisoners at the House by the Indians who had immediately rushed forward on the Report of the Guns.

"The Persons killed were the Colonel, 2 Captains, 2 Lieutenants, one Ensign and 20 Privates. The Prisoners are a Lieut. Colonel, a Lieut., an Ensign, the Surgeon's Mate and 10 Privates.

"The Colours of the Regiment were burnt in the House.

"Although our design of surprising the Fort was thus frustrated, we nevertheless made an Attempt, firing upon it for the space of Ten Minutes at about 70 yards distance, which was briskly returned both by the Musquetry and Cannons, when finding it inaccessible on this part, I moved with the Rangers to explore the other side, destroying in our way a Block House which the Rebels had abandoned on our approach. But perceiving the Indians dispersed over the Settlement, killing and taking Prisoners the Inhabitants, plundering and destroying the Buildings, &c., I found it absolutely necessary to move again with the whole of the Rangers and take possession of an eminence, which commanded the Fort on the side we first attacked in order to prevent a Sally while the Indians were scattered as aforesaid. We remained in this position till late in the evening tho' it rained incessantly; we retired about a mile further and there passed the night; the greatest part of the houses, Barns, &c., in the Settlement being burn'd and a great number of Cattle killed and driven off by the Indians.

"The next morning I sent Capt. McDonald with 60 Rangers, accompanied by Mr. Brant with 50 Indians to compleat the destruction of the place while the other Indians with the weakest of the Rangers went off with the Cattle. I remained myself with the rest of the Rangers to support Captain McDonald in case of a Sally, having men continually going to and from the Fort to give me notice of all the Enemy's motions until Captain McDonald returned after entirely desolating the Settlement and adding a large drove of Horses and Cattle to those already taken. The Garrison all the while cooped within their Breastworks remained Spectators of our depredations which they made no attempt to interrupt.

"After having in vain endeavoured to draw them out of the Fort and finding it not practicable with our Force to take it, we thought proper to retire and leave it, the only remaining building amid the ruins of the place.

"I have much to lament that notwithstanding my utmost precautions and endeavours to save the Women & Children, I could not prevent some of them falling unhappy Victims to the Fury of the Savages. They have carried off many of the Inhabitants Prisoners and killed more, among the latter is Colin Cloyd, a very violent Rebel.

"I could not prevail with the Indians to leave the Women & Children behind, tho' the second morning of our March, Captain Johnson, (to whose knowledge and address in managing them I am much indebted), and I got them to permit twelve who were Loyalists and whom I had concealed the first day with the humane assistance of Mr. Joseph Brant and Captain Jacobs of Ochquaga, to return. The death of the Women & Children upon this occasion may, I believe, be truly ascribed to the Rebels having falsely accused the Indians of Cruelty at Wyomen, this has much exasperated them, and they were still more incensed at finding the Colonel and those men who had then laid down their Arms, soon after marching into their Country intending to destroy their Villages and they declared they would no more be falsely accused, or fight the Enemy twice, meaning that they would not in future give quarters.

* * * *

"It gives me pleasure that I can mention with truth the alertness of the Officers in General and Captain McDonald in particular, whose activity & spirit on every occasion does him much honor and to whose conduct I am much indebted."

Two days after the attack seven men, ten women, and thirty-two children, who had been carried off by the Indians, were liberated and given a letter from

Walter Butler to General Schuyler, in which he stated that this had been done "least the inclemency of the season and their naked and helpless situation should prove fatal to them," and asked him to release "an equal number of our People in your hands amongst whom I expect you will permit Mrs. Butler (his mother) & Family to go to Canada."

The greater part of the Rangers returned to Fort Niagara where they went into winter quarters at "Butler's Barracks" on the opposite side of the river. In May, 1779, another alarm of a projected invasion of the country of the Six Nations brought them again into the field and Major Butler established his headquarters at the Indian village of Canadasaga. As his men were almost starving he began to collect provisions. Thence he wrote to Bolton, on May 24th, that he had sent an officer and forty men to some place on the Susquehanna to drive off cattle, and added:

"I hope in a day or two to be able to send off Captain McDonald & sixty men with a number of Indians to the Mohawk River upon the same Design. I am induced to do this as there seems to be no further Accounts of the Enemy coming into the Country and by the best Intelligence there is the highest probability of their success & great likelihood of their being able to bring off a number of cattle, at the same time these detachments will so diminish the number of the party that such as remain will be more easily supplied."

Walter Butler then arrived from Montreal, bringing many letters, and on May 28th Major Butler again wrote to Bolton:

"Captain McDonald has received a letter from the Major of his Regiment signifying that unless he joins it soon, he will probably be superseded. His leaving this at present will really be a detriment to the Service & it cannot be expected that he will sacrifice his Rank in the Army. I would therefore beg of you to mention it to the General that he may be permitted to remain here this Summer without it interfering with his other views. I have myself wrote to the General on the subject, and if my request be backed by you I make no doubt but he will agree to it. The Indians are very fond of Captain McDonald & upon being told he was going down the Country have particularly requested that His Excellency would allow him to stay."

Information obtained during the first twenty days of July made it tolerably certain that an overwhelming force was being assembled for the invasion of the Indian country, a part of it at Otsego Lake, but the main body at Wyoming on the Susquehanna. Captain Macdonell was accordingly despatched to make a raid upon the west branch of that river, partly to obtain cattle, but partly also to divert the attention of the enemy in that direction and delay their advance. The records of this expedition are sufficiently compendious from Macdonell's own letters and others published in the Pennsylvania Archives. The exact strength of Macdonell's party is not stated, but it was composed of a few men of the 8th Regiment, a larger number of Rangers and a good many Indians. On July 24th he wrote from his camp, "20 Miles from Fort Wallace," to Major Butler:

"I was met here by Samuel Harris's Party of Twenty Warriors, they went off from Shimong two days before my arrival & have taken two Prisoners & three scalps, a little below Fort Wallace.

"That the Enemy mean to attack the Indian Country from Wioming remains no longer a Doubt. All the Accounts I have been able to gather relative to their strength from Prisoners taken at different places & periods seem to corroborate. I have reason to apprehend from the information I have just received that they are about this time in motion.

"The Prisoners say that Genls. Sullivan & Maxwell were arrived with the last Division of the Troops—a long Train of Artillery and a Brigade of Provision Boats, this Division said to contain 5,000 men composed of Continental or standing Forces. Genl. Hand had 2,000 prior to the arrival of this reinforcement, they have 1,000 Pack Horses & 170 Boats. The whole is said to consist of 8,000 men, tho' I cannot allow them above the half nor do I believe they have that.

"I sent off a Scout from Shishiquin to Wyoming to watch the motions of the Rebels till our Return, should they discover them on their Route a Runner is to strike across the woods to me, the rest to return and spread the Alarm, in which case I shall, after doing them all the Injury I can in this Quarter, send off a sufficient Guard with what Cattle I'll be able to collect toward the Mountains to the Nanticoke Town & hang upon the Rear of the Enemy & harrass them as much as possible on their march with a few of the most Active of the Rangers & about 100 of the Indians. You may depend upon it I shall be very cautious to do anything that may have a tendency to dishearten the Indians. I know too well their capricious humours.

"I shall collect all the Cattle of every kind I can, as I am sensible that Provisions will be an object of the utmost consequence when all the Indians are embodied."

After this letter reached Butler, he wrote to Bolton on August 3rd:

"I received a letter from Captain McDonnell the 1st inst., which I sent to Captain Butler, desiring him to forward a copy of it immediately to you as I had at that time no Horse that I could send express with it. It Appears now that the Rebels are firmly bent on coming against the Six Nations with a large Body of men & have made all the necessary preparations. Captn. McDonnell's letter will inform you of the reports concerning the Enemy's strength, &c. at Wyoming. . . . . The Enemy must, I should imagine, have laid aside their Designs against Detroit, if they really mean to come into the Indian Country in this Quarter, and that they will, I think, is beyond a doubt should Genl. Clinton's success not be such as to prevent them. In this case, if Captain McDonnell is not able to drive off a great quantity of Cattle & we cannot be largely supplied with Provisions from Niagara, I do not know what may be the consequences, as it will be impossible without this to maintain any number of People together."

The result of Macdonell's expedition is well described in his letter to Colonel Butler, dated at Tioga Point, on August 5th:

"I have the pleasure to inform you of the success of the Indians and the Detachment I had the honor to command against the West Branch.

"After a very tedious, fatiguing march over Mountains & through Woods almost impenetrable, We came in upon the Settlement the 27th in the evening, continued our march all night & invested a small Place called Fort Freeland, early in the morning, the then Frontier Post occupied upon the River.

"At Ten o'clock the Fort surrendered by Capitulation, a copy of the Terms I have sent herewith.

"The Garrison consisted of one Sergeant & 12 Privates of the Continental Troops and 20 of the Militia, commanded by one of the Commissioners of the County, they had two men killed before the place surrendered. John Montour received a wound in the small of the back, scalping a man under the Pickets of the Fort but is in a fair way to do well.

"About two Hours after we got possession of the Place we were attacked by a Party of Rebels that came up to reinforce the Fort of 70 or 80 men, having heard our Fire. We had no intimation of their approach till they were close upon us. The Scouts of Indians that were sent out having fell in with some Horses which they pursued, neglecting the charge they were trusted with. The Indians upon the first Appearance of the Rebels retired a little, but soon recovered [from] their surprise and came in upon their left Flank with great Fury, while the Detachment of the 8th Regt. & Rangers attacked them in front And put them immediately to the Route with the loss of Three Captains, (two of which belonged to the Continental Troops), & between thirty & forty men killed.

"Few of them would have escaped had they not been favored with a very close Copse, where they concealed themselves. We had only one Indian killed & one wounded upon this occasion.

"I did everything in my power to prevail upon the Indians to pursue their Success but they were so glutted with Plunder, Prisoners & scalps that my utmost efforts could not persuade Them from Retreating to Fort Wallace that night. Next day I returned with about 100 Indians & Rangers, we burned & destroyed five Forts & about 30 miles of a close settled Country.

"They had abandoned their Forts the evening before and fled with Great Precipitation, leaving behind a large quantity of Goods & most of their Cattle. We were within eight miles of Shamokin. I am confident there is not a Rebel on this side of it.

"The Prisoners corroborate the accounts I gave you in my letter of the 24th ulto., & I have no further news.

"The Commissioner, who is a very intelligent man, asserts for certain that the Armies from Wioming & Cherry Valley are destined for Niagara, they were to set off from Wioming the 26th ulto. A Genl. Clinton commands the Army at Cherry Valley.

"Out of 116 Cattle we drove past Wallace's Fort we have only 62 remaining, some we lost, the greatest part were stole from us by the Indians. The Tuscaroras have a separate drove containing, I believe 40 or 50.

"For further particulars I must refer you to Lieut. [Andrew] Thompson, whom I beg leave to recommend to you as a very active, Spirited Officer.

"P.S. Please to send me word as soon as possible what I am to do with the Prisoners & Cattle."

The terms of capitulation consisted of three very brief articles and this document has been preserved in the archives of the State of Pennsylvania:

"Articles of Capitulation ent'd into between Captn John Macdonell on his Majesty's part & John Little on that of the Congress.

"Article 1st. The men in garrison to march out & ground their Arms in the Green in front of the fort which is to be taken in possession of by his Majesty's Troops.
Agreed to.

"2ndly. All men bearing arms are to surrender themselves prisoners of war & to be sent to Niagara.

"3d. The women and children not to be strip'd of their cloathing nor molested by the Indians and to be at liberty to move down the country where they please.
Ag'd to.
John Macdonell, Capt. of Rangers.
John Little."

Letters from the lieutenant of the county and other inhabitants of Sunbury fully corroborate and in some respects amplify Macdonell's account of his raid. Colonel Samuel Hunter wrote from Sunbury on July 28th:

"This day, about twelve O'clock, an express arrived from Capt. Boon's mill, informing us that Freeland's Fort was surrounded by a party of Indians, and immediately after that another express came, informing that it was burned and all the garrison either killed or taken prisoners; the party that went from Boon's saw a number of Indians and some Red Coats walking round the Fort (or where it had been), after that there was a firing heard off towards Chilisquake, which makes us believe that the Savages are numerous, and parties are going off from this Town & Northumb'd to ye relief of the garrison at Boon's, as there is a number of women and children; there was at Freeland's Fort fifty women and children, and about thirty men and God knows what has become of them; by this you may know our distressed situation at this present time."

Francis Allison wrote the same day to the president of the Executive Council of the State:

"At the particular request of Col. Hunter, I inform you that Freeland's Fort, the most advanced Post on the frontiers of the west Branch, had on Wednesday last three of the garrison killed & scalped, (one only shot) within sixty yards of the fort, & two made prisoners; the number of Indians appeared to be upwards of thirty in the open view of the garrison. Relief was sent immediately from Boon's Fort & the two Towns, & additional force was left behind to ye assistance, notwithstanding which, they attacked them this morning, & by intelligence received from persons of credit, sent out as spies, they had surrounded the fort, were walking carelessly around it & the gates were thrown open. This account arrived by express from Major Smith at twelve o'clock, since when Mr. Trigg, sent by Capt. Nelson, informs that other spies had seen the forts and barns in ashes, the mill still standing, & that the Indians appeared very numerous, among whom were some Red Coats, supposed to be Regulars—that thirty-four men had turned out from Boon's Fort to relieve Freeland's Fort, of whom there is not the least intelligence.

"The garrison of Freeland's F. consisted of thirty-two men, fourteen of whom were nine months men, & had in it upwards of forty women & children. The situation of this County is truly alarming & deplorable to the last degree."

Next day Colonel Hunter wrote again to another member of the Council:

"Yesterday morning early, there was a party of Indians & Regular Troops attacked Fort Freeland; the firing was heard at Boons place, when a party of thirty men turned out from that under the command of Capt. Boon, but before he arrived at Fort Freeland the garrison had surrendered and the British Troops and Savages was paraded round the prisoners, & the Fort & houses set on fire. Capt. Boon and his party fired briskly on ye enemy but was soon surrounded

by a large party of Indians; there was thirteen killed of our people and Capt. Boon himself among the slain. The regular officer that commanded was [of] the name of McDonald; he let the women and children go after having them a considerable time in custody. The Town of Northumberland was the frontier last night, and I am afraid Sunbury will be this night. . . . . "There was about three hundred of ye enemy, & the one-third of them was white men, as the prisoners inform us, that made their escape.
"N.B. It must be Butler's party."

John Buyers wrote the same day from Sunbury to the same member of the Council:

"Our situation at this time is very alarming, yesterday morning Freeland's Fort was attacked by not less than 300 British troops & Indians, they acted on the defensive as long as they could well but found it impracticable to hold out any longer after the enemy had sent in three flags desiring them to surrender, the last mentioning if they did not they would put them to the sword every one, the officer who commanded the garrison capitulated on these terms, viz. that the men should be prisoners of war, the women & children were to go to the towns of Northumberland & Sunbury unmolested; the whole killed in the fort was four men. Capt. Boon who went out for their relief fell in with the enemy. Capt. Kempton who observed the first Indian on guard shot him dead on the spot, then a party rallied out of the mill and defeated Boon's company, Killed Boon, Capt. Doherty, Capt. Hamilton & all the rest or took, of the party only 13 escaped. Northumberland is now the frontier, you may judge of the situation. . . . . we do not find there was more than eight or ten of the enemy killed."

In a second letter written that day Francis Allison said:

"Since mine of the 28th we have received particular instructions from Ft. Freeland by women who had been in the Fort. They say the garrison surrendered after making a noble but short resistance & after being thrice summoned they capitulated in form, the copy of it has not yet come to hand. Of the garrison four were killed & thirteen scalps were brought into the fort in a pocket handkerchief, amongst whom were Captain Boon's & Dougherty's, supposed to belong to the party from Boone's Fort wch attacked the British, Indians, &c., & even got among the people who were prisoners, but were obliged to fly on acct of superiority of numbers, 13 or 14 of the party have come in; they (the women of F.F.) estimate the number of the enemy at between 3 & 4 hundred, one-third of whom are Regular Troops. Boone's Fort is evacuated & Northumberland Town is already the frontier. Hurry all the assistance possible with the utmost haste or else the consequences on our side will be dreadful.
"The Commanding Officer is said to be a Capt. McDonald who intimated to the women yt a party was still in the rear."

After the retreat of the raiders, Colonel Matthew Smith, a militia officer, made the following report to the President of the Council:

"I have arrived at Sunbury with sixty Paxtang boys, the neighbouring townships turn out a number of volunteers. Cumberland County will give a considerable assistance, to-morrow at twelve o'clock is fixt for the time of march, provisions are scarce, but we intend to follow the Savages, we hope to come up with them, as the number of cattle is great they have taken from the country & must make slow progress on their return home—I hope to see them on their return & doubt not if we do to give a good acct. I inclose a copy of the capitulation at Fort Freeland, the Capt. McDonald of the Rangers is formerly a sergeant in Col. Montgomery's Regt. of Highlanders, his humanity has appear'd in this one instance—perhaps the first in this war, fifty-two women & children came safe to this place, being the number taken—four old men also was admitted to come back, the enemy suppos'd them not fit to march to Niagara. Inclos'd is a list of the number of Capt. Boon's party killed (11), also the names of persons belonging to the garrison (5). This acct I believe is the fact as the party out yesterday have bury'd the dead & gave me the list. The distress of the people here is great—you may have some conception but scarcely can be told—the town now composes Northumberland County. The enemy have burnt everywhere they have been houses, barns, rye & wheat in the fields, stacks of hay, &c., is all consumed—such devastation I have not yet seen."[1]

---

[1] Pennsylvania Archives, Vol. VII.

The Colours of the Second Battalion Royal Canadian Volunteers in possession of J. A. Macdonell, K.C., Alexandria, Ont.

Macdonell, however, effected his retreat without molestation and rejoined Butler, bringing a considerable drove of the captured cattle and important information respecting the advance of the enemy. On August 10th, Butler wrote to Bolton from "Canadasagoe," reporting his return:

"Captain McDonell is here, from what he has heard of the Prisoners the Enemy mean to Establish a Strong Post at Tioga, this must take them some time, so that we shall probably have sufficient Time to assemble a Considerable Body before they advance any further; this however is uncertain, as they may perhaps come on immediately."

In a letter on the same day to his son Walter, he said:

"Captain McDonell is here, and the Party will be in to-day. By the accounts he has from the Prisoners, the Rebels were to leave Wioming the 26th Ulto—they mean to build small Forts at every 20 to 30 miles as they come along, and Establish a very strong Post at Tioga. They have two companies of Artillerymen and 20 pieces of Cannon and by the Commissary's Return which one of the Prisoners had seen, there were upwards of seven thousand Rations Issued at a time at Wioming.

"I think it beyond doubt that they are very strong and seriously bent upon this Expedition."

This formidable force moved slowly but steadily forward, hewing a road, building bridges, and constructing log forts and supply depots at short intervals. At Tioga point it was joined by a lesser body from Otsego Lake, which had dammed the river and was floated jubilantly down stream upon the flood thus created and suddenly released. Although outnumbered ten to one, Butler made a resolute effort to check the advance of the invaders, by occupying a position the Indians had chosen.

"It was a Ridge of about half a mile in length," he wrote, "to the Right of which lay a large Plain extending to the River, and terminating in a narrow Pass near our Encampment, so that having possession of the Height we would have greatly the advantage should the Enemy direct their march that way—on our left was a steep mountain and a large Creek in our front at a little distance. We threw up some Logs, one upon the other by way of a Breast Work, which we endeavoured to conceal with Bushes, that the Enemy might not perceive it on their approach and extended our Line to the left across the Creek at the Foot of the Mountain, where great part of the Indians were posted.

"Capt. MacDonell with 60 Rangers and Joseph Brant with about 30 white men and Indians lay to the Right and the Rest of the Indians and Rangers with the Detachment of the 8th occupied the centre, where I had placed myself."[1]

Here, however, he was discovered by the enemy's scouts and six guns opened fire upon the breastwork, "discharging Shells, round and grape shot, Iron Spikes, &c., incessantly," which drove out its occupants. "The Shells bursting beyond us made the Indians imagine the Enemy had got their Artillery all round us and so Startled and Confounded them that great part of them ran off." The American infantry was at the same time endeavouring to make a wide circuit round the mountain and cut off their retreat, in which they nearly succeeded. "Many of the Indians made no Halt," Butler continued, "but proceeded immediately to their respective Villages; the different parties of the rest and the Rangers Rendezvoused in the evening at a Village, called the Nantikoke Town, about five miles from the Place of Action, from whence we proceeded with our Baggage a few miles and encamped for the Night. Our Loss in men, considering everything, is much less than could be expected, of the Rangers, we had five men killed and three wounded, and of the Indians five killed and nine wounded."

---

[1]John Butler to Bolton, Seechquago, 31 August, 1779.

The rangers were gradually thrust back beyond the Genesee, and eventually retreated to Fort Niagara, where they were followed by several thousands of distressed Indians, whose villages and cornfields were ruthlessly destroyed by the victors.

A letter from Haldimand to Butler, written in August, gave the required permission for Macdonell to stay with the Rangers. "Captain McDonald," he wrote, "upon your Representation has my permission to remain with you for the Campaign upon which subject I shall write to Major Nairne."

Owing probably to his commercial training, Macdonell was selected to act as paymaster of the battalion and accompanied Walter Butler to Montreal in the course of the following winter to settle their accounts.

On 21st February, 1780, Walter Butler wrote from that town to Captain Robert Mathews, the Governor's military secretary:—

"We do very little else but feasting and Dancing, it has nearly turned my head—I find it as hard as Scouting—in order to change the Scene McDonell and me intend to make the Tour of the mountain every other day on Snow Shoes."

On his return journey to Niagara, Macdonell was apparently entrusted with a letter to Lieutenant-Colonel Butler, proposing a diversion from Niagara to assist an expedition from Montreal to the Mohawk valley, commanded by Sir John Johnson, but he was detained so long at Carleton Island by contrary winds and ice, that this order did not arrive in time to be carried out.[1]

Some time in June, Macdonell was sent off with a strong party of rangers and Indians to bring off the Oneidas from their villages on the Mohawk river, as they had expressed a desire to join the remainder of the Six Nations near Niagara and abandon the rebels with whom they had been acting since the beginning of the war. His first letter to Lieutenant-Colonel Bolton, while thus employed, has not been found. On July 1st, he wrote to that officer from "Onandago":—

"In my last to you from Canadago, I acquainted you that the Indians had changed their first design and that they had determined to fall back upon the Claesbarrack.

"In this resolution they continued till the 21st when I was informed by David, the Mohawk, that they intended to pay the Onidas a visit, as they had great reason to believe that many of them would come off, from the repeated messages they had sent to that effect & that they were resolved to burn the village and oblige those that declined profiting by the opportunity to retire into the interior parts of the Country to be supported by the People whose cause they were engaged in. The Indians after this route was fixed upon were very attentive and alert in keeping out Scouts.

"The 24th we arrived at old Onida undiscovered. I very soon perceived that they had but little intention to put their threats in Execution. The Onida Chiefs were immediately called to a Council, a long Speech was delivered to them of their situation in case they continued blind to their own Interest and did not follow the advice which they had often received to come off and join the rest of the six nations, &c. The Onidas observed in the close of their answer that their hearts felt very sore at the treatment that they heard their Chiefs had received at Niagara in being detained there in captivity.

"The day following the Spruce Carrier arrived with his Party. Another Council was called, the result of which I am happy to inform you was much more favorable than the first, whether the Spruce Carrier's arguments were more forcible or that they had deliberated on what had been told them the day before I cannot pretend to say. They have, however, unanimously agreed to come off. They beg of me to inform you that they are very sorry for their past Behaviour, but that they will for the future behave like dutiful children. They request that their Chiefs may be allowed to return as they have very large Families and no men in them to take care of them, the instant they arrive the whole of them are to set off.

---

[1]John Butler to Haldimand, Niagara, 14 May, 1780.

"We have brought off eleven Warriors, I have not the least doubt from every appearance but the rest will follow.

"I used my utmost endeavours to get the Indians after our return from Onida to pursue our first design as we had not Provision sufficient to bring us to Niagara, but enough to bring us to the Place we intended going to.

"This I explained in the strongest manner I could but to no purpose for I could not get Twenty Indians to go with us. We shall be very much distressed for Provisions before we can possibly get a supply.

"I have had the Fever and Ague these Ten days past to an immoderate degree, and the Rheumatism in my neck, the Ague is just going to attack me, so that I must refer you to Lieut. Bradt for particulars."

A letter from Walter Butler to Captain Mathews, written from Niagara on July 24th, gives a glimpse of the sufferings he endured while on this arduous expedition.

"McDonell has had his own trouble while he was out, and at last could only get the Indians to go to Oneyda, where they did not perform what they promised; he was so ill with the Ague that he was under the necessity of having himself tied on his Horse; they Killed their Horses & Dogs for food."

During his absence one of his brothers was recommended for a commission in one of the new companies being added to the battalion of rangers. "There is a Young Gentleman," Major Butler wrote, "a Mr. Chichester McDonell, son of Capt. McDonell of Sir John Johnson's Regt., & Brother to Captn McDonell of my Corps whom I could wish His Excellency would give a 2nd Lieutenancy in my Corps to. I am informed he is a Volunteer of some years standing."

In August another raid in force was projected against the Mohawk valley under the command of Sir John Johnson, advancing from Oswego, while another expedition was to move simultaneously from Crown Point toward Albany. About the middle of September, Johnson ascended the St. Lawrence from Montreal to Carleton Island, and Colonel Butler was directed to join him from Niagara with detachments of two regular regiments and all the effective men of the rangers. The garrison of Niagara had been weakened to an unusual degree by disease. Walter Butler had gone to Montreal sick; Caldwell had been detached with his company to Detroit; Macdonell was accordingly the senior officer available for this service and took command of the rangers, among whom were a number of convalescents barely able to bear arms. Embarking at Niagara on September 24th, contrary winds prevented their arrival at Oswego until October 1st. Johnson had awaited them there for ten days. Making their way with infinite toil and fatigue through an almost pathless wilderness, they entered the Scotch settlement of Scoharie on the seventeenth day of their march, and, sparing a few houses at its upper end, known to belong to friends, they swept down the valley, torch in hand, with ruthless orders to destroy every building in their path. When they reached the Mohawk river a large party was sent across it to burn the houses near Fort Hunter. When this was done they swiftly advanced up the river, laying waste the settlements on both sides until midnight, when a halt was made at the narrow pass called "the Nose." They had then been constantly in motion for twenty-four hours and their strength was well nigh exhausted. Early next morning Johnson brought over his whole force, with the exception of a few rangers and Indians.

"Two men who had deserted from Fort Stanwix this spring," Johnson wrote in his official letter, "left us and went over to the Enemy at Stone Arabia and informed Colonel Brown, who

commanded there, that the Detachment on that side of the River was very weak, which induced him to march out next morning with three hundred and sixty men to attack them. I meant to have crossed over to them in the night but the Troops were too much fatigued to attempt it till the morning of the 19th when we joined them about sunrise; in a thick fog we marched on to within about a mile of Frey's, a few Indians burning along the opposite shore, we discovered several horsemen watching our movements, who all took the Road to Stone Arabia. We followed and soon fell in with their Advance Guards who immediately retired upon the Indians advancing. When we had gained the heights of Stone Arabia, the Enemy were discovered and attacked by about fifty Indians, who were forced to give way but we immediately supported them with a part of the 8th, 34th, and Rangers, the remainder of the Troops being at some distance, the fire continued very brisk for a few minutes. The Enemy were under cover of a Wood, and a fence on one side of a lane, while we had only a fence and an open field on the other side within thirty yards of them. Finding the Indians were endeavouring to flank them on their Right, I ordered Captain McDonell with the Rangers to attempt their left, at the same time leaping over the fence with the 8th and 34th, the Enemy immediately gave way, when a General pursuit took place in which Colonel Brown and about one hundred Officers and men were slain. Captain McDonell of the Rangers and Captain Brant exerted themselves upon the occation in a manner that did them honor, and contributed greatly to our success. We lost only one private of the 8th and three Indians; Captain Brant received flesh wound in the soul (sic) of the foot near his former wound, and three Rangers were wounded. By papers found in Colonel Brown's Pocket I learned that General Ranslaer with six Hundred Militia and three field pieces was at Fort Hunter the day before and of course then could not be very distant. We therefore without loss of time began to burn the settlement which we compleated in a short time, the Enemy firing upon us from their Fort; from thence we took the Road to Foxes upon the River above Frey's, which being also fortified we shunned, but everything else about it and all the way up to George Klock's near the Fort Hendrick Ford [was burned], there again we were obliged to take to the Woods to avoid three or four fortified houses that entirely commanded the Roads & flatts; that took us till near sunset when we found ourselves opposed in going down to the High Road by the Enemy from behind fences, houses, and Orchards. I immediately ordered a strong Detachment to a height upon our left which Commanded the Road, with the remainder of the Troops I pushed down the Hill, crossed the Road and formed in the open Field, the Enemy firing and Retreating to some distance under their Fort at Klock's where they also formed in some force. The Indians who were all on Horseback were panic-struck and crossed the River. The Enemy Observing them were encouraged to advance upon our left under cover of Woods, houses & fences, and began a heavy fire upon us from all Quarters especially upon our left where I ordered a House, Barn, &c. to be taken possession of, but the Order not being attended to in time, the Enemy took advantage of it and threw in a heavy fire, which forced the 34th and a part of my Regiment to give way, upon which they gave three cheers. I immediately ordered the three-pounder to be fired with Grape shott which was also followed by a discharge of small arms which totally silenced them, but it being dark and the Troops in a good deal of confusion and having every reason to think the Enemy were Collecting from all the Forts and that Ranslaer must be at hand, if not with them, I thought it most for the good of His Majesty's Service to cross the River without loss of time, which was effected, without any interruption. The Indians led us immediately up into the Woods and it being very dark we were separated, Captain Parke with a large Body taking the Road to Fort Herkimer, where they arrived the next morning and fell in with sixty of the Enemy who were returning home. Captain Parke not knowing their numbers ordered the whole to take into the Woods to gain the Road we came down upon, but Captain McDonell with his usual Spirit attacked them with a few Rangers assisted by some of my men, Killed ten and took two of them, driving the rest into the Fort. The front having marched on Captain McDonell lost their track, and was separated from them for two days, when we all met again except Captain Dame and those returned missing in the Enclosed Return who I fear are mostly taken, tho' there were Indians missing, who may bring them in. . . . .
. . . . "Captain McDonell of the Rangers obtained Colonel Butler's leave to come down with me (to Montreal) on account of his bad state of health, he hopes your Excellency will permit him to remain here for the winter, he really merits every indulgence."

Captain Dame with eighteen of the missing men and thirty Indians arrived at Oswego soon after the rest of their comrades had left that place, leaving boats and provisions behind for their use. The Rangers, as in former years, went into winter quarters at Niagara. Captain Macdonell rejoined the regiment in the spring and it would seem was a witness at a General Court Martial on some of the officers. The only reference to this that I have found is contained in a letter from Lieut.-Colonel John Butler to General Haldimand, dated 2nd July, 1781, in which he stated that:—

"On Lieut. Peter Ball's Tryal, it appeared orders had been delivered him, sent by Capt. McDonell, who commanded the Corps last Fall near Fort Harcamer for him to come up with the rear of the Regmt (where he was posted) to support the Main Body of the Corps then Engaged with the Enemy, this he refused to obey saying 'it was too dangerous,' & likewise prevented several of the men supporting Captn McDonell by telling them 'not to go, it was too dangerous,' the Court conceived this would not fall under the Charge of stirring up a Sedition & Mutiny but that it fell under a particular Article of the Articles of war—should Lieut. Peter Ball be acquitted for what he has been Tryed, the Corps will not do Duty with him till he clear up this."

In a postscript Butler added:—

"Captain McDonell says from the separation that took place immediately at the Affair at Fort Harcamer, was the reason he was not Informed Why the Rear did not support him as he would wish, he never, till joining the Corps this Spring Knew the Cause."

Macdonell resumed his duties as paymaster of the regiment and there is a record that he appointed Robert Ellice of Montreal as attorney to receive all subsistence and other allowances due to all ranks. This employment and persistent ill health apparently were the causes that prevented him from taking part in the expedition conducted by Major Ross into the Mohawk valley in October, 1781, in which Walter Butler met his death. This proved to be the last offensive operation undertaken during the war from Niagara, as a large detachment of the Rangers, under Captain Caldwell had been diverted for the protection of Detroit. Captain Macdonell remained in command of his company at Niagara and continued to perform the duties of paymaster. No mention of him occurs in the official correspondence until the 25th of March, 1782, when Brigadier General H. W. Powell, then in command there, informed General Haldimand that "Colonel Butler has applied for leave of absence for Captain McDonell, who is paymaster, to go to Montreal on the Regimental business and also for Captain Dame to go for his Family. Should neither of them be employed on the present occasion I beg to be informed if you approve of their going." The occasion to which he referred was the transfer of the main body of the Rangers from Niagara to Carleton Island to enable Major Ross to establish a new post at Oswego.

Haldimand's reply is dated the 18th May and he remarked that:—

"The beginning of a Campaign is an awkward time for officers, particularly at so great a distance, to leave quarters—should Capn. McDonell's business as a P. Mr. require his presence here I have no objection to his coming down in the Fall. Mr. Dame is by the return detached to Oswego."

On June 1st, Lieutenant-Colonel John Butler wrote from Niagara to the Military Secretary to the Governor:—

"As His Excellency was pleased to order no new Commissions [I] should be very happy that a mistake could be rectified in the dates of Captn McDonell's and Captn Tinbrook's Commissions as it never were my intentions that Captain Tinbrook should take Rank of McDonell, which will appear by the Muster Rolls, &c. as the latter company were raised & mustered prior to the former, And always (until latterly) thought to be the eldest, as Capt. McDonell is the most capable officer in the Corps to command in my absence, which will often be the case if I am to have the care of the Indian Department, he is also the best liked by the Indians who soon after the death of my Son desired in a very pressing manner that he should step in my son's place, [for] the above reasons [I] should be happy the General would comply with my request, the whole of this [I] beg to leave to your better Judgment whether it be proper to mention it to the General or not. Some time ago [I] applied for a Lieutenancy for Captain McDonell's Brother who has been a Volunteer in Sir John Johnson's Corps. I am told he is a very promising Youth, [I] should be much obliged to His Excellency to grant him a Commission."

On June 10th, General Powell wrote to Haldimand that:—

"Captain McDonnell having some accounts of consequence to settle at Montreal as Pay Master to the Corps, and there being no appearance of his being immediately wanted here, I have given him leave to go down for a few days."

Two months later Powell was recalled to Quebec and took his departure from Niagara early in September when he seems to have been accompanied by Macdonell, as on the 2nd of that month Butler wrote to Mathews that:—

"Brigdr. General Powell and Captn McDonell will fully explain every particular [relating to the settlement at Niagara] to His Excellency. The latter has a verbal message from me to you."

On November 4th, Captain Mathews informed Butler that:—

"Agreeably to your Request for the reasons it contained, His Excellency has ordered that Captain McDonell's Commission should bear a prior date to Capt. Tinbrook's, of which Brigr. Genl. Maclean is informed. You will please nevertheless to explain the matter more fully to him."

It would seem that Macdonell returned to Fort Niagara after a short stay at Montreal and continued to act as paymaster until the final disbandment of the regiment. A letter from him to Captain Mathews, dated there on December 3rd, 1783, covering the corrected pay lists and subsistence account, has been preserved. On January 14th, 1784, he wrote to the same officer, asking that Lieutenant John Turney should be allowed deferred pay for six months on account of the distressed state of his wife and family. On May 8th, he wrote again, sending a corrected pay list but stating his inability to answer certain questions as he was entirely ignorant of the manner in which the regimental business had been conducted at the early period to which they referred. He regretted that the bills drawn in favour of Ellice & Co. had not been honoured. He could not clear the accounts of the regiment at its disbandment without hard cash and requested that a temporary warrant should be issued for that purpose.

A return, dated 1st December, 1783, of the Loyalists incorporated in the Corps of Rangers commanded by Lieutenant-Colonel Butler shows that Macdonell's company then consisted of fifty-three men, eleven women, twelve boys, and nine girls, making a total of eighty-five persons, for whom fifty-six rations were drawn. The regiment was finally disbanded at Fort Niagara in June, 1784, with the intention that the officers and men should settle upon lands to be granted to them on the opposite side of the river, but unexpected delay occurred in the survey and assignment of lots. Macdonell was credited with exactly nine years service, beginning on the 14th of June, 1775. The officers were retired upon half-pay and given liberal grants of unimproved land. Captain Macdonell was then only about thirty-four years of age, but the anonymous author of the sketch of his life published in the *Canadian Courant* of Montreal in 1811, states that "the great hardships which he had to surmount undermined a constitution naturally excellent, and entailed upon him a severe rheumatism which embittered the remaining part of his life," but adds that "by his own care and attention, he found himself at the end of the war in the possession of a small independency." He was entitled to a grant of three thousand acres of land; his father had served as a captain in the Royal Regiment of New York, and his brother, Hugh, had been a lieutenant in the same battalion, while his brother, Chichester, had, as already stated, been appointed as subaltern in Butler's Rangers. His uncle, Allan Macdonell of Collachie, had been a captain in the Royal Highland Emigrants, and one of his sons, a lieutenant in Butler's Rangers. The grants of land, to which they were collectively entitled, amounted to fifteen thousand acres. As his father and other members of his family wished to settle with their clansmen and friends on the north shore of the St. Lawrence upon the lands allotted for the loyalists, John Macdonell decided to accompany them, and selected farm lots in townships No. 2 and No. 3, which afterwards received the names of Charlottenburg and Cornwall in what was at first known as the district of New Johnstown.[1] His biographer already mentioned states that "this he considered equally the property of his father, brothers, and sisters as his own, and proved by his generosity, that his filial love and brotherly affection were equal to his other virtues." Here he appears to have begun improving and cultivating part of his grant at an early date. His name, with those of his father, uncle, and his brother, Hugh, is attached to the address of congratulation presented to Lord Dorchester, soon after his arrival in Canada, from the inhabitants of New Johnstown, dated 2nd December, 1786. As a representative of Township No. 3, he signed the petition of the western loyalists, praying for an alteration of the tenure to grants "in free and common soccage, unincumbered with any crown rent whatever." They also asked that a glebe of four hundred acres should be set apart in each township for a clergyman; that some assistance should be given towards the establishment of a school in each district; that the importation of pot and pearl ash and lumber from the State of Vermont should be prohibited, and that a bounty be granted for the production of those articles and of hemp "to stimulate their Industry, and encourage their internal Trade"; that an additional loan of three months' provision of pork should be allowed the settlers to be repaid in three years; that some plan should be adopted to expedite the survey of division lines in the several townships; that a post road should be established from Montreal to Cataraqui with post offices for letters at New Johnstown, New Oswegatchie, and Cataraqui, and that a passage should be opened from "the head of the Bay of Quinty through Lake Huron for the Benefit of the Indian Trade, a Channel which at the same time that it is universally acknowledged to be Superior to the Old holds out a prospect of the most flattering advantages, not only to the Commerce of this Province in general but to this settlement in particular." It also requested that three places should be selected between Point au Baudet and Cataraqui for the purchase by government of the surplus grain grown by the settlers and that they be granted the right to build and navigate boats on the lake, that the Commissioners, appointed to examine the claims of the Loyalists for compensation for their losses during the war, should be urged to visit New Johnstown, New Oswegatchie, and

[1] His name appears in a list of disbanded troops and loyalists settled in Township No. 1, mustered 16th October, 1784.

Cataraqui to take evidence; that the settlers should be confirmed in the right to the free use of the locks and canals on the St. Lawrence, a privilege already granted to them by Lieutenant-Governor Hope; and finally that they should be placed on the same footing as the officers and men of the 84th Regiment in regard to the proportion of lands to be granted them by the Crown. This document was signed by sixteen of the leading residents, each of the eight townships being represented by two of them.

Lord Dorchester at once recommended in the strongest manner an alteration of the tenure of their lands, which was granted by the Canada Act of 1791, and he took measures to comply with several other requests, as far as his authority and means would permit.

An ordinance was passed on 30th April, 1787, authorizing the Governor to form one or more new judicial districts as soon as circumstances would permit and accordingly the "upper country" was divided into four districts by a patent dated 24th July, 1788. The eight eastern townships became the district of Luneburg. Alexander Macdonell was appointed the third Justice of the Court of Common Pleas for the district, the other two being Richard Duncan and Edward Jessup. Sessions of the court were held at Cornwall and Edwardsburg in January, 1789; at Edwardsburg in March; at New Johnstown and Edwardsburg in July; and at New Johnstown and Augusta in October, only Duncan and Macdonell presiding on each occasion. When the court sat at Augusta on 17th May, 1790, John Macdonell took the seat of his father, presiding with Duncan. The next session was held at Cornwall in June. At the court held at Osnabruck in September Jessup was present for the first time. At subsequent sessions held at the same place in January and June, Duncan and John Macdonell attended, and at the session held there in September, Jessup and the latter were present. No subsequent session seems to have been held until 10th December, 1792, when John Munro took the seat of Jessup and all three Justices were present. All of them were present at the sessions held in January and February, 1793, but in May, 1793, Macdonell was absent for the first and only time, probably because of the meeting of the legislature which assembled at Niagara on the last day of that month. Later sessions of the court were held at Osnabruck in November, 1793, and at Cornwall in January and April, 1794, which were attended by Macdonell and Munro only. The court was then abolished by the King's Bench Act of the Legislature passed that year.

In September, 1788, Captain Macdonell was appointed a member of a board of five persons, of which Richard Duncan was chairman, "to examine into the loyalty and character of such persons as may come in and apply for lands in the District of Luneburg" and authorized on "being satisfied of the worthiness of the person applying to give orders on the Deputy Surveyor of the District for a lot to each." This was followed in April, 1789, by the appointment of a land board for the District of Luneburg, of three members, in which Macdonell was associated with Richard Duncan and Jeremiah French. On 3rd March, 1791, the land board for the District of Luneburg was increased by the addition of four new members, and the quorum for the legal transaction of business was changed from three to five members. After the division of the new province of Upper Canada into counties by proclamation on 16th July, 1792, the district

Ruins of "Glengarry House" which was destroyed by fire in 1813.

land boards were abolished and county land boards established. The land board appointed for the counties of Glengarry and Stormont consisted of five members, John Macdonell being one, with James Gray as chairman. An order in council passed on 6th November, 1794, abolished the county land boards and directed that all applications for grants of land should be made to the Executive Council.

A report of the Land Committee of the Executive Council of the Province of Quebec, dated 19th February, 1790, shows that lands had been granted to several persons bearing the same name as Captain Macdonell in the Township of Charlottenburg, without any distinctive designation, thereby causing much confusion.

"The Committee observing in Examining the Index to the Schedule of Grants made in Charlottenburg that under the Letter M, John McDonell appears to possess 2,400 Acres of Land, and on Enquiry of the Deputy Surveyor General, it was found that that quantity does not belong to one, but to many John McDonells, but for want of some mark of Distinction upon the plan, these John McDonells have been considered as one and the same person.

"To correct this and such like Inaccuracies the Committee humbly conceive that it may be expedient to order the Deputy Surveyor of the District to advertise the Grantees of that Name to produce to him their Certificates of Location, and from each learn the Name or Epithet by which he is distinguished from another John McDonell, among his Countrymen, and let that name be added to the name already entered on his Lot or Lots upon the plan, the same will be done upon the Schedule, from which the Alphabetical List, or Index, may easily be corrected."

The report further stated that the lands in question had actually been granted to five different persons, seven hundred acres to one, five hundred acres to each of three others, and two hundred acres to a fifth. The centennial list of loyalists contains the names of fifty-one Macdonells, who received grants of land in the eastern part of Upper Canada and among these not less than eleven were named John.

An ordinance "for better regulating the Militia of this province, and rendering it of more general utility towards the preservation and security thereof," was enacted by the Executive Council of the Province of Quebec on 23rd April, 1787. Sir John Johnson was appointed to the command of all the militia of the new settlements in the upper country. The first return of enrollments in Luneburg, or Point au Baudet, showed a total of 1525 liable for service. It was organized into two battalions and Captain John Macdonell was appointed to the command of that composed of men resident in the townships of Lancaster and Charlottenburg, with the rank of major. The prospect of a war with Spain in 1790 caused the Governor-General to call for a special return with a view to a draft of two thousand men for two years' service if necessary. This showed that Macdonell's battalion consisted of twenty-two officers and 313 other ranks, who had in their possession only sixty-five muskets. A note under the head of remarks states that "by the particular Return made by the Commanding Officer it appears that 71 unmarried men may be drafted from it to serve as the Ordinance requires consistently with the present condition of the District and without any material inconvenience arising to the settlement from such draft." The proportionate number that would be required was only twenty-eight. This return is dated at Montreal on the 6th of October, 1790, and signed by Sir John Johnson as Brigadier-General, commanding the militia of the district. This dispute with Spain over the aggression at Nootka Sound became known as "the Spanish armament," and is said to have cost Great Britain three millions of pounds sterling in the equipment of the navy alone.

An ordinance for promoting inland navigation enacted on 30th April, 1788, granted the privilege of transporting merchandise and peltries on the upper lakes to the owners of vessels under ninety tons, built and launched in Canada and navigated by British crews. Hitherto this right had been restricted solely to the King's ships and was a subject of complaint.

In May, 1789, official announcement was published that a public postal service would be established every four weeks between Montreal and Kingston, conveying letters and parcels addressed to Point au Baudet, Lancaster, Charlottenburg, Cornwall, Osnabruck, Williamsburg, Matilda, Edwardsburg, Augusta and Elizabethtown in the District of Luneburg, and that the first mail would leave Montreal on Monday, the 8th of June.

About this time Captain Alexander Macdonell and his sons seem to have undertaken the construction of the large dwelling on Glengarry Point, which became known as Glengarry House, and is believed to have been the first stone house built in the Eastern District. It is mentioned in his book of travels by Patrick Campbell, who saw it in November of 1791, and stated that it was then nearly completed at a cost of £1,300, which he apparently considered a large sum.

Writing to Mr. W. W. Grenville on 15th March, 1790, and acting admittedly on the advice of Sir John Johnson, whom he proposed for appointment as Lieutenant-Governor, Lord Dorchester recommended John Macdonell as one of thirteen members to compose the Executive Council of the new Province of Upper Canada. As this body was eventually limited to only five members, including the Chief Justice and Receiver General, Macdonell was one of the eleven who were not appointed.

Soon after his arrival at Quebec a correspondence began between Lieutenant-Governor Simcoe and some of the leading residents of the Eastern District, among them being Richard Duncan, James Gray, John Macdonell, and John Munro. None of Macdonell's letters to him have been found. In a letter to Henry Dundas, dated on April 28th, 1792, Simcoe quotes part of a letter from Munro, in which he said: "On my return I found the Lawyers had infused an Idea throughout our district that we had no Law and as many wished to take advantage of this report I sent advertisements all over the district and a copy of your Excellency's letter to Judge McDonell, all which I flatter myself will have the desired effect & I have the pleasure to inform your Excellency that Emigrants are flocking in from the States with all their property."

The next mention of him that has come to my notice is found in a letter to Simcoe from Richard Duncan, written at the Hermitage on 30th April, 1792, in which he said:—

"Your Excellency will pardon me for mentioning to you that I was unwarily betrayed into a promise, when in Montreal, of recommending to your notice a Mr. Chichester McDonnell of Charlottenburg, brother to a worthy character of that name, A Major John McDonnell, one of the Judges of the District of Lunenburg, who wishes to hold some employment either in a Civil or Military Capacity under Your Excellency's auspices, and I must beg leave to add that I know him to be a young man of good deportment and otherwise worthy of notice."

The principal business of the first meeting of the Executive Council of Upper Canada, held at Kingston in July, 1792, was the division of the Province into counties for the purpose of electing members of the Legislative Assembly. The first of these counties was defined as being "bounded on the east by the lines that divide Upper from Lower Canada, on the south by the river St. Lawrence, and westerly by the easternmost boundary of the late township of Cornwall, running north twenty-four degrees west until it intersects the Ottawa or Grand River, thence descending the said river until it meets the divisional lines aforesaid," and in addition to include all the islands in the St. Lawrence, nearest to it, and in the whole or the greater part fronting the county. In memory of the old home in the Highlands of many of its Scottish inhabitants it was given the name of Glengarry.

At the election for the Legislative Assembly held in the following month, John Macdonell and his brother, Hugh, were elected as members for the county, apparently without opposition.

The Legislature met at Niagara on September 17th, when John Macdonell was unanimously elected Speaker of the Assembly. The meagre minutes of that session contain no further reference to him beyond recording the fact that he occupied the chair on each of the nineteen days on which sittings were held, after his election as Speaker.

Soon after the adjournment, Simcoe appointed Hugh Macdonell Adjutant-General of Militia, "an Office," he remarked, "indispensable to the arrangement & management of the Corps, & whom I propose that the Province shall pay whenever they shall raise taxes for the support of Government. I hope," he added, "that it will be thought proper to furnish the Militia with Arms, due provision being made for their preservation in the Act; I have promised to submit to you a request of the MacDonnells of Glengarry, That a competent number of Broad swords, the property of the Crown, & now in store in Lower Canada may be issued to them, as I consider it both politick & just to encourage these settlers, who proved themselves such Loyal Subjects during the late war, I hope, Sir, for a favourable answer to the request."[1]

The second session of the Legislature began on the 31st of May, 1793, and was prorogued on July 9. The Speaker was apparently in the chair every day that the Assembly sat. The two measures to which the Lieutenant-Governor referred with particular approval in his closing speech were the Militia Bill and the Act for the gradual abolition of slavery and prohibiting the importation of slaves.

On July 13, Speaker Macdonell presented an address of the Assembly to the Executive Council asking a loan to pay the salaries and contingent expenses of that House and produced an estimate showing that the sum required amounted to £191 5s. The journals for the remaining sessions of that parliament and the first session of the next are not known to be extant.

In the spring of 1794, Lord Dorchester received instructions to raise "from among the Inhabitants of Upper & Lower Canada Two Battalions, not exceeding 750 Men each to be called respectively the first & second Battalion of the Royal

---

[1]Simcoe to Dundas, 4 Novr., 1792.

Canadian Volunteers."¹ Each battalion was to consist of ten companies with the usual proportion of officers and non-commissioned officers. In the selection of officers, he was advised to "pay particular attention to His Majesty's Canadian Subjects," and to appoint without favour or partiality "such as, from their Military Talents, Character & good conduct, & their attachment to His Majesty's Person & Government, will best promote the Honour and Credit of the Service."

These battalions were to "be merely provincial and for the Service of Upper & Lower Canada only, subject to the Control & Orders of the Commander in Chief in North America," and commissions were only to be granted to British subjects residing in those provinces.

Dorchester replied that the proposal came at "an unfortunate moment, such is the temper which at present prevails among the [French] Canadians that I am apprehensive it would have an ill tendency to make the Proposal known,"² but he transmitted his instructions with little delay to Simcoe and requested his recommendations for officers to command the battalion to be recruited in Upper Canada but at a later date this was limited to four companies to be incorporated in the first battalion.

Simcoe completed his list of officers by the end of June, recommending "Captn John McDonnell on the half pay of Sir John Johnson's Corps and Speaker of the House of Assembly" as major to command and eight other well known gentlemen as captains.

"In recommending Captn. McDonnell for the majority," he wrote, "I do it under the apprehension that he is the most proper person for that appointment upon all considerations within this Province. The Officers are named principally by Gentlemen of the Legislature who know them."³

A little later he wrote again:—

"I have intimated to the Speaker, Mr. McDonnell, whom I have offered to Your Lordship as Major (or Lieut.-Colonel) of the Canadian Corps that it would not be improper could he wait upon Your Lordship—In conversation he might explain many circumstances relative to the Province that cannot be dilated upon in correspondence. In particular his residence and influence with the St. Regis Indians may at present become serviceable; and in respect to the raising of Troops I have but little doubt but that the Highlanders will follow him in numbers, and it might appear to me that as Your Lordship in a particular manner turns your views to the defence of the Communication, somewhere near the County of Glengarry, where the McDonnells reside, would be a very proper station for the Quarters of part of the Provincial Corps, which is to be established."⁴

It would appear that Macdonell went to Quebec to consult with the Governor-General, for on the 26th of October, 1794, he wrote from that place to the Military Secretary:—

"As it will be necessary to bring the recruits raised in the Upper Province, for my Company, in the proposed Battalion of Canadian Volunteers immediately to Montreal, I request you will have the goodness to inform His Lordship that it will be attended with great difficulty, if not impracticable, to march them thither at this season of the year, I have therefore to beg that His Lordship will be pleased to order me a Batteau for this conveyance and a Weeks provision for thirty men.

"I beg leave likewise to suggest that it would be necessary to appoint Drummers for each Company."

---

¹Dundas to Dorchester, 15 Feby., 1794.
²Dorchester to Dundas, Quebec, 28 July, 1794.
³Simcoe to Dorchester, 30 June, 1794.
⁴Simcoe to Dorchester, 10 July, 1794.

A few weeks later a sudden change in policy was forecast perhaps through the uncertainty caused by reports of a treaty of amity concluded with the United States and on the 12th of December Macdonell informed the Military Secretary in a letter from Montreal:—

"In obedience to His Lordship's desire I shall immediately call in my recruiting parties, and cease enlisting any more men until further orders. Yet I should wish that some favourable opportunity offered of suggesting to His Lordship that as the Canadians begin to manifest a relish for the Service, the approaching Holy days would be a seasonable period to profit by. On the first November last Major Duke had approved of forty of my recruits.

"I am flattered by His Lordship's condescension in considering of a Gentleman for the Ensigncy of my Company; altho it may involve me in some embarassment having made a promise of it to a Mr. Ranald McDonell formerly a Lieutenant in the late 84th Regiment, and a Servant of the Crown for forty years nearly—Since I had the Honor of writing you last Lieut. Miles McDonell has joined me here with a party of twenty eight recruits from the Upper Province. Captain Spencer is likewise arrived with about thirty men of his Company."

On 18th December Captain Louis Genevay, the paymaster, wrote that 132 recruits had been approved and assembled at Montreal, ninety of whom had been enlisted by Major Macdonell and forty-two by Captain Spencer.

On the last day of January, 1795, Lord Dorchester transmitted a requisition to London for clothing and light infantry accoutrements for eight hundred men to equip one battalion of the Royal Canadian Volunteers. The uniform was described as a scarlet cloth coat, with blue lapels and cuffs, a red cloth waistcoat, and white cloth breeches, with a round hat, with black binding and a cockade. He reported that two companies were then at Montreal, nearly complete, and that two other companies, still in Upper Canada, were stated "to be in considerable forwardness."

Colonel Macdonell again presided as Speaker at the session of the Legislative Assembly held at Niagara in the summer of 1795, of which the journals have disappeared. On the 10th of August both Houses passed an unanimous vote of thanks in identical terms to Lieutenant-Colonel William Campbell of the 24th Regiment, in recognition of his conduct in command at Fort Miamis when threatened with an attack by an army of the United States the year before.

Colonel Macdonell's letter to Campbell has been preserved and reads:—

"It is with great pleasure that I communicate to you a Resolution of the House of Assembly of this date, by which the thanks of the House are voted to you in the following words, 'Resolved that the thanks of this House be given to Lieutenant-Colonel Campbell of His Majesty's 24th Regiment of foot for his temperate and dignified forbearance, and otherwise exemplary and meritorious Conduct at Fort Miamis during his command of it in the year 1794,' which I am required to transmit to you."

"House of Assembly,
Monday, 10th August, 1795."

The recruits of the Royal Canadian Volunteers seem to have remained at Montreal and Sorel for nearly or quite two years. Before his departure for England Lord Dorchester made a recommendation that they should be employed as garrisons of the frontier posts. Writing to the Duke of Portland on 16th April, 1796, he said:—

"Before I conclude it may not be amiss to observe that it would be of considerable advantage could all the Block-Houses on the Frontier be garrisoned by incorporated Militia; the Canadian Volunteers might serve as a Basis for that purpose; Desertion from the Regular Troops would by this Measure be rendered more difficult, the People in the Provinces would learn that all Disputes and Bickerings on the Frontier are their own immediate Concern; they would thereby be taught to defend themselves and to have a more just Esteem for the Protection which they receive from Great Britain."

The regiment was divided into two battalions on June 1, 1796, and Major Macdonell was appointed to command the second one with the rank of lieutenant-colonel. For some months the headquarters of this battalion was established at St. Jean in Lower Canada.

To enable the preceding proposal to be carried out the second battalion under Lieutenant-Colonel Macdonell was sent to Kingston and the Queen's Rangers then garrisoning the posts on the frontier were gradually relieved by detachments of it. On 23rd June, 1797, Major Hazelton Spencer, second in command, wrote from Kingston that:—

"The Light Infantry and half of the Colonel's Company destined for Fort George, and the two Companies for Amersburgh, (Amherstburg), Embarked on board the ship Mohawk and a small Gunboat, under the Command of Colonel McDonell on the sixteenth instant."

Captain Peter Drummond with forty-two other ranks had already been despatched in September, 1796, to relieve a small party of the Queen's Rangers at Saint Joseph's Island, which was supposed to be in serious peril from the ill temper of the Indians. Drummond arrived at Amherstburg on October 2nd and reached Saint Joseph late in the autumn. The Indians seemed as friendly as usual and readily consented to sell the island to the government. Captain Hector McLean with two companies, one of them being mostly composed of French-Canadians, commanded by Captain Joseph Vignau, did not arrive at Amherstburg until 22nd July, 1797. Apparently two companies were quartered at Kingston and the headquarters with the remainder of the battalion garrisoned Fort George at Niagara with its dependencies, finally including Queenston, Chippawa, and Fort Erie. Here they remained without any change of quarters until disbandment five years later. The officers at the out-stations seem to have received instructions directly through the Military Secretary and reported to him. They were thus made nearly independent of the control of the commanding officer of their battalion. All these garrisons were very weak.

In the course of the winter of 1796-7 information was received that the Spaniards on the Mississippi were planning an invasion of Upper Canada in conjunction with the Indians who were known to be discontented and supposed to be incited to hostility by French emissaries. This report seemed so reliable that the Administrator of the government published a proclamation to the inhabitants warning them to be prepared against an attack. The truth of the matter was that the Spaniards themselves were so much in fear of an attack that a considerable force was assembled for their own defence.

The conduct of Joseph Brant at this time was so suspicious as to cause much alarm. After delivering an inflammatory speech at a council held at Niagara in November, 1796, in which he strongly denounced the Executive government of the Province, he went to Philadelphia for the purpose of making a complaint to the British Minister, who was told that he had threatened that if he did not obtain redress through him, "he would offer his services to the French Minister Adet, and march his Mohawks to assist in effecting a Revolution and overturning the British Government in the Province."

The Minister was so much influenced by his statements and considered him "so determined, so able, and so artful," that he promised to transmit his complaints to the British Government in the hope of "averting a possible insurrection."[1]

The Governor-General took the precaution of sending two thousand muskets to Upper Canada to arm the militia and advised President Russell that "pointed regard" should be paid to the Indian nations, "particularly when it is known that evil-disposed persons are tampering with them and may endeavour to estrange their affections from the British Government and join its Enemies."[2]

Russell took the hint and at the end of June assembled the Executive Council which decided that the demands of the Six Nations to be permitted to sell a large part of their lands on the Grand River should be complied with. This concession seemed to allay their discontent and they professed strong attachment to the King. One company of militia in each battalion was warned to be in readiness for actual service, for which purpose the men were selected by a general ballot of the whole.

Meanwhile at the general election in 1796, John Macdonell had been re-elected as member of the Assembly for the second riding of Glengarry, and his sister's husband, Richard Wilkinson, had succeeded Hugh Macdonell as member for the first riding. The journal for the first session of the Legislative Assembly in that parliament has been lost, but it seems evident that Colonel Macdonell failed to attend. The reasons for his absence can only be conjectured. The second session began at York on the 6th of June, 1798, when the House was obliged to adjourn for want of a quorum. Many members were absent next day and a motion was passed that a call of the House should be taken on the 9th and that the clerk should be instructed to write to the absentees requiring their attendance. When the call was made three times in succession six members failed to respond of whom John Macdonell was one. Two were excused by motion on the ground of illness and it was then moved by the Solicitor-General, R. I. D. Gray, the member for Stormont, and seconded by Captain Thomas Fraser, member for Dundas, "that Colonel John Macdonell do stand excused for his non-attendance by reason of indisposition and of the strong probability of his arrival to take his seat in the course of the day should the state of his health permit." The motion was adopted and after the transaction of some further business Macdonell came in, made and subscribed the oaths, and took his seat. Before adjourning the Speaker, D. W. Smith, addressed the House, saying:—

"As you have done me the honour to call me to the Chair of this House I feel it a duty I owe to the recollection of the services of Colonel Macdonell to move you that in order to mark the sense I entertain of his former situation as Speaker a place be considered as appropriate to him during the present Session being the first next the Chair on the right hand." The House unanimously agreed to this recommendation.

The minutes do not show that he took a very active part in the subsequent proceedings. On June 12th, he seconded a motion for the adjournment and on the 13th seconded a motion by the Solicitor-General for the second reading of

---

[1] Robert Liston to Prescott, 8 April, 1797.
[2] Prescott to Russell, Quebec, 11 May, 1797.

a bill to amend the Act respecting the practice of the Court of King's Bench. On June 18th he seconded a motion to adjourn and on the 20th his name appears first among the yeas in a division in favour of the third reading of a bill "to authorize and allow persons coming into this Province to settle to bring with them their Negro Slaves," while his friend, the Solicitor-General, and his brother-in-law, Captain Wilkinson, both voted in the negative. Macdonell's name was then added to a committee appointed to carry up the bill to the Legislative Council. On June 22nd a motion was passed granting him leave of absence for eight days from the 25th, and as the Parliament was prorogued on July 5th, it does not appear that he again attended during that session. The Committee on Public Accounts reported that they had observed in the Treasurer's statement a payment of £100 to Colonel Macdonell "for a Commission into Lower Canada in the year 1796 and another in 1797, which they anticipate to be a clerical mistake, as by the Journal it should appear to be in 1794," and they recommended the payment of a balance of £200 due to him as salary while he was Speaker.

In the autumn of 1798 the alarm of an impending attack from the westward was again renewed. On October 5th General Prescott wrote from Quebec to President Russell:—

"I received very lately confidential Information that a French General named Collot, who was amongst others engaged in a Plan for Stirring up a Rebellion in Canada, went into the Western Country in the Summer of 1796 & 1797 to prepare the Indians to make an attack upon Upper Canada, at the same time that a French force should come into Lower Canada. When he (Collot) left that Country, he promised the Indians that he would return in 1799, and they expect him accordingly. He was to sail for France in the beginning of July to assist in concerting measures for renewing the above Plan.

"The above Communication is to be relied upon, and I take the liberty of handing it over to you; that if possible you might discover what Tribes of Indians in the Western Country have been tampered with by the before mentioned Frenchman, that measures may be taken to prevent the intended mischief."

Similar information was no doubt sent to Colonel Macdonell and the officers commanding the frontier posts. Captain Hector McLean, who commanded at Amherstburg, had quarreled fiercely with Mathew Elliott, the local superintendent of Indian affairs, and succeeded in having him dismissed, but he assured the Military Secretary that "every attention" would be paid to the Indians and "that there will be no cause for discontent, they are perfectly satisfied & the officer Capt. McKee who has the direction of them appears to have the Kings interest at heart & to be perfectly reasonable & totally disinterested if left to himself & not under the influence of his father."

Russell received Prescott's letter on November 2nd and replied the same day that the information contained in it and another from the Duke of Portland, received on September 27th, combined with a conversation he had lately had with Brant, convinced him that "a very dangerous cloud hangs ready to burst over the Province. And I am sorry to mention in Confidence to Your Excellency that I have not at present the means of discovering with any degree of certainty in what Tribes of Indians we may place an implicit trust." The Indians of the Grand River he thought would prove faithful, but Brant had told him that he had no doubt of the hostile feeling of the Caughnawagas and others of the Seven Nations of Canada whom he believed to be "strongly in the french Interest." Russell asked for an increased regular force and stated that he had given orders

Glengarry House Cairn.

to all the Lieutenants of Counties to arm and keep one hundred men in each battalion of militia "in constant Preparation to attend the first summons." The arms and ammunition sent up the year before had been distributed among them equally. The militia of Long Point and the County of Lincoln numbered almost a thousand men who were "Staunch old Soldiers and may be depended upon."

At Russell's request an Indian was sent by Brant to Detroit to gain information, who reported that an Ottawa chief called the Otter had shown him a belt which he said he had received from the Caughnawagas the last summer and explained its meaning in the following words:—

"That there were about four thousand Indians friends to the Spaniards met in a Body at the mouth of the Mississippi who were to begin their march in four months time to meet the Indians to the Westward at White River and this is what they say—If you meet us at the White River according to our request we shall consider you as friends—but if not take care and go out of the way—for we have a big Stick and a Broad Foot, and in case you interfere with our plans or designs we will knock you down and tread you under foot." The messenger added that on his way back a Muncey chief had told him that nearly all his tribe had decided to leave the Thames and join the Spaniards at the White River.

Russell sent this information to McLean, telling him that "in case the Invasion of this Province turns out to be more serious than I at present Judge it to be," he would order a body of militia to do garrison duty at Amherstburg.

McLean bluntly pronounced the whole story to be an invention, "totally void of foundation." He stated that the Otter positively declared that the messenger had never seen him and that no belt had ever been sent to him by anybody. "I have written to the officer Commanding at Detroit," he added, "and he treats the idea with the utmost ridicule. These reports have without doubt originated with the Dept. themselves and supposed Calculated Chiefly with a view to impose a belief on the President that the importance of the Crisis on the eve of a pretended invasion required that the office of Dep't Superinten't Gen'l of the Indians should be filled up immediately, lest otherwise it should be thought so unnecessary as to be discontinued and their consequence thereby diminish'd, and to add to their weight and influence in Upper Canada it was thought good policy to recommend two members of the Council to the succession."[1]

Alexander McKee, the capable Deputy Superintendent of Indian Affairs, had lately died, but his secretary, Selby, sent messengers to the Mississippi, who reported on their return that the Indians showed no inclination to be hostile. Brant, however, asserted his belief that "the French are busy among the Indians and they will (if possible) Invade the Country."[2]

By the middle of May Russell was convinced that the report of preparations for an attack from the west was "a mere fabrication for selfish Purposes," but at the same time he was able to state that "this little Alarm has however had the pleasing & satisfactory Consequence of evincing the loyal zeal of His

---

[1] Captain Hector McLean to Captain James Green, Military Secretary, Amherstburg, 21st March, 1799.
[2] Joseph Brant to Peter Russell, Grand River, 27th Jan., 1799.

Majesty's Upper Canada Subjects & the Capability of the Province to repel any Indian hostile attempt against it as two thousand Volunteers immediately offered themselves as Detachments from the Militia ready to march with Arms in their Hands to any part whither I should judge proper to order them, & have ever since held themselves in a State of readiness for that Service."[1]

He repeated this statement in a speech to both Houses of the Legislature on June 12th. The first mention of Colonel Macdonell's presence occurs in the Journal on June 13th, when he seconded a motion for the second reading of a bill to revive and continue an Act for the better securing the Province against the King's enemies, and on the following day he was appointed the chairman of a committee to carry that bill up to the Legislative Council and inform them that the Assembly had concurred in passing it without any amendment. On June 22nd he seconded a motion of the Solicitor General that a bill to improve and amend the communication between Lakes Ontario and Erie by the construction of a canal with locks at the rapids near Fort Erie should be considered in a committee of the whole. His name does not appear in a division taken on June 27th, nor does it occur again in the Journal of that session which ended on June 29th. The President in proroguing the Legislature urged the members to recommend "their constituents not to relax in their attention to Militia duties, and to keep that portion of each battalion (which has been selected by my desire for active service) in a constant state of readiness to go wherever wanted."

A return of the state of the second battalion of the Royal Canadian Volunteers, dated 3rd April, 1799, shows a total strength of thirty-five officers and 476 other ranks, and a subsequent statement made on the 1st September in the same year shows a total of thirty officers and 502 others and a deficiency of 289 rank and file wanting to complete the establishment. Another return, dated 1st October, showed that between 1st July, 1796, and the 1st September, 1799, one hundred and twenty-seven men of the battalion had deserted, of whom twenty-seven had returned.

The Legislative Assembly was called to meet on the 2nd of June, 1800, but was adjourned for want of a quorum until the 5th, when Samuel Street was elected as Speaker on a division, to succeed D. W. Smith, who was absent. Colonel Macdonell voted in the negative. He appears to have attended regularly as his name is recorded in the Journal as having been present on sixteen days, and on one occasion when a call of the House was taken, he was one of the four members who answered their names. The meagre report shows that the business transacted was unimportant.

The Duke of Kent had been lately appointed Commander in Chief in British North America, and he had suggested that much advantage might be gained in the event of an invasion by placing all the provincial regiments on the footing of fencibles for service anywhere in North America. The Colonial Secretary approved this proposal on the condition that "the Extension of their services, if it shall take place, shall be purely voluntary on their part, in the strictest sense of the word."

---

[1]Peter Russell to the Duke of Portland, York, 18th May, 1799.

When it was made known to the officers and men of the Royal Canadian Volunteers stationed on the Niagara, they promptly agreed to it, and the result was reported by Colonel Macdonell in a letter to Lieutenant General Peter Hunter, dated at Fort George on 20th February, 1800:—

"The suggestion that the services of the Second Battalion Royal Canadian Volunteers might be usefully extended to the different parts of North America in general was no sooner known to the five companies forming the garrison in this post, Fort Erie, and Fort Chippewa, than they most cheerfully offered and generally showed a desire to extend them to any part of His Majesty's dominions.

"The officers (as might be expected from such Loyalists) expressed satisfaction at having an opportunity of testifying their zeal and attachment to their King by tendering their services in any part of the globe to which they might have the honour of being called. I shall have the honour of reporting to you as soon as possible the sentiments of the other four companies at Kingston, Amherstburg, and St. Joseph. I think, however, I can vouch that their zeal to His Majesty's service is not less than the companies I have already mentioned. The example of the Nova Scotia and New Brunswick Corps is certainly highly meritorious, and would no doubt operate strongly in exciting an emulation in others, but I have the vanity to believe that the Second Battalion of Royal Canadian Volunteers would have offered their services even had the other Provincial Corps not shown the example."

At a later date he was able to state that the remainder of the battalion had also volunteered for general service.

On the 1st of September, he made his first application for leave of absence in the following terms:—

"Not having it in my power to examine into the state of the Militia of the County of Glengarry, nor of my private affairs since the first raising of the Royal Canadian Volunteers, I take the liberty to request of Lieutenant General Hunter leave of absence for a few weeks for those purposes.

"Captain MacMillan has requested me to apply for leave of absence for him on private affairs in Glengarry, he not having been absent since he first joined."

Before leaving his headquarters Colonel Macdonell succeeded in making the arrest of a person who was believed to be an active agent of the French Government in its designs against Canada. During the summer of 1798 the British Minister in the United States received confidential information from reliable sources that a number of agents of the French Directory residing in that country were in correspondence with disaffected persons in Canada, with the intention of promoting an insurrection. Among these was named a certain Louis Le Coulteulx, who had announced his intention of visiting Upper Canada and Detroit, it was supposed, in connection with this design. Mr. Liston reported this to the Foreign Office and also to the Governor General. It was to some extent corroborated by Dr. Nooth who had visited Albany and had conversations on the subject with John Jay, then Governor of the State of New York, and other friendly persons, whose suspicions of the conduct of some of the French emigrants were frankly stated. A letter on the subject from the Military Secretary had been received by Macdonell as early as the 5th of April, 1799.[1] Replying to this on May 24th, he remarked:—

"Aware of the probability that attempts might be made by the French to disturb the quiet of His Majesty's Subjects in this Province, I have been particularly cautious and attentive to the Orders respecting the admission of Frenchmen or other Aliens. But it affords me the greatest

---

[1]FROM JAMES GREEN TO OFFICERS COMMANDING AT KINGSTON, FORT GEORGE, AND AMHERSTBURG.

Quebec, 28th Feby. 1799.

SIR,
The Cautions so frequently given respecting the Admission of Aliens, and particularly

satisfaction to say with Confidence that I think the Loyalty of the Inhabitants of this Province in general is such as to render the success of any attempts of this nature highly improbable."

He had obtained a description of Le Coulteulx, probably from a correspondent in the State of New York, which he sent to Captain McLean at Amherstburg. Nothing more was heard on the subject until 7th October, 1800, when Le Coulteulx landed from a boat at Niagara. He was met at the wharf by the adjutant, who recognized him from the description given, and conducted him to Colonel Macdonell, who at once ordered his arrest and seized his baggage and papers. Le Coulteulx appealed for protection to Major Rivardi, the commandant at Fort Niagara, also a native of France, who very courteously enquired the reason of his detention and forwarded a letter of introduction of Le Coulteulx to him, from Timothy Pickering, the Secretary of State, describing him as a naturalized citizen of the United States. Macdonell replied that as he was a Frenchman, who had left France since the period designated in the Alien Law, and was unprovided with a passport from one of the British Secretaries of State, it was his duty to detain him until the pleasure of the Commander in Chief was known. The arrest was reported by him in a letter to the Military Secretary in the following terms:—

"Agreeably to the directions contained in your letter of the 28th February, 1799, I have been continually on the look out for Mr. Le Coulteulx, and on the 7th Instant had the satisfaction of securing him in this Post—having had notice of his being on the way some days before he arrived, he was met at the moment of his landing on this side by the Adjutant and after having informed him that he had Orders to conduct him to the Commanding Officer, He answered yes that he was then on his way to pay his respects to the Commandant of the Garrison. Having ascertained him to be the identical Person described in your letter, I had him confined in the Officers Guard Room, until an opportunity to send him on to Head Quarters—as the season is so far advanced that I could not reasonably expect further instructions in time to put them into execution before the closing of the Navigation on Lake Ontario—I therefore judged it proper to send him to Kingston in charge of Lieut. Malhiot on Board of the Schooner Speedy to be forwarded in such manner as Lieut. Col. Smith may think necessary from thence—The Style of his travelling is not such as is commonly adopted by Indian Traders—His Private Baggage consists of a Vast quantity Frenchmen, have hitherto rendered abortive many plans conceived by Individuals for disturbing the tranquillity of the Province.

A vigilant attention to the orders on that subject, on your part, is at the present moment as necessary as ever, and perhaps more so, when we consider that from the late Successes of His Majesty's Arms, the Enemy has been considerably foiled in his endeavours elsewhere, and may turn his thoughts towards this Country. The relative situation of America is another circumstance which may induce the French to endeavour at forwarding disturbances here.

For the above considerations the Commander in Chief relies on your unwearied attention to these objects, and directs me to acquaint you, that he has received information that a Frenchman, named La Couture or Couteulx, an Agent from the French Directory, resident at Albany, and hitherto engaged in Mercantile pursuits there, is on the point of, or has already perhaps set out for Niagara and Detroit. His Excellency desires that you will use your best endeavours to ascertain his arrival, and should he cross over to the Post or dependencies under your Command, that you will secure him; and either send him to Head Quarters under sufficient Escort, or Report for further Instructions—We have unfortunately no description of his Person—It is not impossible but he may mask his hostile intentions, under pretence of being an Indian Trader.

I am &c.
JAMES GREEN, M.S.

(Postscript to Major Spencer at Kingston.)
The above letter was written to the Officers in Command at Fort George and Amherstburg, but the principle respecting Aliens being applicable to every Post, and it being possible the Person therein described may elude the Vigilance of the Officers above, and visit Kingston with a view of descending to Lower Canada by that Route, His Excellency has directed me to send it to you for your guidance and information.

J. G.

of Linnen and other Household Furniture which have been examined with his Goods and Papers by a Board of Officers appointed by a Magistrate but nothing material has been discovered. This goods and Baggage are secured here in Store But all his Papers are sent along with the Prisoner under lock & Key—His Examination taken before a Magistrate, and three other Papers regarding Mr. Le Coulteulx's Cargo, are enclosed herewith. I take the liberty also of enclosing a Copy of a letter I received from Major Rivardi on the subject of Mr. Le Coultculx's detention with my answer thereto."

After the prisoner arrived at Quebec, his papers, of which there was a great quantity, were examined and copies of letters written by him, which he had been so unwise as to bring with him, were found, expressing intense hostility to Great Britain and advocating the invasion and reconquest of Canada by the French. Other letters indicated that he was on terms of intimacy with the Duc de La Rochefoucauld-Liancourt and M. Volney, both of whom seem to have visited him at Albany, where he was then established as a merchant.[1] The question of his disposal was at once referred to the Attorney General of Lower Canada, who gave an opinion that the papers found in his possession and other information respecting him did not warrant his detention by the civil power, but being an alien enemy he might be legally detained as a prisoner of war until the pleasure of the King was known. As Mr. Le Coulteulx was well educated and influential, great efforts were made to secure his release. John Marshall, then Secretary of State for the United States, made a direct application for it, at the request of the President, to the British Minister, who was induced to intercede on his behalf. Writing to General Hunter on November 19th, 1800, he said:—

"I look upon him as being by no means the dangerous Man he has been represented to be, and the manner in which he entered the Province is a species of Proof that he had no design to act as a Spy, or to attempt to endanger the tranquillity of the Government. On the other hand I have the best authority for saying that he is a Person of a humane and liberal disposition, and in his private Conduct deserving of general approbation. I therefore flatter myself that you will have the goodness to allow the poor Man to pursue his journey to Detroit (which seems to have been his object) and I shall regard your obliging attention to my interference on this occasion as a personal favour conferred on me."

Before this letter had been received, General Hunter's report on the subject with the Attorney General's opinion and copies of the most incriminating documents had been forwarded to the Colonial Office. Subsequently a letter was received from Alexander Hamilton, pleading for Le Coulteulx's liberation on the ground that he was a naturalized citizen of the United States, which was likewise forwarded. The case was then submitted to the Law Officers of the Crown in England for a further opinion. They advised unanimously that he should be detained as a prisoner of war during the continuance of hostilities with France, if sufficient evidence was not obtained to ground proceedings against him in the civil court. In consequence he was held in confinement at Quebec until 29th July, 1802, when he was released after the ratification of peace.

[1]Mr. Le Coulteulx afterwards became a resident of Buffalo, N.Y., where he died in 1840 at the age of eighty-four. A careful memoir of his life by Miss M. J. F. Murray has been published in the ninth volume of the Publications of the Buffalo Historical Society, pp. 431-453, to which is appended translations of extracts from the letters which led to his detention as a prisoner of war, and the letters from Pickering to Rivardi, from Rivardi to Macdonell, from Macdonell to Rivardi, the opinion of Attorney General Sewell, and letters from General Hunter to the Duke of Portland, referred to above, and now in the Colonial Office Records. As the letters from Mr. Liston and Edward Thornton, his Secretary, to General Hunter, the opinion of the Law Officers of the Crown in England and the subsequent letter from the Duke of Portland to Hunter, have considerable interest and have not hitherto been printed, they are now included in an appendix to this sketch.

The service of the battalion at the frontier posts was uneventful and it was finally disbanded after the ratification of the treaty of Amiens on the ill-founded belief that what was actually only a temporary suspension of warfare would prove to be a permanent peace. Probably it had never been completed to the full establishment. One company, and perhaps more than one, consisted chiefly of French Canadians. Among the officers appear the historic names of Chaussegros de Lery, de Hertel, Taschereau, Malhiot, Duchesnay, Boucherville, and Lorimier. The actual discharge of the men at Fort George took place on 30th August, 1802. On the 12th of that month, a council of the sachems, chiefs, and warriors of the Six Nations at the Grand River was held at the council house in the town of Niagara. They took advantage of the occasion to conclude their speech to the Deputy Superintendent General, Colonel William Claus, with the following words of farewell to Colonel Macdonell:—

"We have a few words more to say. We have already mentioned our attachment to our ancient forms and customs; it is one of them to lose no opportunity of expressing our gratitude at least by our thanks; and we take this occasion of thanking our friend, Col. Macdonell, (whose intention, we understand, is soon to leave this place) for his long friendship for the Six Nations, and his ready compliance with all their requests, whilst in command here. May the grateful remembrance in which he shall ever be held by the Six Nations on the Grand River be a pleasant reflection to him wheresoever he may be."

To this message Colonel Macdonell next day replied:—

"Brothers,
"Indisposition, which prevented me from meeting you yesterday in council, hinders me also to-day from returning my thanks in person, for the affectionate and kind mention which you were pleased to make of me in your speech.
"Brothers,
"The affection and esteem which attaches me to your nations, are too firmly rooted in my breast ever to be eradicated; they were formed in the hour of common danger and common service, and shall accompany me wheresoever I may be."

Many of the principal inhabitants of the town and district, having assembled for that purpose on August 28th, presented the following complimentary address to Colonel Macdonell:—

"The magistrates and the principal inhabitants of the district of Niagara, fully sensible of the many advantages that attend a proper understanding between the military and the civil parts of society and having now the prospect of parting with you and the regiment under your command, request to say that we never, in this respect, have experienced greater satisfaction and comfort than during the five years you have commanded the Royal Canadian Volunteers in Fort George and its vicinity.
"We are happy in recollecting that during all this period, no sort of disturbance, that hardly any cause to complain has occurred between them and the inhabitants, whose persons have been as free from anything like insolence or insult, as their property has been safe from any sort of depredation. We with justice ascribe this to your unremitting care of the discipline of the regiment, to the friendly attention of the officers, and to the character of the men.
"For these comforts we thus personally request that you will accept of our grateful acknowledgements, and that you will have the kindness to communicate these our sentiments, accompanied with our best thanks to the officers, non-commissioned officers, and to the men of the corps, that they will carry with them our warmest wishes for their happiness and success, in whatever situation they may be placed; and we most sincerely pray that health and every other blessing may attend you and them."

Colonel Macdonell replied:

"The very flattering mark of your attention, with which you have been pleased to honour me, is altogether as unexpected on my part as it is unmerited.
"I have always conceived it to be the duty of a Commanding Officer to employ the authority which our gracious Sovereign hath committed to him, for the protection of the persons and civil rights of all fellow-subjects within his command. Give me leave, however, to say that it

will always be a matter of the most grateful recollection to me, that the gentlemen of the district of Niagara have given this public testimony of their approbation of my conduct during five years command among them.

"I am about to retire to a private station, and cannot help expressing my most hearty wish that the district may enjoy every blessing which a brave, loyal, and industrious people can never fail to possess while fostered by the kindness and protected by the power of the United Kingdom of Great Britain and Ireland.

"I shall take the earliest opportunity of communicating to the officers, non-commissioned officers, and men of the second battalion of the Royal Canadian Volunteers, your very favourable sentiments and approbation of their conduct."

Upon disbandment taking place, Colonel Macdonell prepared a careful and strongly worded memorial on behalf of the officers to be placed on the half-pay list. Most of the senior officers, including himself and all the staff officers, were already entitled to this, from their former services, according to the rank they then held, but one captain, and all the subalterns with two exceptions were excluded from any claim by the terms of their engagement. The memorial urged, however,

"That the destructive ambition of His Majesty's enemies having, contrary to all expectations, protracted the war to such a length, your memorialists have now remained embodied nearly eight years; the consequence has been that the domestic affairs of your memorialists of the first description [half pay officers] have in that long interval of absence and unavoidable neglect been materially impaired, and they will be now obliged (unless His Majesty's gracious favour be extended to them) to return to their homes at a more advanced period in life and with prospects less favourable both for themselves and their families than when the War began. Your memorialists of the latter description [sons of half-pay officers] are involved in a still more gloomy situation, for having dedicated the flower of their years to a military life, and having passed in His Majesty's service that period of their lives during which they might have embraced other professions, unless some provision be made for them by the munificence of their Sovereign, having no resources of their own, it is painful to foresee the hardships and difficulties which must await them.

"Your memorialists therefore most humbly pray of Your Excellency that you will lay them at His Majesty's feet, beseeching him that he will be graciously pleased to place them upon the half pay list according to rank which they at present hold in his service.

"And that His Majesty will also be graciously pleased to extend to the Battalion the same gracious bounty in donations of waste lands of the Crown which was extended to the Provincial Corps at the end of the American War—a measure which, besides filling the hearts of your memorialists with additional gratitude, would at the same time place at the disposal and within the immediate call of His Majesty's representatives in this Province a body of loyal disciplined men, attached to the country, and proud of transmitting their own principles and sentiments unimpaired to their posterity, and your memorialists as in duty bound will ever pray."

In respect to half pay this petition was unsuccessful, but the non-commissioned officers and men seem to have been awarded the grants of land asked for them.

Colonel Macdonell then returned to his residence at Glengarry House in ill health and considerably impoverished in estate. War with France was again declared in May, 1803, and three years later relations with the United States had become very alarming. Colonel Macdonell then made a proposal to raise a battalion of volunteers for local defence in the following letter addressed to Mr. Windham, then Secretary of State for the Colonies:

"County of Glengarry,
Upper Canada,
9th July, 1806."

"SIR,

"I have the honor to forward to you the accompanying proposals for embodying a corps of Volunteers in the County of Glengarry of which I have the honor to be Lieutenant. Our settlers are all to a man Scots Highlanders, either loyalists who fought for their King & Country during the American Rebellion & their children, or emigrants whom the conduct of the Highland proprietors at home, or the invitation of their friends here, have induced to quit their native country & settle in this Province. We can raise at the shortest notice a Corps of 500 Men independently of our Militia which are 730 strong. With every sentiment of loyalty & attachment to the person and government of our Sovereign in common with our fellow subjects we consider ourselves peculiarly bound in gratitude and affection to the munificence of our Royal benefactor who has been graciously pleased to confer upon us valuable landed properties in this country, from which we already derive ease & comfort, as well as weight & consequence in the state; & we are not only determined to defend those with the last drop of our blood, but feel eager to contribute our share to the general defence of the British Empire. With the accession of strength which we receive from the numbers of our countrymen that annually arrive amongst us and the advantageous situation of our settlements bordering upon the lower Province, and occupying almost the whole space between the Great Rivers Ottawa & St. Lawrence, we might form a strong and effective barrier to this part of the Province & frustrate any attempt of an external enemy. Should these proposals, however, not answer the views of Governt we shall be always ready to enter into any other that may appear more calculated to strengthen the hands of administration, & render essential service to the Country.

I have the honor to be &c.,
J. McDonell, Lieutenant of the County of Glengarry."

"Rt. Honble William Wyndham."
"Proposals to raise a Corps of Highland Volunteers in the County of Glengarry, Upper Canada.
"To consist
of 1 Colonel, 1 Lieutenant Col., 1 Major, 7 Captns., 10 Lieutenants, 10 Ensigns, 1 Surgeon, 1 Chaplain, 1 Qr. Master, 1 Adjutant, 1 Serjeant Major, 20 Serjeants, 30 Corporals, 20 Drummers & 470 Privates
on the following Conditions—
"1st. That the Corps be completed in 3 months without any Levy.
"2d. That it receive arms & cloathing from Governt immediately after the Inspection.
"3rd. That it be embodied only for 3 months of the year & serve in their own district, except in case of Invasion or threatened Invasion when they shall serve in any part of the Province & while the danger continues to exist.
"4th. That such of the officers as have been formerly in the service be put upon the full pay of their respective Ranks & those who have not served before receive the full pay of their Ranks during the time that the corps continue embodied."

This proposal received the warm support of Colonel Isaac Brock, then commanding the regular troops in Canada, but was not adopted at that time, "on the ground that every attempt of this nature has generally failed and at this moment the Canadian Fencibles, though endeavouring for nearly three years to compleat, consist of only 124 Men by the last Return."[1]

The project was revived in a different form in 1811 and led to the formation of the Glengarry Light Infantry, which rendered such remarkably distinguished services in the war with the United States.

Colonel Macdonell's marriage with Miss Helen Yates, of Schenectady, it is stated, occurred while his battalion was stationed at Fort George. His wife belonged to an influential family, several of whom have been considerably distinguished in the professional and political history of New York, and one of her brothers took an active part in promoting the construction of the first Welland Canal. They had one son, Alexander, who served as major of the Lancaster regiment of Glengarry militia in the suppression of the rebellion of 1837-8, and two daughters, all of whom died without leaving children.

---

[1]Charles Stewart, secretary to Lord Castlereagh, to Colonel Brock, Downing Street, 25th April, 1807.

Tablet to mark the site of Glengarry House, near Cornwall, Ont.

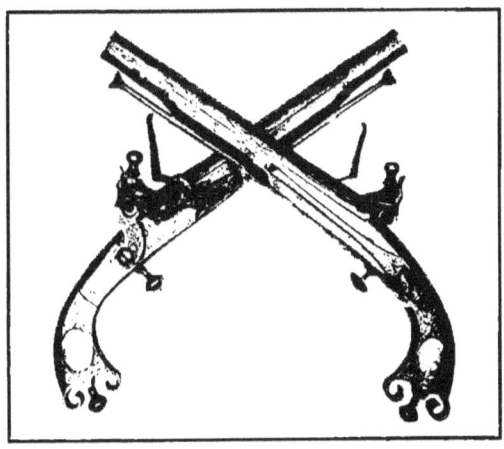

Silver-mounted flint-lock pistols which belonged to Colonel John Macdonell, of Glengarry House, now in possession of J. A. Macdonell, Alexandria, Ont.

A MEMOIR OF LIEUTENANT-COLONEL JOHN MACDONELL 57

Mr. J. A. Macdonell quotes a letter from Mrs. Ross, Colonel Macdonell's sister, to her brother Hugh, who was then Assistant Commissary General at Gibraltar, which seems to have been written some time in 1809:

"By a letter from Chichester [Macdonell] who had letters from Canada, I am sorry to find that our brother John's health has been on the decline, and I fear his means also. Chichester has procured him the paymastership of the Tenth Veteran Battalion, which will be something in the meantime. Had he not trusted so much to other people, he would not have been under the necessity of accepting of such a trifle. Poor fellow, he thought all the world as honest-hearted as himself."[1]

His anonymous biographer, in a Montreal newspaper, also remarks:

"The Colonel's active benevolence was known to all and experienced by many of his Friends. There was something so generous, so noble in his manner of doing a kindness of this sort, as to give it a double value. In 1807 he was appointed Paymaster to the Tenth Royal Veteran Battalion, a situation certainly far below his merits, but his circumstances which, owing to his generous disposition, were by no means affluent, induced him to accept."[2]

No military rank was attached to that appointment, but it was by no means undesirable, as the battalion had been lately sent to Canada for garrison duty, and its headquarters were established at Quebec. In the Quebec almanac for the year 1808, the name of John Macdonell of Glengarry House appears as lieutenant of the county of Glengarry, heads the list of commissioners of the peace for the Eastern District of Upper Canada, and is first of the three commissioners in the same district for administering the oath to half pay officers. In the following year it is no longer on the latter list. He figures in that publication as paymaster of the 10th Royal Veteran Battalion in 1808, 1809, and 1810.

His contemporary biographer concludes his sketch with the following words:

"He had been exceedingly infirm for many years and perhaps the severe climate at Quebec was too much for his weak constitution; certain it is, that this City has been fatal to several respectable characters from the Upper Province. He caught a severe cold in the beginning of November, 1809, accompanied with a violent cough and expectoration, he was not indeed thought dangerously ill till within a short time of his death, but his feeble constitution could not support the cough and he expired on the twenty-first. Such are the scanty materials which I have been able to collect respecting the life of a most excellent officer and honourable Man, who became dearer to his friends and acquaintances the longer he was known to them. He was rather below the middle size, of a fair complexion, and in his Youth, uncommonly strong and active. For some time past his appearance was totally altered; insomuch so, that those, who had not seen him for many years, could not recognize the swift and intrepid Captain of the Rangers. An acute disease made it frequently painful for him to move a limb, even for days and weeks together, but though his body suffered, his mind was active and benevolent, and his anxiety to promote the interests of his Friends ceased only with his life."[3]

---

[1]Sketches of Glengarry in Canada, pp. 102-3.
[2]*The Canadian Courant and Montreal Advertiser*, 28th January, 1811.
[3]Ibid.

APPENDIX.

I

City of Washington
19th November, 1800.

Sir:—

General Marshall, the American Secretary of State, has informed me that Mr. Lewis Le Coulteulx, has been detained as a Prisoner by Colonel McDonnell, the Commanding Officer at Niagara, on suspicion of his having entered Canada with some improper intention; and General Marshall has in the name of the President requested my interposition to obtain his liberation.

I am far from being ignorant of the notices which have from time to time been communicated to his Majesty's Government respecting the Character and the Views of Mr. Le Coulteulx; I even transmitted some of the information in question myself But I am now convinced that those notices were, if not erroneous at least much exaggerated; I look upon him as by no means the dangerous Man he has been represented to be, and the manner in which he entered the Province is a species of Proof that he had no design to act as a Spy, or to attempt to endanger the tranquillity of the Government. On the other hand I have the best authority for saying that he is a Person of a humane and liberal disposition, and in his private Conduct deserving of general approbation. I therefore flatter myself that you will have the goodness to allow the poor Man to prosecute his journey to Detroit (which seems to have been his object) and I shall regard your obliging attention to my Interference on this occasion as a personal favour conferred on me.

I have the honour to be, etc.,

Rob. Liston.

A true Copy of the Inclosure contained in Mr. Thornton's letter of the 4th December, 1800, to me.—Rob't. S. Milnes.

II

Philadelphia, 4th Dec'r. 1800.

Sir:—

I have the honor of informing you that Mr. Liston left this city on the 2nd Inst., on his way to Norfolk in Virginia where he will embark for the West Indies, and that I have taken the liberty of opening the letter relating to Mr. Le Coulteulx which you did him the honor to address to him on the 6th of last Month.

During his last visit to the new seat of Government at the City of Washington application was made to him in behalf of Mr. LeCoulteulx by the American Secretary of State; in consequence of which he addressed to Gen'l Hunter a letter of which I have the honor of enclosing a copy—It would be presumptious in me to say more on this subject than to express my hope that you will be pleased to allow Mr. Le Coulteulx to return into the United States unless there have been produced against him proofs of improper practices, of which Mr. Liston was not aware, and to which I am persuaded the members of the American Government would be as little disposed as himself to give countenance by their interference.

I take opportunity of informing Your Excellency, that the Charge of the King's affairs has been committed to me during the absence of His Majesty's Minister and that I shall take particular pleasure in executing any commands whether of a public or private nature which you may be pleased to lay upon me.

I have the honor to be, etc., etc.,

Edw'd. Thornton.

III

10th February, 1801.

My Lord Duke,

We are honored with your Grace's letter of the 14th Ult., transmitting to us Copies of a letter and its Inclosures from Lt. General Hunter dated Quebec 19th Nov'r, 1800, and desiring us to report to your Grace our opinion whether, under the circumstances mentioned therein, His Majesty is authorized during the continuance of the War between this Country and France, to retain Mr. Le Coulteulx as a Prisoner of War. We conceive that according to the strict rule of Law every native of an Enemy's Country may be considered and treated as an Enemy and may therefore be seized and detained as a Prisoner of War—It is true that Nations do not in practice act up to the rigour of this right—But where a particular motive for enforcing it happens in any case to exist, it may undoubtedly be exercised—The Government appears to have such a motive in the present instance from the knowledge it possesses of Mr. LeCoulteulx's designs and conduct— The circumstance of Mr. LeCoulteulx having been naturalized in the American States does not, as we conceive, in any manner affect the right of arresting and detaining him when found within His Majesty's Dominions—For altho' an Enemy born is when domiciled in a Neutral Country, considered to certain purposes, as one of the people of that Country, yet no inference can from them be drawn that an Alien Enemy is entitled to claim within the British Territory all the Privileges of Personal security, which a mere neutral might be entitled to enjoy—The Act of another Country cannot deprive this of the right of taking such Precautions as it may judge necessary to guard against the Hostile disposition of any of its Enemies.

We are therefore of opinion that His Majesty is authorized during the continuance of the War between this Country and France to detain Mr. LeCoulteulx as a Prisoner of War in Canada, in case there should not appear sufficient evidence to ground a proceeding against him by the Civil Power.

We have etc.,

J. NICHOLL.
J. MILFORD.
WM. GRANT.

IV

Whitehall, 12th February, 1801.

SIR:—

I lost no time in submitting your letter of the 19th of November last, relative to Mr. Le Coulteulx, to the Law Officers of the Crown for their consideration and Opinion, whether, under the circumstances therein mentioned, His Majesty is authorized during the continuance of hostilities between this Country and France, to retain Mr. LeCoulteulx as a Prisoner of War, and I take this opportunity of transmitting to you a Copy of their Report upon that subject—I have only to add that His Majesty's Servants perfectly concur with the opinion expressed therein— You will therefore consider yourself as authorized to detain Mr. LeCoulteulx at all events as a Prisoner of War as long as Hostilities continue between this Country and France, in case there should not appear upon Inspection of the Papers which you state to have been found upon him, sufficient Evidence to ground a Criminal Prosecution against him; but should anything be discovered of a nature to Warrant such a Proceeding, you will not fail to take such measures as will ultimately lead to his conviction.

I am Sir,

Your most obedient humble servant,
PORTLAND.

Lieut. General Hunter, etc., etc., etc.

V

THE INCEPTION OF THE WELLAND CANAL
By Brig.-General E. A. Cruikshank, LL.D., F.R.S.C., F.R.Hist.S.

The labour, expense, insecurity, and uncertainty attending the transportation of supplies from Montreal by way of the St. Lawrence, Lake Ontario, and the Niagara had been forcibly brought to the attention of the public in Upper Canada during the protracted period of hostilities with the United States in 1812–14, lasting upwards of thirty months. As no roads fit for the conveyance of heavy articles were in existence, except in the winter, when not blockaded by snow, and a sufficient number of horses or carriages were not available if they had been passable at other seasons of the year, there was no alternative highway. The cost of taking a single 24-pounder gun from Quebec to Amherstburg was estimated to be six hundred pounds, and it was stated that the fortunate contractors for the transportation of government stores from Montreal to Kingston, in the winter of 1814–15, cleared a profit of £30,000. In time of war the danger of interruption was very great. To obviate this an alternative route from Montreal to Kingston by the Ottawa and Rideau rivers was proposed and explored by Lieut.-Colonel George Macdonell, of the Glengarry Light Infantry, and Captain Reuben Sherwood, assistant quartermaster-general of militia, who was a land surveyor. The invasion of the Niagara peninsula in 1813 had compelled the British commander to send supplies for the forces defending the Detroit frontier in the first instance from the head of the lake overland to the Grand River, and finally to Oxford on the Thames. The feasibility of connecting Lakes Erie and Ontario by a canal was suggested. As it seemed evident that the construction of such artificial channels for navigation would contribute greatly to the security of the Province, it was not unreasonably believed that assistance might be obtained from the British treasury.

After the war, the rapid progress made in the construction of the Erie canal not only attracted much interest but excited positive alarm lest the whole commerce of the lakes should be diverted by it. In his speech on opening the session of the provincial legislature on 4th February, 1817, Lieutenant-Governor Gore, after referring to the "liberal appropriation made by the last session for the improvement of the roads," added that "the water communication of the River St. Lawrence below Prescott is also deserving of your serious consideration." An appropriation was made in consequence for a survey of that part of the river. A petition was presented from Adam Dixon, a merchant of Cornwall, praying for authority to construct locks at Moulinette and Mille Roches, as a means of "facilitating the intercourse between the two Provinces, particularly at a time when in a neighbouring country every effort is made at internal improvements for the purpose of diverting into new channels that trade which we have hitherto enjoyed." His petition was supported by a dozen merchants of Upper

THE INCEPTION OF THE WELLAND CANAL

Canada and by seventeen companies in Montreal, but was opposed by Alexander Hover, who had already built a lock at the Moulinette, and by David Sheek, who was constructing another at Mille Roches.[1]

At the session of 1818, a joint address of the two houses was adopted, declaring the improvement of the navigation of the St. Lawrence to and from Montreal to be a subject of "the first importance," and stating a "desire that concurrent means may be adopted by both Provinces for effecting so desirable an object on liberal and united principles, essential to the interests of each Province in a commercial, and to our Parent Country, in a political view."[2]

Thomas Clark and James Crooks were appointed commissioners to confer with George Gordon and Joseph Papineau, who had been selected to represent Lower Canada, whose legislature had voted five hundred pounds to commence improvements in the navigation. A joint report was made in which the commissioners declared:

"First. That they are fully convinced that no Public undertaking will be more conducive to the progress and prosperity of the agriculture and commerce of both Provinces, to the augmentation of their wealth in time of peace, and to their security and defence in time of war, than by facilitating the communication of their internal Navigation.

"Second. To secure to these Provinces the advantages of the Trade they already possess, it is urgent that no time should be lost in forwarding the work necessary to facilitate such water communication before the United States may have completed their grand Canal from Lake Erie to the Hudson River, in the State of New York; which canal when so completed will carry to New York the numerous and precious cargoes which would continue to be exported by the Province of Quebec if both Canadas availed themselves of the means they have to carry the same at a smaller expense and in a shorter time by the natural outlet of the St. Lawrence."

They agreed to recommend to their respective legislatures that the construction of any public canals on that route should be prohibited by law, in which the locks were of less size than those of "the Great Western Canals in the State of New York."

The Commissioners for Upper Canada recommended the appointment of commissioners from each Province "with adequate means to act in conjunction, for procuring with all possible dispatch accurate surveys, both of the St. Lawrence and Ottawa Rivers, together with estimates of Canals and Locks for boats and vessels of different constructions, to be laid before the two Legislatures for their selection and approval."[3]

Within a week after the presentation of this report a plan to connect Lakes Erie and Ontario by a canal was brought to the attention of the Legislature by a petition to the House of Assembly from the inhabitants of the District of Niagara, dated at Niagara, 14th October, 1818, which stated:

"Your Petitioners, viewing the great benefits these provinces will derive from having a Canal made between Lakes Erie and Ontario, have examined

---
[1] Journals of the Assembly, 21st February, 1817; 24th February, 1818.
[2] Ibid., 10th March, 1818.
[3] Journals of the Assembly, 30th October, 1818.

the Report on levelling the land between Chippawa and the source of the Twelve Mile Creek, and have every reason to believe a communication can be effected at a trifling expense, from the accompanying plan which will be submitted to Your Honorable Body. From the source of the Twelve Mile Creek where the excavation will end, to the brow of the Mountain at Captain De Coo's is a gentle descent, not a lock will be necessary; after descending the Falls it will be necessary to make locks to pass four or five Milldams, and the navigation will be complete for boats to Lake Ontario.

"The grand object of the American people appears to be opening a navigation with Lake Erie, which design our canal, if effected soon, would counteract and take down the whole of the produce from the Western country.

"Your Petitioners therefore beg that you will appoint some scientific men to view the country between Chippawa and Lake Ontario, and adopt such measures for carrying the above objects into effect as you in your wisdom may deem meet."[1]

This petition was signed by Thomas Dickson, Chairman of Quarter Sessions in Sessions, and seventy-four others. It soon became evident, however, that local opinion was not unanimous in its support.

On 17th September, 1818, the *Gleaner* newspaper, published at Niagara, by Andrew Heron, a leading merchant, had warmly supported the improvement of inland navigation, in an editorial, which said:

"We are glad to find that one of the first acts of His Grace, the Commander in Chief [the Duke of Richmond] has been to appoint Commissioners to meet those on the part of Upper Canada to report what measures are necessary for the improvement of the water communication in Upper and Lower Canada. We do think that the greatest part of the surplus money belonging to this province ought to be devoted to that purpose. It is a large field and will immortalize the name of its patrons. It is to be hoped that what is done will be done on a large scale. Nothing less than a line of navigation from Quebec to Lake Huron ought to be contemplated, 6 or 7 feet water will carry vessels large enough to navigate the lakes, less would be throwing away money. But is it not strange, passing strange, that upwards of £50,000 was by the Assembly of Lower Canada appropriated for the purpose of making a canal from Montreal to Lachine 5 years ago and not one pound has yet been expended. Surely no time could have been more proper for commencing a work of the kind. Vast numbers of emigrants have arrived every year at the port of Quebec for several years, who would have been glad to be employed in such a work, many of whom went to the United States to work on the north and west canal in the State of New York and are lost forever to the population of Canada. We have always considered the public money laid out on the highways in this province as more usefully applied than to any other purpose, some may still be necessary for that purpose but we consider the improvement of the water communication now to be the most necessary. Nature has done much; a little assistance of art is only necessary to complete an inland navigation of 1,000 miles from Quebec through the centre of as fine a country as any in the world.

---

[1] Journals of the Assembly, 4th November, 1818.

"Should the State of New York succeed in their intended canal (as no doubt they will) a barrel of flour or pork will never be sent from Lake Erie to Montreal unless a water communication is made between Lake Erie and Lake Ontario and the navigation from Prescott to Montreal improved. This, our friends in Lower Canada will perhaps find to be the case when too late."

But some six weeks later, the same newspaper expressed its disapproval of the suggested route.

"We have perused a communication in the Niagara *Spectator* of the 22nd inst., respecting the advantages of a canal from the waters of Chippewa to Lake Ontario by the way of 12 Mile Creek. We understand that a petition will be presented to the Legislature for funds to carry it on. Should that body have funds for that purpose we presume they would consider it necessary to have surveys of the different routes and adopt the best.

"If the intention is to bring the canal down the mountain in the channel of the 12 Mile Creek, we consider that impracticable as the great freshets that come down that stream collected on the high lands would impede the navigation at times and injure the locks. It would also be very difficult to form a harbour on the banks of the lake even for boats, the great body of loose sand would render it very difficult upon a large plan. We are decidedly of opinion that the canal should come into the Niagara river, where every vessel would be sure of a good harbour and a lock could be constructed to receive vessels of 100 tons burthen. We have little doubt but a canal could be cut from the mouth of the Chippawa and be constructed near the banks of the river to Queenston or St. David's; besides other advantages it would save 15 miles of water carriage from the mouth of the Chippaway to where the canal (from the 12 Mile Creek) would enter.

"We understand surveys will be laid before them of the best way of improving the line of navigation from Lower Canada to Prescott. We presume it will take all the funds to be spared for some time. Whatever is done we hope it will be done on a large plan; paltry improvements are only throwing away money."[1]

The petition was considered in a committee of the whole House and referred to a select committee of four members, of which James Durand was chairman, as "containing matter of great national importance."[2]

The Province had little surplus revenue and no credit. The select committee could scarcely do more than express sympathy in general terms.

"It is the opinion of your Committee," their report stated, "that a canal cut agreeably to the plan proposed by the Petitioners alluded to would be of great benefit to the Commercial Interests of this Province, and ought to be encouraged by every means of furtherance by Your Honorable House.

"And your Committee are further of opinion that should any number of persons be disposed to associate themselves for the purpose of carrying such a project into execution, it would comport with the true interests of this Province to give to such an incorporated body the authority and sanction of law, and to provide for their obtaining the use of such lands as may be required for the cutting

[1] *Gleaner*, 29th October, 1818.
[2] Journals of the Assembly, 6th November, 1818.

of said canal in a manner similar to that already pointed out by the Statute for the improvement and altering of Highways and Roads throughout this Province."[1]

A joint address of the two Houses was adopted praying for the appropriation of a portion of the "waste lands of the Crown for the purpose of improving the navigation of the River St. Lawrence, and for cutting canals through this Province," and an Act was passed granting two thousand pounds for making surveys of that river and other purposes, but no measure was taken to provide the money.[2]

Two steamships were than plying on Lake Ontario and one on Lake Erie. The revolution in lake traffic had begun. The commerce of the upper lakes had greatly increased but was mainly carried on by citizens of the United States. In December, 1818, Sir Peregrine Maitland reported that "there are at present 80 schooners employed in navigating Lake Erie, vessels capable of carrying in the event of war, either one or two guns of the larger calibre, of these not more than ten belong to, or are navigated by, subjects of His Majesty."[3]

In transmitting the joint address of the Houses of the Legislature for the grant of crown lands for the improvement of navigation, he remarked that this would be inexpedient except with great circumspection, and advised that, in any event, the reserves should not be alienated as that would materially "injure the interest of the Crown."[4]

Probably no one in or out of the Legislature had a more intimate personal knowledge of the difficulties of transport to and from Montreal than Lieutenant-Colonel Robert Nichol, who had been quartermaster-general of militia during the war, and since 1812 a member of the Assembly. He had been absent in England during the two sessions of the provincial parliament held in 1818. As chairman of the select committee on public accounts in the following session in the summer of 1819, he presented a report, which showed a deficit of £16,600 to be provided for by new taxation, and made the suggestion that "of the above deficiency the sum for the survey of the River St. Lawrence may not be called for, and with a view of relieving the Provincial Revenue from the present pressure, it might be desirable to address His Excellency, the Lieutenant-Governor, requesting him to suspend the operation of the Bill until the funds are provided to meet the expense."

It further remarked rather ruefully: "With heavy appropriations, and without sufficient funds to meet them. the Executive Government would be placed in a most embarrassing and degraded position, from which they cannot be effectually relieved without the interposition of Your Honorable House. These difficulties will doubtless suggest the propriety of some legislative provision to meet every exigency of service for the current year, as well as to place the Revenue of the Province on such a footing as will prevent a recurrence of the evil."[5]

---

[1] Journals of the Assembly, 17th November, 1818.
[2] Ibid., 19th November, 1818.
[3] Maitland to Bathurst, No. 13, York, 8th December, 1818.
[4] Maitland to Bathurst, No. 11, York, 7th December, 1818.
[5] Journals of the Assembly, 25th June, 1819.

Old Welland Canal at Thorold.

Newly constructed Welland Canal (1881) at Thorold, looking north.

Two views marking two stages in the development of the Welland Canal in the transition of half a century ago. Preserved in "Water Routes from the Great Northwest," Harper's New Monthly Magazine, August, 1881, Vol. LXIII, p. 415.

The delay in proceeding with the surveys was therefore entirely due to the lack of money to carry them on. Political discontent and economic distress among the scanty population had found an indiscreet and voluble spokesman in Robert Gourlay, whose letters and speeches provoked the wrath of the Legislature and alarmed the government. A special Act was passed for the suppression of seditious meetings, which probably increased the former discontent. The lieutenant-governor himself reported that Gourlay was "sinking into insignificance" when he was unwisely arrested and ordered to leave the province. On his refusal he was committed to jail, which Maitland predicted would give him a "new interest for a time." Yet he allowed the prosecution to proceed and even dismissed two sheriffs for having taken part in public meetings prohibited by the Act.[1] This agitation tended to divert public attention from the proposed improvements of internal navigation. Yet the scheme of connecting Lakes Erie and Ontario by a ship canal had still some zealous advocates. Early in 1819, William Cosgrave addressed a long letter on the subject to Hon. Henry Goulburn, then Under Secretary of State, in which he said:

"The distance between Lakes Ontario and Erie at the utmost is not above 20 miles and in some parts a junction might be found at from 12 to 15 miles by a Canal connecting these lakes formed sufficiently capacious for Vessels of 100 Tons Burden who might then sail from Montreal for a distance of 1,000 miles without interruption or unshipping as at present. By this Portage the Upper Settlers are totally prohibited from bringing down their Timber in rafts or Staves to the Montreal Market, whereby much valuable timber (especially oak and pine Masts fit for Naval purposes) is prevented being exported to the Mother Country who is compelled to buy in Foreign Markets.

"I beg to state that unless this Canal was formed sufficiently large for Vessels of 100 Tons Burden it would be almost useless for in that case the small Vessels would have to load and unload into the larger which would be attended with very nearly the same expense as is now paid at the portage and another strong argument for having a capacious Canal is to allow Rafts of Timber and of Staves to be floated to Montreal that being one of the Settlers Staple Commodities, and on which they must bring down Flour, grain, &c."

He urged the employment of the soldiers stationed in Canada upon this work, and predicted that the completion of the canals in the State of New York connecting Lakes Erie and Champlain with the Hudson River would seriously injure the trade of Montreal unless counterbalanced by the canal he proposed[2].

A reply to the address asking for a grant of crown lands in aid of the improvement of navigation was laid before the Legislature at the session held in 1820, stating that assistance would be "readily afforded," but requesting information as to the extent of grants of money which would be voted for this purpose, before entering into a discussion on the subject. As the deficit for the year amounted to nearly twenty thousand pounds, the Committee of Finance expressed the opinion that the sum appropriated for a survey of the St. Lawrence "cannot be considered an urgent demand."[3]

[1] Maitland to Goulburn, 22nd July, 1819; Maitland to Bathurst, 4th March, 1820.
[2] Cosgrave to Goulburn, 18th January, 1819, printed in full in Dr. Brymner's Report on the Canadian Archives for 1897, pp. 63-5.
[3] Journals of the Assembly, 24th February, 7th March, 1820.

In his speech on opening the first session of the eighth provincial parliament of Upper Canada on February 2, 1821, Sir Peregrine Maitland asked the members not "to overlook the means which tend to increase the wealth and power of the country. The last objects," he said, "have been unusually advanced by the late emigration from the Parent State, but still a great augmentation of wealth and population from this source must be counted among the numerous advantages that would attend on the improvement of our land and water communications, thereby rendering access easy to a country that offers to capital and skill a wide field for agricultural improvement, and ample materials for many purposes of commercial enterprise."[1]

A select committee of eight members of the Assembly was at once appointed "to take into consideration the Internal Resources of the Province in its agriculture and exports, and the practicability and means of enlarging them; also to consider of the expediency of granting encouragement to domestic manufactures." Robert Nichol was elected as chairman of this committee, although James Crooks, who had been a commissioner to Lower Canada in 1818, was a member.[2]

On the last day of March a lengthy and carefully prepared report was presented, which made some definite recommendations for the construction of canals.

"The great and indeed only efficient measure by which, in the opinion of your committee," this report said, "a permanent relief can be afforded to the commerce of Upper Canada, 'and the safe, easy, expeditious and economical exportation of our staples to the markets to which we have access can be secured,' is the improvement of our inland navigation.

"This is a measure, which in the opinion of your committee, claims the earliest and most profound attention of your Honorable House. It is a measure deeply involving the national interests as well as the commercial prosperity of the Province, and one, which if entertained by your Honorable House, should in the opinion of your committee be undertaken on an extensive scale, a scale commensurate with the increasing power and rapidly accumulating commercial resources of the Province.

"That it is perfectly practicable to connect the Lakes Erie and Ontario with Montreal by canals of sufficient depth to enable vessels of burthen to sail without unloading directly to that port cannot be doubted. The successful enterprise of our jealous neighbours sanctions your committee in forming this opinion, and is an example that ought to excite us to similar exertions.

"We ought not to allow ourselves to be deterred by the magnitude of the undertaking from undertaking at all. Difficulties there are no doubt, but they are not insuperable, and will be found to be comparatively insignificant when encountered by perseverance and determination.

"That the Province is without funds for carrying on a work of this nature, upon even the most moderate scale, your committee most readily admit, but they are also inclined to believe that by a proper representation of the subject to His Majesty (whose gracious intentions have already been communicated

---
[1] Journals of the Assembly, 2nd February, 1821.
[2] Ibid., 5th February, 1821.

to the House) and to the imperial Parliament, setting forth the real and substantial advantages which the opening a water communication upon a grand scale from Lake Erie to the sea, would produce to the interests of the Mother Country and the colonies, that His Majesty and His Imperial Parliament would concur in enacting such laws, and in giving such facilities and encouragement to this stupendous undertaking as would ensure its success.

"To entitle ourselves, however, to the active aid of the Imperial Government in this great measure we must evince a disposition to contribute to it to the extent of our means; for we ought not to expect our Mother Country to expend her resources for our benefit, while we, who will so immediately reap the advantage are restrained by cold, narrow, selfish feeling from giving our fullest support to the measure necessary to its success.

"By the report of the American Canal Commissioners in January, 1817, it appears that the great Western Canal, when completed, will be in length 353 miles 29½ chains; in width on the water surface 40 feet, in width at the bottom 28 feet, and in depth of water 4 feet. That the length of the locks is ninety, and their width in the clear twelve feet. That the estimate of the total expense for completing the said canal is four millions eight hundred and eighty-one thousand seven hundred and thirty-eight dollars; or, at the average rate, including the expense of constructing seventy-seven locks, of about \$13,830, or a little more than £3,000 sterling per mile. And from subsequent reports of the same commissioners it appears that hitherto the work has been done at a rate greatly within the estimate. This then is data for us to go upon, and by which we may be enabled to form a tolerably correct estimate of the sum it would require to complete a work of such vast utility. Your committee in this first report, do not consider it necessary, neither are they prepared to go into any detail respecting the canal. They wish merely to draw the attention of the Government and the House to the subject. The views, however, of your committee generally are that a work of this description should not be on an exposed frontier, but should be, wherever circumstances admit of it, inland. Could it be completed on a scale which would enable the Government to bring the smaller-sized vessels of war right into the lakes, it would prove in the opinion of your committee the best barrier against the future hostile attempts of the United States of America that could be formed. Military protection and commercial facility would thus be united, and the Province of Upper Canada, instead of being as it is at this particular time a dead weight upon the Government and commerce of Great Britain, would be one of her most flourishing colonies.

"Your committee, therefore, respectfully recommend to your Honorable House to pass a bill appointing commissioners,

"First.—To devise and adopt such measures as shall be requisite to facilitate and effect a communication by canals and locks between the Lakes Erie and Ontario, and Lake Ontario and Montreal.

"Second.—To examine and explore the country for the purpose of determining the most eligible routes for the contemplated canals; to cause surveys and levels to be taken, and maps, field-books, and draughts to be made, and to adopt and recommend proper plans for the construction and formation of the said canals, and also of the locks, dams, embankments, tunnels, and aqueducts, and to cause all necessary plans, models, and draughts thereof to be executed.

"Third.—To calculate and estimate the expense of the above operation.

"Fourth.—To devise and recommend ways and means for carrying the above purposes into effect."[1]

This report was adopted and an Act passed for the appointment of commissioners to carry out these recommendations. In his speech on proroguing the Parliament, Maitland declared that this bill "may be considered as the commencement of an important undertaking eminently calculated to advance the prosperity and greatness of Upper Canada."[2]

John Macaulay, a member of the Legislative Council, and Charles Jones, James Gordon, and Robert Nichol, members of the Assembly, were appointed commissioners. They employed Samuel Clowes and James Clowes as engineers, and Reuben Sherwood as surveyor, and a route from Kingston to the Ottawa river was explored in the summer of 1823, and an estimate prepared for the construction of a canal one hundred and twenty-five miles in length, seven feet in depth, forty feet in width at the bottom and sixty-one feet in width at the surface of the water at a total cost of £69,785. Estimates were also submitted for a canal to connect Lake Ontario with Burlington Bay for the establishment of a safe and commodious harbour at the head of that lake, in which it was suggested that aid might be obtained from the Admiralty. The two reports of the commissioners on these subjects are dated December 20, 1823.[3]

Meanwhile an engineer, who had been engaged in making a survey for a canal around the Falls of Niagara on the New York side of the river, was engaged by Captain William Hamilton Merritt and some of his friends to make a preliminary survey for a canal to connect Chippawa Creek with the west branch of the Twelve Mile Creek. An estimate was made for a canal designed for the navigation of large boats, which were to be conveyed up and down the escarpment by wooden railways, and additional water-power would be supplied for the mills on the latter stream. "The whole expense of the route," the engineer reported, "exclusive of railways is $34,550, and boats of 20 to 40 tons will navigate it with ease from Lake Ontario to Chippawa in a day or a day and a half at farthest."

A public meeting was held and arrangements were made for printing the engineer's report, and it was resolved to apply to the Legislature for the passage of an Act of incorporation for a company to carry out the construction of the proposed canal and railways to be operated by water-power.

A good many years afterwards Mr. Merritt prepared a narrative relating the early history of this company, a copy of which is preserved in the collection of manuscripts made by George Coventry, now in the Library of Parliament in Ottawa. This copy contains some obvious clerical errors, which have been corrected as far as practicable in the following transcript.

---
[1] Journal of the Assembly, 31st March, 1821.
[2] Ibid., 14th April, 1821.
[3] Report of the Commission on the Improvement of Internal Navigation, Colonial Office Records, Q. 335-2, pp. 299-323.

It may be proper to observe that Mr. Merritt had actually attempted the manufacture of salt at a considerably earlier date than that mentioned in his narrative, as the *Gleaner* under date of January 1, 1818, contained the following statement:

"We learn with pleasure on perusing the *Spectator*, that Mr. Merritt has succeeded in obtaining a supply of water sufficient to make a quantity of salt. It is earnestly to be wished that all those who have springs of the same kind would make exertions to make salt enough to supply the country. Besides the neat price paid for salt imported from the State of New York, a duty of 62½ cents is paid to the state which ought to be an inducement to farmers to purchase what is made in the country, if it can be done on nearly equal terms."

THE NARRATIVE OF WILLIAM HAMILTON MERRITT.
(*Coventry Manuscripts, U. E. Loyalists, pp. 261-302.*)

I purchased a Mill site on the 12 Mile Creek, built a House in [the] village of Saint Catherines and erected a flour mill.

On examining and preparing the foundation and water capabilities, I discovered a salt Spring, which was looked upon as a great boon to the vicinity as Salt was a scarce and dear article, having to procure it from the Onondaga Government Salt works in the States.

At one period during the War, it was sold as high as $10 to $15 per Bushel and since has varied from 5, 6, to 7$ per barrel.

Governor Simcoe Considered Salt so essential to Farmers that he took considerable pains to procure without being dependant upon the States for a supply.

Accordingly a Salt Lick having been found at Louth in 1793 some Government Works were established on a small Scale, which as far as they went, were of considerable utility to the neighbourhood, but the demand in time was so great that Onondaga was obliged to be resorted to and the Government works not paying the expenses, they were abandoned.

On the 23 June, 1820, I commenced digging at the centre Spring 12 Mile Creek, assisted by Messmore Williams. The ground was very salt, yet firm, being a blue sand mixed with clay. About 12 feet down we came to Red Clay.

The same distance as at Lower Spring. Three feet lower down came to what was supposed to be Rock.

On the 1st July commenced boring through Red Clay.

After considerable difficulty got the well lined with Timber and a Tube fixed for boring again.

On the 10th July at 25 feet from the surface we came to Rock and 6 inches further a strong vein of salt water; had much difficulty in keeping out the clay.

Stopped boring at a distance of 64½ feet. The works were continued, and the following year Salt was for sale to the farmers and others around at one Dollar per bushel.

They were carried on for many years by Dr. Chase on a considerable Scale.

Still they could not cope with the Government works at Onondaga in the States and were consequently abandoned.

The Land was afterwards sold to E. W. Stephenson who erected upon the Scite a magnificent Hotel, and converted the Salt works into Baths which have been of great service to Invalids from all parts of the Country, and United States.

The boring was continued to the depth of 500 feet, so that the supply never fails; the strength of the water is about 11 per cent. similar to that of natural sea water.

From the brine a chemical residuum is produced called Calchism [sic] which is efficacious in most internal complaints.

Although Canada abounds in Salt Licks the former resort of Deer and Cattle, there does not appear to be any Spring so powerful as that of Onondaga, consequently the Salt manufactured in the Country is on a small scale.

No Rock Salt has hitherto been found although it abounds in the Columbia River towards the Pacific, but hitherto has been of no practical use to the Community.

As the Western Country opens no doubt many things will be discovered that have hitherto escaped notice.
God has provided everything available for man's use, and it remains for his labour to convert them into some tangible use.

* * * * * * * * *

The Water intended for the working of my Mill was supplied by the 12 Mile Creek, which took its rise on high grounds in the vicinity of Beaver Dams, Short Hills, and up the valley.
Finding that the supply was too limited in the summer months from that source, I first conceived the Idea of obtaining a further supply from the Chippewa, the summit of which was but 2 miles distant. This being impracticable to be accomplished by one individual, I applied to various others suggesting my Ideas on the subject.
For my own satisfaction I took the levels, having at School learned the principles of Surveying.
In this important step I obtained the assistance of practical men as witnesses to the final result; it was accomplished with a water Level in the country.
This trivial affair shews what Stupendous works arise from small beginnings; As the Welland Canal was the final result.
The preliminary proceedings were kindly noticed by the *Gleaner*, a paper then rising into public Notice.

WELLAND CANAL PROJECT.

April 12th, 1823.

A subscription has been opened in this District for the purpose of Surveying and taking the Level of the Land lying between the Chippawa River and the source of the nearest stream leading into Lake Ontario, with a view of connecting these Waters that they may become Navigable.
We are happy to see the names of our most respectable and Influential Inhabitants at the head of the list, and trust they will be liberally supported.
The subscription paper will be left with Mr. John Crooks of this Town.
We are credibly informed that the distance between the Chippawa and the source of the 12 Mile Creek is no more than 2 Miles. In a month or two we hope to publish the report of the Engineer on this interesting subject.

NOTICE.

A public Meeting of the Inhabitants of this District of Niagara will take place at Mr. McLelland's Inn, Broadham, on Saturday the 28th [June] at 10 O'Clock, to take into consideration and adopt measures to facilitate the opening of the proposed canal between Lakes Erie and Ontario.
Every person interested in the prosperity of the Country it is hoped will give their attendance.

July 5th, 1823.

To the Editor of the *Gleaner*

I fear your remarks in the last *Gleaner* relative to the Canal route by the 12 Mile Creek may have a tendency to weaken the public confidence at a distance, and deter those from taking Stock who would otherwise have been inclined to do so.
There is no analogy whatever between the Mohawk River and the 12 Mile Creek.
You will see by the Engineer's report, that a very small sum will make this stream a regular Canal.

W. H. Merritt.

THE INCEPTION OF THE WELLAND CANAL

PUBLIC NOTICE.

We the undersigned Freeholders of the District of Niagara intend petitioning the Legislature, the next Session of Parliament, for the purpose of connecting Lake Erie with Lake Ontario.

George Keefer.
William Chisholm.
George Adams.
Job Northrop.
Jos. Smith.
J. Decow.
Thomas Merritt.
P. Shipman.
Wm. Hamilton Merritt.

Nov. 8, 1823.

Mr. Editor,

In looking over the New York *Spectator* of a late date, the celebration of the grand American Canal, in the State of New York, at Troy and many other places, naturally drew my attention to the grand object which our enterprising and persevering neighbours are about completing and have nearly finished.

In viewing the probable rate of transportation on the said canal from Buffalo to New York, it must afford every person or inhabitant of this Country, no small share of satisfaction, in perceiving that the rates for conveying each and every barrel of flour, and any other kind of produce of equal weight, far exceeds the actual rate from any part of Lake Ontario to Montreal —in this point we have to congratulate ourselves upon the unexpected event, for it was the opinion of many individuals, that after the entire completion of the Canal mentioned, the freight of produce and other articles would be much lower than it is in reality.

The inducement, however, which an open communication will hold out, between New York and Upper Canada must be flattering to the people of the United States and although real apprehension may be entertained on the commercial trade on the part of this Province, Lower Canada has nevertheless still more to fear if the Merchants are not more conciliatory towards us from the growing intercourse between the United States and this Country, and it will without the slightest doubt, increase to an alarming degree, and prove particularly injurious to our trade with Lower Canada.

Therefore in order to alleviate the many impending(?) evils, which every intelligent mind must easily see, are about to arise, both to the revenue and to the Country, it becomes our duty and should be our sole aim to endeavour to draw the whole trade from the Western District and keep it within ourselves, by means of Canal and other improvements, we have remained too long in a dormant state, but we should rejoice to perceive that a few spirited individuals have at length taken the welfare of the District into consideration by exerting themselves in order to facilitate the opening of a Canal from the Grand River to the Chippawa Creek, and from thence across to the Beaver Dams, where it will intersect the Twelve Mile Creek, and continue on to Lake Ontario.

As to the whole distance which it will be necessary to cut, it is not possible for the present to speak with certainty; the cut through the whole route cannot, however, exceed seven miles altogether. It may be stated with confidence that that part from the Chippawa to the brow of the mountain where it meets the Twelve Mile Creek, requires an artificial cut of two miles only.

AN OBSERVER.

Thorold, 25 Nov., 1823.

On reading the *Gleaner* of the 8th Instant I observed a communication signed by a gentleman who composed the committee chosen at the meeting held at the Beaver Dam, on the 5th July, stating that they intended to apply to the Legislature of the present Session for an Act to carry the Canal through any route between the two Lakes, that might be found most advantageous, this is liberal, this is as it ought to be, I shall therefore beg leave to lay before the public my opinion on the subject, if you will be kind enough to give it an insertion in your useful paper. I find after repeated attempts, no place can be found near so convenient to bring the waters of the Chippawa over the high lands called the mountain, as that in the middle branch of the Twelve Mile Creek, as far as the face of the mountain.

The greatest objection to its proceeding down the Channel of the Twelve Mile Creek to the West or main branch, is the great freshets some times in that Creek, and the want of a harbour for vessels at its mouth.

The idea of a Railway in the middle of a Canal, I consider as a bad plan. Was it at one end where the goods had to be unloaded, it might answer, but to haul loaded boats over a Railway would be a bad plan, besides it would put a stop to all rafts of timber coming down, which might be a great branch of trade.

Now to obviate all those difficulties, I would propose the following route. Let the Canal descend the east branches of the Twelve Mile Creek to the face of the Mountain, eastward, which would bring it near to the rivulet called the Ten Mile Creek, then down the Channel of that Creek which I believe is almost on a dead level to the cross roads on E. Vanderlip's lands, from that to the town of Niagara is eight miles, I believe very near level, in that route there are no stones, some parts are clay, and some parts sand. It might extend most of the way on the side of the road, which is streight to the Town, where there is a spacious harbour, which can be entered by night or day.

This would not prevent the people on the Twelve Mile Creek from receiving an additional supply of water, which appears to be the principal object of the present plan.

Many are the Advantages of this route, besides having a good harbour, the Town of Niagara is the only market for all the produce of our farms, wheat excepted.

We could then easily carry not only our butter, Oats, &c., &c., but our Wood and even stones, the finest of any in Canada, are in abundance in that route.

The benefits to you and to us would be reciprocal.

We would carry to Market articles of no use to us, and you would be supplied with timber, both for fuel and building, and stone fifty per cent. less than they now are. Should the plan proposed find a corner in the *Gleaner*, I may offer something more on the same subject another time. I have conversed with several neighbours on the subject, who are much of my mind.

Decr. 8th, 1823.

Mr. Editor,

Under the head of communications in the *Gleaner* of the 29th last, I note the sentiments of a Gentleman upon the subject of the contemplated Canal in the lower part of the District.

I should not have replied to this communication, were it not that it savours something of an answer to my former Address, from one upon the same subject, and as we do not fully agree upon many points I now take the liberty of making a few remarks thereto.

In the first place our correspondent states that no place can be found so convenient as the present route lately laid down by an eminent Engineer from the Chippewa to the brow of the Mountain, intersecting the 12 Mile Creek.

So far I am willing to acquiesce with him, but as to the frivolous objections which he has brought forward, I must certainly beg leave to differ with him, for they are founded upon such grounds as the nature of the case cannot possibly admit under the argument which he advances.

The objection to its proceeding down the Mountain under the construction of the Railway is erroneous in the extreme—is it reasonable for a moment to think that the Directors of the projected Canal would allow the ascent of boats and their contents to interfere with the progress of produce, lumber, &c., coming downward.

It is a very easy matter to construct it upon such a principle, as to prevent the carriers of various kinds of commodities to pass each other without the least necessity of interfering or meddling one with the other.

It has been suggested according to the original intention that any craft of whatever shape or form if capable of navigating the Canal, will be propelled by a water-wheel of sufficient power to convey it bodily, if compatible with safety, to its destination.

If it is not convenient to take a Boat up bodily the Cargo may follow immediately in a machine adapted for the conveyance of Goods. And may be so arranged that in the event any two (or more) meeting one another, the one may continue on her descent whilst the other is ascending.

This can be done free from any inconvenience or danger.

Should this not meet the approbation of "A.B." and his neighbours we can then as a substitute for the Railway have a regular line of Locks, through the ravine which has an easy and gentle descent. Nature has been prolific in this respect, and, as it were, designed for the purpose to which I trust it may be applied.

I consider his plan of constructing the locks along the face of the Mountain as a bad design, for it would not only require an additional number of locks from what might be intended in the ravine, but create further expense which would be quite unnecessary and would add to the delay in the ascent.

Many impediments will here present themselves which we will not have to contend with in the intended route, and it is a matter of doubt whether it is practicable to complete his design.

Locks would in my estimation claim the first right, were it not that they are attended with much trouble, difficulty and expense, but possibly be the cheapest in the end.

January 3d, 1824.

We have the pleasure of informing our readers that a bill to incorporate a Company to make a Canal from the waters of Lake Erie to Ontario has passed both Houses of Parliament, and no doubt is entertained but it will receive the Assent of the Lieutenant Governor. Books will no doubt soon be opened to receive subscriptions.

We hope every person who has the means will not only come forward but encourage others.

We have reason to believe that there are many who do not approve the route down the main branch of the 12 Mile Creek, and on that account are backward in supporting the measure.

We have the pleasure of informing the public that the route will be determined by the Company, when every stockholder will have a vote.

EDITOR.

St. Catharines, 1st January, 1824.

Mr. Editor,

A Bill having passed both Branches of the Legislature, and now only awaiting the sanction of His Excellency the Lieutenant Governor to become a law for the purpose of incorporating a Company to unite Lakes Erie and Ontario by a Canal, and for the erection of machinery for hydraulic purposes thereon:

I shall venture to make a few remarks on the subject, confining them principally to the route already levelled, and laid down by Mr. Hiram Tibbet. Whoever has taken the trouble to read his report, will find the only serious obstacle we meet with is a cut of two miles on leaving the River Welland, from the termination of this cut to the brow of the Mountain we have almost a dead level, only one lock at most will be necessary.

To descend the mountain we shall be under the necessity from our limited means to make use of Railways.

These can be so constructed as to take up or let down Boats with their entire loading at pleasure, as we have unlimited power at command, and from the gentle, even, and easy descent of the Mountain they can be made at a very trifling expense, I will refer those who wish to understand the nature and effect of them to the Encyclopædia, where they will find they have been used to advantage on the Duke of Bridgewater's Canal.

They are likewise in successful operation in the Coal and Iron mines in different parts of Great Britain, and take up from 60 to 80 tons burthen at a time.

From under the Mountain we take the Canal to the West or main branch of the 12 Mile Creek, Thomas's Mills, here another Lock will be necessary, lift 13 feet 8 inches.

From this it will be taken on the bank to Colonel Johnson's farm a distance of 100 & 18 chains. Another Lock of 8 feet 4 inches lift—then take the channel in Mr. Campbell's mill-pond to his Mill, another lock 7 feet 10 inches lift, from thence on the bank again to the St. Catharines Bridge, distance 100 & 39 chains; another lock of 9 feet 2 inches lift, which brings us on a level with Lake Ontario, the distance to which is four miles.

Mr. Tibbet's plan is to take the bed of the Creek the whole way with the exception of three miles and 17 chains in the two cuts before mentioned.

An Engineer can be the only competent judge whether the bed of this stream will answer every purpose for navigation, and I much question whether any of them will differ on the subject after examination.

A tow path on the bank will be necessary to float down lumber, staves, &c., and if on experiment it does not answer the desired effect, it can be carried on the bank the whole way as suggested by our friend "Observer," who has said everything on the subject of the Harbour that is necessary. I hope he will continue his remarks.

The distance from the mountain to the Lake is 9 miles and the descent 50 feet, which can be made navigable for the following sum:

Lock at Mr. Adam's Dam	$350
Merritt's	500
St. Catharines Bridge	500
Cut to Campbell's Mill	1,000
At Do's Mill	500
On Johnson's farm	500
Cut to Thomas's Mill	1,000
	$4,350
Cut	4,355
Lock at Thomas's	1,000
Cleaning the Creek	400
Tow path 50 yds wide pr. mile	450
	$6,350
Lock on Mountain	1,000
Cut from Welland	30,000
	$37,350

Railway will cost from 3,000 to 5,000 dollars.

When it is considered that all our exports consist of cheap, heavy, bulky Articles, and our imports of light valuable ones we must infer that at least 40 tons will go down for one that returns, the current will be rather in favour of navigation than otherwise. Take the whole route together, nature never presented fewer obstacles, not an aquaduct, extra embankment, or other artificial section except the Railway in the whole distance.

To remove the doubts of those who still affect to believe the Canal will not be carried into operation, I will observe that a cut can be made through the two for the sum of 12,762 dollars, twelve feet wide on the surface and six feet wide at the bottom at ten cents the yard. It is the opinion of Mr. Tibbet and others who understand the business that it can be done for six cents the yard from the favourable situation of the ground all the earth can be removed in boats and deposited in the river Welland; if so it will reduce the sum proportionably less. I mention this to shew were we supported by individuals from a distance we could accompiish this much of ourselves the ensuing summer, and finish the remainder to Lake Ontario the year following. However we do not anticipate such backwardness, but from the probable and durable nature of the Stock, have every reason to believe it will all be taken up in two months after the passing of the Act and the Canal completed from the Welland to Lake Ontario the present year.

Many of the inhabitants now lying on the route, say the first design of bringing the Chippawa into the Twelve Mile Creek was suggested by the late Hon. Robt. Hamilton at a very early day; the Country have reason to deplore the loss of that public-spirited Gentleman, for although at the time he was opposed by selfish and narrow-minded individuals as well as short-sighted politicians in our Legislature, his perseverance would have enabled him to succeed in effecting a Canal from the Bay of Quinty to Lake Ontario, a track-way or tow-path from Chippawa to Lake Erie, as well as draining the Cranberry Marsh or swamp in Wainfleet. He was the projector of all those improvements, which if then carried ahead, would have placed the Country twenty years farther ahead than it is at the present day.

I forbear making any remarks on the route to Niagara. After it is levelled by a competent Engineer it will be a subject of discussion. However, as you are all so desirous that the Canal shall terminate at that place (and very naturally) a fair opportunity will be offered to effect your object. Immediately after the passing of the Act, Books of subscription will be opened in the Town of Niagara where you have a good harbour and other advantages that we do not at present possess.

People in general are too much in the habit of deciding on any subject as they conceive their interest leads them, without reflection or endeavouring to ascertain the truth.

The above remark was never more fully verified than in the illiberal manner individuals have discussed the present subject—not one in twenty of our Merchants but have represented it altogether chimerical, and have been very assiduous in Montreal, where it has had its full effect as they have not an opportunity of seeing and judging for themselves, but must naturally be guided by the reports which reach them.

Most of you say, in case the Canal terminates at the mouth of the Twelve Mile Creek it will be prejudicial to the interests of Niagara. This is not only a narrow-minded, but I conceive a very erroneous idea of the subject—drawing a population to this and other situations on the Canal for manufacturing purposes will not lessen yours but from the constant effort we must of necessity keep up, be a means of increasing it and enhancing the value of every man's property between the two places.

If the intrinsic value of land is to be determined by the nett proceeds realized from it, the flouring Mills to be erected on the line of this Canal will double the value of every man's farm in this District; for instance, suppose all the farmers now clear over and above all expences 1/3 currency on each bushel of wheat he now raises and afterwards realizes 2/6, we must admit his yearly income is doubled, consequently the value of his property, to prove the article, will immediately rise in the proportion I mention to the past price of wheat at Rochester, 80 or 90 miles distant, and contrast them with the prices here. They have been paying 9/ per bushel for this article, at the same time we could not afford to pay 5/6 or 6/ per bushel, when we have better markets and cheaper transportation.

The reason is obvious. For the want of those Mills our Merchant now gets his return for produce from Montreal once in the year, whereas had we a sufficient number of them, as at Rochester, flouring Merchants would purchase wheat with cash, have it ground immediately, shipped, and get their returns monthly, or within six weeks during the navigable part of the season, and have it of the best instead of the most inferior quality as heretofore.

I will not dwell on the immense Wheat Country that will be opened for us on the borders of the Grand River, and to Westward of it, nor on the advantages of transportation.

The benefit of Canals are now so well understood, that all Governments have not only given them their sanction, where practicable, but contributed their Aid to carry them into effect. My object in this communication is to endeavour to shew the ease and facility with which the Canal can be completed.

The great advantages our agricultural and commercial interest must derive from it, and that we are equally concerned, according to the value of our individual property.

In its speedy accomplishment it therefore behooves us all to make every exertion, and take as many shares as our means will admit. I wish particularly to draw the attention of farmers in the immediate neighbourhood, any one of them can take from five to ten shares. Ten per cent. is requested to be paid on commencement of the work and not more than ten per cent. per month, until the whole is completed. They will not only feel a particular interest in going to their own Mills and Machinery, but from the profitable nature of the Stock, will be induced hereafter to embark in further improvements, and if we can once encourage a sufficient spirit of enterprise, to keep whatever little Capital we have afloat, it will tend to the general and rapid improvement of the Country, and prevent an individual from monopolizing too great a share.

W. H. MERRITT.

NOTICE.

January 24, 1824.

A meeting of the Petitioners of the Welland Canal will take place at Mrs. Rogers' Hotel, in the Town of Niagara, on Saturday the 31st Instant. For the purpose of appointing some person to each County town, in the several Districts of this Province, to open Books of subscription, as provided by the Act, and to devise measures for the speedy formation of the Company.

St. Catharines, January 24, 1824.

WM. HAMILTON MERRITT,
One of the Petitioners.

Gleaner, FEBRUARY 7, 1824.

At a numerous meeting of the Inhabitants of the District of Niagara Assembled at the House of Mrs. Rogers in the town of Niagara on Saturday, January 31st, convened under Authority of an Act of the Provincial Parliament of this Province, passed last session, Entitled an Act to incorporate sundry persons therein mentioned under the style and title of the Welland

Canal Company, whereof certain of the original Petitioners being then and there present. A Chairman and Secretary to such meeting were duly appointed, and the object of the meeting explained, it was then

Resolved.—That in conformity to the Provisions of this Act, Books be provided by the Agents hereafter named, and transmitted to certain persons in the different Assize Towns in this Province, for the purpose of receiving subscriptions for Stock, in the said incorporated Company.

2d. Resolved.—That George Keefer, W. H. Merritt, Rd. Woodruff, Geo. Adams, R. M. Crysler, John Lafferty, Esqrs., be a board of Managers in behalf of the Petitioners, to make all necessary arrangements until the Company is duly organized.

3d. Resolved.—That William Hamilton Merritt, Esquire, of Grantham, be an Assistant general Agent, to obtain subscriptions for Stock in the said Company and that it will be recommended to him to proceed to the Lower Province, with as little delay as possible, and solicit subscriptions for stock therein from those who may be inclined to further an object so momentous and beneficial to the future prosperity of both Provinces.

4th. Resolved.—That the Chairman on behalf of the Petitioners Address letters to such Gentlemen in either Province, as he may consider would take an Active interest in promoting any laudable and enterprising undertaking of the kind, particularly the Hon. J. H. Dunn, His Majesty's Receiver General, at York, the Hon. George Markland of Kingston, the Hon. John Richardson of Montreal, and the Hon. James Irvin of Quebec, soliciting their support and assistance in aiding Mr. Merritt in recommending subscriptions in the said Corporation.

WILLIAM DICKSON, Chairman.
THOS. BUTLER, Secretary.

EDITORIAL.   Saturday, February 28, [1824].

We are glad to find by the following paragraph that Mr. Merritt, Agent for the petitioners for the Welland Canal, had met with much encouragement in York.

We understand he was much discouraged when he set out from this place, owing to the backwardness of many in this District.

Funds have been raised by subscription and commissioners appointed to endeavour to find a route to the river.

The Agent of the petitioners of the Welland Canal passed through this Town to-day, on his way to Lower Canada.

Hon. J. H. Dunn, H.M. Rec. Genl.

WELLAND CANAL.   (Quebec,) Saturday, April 3, 1824.

A meeting in conformity to an Advertisement by the Committee of Trade took place at the Exchange on Thursday last to consider of the union of Lake Erie and Ontario by this Canal.

The Hon. Jas. Irvine in the Chair. The Honble Chairman explained the object of the meeting and proposed Resolutions declaring the undertaking of the highest importance to the commercial and agricultural interests of the Canadas which was unanimously adopted.

A Committee to assist Mr. Merritt to obtain subscriptions in this District, composed of N. Freer, J. Steward, A. Patterson, —. Jamieson, Esqrs., and the Hon. Mr. Irvine, was then appointed.
—*Quebec Gazette.*

WELLAND CANAL.   Quebec, March 11th, 1824.

In conformity with a notification previously given by John Steward, Chairman of the Committee of Trade, a general meeting of the Merchants and other inhabitants of Quebec was this day held at the Exchange Reading Room for the purpose of taking into consideration a communication relative to a contemplated Canal in Upper Canada, to be called the Welland Canal.

The Honble J. Irvine was called to the Chair.
The following Resolutions were proposed and unanimously concurred in.
1. Resolved.—That this meeting views with great satisfaction the proposed undertaking by our fellow-subjects in Upper Canada of a canal communicating between the Waters of Lake Erie and Ontario to be called the Welland Canal.
2. Resolved.—As the opinion of this meeting that the Welland Canal when in operation would tend to draw forth the commercial and Agricultural resources of the extensive interior of the Upper Province and become the means of preserving to the Canadas a valuable trade which without such a Channel of communication would be lost to these Provinces and pass to the United States.
3. Resolved.—As the opinion of this Meeting that the completion of the said Canal is an object of the first importance and would be productive of the greatest benefit and advantage to the commerce of the Country—not less to this Province than to that of Upper Canada.
4. Resolved.—As the opinion of the meeting that the said undertaking merits every encouragement, and the aid of every inhabitant of this Province who feels an interest in the agricultural and commercial prosperity of the Canadas.
Resolved.—That Books be immediately opened for the purpose of receiving the subscriptions of those persons who are or may be desirous to become Stockholders in the incorporated Company styled the Welland Canal Company.
Several subscriptions were then put down, amongst the first was Colonel Johnson of H.M. 68th L.I. Regt., who honoured the meeting with his presence, and who is intimately acquainted with the locality of the situation through which the Canal is to run.
It was then resolved that with a view of carrying into effect the object of the foregoing resolutions, it is highly expedient and desirable that a committee of five gentlemen be appointed to assist the exertions of Wm. H. Merritt, Esqr., the gentleman who has been named as General Agent from Upper Canada to visit this Province for the purpose of obtaining subscribers to the Welland Canal, and that the following gentlemen be requested to Act as the Committee for the City and District of Quebec, viz., Capt. Freer, Wm. Johnson Stewart, Mr. Andrew Patterson, Mr. Jamieson and Jno. Irvine.

April 10. [1824]

EDITORIAL.

On the debates in Congress about charging 25 per cent. on Canada Wheat—113 lost 71.

Notice of a meeting at Mrs. Rogers' 15th May to choose Directors.

Notice.—J. Clowes employed in levelling. Contractors may have an opportunity of examining previous to viewing proposals.

Saturday, May 24th, 1824.

Agreeable to public notice given a meeting of the Welland Canal Stockholders was held in this Town on the 15th Inst., when the following Gentlemen were chosen Directors: Hon. J. H. Dunn, W. H. Merritt, George Keefer, John Decow and Saml. Clowes, Esq.
At a meeting held by the four latter gentlemen we are credibly informed, the Directors have determined to obtain the opinion and estimate of one of the most experienced Engineers they can find, of the whole route necessary to connect the two Lakes by way of the Grand River and obtain the whole amount of Stock necessary to complete the Canal from Chippawa to Lake Ontario, previous to commencing part of the work; this is as it ought to be.

TO THE DIRECTORS OF THE WELLAND CANAL COMPANY.

York, May 30 [1824].

Gentlemen,
I had the pleasure to receive your letter and beg leave to express thanks for the honour conferred on me by nominating me President of the Welland Canal Coy.
The situation which I have the honour to hold in the Province leaves it quite out of my power to give any personal attention to the object. My duty requiring my constant presence

at York—this together with my want of experience in filling such an Office, renders me under the necessity of requesting you will be pleased to find some more disposable and fit person as your President.

I feel highly gratified with the Report of Messrs. Samuel and James Clowes, Engineers, which is so highly satisfactory that I highly recommend your publishing the same for the information of your friends in the Provinces.

I cannot view the proposed Canal in any other light than a public benefit and it would have afforded me very great pleasure if I could with propriety comply with your wishes, but rest assured I shall do all I can to promote it and from the easy mode you propose calling in your installments, I beg you will permit me to double my number of shares.

I have the honour to be, gentlemen,
Yr. obt. Servt.,
JOHN H. DUNN.

(Niagara), Saturday, 14th August, 1824.

WELLAND CANAL.

We are informed the whole intended route of the Canal is now surveyed. From the Grand River to Chippawa is ten miles, along the Chippawa to Lake Ontario by the Twelve Mile Creek, or to the river at this Town, twenty miles.

There is but little difference in the length from the Chippawa to the mouth of the Twelve Mile Creek or to the River at this Town.

There is also but little difference in estimated expense of the route to those two places. That to this Town, we understand is estimated at about £2,000 more than that to the mouth of the Twelve Mile Creek; in the last route, however, there is a much greater part to be done on perishable materials than the former, besides the greater superiority of the noble harbour, formed by nature in the River, and the superficial one to be made at the mouth of the Twelve Mile Creek.

This will, we have no doubt, induce the Directors to bring it to Niagara.

In the meantime the first thing to be done: From the Grand River to Chippawa the intended route of the Canal passes through a very extensive swamp, containing many thousand acres of land, at present of no use and is a great injury to the neighbourhood from the unhealthy vapours that proceed from those stagnant waters in the summer, and being a harbour for wolves and other beasts of Prey.

The level of the swamp is higher than the Grand River and about ten feet higher than Chippawa; so that extensive tract of Land in place of being a nuisance to a neighbourhood might be converted into fruitful fields.

We understand that a petition will be made to His Majesty through the Lieutenant Governor for a grant of the said tract to the Stockholders of the Welland Canal. Should that be granted (of which we can hardly doubt) it will go far in defraying the expense of the cut from the Grand River to Chippawa.

Much credit is due to the Directors and a few individuals for their great and persevering exertions in pushing forward the business under many discouraging circumstances. It is melancholy and surprising to find such backwardness in the most influential and wealthy people in the District to that great work.

EDITOR OF *Gleaner*.

Gleaner. Saturday, November 20, 1824.

We consider it a compliment paid to the sons of Caledonia, that the Commissioners of the Welland Canal have appointed the 30th Inst., being St. Andrew's Day, for breaking ground on that important work.

At the end of many years to come, when that Canal is in complete operation, it must be pleasing to any person that he witnessed the first shovel full of earth that was removed on the route. We therefore hope that a number will attend.

THE INCEPTION OF THE WELLAND CANAL

REPORT OF THE PRESIDENT AND DIRECTORS OF THE WELLAND CANAL COMPANY, OF THE PROGRESS AND STATE OF THE SAID CANAL.

Aware of the importance of their trust the Directors have on all occasions been alive to the general interest of the Company and public good and used their best efforts in the vigorous prosecution of the work confided to their management—they conceive it a point of duty to submit to the Shareholders generally their proceedings up to date.

Sufficient Amount of Stock having been subscribed, 1st November last, to warrant the commencement of the undertaking, due notice was given and contracts closed on the 15th for the Completion of the Canal from the River Welland to New Holland, being three miles, two of which are to be excavated, and which was commenced on the 30th of that month.

Those contracts have been made with able Engineers and experienced men, every way equal to the task and (though no preparatory arrangements could have been made) buildings and machinery were soon erected, tools and implements procured and as many men employed as can work with advantage and from the very favourable nature of the soil and uncommon fine weather, they have been enabled to forward their different sections with unusual rapidity and a zeal that reflects credit on their ingenuity and exertions; both tunnel mouths have been taken out to *bottom level* and will be finished full Canal size by 1st May next, at the latest.

A shaft has also been sunk to the same depth in the centre of the tunnel, and enabled the contractors to test the quality of the earth with certainty, which proves to be a strong adhesive clay in regular stratums from beginning to end, peculiarly adapted for a safe and expeditious prosecution of the work—no water or stone here or at either end being met with, until below water level. We can confidently assert that no serious obstructions will intervene.

The original plan of this canal was a nine feet wide tunnel, eight feet lock and sixteen feet bottom. The propriety of enlarging it to fifteen feet wide, fourteen feet high and eight feet water, the size of the Erie Canal, was suggested to us and has been adopted with the general concurrence of the Stockholders, the advantage of which is apparent, expecially from our proximity to the American Canal, as Boats from thence may pass through this Canal, without the inconvenience and expense of shifting cargoes.

When the tunnel was first contemplated it was thought two years would be occupied in its execution. Experiment has now satisfied us that it may be completed the present season.

Mr. Harvey the contractor is making extensive preparation to that effort and from his plan submitted to us for the prosecution of this work, we are convinced that it will be navigable by the first Novr. next.

Arrangements have been made with the Stockholders in New York and Lower Canada for the prompt and regular payment of their monthly installments, and in their communications to us, they express a desire to have the work forwarded with the utmost expedition.

We have great satisfaction, therefore, in being able to assure the Stockholders that the Canal which was supposed a work of so great magnitude has been found simple and easy—the greatest difficulty (its commencement being overcome), and that it is progressing under the most favourable circumstances and were a moderate share of public patronage given to the undertaking we should anticipate the completion of the whole line from the Grand River to Lake Ontario, the present year.

GEORGE KEEFER,
President Welland Canal Co.

Welland Canal Office,
St. Catharines, 1st February, 1825.

One Hundred Dollars Premium will be paid by the Board and Directors of the Welland Canal Company for the best Model of a Wooden Lock, or Stone and wood connected, that may be presented at their Office in St. Catharines on the 5th October next.

The object of the Board is to obtain the most perfect plan to combine solidity and duration and be constructed on the most simple and cheapest method.

The dimension to be One hundred feet long and twenty-two feet in the clear and ten feet lift. A minute specification to accompany each.

By order of

WM. HAMILTON MERRITT,
Agent W.C.C.

Welland Canal Office,
St. Catharines, 4th July, 1825.

Brief Review (Extracts).

As few public works in any country have, under similar circumstances, been attended with the like success, it is desirable that the public should be placed in possession of a brief narrative of the facts connected with the Welland Canal as recorded from time to time in the Journals of the Province.

1823.

The first active movement towards the accomplishment of this great National Work, was in obtaining a survey of the Country lying between the Chippawa river and the waters running into Lake Ontario, by Hiram Tibbetts, Esq., who reported thereon.

1824.

On the 10th of May [1823], a petition for an Act of incorporation was presented to the Legislature, and on the 19th day of January, George Keefer, Thomas Merritt, George Adams, William Chisholm, Joseph Smith, Paul Shipman, John Decow, William Hamilton Merritt, and others were incorporated by the name of the Welland Canal Company with a Capital of £40,000 divided into shares of £12. 10s., each.

The Stock was subscribed and the work commenced on the 30th of November, the same year.

One of the most striking features in the history of this work is, that notwithstanding the want of means, opposition, and endless embarrassment, its prosecution was not discontinued a single day until two vessels passed from Lake to Lake, five years after.

The first project completed only the connexion of the Lakes by means of a Boat Canal, passing up the valley of the 12 mile Creek to the foot of the mountain ridge—ascending from thence by a railway to the Beaver Dam and thence to the Chippawa, by a second Boat Canal tunnelled through the high land on the site of the present Deep Cut.

1825.

As public attention was soon directed to the importance of connecting Lakes Erie and Ontario by a Ship Canal of enlarged dimensions, for which the amount of the original stock was quite inadequate, on the 13th day of April, the Act of 4th George IV, was amended by the 5th George IV, and the Capital increased to £200,000.

Every inducement was held out to capitalists to invest money in the undertaking.

As an instance the 13th clause of the amended Act provided, "That it should not be lawful for His Majesty, his Heirs or Successors, at any time to assume the said Canal, unless it should appear from the accounts of the said Company laid before the Legislature, that the Stockholders shall have received every year, upon an average twelve and a half per cent. for every one hundred pounds which he shall be possessed of in the said concern."

. . . .

The present Lord Bishop of Toronto, Dr. Strachan, who was then a member of the Legislative Council, took a warm interest in this magnificent undertaking, from the first, and did all that was in his power to assist and encourage those who were labouring for its accomplishment.

As early as 1825, when the work was in its infancy, bitterly opposed by some, and distrusted and thought lightly of by others, he drew up a paper setting forth the inestimable advantages it must produce to the commerce and agriculture of the Country, and urging its accomplishment by every effort and at whatever cost. The Directors, partaking those sentiments and opinions, were happy to introduce, with his permission, his eloquent appeal into their Report, and the paper I have last referred to, with the exception of such passages which relate to the details of the company's proceedings, contains Dr. Strachan's sentiments and his early views, and objects of this great work in his own language. They are introduced here from a conviction that it will be no less gratifying to the venerable Prelate than to his many friends, as well as interesting to the public, to observe how clearly he predicted, when the Company was struggling with its greatest difficulties, the inevitable progress and success of the noble work they were engaged in, and the splendid results it must produce throughout a country which forms a large portion of the globe. When he remarks in language which many at the time may have thought extravagant, that the Welland Canal will, in time, yield only in importance to the Canal which may hereafter unite the Pacific with the Atlantic Oceans, through the Isthmus of Darien, it is interesting to reflect that he was contemplating a work, which after an interval of twenty-six years, we now find engaging the attention of the business world in both continents.

THE INCEPTION OF THE WELLAND CANAL

A summary of the List of Stockholders in the Welland Canal Company, in the year 1825, giving their names and residence the number of shares held by each, and the total amount of the subscriptions, for which each individual stockholder was liable.

1825
Welland Canal Office,
St. Catharines.

NEW YORK.

Shares	Amount
1125	£14,062

J. B. Yates held 700 shares, amounting to £8,750.
Thomas Dixon held 200 shares, amounting to £2,500.

QUEBEC.

344 shares	£4,300

The Earl of Dalhousie and the Hon. James Irvine had each taken 20 shares, amounting to £250.

Montreal, 185 shares	£2,312. 10s
Kingston, 19 shares	237. 10s
York, 139 shares	1,737. 10s

Hon. J. H. Dunn took forty shares, amounting to £500.

Amherstburg, 18 shares	£225
Niagara District, 816 shares	£10,200

Andrew Harvey, the contractor, took 200 shares, £2,500.
Eight of the Niagara subscribers, holding sixty shares, £750, have refused to pay their subscriptions.

Jas. Gordon,
Treasurer.

———

Total amount of all subscriptions at that date, £33,074. 10s.

During the summer of 1824, the directors of the Welland Canal, as had been foretold in the *Gleaner*, presented the following petition to the Lieutenant-Governor, asking him to recommend a grant of the Crown Lands in the township of Wainfleet to enable them to extend the canal to the Grand River.

PETITION OF THE WELLAND CANAL COMPANY.

To His Excellency Sir Peregrine Maitland, K.C.B., Lieutenant-Governor of Upper Canada and Major General Commanding His Majesty's Forces in North America, &ca., &ca.
In Council Assembled.

The Petition of the President and Directors of the Welland Canal Company.
Humbly Sheweth.

That your Petitioners have succeeded in the formation of the Welland Canal Company, according to the Act of the last Legislature of this Province, have obtained stock to the Amount of twelve thousand five hundred Pounds, and have completed the surveys of the said Canal from Grand River on Lake Erie to Lake Ontario by the most experienced Engineers in the Province, reports of which are herewith submitted, and altho' the sum is trifling in the extreme, compared with the advantage to be derived by the completion of the Canal, still your Petitioners find the greatest difficulty in getting the remainder of the stock subscribed from the supposed magnitude of the undertaking and the extreme scarcity of money.

Your Petitioners therefore pray that Your Excellency may be pleased to recommend to His Majesty's favorable consideration to grant the Welland Canal Company all the waste lands of the Crown now in the Township of Wainfleet, or any other your Excellency may please to recommend on condition that the Company complete the said Navigation.

It is needless for your Petitioners to recapitulate the advantages the Country must derive from the measure, and the increased value it must place on all the unlocated lands of the Crown that will be connected by this navigation.

And as in duty bound your Petitioners will every pray.

GEORGE KEEFER, President.

St. Catherines,
8th August, 1824.

CHANCEY BEADLE,
THOMAS BUTLER,   } Directors.
JOHN DE COW,

Sir Peregrine Maitland was then residing in the township of Stamford, near Queenston, where he had unusual opportunities for gaining further information. He delayed action for more than two months, undoubtedly for that purpose. It was then confidently expected that the canal would enter Lake Ontario at Niagara. Disappointed in obtaining the financial support they hoped for in Canada, the directors sent Mr. Merritt to New York, where he was more successful. A newspaper, published in that city, announced that $50,000 had been subscribed in a single day. The largest subscriber was a wealthy politician, who then held an important public office. This information caused Maitland to become distrustful of the project. He had also lately received a letter from Captain Robert Barrie, commissioner of the Royal Navy at Kingston, on the subject of the canal to connect Burlington Bay with Lake Ontario, stating that the Navy Board would not authorize any action until after a full explanation and consultation with the government of the province. He then decided to transmit the petition of the Welland Canal Company, with a letter which made its rejection almost certain.

FROM SIR PEREGRINE MAITLAND TO LORD BATHURST.

Miscellaneous
No. 163
My Lord.
Upper Canada.
Queenston, 9th November, 1824.

At the solicitation of the President and Directors of the Welland Canal Company, incorporated under a Statute of this Province, I have the honor to forward to your Lordship their petition for the grant of an extensive tract of land for the purpose of assisting in their object, namely, the construction of a Canal between the Lakes Erie and Ontario.

I am fully aware of the great importance to this Province of a secure water communication between these Great Lakes, but the line proposed by this company does not embrace many of the advantages that might be realized by the execution of such a project.

If the Canal were conducted into Lake Ontario as was originally intended, through any one of the several streams that run into the Lake to the Westward of the Niagara River, it would afford in the event of hostilities with the United States, a secure line of communication for Troops, Stores, &c.—but as by the present plan it is to be brought into the Niagara River immediately under the Guns of the American fort, this object, which must to the Government be of the first importance, is entirely lost; and I feel it right, in transmitting the present application, that this observation should at the same time be presented to your Lordship's notice.

The public impression in this Province with regard to the proposed Canal is not so great but that the projectors have been compelled to seek for subscribers in the United States of America, where half the stock subscribed has been taken up and your Lordship may perhaps be disposed to doubt whether it be advisable to subject a considerable tract of Landed property in this Country to the Control of a Company so constituted. It is moreover believed that with the aid of their foreign subscriptions the undertaking will be attempted whether the assistance now prayed for from the Government be conceded or not.

I have the honor to be &c.

P. MAITLAND.

The Earl Bathurst, K.G., &c., &c., &c.

At the following session of the provincial parliament a joint committee of the two houses was appointed to confer on the subject of the improvement of the internal navigation, of which the two leading members were John Beverly

Robinson on the part of the Assembly and the Reverend Dr. John Strachan on behalf of the Legislative Council. The report for the drafting of which Dr. Strachan as chairman seems to have been mainly responsible, referred favourably to the new proposals of the Welland Canal Company, who had definitely decided to enter Lake Ontario by way of the Twelve Mile Creek and were asking authority to increase their capital to £200,000 to enlarge the canal and continue it to the Grand River.

The Honourable John H. Dunn, the Receiver General of the Province, had consented to act as President of the Company, and on the day following the passage of the amended Act, he presented another petition to the Lieutenant-Governor, renewing the former application for a grant of Crown lands, which although forwarded without unfavourable comment, met with no better success than its predecessor.

REPORT OF THE JOINT COMMITTEE APPOINTED TO CONFER UPON THE IMPROVEMENT OF THE INTERNAL NAVIGATION OF THE PROVINCE OF UPPER CANADA.

. . . .

Tho' many of the improvements of which the Inland Navigation of this Province is susceptible are perfectly obvious, and they had therefore been very early the subject of discussion, the first attempt to direct attention to them, by any public measure (if we except the provision made by the Legislature in 1817 for surveying the waters of the Saint Lawrence), was by the Act of 1821 appointing the Board of Commissioners whose labors are comprehended in the subjoined reports.—It is due to the memory of the late Col. Nichol, formerly an active and very intelligent Member of the Legislature, to remark that his zeal in the cause of public improvements occasioned this measure to be brought forward at an earlier period than it would otherwise have been, and that so long as he lived he persevered very faithfully in carrying it into effect.

When the State of the Province, even at the present moment, is considered with regard to its population and its resources, it must be acknowledged, that it was at an early stage of its advancement that attention was thus turned to objects so important.—It has been not unusual to reproach the people of Upper Canada, with a want of enterprize and exertion in not having sooner applied themselves to works of this description—a comparison not very strict, with the neighbouring States, has appeared to give occasion to such reproaches, but they are in truth, undeserved.

When the State of New York contained four times the present population of Upper Canada, and when its resources from its commercial advantages and the greater general opulence of its inhabitants, exceeded those of this Province in a proportion infinitely greater, no work of the magnitude of some of those which we now venture to contemplate, had been undertaken or even thought of.

When in very recent years the patriotic zeal of a few men of more than ordinary talents inspired them with courage to propose the wonderful undertaking which the State of New York has now carried nearly to its completion, it appeared to most persons so far above the means of the Country to accomplish, that it was with difficulty, the plan could be at first supported against the prejudice of public opinion, but it is obvious that when it was determined to proceed in its execution, it was in the power of that State to furnish great resources for the undertaking.

It cannot with any reason be thought to reflect shame on this Country that it has hitherto felt itself unable to commence works of even far less cost.

It must be remembered that with more than a million of inhabitants, whose circumstances are, generally speaking, much more opulent, the State of New York possesses a very flourishing Seaport, which attracts the riches of Commerce and affords the means of raising with ease and certainty a great revenue by indirect taxation,—and that her more advanced State with regard to population and trade, not only makes her infinitely more equal to any great undertaking like that alluded to, but affords a more certain prospect of an immediate and profitable return.

It is in one respect fortunate for this Province that the State of New York has found itself able, at so early a day to attempt the completion of an Inland Navigation, which might well have been thought to exceed its power, an example has in the progress of this great work, been afforded to the people of Canada, sufficiently applicable in all essential points to form the ground of satisfactory calculations.

. . . .
. . . . . .

That a Canal from Kingston to the Ottawa River would in the event of a War not merely diminish beyond measure the Charge of our defence, but render its success greatly more certain, admits of no doubt. Happily present appearances indicate no interruption of the good understanding between Great Britain and America, on the contrary, they afford a well grounded hope of its permanence, but without bringing probabilities into discussion, it may be affirmed that it would be most imprudent to reckon securely on a very long continuance of peace.

In the event of a war protracted as the last, the safety and the saving of transport, conducted by such a channel, would, it is believed, fully compensate to the nation the charge of the improvement,—and it is most evident that to give full effect to the sound and liberal policy which has created the Military Settlements on the Rideau and introduced since the war a loyal population of more than 10,000 souls where there was before no Inhabitant and which is now surmounting at a considerable expense the interruption of the navigation of the Ottawa, it is necessary to perfect the Water Communication removed from the Enemy's Frontier, and leading in truth from the Ocean to Kingston which is the key to Lake Ontario and the principal Military Station in the Province.

The same reasoning applies in a less degree to the proposed Canal, connecting Lake Erie and Ontario.—Such a work would undoubtedly facilitate military operations in defence of the Province, to a greater extent under any probable circumstances, but it would not so decidedly ensure the safety of the Western portion of the Province, as the first mentioned Canal would the Eastern because the Enemy, if in possession of the Lake, might still cut off resources from below and render the benefit of such a Work partial and uncertain.

With respect to the advantages to Trade and Commerce which the projected communications would secure, little can be said that has not been urged and nothing that observation in a neighbouring Country does not readily suggest.—In this view the improvement, which would connect the waters of Lake Erie and Ontario, is undoubtedly the most important—because the more remote that portion of the Province is from the Ocean, the more ruinous to its Commerce, and consequently to its agriculture is any natural obstruction which increases materially the difficulty of transport.

To a Country so situated, the manufactures its inhabitants consume come at a higher charge, and if the only articles they can furnish in return are subject to disadvantages which almost exclude them from the Markets, there is reason to fear a depression of circumstances, a discouragement to exertions, and ultimately perhaps, even a consequent inferiority in moral character amidst great positive advantages of climate and soil.

When the great importance in a commercial point of view of an uninterrupted navigation from the Country bordering on Lake Erie, is thus considered, it is very gratifying to find that a hope is held out of its speedy accomplishment by the exertions of a private Company at a much less expense, than that contemplated by the Commissioners, but by a route, which may perhaps as effectually serve the interests of the Country in time of peace.

If the Welland Canal should proceed upon the scale now contemplated by the Company, admitting of sloop navigation, it is to be supposed that for all purposes of Commerce, the execution of the plan reported by the Commissioners might be postponed till the population of this Country should become such as to warrant its being entertained for the reasons that it would serve the interests of a much greater extent of interior country and would terminate at a safer and more commodious harbor. The latter reason would undoubtedly indicate the Canal projected by the Commissioners, as that which would best conduce to the Military defence of the Country—but if the Welland Canal should be carried successfully through, it is conceived that no sufficient motive would remain for desiring the completion of the other until many more necessary improvements of a similar kind had been first executed.

. . . .

The question on what scale it would be expedient to undertake either of the canals projected seems to have appeared very doubtful to the Commissioners, and it certainly is one which admits of much discussion and calls for great consideration.

Beginning in the westward, it is certainly most important that the lakes should be connected by a Navigation which will allow of the same vessels continuing their voyage without discharging their cargoes, so that a schooner laden at Amherstburg could proceed without breaking bulk to Kingston or Prescott. The present design of the Welland Canal Company admits of this to the fullest extent contemplated by the Commissioners, and it is therefore for the moment unnecessary to discuss the point as regards that part of the communication.

. . . .

JOHN STRACHAN,
Chairman of the Committee from the Legislative Council.
ANGUS MACKINTOSH.

Joint Committee Room,
April 6th, 1825.

JOHN B. ROBINSON,
Chairman of Committee of the House of Assembly.
WILLIAM MORRIS,
JAS. GORDON.

THE INCEPTION OF THE WELLAND CANAL

Memorial of the Welland Canal Company.

To His Excellency Sir Peregrine Maitland, K.C.B., Lieutenant Governor of the Province of Upper Canada, and Major General Commanding His Majesty's Forces in North America, &ca., &ca.

The Memorial of the Welland Canal Company
Respectfully sheweth,

That by an Act passed during the last Session of the Provincial Parliament, the capital stock of the said Company has been increased from £40,000 to £200,000 for the purpose of inabling them to encrease the dimensions of the said Canal and render the same navigable for such vessels as are usually employed upon Lakes Erie and Ontario, and to make secure and convenient harbours at the mouth of the Grand River and the twelve-mile Creek.

That a Canal of such encreased dimensions, your Excellency will no doubt perceive, must be of great public utility and tend very much to the military strength of the Country in time of war and will also encrease the facilities of transporting His Majesty's Naval and Warlike Stores.

That from the discussions which took place in Parliament during the passing of said Act and also from certain Resolutions which passed the House of Assembly, Your Memorialists were led to hope, that their exertions would have been aided by the fostering of the Government either by a Loan of Money to aid the Company in its commencement or by the Government giving its countenance to the undertaking which would have been more valuable by taking a certain number of shares in their capital stock, which hopes however, your Memorialists are sorry to find have not been realized, although they are persuaded that failure has arisen altogether from fortuitous circumstances and not at all from any want of disposition either in the Legislature or His Majesty's Government to further the objects of the undertaking.

That in the absence of either of the means of support from His Majesty's Government, which your Memorialists have noticed, a Grant of a portion of the Waste Lands of the Crown would materially tend to produce public confidence in the undertaking by shewing the interest the Government felt in its success, and would also by encreasing the value of the stock, make it a greater object of desire to capitalists.

That the value of landed property in general to the Westward of the said Canal must thereby be enhanced, and of course the Lands of the Crown will benefit in the same proportion with that of individuals.

That immediately upon the route of that part of the Canal which is to connect the Grand River with the Welland in the Township of Wainfleet, there is a large tract of Marsh Land wholly useless until drained, forming a Harbour for vermin of all descriptions, and being the cause of agues and other local diseases, which by the construction of the Canal will be rendered available for the purposes of husbandry and salubrious to the surrounding neighbourhood.

Your Memorialists therefore humbly pray that Your Excellency will be pleased to grant them whatever Lands of the Crown may still remain unconceded in the Township of Wainfleet together with such other portion of the Waste Lands of the Crown in the western part of the Province as to Your Excellency may seem a sufficient encouragement to this great national undertaking, and Your Memorialists as in duty bound will every pray.

JOHN H. DUNN,
Presidt. in behalf of the Compy.

York, 14th April, 1825.

In 1819, Lieut. J. E. Portlock was employed in making surveys with the object of forming a harbour and naval station at Mohawk Bay or the mouth of the Grand River, for improving the navigation of that river, and connecting it with Chippawa Creek.

He prepared three plans on the subject, the latter being drawn to illustrate the communication between those streams by a canal or a road, and submitted the following document.

Remarks to Accompany Plan No. 3.

From the mouth of the Grand River as far as Huff's settlement, the banks are alternately moderate and low, the latter bound natural meadows, and in many places are excessivly marshy. Corn is raised on several of these meadows, and if drained, as with some exceptions they might be, their rich soil would become highly fertile, and they would cease to be as at present a constant source of sickness.

The general soil of the river is a sandy loam, resting on Clay and the bed of the river is here clay.

After passing Huff's, the banks become more elevated—at the Delaware Village they are high and occasionally stony.

At the rapids the banks are generally moderate, alternating with occasional eminences, and rich flats, the former crowned with Indian Cottages, and the latter covered with corn surrounding the rude dwellings which are scattered through it. The bed of the river abounds with Lime Stone, either in a continuous stratum or in broken pieces. Beyond the rapids the scenery still improves; the water is generally deep—the flats are richer and the villages are planted in situations still more picturesque—at every step the beauty of the river is felt—but on ascending the high bank at Birch's and crossing a neck of land towards the Mohawk village a scene more beautiful bursts on the sight before the observer raises nearly two hundred feet is spread a wide plain through which the river, dwindled in appearance to a brook, pursues its meandering course, as it were, seeking the Indian Cottages which everywhere stud its banks, whilst the Mohawk village terminates well the view, is it possible to refrain predicting the fertility which will reign hereafter over this delightful region?

My reason for commencing my sections from Lymburner's farm are that they would thereby strike both the Grand and the Chippawa rivers at navigable points and that the distance between the lakes would be shorter than from any other point. By an inspection of the first section it will be perceived that were even the Oswego Creek sufficient to supply a Canal with its locks; when seen by me I do not conceive it was—a deep cutting of 17 feet would be necessary after allowing the height of the Mill dam, and such an excavation would cost far above any allowable maximum of expense with three locks to the Chippawa, it would cost upwards of £40,000, some part of the excavation might be saved by following the course of Lummis's Creek and then that of the Oswego but with a great encrease of distance.

The Oswego might also be cleared out and made use of from Major Robinson's mill did not its very circuitous course form a serious objection. The impracticability of continuing the canal to the 20 Mile Creek renders it useless to dwell longer on this subject.

It appears from the second section that the 20 Mile Creek is 35 feet higher than the Chippawa at a navigable point and that the land rises so much between the two as to preclude their connection by a canal. As the dividing ridge cannot be avoided and indeed the 20 Mile Creek with Taylor's would not furnish a sufficient quantity of water I fear this obstacle is insurmountable. A Canal from a point above the rapids of the Grand river would meet with nearly the same difficulty—the land is indeed there more level, but a certain height must be attained before it is, so a section however in this direction would not be useless.

The obstacles I have pointed out all arise from the nonexistence of any considerable stream between the principal rivers and the necessity in consequence of assuming a constant level. These difficulties in so short a distance do not occur in the whole Grand American Canal, for proof of which I refer to the Canal Commissioners report.

A road is the next and best method of connecting Lake Ontario with the Grand River, by following the direction marked in the plan to the Chippawa and then proceeding in a straight line to the 40 Mile Creek the distance would be about 20 miles over a soil excepting the last three miles excellent for the purpose. This road should be about 60 feet wide and have a ditch on each side, by which the small marshes marked on the section would be effectually drained,—such a road might be made for £18,000 and would greatly advance the prosperity of the Country through which it passed. An inclined plane formed in one of the ravines of the mountain and provided with machinery would facilitate much its ascent. The additional expence would be trifling.

A port at the Lake is the last desideratum, and that of most difficult attainment. No favorable point for a pier occurs at the 40, and indeed, I know of no place so advantageous,—were there an opening sufficient at the outlet, as Burlington Bay and the inner Lake. Within the latter vessels might shelter themselves immediately under the strongest military position in this part of the Country. To make an opening at the outlet to prevent the accumulation of sand by Piers would be equally difficult as the formation of the latter at the 40, if therefore a harbour is not a first consideration, the 40 Mile Creek obtains the preference as a road communication by combining a good Military position with short distance and a most healthy situation. In the last particular Burlington is most dreadfully defective.

As a last remark it must be observed that all the rivers were exceedingly low, when seen by me—the Beaver Creek being absolutely dry. Taylor's Creek empties itself in the 20, Beaver Creek in the Chippawa.

J. E. PORTLOCK,
Lieut. R. Engrs.

With regard to the 20 and 30 Mile Creeks, they display the same difficulties as to a harbour, and of course being nearer the frontier are necessarily rejected.

(Dominion Archives, C. 39 pp. 96-103.)

Five years later the Commissioner of the Navy addressed the following letter to the Lieutenant-Governor, while the report of the Commissioners on Inland Navigation was still under consideration and the surveys for the Welland Canal Company were in progress:—

FROM CAPTAIN ROBERT BARRIE, R.N. TO SIR PEREGRINE MAITLAND.

Kingston Dock Yard,
U.C.
15th June, 1824.

Sir,

I beg leave to submit to your Excellency, the Copy of a Letter I some time since received from Mr. Macaulay the President of the Commissioners of Internal Navigation &ca. on the subject of cutting a Canal between Lake Ontario and little Burlington Lake. It may be in Your Excellency's recollection that so far back as October 1819, I wrote to Your Excellency on this head, and about the same time, I also wrote to the Navy Board, strongly urging the necessity of such a Canal, as its completion on a scale large enough to admit our Ships of War would not only afford us a Secure Harbour, where at present we have no Harbour, or safe anchorage at all, but would also by opening a back communication from the Store houses on Burlington heights to Grand River, and the settlements beyond it, render us independent of the risk, and absolute loss, which has heretofore been incurred in the transport of Stores by the Niagara frontier.

I shall not presume to intrude my opinions on the advantages which in a Military point of view would probably result from the possession of such a Canal. Your Excellency's local and general knowledge will enable you to decide on this subject.

In February, 1823, the Navy Board in reference to my Letter of October, 1819, acquaint me that my Lords Commissioners of the Admiralty would not authorize any steps being taken (independent of their unwillingness to incur any expense at present) respecting the proposition for opening a communication between Lakes Ontario and Burlington, except after full explanation and consultation with the local Authorities, to its necessity and general benefit in a Military as well as Naval point of view.

I have had the honor of submitting verbally to Your Excellency my opinions on this subject in a Naval point of view, with them I understood Your Excellency entirely to agree. May I request before I submit Mr. Macaulay's letter to the serious consideration of the Navy Board, that your Excellency will furnish me with such explanations as your Judgment shall direct on the utility and necessity of the measure, both generally, and in a Military point of view.

It may be proper for me to add, that I have had the honor verbally to submit my opinions on this head to His Excellency the Commander in Chief, the Earl of Dalhousie, in the presence of Lieutenant Colonel Harvey, Deputy Adjutant General, at his Lordship's request I furnished him with memoranda on this subject previously to his departure for England, Lieutenant Col. Harvey, whose local knowledge was obtained during the late War, expressed himself most highly in favor of the Canal, both in a Naval and Military point of view.

As this Officer will be in London, when my dispatches arrive, I shall refer the Commissioners of the Navy to him for any local imformation they may require.

I have the honor to be, &c.

ROBT. BARRIE,
Acting Commissioner.

His Excellency
Sir Peregrine Maitland, K.C.B.
Commander of the Forces, &c., &c., &c.
(Dominion Archives, Q 336-2, pp. 290-2).

It is evident that in the opinion of the Lieutenant-Governor and the naval and military officers, who were consulted, the foremost consideration was the creation of safe harbours and naval bases near the head of Lake Ontario and on Lake Erie and an inland line of communication between them. They were still haunted by the fear of an invasion and believed it their paramount duty to take every precaution for making a successful resistance.

The subjoined letter shows that it is almost certain that Maitland had examined the plans of the Welland Canal Company before writing on the subject of their application for a grant of lands.

FROM WM. HAMILTON MERRITT TO LIEUT. MAITLAND, A.D.C.

St. Catharines, 30th July, 1824.

Sir,

As agent for the Welland Canal Company, I am desired by the President and Directors thereof to inform His Excellency that the different surveys from the Grand River & Lake Erie to River Welland & from thence to Lake Ontario are now compleated.

May I request you will please intimate the same to His Excellency & say I should be happy to attend with the plans & submit the same to his consideration at any time he may be pleased to bestow a few Minutes on the subject.

I have the honor to be, &c.,

WM. HAMILTON MERRITT.

Lt. Maitland, A.D.C.

(Dominion Archives, C 41, p. 34).

VI.

AN ADDRESS ON TURNING THE FIRST SOD OF THE PIONEER MONUMENT.

WATERLOO COUNTY PIONEERS' MEMORIAL, SCHOERG FARM NEAR KITCHENER, ONTARIO, 24 JUNE, 1924.

By Brigadier-General E. A. Cruikshank, Chairman of the Historic Sites and Monuments Board of Canada.

Mr. Chairman, Ladies and Gentlemen:

It is a great privilege and pleasure to be here and to be permitted to take a minor part in this interesting ceremony. Our first duty is to offer our hearty and sincere congratulations to Mr. W. H. Breithaupt and his worthy colleagues, the ladies and gentlemen of the Waterloo Historical Society and the Waterloo County Pioneers' Memorial Association on their notable success in the discovery, publication, and preservation of so much valuable historical material and the public spirit, energy, and perseverance they have so finely displayed in the acquisition of this noble site and in making plans for the due commemoration of the labours and virtues of the Pioneers of this good County by an appropriate monument. These efforts, indeed, deserve our utmost commendation.

It is scarcely possible after the lapse of a century and a quarter, to imagine, and still less to describe in fitting terms, the perils and hardships so courageously and resolutely faced and overcome by those early pioneers who threw themselves fearlessly into the heart of an unbroken forest, haunted by wolves, wild cats, and other beasts of prey, as well as innumerable lesser animals that ravaged their fields and gardens and stacks of grain. They were completely isolated, far beyond the verge of civilization. Along the banks of this river below were the warlike tribes of the Six Nations, whose goodwill was by no means assured; and in the unexplored and mysterious woodlands, extending northward to the shores of the Georgian Bay and westward to Lake Huron, roved many lawless bands of Chippewas and Mississaugas, whose appearance was decidedly unwelcome to the lone white settler. They seldom had a visitor and seldom had a message from their former homes. When they came hither, the nearest post-offices and probably the nearest stores and markets were at Niagara or at Sandwich, and the nearest mills were certainly many miles distant. They were obliged to build their own houses, weave their own cloth, make their own clothing and shoes, fashion their own tools, and grind their own flour. Newspapers, in the modern sense of the word, there were none.

Courage they certainly had, and the staunch qualities of energy, undaunted industry, determination, patience, and sobriety, which lay such sure foundations for social progress and national prosperity. This province, and in fact Canada as a whole, owes much to them.

The whole history of your county has happily been constructive, and is a record of steady industrial and social advancement. Elsewhere it has been so frequently a chronicle of calamity and destruction in one form or another, which you and your ancestors have so fortunately escaped.

I can speak with some assurance of the admirable qualities of our fellow-citizens of German origin; particularly of the descendants of those people whom we were wont to call the Pennsylvanian Dutch. In the Township of Bertie, in the County of Welland, where I was born and lived for the greater part of my early life, they, at that time, formed the great majority of the inhabitants. There had been, I may say, three successive waves of such immigrants. First of all, about 1784-5 came the disbanded loyalists, most of whom had served for several years in the famous regiment known as Butler's Rangers. Of these I may recall the names of Anger, Anguish, Benner, Cregar, Haun, House, Huffman, Plato, Riselay, Sypes, Seager, Windecker and Wintemute. Many of them came from the valley of the Mohawk river, being descendants of Protestants driven from the Rhenish Palatinate by the French invaders. They in their turn had deliberately sacrificed their homes and property to demonstrate their fidelity and loyalty to the government that had given them an asylum in the new world. Others at the same time had fled from the banks of the Susquehanna to fight under the old flag.

Next from about 1796 onwards for ten or twelve years came a steady though not very large tide of immigrants from Lancaster and neighbouring counties in the older settled portion of Pennsylvania. These were essentially men of peace, mostly Mennonites and Tunkers, whose principal motives in removing seem to have been a desire to escape excessive taxation and compulsory military service. Among them I can recall the names of Baker, Bitner, Boehm, Buerger, Climenhage, Fretz, Hershey, Morgenstern, Mueller, Noxsell, Sherk, Shisler, Troup, Winger, Zavitz and others, some of which may be familiar to some persons present.

Then still later, from about 1840 to 1855, a good many emigrants came directly from Germany, bearing such names as Bauer, Bossert, Claus, Critz, Deterling, Eisengott, Koebel, Kohl, Lichtenburg, Loeffler, Mann, Ott, Rheinhardt, Sauerwein, Weiss, Wilhelm, Woehl and Zimmermann. Hard times, the disturbed political state of their native land, the hope of bettering their conditions, and in a very few cases participation in a revolutionary movement, were the chief causes of their emigration. Carl Schurz, in his "Reminiscences," names one of his trusted revolutionary comrades, who found an asylum there, Augustin Loeffler, whom I well remember as a very quiet, sedate, old farmer, not in the least resembling the ideal of a rebel, and steadily voting for the Conservative candidate in every election.

With very few exceptions these people were eminently sober-minded, hard-working, steady-going, honest and upright men and women, who bore a good name everywhere, and whose lives were an example to all who knew them.

They were most certainly the type of men and women Walt Whitman had in mind when he wrote his memorable verses:

"Have the older races halted?
Do they droop and end their lesson, wearied over there beyond the seas?
We take up the task eternal, and the burden and the lesson,
Pioneers! O pioneers!

"All the past we leave behind,
We debouch upon a newer mightier world, varied world,
Fresh and strong the world we seize, world of labour and the march,
Pioneers! O pioneers!"

It gives me great pleasure to announce that the Department of the Interior, acting on the advice of the Board of which I have the honour to be a member, will accede to the request of the President of the Waterloo County Pioneers' Association, and supply a standard tablet to be placed upon this monument, when it is completed.

VII.

JOHN DE COU, PIONEER.*

By Ernest Green.

On the low-lying, sandy and deeply-indented west coast of France, anciently in the province of Saintonge, now in the Department of Charente Inferieur, lies a region made forever famous by the Huguenots. LaRochelle was its stronghold. There, also, stood the venerable village of Coux from which, it is believed, the family of "des Coux" got its name. They were Protestant folk and incurred all the penalties that fell upon the followers of that faith in France in the early part of the seventeenth century. Some of them lost their lives, while others abandoned their possessions and fled to more tolerant lands. Traditions of the sufferings and losses sustained by their ancestors of three centuries ago are still related in accents of bitterness by members of the oldest generation of the family surviving at this day. Documentary records of their pecuniary losses are extant. (1)

In England, at that period, the great Dutch engineer, Vermuyden, was draining the Lincolnshire fens, in which work he employed many emigrés from continental countries, including the fugitive Huguenots from France. At Sandtoft, in Lincolnshire, these established a colony, about 1630, and there lived "Leuren (Lawrence) desCou," the remotest ancestor to whom the "deCou" family of America can trace descent. The family name appears in the registers of several of the old Huguenot churches in England and displays many of the variations in spelling that are still in common usage, including the forms "Decou," "DeCow," "Decow," "DeCowe" and "Decamp." In the fen country it is still to be met with as "Descow." (2) The Society of Friends absorbed great numbers of the French Protestants, including the deCou family, and it is probable that some of the American branches still adhere to the Quaker faith.

William Penn's American colonization scheme attracted the younger generations of the time and in 1685 Isaac and Jacob "DeCow" (sons of "Leuren") purchased the 2,500 acres of land in Bucks county, Pennsylvania, that is still

---

*The family name is now spelled in so many different ways that it is impossible to say that any particular form is the "correct" one. The original spelling was probably "de Coux" or "des Coux." There is a tradition that "de Ceaux" was the ancient form, but this is not supported by any documentary evidence, and as such a spelling would entail a different pronunciation this old story is open to serious question. When used as a place-name in Canada, the spelling is always "DeCew," (DeCew Falls, DeCewsville, etc.), while members of the oldest living generation of the family use both "DeCew" and "DeCeu." Old documents frequently have it "DeCow." I have adopted the spelling "DeCou" for my subject because it is the modern form most similar to the original spelling and also because it is the spelling in Captain John DeCou's signature to documents now in the Public Archives, Ottawa. Captain DeCou was very particular to have his name pronounced "DeKoo,"—with the accent on the "De." The frequent mispronunciation "DQ" vexed him greatly. It was in the endeavour to escape this mispronunciation that his children and grandchildren adopted certain spellings and they varied these in the hope of distinguishing one branch of the family from another, in which they were largely unsuccessful.

known as "the DeCou tract." They finally sailed from Hull on March 8, 1686, on the ship "Shields" of Stockton, and established themselves in the New World, to become the founders of a large and widely-distributed family. Its members have always been numerous in New Jersey and have held many high offices in that state, both in Colonial and post-Revolutionary times. The name is also found in Maryland, Pennsylvania, New York, Vermont and elsewhere.

Isaac DeCow died soon after his arrival in America. A line of descent is traced from him through Jacob (1668-1735), Jacob (1710-17..), and a third Jacob, to John, born in Vermont in 1766, who is the subject of this memoir. (3)

The only connected record of John DeCou's career is a compilation of his reminiscences, prepared by his sons, Edmund and Robert, some years after the death of the narrator. It is an interesting, if simple, relation and offers so excellent a frame-work for a fuller story that no apology is offered for making use of it in that way, adding, in course, the further information that has been collected and making the "reminiscences" again available to all who may be interested in them. (4)

REMINISCENCES OF AN OLD PIONEER.

> My forefathers were Huguenots, and fled from France to England on account of their religion, and at an early day came to America and settled in Vermont, where I was born in 1766. When a boy I took great delight in rambling along the sides of the Green Mountains. At one time as I stooped down to look under a rock a rabbit sprang out and into the open bosom of my blouse.

February 3, 1766, was John DeCou's birthday. The "Genealogy " (see Note 3) gives Oxford township, New Jersey, as his birthplace and reproduces the description attached to a parole of 1813 in which it is so stated. However, this document gives his age as thirty-five years, whereas he was forty-seven years old at that time. It is suggested that the description may be that of another man of the same name, or that it contains deliberate mis-statements designed to deceive the enemy. Be that as it may, the year of his birth was undoubtedly as above stated and his repeated references to Vermont as his native State and to the Green Mountains as the scene of his boyhood can hardly be denied.

> At the close of the American Revolution my father and family removed to Upper Canada, crossing the river at Queenston.

From numerous references in the Land and State Books of Upper Canada it appears that Jacob DeCou took up his residence in the Niagara district in 1790, removing later to Burford, accompanied by his sons, Abner and Abraham, while the other two sons, John and Edmund, remained in Thorold township. In 1794 Jacob asked for a grant of land in the Short Hills and was recommended for 200 acres, the location not being stated. In 1797 he was recommended for 200 acres as a Loyalist and 350 acres "family lands." Later, a committee of the Executive Council, who had been appointed to purge the "U.E. List" of names wrongfully recorded thereon, recommended that Jacob DeCou be struck off, along with several hundred others. In 1804 his son, Edmund, petitioned for land as the son of a Loyalist and filed an affidavit of Isaac Swayze establishing that "Jacob DeCow" had served in the first Battalion of Jersey Volunteers under Colonel Barton during the "American war." The Board thereupon restored Jacob DeCou's name to the U. E. List, expressing the opinion that it should not have been suspended therefrom. Edmund, Abner and Abraham DeCou each received 200 acres of land, in 1806, as sons of a Loyalist. The status of the DeCous as Loyalists is thus established beyond question. (5)

While 1790 appears to be the year in which Jacob DeCou came to Upper Canada, his sons, John and Edmund, must have been here earlier, for there is record of their employment in survey work in township No. 7, District of Nassau, in July and August, 1788. (6) Such employment would give special facilities for a reconnoissance of the virgin country.

> I commenced exploring, and, led by my early predilections, finally selected a property to my liking in the Townships of Thorold and Grantham, covering what is now called DeCew's Falls, on the Beaverdam creek.

When he first saw this branch of the Twelve Mile creek pouring its beautiful cascade over the Niagara escarpment into the deep gorge that its waters had carved out, he ceased his search for a home-site, feeling that he could find no place more pleasing. He spent the following night in his blankets, close to the cataract that was thenceforth to bear his name, lulled by its music and dreaming of the industrial as well as the agricultural possibilities of the place.

> I purchased one man's right to a hundred acres for an axe and an Indian blanket, and another hundred acres for a gold doubloon.

Prior to 1791, when Upper Canada became a separate province, with freehold land tenure, settlers received "allotment tickets" from the District Land Boards for the quantity and location of lands assigned to them. These were transferable when the transactions were approved and recorded by the Boards. A discharged soldier receiving 200 acres of land as the reward of his loyalty and services, and having the choice of only remote locations in the midst of a forest that he had not the means to clear away, naturally sought a purchaser at the best price he could get. With hundreds of such lots offered, values were low. John DeCou probably paid a very good price for the two "rights" that he purchased. Merchants and traders took many "rights" in exchange for goods. In this way, Hon. Robert Hamilton, of Queenston, and others became great landowners. This speculation in "rights" has a modern parallel in the South African Veteran Land Scrip scramble of fifteen years ago.

John DeCou's "purchase" of land at DeCew Falls does not imply that he was not entitled to a free grant. He probably preferred to buy choice "rights" near the Niagara frontier, cheaply, to taking residence upon free land in a remote locality. Official records show that, in 1796, he petitioned and was recommended for 200 acres "in addition," indicating that he had had a previous grant. In 1797 he was allowed a town lot in Newark, his petition stating that he had the frame of a house ready for erection. (7)

> I endured many hardships but worked away happily. One of my first wants was a grindstone, which I supplied by discovering a quarry not far below the falls from which I selected a stone of suitable size and quality, and having partially

shaped it with a pick, I started home with it. On becoming tired I would lay it down and resume picking; resting, lightening my load and bringing the stone nearer the required shape at the same time. Whilst thus engaged at one time I thought I heard a rustling in the leaves behind me, and on turning my head I saw an enormous blacksnake reared up and looking over my shoulder. As quick as thought I discharged my pick at his head, and laid him dead at my feet. I suppose he took me for a stump and thought there was a woodpecker on the other side, of which he might make a dinner.

I used a good many devices to accomplish as much work as I possibly could with as little means as possible. One trouble I had was to get rid of big logs, and in my first clearing nigh the road-line stood a gigantic hemlock, which I was perplexed to know how to dispose of; if I cut it down I had not a team that could move it. Finally I took my axe and climbing to nigh the top, commenced cutting away the limbs, leaving myself enough to stand upon. Burning the brush effectually killed the tree, and the blackened skeleton was a sort of way-mark for several years and was known as the "big hemlock stub."

I, at length, resolved to build a sawmill and an oil mill, there being none at the time between the two lakes. I was aided in my enterprise by Colonel Hamilton, of Queenston, who imported the necessary ironware for me from Scotland.

The phrase "none...between the lakes" has reference to the oil mill only, for sawmills had been erected as early as 1786 by private enterprise, and under government control at an even earlier date. (8)

On November 7, 1792, D. W. Smith, surveyor-general, made a report upon the various mills then constructed or under construction in the Niagara district. There were twenty in all, No. 14 being "A sawmill now erecting on one of the branches of the creek called the Twelve-mile in township No. 9, Lot 16, in 5th Concession, by John DeCow; the lands were granted to him as only fit for husbandry." (9)

The original sawmill stood about three-quarters of a mile back from the crest of the falls, there being a small cascade or rapid there in a location where a dam and raceway could be easily constructed. The building has been gone for many years, but its great oak sills are still in the place where the builder laid them down, now covered by the waters of an artificial pond.

It is not known when the oil mill was built. Flax was an important crop in the early days of the colony, the settlers performing in their homes, with hand implements, all the processes required in producing linen thread from flax straw, and finally weaving their own linen cloth or "linsey-woolsey," the latter combining linen and wool. Buttons for garments were made from knots of flax fibre. The flax seed, as a by-product, brought only a small price until the establishment of DeCou's oil mill created a local industrial market for it and added something to the scanty income of the struggling pioneers.

"Colonel" Robert Hamilton was the Hon. Robert Hamilton before referred to. He was the greatest man of his time in the Niagara region and lent his aid to John DeCou in several enterprises for the development of the locality.

By 1800, settlers had become so numerous in Thorold, Stamford and Pelham townships and so much land had been cleared and drained that the character of the small streams had greatly changed. They rose to floods in rainy seasons but dwindled to nothing in dry times because the woods, swamps and beaver-meadows that had been the storage reservoirs for their waters were largely gone. The owners of mills on such streams were seriously affected, for as the production of grain in their neighborhoods increased the annual grinding capacity of their mills was reduced, the periods of shut-down for lack of water growing longer and longer. In this dilemma they naturally turned to the larger and unfailing streams for mill-sites and power,—to the Niagara most of all.

On August 28, 1800, John DeCou and Robert Ker laid before Lieutenant-Governor Peter Hunter a petition for a strip of land on the banks of the Niagara river "above Canby's and Margill's" for a mill-site. Their declaration that the drying-up of streams had crippled many existing mills was confirmed by a supporting petition signed by forty-six of the principal inhabitants near the frontier, who further declared that the two existing mills on the Niagara were insufficient for the needs of the country and pointed out that the proposed new mill would be accessible to boats.

The enterprise was officially objected to on several grounds and finally disapproved. Doubtless it was opposed by the wealthy and influential men already established in the milling business along the Niagara. (10).

It might be inferred that John DeCou had been operating a grist-mill prior to this time, but the date when he began grinding grain at DeCew Falls has not been established. He had such a mill in 1801.

We must now turn back two years in order to record a most important event in John DeCou's career—his marriage, which took place on August 9, 1798. Although the date is a matter of family record, the place and the name of the clergyman or magistrate officiating at the ceremony are unknown. The lady of John DeCou's choice came of stock typical of the times and the people. Catherine Docksteder was born at Fort Niagara on January 9, 1781, the daughter of Frederick Docksteder, a Loyalist soldier, then newly-appointed to a commission in Colonel John Butler's famous corps of Rangers. Before she was a year old her father lost his life while on service against the enemy, leaving his widow and infant in impoverished circumstances. To the care of an uncle, Lieutenant John Docksteder of the Indian Department, these helpless ones owed protection in the later years of the Revolution, for a pension had been denied them. (11) Where the orphan spent her girlhood years is now unknown. Her mother married again (date unknown) to John Vanevery, also a Loyalist. John DeCou's seventeen-year-old bride, born amid the tragic circumstances of the Revolution, was destined to experience, as a soldier's wife and the mother and protector of a young family in the enemy's hands, all the trials and anxieties that war brings to women. (12).

Upon locating at the Falls, John DeCou erected a log dwelling, facing his mill and the stream that furnished its power. The rattlesnakes came into it in such numbers, before he had the floor laid and a door put up, that he was forced to sling his hammock from the rafters from fear of being bitten in the night. Prosperity and the married state turned his thoughts to the erection of a more fitting domicile and he determined to make his new house the finest in all the region round-about.

By this time a road had been opened through his property, leading westward to "the Head of the Lake" and dividing at Beaver Dams, a few miles east of DeCew Falls, into two branches, one of which connected with Lundy's Lane and

THE DE COU HOUSE
at De Cew Falls, showing the original portico, and the old lilacs and pear tree.

the other, following the crest of the escarpment, reached St. Davids and Queenston. This became the principal east-and-west highway of the Peninsula, adding greatly to the value and importance of the localities through which it passed. The road was opened north, and in the rear, of the first DeCou house, but a commanding site on its further side was chosen for the new structure so that, facing southerly, it would overlook the highway, the mill and the stream. Stout walls of the hard limestone of the vicinity, bound with clay and straw, rose from deep and broad foundations to the height of two lofty storeys. Great stone chimneys were built into the walls in each gable end, providing cavernous fireplaces in the principal rooms. The dignified entrance gave access to a spacious hall, from which rooms opened on either hand and stairs led to the floor above. The interior finish was of heavy black walnut, and all the furnishings were of the best in design and workmanship. The stone-flagged basement contained the fireplaces for cooking and the bake oven, as well as the cheese-press and other domestic machinery. A small portico sheltered the front door, looking out upon a terrace with stone steps. The grounds were tastefully laid out and ornamented in a fashion appropriate to the building. This mansion (for so it was regarded in those days) was the wonder of the countryside and the admiration of travellers. The dwellers in log huts came from miles around to view it, while other men of means were inspired to erect for themselves dwellings of a size and style that had not previously been contemplated. The suns and storms of a hundred years have beat upon it, and its lofty gable has attracted the thunderbolt, but still the DeCou house stands a monument to the thorough methods of its builder, as solid as when he and his bride threw open its doors for a grand house-warming.

The building of mills and a fine house were not by any means the whole sum of John DeCou's activities at this period. His lands were well cleared and thoroughly cultivated, and he imported, at considerable cost and difficulty, a variety of fruit trees and ornamental shrubs for the beautification of his estate and the extension and improvement of its products. Clumps of sturdy lilacs that still surround the old house are from roots that he planted, and the remnant of a great pear tree, that still bears fruit on its one vigorous branch, is the sole monument of the orchard that he set out more than a century ago.

The hospitality of the DeCou house was known, not only to those who travelled the great highroad, but also to those who passed silently along the dim forest trails. In those days numbers of Indians were constantly going back and forth between the Grand River and Niagara. DeCou's was one of their regular resting-places and often, on a stormy night, the floor of the great west room would be so crowded with blanketed forms that no more could be accommodated.

There was a small family burying-ground in what is now called "the old orchard," on the south side of the road, near the site of the original house. All traces of it have long been obliterated. It is said that there never were any grave-stones, and no record of interments there is discoverable. The last burial, many years ago, was that of a young grandchild of John DeCou. Whether the earlier graves were those of adults of the first generations of the family in Canada can only be conjectured.

In 1804 John DeCou was elected a director of the Niagara District Agricultural Society, the pioneer organization of its kind in Upper Canada.

The earliest municipal records of Thorold township are those for the year 1799, although there was some organization at an earlier date. In the year mentioned, John DeCou was collector; in 1810, 1816, 1818, 1819 and 1835 he was assessor; and in 1815, 1820 and 1822 he was warden of the township. (13)

Traditions preserve the memory of the substantial assistance he gave to the earliest schools established in the vicinity of DeCew Falls and a further evidence of his interest in education appears in the records of the Niagara library. He was one of the forty-one original "proprietors" at the founding of this venerable institution, in June, 1800, each member paying twenty-four shillings into the fund. (14)

> A kind Providence crowned my undertakings with success, and by the year 1812 I had built a substantial stone dwelling, which, on the war coming on and our men being obliged to retreat from Niagara, was used as a military storehouse. By that time the country had become pretty well settled, and I was appointed Captain of a company of Militia, and, being thoroughly British, I turned out with my men, although conscious that we had to fight against great odds, yet determined to make up in courage and determination what we lacked in numbers. After engaging in several skirmishes I was among the few made prisoners at the taking of Niagara, and at once hurried across the river and to Batavia, where we were joined by some of our regulars.

In three sentences the "Reminiscences" summarize a range of time and occurrences of which a detailed record would be of great interest and value. In 1808 the Legislature of Upper Canada passed a new Militia Act, entirely remodelling the plan on which the men of the province were organized for its defence against invasion. Brock had been in command of the military forces of the province for more than a year previously and it seems certain that his wide experience and shrewd judgment had much to do with the framing of the measure.

In 1809 "John Decoe" was commissioned "Lieutenant of a company of militia in the Second Regiment of Lincoln, District of Niagara." The commission, signed by Francis Gore, lieutenant-governor, was dated at York, on January 2. (15)

At that time the *Chesapeake* and *Leopard* affair was a very recent occurrence and far-sighted men realized that the embers of enmity left from the Revolution would sooner or later be fanned into flame and that the inland frontiers would again be the scenes of bloody campaigns. John DeCou was one of those who actively co-operated with Brock in preparing for the storm which they believed to be inevitable. The encouragement, arming and training of the militiamen, the making of such provision as was possible for commissary and transport services during hostilities and the surveillance of the numerous enemy aliens who had been permitted to settle in the country under too lax immigration laws, were all subjects of numerous consultations between the General and his most earnest assistants among the militia officers. Very often the "east room" of DeCou's house was the scene of grave councils that were to bear fruit in succeeding years.

No record has been found of Captain DeCou's part, if any, in the actions at Queenston Heights, Frenchman's Creek and Fort George,—the only fights that occurred on the Niagara frontier before he was made prisoner. He would not be likely to refer to Queenston Heights or Fort George as "skirmishes" and it may be surmised that he was engaged at Frenchman's Creek (November 28, 1812). This belief is strengthened by militia records showing that he was continuously on duty from September 13 to December 5 in that year; that from October 13 to 24 he was with a large detachment of the 2nd Lincoln in Willoughby township, and that from October 25 to November 24 he was with a detachment of several companies stationed at Dr. Hersey's house, which was in Bertie township, very near to the scene of the Frenchman's Creek affair. (16)

When, on May 27, 1813, Niagara and Fort George were abandoned, after gallant but futile defence, the survivors of Vincent's force retired, gathering, as they went, the guards and pickets that had been stationed at various points, and carrying all the ordnance, arms and stores for which transportation could be provided. At nightfall the little army reached "DeCou's" and there halted to rest. (17) The house accommodated headquarters, outbuildings sheltered the wounded, and regiments bivouacked in the fields. Before morning they were joined by the regulars that had formed the garrisons of Fort Erie and Chippawa and by Commodore Barclay and his sailors, *en route* for Malden. (18) It was but the first of many stirring experiences of the war-time that "DeCou's" was destined to pass through. When morning came, the retreat was resumed. No encouragement was given the militiamen to remain with the army. (19) Their natural desire to remain in their homes for the protection of their families and property agreed with Vincent's anxiety to ease the drain upon his scanty stores.

With sinking hearts the loyal inhabitants saw the rear-guard of the British forces disappear on the road to Burlington, and turned their eyes eastward to watch for the first scouts of the victorious army of invasion. They had not long to wait. The enemy's patrols were at the line of the Twelve Mile creek and "DeCou's" the next day, and on June 1 that position was occupied in force. (20)

While the commander of the United States forces published reassuring proclamations, his ill-disciplined militia and volunteers soon began to ravage and plunder the helpless settlers, giving them their first experience of what was to occur again and again during the rest of the war. They believed that they were abandoned to their ancient foes and were plunged in black despair, when the first rumours of the event of Stoney Creek began to circulate. Such news seemed incredible, but soon a retrograde movement of the enemy forces was observable and by June 9 their heavy columns had all passed eastward once more, and the British dragoons, following hard upon the heels of the rearguard, routed them from the Twelve Mile creek line. The militia, smarting from the experiences of the last ten days, sprang to arms and joined the van of the British advance. The enemy were fairly chased into Fort George, but Vincent's main force was not strong enough to risk an advance beyond the Twenty Mile creek. A large area of the best of the Niagara settlements remained debateable ground, not fully occupied by either army, and exposed to incursions from both.

Under such circumstances there were, no doubt, numerous violations of the laws of war and neutrality on both sides. The invaders had plundered civilians, and, perhaps, some militiamen took up arms after having been paroled. The enemy now realized that the inhabitants in general were strongly attached to the British cause and that expectations of seducing them from their allegiance by either cajolery or fear were very ill-founded. General Dearborn now put into effect orders, received from Washington, that were quite at variance with the spirit of his former proclamations. Parties were sent out to arrest and bring into the United States lines a number of the leading men of the frontier country. This was accomplished by fast-riding mounted detachments, sometimes dashing out in the night, and often guided by renegade inhabitants of the locality. The victims were taken by surprise, placed upon horses and whisked away without opportunity of evasion or resistance. The swift movements of the raiders defied attempts of the British scouts, who were sometimes witnesses of the forays, to organize a counter-attack or effect a rescue.

One of the victims of these seizures was Captain John DeCou. Records show that he was among the twenty-one men seized on the 19th, 20th and 21st of June. It would be correct to say that he was made prisoner "after" the fall of Niagara, rather than "at" that occurrence, as the "reminiscences" compiled by his sons express it. Of the place and manner of his capture, or the experiences of his wife and young children during those days of trial, tradition has preserved no account. Official and other contemporary records indicate that the prisoners were removed from the Canadian side of the Niagara river to Fort Niagara on June 22, and were kept in that stronghold three days before commencing their long journey into the interior of the States. (21)

Already events were taking form that were to make DeCou's house a place of note in national as well as in local annals. On June 12, Lieutenant James FitzGibbon, of the 49th regiment, had sought and obtained permission from General Vincent to organize a troop of mounted volunteers to do scout and patrol duty in front of the British position and to counter the activities of United States raiding parties, especially the gang of plunderers led by Cyrenius Chapin of Buffalo, and the renegade Willcocks' so-called "Canadian volunteers." In three days the troop was completed and outfitted, and on the 16th they advanced and took up headquarters at "DeCou's." Immediately they entered upon a career of the most daring, picturesque and useful character. They struck the foe at many and widely-distant points, routed his patrols, ambushed his wagon-trains, seized his spies, raided his depots and so circumscribed the area within which small bodies of his troops could operate that the United States general decided that such tormentors must be destroyed without delay. On June 23 he ordered Lieut.-Col. Charles G. Boerstler to take a force of 500 men and two field guns, advance to DeCou's house, which he knew to be FitzGibbon's headquarters, and destroy it.

At "DeCou's" nothing was known of the impending attack. Mrs. DeCou and her children, living in one or two rooms while the soldiers occupied the rest of the house and its dependencies, rejoiced to have so many gallant protectors about them when the head of the family was a prisoner in the enemy's hands. In DeCou's fields, to the eastward, a large party of Caughnawaga Indians were encamped. Such rude and savage neighbours made the presence of disciplined white soldiers doubly welcome. This sense of security was rudely disturbed on the morning of June 24, when a party of the redskins came to the house, having in their custody Laura, wife of James Secord, of Queenston, whom they had seized when she strayed into their camp in the darkness. The story of Laura Secord's pilgrimage is too well known to require repetition here. While she was describing to FitzGibbon the strong enemy column that was moving against him for his destruction, Indian runners brought tidings that the foe had already passed St. Davids and was even then in conflict with their pickets.

Then ensued a time of wild excitement at "DeCou's." The whole body of Indians rushed away to ambush the advancing column, couriers galloped to appraise DeHaren at the Ten Mile creek, and Bisshopp at "the Twenty," of the sudden developments in the situation, while FitzGibbon's men dragged out all the stores that would stand such treatment and sank them in the waters of DeCou's mill-pond. Accompanied by a handful of his men, the commander himself went forward to the scene of conflict.

Meantime, Mrs. DeCou and her daughters were doing what they could to relieve the exhaustion and sufferings of the woman who had dared so much and struggled so heroically to serve her adopted country and save its defenders. Food was set before her, her bare and lacerated feet and limbs were bathed and bandaged and the shoes and stockings of Catherine DeCou replaced those lost in the jungle and the bog.

Mrs. DeCou and her children were resolved to remain in their home until it should be actually assailed by the approaching foe, but Mrs. Secord was unequal to facing any additional trials of strength or courage that day, and she desired to be taken to the home of her friends, the Turneys, below the mountain, a mile or so distant. Her exhausted body was incapable of any further exertion, so a hammock was made by fastening a long blanket to a pole, two Indians took her light weight upon their shoulders and one of the DeCou boys walked beside, as guide and protector. So Laura Secord went to a place of comparative safety while the inmates of DeCou's house trembled at the boom of artillery, rolling through the woods and fields from the direction of the Beaverdams.

The tale of "the fight in the Beechwoods" has been often and well told. (22) Ere the sun had set, "DeCou's" saw, with inexpressible delight, the long column of enemy prisoners plodding along the highway towards Burlington, protected by redcoats from the enraged and vindictive Indians. Captain DeCou, prisoner in Fort Niagara, only twenty miles away, knew nothing of the stirring events of that day nor the perils from which his wife and little ones had so providentially escaped. He was to pass through even greater perils himself ere he could listen to the tale from their own lips.

During the remainder of 1813 and for many periods in 1814, "DeCou's" was a military post. Stores were collected there, the mills ground grain for the army, detachments proceeding to or from the frontier halted there for rest or refreshment and it was constantly a centre of military activity. In the autumn of 1813, and again in July, 1814, when temporary misfortune forced the British to abandon the field in the peninsula, enemy parties ransacked the place and the family were subjected to hardship and indignity. So commonplace, however, were experiences of that kind in the Niagara region in those days that details of the occurrences did not even become subjects of tradition. (23)

Captain DeCou's story of his adventures from the time of his arrival at Batavia, N.Y., with other prisoners of war, is much more detailed. He said:

> We now numbered in all about fifty prisoners, with but a small guard placed over us. We discovered in the place an arsenal containing arms and ammunition, and resolved to capture it, arm ourselves and make our way back home. Our plans were matured and the time appointed when at a given signal, to be given at night, when we would have less to fear from the inhabitants, our designs were to be put into execution. But before the hour arrived our wild scheme was frustrated by one of our regulars who divulged our secret to the enemy. Our indignation against the traitor was so marked that our guard had to rescue him, but his red coat could not be found and on inquiry being made after it one of his old comrades exclaimed, "he deserted his colors and his coat deserted him." An opportunity was shortly after presented, when said coat was placed on a post and whipped to shreds. Shortly after this we were carried from place to place, nothing of particular interest occurring more than that we were a sort of free show that attracted general attention. At one place an old lady came hurrying out, exclaiming, "Where are they? Where are they?" When one of our men pointed out a couple across the street, she, with a wondering look said: "Why, law me, they are just like men; they look like our folks." At another place we halted for a few days at the foot of a mountain, and were allowed to go on parole. I took a chisel, and finding a rock with a smooth face, I cut my name on it, "Capt. John DeCew, II Lincoln Militia." This excited a good deal of query; they could not conceive what Lincoln meant; finally it was decided to mean Linken which implied that they were all linked together as one man, and would consequently prove formidable antagonists. I did not contradict this exposition.

From Batavia, these prisoners were marched via Canandaigua, Geneva and Utica to Albany,—a circuitous route of about 300 miles, occupying about eight weeks' time. (24.) Some of them, including Captain DeCou, were subsequently sent on to the internment camp at Burlington, Vt. At that place, Captain DeCou was given a parole and pass, on January 28, 1814, to proceed by way of Vergennes, Middlebury, Rutland, Manchester and Bennington, Vt., and Williamstown, Mass., to Cheshire, Mass., where he was to report to Captain David B. Brown not later than February 5. Cheshire is but a dozen miles north of Pittsfield. (25.)

Meantime, negotiations had been opened for an exchange of prisoners of war, including those in the depot at Burlington, Vt. "John De Coe," captain, and Wm. H. Myers, ensign, were included in a proposed exchange list dated January 8, 1814, but circumstances intervened to prevent the carrying out of the arrangement. (26.)

> We at length arrived at Pittsfield, where twelve officers, I being one, were selected as hostages—to be sent to Washington and executed in retaliation for the execution of some of their men, who proved to be deserters from our army and captured bearing arms against us. After travelling eight days towards the place of execution, the orders were countermanded, Sir George Prevost having informed them that he had caused twenty-four of their subjects to be placed in close confinement, and would put two for one to death if they persisted. During the final adjustment of this, to us a vital question, we were ordered to be kept at Philadelphia, and were placed in what was not appropriately called the Invincible prison—a large three-storey building, the third flat of which contained a spacious hall, to which we all had access during the day, but confined in several apartments during the night.

The "final adjustment" involved a long correspondence between the government of the United States and the Commander-in-Chief of the British forces in Canada, during which threat was followed by counter-threat until the United States authorities were holding seventy-seven British prisoners as hostages, and the British were, apparently, detaining twice as many United States officers as sureties. In this game of "doubles or quits," with prisoners as pawns, the British were sure to win out in the end, as there were many hundreds of United States soldiers in their hands, while the enemy held a much smaller number of British prisoners. Happily, the contest was not pushed to extremities, but during its continuance the unfortunate hostages were in sore mental distress. (27)

> We were humanely treated, and for a time had liberty to traverse a portion of the city, on parole. This privilege was utilized by a young Ensign named Myers in making the acquaintance of a young lady, which he afterwards turned to good account. During our parole we were frequently invited to the tables of the more wealthy inhabitants, when the subject of the war and its injustice was frequently the topic of conversation, and at one of the dinners our host became so excited in his condemnation that, bringing his knife down with emphasis, he cut a large hole in his table cloth.
> On returning to our restricted position, our longings for home, together with the uncertainty that hung over our ultimate position, caused us to plan an escape. There was a fire-place at the end of our hall nighest the street, the chimney of which was sufficiently large to admit of our escape through it, but it was so grated with iron bars as to require the removal of two in order to permit of our egress. We knew the hours when we were usually left alone, and commenced operations on the grates by using the mainsprings of our watches for saws, placing them in frames for that purpose.

There is a tradition that one of the prisoners had a fife upon which he played during the sawing operations, its shrill notes drowning the sound of the tools. Lusty choruses were also sung to assist in the hoodwinking of the guards.

> But the work was not completed before our tools were worn out, and then the young lady before mentioned furnished her friend with a clean pocket-handkerchief containing a phial of aqua-fortis, which soon completed the work. To provide against detection, the chimney was inspected every day, we found it necessary to replace the grate we had removed when we were not engaged at the work. This we did by securing it in place by wrapping it with paper which we had first rubbed on the sooty chimney in order to give it the proper color. We next made a rope of bedding, tying the strips together, and chose the hour between eight and nine in the evening, we being then usually alone and the streets not much frequented. I was the last to escape, and unfortunately for me the rope had broken in the descent of the man that had preceded me, so I found myself at the end, not knowing how far I was from the ground, but let myself fall, and found myself supported by two comrades, the blood running from my mouth. With difficulty I prevailed upon my friends to leave me, and make their own escape, as it was impossible for me to travel. (28) After remaining alone for some time, rain commenced pouring down, and I recovered so as to be able to walk, which I did in a direction leading from the prison; but, by a strange mishap I, in the darkness, fell into an unoccupied cellar in which stood nigh a foot of water, losing my hat in the fall. I waded around a good while before I found my hat and still longer before I found my way out, and in the meantime I heard the patrol of dragoons pass by on the street. I continued my journey notwithstanding my accumulated bruises, slowly and silently, and at length saw a light from a window, towards which I proceeded, directed, as I believe, by a kind Providence. On reaching the house from whence the light proceeded, and gaining admittance, I found a gentleman and lady occupied with books and I addressed myself to them saying, "You see before you an unfortunate prisoner of war, who has just escaped from the Invincible, in which I have been confined as a hostage, with the possibility of execution. I have a wife and five children on the frontiers of Canada, exposed to all the ills of a bloody war. I am maimed and bruised in effecting my escape and am wholly dependant upon what your mercy may induce you to do." The young man seemed lost in astonishment and the lady sat in silence, but I saw tears in her eyes and a glow of generosity beaming in her countenance as she exclaimed, "I would risk everything rather than see him given up." They proposed to put me upstairs, but I advised them to let me go to some outhouse, so that if discovered I could say that I had secreted myself there without their knowledge. This they did, and I crawled into a hayloft over a stable. My

present anxiety being now somewhat relieved, I was given to feel the full force of the pain caused by my bruises. The young lady visited me in the morning with refreshments and wept over me in my sad condition. I came nigh being discovered one day by some children, but I covered myself up effectually with hay as I heard them coming. They soon found some pretty buttons which I had bought in the city (for I never forgot my boys) and ran to the house with them. This aroused the watchfulness of the owner of the premises, and father of the young lady, and he afterwards himself stood watch over the buildings when the children were about. He was a Quaker, and was engaged in publishing a bible. I was presented by him on the day following that of my concealment with a printed bill offering one hundred dollars reward for the capture of each of the escaped prisoners and also announcing that if anyone was known to harbor or in any way assist in their escape their property would be confiscated and they tried for high treason. In view of the immense risk, I requested him to give me up and receive the reward, but to this he would by no means consent, preferring, as he said, a good conscience before his estates, although they were considerable. The escaped prisoners were all re-taken the first forenoon, but myself and two others who had friends in the city. (29) I remained in my concealment for several days, during which I received every possible kind attention and was then furnished with a change of clothing to prevent detection and money for my journey. I set out as a drover returning from market and fell in with a couple of that craft from whom I obtained a great deal of information respecting the business as well as the roads and country through which I was to pass. I had great pain in one of my feet which was injured in my fall, but I accounted for it by saying it was affected with rheumatism. Knowing that I would not be able to cross the Niagara River, I took my way to Lower Canada through Vermont, my native place, where I found some of my relatives living nigh Bennington to whom I made myself known and received assistance from them; continued my journey *via* Rutland to Burlington where I took the steamer to Plattsburg. At Burlington I was startled by a young man eyeing me narrowly and who afterwards, on lighting me to bed, exclaimed, "Here you will be safe." He called me in the morning and conducted me to the boat, when he inquired if there were any officers on board. He probably mistook me for a deserting soldier. From Plattsburg I made my way towards the Canadian lines, on nearing which I cut a stout cane or cudgel and resolved not to be captured by less than five men. I found myself sadly perplexed to know how to avoid the American and how to fall in with the Canadian outposts, for I durst not inquire. I, however, entered a cottage and found an old lady making johnnycake, of which I got a share, and praised it all it was worth, which was not a little. She became very talkative and told me all I wanted to know, and in a few hours thereafter I found myself in a British camp surrounded by red coats and under my beloved Union Jack.

Here, again, we have to regret that the "Reminiscences" give only the briefest of summaries where a circumstantial narrative would have been of the greatest interest. From Philadelphia to Burlington, Vt., in a straight line, is about 325 miles. The half-disabled fugitive may well have covered double that distance. The broken bone in his foot rendered walking slow and painful and necessitated long rests. On one occasion he concealed himself in a swamp. The foot was greatly inflamed and in the hope of easing the agony he thrust the injured member deep into the black muck. To his joy he discovered that this acted as a sort of natural poultice and, after some hours of the treatment, he was able to resume his weary journey.

The old lady who fed him with johnnycake was a negress. He carefully remembered her name and locality and, in later years, when the war was over and communication between the countries was free of censorship, he always sent her a broad gold piece at Christmas time.

These are the only remembered incidents of one of the most difficult journeys every accomplished by a Canadian soldier in time of war. It must have been replete with adventure but its details are lost forever.

The injury to Captain DeCou's foot, having had no skilled attention during weeks of constant irritation, was beyond repair when he reached home. He continued to suffer its pain and inconvenience for more than forty years.

> I was shortly afterwards sent for by the General who supposed that I might have broken my parole, but on hearing my story gave me credit for tact and endurance, paid me my arrears and gave me a free pass home, where I arrived just two weeks after my friends whom I had left behind, an exchange of prisoners having taken place in the meantime. (30)
>
> On my arrival at home I learned that they had had some hot times. The enemy learning that there were military supplies stored in my house sent an army with cannon to capture the stores and knock the house down. They got as far as the Beechwoods, two miles East, where they were intercepted by a band of Indians lying in ambush, who opened fire upon them from behind the trees, yelling in most approved Indian style and killed several of them. They, however, returned the fire, and even brought their cannon to bear upon the unseen foe, but without effect; they, however, sent one of their grapeshot into a pine tree which afterwards almost ruined one of my saws. In the meantime, Colonel Fitzgibbon, having disposed of most of the stores, and hearing the firing, set out on horseback for the scene of action, carrying a white flag. On his arrival he told their commander that their enterprise was hopeless, that he had a sufficient number of men to capture them. He gave an exaggerated account of the number of Indians and gave them the choice of surrendering to the whites or Indians; they chose the former and were marched by here with one red coat to ten blue ones.
>
> I was present at the battle of Lundy's Lane but having charge of the commissariat I was not in the fight. I shall never forget the cheering when our reinforcements arrived, and how some of the prisoners taken by us said it went down them like rain. We followed the enemy to Chippawa, and found some stores abandoned by them. These Colonel FitzGibbon declared legal plunder and asked if I could not take part of it home, but I declined, being resolved that no one should ever say that I had gone out plundering.

Captain DeCou was on duty with his company of the 2nd Lincoln from June 30 to August 24, 1814—that is, from before the invasion of that year until after the retirement of the United States forces into Fort Erie. This period included the battle of Chippawa, where the regiment distinguished itself and lost heavily; the British retirement into the Niagara forts, the Short Hills and Burlington; and the final British advance, culminating in the battle of Lundy's Lane. It is very probable that his services in that year were for a much longer period, but the regimental records have been lost. (31)

> The war is over now and we see little to remind us of it, but now and then an old bayonet or gunbarrel, or an occasional cannon-ball or bombshell, relics of the arms destroyed to save them from the enemy.

To no Canadian family could the conclusion of the war have been more welcome than to the DeCous. While all of them had escaped its perils with their lives, they had suffered very greatly from anxieties, military occupation, pillage and privation. Captain DeCou was handicapped by an injury that would never heal, his horses and cattle had disappeared, his fields were suffering from neglect, his fences were in ruins, his vehicles were gone and his mills were in a state of dilapidation from constant usage and lack of repairs. The army pay of himself and his company was in arrears, due to lack of returns for the period during which he had been a prisoner of war. (32)

With characteristic energy he set about the work of restoration and not only made all as good as before, but also rebuilt or enlarged his grist-mills. He acquired several hundred acres additional of land, resumed his municipal responsibilities and was active in all movements for the development of the country. He was one of the signers of the report furnished from Thorold township in response to Gourlay's inquiry in 1817.

Tradition says that, when a prisoner in Philadelphia, he procured the seed of teasels, which plants were essential to the working of wool, but which had been difficult to procure in Canada. This seed he carried with him during his escape and journey home. He planted it, with good results, and, on his removal to another location, twenty years later, he carried seed of the same stock with him.

At some period, for which no approximate date can be assigned, he secured a large number of young cherry trees of a good sort and planted a row of them along the high-road from his house to the Falls, a distance of about half a mile.

His numerous enterprises gave employment to a considerable number of men. Houses were erected for them near the mills and, with its school, church, blacksmith shop and other usual conveniences, the settlement became a recognized hamlet with the name "DeCew Town." To the establishment of the church, as well as the school, he gave substantial aid. Tradition says he "built the church."

But all the fruits of his enterprise were doomed to early destruction. Success was but the forerunner of misfortune. The lack of water, at certain seasons of the year, for the operation of the mills, was a constant source of trouble, and John DeCou associated himself, at an early date, with William Hamilton Merritt in investigating the practicability of uniting the headwaters of the Welland river and Twelve Mile creek by a canal, so that a greater volume of water could be diverted into the latter. They, with other associates, borrowed a crude waterlevel from Beckett, the miller of the Short Hills, and, in 1818, made a survey of the height of land dividing the streams. Their lack of skill and equipment led to their estimating the ridge at thirty feet, whereas it was actually sixty feet in height. Perhaps the error was a fortunate one. Had they appreciated the full extent of the obstacle, the great enterprise might have been abandoned at once. As it was, the idea of a ditch to bring water to the mills led to the vision of a barge canal. Already there had been talk of a waterway around the Niagara cataract. Colonel Robert Nichol had laid such a scheme before the Legislature of Upper Canada in 1816. Although a government engineer surveyed an impracticable route, Merritt and his associates were not dismayed.

In January, 1824, the Welland Canal Company was formed, John DeCou being one of the incorporators named in the Act. On May 15th, the first meeting under the charter was held at Mrs. Rogers' hotel in Niagara town and DeCou was one of the five who were elected directors. He had subscribed for seven shares and was one of the first four to make payment on his allotment. Six other members held an equal number of shares, three others held nine shares each; all other holdings were smaller.

While exact data as to the original canal plan is hard to procure, its course evidently was *via* DeCew Falls, where it would reach the crest of the escarpment. An engineer named John Clowes laid out the route from there to the Beaverdams flats. Merritt, writing to Sir John Harvey, in May, 1824, said:

"I can bring every part of this route forcibly to your recollection. It "commences ten miles up the Chippawa (Welland) river; passes DeCew's (the "house we retreated to after we were beaten from Fort George) and terminates "at the Twelve Mile creek, the place where our boats generally landed during "the war." (33)

Had the canal been constructed on this line, a great industrial area would have developed at DeCew Falls and along the branch of the Twelve Mile creek from there to St. Catharines, while Thorold town and Merritton would not have come into existence.

The first sod of the canal was turned on the last day of November, 1824. Before, or soon after this event, material alterations were made in the plans for the undertaking, this action precipitating the first of the many storms in the Legislature that marked the whole history of the canal company. The route on which the canal was constructed did not come within two and a half miles of DeCew Falls and it had the effect of diverting water from the streams supplying DeCou's mills, rather than adding to their flow, as was the aim of the original scheme.

These alterations completely estranged John DeCou's support. In June, 1825, he wrote to the company asking for refund of the amount he had paid in, as was provided for in the amended charter. He stated that he had taken stock "merely for the purpose of promoting that desirable work . . . as I should not have subscribed thereto under present circumstances." (34)

When the canal was completed and opened the DeCou family suffered from it in several ways. The old falls nearly went dry; the new canal towns drew population and business from DeCew Town. In 1830 Abner DeCou petitioned the Legislature for relief because the canal company had built a dam causing flooding of his lands. (35) In 1834 John DeCou petitioned for compensation for damages sustained by the diversion of water from his mills. (36) In 1835 he petitioned again, and his plea was referred to a special committee. (37)

In 1836 a special committee of the Assembly reported upon their investigation of the affairs of the canal company. In the evidence given by William Lyon Mackenzie it was stated that John DeCou had been awarded £625 for injury done to his property by the canal, with the comment "the award is on "the minutes, but he has no credit in the ledger for the amount." (38)

John DeCou was evidently identified, at this time, with those who were fighting the canal company on many grounds. In 1835 he headed a petition to the Assembly asking that the company be not given the right to erect a toll bridge across the Welland river at Chippawa, but that if any such bridge was to be erected the inhabitants of the village should have the preference. (39)

But before these claims and actions had been so far advanced, the contest had also been waged in quite a different field. In 1832, John Warren, member of the Assembly for Haldimand, died of the cholera. William Hamilton Merritt, believing that he could advance the interests of his great enterprise more effectively if he were a member of the provincial parliament, offered himself for the vacant seat. John DeCou was also placed in the field and the appearance of William Johnson Ker and C. Richardson as candidates developed a "four-cornered" contest which was waged with great bitterness.

Captain DeCou's avowed aim was to air his grievances on the floor of the House. He had the support of David Thorburn of Queenston, W. and R. Woodruff and A. Brown, all of whom Colonel Clarke described as being "for the frontier interest"—which was bitterly hostile to the canal and to everyone connected with it. (40) The polling took place on the closing days of October and the first days of November, 1832. At one stage Merritt and DeCou had received equal numbers of votes, and Ker was just a few behind. (41) When the poll closed, Merritt was declared elected. (42) There is a tradition that disorders occurred at the close of the voting and that certain of the election records were destroyed. Some of DeCou's supporters declared that their candidate had received the greater number of votes and that the trouble was intentionally provoked in order to obscure the result.

Haldimand was considered to be a Reform constituency in those bitter pre-rebellion times. Merritt placed the interests of the canal above all political considerations, and when he found that the Family Compact party would support his plans he voted with them in the Assembly. Nevertheless, he held the support of his constituency, for the construction of the Welland canal feeder had given a direct navigable route from the Grand River to Lake Ontario and the prosperity of Haldimand was considered to be largely dependant on the welfare of the canal.

Captain DeCou continued to be active in political affairs. On June 15, 1833, a meeting was held at the Black Horse Inn at Allanburg to select a candidate for the Third Riding of Lincoln (Stamford, Thorold and Pelham townships) for the ensuing election. A committee was appointed to name a candidate, John DeCou being a member of it from Thorold township. (43)

An election was held on October 6 to 11, 1834, the polling place being at Stamford village, with Alexander Hamilton, sheriff, as returning officer. The candidates were Dr. John Johnson Lefferty of Lundy's Lane, who had been the member for several parliaments, and David Thorburn of Queenston. Captain DeCou now supported Thorburn, who had assisted him two years before.

By the amazing, and apparently deliberate mismanagement of the returning officer, the poll was kept open beyond the lawful hour on the last day of polling, and Lefferty himself recorded the last vote, in his own favour, after the proper closing time, thereby tying the score. Hamilton made a "double return," which prevented either contestant from taking the seat. Thorburn presented his claim to the Assembly at the session of January, 1835, while John DeCou and his son Frederick were among the eight electors presenting a petition in support of the claim. A special committee found in Thorburn's favour, and Hamilton was summoned to the Bar of the House and required to amend his return, which he did very much against his will. (44)

The whole incident reflects the incredible conditions that existed in this province in the days when it was drifting into rebellion. Hamilton and Lefferty were stalwarts of the "ruling caste," while Thorburn, a man of the highest character, was known to be independently liberal—an attitude which resulted in his being called "disaffected" in 1838. He had a long and honourable career in parliament and in other public capacities.

Captain DeCou was thoroughly identified with the struggle for parliamentary reform. In 1836 he headed the petition from the inhabitants of Thorold township to the Assembly, protesting against the character and conduct of the government of the day, asking that an address be sent to the King praying for the removal of the advisers of the Crown in this colony, and requesting the Assembly to withhold supply until the grievances were remedied. They further prayed the Lieutenant-Governor to remove the members recently appointed to the Executive Council, they being "persons unworthy of trust." (45)

DeCou's strong animus against the governing party was due to many causes. At the beginning of the century his milling enterprise on the Niagara river had been nipped in the bud because, he suspected, it would rival the establishments of Samuel Street, and other strong government men. His claims for compensation for property destroyed and used up during the war had never been settled; his DeCew Falls mills had been ruined by the Welland canal, which was now a Family Compact affair; his political ambitions had been defeated by alleged unlawful means, and he had other causes for bitter opposition. Among them was the failure of a glass manufacturing enterprise which he had endeavoured to launch in 1833. He asked for protection for his industry. But his application was lost in the intricate legislative channels, although the noted reformer, Robert Randal, was one of the committee upon it. In 1834 a bill to incorporate John DeCou and nine others as "The Upper Canada Glass Manufacturing Company" passed the Assembly, but was amended and returned by the Council, being finally lost. It may be noted here that DeCou renewed his efforts in this direction as late as 1841, his bill at that time passing both Houses, but being "reserved for Her Majesty's pleasure" and never heard of again. It may be significant that a noted Family Compact man with whom DeCou had long been in rivalry, was also promoting a glass manufactory at this time. (46) Other rebuffs suffered by DeCou at this period will be noted at a later point in the story.

Colonial misrule persisted and intensified until the inevitable explosion resulted. Few men in the Niagara district had more causes for hatred of the Family Compact, and few had worked harder to bring about fairer conditions and secure better representation in parliament than John DeCou, but he was still "thoroughly British," as he had been in 1812, and he would not countenance the taking-up of arms. He was far beyond the age of military service, but his sons took their places in the militia ranks and served until peace was restored. John DeCou, junior, was an officer of his father's old regiment, the 2nd Lincoln, at this time, (47) and Frederick DeCou was also in its ranks. When the rebellion was over and the victorious ultra-loyalists were busy hunting every thoughtless lad against whom any evidence could be brought of even having attended one of Mackenzie's public meetings, the DeCous were among those who strongly denounced the savage persecution. Frederick, who was a man of high temper, had removed to Cayuga at the close of hostilities, and there his outspokenness in compassion for the fugitives came near to involving him in serious consequences.

In following the political thread of this story it has seemed expedient to skip, for the moment, the opening of an important and, indeed, the last active phase in the career of Captain John DeCou. Disheartened by the sight of his mills at DeCew Falls standing idle for lack of water to turn their wheels, despairing of justice in his claims for redress, and recognizing that the industrial activities of the Niagara frontier would thereafter be centralized along the Welland canal, he resolved to once again take up the role of pioneer and devote himself to the development of another virgin locality. Accordingly, in 1833, or earlier, he purchased 600 acres of wild land on Derquania creek in the township of North Cayuga, Haldimand county, the property including mill sites and privileges. Here, when more than sixty-six years of age, he undertook a new industrial development.

A dam was thrown across the creek and the pent-up waters were led to a series of two sawmills and a grist mill, all of which were under the direct management of his sons. Captain DeCou also acquired another 600 acres in South Cayuga and Oneida townships, upon which lands lumbering, quarrying and other industries were established.

He now disposed of his holdings in the vicinity of DeCew Falls, partly by sales and partly by gifts to his children. The famous old house was sold. By a strange irony of fate, the purchaser was one who had made a small fortune out of the Welland canal works which had nearly ruined DeCou. The new owner was David Griffiths, a Welshman, who had resided in London, England, but who came to Canada and secured a contract on the "deep cut" of the canal. The DeCou homestead is still owned by his descendants.

The natural flow of the Beaverdams creek has been wholly diverted, but its channel receives the small overflow from a power company's reservoir, so that a thin veil of water is usually passing over the falls. Of DeCou's mills, only ruins are to be discovered. A mill now standing dates only from 1872.

John DeCou's activities in his new location are reflected in old official records. His mill dams flooded some wild land and he asked that it be granted to him to save him from damage claims by possible future grantees. His petition was refused. (48) In the same year he petitioned the governor, Sir John Colborne, for grants of landing-places on either side of the Grand River, proposing to establish a ferry at his own expense, as it was necessary for the convenience of the new town and for the development of the locality. His petition was refused, as the lands were in the Six Nations reservation. (49) In 1835 he was among those who petitioned the Legislature for money to build a bridge across the Grand River at Cayuga, dams on that stream having rendered the ford impassable and thus interfered with travel on the great road from Niagara Falls to Sandwich. (50) In 1841 he headed one of the petitions asking that Haldimand be erected into a separate district. (51)

Meantime, he had been going ahead with his own enterprises. A hamlet sprang up in the vicinity of his new mills, he having subdivided some land for the accommodation of the settlers. Thus the village of DeCewsville came into existence—the second community of which he was the founder and which took his name. He erected for his own occupancy one of the first stone dwellings in Haldimand county. While the mills that brought DeCewsville into existence have disappeared, as have those of DeCew Town, only the ruins of the dams remaining, this later stone house, like its famous predecessor at the Falls, still stands, though much altered.

With his old-time liberality towards public improvement, Captain DeCou sold a site for a common school for five shillings and also set apart half an acre of land for a public burying-ground. (52) He also gave substantial assistance to pioneer religious organizations in that locality, two or three of his sons being either fully-ordained ministers or "local preachers."

He was active in many affairs when long past the allotted span of years, but when four score winters had whitened his head he relinquished his business cares to his sons. An addition was built to his residence so that the youngest son, William, and his family might make their home there, still leaving the old couple their separate apartments. Some aged persons still living, including several of his grandchildren, picture John DeCou as a venerable man standing at his gate on fine days and bidding weary wayfarers on the great road to come within his house for rest and refreshment (much to the disgust of his women-folk who disliked having "tramps" in their immaculate kitchens). When nights drew on, or weather was unkind, he sat in his chair before the open fire, poring over old books or baring his wounded foot to the comforting heat, and telling eager listeners stirring tales of pioneer days and "the war of 'twelve."

One more notable event was to come within the compass of his years and disturb, in some measure, the serenity of his surroundings. William Lyon Mackenzie, pardoned of his treason, had returned to Canada and, in 1851, sought re-entry into public life by candidacy for the parliament of United Canada in the county of Haldimand. Seventy years have dimmed the annals of the famous contest that he waged with George Brown. Partizan feelings ran to dangerous heights, and there was bitter resentment when Mackenzie triumphed.

In this political battle the younger DeCous strove strenuously against Mackenzie, William being especially active in his opposition. After the election Mackenzie desired to see, once more, the old reformer who had given him staunch support in pre-rebellion days, so he called at the DeCou residence. To William's family the one-time rebel was a man to be scorned, and there was a disposition to forbid him admission to the house. Happily, milder counsel prevailed, and the children stood in amazement to see their revered grandfather extend a welcoming hand to the man whom their father declared to be the most detestable in the Queen's dominions.

On the twenty-fifth of March, 1855, John DeCou laid him down to rest, having completed eighty-nine years. He was buried in the DeCewsville cemetery, which he had donated to public use. There, a few years later, Catherine Docksteder was laid beside him and there several of his children and grandchildren also are interred. (53)

John DeCou's life was of extraordinary span as measured by the history of this country. When he was born, Canada, but three years a British possession, was still under military rule and this Province was an unbroken wilderness. He was nine years old when the first shot was fired at Lexington; he fought in the war of 1812-14 as a middle-aged officer. He was past the allotted span when Mackenzie took up arms, yet he lived to within a dozen years of the formation of the Dominion.

Through the whole long story of transformations he was a pioneer. He was with the first surveyors in the Province; he became a pioneer settler; he built some of the earliest mills; he led in the betterment of agriculture, housing and means of communication, and in the encouragement of education and religion. He held a commission in the first complete militia organization; he was a projector of the first Welland canal; he was one of the first municipal officers. He struggled for parliamentary reforms; he was in the van of every movement for the development and improvement of the country. I know no better title for him than "John DeCou, Pioneer."

APPENDIX

Selections from "The Haldimand Papers" in the Public Archives of Canada, Ottawa.

Series B., Vol. 85-1, p. 69: (Precis)

Frederick Dockstedder received a commission as lieutenant in Lieut-Col. John Butler's corps of Rangers on February 19th, 1781.

Series B., Vol. 101-2, p. 7:

Brig.-Gen. H. Watson Powell to General Haldimand: Niagara, 19th February, 1781. (Extract).

"Lieutenant Dockstader is the bearer of these Despatches, he was a Sergeant in the Rangers till the late promotion and is particularly recommended."

Series B., Vol. 105, p. 304:
Lieut-Col. John Butler to Captain Mathews, Military Secretary.

Niagara, Dec. 7th, 1781.

DEAR SIR—

I Request that you will please to lay the enclosed Memorial from Lieut. Docksteder of the Indian Department before His Excellency the Commander in Chief in behalf of his Sister in Law. I beg to recommend her to the General as an object of great distress—If the promotion of the Captain Lieutenancy goes in the Rangers I hope that the eldest Lieut. will succeed to it.

I beg leave also to recommend Sergt. Solomon Seacord to His Excellency for a 2d Lieuty. I remain, Dear Sir, your most obt. & most h. St.

JOHN BUTLER

Capt. Mathews
Endorsed: A 1781.
    From Lieut. Colonel Butler
       7th decr.—Recd. 25th.

Series B., Vol. 105, p. 305:

MEMORIAL OF LIEUTENANT JOHN DOCKSTEDER

To his Excellency Gen[era]l Haldimand, Commander in Chief of all His Majesty's Forces in the Province of Canada and Frontiers depending thereon &c. &c. &c.

· The Memorial of John Docksteder humbly sheweth:—

That the Brother of your Memorialist from his Attachment to Government, and Zeal for His Majesty's Service left his Family and Friend on the Mohawk River where he lived in easy circumstances, and came to this post in the year 1776, where he served some time in the Indian Department, and afterwards as Sergeant in Lieut.Colonel Butler's Corps of Rangers, in which station he behaved so as to procure a Recommendation from the Commanding officer, in consequence of which Your Excellency was pleased to appoint him to a lieutenancy in the said corps. He was called out in the detachment of that Corps on the late Expedition to the frontiers under

Major Ross, & on the march against the Rebels was attacked by a violent Disorder which Deprived him of life, and has left his widow and a young child in distresst circumstances, and without any means of present subsistence or support but from Your Excellency's well known Bounty & Benevolence which your Memorialist hopes will be incited to afford her some relief.
And your Memorialist, as in duty bound, shall every Pray.

JOHN DOCKSTEDER,
Lieut. of the Indian Dep[artmen]t.

Niagara, December 7th, 1781.
Endorsed: Memorial Mr. Dackstadder.

NOTE.—Lieutenant Frederick Docksteder died on October 19th, 1781, when the expedition commanded by Major Ross was somewhere near Otsego Lake, in central New York. Details respecting this expedition will be found in Cruikshank's "Story of Butler's Rangers" and in the memoir, "Gilbert Tice, U.E.," appearing in Vol. XXI of the Papers and Records of this Society. Gen. Cruikshank refers to Lieutenant "Dochsteder" as having "distinguished himself on . . . many occasions."

NOTES

(1) "The Huguenot Emigration to America," Charles Washington Baird, D.D. Les Archives National, Paris, Manuscript TT232, p. xix.

(2) "Lives of the Engineers," Samuel Smiles.

(3) In these introductory paragraphs I have made much use of data from "The Genealogy of the DeCou Family, Showing the Descent of the Members of this Family in America from Leuren desCou of the Sandtoft Colony, a Huguenot Settlement in Lincolnshire, England, founded about 1630,"—a large work compiled by S. Ella DeCou, of Trenton, N.J., and John Allen DeCou, of Moorestown, N.J., and printed by the Franklin Printing Company of Philadelphia. In this book the compilers have dealt very fully, and in an authoritative manner, with the origin and early history of the family, but, unfortunately, they were not well-served by their collaborators who prepared the charts of the later generations of the Canadian branches. These contain many regrettable errors.

(4) These "reminiscences" were first published in the *Haldimand Advocate* newspaper, of Cayuga, Ontario, in 1888. A large portion of the story was reprinted in the "Jubilee History of Thorold," and selections have also appeared in other publications.

(5) Land Books of Upper Canada in the Public Archives, Ottawa: "A," p. 180; "B," p. 261; "D," p. 789; "F," p. 22; "G," p. 75. Reville's "History of Brant County."

Jacob DeCou had three brothers, Abner, Abraham, and John. One of them at least, Abner, also came to Canada. He settled in Norfolk county.

The family of Jacob DeCou and Elizabeth Bloome, his wife, consisted of seven children,— John (the subject of this memoir), Abner, Abraham, Edmund, Jane, Patience, and Sarah. The younger Abner married Catherine Hyslop. Patience married (. . . . .) Skinner. Jane married John Losee, a Loyalist settler in Stamford township, near Lundy's Lane. They had no issue. No genealogy of the Canadian branches of the DeCou family is here attempted. Its preparation would be a formidable task because of the several distinct but closely-connected branches and because of the amazing similarity of names in all of them. In two generations there were at least five Johns, four Sarahs, four Janes, three Jacobs, three Abners, and two each of Abrahams, Annas, Elizabeths, and Marys.

The Abner DeCou who returned to the United States during the war of 1812-14 was probably a son of Abner, the brother of Jacob, and, consequently, cousin to Captain John. A strong enmity which formerly existed between certain families of the name may have had its rise in this circumstance. Later generations have dropped the "feud" and even forgotten its origin. Another Abner "DeCow" was an officer of militia but volunteered and served as a private in the second flank company of the 2nd Oxford in 1812. An Abraham "DeCow" was in the 1st Oxford under Colonel Bostwick.

(6) Ontario Archives Report, 1905, p. 345.

(7) Upper Canada Land Book "B," pp. 66, 196.

(8) Cruikshank's "Ten Years of the Colony of Niagara," pp. 9, 20.

(9) Cruikshank's "Notes on the History of the Niagara District, 1791-1793," p. 49. Ontario Archives Report, 1905, p. 335.

(10) MSS. in The Public Archives, Ottawa. Upper Canada Land Book "D," p. 542.

(11) See Appendix. No financial provision had been made for military pensions to the dependants of deceased officers of such corps as Butler's Rangers. In 1795 the widow of Lieutenant Frederick Docksteder was granted 1,200 acres of land in consideration of her late husband's services and death. (Upper Canada Land Book "I," pp. 119-120.) In 1804, "Catharine DeCow, wife of John DeCow of Thorold and only child of Lieutenant Dochteder, deceased, late of Butler's Rangers", petitioned the Executive Council for a part of "her father's lands." This claim, it was ruled, should have been made before the Commissioners for ascertaining titles to lands and the Council could not consider it. However, they granted her 200 acres of land as the child of a U. E. (Upper Canada Land Books "E," p. 400; "F," p. 22.) In 1810, the heirs (including Mrs. DeCou) of certain officers who had been killed or died on service in "the American war" took action to secure lands in the township of Binbrook which had been set aside in 1789 for "reduced" officers. A plan filed at Quebec by the Deputy Surveyor for the District showed several allotments in the names of officers who had lost their lives, including 1,000 acres to "Lieutenant Frederick Docsteder." The claims were dismissed on the ground that there had been no authority for granting lands to dead men. (Upper Canada Land Book "H," p. 320.)

(12) See Appendix. Lieutenant (later Captain) John Docksteder married a woman of the Six Nations and was "adopted" into one of the tribes. His children (cousins to the wife of Captain John DeCou) were, of course, half-breeds. From this circumstance, probably, arose the old tradition of "Indian blood in the DeCous," which the closest search has failed to substantiate (at least, so far as Captain John's branch is concerned) and which the best informed among the oldest living members of the family declare to be without any foundation in fact. The tradition has, quite possibly, been strengthened by the physical characteristics of many of the family. Their French ancestry is reflected in the dark skins and hair and brilliant black eyes. "The Decou eyes" are well-known, but they are characteristically French and lack the peculiarities of Indian eyes.

Captain John Docksteder received a lease from the Six Nations of the lands now comprising the township of Canboro, in Haldimand county. He was subsequently given a complete title to the tract in order that he might sell it to Benjamin Canby. The purchase price of $20,000 was to be secured by mortgage, but the execution of the security was evaded and the purchase money was never paid. As late as 1835 John Docksteder's children were still endeavouring to recover something from their dead father's lost estate. (Historical sketch in Atlas of Haldimand County, 1876.)

(13) "Jubilee History of Thorold."

(14) Miss Carnochan's "Names Only, But Much More," p. 19; "Niagara Library, 1800-1820," p. 7.

(15) DeCou Genealogy.

(16) MSS. rolls of 2nd Regiment of Lincoln Militia, 1812-14, in Public Archives, Ottawa.

(17) Cruikshank's "Battle of Fort George," p. 32. Narrative of Colonel William Claus (Niagara Historical Society publication No. 9, p. 26).

(18) Narrative of Captain William Hamilton Merritt.

(19) Narrative of Captain William Hamilton Merritt. Cruikshank's "Blockade of Fort George," p. 5.

(20) Cruikshank's "Blockade of Fort George," p. 8.

(21) Correspondence of William Dickson (one of the prisoners) with Major-General Dearborn. (Public Archives, Ottawa, Series C. 690.) Ibid.: Dickson to Thomas William Moore, agent for British prisoners in Albany, 14th August, 1813.

(22) Cruikshank's "Fight in the Beechwoods" and "Documentary History," Part VI.

(23) Cruikshank's "Documentary History," Parts I, V and VI (numerous references). Narrative of Colonel William Claus.

(24) Dickson to Dearborn. Public Archives, Ottawa, Series C. 690.

(25) DeCou Genealogy.

(26) Public Archives, Ottawa, Series C. 692, p. 44.

JOHN DE COU, PIONEER

(27) Cruikshank's "Documentary History," Part V, p. 288.

(28) The escape took place on April 20, 1814. The Salem *Gazette* of April 29 gave a list of those who escaped, as follows: Capts. McEwen, DeCoe, Lorimier; Lieuts. Williams, Humberlin, Stewart, Luke, Duval and Lamont; Ensigns Myers and Kerr; Midshipman Lawe; Sailing-Masters Campbell and Barwis; Seamen Rogers, Byles and Wood. (Cruikshank's "Blockade of Fort George," p. 24.)

(29) The Salem *Gazette* of above date said that Myers, Kerr and five others had been retaken.

(30) Reciprocal arrangements for a three-months' parole, with privilege to return home, for the seventy-seven hostages held by the United States and an equal number of their officers held in Canada, were concluded about the time of the escape from the Invincible prison. The orders reached Philadelphia two or three days too late. The arrangement was, however, carried out for the prisoners held elsewhere and, after a short delay, the recaptured fugitives from the Invincible also received its benefits. (Correspondence of J. Mason, Commissary General of Prisoners at Washington with Brig.-General Winder at Quebec. Public Archives, Ottawa, Series C. 692, p. 267.)

(31) Muster rolls and pay lists of 2nd Regiment of Lincoln Militia in Public Archives, Ottawa. Green's "Lincoln at Bay" (Appendix).

(32) Public Archives, Ottawa, Series C. 688E, pp. 228-9.

(33) Merritt to Harvey, May 24, 1823. (Biography of the Hon. W. H. Merritt, p. 54).

(34) Journals of the Legislative Assembly of Upper Canada, 1836 (Appendix), p. 285.

(35) Journals of the Legislative Council of Upper Canada, 1830.

(36) Journals of the Legislative Assembly of Upper Canada, 1834, pp. 45, 72.

(37) Journals of the Legislative Assembly of Upper Canada, 1835, p. 67.

(38) Journals of the Legislative Assembly of Upper Canada, 1836, Appendix No. 90, Report of Select Committee on Welland Canal, p. 112.

(39) Journals of the Legislative Assembly of Upper Canada, 1835, p. 238.

(40) Merritt Biography, p. 137.

(41) *Cobourg Star and Newcastle Advertiser*, Nov. 7, 1832.

(42) The official return is said to have given Merritt a majority of five votes over DeCou.

(43) *Colonial Advocate*.

(44) Journals of Legislative Assembly of Upper Canada, 1835, p. 21, *et seq*.

(45) Journals of the Legislative Assembly of Upper Canada, 1836.

(46) Journals of the Legislative Assembly of Upper Canada, 1833 (January 10th and 12th), Ibid., 1834, pp. 59, 98, 111. Journals of the Legislative Assembly and Legislative Council of Upper Canada, 1841.

(47) Militia records in the Public Archives, Ottawa.

(48) MSS. in the Public Archives, Ottawa.

(49) MSS. in the Public Archives, Ottawa.

(50) Journals of the Legislative Assembly of Upper Canada, 1835, p. 136.

(51) Journals of the Legislative Assembly of Upper Canada, 1841.

(52) Records in Haldimand County registry office, Cayuga, Ontario.

(53) The children of John DeCou and Catherine Docksteder were eleven in number,—John, Robert, Frederick, Edmund, William, Elizabeth, Catherine, Mary, Phoebe, Eva Caroline, and Eliza Jane.

JOHN (1801-1886) was a farmer, storekeeper and lime manufacturer. He was a local preacher of the Methodist Church and at the period of the rebellion of 1837 held a commission in the 2nd regiment of Lincoln militia. He married: (1) Sarah Ann Cowel, (2) Maria Larraway.

ROBERT (1807-1878) was a miller and farmer at Decewsville. He married Margaret McClellan.

FREDERICK (1809-1884) was a farmer, served in the 2nd Lincoln in 1837, and married Elizabeth, daughter of George and Elizabeth Lacey, of Thorold township. He lived in Thorold, Stamford, Cayuga, and Port Burwell. One of his grandsons, A. C. Garden, has had better success in politics than the early generations of Decous and is now a member of the Ontario legislature.

EDMUND (1812-1892) was one of the first members of the family to take up his residence in Haldimand. He was the first warden of that county (1850) and reeve of North Cayuga in 1851. His wife was Sarah Ann Fawell. After serving an apprenticeship with Mahlon Burwell, he was licensed a Provincial land surveyor in 1836 and practised his profession in Bertie, Binbrook, Canboro, Crowland, Pelham and Thorold townships. With his son, John (1835-1884), who was a Provincial and Dominion land surveyor, he did a great deal of geological field work and made valuable collections of specimens which were donated to various public institutions. His son wrote several geological treatises of note and the fossil "pleuronotis DeCewi" was named in his honour. Both father and son were Methodist local preachers. (See biographies by Willis Chipman, C.E., in Annual Report of Ontario Land Surveyors' Association, 1922).

WILLIAM (1818-1890) ran the sawmill built by his father at Decewsville, was the village postmaster, member of the first council of North Cayuga (1850) and reeve of the township in 1853 and 1854. He also operated stone quarries. He was a prominent politician and an unsuccessful candidate for parliament. In 1856 he bought the *Sachem* newspaper of Cayuga, changing its name to the *Sentinel*, but as this was merely a political enterprise, he soon sold out again. He was an officer of the Haldimand militia. His wife was Caroline VanLoan.

ELIZABETH (1799-1804).

CATHERINE (1803-1881) married William Young, of Indiana, Haldimand county.

MARY (1805-1806).

PHOEBE (1814-1876) escaped in the night, by a rope ladder, from an upper window of her father's house at Decew Falls, to marry Rev. Robert Wilde, a Baptist, whom Captain DeCou had forbidden to come upon his premises. The daughter's disobedience threw her high-tempered father into a severe illness of long duration.

EVA CAROLINE (1820-1861) married Robert George Hagar of Allanburg.

ELIZA JANE (1823-   ) married Henry Young.

VIII

THE CONSTRUCTION OF THE RIDEAU CANAL, 1826-1832.[1]

By Hamnett P. Hill, K.C.

During the War of 1812-1815 the British authorities experienced much difficulty in attempting the defence of the western part of the Province. This was owing to the difficulties of transporting men and supplies from Montreal to Kingston, because of the rapids on the St. Lawrence River. They were also faced with the danger of a U. S. army blocking progress up the river by seizing some of the islands near Kingston. The cost of transport from Montreal to Kingston was also excessive, being fifty-four shillings per cwt. It is stated that to ship a 24-pounder this distance cost 200 pounds.

In 1815 one Lieutenant Jebb was detailed to make a report on the possibility of a back route to Kingston by means of the Ottawa River and the various waterways flowing into this river and into the St. Lawrence. Nothing was done following the receipt of his report as peace was shortly afterward declared.

After the war the British authorities adopted the plan of establishing military settlements in the eastern portion of the Province, it being thought desirable to establish colonies of disbanded soldiers with a view to insuring a loyal settlement in this area. Accordingly, settlements were founded at Perth, Lanark, and Richmond, and in the Township of March. As a result there sprang up an agitation for the building of roads or the improvement of the water communication.

In 1821 the Upper Canada Government took measures to improve the internal navigation in the Province, and in 1824 Mr. Samuel Clowes, an engineer who had been appointed by the Government to make reports on the various waterways, made his report recommending the improvement of the Rideau River and the Cataraqui Creek to enable boats to pass from the Ottawa River to the Great Lakes. This report was made in great detail, and the cost of the improvements was estimated at 145,802 pounds. The report was presented to a joint committee of the Legislative Assembly and the Legislative Council, who, in April, 1825, issued a report dealing with the proposal. The report dealt with the project from a military point of view. An excerpt from this document may be of interest:

"That a Canal from Kingston to the Ottawa River would, in the event of war, not merely diminish beyond measure the charge of our defence, but render its success greatly more certain, admits of no doubt. In the event of a war protracted as the last, the safety and the saving of transport conducted by such a channel would, it is believed, fully compensate to the nation the charge of the improvement, and it is most evident that to give full effect to the sound and liberal policy which has created the military settlements on the Rideau and introduced since the war

---

[1]This address was delivered before a joint meeting of the Kingston Historical Society and the Kingston branch of the Engineering Institute of Canada, in Convocation Hall, Queen's University, November 4th, 1924.

a loyal population of more than ten thousand souls where there was before no inhabitant, and which is now surmounting, at a considerable expense, the interruptions of navigation on the Ottawa, it is necessary to perfect the water communication removed from the enemy's frontier and leading in truth from the ocean to Kingston, which is the key to Lake Ontario and the principal military station in the province."

This report was in due course forwarded, through the Governor-General, to the military authorities in London. The British Government offered a loan of 70,000 pounds if the Upper Canada Government would undertake the work, but this offer was refused, as the Legislature favoured improving the St. Lawrence route.

The Duke of Wellington, who was at that time Master-General of Ordnance, appointed a commission of military engineers to visit Canada and to report to him on the feasibility of the Clowes plan. This commission traversed the proposed route and approved of it, and advised the building of the canal by the British Government for military purposes, of a size to permit gunboats to pass. It questioned the correctness of Clowes' estimate and reported that the cost would be 169,000 pounds.

It is interesting to note the attitude of the Canadian authorities at this time, having in mind the fact that the joint committee of the Legislature and the Council had recommended the undertaking in such strong language. The commissioners' report states:

"In compliance with Your Grace's command, we have endeavoured to ascertain what assistance, if any, could be procured from the Provincial Government towards carrying this important work, whether viewed from a military or political point of view, into effect. We regret, however, to say that there does not appear to be the slightest chance of any pecuniary aid from the Province of Upper Canada. The settlers are very poor and the Province is still in its infancy. Excepting it is undertaken by His Majesty's Government we are afraid it will never be executed. Companies are forming and cheap and temporary expedients are likely to be resorted to for improving the navigation of the St. Lawrence in order to enable the produce from Lake Ontario to be forwarded to Montreal and Quebec with less trouble and risk than at present. The important advantages of such a communication in the rear of the frontier are not likely to be appreciated by the great bulk of the inhabitants of the Province; nor is it probable that for the attainment of a remote good they will agree to any tax or immediate pecuniary loss."

On the receipt of this report the military authorities decided to undertake the construction of the waterway, and Lieutenant-Colonel John By was selected to be the officer in charge. Colonel By was born in London in 1781. After passing through the Royal Military College at Woolwich he became a lieutenant in the Royal Artillery, but shortly afterward was transferred to the Royal Engineers. In 1802 he had been sent to Canada as a captain, where he remained for nine years. At Quebec he had been entrusted with the construction of Martello towers and the rebuilding of the Citadel, and he had also superintended the building of the Cedars Canal, near Montreal.

In 1811 he returned to England and was sent to Portugal, where he served under the Duke of Wellington in the Peninsular War. From January, 1812, until August, 1821, he was in charge of the Royal Gunpowder Mills at Faversham, Purfleet, and Waltham Abbey. In 1821 he was placed on the unemployed list. He was accordingly forty-five years old when he was selected for the Rideau River undertaking.

By's instructions were to complete a water communication having a uniform depth of five feet from the Ottawa River to Kingston, along the line already recommended by Clowes. Work had commenced on the Grenville Canal on the Ottawa River about midway between the city of Montreal and the present city of Ottawa, and the locks on the Rideau and on the Grenville Canal were to be constructed of the same size as the locks at Lachine, namely, twenty feet wide by 100 feet long. It is interesting to note that By was warned not to bring the canal down to the St. Lawrence River by way of Cornwall, as he would be pressed to do by the merchants and other parties interested in the development of the St. Lawrence River. Owing to the danger of any hostile army from the United States stopping all navigation on the St. Lawrence in a comparatively easy and simple manner, the work was to be constructed from the Ottawa River to Kingston, which was on Lake Ontario and well fortified.

The question of how the work was to be done was carefully considered by the Ordnance Department and By was instructed to have it done by contract. It was pointed out to the Board of Ordnance that the only inconvenience attending the execution of the work by contract was that in such case the whole of the cost should be asked for from Parliament at once, as the contractors should be at liberty to commence as early as the season would permit, without waiting for the passing of the annual grant. The year before, the Ordnance Department had had inserted in the estimates which had been presented to Parliament an item of 5,000 pounds for preliminary work on the Rideau River. This item had passed the House of Commons apparently without any particular attention being called to it, and the Ordnance Department then assumed that, this item having been approved of, Parliament was committed to the work being proceeded with, and that therefore there would be no objection to proceeding with the work without waiting each year for the notification of the building grant. No estimate of the cost of the work had been presented to Parliament at the time of the adoption of the small item mentioned above, and Parliament had no opportunity of either approving or disapproving of the Government entering into such a large undertaking as the building of the canal ultimately turned out to be.

The War Office communicated with the Colonial Department, and the Secretary of State for the Colonies wrote the Lieutenant-Governor of Upper Canada to afford every aid and assistance in the carrying out of the undertaking.

Colonel By arrived in Montreal in August, 1826, and a few days later he wrote the Department that the canal could not possibly be built for 164,000 pounds, and, although he had not been on the ground, from the information that he had he was sure that it would cost at least 400,000 pounds.

By came up the Ottawa River to the little settlement of Hull, on the Ottawa River, on September 21, 1826, and decided that the entrance of the canal into the Ottawa River should be in a little bay, well protected from the winds, about half a mile east of the Chaudiere Falls. The land on the high banks of the river had previously been purchased by the British authorities, and By proceeded to subdivide this property. Ultimately a village sprang up, which was known as Bytown and later became the city of Ottawa. At that time the site of the city was a forest, with the exception of a little clearing on which a Mr. Nicholas Sparks was endeavouring to eke out a living by farming.

The undertaking by the British Government of this public work in a self-governing colony raised interesting legal questions. The Imperial Government had no authority by law to undertake any such work and it was necessary for the Legislature of Upper Canada not only to give permission to the British authorities to carry on this work, but also to invest them with necessary power. Accordingly the Rideau Canal Act was passed. This Act gave to Colonel By all the powers which the Upper Canada Government itself would have possessed had it undertaken the work. The view of the Legislature is set forth in the recitals to the Act:

> "Whereas His Majesty has been most graciously pleased to direct measures to be immediately taken under the superintendence of the proper military department, for constructing a canal uniting the waters of Lake Ontario with the River Ottawa and affording a convenient navigation for the transport of naval and military stores;
>
> "And Whereas such a canal when completed will tend most essentially to the security of this province by facilitating measures for its defence;
>
> "It is therefore expedient to provide by law every necessary facility towards the prosecution of so desirable a work. . . . . . .
>
> ". . . . that the Officer employed by His Majesty to superintend the said work shall have full power to explore the country lying between Lake Ontario or the waters leading therefrom and the River Ottawa, and to enter into or upon the lands or grounds belonging to any person or persons, bodies, politic or corporate, and to survey and take levels of the same, and to dig, get, remove, take, carry away and sell earth, soil, clay, stone, rubbish, trees, roots of trees, beds of gravel or sand, or any other matters or things which may be digged or got in or out of any lands or any grounds."

These were very unusual powers to be given to any party, and were seemingly very comprehensive. Despite this, By was during the whole time he was carrying on the work impeded and hindered by lawsuits. The ingenuity of lawyers in Brockville, Cornwall and Perth was easily able to discover By doing things which he was not authorized to do by the Act.

It will be noted that despite By's protest, and despite the fact that the canal was being built for military purposes, no power was given him to expropriate any land for the defence of the canal.

By, with his accustomed energy, had a preliminary survey made of the route and in the spring of 1827 contracts were let covering the whole route. During the summer and autumn of 1827 the route was more carefully surveyed and estimates prepared, and in December, Lieutenant Pooley, who was on By's staff, was sent to London with a full report, the cost being estimated at 475,000 pounds. By strongly recommended that the locks should be increased in size in order to pass steamboats of sufficient size to navigate the lakes, and also spars that were required for the Royal Navy. This report, with its increased estimate, apparently caused consternation in the Ordnance Department and it was intimated from a high source that the original estimate made by Clowes had been "made out from the reprehensible motive of endeavouring to benefit the Colony by embarking His Majesty's Government in this undertaking upon the faith of an estimate which the author of it, himself, admits he considered to be fallacious and inadequate." The reports and plans were referred to a committee of engineers with instructions to examine same and to ascertain if Colonel By had not completely lost sight of the original proposal and was not indulging in one of his own invention. The committee, after making its examination, reported that Colonel By had not deviated from his instructions and that they could find nothing to criticize in either his plans or his estimates.

One paragraph of its report is interesting as showing the magnitude of the undertaking:

> "With regard to the dams proposed by Colonel By for raising the water in the rapids to render the Rideau navigable, we would observe that this is by no means a novel expedient, having been much practised in the old and new hemispheres under the usual denomination of waste weirs. The principle in use, however, is the same, but we have not learned that any have been constructed so high as Colonel By has proposed at Hog's Back and at Jones Falls, these being 45 feet and 48 feet, respectively. The Americans have one 28 feet high."

The Government, however, were not satisfied with the report of these engineers, and a commission of military engineers were sent out from England, under the chairmanship of Lieutenant-General Sir James Kempt, their instructions being to personally examine and consider the plans and estimates of By in detail, and if they found them practicable and calculated to give secure communication, and if prepared with due regard to the great interest of the colony and to local circumstances and with due attention to economy, they were to authorize Colonel By to continue with the work. Otherwise he was to be stopped. If the commission concurred with Colonel By on the question of enlarging the locks, they could authorize him to enlarge them in the manner that he had indicated in his report.

The report of this commission, which was made in June, 1828, refers to the uncleared state of the greater part of the country and the nature of so difficult a work. The estimates and specifications had been checked over and were found correct. In connection with the cost they reported as follows:

> "Economy had not been lost sight of by Colonel By, and he has, in accordance with what he believed to be the spirit of his instructions, pushed forward the work and excited a degree of exertion throughout the Department which few individuals could have accomplished."

The commission recommended that the locks should be increased to a width of thirty-three feet and a length of 134 feet. Meantime, however, Colonel By had been obliged to revise his cost, and now estimated the probable expense at 576,757 pounds. The commission reduced this estimate to 558,000 pounds, and this sum "they have every reason to believe, will be found ample to meet any probable contingency that may occur." They also reported that they had instructed Colonel By to proceed with the work.

In connection with the contracts which were awarded for the work, it should be borne in mind that these contracts were prepared, not by Colonel By, but by the Commissariat Department at Quebec, and that Colonel By had no control over the amount of work done by the contractors each year. All the contracts provided that the contractors should be paid as the work progressed, on a unit basis; that is to say, so much per cubic yard for excavating earth, or excavating rock. The masonry work in connection with the locks and the dams was similarly treated.

It should also be recalled that this work was being done through uninhabited country. The lakes in the interior were originally not much more than swamps. Malaria or lake fever broke out amongst the labourers employed, and hundreds of Irish immigrants who had been brought out for the work died. Colonel By himself was at death's door for some time, and all his officers and clerks of works similarly suffered. In addition to this, the litigation to which I have already referred resulted in By being obliged to devote time in the courts which he would otherwise have been able to apply to the work in hand. Many of the contractors discovered that their figures were much too low, and in consequence they discontinued their contracts, thus causing delay and adding materially to the cost. The extraordinary rise of the waters in the spring was a factor which had not been properly estimated. In April, 1829, the Hog's Back Dam, just as it was nearing completion, was carried away, entailing much additional expense.

In the spring of 1830, By's estimate had increased to 762,679 pounds, with a suggestion that the cost would probably be greater than this. In transmitting this report to London, Lieutenant-Colonel Durnford, the head of the Ordnance Department in Canada, reported that if the cost was greater, General Mann, the Master-General of Ordnance, "may rely on its not being attributable either to Colonel By, his officers or contractors, of whose unremitting assiduity and perseverance I cannot speak too highly."

By, in his report, referring to estimates of cost, wrote as follows:

"I beg to observe that any calculations must not be considered as the positive sum required; for though myself and my officers are using every exertion to bring them as near the sum required as possible, yet the clearing and deepening of various parts of the river, Cranberry Marsh and Lake, as also clearing and deepening Cataraqui Creek, are services so interwoven with unforeseen contingencies that the expenses of them must remain uncertain until they are completed, and the utmost that can be done is to state the probable amount required."

The large sums of money being voted for the work aroused considerable criticism in the British House of Commons and in the spring of 1831 a select committee was appointed to enquire into the matter. The report which this committee made is most interesting as it throws much light on the attitude of the military authorities when they had decided to embark on the undertaking. It can be presumed that the House of Commons was not enamoured of expenditure for military purposes, and accordingly the military authorities were obliged to adopt dubious methods to enable them to carry on such undertakings. The report calls attention to the fact that on a vote of 5,000 pounds, and without any mention to the House of Commons, By had been authorized to enter into contracts without limitation of annual grants and without the consent of Parliament, given after being furnished with an estimate of total cost; that, despite By's letter to the contrary, the original estimate of 167,000 pounds had later been presented to the House as the probable cost of the work. The committee also referred to numerous other cases where the military authorities had acted likewise. "The various works were begun and moderate sums were called for from year to year; the grant of every former session became a reason for granting more in the succeeding session, in order that the first sum might not be expended in vain or the work left incomplete."

The committee expressed itself as being quite satisfied with By's explanation of the impossibility of confining his annual expenditure to the sum specified in the estimate.

It made a number of recommendations, one of which was that no work of any magnitude be hereafter undertaken except on a survey and an estimate made by an officer acting under the orders of some responsible Department; this apparently being due to the Department having acted on the fallacious estimates of Mr. Clowes.

By was not disturbed by the action of the committee. In a letter to Lieutenant-Colonel Durnford he says:

> "I have always reported the sum estimated for the Rideau Canal as the probable, not the positive sum, as it was, and still is, utterly impossible to state the exact sum required to complete the work.
> "When this service was first mentioned to me, I said the estimate was absurd, and on 13th August, 1826, I wrote General Mann that from information I had obtained in Montreal, the work would cost 400,000 pounds at least, and this was before I had ever been on the ground. The contracts were all made by the Commissariat Department at Quebec, and I am obliged to pay the money as the work progresses. If I had interfered with contractors I would have been sued for damages. I have no control over the expenditure, and in consequence, owing to contractors rushing the work in order to escape lake fever in the spring and fall, I had to pay in one year 211,354 pounds instead of 130,000 pounds, allowed in the estimate."

In February, 1832, By reported that the total expenditure was 715,408 pounds, being 22,700 pounds more than had been voted by Parliament, and that a further sum of 60,615 pounds would have to be expended to complete the work. The excess of cost over his original estimate made to the commission of which Sir James Kempt was chairman, was only 30,134 pounds. The balance was for additional work which experience showed was necessary, such as the adoption of waste weirs, the enlargement of the dams and the embankments, etc., owing to the experience gained at Hog's Back. The costs of the civil and military establishment were also not included in the original estimate, but were included in the expenditure as reported.

On May 29th, 1832, the steamboat *Bumper* was able to pass through the canal, with a large party of military and civilian officials, and By had the satisfaction of knowing that the waterway had been completed.

Just four days before this happened, the Lords of the Treasury, in London, had considered By's last report and had written a peremptory memorandum to the War Office that Colonel By be immediately removed from the work and be forthwith ordered to return to England, that he might be called upon to afford such explanations as the Lords of the Treasury might consider necessary upon the important subject of the cost of the canal.

On his return to England By appeared before a third committee of the House of Commons. The committee, while admitting that the work had been carried out with care and economy and had been well performed, concluded their report with a strong expression of regret at the excess expenditure over the estimate and the Parliamentary votes. By, who had expected high commendation on the completion of this magnificent work in so short a time and under so many difficulties, and at a cost by no means extravagant, felt himself extremely ill used, and never recovered from the disappointment.

It must be conceded that By was a victim of circumstances and of politicians. Every commission and committee of the House of Commons had approved of the work, in some cases highly praising Colonel By, and in other cases expressly excepting him from any criticism. Every engineer who had gone over the work had approved of it. During the whole progress of the work not one word of disapproval had emanated from the Ordnance Board, under whom By was carrying on the undertaking. Owing to the Commissariat Department making the contracts, By had no control over the expenditure. A scapegoat, however, had to be found to satisfy the politicians, and By was allowed by the military authorities to bear this stigma. No one can read the letters and reports in the Government Archives at Ottawa without sympathizing with By in the disappointment he suffered and the indignation he felt.

By retired to his estate near Frant, Sussex, and there died on February 1, 1836. On his tombstone is engraved the following pathetic obituary:

"Sacred to the Memory of Lieutenant-Colonel John By, Royal Engineers, of Shernfold Park in this Parish, zealous and distinguished in his profession, tender and affectionate as a husband and a father, charitable and pious as a Christian, beloved by his family and lamented by the poor. He resigned his soul to his Maker in full reliance on the merits of his Blessed Redeemer on the first of February, 1836, aged 53 years, after a long and painful illness brought on by his indefatigable zeal and devotion in the service of his King and Country in Upper Canada.

"This stone is erected by his afflicted widow in remembrance of every virtue that could endear a husband, a father and a friend."

The Rideau Canal for many years was an important artery for the transportation of immigration to Western Ontario. It very materially assisted in developing not only eastern Ontario, but also the western part of the Province. While it was fortunately never called into use for the purpose for which it was originally designed, the Province owes a deep debt of gratitude to the Mother Country for what at that time was a truly magnificent work and one of very great magnitude. The subsequent building of the canals on the St. Lawrence River and the development of railways rendered it obsolete, and it is now a relic of the past. The Dominion Government still maintains the locks and the dams, and apparently will always be obliged to do so, as, if the dams were allowed to deteriorate, the flooding which would occur would be of tremendous damage to the numerous towns and villages which have grown up along its course.

IX

HISTORICAL NOTES ON FINANCE IN THE GREAT WAR, AND AFTERWARD

By A. F. Hunter, M.A.

Throughout the progress of the late Great War, the writer gathered newspaper clippings and jotted down notes respecting the outstanding naval and financial events, both of which factors were of prime importance in the great conflict. The military operations were, of course, of the first importance, but as their details were endless and furnished a more voluminous budget than the writer's time permitted him to collect, they were left for other hands and authorities better situated and better versed in the subject.[1]

As everyone knows, if there had not been supremacy in naval and financial affairs on the side of the Allies—the one to gather on short notice from the remotest colonies the fittest soldiers to help at the various fronts, with supplies for their maintenance, and the other to speed forward the wheels of commerce for the supplies needed in those fields of war, the results on the western front could not have been very different from what they were on the eastern front. These two factors—naval and financial strength—represented the departments in which our own British nation was in a condition of preparedness and held the foremost place.

This paper, accordingly, sums up the above mentioned financial items and the material collected in those notes and clippings of the war years, leaving the naval material, possibly, for some future time; and it attempts to weave them into a consecutive story of the struggle in the language of national currency. Fewer articles have been published on the financial transactions of the war than on the military and the naval events, and as none of any kind have hitherto appeared in this Society's publications, no further apology is needed for submitting it.

It deals with the financial factors only—without an equipment in which, there would have been no success to the Entente Allies, and which especially, as the source of the subsequently resulting financial problems, continue to confront us long after the military and naval operations have ceased. A thorough knowledge of the course of events in financial affairs during the war, and the predicaments left by them at the close, helps one to understand better the after-war complications, with their economic consequences.

The outstanding features of the subject fall under two headings, presenting separate phases, and they are set forth in two parts, viz.:—

1. The course of international exchange, including the fluctuations and perturbations of the various national currencies in the stock exchanges of foreign

---

[1]Various general sketches of the military operations have appeared in Canada. In the Canada Year Book for 1919, for example, Brig.-Gen. E. A. Cruikshank has given a summary of the military events throughout the whole course of the hostilities, with some references to the economic and financial disturbances. In Nelson's Looseleaf Cyclopaedia, available in all public libraries, a detailed sketch appears under the heading "European War."

countries, first in the case of the currency of Germany and her eastern coadjutors, and afterward in those of the victorious Allies.

2. The financial efforts and transactions of the countries participating in the great struggle, one by one, whereby they maintained their internal affairs and kept armies in the various fields.

The figures employed throughout the text have been reduced to dollars in every case, although sometimes also they are given in some other particular currency with the Canadian equivalent.

PART I

THE WAR VAGARIES OF MONEY AND EXCHANGE

The story begins with the forced shipment of gold from the United States to Europe in the years prior to the war. This movement attained its maximum two or three years before the outbreak. The flow of gold continued for months and even for years, toward Germany, chiefly out of the United States, and mostly to Great Britain as a foil, or to Holland, and thence ultimately more or less directly to Germany. Scarcely anyone then understood the reason for this singular movement, and did not until after the crash came, nor did anyone even suspect what it meant at the time. But it became clear at once that it had been a systematic preparation for war, which had been going forward for a long time. Notwithstanding that German imports far exceeded their exports in those years of gold acquisition (and for many years prior to the war the trade balances were unfavourable to Germany), yet the receipts of bullion and specie by Germany for its war chest, and for the gold reserve in the Reichsbank, were the outstanding feature of its finance for a dozen years or more. At the time of the outbreak the German military chest contained a surplus of about $60,000,000 in gold, besides silver, and the gold reserve in the Reichsbank had increased to $339,000,000 in July, 1914.

Under the circumstances, the only possible conclusion that one can fairly reach as to these transactions, must be that by the forced issue of paper currency, the sale of German Government bonds in foreign countries, and the sales of such notorious stocks as the Krupp gun and steel works at Essen to foreign purchasers, they produced the influx of gold to the conspiring nation. These were outstanding examples of their clandestine methods; there were others. Throughout the United States especially, there are now great quantities of German paper money dated from those pre-war years; for example, the issue of April 21, 1910, which gives the date when Germany, as a nation, actually conceived the idea of making a war. And the alien brokers of Toronto can now also furnish such paper money in abundance.

British financial institutions likewise had been loaded up with German securities—to the estimated extent of $950,000,000—and had thus been used unwittingly as financial outposts of the German Empire.

What is known in England as the Suspension of the Bank Act, and has been rarely applied—only two or three times, indeed—was a regular operation in Germany. The Reichsbank, on payment of five per cent. to the Government on the amount of over-issue, might inflate the paper currency, and regularly did so, in full accordance with the law. In other words, there was legalized financial crime provided for in the statute book. With the outbreak of the war, the Reichsbank was entirely relieved of any necessity to maintain a supply of gold to cover its paper notes.

THE COMPLETE COLLAPSE OF GERMAN FINANCE

As the war continued, the Reichsbank exported gold to Holland and to the other neutrals for foreign supplies such as the Germans required, and thus the value of the mark remained at a nominal figure in foreign countries. But exhaustion of the gold reserve in Germany ultimately became visible. And with the exhaustion a decline of the mark soon began in the exchanges of the neutrals.

Following the ultimate depletion of the gold reserve of Germany and its Central Allies, which came about in due course of time, there was an amazing decline of the mark to a very low figure, especially after the war. This decline produced the inevitable inflation of prices of foodstuffs in Germany and of everything else. The rouble of Russia, and the standards of other eastern nations, all followed the same course, or declined, in some cases, even in advance of the mark. So great was the influence of the prolongation of the war beyond the expected length in producing the decline of currency in several nations— Germany and eastward—and the enormous inflation of prices in some of them, that it became the outstanding feature of finance. After the war anyone wishing to draw money from a bank in Germany had to take a suitcase with him for the paper currency, there was so much of it. This might be called an extreme case of circulation.

Nearly all recent wars had been short and decisive, like the Spanish-American war, the Russo-Japanese war (1904–5), the Balkan wars in 1913, and the Itallo-Turkish war. It was inevitable that the World war, which was prolonged beyond the usual period of other recent wars, and attained to such a length as to be an exhausting one, would effect the financial obliteration of one, or perhaps both, sides. It became a war of attrition and extermination, and Europe, where the chief portion of the conflict was waged, might be looked upon to furnish a scene of financial destruction. It was an industrial and economic struggle—a convulsion in which many great works of civilization were overthrown by the uncontrolled deeds of men who had relapsed into ferocious beasts for the time at least. The havoc of such cannot soon be repaired, and as everyone foresaw, many years must pass away before the countries overrun in the conflict can recover their prosperity from the war's ravages. While the sole aim of many of the Allied participants was merely to put Germany out of the menacing military attitude for all time, this could not be done without great sacrifice of life and money. The Russians, after ridding themselves of autocracy at a comparatively early date in the conflict, went out of the military business for the remainder of the war at least, and the Germans also grew sick of it and wanted to quit long before it was over, but they did not get the permission. As a result of the prolonged drain upon their resources, and the consequent money inflation, the eccentric courses of their national currencies in international exchange since the war were never paralleled in the history of the world. Germany, by inventing new devices for inflation, had prolonged existence for a time, but inflation must end; the bubble had to burst, and their old currencies practically ceased to exist.

In this war, for the first time, we had to begin the staggering effort of thinking and reckoning in billions, whereas prior to the war it was sufficient to count in millions. It has been quite as bewildering as trying to conceive astronomical distances when expressed in our finite measurements of length and time. The task of counting in billions has had to be undertaken in order to understand.

Moreover, when Europe went into the war, its twenty-five nations were classified as five republics, seventeen limited or constitutional monarchies, and three despotic monarchies.[1] It came out of the war minus the last three, which the ordeal, amongst many changes, had converted into constitutional governments. Besides this transformation, numerous German confederate kingdoms, grand duchies, duchies and principalities were also all wiped out. What was really upon trial was the form of government which should endure, and especially those of Germany, Austria, Russia, and Turkey. If our own form of democracy and constitutional government had been a weaker system of government, it would have failed before the despotisms of those countries. The war itself was set in motion without the decision or consent of a parliament (the Reichstag), was, in fact, begun in an unconstitutional way, as we understand government—because the nation (Germany) which began it, was at that time a despotism.

Speaking, then, in a general way, in the formerly autocratic nations, the paper currency became enormously inflated and depreciated in value. A chief reason for this was to maintain their stability as long as possible. They feared first a revolution against Imperialism, as their people would not bear taxation as the others do, and then, having revolted, feared a relapse to Imperialism.

In the nations that underwent most transformation—Germany, Austria, Russia, and Turkey—their currencies soon ceased to be recognized by other nations as media of exchange, and they emerged from the contest without credit. Their old forms of money soon became unquotable in the foreign exchanges. In a few of the others, smaller but nominally classed as constitutional, though really despotic, monarchies, because inexperienced in democracy, the condition of finance became almost equally bad.

Notwithstanding the plight of German finance from the decline of the mark described above, by the participation of Hugo Stinnes, Thyssen, and other industrialists desperately driven toward the end of the conflict, the German national bonds were internally cared for, leaving the reparations, inherited at the close, to bankrupt Germany, or rather to bring about the insolvency of its national currency.

The Reparations payments due by Germany were finally fixed in January, 1921, at 132 milliards or billions of gold marks, or about $30,000,000,000. As the total gold in the world in use as the basis of currency does not exceed $10,000,000,000, approximately, it may be seen that the Reparations alone, due by Germany, in the forty-two years prescribed, amount to three times

---

[1] Duchesne—"Democracy and Empire," 1916—with additions. Austria-Hungary was therein classed as a limited monarchy.

the total gold in use in the world as currency, and that it would require the acquisition of that amount three times in succession. Viewed in this light, there is little prospect that Germany will pay 100 cents on the dollar if it can be evaded, as the sum is large, and there is the cost of the German side of the war burdening her besides. But it is not necessary to reckon in this way. And on the other hand, Great Britain raised much more than the amount of the Reparations account in a little more than four years of war.

As a consequence, much trouble has arisen since the war over the adjustment of the Reparations payments by Germany, and the method of payment; theorists, without wishing to minimize the guilt of Germany, have imagined difficulties in the way, and their writings have encouraged Germany in a resentful course. Whether as gold payments or guarantees, or as an agreement like the Stinnes-Lubersac contract for deliveries of reparations in industrial products, the amounts could be paid if Germany really wanted to do so.

Payments of Reparations by Germany, as expected, since the Treaty provisions went into force, have been unsatisfactory. Under Article 233 of the Treaty of Versailles, the amount of the damage for which Germany was to make compensation had to be determined by an Inter-Allied Commission, to be called the Reparation Commission. This Commission on March 8, 1922, issued a return of payments by Germany, under three headings, as follows, from the Armistice to December 31, 1921:—

1. In Cash (Gold and Foreign currencies).

	Dollars	Dollars
(a) Direct payments made by Germany to December 31, 1921.................	249,940,560	
(b) Receipts from other sources on German account:—		
1. Payment by Denmark for cession of part of Schleswig............	15,600,000	
2. Destroyed War Material sold.....	9,830,400	
3. Sundry items...................	157,680	
(c) Proceeds of British Reparation Recovery Act...........................	8,672,640	
		285,201,280
2. Provisional Estimate of the value of deliveries in kind (coal, etc.).		
(a) Supplied to Allied and Associated Powers	662,460,144	
(b) Sold to Luxembourg, to Textile Alliance of the United States, etc............	9,382,080	
		671,842,224
3. Cessions of State Properties in Ceded Territories. Estimated, excluding the Schleswig properties shown in item (b) 1, and not including any valuation of the area awarded to Poland.................	600,042,080	
		600,042,080
Total.................................		1,557,085,584

(The French occupation of the Ruhr and the acceptance of the Dawes plan of recovery of Reparations have both taken place since the compilation of this paper.)

DIFFICULTIES AND ULTIMATE SUCCESS OF THE FINANCE OF THE ENTENTE ALLIES

For the first few months after the war began, the course of foreign exchange amongst the Allies and their friends was erratic. Great Britain and France were extensive creditor nations, having invested largely in foreign countries. It has been estimated that the British foreign investments at the beginning of the war amounted to $20,000,000,000, and those of France to $8,000,000,000. At the outbreak citizens of these two nations in particular set about collecting some of their outside investments, and so the sterling pound and the franc rose in the foreign stock exchanges and sold at high premiums. In the New York exchange, for example, a price of $7.00 was reached for the pound at the beginning of August, British investors having held large amounts of U. S. securities, which they wished to convert and use at home.

In order to eliminate the danger of shipping gold from New York, in the first few months of the war, a consignment of gold was sent to Ottawa and deposited in the Bank of Ottawa to the credit of the Bank of England. This measure relieved the exchange situation very materially. But soon the movement of gold was reversed, and altogether $1,300,000,000 in gold reached Ottawa during the war.

For more than a year after the outbreak of the war, viz.: until December, 1915, British investors in the industrial and the commercial enterprises of the United States thus sold their stocks heavily. They possessed U. S. securities to the extent of about $3,500,000,000 at the beginning. Thereby the British maintained in some degree their necessities in the war, but the conversion of the stocks affected sometimes sharply the international exchange between the two countries. Finally, in December, 1915, there was effected an agreement between them by which the pound sterling became fixed in value and this arrangement lasted for more than three years. In other words, from December, 1915, long before the declaration of war by the U. S. against Germany, the U. S. dollar was fighting shoulder to shoulder with the Canadian dollar in the great struggle, and this important fact is one that should be kept in view. This agreement was brought about in various ways but chiefly from the abnormal fluctuations of exchange, and it was in reality a relief to both nations.

This financial arrangement of such benefit to the Entente Allies, just referred to, was in effect an agreement between Great Britain and the United States to stabilize the value of the pound sterling. By arrangement between the two countries, the quoted price of the pound sterling remained uniform in America at $4.76 7/16 from December, 1915, as stated above, to March 21, 1919, at which date the agreement ended. Then the pound sterling dropped in price in New York and other financial centres in the United States, and in February, 1920, the maximum premium on U. S. money was reached, viz.: 17½, as compared with British standards. In other words, the pound sterling fell to a little below $3.20 in value. The Canadian dollar was at a discount, too, but not so large, the lowest quotation having been slightly less than 85 cents. Our credit paper had increased in comparison with that of the United States, and thus a condition prevailed in Canada the reverse of what had occurred in the time of the U. S. internal war of 1861-5, when greenbacks went down to

40 cents on the dollar of our Canadian money. (Confederate bank notes of the South went to nothing, just as the pre-war German mark has gone out of sight since the war.)

The recovery of the pound sterling from February, 1920, onward to 1922 was rapid. The exchange rate having been fixed for more than three years with the United States, many Canadian and British securities, especially the former, were placed in that country during the three-year period, but the pound sterling has already risen above that figure ($4.76 7/16). On two occasions since the war the Canadian dollar has been at a premium in New York.

Closely connected with the fluctuations of exchange were the rates of interest. Wide fluctuations occurred in the rate of money from the beginning. When the crisis came, on the impulse of the moment the Bank of England advanced its rate from 3 to 10 per cent. on August 1, 1914, which was the highest in the history of the bank. Nearly similar high rates had been charged upon only two other occasions, viz.: during the panics of 1857 and 1866. But within a few days after August 1st, the rate was reduced to 6 per cent. and soon to 5 per cent. It remained steadily at that figure until July 1, 1916, which may be looked upon as the critical point of the whole war, from the military standpoint, when an advance took place to 6 per cent., but it lowered again to 5 per cent. in April, 1917, when the United States entered with the Allies. On November 6, 1919, in order to retard the inflation of paper money and credit, the Bank of England adopted a dear-money policy, and the rate was raised to 6 per cent., and after remaining there until April 15, 1920, a further advance took place to 7 per cent. (The Federal Reserve Bank in the U. S. had adopted a dear-money policy in January, 1920.) On April 28, 1921, there was a reduction by the Bank of England to $6\frac{1}{2}$ per cent., on June 23rd to 6 per cent., on July 21st to $5\frac{1}{2}$ per cent., and finally on November 3rd to 5 per cent. These rates, although declining step by step, had been larger than the rates in the ordinary money market, the whole decline in the year 1921 giving an advantage in commercial matters. At July 1, 1921, money in the London market ruled at 5 per cent., but in New York at the same date it was quoted at 6 per cent. Hence there could arise a wide difference in the foreign exchange, as money owners would not send away money to another country to get a lower per cent., but it gave Great Britain an advantage in trade. By giving a high rate on deposits, moreover, the London banks attracted money to themselves and defended their status as a money centre. The Bank rate, however, was reduced from 5 to 4 per cent. in February, 1922, and again to 3 per cent. in midsummer, but in July, 1923, it was advanced to 4 per cent.

The amounts borrowed by one nation from another amongst the victorious Allies, making what are called the inter-Allied debts, with the question of who should ultimately bear them in the final adjustment, soon after the close of the war began to attract notice, and has continued to the present time. It is worthy of note that Allied countries are indebted to Great Britain for loans to the extent of $10,000,000,000, which does not include the loans to the British dominions in the early part of the war. The recovery of the greater part of this sum from the debtors is uncertain, and the slow rate at which Germany has been meeting its obligations makes it doubtful whether redress can ever be obtained in that direction.

Another noteworthy feature of war finance was that bank deposits everywhere had almost trebled by the end of the struggle, owing to the world-wide inflation and the enormous increase of paper currency. There were also important effects upon the inflation itself by the numerous loans in the countries engaged in hostilities.

Measures for the urgent relief and extension of credit, which had broken down everywhere at the commencement of the war, took the same three forms in all the various countries engaged in the contest, although the use of each of the three was differently manifested in each country, viz.: moratoria, protection of gold reserves, and enlarged issues of the media of exchange especially of paper currency. Accordingly, they need not be further mentioned under the different countries in the following survey of their financial efforts, but only where exceptional instances occurred.

PART II

THE FINANCIAL EFFORTS, NATION BY NATION

Great Britain.

The total effort of the United Kingdom in the war was the stupendous sum of £9,000,000,000, or about $43,000,000,000, which amounted to something like $1,000 per capita. This was the largest financial effort of all the nations.

This amount far exceeds the penalty which Germany was afterward asked to pay, and equals the total burden upon the Germans per capita when their own war costs are added, theoretical economists having agreed that Germany could pay at least the sum of $30,000,000,000 and recover a place in the world. The British effort was raised in less than five years and without a murmur, but Germany has been given forty-two years in which to make up the Reparations, and has been doing little else than side-stepping and whining. Moreover, the pre-war population of the United Kingdom was 46,499,000, whereas that of Germany was 68,442,000, or nearly 50 per cent. greater. These comparisons show how much more the British were penalized by the war than the Germans. The winners were actually the greatest losers, and the same result happened in connection with the Bonaparte wars a century earlier. Unfortunately, only in subsequent years the United Kingdom has been finding out the actual condition of its affairs.

The British fiscal year ending with March 31, the gross expenditures made by the United Kingdom in each year of the war, and the net totals of loans during the same periods, were:—

Year	Gross expenditures (dollars)	Net debt from loans, etc. (dollars)
1914–5	2,802,367,665	2,841,438,115
1915–6	7,795,791,888	5,977,159,165
1916–7	10,990,563,550	8,149,508,125
1917–8	13,481,107,025	10,196,769,005
1918–9	13,896,505,940	8,574,436,860
	48,966,136,068	35,739,311,270

(These are the computations by Prof. Bogart, with reductions to dollars.)

In the United Kingdom there was no suspension of specie payments throughout the entire duration of the war—the only one of all the European countries engaged in the conflict to make this achievement. Moreover, the Bank of England, which is the authorized bank of issue, did not take advantage of the suspension clause in the Bank Act to issue an undue amount of paper currency.

The mobility and strength of British finance were materially increased during the war years by the formation of bank mergers. These amalgamations of the larger joint stock banks in London formed one of the outstanding features. In this way the ten largest London banks of deposit were reduced to six, and ultimately to five, now known as the "Big Five." These show much larger combined financial resources and deposits than the total of all the British banks in 1914. The five of the larger sort which remain in the field are Barclay's, Lloyd's, Westminster, London Joint City and Midland, and the National Provincial & Union. (The Bank of England itself is chiefly a bank of issue.) The consolidation gave them greater mobility and strength, just as a long rod or beam has more combined elasticity, and can bend by a greater amount than a short one, and besides, being bound together they were made stronger and stiffer. The chief of the noteworthy unions were those brought about by Sir Edward Holden of the Midland, who died August, 1919. The deposits in his London City & Midland Bank grew from $450,000,000 in 1915 to $1,600,000,000 in 1919, largely by means of consolidations.

Of the financial corporations other than the banks, the enormous power of the British system in sudden financial demands came into view on various occasions. The allotment of $100,000,000 by the Prudential Assurance Co. in a then recent British war loan, as announced in the public press of January 13, 1917, was instructive. It enabled us to realize the efficacy of free institutions, such as those of Great Britain, and showed a proof of their value as contrasted with those under state control in a time of crisis. If insurance operations had been an official state effort, this allotment would not have been possible, but the flexibility of the British system was able to cope with the formidable situation.

Great Britain and the United States mutually stabilized their respective currencies as already stated, in December, 1915, by an arrangement of great utility to the Allies, the value of the pound sterling being fixed at $4.76 7/16. This lasted until March 21, 1919, and might have lasted longer, but the British, it is said, advised its termination. Although it was well understood that, when the fixed exchange ceased, the value of the pound sterling would run down to an unknown figure in the foreign exchanges, the British financiers said in substance, "Pull out the peg and let matters come to the worst." They were perhaps buoyed up by the notion, rightly or wrongly, that a low value of the pound sterling in the foreign exchanges would draw new trade to the United Kingdom. The peg was drawn, and the pound ran down, reaching its lowest record in New York at about $3.17. Its recovery in the foreign exchanges has been one of the most outstanding features of the subsequent years to the present time.

A new departure in British finance, soon after the outbreak of the war, to increase their media of exchange, was the extensive issue of Treasury notes for short term obligations. The issues of these Treasury notes continued throughout the war and formed the main item in the floating debt. A considerable time after the close they had reached a total of $5,354,935,000 in outstanding Treasury bills.

Enormous as the British effort was, the reduction of their debt has been going forward at a rapid rate. From a compilation of figures for the various countries in 1922, the per capita taxation in Great Britain was £17, or say $75,— which was a greater amount than in any other country. This high taxation has borne heavily upon the classes who possessed savings.

The United States.

The financial effort of the United States in the war totalled about $24,000,000,000, or approximately, $240 per capita. In addition to this, in war loans to the Allies, further sums amounting to about $10,000,000,000 were raised.

The fiscal year of the United States begins on July 1. An estimate of its war expenditures is as follows:—

Fiscal Year	War Expenditures.
First three months of war, April 6 to June 30, 1917	$423,405,993
1917–18	8,242,039,268
1918–19	14,312,821,707
Net Total	$22,978,266,968

The advances to Allies made by the United States to June 30, 1920, are given as follows:—

Country	
Belgium	$350,428,794
Cuba	10,000,000
Czecho-Slovakia	67,329,041
France	3,047,974,777
Great Britain	4,277,000,000
Greece	48,236,629
Italy	1,666,260,180
Liberia	5,000,000
Roumania	25,000,000
Russia	187,729,750
Serbia	26,780,465
	$9,711,739,636

The Federal Reserve Bank which had its origin in 1913, and was further developed after the war had begun, gave greater mobility to the financial system of the United States in war time, as Federal Reserve banks were opened in November, 1914. But it added further inflation by credit documents, and doubled the national currency. This, however, was scarcely felt on foreign exchange, as most of the other nations, had also doubled, and some of them more than doubled, theirs by similar methods. The Federal Reserve Bank gave the U. S. system a resemblance to the British system—the bank holding a somewhat similar relation to the other banks of the U. S. that the Bank of England with its issue department, in which there was always a gold reserve of $600,000,000 or more, does to the other banks of England.

A feature of U. S. finance was the growth of its foreign trade as a neutral nation after the war began. Its exports to the five leading countries of the Allies grew from $927,000,000 in the year 1914 to $2,432,000,000 in 1915, and to $3,012,000,000 in 1916. So profitable was the export trade, mostly in war necessities, carried on in enormous quantities and at the top of the market prices, that the U. S., about the time of its entry into the war, April 6, 1917, had paid its debts to foreign countries and had become a creditor nation for the first time in its history.

France.

The total expenditures of France during the war, according to the estimate of the Chamber of Deputies in February, 1919, amounted to $36,400,000,000.

The votes of that Chamber give approximately the total amount not provided for in current taxation, as follows:—

Year	(Dollars)
August 1 to December 31, 1914	1,779,717,000
1915	4,560,895,000
1916	6,589,029,000
1917	8,374,185,000
1918	9,217,961,256
	30,521,787,256

The above amounts do not include advances which France made to some of the other Allies, to the extent of $1,547,200,000 during the war.

The credits voted by the Chamber of Deputies, given above, to the end of 1918, were raised as follows, according to a subsequent estimate:—

Source	(Dollars)
Total sums borrowed in France	11,012,200,000
Advances from U. S. Government	2,436,427,000
Advances from Great Britain	2,170,000,000
Collateral loans in the U. S.	686,000,000
Collateral loans in neutral countries	150,000,000
Advanced by Bank of France	3,430,000,000
Advanced by Bank of Algeria	17,000,000
Floating Debt in 1919	4,483,750,000
	24,385,377,000

Much as we may regret that there was currency inflation as a result of the war in all the English-speaking countries, it is but fair to state that inflation of the currency in France was somewhat greater. The paper circulation at the outbreak of the war was nine billion francs, or $1,800,000,000, and at the end of 1918 it reached thirty billion francs, or $6,000,000,000. Short-term treasury bills for immediate needs (*bons, obligations*, etc.) were the principal dependence of the French Government, as elsewhere. This inflation resulted in the low figures at which the franc has since been quoted in foreign exchanges, and in the higher prices of food, etc., in France. Taking the same course which had been pursued in Germany just after the outbreak of the war, to increase the gold reserves in the national bank of issue, an appeal was made throughout France in 1915 to the people to exchange their gold for paper currency, and there was a flocking to the banks with gold jewellery and keepsakes for deposit. The result was an increase of the gold reserves by over $1,000,000,000, half of which was sent abroad for the negotiation of loans.

At the war fronts France was numerically the greatest sufferer. And financially, she has suffered to a corresponding degree. The expenditures of France were numerically less than the outlays of Great Britain, because France had less wealth at the beginning of the war, speaking comparatively, owing to the misfortunes in war forty years previously.

The emergencies of the war crisis laid a great strain upon the Bank of France, but it acquitted itself fairly well. As one can see from the above figures, the bank met the appeals of the Government by the issue of paper currency rather than by credit loans to the same extent as in Great Britain, where the credits of this kind totalled $35,739,311,270 as against $11,012,200,000 in France. Yet, in view of all its misfortunes and trials, one cannot fail to view with regret the hardships of France, and to admire the patriotism of her people.

Russia.

At the outset Russia at least divided the attention of the German prepared forces, and thus diverted the full weight of their blow from the western front. For this favour alone Russia is entitled to brotherly treatment from the Allied nations, notwithstanding the misguided course of that country in the latter part of the struggle, and subsequently. The war expenditures of Russia during the time that country was active as one of the Allies have been estimated by a financial authority of that nation as follows:—

Year	(Dollars)
August 1 to December 1, 1914	1,273,000,000
1915	4,687,450,000
1916	7,633,500,000
1917 to September 1	7,102,407,500
	20,696,357,500

This estimate rather understates the Russian expenses, as the soldiers received low pay, there were government-owned railways making transportation at nominal amounts, and foods were at low prices in the early years of the war.

The above total was raised in the following ways, so far as it was not provided for in current taxation:—

Source	(Dollars)
War loans by the Russians (7)	6,176,000,000
Advances by Bank of Russia	7,239,663,000
Advances by Great Britain	2,840,000,000
Advances by France	1,085,000,000
Advances in the United States	350,229,750
Advances by Japan	333,000,000
	18,023,892,750

At the beginning of the war, strange to say, the specie deposits in the Imperial Bank of Russia, viz.: $824,600,000 in gold, and $36,910,000 in silver, were larger than in any other country, and at the end of 1913, there had been commercial deposits in the same bank amounting to $610,650,800, which were the largest, at the time, of any bank in the world. Accordingly, large bank deposits do not always give an exact idea of a country's financial strength, but sometimes furnish evidence of stagnation of commerce.

When the sudden enormous demands on the resources of the bank came from the Government, the Russian people were not prepared to furnish credits in loans or other advances, as their wealth was small in comparison with that of the British and French people, for example. Accordingly, from the beginning, Russia made up, through the Imperial Bank of Russia, its war expenditures more completely from paper currency than did any other of the Entente Allies. From the last published report of the bank in October, 1917, it appears the note issues had been inflated to $9,458,500,000 against a gold reserve of less than the initial sum given above by about 25 per cent. reduction. The seven internal war loans amounted to $6,176,000,000 up to the time of the first revolution in March, 1917, after which the disturbed military and political conditions of Russia gave its national financial transactions an insignificant character, although the amounts were nominally large, but the currency by that time had been so much inflated as to give an incorrect idea from comparisons with currencies of the nations of Western Europe. Subsequently, the Bolshevists overthrew the first revolutionists and repudiated all debts to foreign countries, and the financial affairs of Russia thenceforward became, for all practical purposes, worse than a pitiable blank.

Italy.

Italy's entrance into the war took place on May 24, 1915. The fiscal year begins with July 1, and the annual expenditures were:—

Year	(Dollars)
1914–15	607,840,000
1915–16	1,670,300,000
1916–17	2,826,440,000
1917–18	3,946,920,000
1918–19	1,345,120,000
Outstanding	2,127,200,000
	12,523,820,000

There was a rapid expansion of the bank note circulation in Italy, as in many other countries, and at the close of the war the total paper currency was $2,350,100,000; hence, the decline of the lira was the outcome.

Belgium and other Entente Allies.

The expenditure of Belgium was estimated officially at $1,154,467,914; that of Roumania at $1,600,000,000; while that of Serbia, Greece, Japan, and the European Entente Allies not already mentioned above, did not exceed $400,000,000 each in any instance.

The plight of Belgium in being almost entirely overrun by the German invasion in the early part of the war leaves little to be said respecting the financial transactions of that country after the first few weeks. Her war expenditures were met mainly by advances from the larger allied nations—Great Britain, France, and the United States. The brave stand of the Belgians and their subsequent sufferings have materially obscured the financial difficulties of that nation, which were, comparatively, very great.

Germany.

There were twelve votes of credit by the Reichstag from the beginning of the war to the armistice, aggregating a total of $34,750,000,000, but the actual expenditures for war purposes were in excess of these credits, just as in the nations of the Entente Allies. These actual expenditures may be derived from the statement of the New Minister of Finance after the revolution and the formation of the republic. According to his estimate, the war expenditures of Germany by years were as follows:

Year	Dollars
1914 (part)	1,875,000,000
1915	5,750,000,000
1916	6,650,000,000
1917	9,875,000,000
1918	12,125,000,000
	36,275,000,000

In addition to the inflation of paper currency by bank notes and treasury bill issues, similar to those of other countries and already sufficiently referred to, Germany had a third device for inflation—cash loan-office notes (Darlehenskassenschein). These loan offices had been devised in advance of the war, amongst other preparations for it, in order to relieve the sudden demands for cash after the war had got under way. They were operated according to the method of the pawnshop by loaning to traders and others on the security of merchandise or other kinds of collateral.

Nine war loans issued in Germany up to September, 1918, raised an aggregate of $24,640,419,925 for the settlement of their war expenditures.

The total circulation of bank paper currency in Germany had increased, by December 23, 1918, to $5,281,080,000, and there was a floating debt by Government which raised the total liabilities of the Reichsbank to the alleged total of $8,536,040,000 at the same date. In addition to these bank notes, there were treasury notes and other similar Imperial obligations outstanding at the close of the war to the enormous amount of $18,000,000,000, making a formidable floating debt. The existence of this had been concealed from the German people generally, as far as possible, until July, 1919, when further concealment was impossible. In their fiscal war policy, the German Imperial Government had not resorted to war taxation during the continuance of the conflict in the expectation of victory, and this naturally made the final burden greater than it would have been if taxation had been practised during the contest.

As an example of the selfish policy of Germany, financially, toward the other Central Powers allied with her, it may be cited that the gold reserves of the Austro-Hungarian Bank almost totally disappeared during the war, at least to the extent of about $200,000,000, and in a similar way the gold reserves of the Bank of Turkey vanished during the same period, while there was a corresponding accession to the gold in the Reichsbank of Germany as the others dwindled.

Austria-Hungary.

Estimates of the Austro-Hungarian war expenditures result in the following aggregates, all information regarding military expenditures having been purposely suppressed (the fiscal year ending with June 30th):

Year	Dollars
1914-5	2,856,200,000
1915-6	3,644,600,000
1916-7	4,200,000,000
1917-8	4,433,000,000
1918-9	4,866,400,000
	20,000,200,000

To meet the obligations incurred in the above expenditures, Austria raised, in eight war loans, a total of $6,957,914,200, and Hungary raised, in eight war loans, a total of $3,665,546,400. As there was but little deposit banking in Austria-Hungary, in comparison with Great Britain, for example, and as the internal war loans made up only about half of the whole expenditure, settlement of the other half took the form of paper currency. Bank note issues, by January 23, 1919, made up the stupendous aggregate of $6,434,400,000. As a result, prices of everything became enormous, and the cost of living was fabulously high.

Australia.

The total expenditures of Australia were given officially as $1,423,208,040. The amounts raised in seven internal loans and new currency issues were given as $961,249,875.

New Zealand and the Other Colonies.

The expenditure of New Zealand was given as $378,750,000, while the amounts raised by three internal loans and war currency amounted to $209,830,000.

The expenditure of India was given as $601,279,000, and the amount raised locally in the colony was $275,000,000 in two war loans.

The South African Union had an expenditure of $300,000,000, while the Crown Colonies had $125,000,000, altogether.

Canada.

The two billions and a quarter spent by Canada in the war amounted to more than $250 per capita. But, as we have seen, the people of the United Kingdom contributed nearly four times that amount per capita. For interest and pensions, the annual burden inherited by Canada as a legacy of the war, not to speak of anything but finance, is about $150,000,000, or about $20 for every man, woman, and child. It is this burden which produces our political troubles in which one class of persons tries to shuffle the burden off their shoulders upon some other class or classes.

The Canadian war loans tell the story of the efforts by the people to subscribe amounts not provided for in current taxation, thus:

Loan	Date	Accepted
First	November, 1915	$100,000,000
Second	September, 1916	100,000,000
Third	March, 1917	150,000,000
Fourth	November, 1917	398,000,000
Fifth	October, 1918	690,000,000
		$1,438,000,000

The responses of the Canadian people were prompt and sprightly. When the Government asked for the first loan, to aggregate fifty millions, the people offered one hundred and thirteen millions, of which the Government accepted one hundred. On the second occasion, the Government asked for one hundred millions, and the people offered two hundred and one millions. For the third loan, in March, 1917, the Government asked for one hundred and fifty millions, and the people subscribed two hundred and sixty millions. Again, in the following November, another hundred and fifty millions was requested, and the response came of four hundred and nineteen millions. Finally, the Government increased its request to five hundred millions, and the answer was unmistakable— six hundred and ninety millions.

The above aggregate of a billion and a half in internal loans takes no account of a continuous procession of debenture issues, increased postage, income taxes, sales tax and various other devices for raising money, all of which have contributed their share to raising prices of food and everything else. Nor does it take any account of borrowings by the Canadian Government in New York, and by other Canadian Corporations, public as well as private, for ends more or less directly connected with the war, to the extent of half a billion. Previous to the war, Canada had mostly secured in Great Britain the borrowed capital it needed. But after the outbreak of hostilities, it turned from the London stock market to that of New York almost entirely. The superior credit of Canada abroad became of assistance to the mother country in the time of need, for its chartered banks loaned to the British Government, for the purchase of foodstuffs, munitions, etc., two hundred millions, and Canada extended to Great Britain a commercial credit for the same purposes of more than half a billion.

On the fatal day when Austria-Hungary declared war against Serbia (July 28, 1914), the stock exchanges at Montreal and Toronto closed their doors, and they remained closed for several months. With the opening again of the exchanges of the world at the end of 1914 and in the early part of 1915, a more steady condition of international exchange ensued. The priority of the leading exchanges of Canada to close their doors was apparently due to this country being a debtor nation. It was significant that the Montreal and Toronto stock exchanges should be the first in the world (along with that of Madrid) to close, and shows the frailty of a borrowing nation in time of crisis—a circumstance we should not lose sight of in the midst of optimism regarding Canada's part in the war. The commercial credits of half a billion advanced by Canada to the Imperial Government, as stated in the preceding paragraph, were balanced by similar advances made by Great Britain to the Dominion for maintenance of Canadian troops.

As in London, the financial centre of the world at that time, so in Canada, a series of bank amalgamations took place during the war and since. The Metropolitan Bank and the Bank of Ottawa were absorbed by the Bank of Nova Scotia in 1914 and 1919, respectively; the Traders' Bank was absorbed before the war by the Bank of Hamilton, and the latter more recently in 1923 by the Canadian Bank of Commerce. In a similar way there was absorption of the Bank of British North America in 1919 and the Merchants' Bank in 1921, by the Bank of Montreal; and of the Quebec Bank in 1917 and the Northern Crown Bank in 1918 by the Royal Bank. Concurrently with these bank amalgamations, the bank deposits of Canada underwent an increase of three hundred millions.

From the very outset Canada creditably pulled herself together for the great conflict, and took a visible part in the war operations of an empire that so conspicuously swayed the world conflict. Our mother country had no concern in the Serbian misfortune which Germany used as an excuse for forcing on the war, but now, though not murmuring, stands mulcted of a larger financial amount per capita than any other nation, even than Germany, with a programme of debt and taxation as the only asset. She had no direct part in the causes that brought the war about, yet for the sake merely of honour drew the sword in the defence of wronged humanity from the German invasion of Belgium, and it should be with some feeling of humble pride that we can call ourselves British subjects.

Articles and Books used for Reference and for Revision of Newspaper data.

Effects of the War on Credit, Currency, Finance, and Foreign Exchanges. Reports of a Committee of the British Association for the Advancement of Science, 1921, 1922.

French Points of View, By Henri Brenier. (1921), Comite de Relations Internationales (Marseilles).

The Statesman's Year-Book, 1922. (Macmillan.)

War Finance, as viewed from the Roof of the World in Switzerland. By Clarence W. Barron (1919). (Houghton Mifflin.) (Contains many nuggets of information but mixed with U.S. bombast. Fairness is generally shown to other nations.)

A World Remaking; or, Peace Finance. By Clarence W. Barron (1920). (Harper.) (A sequel to the preceding volume.)

War Costs and their Financing. By Prof. Ernest Ludlow Bogart. 1921. (Appleton.) A Study of the Financing of the War and the After-War Problems of Debt and Taxation.—(One of the best studies of the subject issued on this side of the Atlantic.)

Reichs-Arbeitsblatt. Berlin, 1914. Industrial and Economic Statistics of Germany at the beginning of the War.

Treaty of Peace between the Allied and Associated Powers and Germany. Signed at Versailles, June 28th, 1919. London, 1919.

Democracy and Empire. By A. E. Duchesne. (Royal Colonial Institute Monographs, 1916.) Appendix 3, for classification of European nations.

The International Whitaker, 1913, for excess in imports of bullion by the German Empire from 1902 to 1911, under "external trade."

London Statist, May, 1914 (Sir George Paish, editor). An article on World Finance, showing the 34 largest banks in the world each with deposits in excess of $150,000,000.

History of the Great War, 1914-18. By Brig.-Gen. E. A. Cruikshank, LL.D., F.R.S.C. In Canada Year Book, 1919, also reprinted in separate form by the Dominion Bureau of Statistics.

Reconstruction in Canada. By S. A. Cudmore, M.A., F.S.S. In Canada Year Book, 1920. In Part I (War-time activities of Government and people) there are sections on war finance, war loans, and war taxation in Canada.

Canada's War Effort, 1914-1918. Issued by the Director of Public Information, Ottawa, 1918. Section 3 gives Finance.

Canadian Trade and Finance During the War. Address by the Hon. (later Sir) W. T. White, Nov. 2, 1915.

How the Fight was Won. A General Sketch of the Great War. By D. E. Hamilton, M.A. Issued by the Department of Education of Ontario, 1920, for use in the secondary schools of the Province.

X

SOCIAL CONDITIONS AMONG THE NEGROES IN UPPER CANADA BEFORE 1865

By Fred Landon, M.A.

When the government of the United States emancipated the Negro slaves in the seceded states in 1863, there was instituted a Freedmen's Inquiry Commission to consider generally what should be done both with slaves who had been freed by the operations of the war and those who should later become free. The members of this commission were Dr. Samuel G. Howe, Robert Dale Owen and James Mackay. Dr. Howe, soon after his appointment, visited Upper Canada and later made a report to Secretary of War Stanton[1] which presents much information on the condition of the refugees who had entered the British province and were there making their home. His findings were highly favourable to the fugitives and one sentence of the report has been frequently quoted, where, after noting some of the advances made by these people in their new home, he adds: "The refugees earn a living, and gather property; they marry and respect women; they build churches and send their children to schools; they improve in manners and morals—not because they are picked men, but simply because they are free men."

Dr. Howe was deeply impressed with this idea, that it was freedom which improved the Negro. In Canada he found the black man facing severe hardships in many cases. The climate was harsh as compared with the South, sometimes there was difficulty in making a livelihood, and there was occasional prejudice. On the other hand, there was justice and opportunity and, above all, freedom. In the preface to his report Dr. Howe says: "When everybody is asking what shall be done with the Negroes—and many are afraid that they cannot take care of themselves if left alone—an account of the manner in which twenty thousand of them are taking care of themselves in Canada may be interesting, even if it be imperfect, and contain superfluous speculations."

Dr. Howe's estimate of the number of Negro refugees in Canada was between 15,000 and 20,000.[2] This is but one of many estimates and it is rather difficult to arrive at any definite figure. The question is of some interest, however, as showing the effect of the refuge offered by Canada upon slave holding in the South. For more than thirty years before the Civil War came, the slaveholders had protested against the British policy of protecting Negroes in Canada against their efforts to return them to slavery. The Canadian census figures are quite unreliable with regard to this class of people. Rev. S. R. Ward, himself a fugitive, says that the enumerators ignored the portion of their report designating colour.[3] Thus we are left to draw some conclusion from the many

---
[1] Refugees from slavery in Canada West, report to the Freedmen's Inquiry Commission, by S. G. Howe, Boston, 1864.
[2] Howe, Freedmen's Inquiry Commission report, p. 17.
[3] Ward, S. R., Autobiography of a fugitive negro, London, 1855, p. 154.

and varying figures given by travellers, by the fugitives themselves, and by others who were interested. R. J. Hinton, biographer of John Brown, makes the highest estimate when he says that in 1858 there were at least 75,000 fugitives in Canada.[1] It is quite certain that this figure is far too high. Rev. W. M. Mitchell, a Negro missionary resident in Toronto, made an estimate of 60,000 in 1860,[2] and this estimate is supported by Rev. Dr. Willis, president of the Anti-Slavery Society of Canada, and by Rev. Hiram Wilson, a missionary among the fugitives.[3] Levi Coffin, when he visited Canada in 1844, was told that there were 40,000 Negroes in the country,[4] and this figure is also given by Rev. S. R. Ward in 1850.[5] The first annual report of the Anti-Slavery Society of Canada estimated the Negro population at 30,000, of whom about one-fifth had arrived in the last two years.[6] Josiah Henson, in 1852, put the figure at between twenty and thirty thousand,[7] "daily increasing," while James B. Brown, a British traveller, made an estimate of 30,000.[8] A resolution passed at a public meeting at Sandwich in 1852[9] speaks of the 30,000 Negroes in Canada, and this figure is also given by John Scoble, writing in the *Anti-Slavery Reporter* in 1852.[10] *The National Anti-Slavery Standard* of September 5, 1850, quotes an address issued by fugitive slaves meeting at Cazenovia, the home of Gerrit Smith, in which they say: "Including our children, we number in Canada at least 20,000. The total of our population in the free states far exceeds this." *The Voice of the Fugitive* of July 29, 1852, quotes from *The Liberator*: "It is stated that there are now in Canada about 30,000 of these poor refugees, 8,000 having been driven from the free states through the panic occasioned by the Fugitive Slave Law."

Henry Bibb, writing in *The Voice of the Fugitive* of May 21, 1851, says: "From the best information we can get on the subject, there must be about 35,000 here now, more or less." He adds that before the passing of the Fugitive Slave Act there were about 30,000 Negroes in Canada, of whom at least 20,000 were refugees from slavery.

Rev. S. R. Ward, in making his estimate of 40,000, states that the majority were refugees from slavery. Apart from children born in Canada, he did not think that there were 3,000 free born Negroes in the country, though this class came in after 1850 in considerable numbers.

Figures of population for separate places show clearly that the majority of the Negroes were in the western part of the province. Windsor, Sandwich, Amherstburg, Chatham, Buxton, Dawn, and Colchester were all in the Detroit River district. Elsewhere the Negroes were found in numbers in London,

---

[1] Hinton, R. J., John Brown and his men, N.Y., 1894. p. 171.
[2] Mitchell, W. M., Underground railroad, London, 1860, pp. 127, 166.
[3] See Siebert, W. H., Underground railroad, N.Y., 1899, p. 221.
[4] Coffin, Levi, Reminiscences, Cincinnatti, 1876, p. 253.
[5] Ward, Autobiography, p. 154.
[6] That is, following the passing of the Fugitive Slave Act of 1850.
[7] Life of Josiah Henson narrated by himself, London, 1852, p. 97.
[8] Brown, J. B., Views of Canada and the Colonists, Edinburgh, 1851, p. 353.
[9] *Voice of the Fugitive*, June 4, 1851. This paper was published by Henry Bibb, himself a fugitive, at Sandwich. Files for 1851-2, being Vols. I and II, are in the library of the University of Michigan, and also in the Burton Library, Detroit.
[10] Quoted in the *Voice of the Fugitive*, May 20, 1852.

Ingersoll, Norwich, St. Catharines, Hamilton, Toronto, and in the Queen's Bush. The first annual report of the Anti-Slavery Society of Canada says that around 1852 there was a coloured population of 500 in Dawn (now Dresden), 1,200 to 1,500 in Colchester, twenty families at New Canaan, 300 families at Sandwich, 2,000 in the Queen's Bush, 800 at Hamilton, 800 at Toronto, 1,500 at St. Catharines and Niagara, twenty families at Wilberforce, north of London, and fifty actual settlers at Buxton.

Benjamin Drew[1] made the following estimates in 1856: Toronto, about 1,000; St. Catharines, 800; Hamilton, 274; Galt, 40; London, 350; Chatham, 800 in the town and probably 1,200 more nearby; Buxton, 800; Dresden, 70; Windsor, 250.

Rev. W. M. Mitchell gave the following figures in 1860: Toronto, 1,600; Hamilton, 600; St. Catharines, 200 to 250; London, 500; Chatham, 2,000; Windsor, 2,500; Sandwich, 2,000; Amherstburg, 800; Buxton, 800. He refers to Chatham as the headquarters of the race in Canada.

The twenty-eighth annual report of the American Anti-Slavery Society (N.Y., 1861), refers to "the thousand refugees" in Toronto, and quotes from the Philadelphia *Friends' Review* an account of the visit of Joseph Morris, an Ohio Quaker, to Chatham, where he found 2,000 coloured people, one third of the whole population of the place. Their homes, he thought, compared favourably with those of the whites and there were no cases of extreme destitution. He visited the Buxton colony which presented an impression very agreeable and encouraging and "he never saw any people more willing to rely on their own resources." Shrewsbury, on Lake Erie, was also visited, and here the coloured people "manifested a spirit of independence in respect to obtaining the means of living and educating their children. He thinks the unrestricted enjoyment of the privileges of citizenship largely promotes their improvement." All in all, this Ohio Quaker was much impressed by what he saw in Upper Canada.

The presence of the Negro refugees in Canada does not seem to have attracted any special attention until late in the forties. The Negro created no special problem either for the government or for the local authorities. His status in Canada differed in no material respect from that of any other citizen. He had to work or starve, therefore he worked. If he transgressed the laws of the land he was punished, though there does not seem to have been any unusual amount of crime among the Negroes. The black man had the same civil rights as the white man, he exercised the franchise and could participate in politics.

Under the Canadian law the Negroes were allowed to send their children to the common schools, or to have separate schools provided for them out of their share of the school funds. Separate schools were so established at a few places where prejudice had been manifested. There were also one or two private schools for Negro children maintained by religious societies,[2] and in the distinctly Negro settlements, such as Buxton, Dawn and at the Refugees' Home

---

[1] Drew, Benj., Refugee, or the narratives of fugitive slaves in Canada, related by themselves, with an account of the history and condition of the colored population of Upper Canada, Boston, 1856. The author gathered his narratives from persons whom he met in the course of a tour through the western part of the province.

[2] The Colonial Church and School Society had a school in London in the fifties which Benj. Drew in 1855 noted as caring for the bulk of the Negro children.

settlement in Essex county, there were special schools. That at Buxton drew students from the northern states. The best work seems to have been done by the mission schools and those located in the colonies. An indication of the general interest taken in education is shown by the incorporation in 1859 of "The Association for the education of the coloured people of Canada," which succeeded and continued the work of "The Provincial Association for the education and elevation of the coloured people of Canada," the object of which was to provide education for the coloured youth of the country.

Dr. S. G. Howe, when he visited Canada, noted that a surprisingly large number of the fugitives could read and write. In Chatham he thought that the coloured children stood as well as the whites, while in the matter of attendance there was also little difference, except that the coloured children left school at an earlier age. The coloured children seemed to be dressed about as well as the white children in the mixed schools, but did not make as good an appearance in the separate schools. Howe thought the separate schools were ill advised and thought it a still greater mistake to ask for coloured teachers. The principal of the Chatham schools told him that Negro children learned about as rapidly as the white children but needed more attention.

Dr. Howe's criticism of the separate schools agreed with the view of some of the more intelligent of the refugees themselves. Henry Bibb was distinctly antagonistic to any separation and made frequent references to this matter in his paper. This was partly due to the occasional manifestations of prejudice against the Negroes in the matter of schools. Rev. William Troy, of Windsor, states that his children were turned out of the common school along with other coloured children,[1] and Patrick Shirreff, a British traveller, refers to Negro children being kept out of a school near Chatham.[2]

Prejudice was almost sure to manifest itself occasionally in view of the nearby American influences. When the Elgin Association settlement in Kent county was beginning its work in 1849 there was considerable opposition manifested, and the Western District council in October of that year issued a resolution[3] reading, in part, as follows:

"The increased immigration of foreign Negroes into this part of the province is truly alarming. We cannot omit mentioning some facts for the corroboration of what we have stated. The Negroes who form at least one-third of the inhabitants of the township of Colchester attended the township meeting for the election of parish and township officers and insisted upon their right to vote, which was denied them by every individual white man at the meeting. The consequence of which was that the chairman of the meeting was prosecuted and thrown into heavy costs, which costs were paid by subscriptions from white inhabitants. As well as many others, in the same township of Colchester, the inhabitants have not been able to get schools in many school sections in consequence of the Negroes insisting on their right of sending their children to such schools. No white man will ever act with them in any public capacity, this fact is so glaring that

---

[1]Troy, Rev. Wm. Hair-breadth escapes from slavery to freedom, Manchester, 1861, p. 26. There is a copy of this book in Princeton University Library.
[2]Shirreff, Patrick, Tour through North America, p. 207.
[3]Quoted in *The Voice of the Fugitive*, Oct. 21, 1852. This resolution also suggested that the government consider the propriety of laying a poll tax on American Negroes coming into the province together with an enactment against amalgamation, and the introduction of regulations whereby all foreign Negroes should be compelled to furnish good security that they would not become a burden on the community. The question of further allowing the suffrage to Negroes was also mentioned.

no sheriff in this province would dare to summon colored men to do jury duty. That such things have been done in other parts of the British Dominions we are well aware of, but we are convinced that the Canadians will never tolerate such conduct."

Rev. S. R. Ward, who was ever a doughty champion of the rights of his race, had a letter in reply to this resolution in which he denied that there was bad feeling between the two races in Colchester township, and stated that the references to Negroes being kept off juries were untrue as they had served in such a capacity in Toronto and elsewhere. The whole resolution was, in his opinion, an attempt to stir up racial hatred and influence Lord Elgin against the refugees. Referring to the outcome of the Colchester incident he said: "Such is the even-handed justice and impartiality of British law, such the purity of the British courts. Thank God for this. There is a resort to which we may go when robbed and insulted."[1]

The attempt to block the granting of land to the Elgin Association was rebuked by the Montreal Pilot, which, reproducing correspondence which had passed between Hon. Malcolm Cameron and the stockholders of the Association, said: "We have on more than one occasion advocated the rights of our coloured fellow-citizens in this province and expressed our surprise and indignation at the attempt made to take them away. The opponents of free settlement may be reminded that we are not yet annexed and that it is far too soon to anticipate by an anti-British policy an event the probable occurrence of which is contemplated by the lovers of genuine freedom and independence with strong feelings of aversion. The prejudice against colour is a moral weakness, to say the least, of which an Englishman should be ashamed. It ought to have no place among us."[2]

Elsewhere,[3] Rev. S. R. Ward drew attention to cases of prejudice shown against Negroes, refusal to provide accommodation in taverns and on steamboats being the most glaring. J. T. Fisher of Toronto also complained of discrimination in the choosing of juries in Toronto.[4] *The Liberator* of January 3, 1851, has a reference to excitement in Canada West over the drawing of a colour line by the Sons of Temperance. There appears also to have been some trouble in 1852 at the annual militia training at St. Catharines, a Negro settlement being attacked.[5] On the other hand, Frederick Douglass could write to *The Liberator* stating that he had been received kindly at a hotel on the Canadian side at Niagara in marked contrast to treatment received in American cities. "Were it not cowardly, and perhaps selfish," he said, "I could wish to leave the United States and become a resident in Canada."[6]

---

[1] *Voice of the Fugitive*, Sept. 9, 1852.
[2] Quoted in *National Anti-Slavery Standard*, Feb. 21, 1850. A reflection of the annexation movement of 1849 can be seen in the Pilot's comments. One of the chief fomentors of prejudice against the Negroes was one Edwin Larwill, of Chatham, a tinner by trade and a typical brawling Tory politician.
[3] *Voice of the Fugitive*, Nov. 4, 1852.
[4] *Voice of the Fugitive*, May 21, 1851. In his letter Fisher makes open protest to the Chief Justice of the Court of Common Pleas. His charge is that one Thomas Tilly, a coloured man, was dismissed from jury service because of his colour. On the other hand the *Voice of the Fugitive*, in its issue of July 2, 1851, noted that a Negro was foreman of the jury three times in one day in a Toronto court. The incident was quoted from the Toronto *Patriot*.
[5] Toronto correspondence of N.Y. *Tribune* quoted in *Voice of the Fugitive*, July 29, 1852.
[6] *The Liberator*, July 13, 1849.

There are numerous references by travellers and others to the condition of the Negroes in Canada at various times and it is quite clear that the presence of black people in this province was a matter of some interest to those who came examining the country. Reference has already been made to the visit to Upper Canada of Joseph Morris, an Ohio Quaker, who wrote his impressions for the Philadelphia *Friends' Review*. A correspondent of the New York *Tribune*, who also visited this province at about the same time (1860), says in his article: "Many of the coloured people are amassing wealth. All parties testify that the coloured man's condition is as good as that of any other emigrants."[1]

The Liberator of April 6, 1849, reprinted from *The True Wesleyan* the observations of one, E. Smith, under the heading, "Freed slaves, how they prosper." The writer, on his visit to Canada, found the greater portion of the refugees engaged in farm work, not waiters, barbers, etc. They had been represented in the United States as lazy and improvident, but he saw evidence to the contrary.

"I saw quite a number who had pretty good farms and everything necessary for life and comfort around them. Some are worth hundreds and others thousands of dollars. The laws there make no distinction on account of color. The colored man can take rank and place with his white brother and the fugitives may become a part of the community and share their portion of its benefits."

About 1850 the Board of the Baptist Missionary Convention of the State of New York sent two representatives, Messrs. Wheelock and Sheldon, to ascertain the condition of the coloured people, particularly those of the Baptist faith, in Canada West. They found the white testimony quite favourable to the Negroes, who were described as generally moral and industrious. They urged in their report that the coloured Baptists in Canada should be aided in maintaining schools and churches, but with regard to other forms of aid they say:

"We found in all the places we visited that respectable colored people, in churches and out of churches, were united in their testimony that contributions of clothing and provisions, except for the aged and the sick, would prove a curse rather than a blessing. In the States there has been much said about the destitution and sufferings of the fugitives, and much has been done for their relief. This reported destitution and suffering, we find, has been greatly exaggerated. None need assistance of this kind but the aged and the sick."

The report adds that there has been much imposition practiced upon benevolent persons, collections having been taken up for the refugees which never reached them.[2]

In *The Liberator* of July 30, 1852, appears a statement with regard to the refugees signed by Rev. Dr. Willis, president of the Anti-Slavery Society of Canada,[3] and by Messrs. Henning and Hamilton, officers of the society. Their communication estimates the coloured population at the time of the passing of the Fugitive Slave Act at 20,000, but says that this was increased by from four to five thousand within a few months after the passing of the Act. Charges of mistreatment of the fugitives by Canadians are denied. "Every coloured man,

---

[1] American Anti-Slavery Society, 28th Annual Report, N.Y., 1861, p. 171.
[2] Quoted in the *Voice of the Fugitive*, Nov. 5, 1851. These visitors made the vastly exaggerated estimate of 80,000 as the Negro population.
[3] An account of the history of this Society will be found in *The Journal of Negro History* for January, 1919, vol. IV, No. 1, pp. 33-40. Rev. Dr. Willis was principal of Knox College, Toronto.

as is well known, the moment he sets his feet on the Canadian soil, is forever free and not only free but he is on a level, in regard to every political and social advantage, with the white man. He can vote for members of Parliament and for magistrates and in every other popular election."

The communication states further that the Negro fugitives have their own churches, though they are not discriminated against in others; that they are not segregated in coaches or on steamers and that they can have their separate schools. "The coloured people in Canada have no grievance of any kind," is the conclusion of the communication.

The American and Foreign Anti-Slavery Society kept a friendly eye on the Canadian fugitives. The report for 1851 says: "Several agents have, during the past year, proceeded to Canada to exert the best influence in their power over the fugitives that have flocked to the province in years past and especially those who have gone the past year. They are supplied with the means of instructing the colored population, clothing some of the most destitute fugitives and aiding them in various ways to obtain employment, procure and cultivate land, and train up their children. Our friends in Canada are exerting a good influence in the same direction. It may not be improper for us to suggest that it is highly important that a plan, on a large scale, should be devised for the permanent employment of the people of color in Canada under the direction of competent agents in agricultural and mechanical pursuits."[1]

The American Missionary Association also received regular reports from its workers in Canada. The annual report for 1855 says: "In general those who have gone there from the United States may provide for the wants of their families after a short residence there, especially if they meet a friendly hand, and, more than all, good counsel on their arrival."[2]

Rev. Wm. Troy, of Windsor, writing about 1860, stated his belief that nine-tenths of the fugitives in Canada had received no aid for their physical wants from any source whatever. They showed a marked disposition to help each other, of which he gave several instances.[3]

An article by John Scoble in *Anti-Slavery Reporter*[4] entitled "Refugee slaves in Canada," estimates their number at 30,000, and increasing. He says: "By not a few of the French-Canadians, the Irish, and, though in not so great a degree the Scotch and English, they are regarded as an inferior caste and a degraded people, and, therefore, but little social intercourse exists between them. As a consequence of this unhappy state of things the colored people are found mostly in isolated communities." Their needs, he thought, were chiefly a well regulated body of schoolmasters, a superior class of religious teachers and easy

---

[1] 11th Annual Report, 1851, p. 100.
[2] 29th Annual Report, 1855, p. 47. For an account of the work of this missionary organization among the Negroes in Canada, see Ontario Historical Society, "Papers and Records," vol. XXI, pp. 198-205.
[3] Troy, Wm., Hair-breadth escapes from slavery to freedom, pp. 108, 122.
[4] Reprinted in the *Voice of the Fugitive*, May 20, 1852. John Scoble was the secretary of the British and Foreign Anti-Slavery Society and had visited Canada in 1851, to see the condition of the refugees. He later advocated emigration from Canada and the United States to the West Indies as offering best opportunity for the Negro.

means of procuring land. He doubts the wisdom of sending in much material aid and says that the Negroes have themselves exposed gross cases of misappropriation of charity.

"It may be regarded as a fact," he says, "that every industrious colored person in West Canada may obtain employment in one form or another and be fairly remunerated for it, and that consequently aid is only wanted to meet temporary necessities, more particularly when the flight of the fugitive has been in the winter."

This writer stresses the need of better educational facilities for both races. "In many districts of Canada West," he says, "the means of instruction are very scanty, and in some they do not exist at all." There is also need of a better qualified ministry among the coloured people. "Many of the coloured preachers in Canada West are wofully ignorant," he says, "thoroughly illiterate and much wanting in the reputation of good manners and a holy life. . . . . It is sad to hear the things which are said and to witness those which are done by these people and which furnish subjects of jest and sport to the profane." He adds that this class of preacher tries to keep his people away from the whites.

In preparation for a state convention of coloured people held at Cincinnati in January, 1852, information was sought from Canada as to the success that was attending the fugitives there. Henry Bibb being asked to make a statement. This he did and published it in his paper,[1] giving much interesting information concerning the refugees at this time. He was asked particularly with regard to the moral standards of his people and his answer was that the morals of the fugitives in Canada were as high as among their people in the northern states, and compared favourably with the white population, though there was still need for improvement. "Mentally, we find our people far behind the intelligence of the age," he says in his statement. "Just as in the States, we have scarcely any professional men among us, while we are well satisfied that they would be well supported in Canada West. We are sorry to be compelled to admit that along the frontier we have to contend with Yankee prejudice against colour, although unlike that which is so formidable in the United States. There it is bolstered up by law—here it has no foundation to stand upon and we can live it down. As to there being legal obstacles in the way of our advancement, we know of none. The laws that apply to the black men apply with equal force to the white men also, and there is no distinction here among men based on the colour of the skin so far as law is concerned, with but one exception, and that was asked for by the coloured people and the Roman Catholics, and their prayer was granted. The request, however, was not made by the intelligent portion of the coloured population, but by a lot of ignoramuses who were made tools of, and who knew not what they were doing. Such men are hardly fit to live or die. The prayer of the petitioners was that coloured persons might have separate schools for their children if they asked for them, and that the Catholics and Protestants might do the same—not that they shall have these distinctions but that they may have them if asked for. We are happy to inform you that there is no compulsion or necessity in Canada for coloured schools or coloured churches and that every man who respects himself will be respected.

[1] *Voice of the Fugitive*, Jan. 1, 1852.

"It would be impossible for us to state adequately the pecuniary condition of the people of color in Canada, but we should think they were worth not less than $200,000. . . . Wild lands may be bought within five miles of the Detroit River at from $3 to $5 an acre, such as will produce from 25 to 40 bushels of wheat to the acre and on which anything will grow and do well that will do well in Ohio soil. There is no difficulty in selling any kind of produce here that the farmer can produce and that without travelling over a distance of 10 miles with it. Corn is worth 50 cents per bushel, wheat 65, oats 31, potatoes 50, butter 15, lard 10, pork $4.50, beef $3.50, eggs 20 cents per dozen and chickens $1.50 per dozen the year round. The farmer who cannot live in Canada West with rich and fertile soil beneath his feet, with a mild climate and with an anti-slavery government over his head, possessing commercial advantages inferior to none in North America, must be a little too lazy to work and would die a pauper should he be placed in a country flowing with milk and honey."

A picture rather less favourable is presented in a letter from Isaac J. Rice missionary at Amherstburg, appearing in *The Liberator* of November 23, 1849. He is concerned over the helplessness of the people coming in. "Whole families reach us," he says, "needing clothing, provisions, a home for a few days until arrangements can be made for life, and all this amid strangers, the prejudiced. They are driven from schools in the States, they are no better here. If they go in schools by themselves, their portion of public money is allowed; but Canadians will not teach them, so that your teachers from the States must do it and aid them also about getting land and various other ways. We have received at our house and clothed more than 50 from the South."

Conditions among the fugitives on the Detroit River at the end of 1850 and early in 1851 are described by A. L. Power, of Farmington, Mich, in a communication to Henry Bibb's newspaper and published in the issue of February 12, 1851. Mr. Power, with a Mr. Benham, crossed over to Windsor about the middle of January, bringing a team load of provisions, bedding and wearing apparel collected at various points. They proceeded to "the barracks" near Windsor, where sixteen or eighteen families were sheltered. "Most of them were in want of food and clothing; some were sick, and others could not get employment." They proceeded from Windsor to Sandwich. "There we found some families in the most deplorable state of destitution that I ever saw. Some of them were sick, in miserable huts, without food or clothes sufficient to cover their shivering limbs; one family of eight or nine children, some of whom were almost in a state of nudity, without a bed in the house and the weather intensely cold. I was favorably impressed with the effort Mrs. Bibb has put forth in commencing a school for the education of the colored children around her. We visited her school, some of the children read and spelled very well. . . . The room is badly constructed for a school, there being but one window and no desks or table and poorly seated."

Negro refugees were found enrolled in the Canadian militia from an early date. There were coloured men on the Canadian side in the War of 1812 and during the troubles of 1838 they were much in evidence. Sir Francis Bond Head speaks of their promptness in answering the call to arms,[1] while Rev. J. W.

[1] Head, Sir F. B., A Narrative, London, 1839, p. 392.

Loguen says that he was in command of a black company in 1838.[1] Rev. Josiah Henson, the founder of the Dawn colony, was on active service during 1838 and did garrison duty at Amherstburg for several months. He was present when the schooner *Ann* affair took place in January, 1838. "The coloured men," he says, "were willing to defend the government that had given them a home when they had fled from slavery."[2]

A somewhat unusual comment on the loyalty of the Negroes in Canada, from no less a personage than William Lyon Mackenzie, is to be found in the fourth annual report of the American Anti-slavery Society,[3] being a reply to an agent of the society who visited Canada at the beginning of 1837 and solicited from certain of the public men of the province their opinion of the Negroes as citizens. Mackenzie writes under date of January 30, 1837:

"Sir, In reply to your inquiries I beg to offer as my opinion with much diffidence, 1st, That nearly all of them are opposed to every species of reform in the civil institutions of the colony— they are so extravagantly loyal to the Executive that to the utmost of their power they uphold all the abuses of government and support those who profit by them. 2nd., As a people they are as well behaved as a majority of the whites, and perhaps more temperate. 3rd., To your third question (regarding crime), I would say, not more numerous. 4th., Cases in which colored people ask public charity are rare, as far as I can recollect. I am opposed to slavery whether of whites or blacks, in every form. I wish to live long enough to see the people of this continent, of the humblest classes, educated and free, and held in respect, according to their conduct and attainments, without reference to country, color, or worldly substance. But I regret that an unfounded fear of a union with the United States on the part of the colored population should have induced them to oppose reform and free institutions in this colony, whenever they have had the power to do so. The apology I make for them in this matter is that they have not been educated as freemen.

I am, your respectful, humble servant,

W. L. MACKENZIE

In this report there appear also letters from Capt. R. G. Dunlop, M.P. for the county of Huron, and from Hon. John H. Dunn, Receiver-General for Upper Canada. Both speak well of the refugees. Capt. Dunlop says that "there are not in His Majesty's dominions a more loyal, honest, industrious, temperate and independent class of citizens than the coloured people of Upper Canada," while Hon. Mr. Dunn speaks of them as "truly loyal subjects of the government . . . both temperate and well behaved."

It was hardly to be expected that the refugees in Canada would be left entirely undisturbed by their former masters. There were several attempts to find some flaw in the Canadian laws which would enable fugitive slaves to be recovered by their masters. One of the earlier cases of this kind is that of a Negro named Moseby, who arrived at Niagara about 1836. His former owner traced him to Canada and applied for his surrender on the ground that he had stolen a horse to make good his escape. The case came before the governor, Sir Francis Bond Head, who thought that the owner's application was in order. Moseby was arrested and lodged in Niagara jail. There was widespread sympathy manifested for the unfortunate Negro and petitions came to the governor on his behalf. Sir Francis replied that he must give the man up as a felon,

---

[1] Loguen, G. W., Rev. J. W. Loguen as a slave and as a freeman, Syracuse, 1859, pp. 344-5.
[2] Henson, J., An Autobiography of Rev. Josiah Henson, London, 1881, p. 176.
[3] Reprinted in the Quarterly Anti-Slavery Magazine, July, 1837, vol II, No. 4, pp. 350-351.

though he would have armed the province to protect a slave. The Negroes in the Niagara district were particularly aroused and declared that they would oppose by force any attempt to take Moseby out of Canada. The order finally came for the delivery of the prisoner to his owner, but when the Negro was brought out of the jail a mob attacked the officers and a fatal encounter resulted. In the resulting confusion Moseby escaped and was not pursued. William Kirby is authority for the statement that he resided until his death at St. Catharines and Niagara.[1]

Another case of similar nature also came before Sir Francis Bond Head, that of a slave named Jesse Happy,[2] who had run away from his master in Kentucky, also taking a horse to aid his escape. His return was demanded on a charge of horse-stealing, but before giving a decision the governor referred the case to the Colonial Secretary in a memorandum dated at Toronto, October 8, 1837, and asking instructions as to general policy.

"I am by no means desirous," he wrote, "that this province should become an asylum for the guilty of any colour; at the same time the documents submitted with this despatch will, I conceive, show that the subject of giving up fugitive slaves to the authorities of the adjoining Republican states is one respecting which it is highly desirable I should receive from Her Majesty's government specific instructions." Proceeding, the governor said:

"It may be argued that a slave escaping from bondage on his master's horse is a vicious struggle between two guilty parties, of which the slave owner is not only the aggressor, but the blackest criminal of the two. It is the case of the dealer in human flesh versus the stealer of horse flesh; and it may be argued that if the British government does not feel itself authorized to pass judgment on the plaintiff neither should it on the defendant. The clothes and even the manacles of the slave are undeniably the property of his master, and it may be argued that it is as much of a theft in the slave walking from slavery to liberty in his master's shoes as riding on his master's horse; and yet surely a slave breaking out of his master's house is not guilty of the same burglary which a thief would commit who should force the same locks and bolts in order to break in."

Sir Francis urged as a further objection to the rendition of fugitive slaves that even if acquitted of crime by a state court the fugitive would be no better off, for he would at once be seized and forced back into slavery. His conclusion was that

"the slave states have no right, under the pretext of any human treaty to claim from the British government, which does not recognize slavery, beings who by slave law are not recognized as men, and who actually existed as brute beasts in moral darkness until on reaching British soil they heard, for the first time in their lives, the sacred words 'Let there be light and there was light.' From that moment, it is argued, they were created men, and if this be true, it is said that they cannot be held responsible for conduct prior to their existence."

The same question was brought before the British Colonial Office in 1840 in a communication from the coloured people of Upper Canada through Mr. E. de St. Remi.[3] A decision had been given by the British government in

---

[1]See Severance, F., Old Trails at Niagara, pp. 190-191; Niagara Historical Society, Transactions, No. 2; Head, Sir F. B., A Narrative, pp. 200-204; also Mrs. Jameson's Winter Studies and Summer Rambles, N.Y., 1839, vol. I, pp. 246-250; Sir Francis Bond Head says that two men were killed and others wounded in the riot in which the prisoner Moseby escaped.
[2]See Head's Narrative, pp. 200-204.
[3]Public Archives of Canada, Colonial Office Records, Series Q, vol. 430, part 3, p. 415.

THE NEGROES IN UPPER CANADA BEFORE 1865   155

1839 relative to the surrender of criminals and fugitives escaping from the Danish West Indies into the British possessions nearby, and the despatch relating to this contained the following declaration:

"Where the criminals, whether male or female, shall be satisfactorily proved to the British colonial authorities to have been guilty of murder or any other heinous crime which the laws of all nations visit with extreme punishment, the safety of society demands that such a criminal should be brought to justice, and it would become the duty of governors of colonies to afford every assistance for his apprehension and restitution to take his trial in the foreign colony in which his crime may have been committed."

The Canadian Negroes were suspicious that this seemingly fair instruction might have a bearing on their status as citizens in Upper Canada. What if charges were trumped up which would be accepted by the Canadian courts? They presented their point of view as follows:

"The colored population of Canada distinctly disavow the desire of being screened from the punishment due to any offence cognizable by the regular tribunals, and which would give them the benefit of trial, although they might reasonably dread a surrender, even in such a case, from the consciousness that if acquitted they would again be involved in cruel, irremediable slavery; and they pray to be sheltered from the fabrications of masters who charge them with crimes of which they are themselves accusers, judges, juries and punishers."

Further supporting their claim, the petitioners pointed out the discriminations against Negroes in American courts of law and asked that there should be the most thorough sifting of evidence in any case where the surrender of a fugitive Negro was asked.

Two other fugitive cases may be noted briefly. In 1847 a Negro was arrested at Sandwich charged with murder. An American philanthropist named Young interested himself in the matter and it was shown that while the Negro had escaped from slavery the murder charge was a fabrication. He was consequently freed.[1] In 1856 a Negro named Archy Lanton was arrested in southwestern Ontario charged with horse stealing. By the connivance of two magistrates, whose names are given as Wilkinson and Woodbridge, he was spirited away and probably taken back to slavery. The two magistrates were at once discharged from office. This appears to be the only case on record where the Canadian law did not protect a fugitive.[2]

The most famous fugitive case in Canadian annals was that of the Missouri Negro, Anderson, in 1860.[3] Anderson was arrested in Canada charged with the murder of a Missouri planter, whom he had stabbed while attempting to make his escape from slavery. The alleged crime had happened seven years before, but the friends of the murdered slaver seem to have been steadily on the trail of the Negro. The trial attracted much attention in Canada, was dragged into the politics of the day and even became the cause of a difference of opinion between the British and Canadian authorities over a question of jurisdiction of courts. Anderson was first brought to trial in Brantford, where ugly charges were made against the presiding magistrate. Following the trial at Brantford, an appeal was made for the release of the prisoner. This was

---

[1] *The Globe*, Toronto, December 24, 1860.
[2] Ibid.
[3] For a fuller account of the Anderson case, see the *Journal of Negro History*, for July, 1922, Vol. VII, No. 3, pp. 233-242.

refused and the case came up before the Court of Queen's Bench, where the judges divided, Chief Justice Robinson and Justice Burns pronouncing against Anderson, with Justice McLean dissenting. At this stage a writ of habeas corpus was issued by the Court of Queen's Bench in London, England. The right of a British court to interfere in this way was at once challenged by the Canadian government, but while the dispute was raging Anderson's case was brought before Chief Justice Draper in the Court of Common Pleas. Here the prisoner was freed on the basis of certain technicalities. Anderson then disappears from view.

This attempt to secure the return of Anderson to his former state was brought under the extradition clause of the Webster-Ashburton Treaty of 1842, though it seems to be quite clear that the British government had not intended that this clause should ever be a means of rendering slaves back to their masters. At a public meeting held in Toronto on December 19, 1860, John Scoble, to whom reference has already been made, told of interviewing Lord Brougham and Lord Aberdeen when the bill was before Parliament and when Scoble was secretary of the British Anti-Slavery Society. Lord Ashburton had told him that "the article in question was no more designed to touch the fugitive slave than to affect the case of deserters or parties charged with high treason." Lord Aberdeen also told Scoble that instructions would be sent to Canada that in the case of fugitive slaves great care must be taken to see that the treaty did not work their ruin. When this was communicated to Lord Metcalfe, the governor of the day, he declared that he would never be a party to wronging a fugitive.[1]

The position of the British government on this question is further shown by the fact that in moving the second reading of the bill to ratify the treaty, Lord Aberdeen stated that it was not intended to deliver up fugitives found in Canada. To escape from slavery was not, he felt, a crime; on the contrary, the condition of the slave attempting to escape was to be regarded with much sympathy. Lord Brougham agreed with this view, regarding it as a settled fact that a slave arriving in British territory would not, under any circumstances, be claimed or rendered liable to further service. Lord Ashburton's own view was set forth in a letter to Thomas Clarkson, president of the British Anti-Slavery Society, in which he stated that Negroes would be given up only for the crimes specifically mentioned in the treaty. The use of a boat or any means of escape was not robbery and could not be so construed. Clarkson lost no time in communicating this view to the Canadian authorities, pointing out that Great Britain would watch with some anxiety the outcome of the treaty when brought into operation, and expressing the hope that Canadians would exercise all possible humanity towards the fugitives.[2]

Most of those who inquired into the condition of the refugees in Canada West noted a desire for economic independence. This is reflected in the steady succession of protests from their leaders against the sometimes unwise philanthropy on their behalf. It is rather interesting to note these protests against gifts of food, clothing, etc., except for the sick and aged. There are strong

[1] *The Globe*, Toronto, Dec. 20, 1860.
[2] *Chicago Western Citizen*, Aug. 10 and Dec. 18, 1843, quoted in Transactions of Illinois State Historical Society, 1917, pp. 93-94.

condemnations of "begging" by Rev. S. R. Ward, Henry Bibb and others. Bibb frequently draws attention to the "begging" propensities of Rev. Isaac J. Rice, the missionary at Amherstburg. At the beginning of 1852 Rice printed a little paper called the *Amherstburg Quarterly Mission Journal*, of which 5,000 copies were to be distributed and in which he appealed for clothes, bedding, provisions, etc., setting forth a grim picture of the needs.

"Nothing can be more false than such a misrepresentation of things," is the comment of Bibb. "How long are we to be represented as a nation of paupers, in nakedness and starvation? There is no respectable missionary who has not given his protest against the begging system, as derogatory to our character and a hindrance to our advancement, and the time has come when all such beggars should be considered and treated as imposters."[1]

At about the same time a meeting was held at Ann Arbor, Mich., where there were many refugees and many friends of refugees, also protesting against agents coming from Canada unless they had the personal guarantee of the editor of *The Voice of the Fugitive*. It was stated that there were then five able-bodied men out begging for "the poor fugitives in Canada."

The desire for improvement expressed itself in various ways. At St. Catharines there was established a "Refugee Slaves' Friends Society," to bear testimony against slavery and to promote the education of the fugitives. Several influential men were associated with this society, including Wm. H. Merritt, M.P.P., and Mayor Elias Adams. Temperance societies were formed in several of the settlements. At New Canaan almost every man, woman and child was a member of the temperance society. The same was true in almost as great degree at Windsor and Sandwich. At Amherstburg there was a Young Men's Educating and Temperance Society for some years.

During the fifties the industrial conditions of Canada West were favourable to the refugees, railroad building providing work at good wages for many. Bibb's little paper contains the advertisements of railroad contractors and others for labourers. A typical advertisement (May 7, 1851) offers $10 a month and board. The issue of November 5, 1851, reports that over 2,500 Negroes are at work on the Canada Railway, the work being driven ahead rapidly in the expectation of trains being running between Niagara Falls and Windsor within fifteen months. The issue of Bibb's paper of April 22, 1852, carried an advertisement for 1,000 labourers to work on the Great Western Railway near Windsor. Many others turned their attention to agriculture and market gardening. The Detroit market, then as now, offered opportunities to Canadian producers of food stuffs and the refugees on the Canadian side of the river were quick to avail themselves of this. "We saw a colored friend of ours to-day cross on the ferry boat with about 200 dozen of eggs, six or eight turkeys, with chickens and butter also, and they are continually going over with loads of a like character." So writes Bibb in his paper in June, 1852, supporting his earlier contention that "Canada

---

[1] *Voice of the Fugitive*, Feb. 26, 1852. The Weekly Toronto *Globe* of Dec. 27, 1861, reports a mass meeting of coloured people at Chatham protesting against begging for refugees and institutions. Mary Ann Shadd Cary is denounced in particular for her begging on behalf of a mission school.

is no place for barbers, bootblacks and table waiters. . . . We want farmers, mechanics and professional men." Elsewhere he speaks of crops of tobacco and sweet potatoes satisfactorily raised and sold.[1]

The morality of the Negro refugees in Canada was commented upon by several observers of some note. The frequent violation of domestic relations in slavery conditions inevitably reacted upon the home life and took away one of the incentives to constancy. But, on arriving in Canada, one of the first things many married slaves did was to have their plantation union reaffirmed by the form of marriage legal in Canada. Dr. Howe noticed that the refugees were settled in families, that marriage meant something to them and that sensuality seemed less in freedom. Mrs. Laura S. Haviland, who was engaged in missionary educational work among the refugees for some time, has much to say about the morals of the race in her book, "A Woman's Life Work."[2] She found a keen desire for education among the refugees and on Sundays the coloured people came in great numbers to her Sunday school. The reading of the Bible was apparently a real delight to these people, most of whom, if they could read at all, could only spell it out laboriously word by word. Dr. Howe notes that in Canada the religion of the Negroes was "less nasal and more practical" than among their race in the South. Their religious instincts were displayed in charity to the sick and to poverty-stricken newcomers. Their attitude toward women was courteous and honourable. Dr. Howe was pleased to find no spirit of vengeance against the old masters. Rather, there was a desire to forget the past now that they had begun life anew.

Occasionally there were echoes in Canada of the colonization projects that were for so many years held up in the United States as the solution for the future of the black race. In 1858 there was a convention held in Chatham, attended by delegates from the Northern States at which emigration to Africa was discussed and a decision reached to send Martin R. Delany to spy out the land. There was little inducement, however, for the refugees in Canada to leave their new-found freedom. They were themselves colonizationists by their own free will and could see their numbers increasing every year. Had the Civil War held off for another five years the continued immigration of the black race might have become more of a problem for the country since even in the fifties there were some who thought that more Negroes were coming in than could be properly looked after. With the opening of the war, however, the migration visibly slackened and when the war was over quite a number of refugees left Canada, many returning to the South where their relatives had remained. Thus, only a portion of those to whom Canada had offered freedom and security remained, and it is their descendants chiefly who are now found in the cities and towns of Ontario. In recent years the number of coloured people in the province has not increased noticeably although there has been an infusion of the race from the West Indies that differs slightly from the older stock whose coming to Canada forms so romantic a page in our history.

---

[1] *Voice of the Fugitive*, July 30, 1851.
[2] Published at Grand Rapids, Mich., 1881. See p. 193, particularly.

THE NEGROES IN UPPER CANADA BEFORE 1865   159

A Selected Bibliography on the Negro in Canada

There is, as yet, no comprehensive sketch of the history of the Negro in Canada, although there exists a considerable body of material in the slave narratives of the period before 1860, the observations of travellers in Canada and the more serious studies that have been made by some Canadian investigators in the last few years. Incidental references to the presence of Negroes in Canada are numerous in the narratives of Europeans and others who visited Canada in the first half of the nineteenth century. There are a few documents in the federal archives at Ottawa dealing with questions that arose over the presence in this country of escaped slaves. Through the files of *The Globe* and other newspapers there are occasional references and articles and the reports and publications of church and missionary bodies yield an occasional fact.

The list of books and articles given below is not intended to be more than a selection. Scores of short references to the Negro in Canada might be brought together without value to other than the few who are deeply interested in the subject and who have probably made their own bibliographies. Most of the items listed are easily accessible in the larger libraries of the province. One of the largest collections, if not the largest collection in Canada on slavery and the Negro in Canada is found in the library of the University of Western Ontario at London.

The titles given below will be found to include the best that has appeared in print on the subject:

Anti-Slavery Society of Canada, annual reports, Toronto, 1852, and later. (Partial set in Toronto Public Library.)

Anti-Slavery Society of Canada, constitution and by-laws, Toronto, 1851. (Copy in Toronto Public Library.)

"Banishment of the people of Colour from Cincinnati," *Journal of Negro History*, July, 1923, Vol. VIII, No. 3, pp. 331-2. The enforcement of the Ohio Black Laws in 1829 drove many Negroes to Canada.

Bibb, Henry: "Narrative of the life and adventures of Henry Bibb," New York, 1849. Bibb was editor of *The Voice of the Fugitive*, published at Sandwich, C.W., and was also the chief figure in the movement for the founding of the Refugees' Home Settlement in Essex county, near Windsor.

Bibb, Henry (editor): *Voice of the Fugitive*, (Sandwich, C.W.), a newspaper issued every two weeks during 1851-2 and possibly later. It constitutes a most important record of the activities and interests of the Canadian Negroes of this time and was a well-edited paper. There is a file for 1851-2 in the Burton Collection of the Detroit Public Library and a similar file in the library of the University of Michigan at Ann Arbor.

Bradford, Sarah: "Harriet, the Moses of her People," New York, 1901. The story of Harriett Tubman, who, as a "conductor" on the Underground Railroad, brought many fugitives to Canada. An earlier edition, printed at Auburn, N.Y., in 1869, bears the title "Scenes in the life of Harriet Tubman."

Canniff, William: "History of the Province of Ontario," Toronto, 1872. There is a chapter on slavery in Upper Canada.

Carnochan, Janet: "A Slave rescue in Niagara sixty years ago," Niagara Historical Society, publication No. 2. Deals with the Moseby fugitive case.

Coffin, Levi: "Reminiscences," Cincinnati, 1876. Levi Coffin was closely associated with the Underground Railroad, being sometimes spoken of as its "president." He visited Canada to see the condition of the escaped slaves.

Drew, Benjamin: "North side view of Slavery: The refugee, or the narratives of fugitive slaves in Canada related by themselves, with an account of the history and condition of the coloured population of Upper Canada," Boston, 1856. (A most valuable survey of the Negro in Canada in the fifties, largely made up of the statements of fugitives in the various towns.)

Edwards, S. J. C.: "From Slavery to a Bishopric, or the life of Bishop Walter Hawkins," London, 1891. Bishop Hawkins was in his later years head of the A.M.E. Church in Canada.

Gregg, Wm. R.: "Mrs. Stowe's Originals in Canada," Toronto *Sunday World*, July 6, 1924. An account of Rev. Wm. King and the founding of the Elgin settlement in Kent county, near Chatham.

Hamilton, J. Cleland: "John Brown in Canada," *Canadian Magazine*, May, 1895, Vol. IV, pp. 119-140. John Brown visited Canada in May, 1858, and at Chatham planned the blow at slavery which eventually took the form of the Harper's Ferry raid.

Hartgrove, W. B.: "Story of Josiah Henson," *Journal of Negro History*, January, 1918, Vol. III, No. 1, pp. 1-21. Josiah Henson is famous as the reputed original of Mrs. Stowe's Uncle Tom. He was an influential Negro among his own people in Western Ontario in the forties and fifties.

Haviland, Laura S.: "A Woman's Life Work," Grand Rapids, 1881. Mrs. Haviland engaged in educational and missionary effort among the Canadian negroes near the Detroit river in the early fifties.

Head, Sir Francis B.: "A Narrative," London, 1839. Contains some references to fugitive slave cases that came before him as governor.

Henson, Josiah: "An Autobiography," London, Ont., 1881. Issued in various editions and from various places with slight changes. An edition issued at London, England, in 1852, has the title "Life of Josiah Henson."

Howe, Samuel G.: "Refugees from Slavery in Canada West: report to the Freedmen's Inquiry Committee," Boston, 1864. Dr. Howe came to Canada to investigate the condition of the refugees and was highly gratified at the progress they were making in freedom.

Jack, I. A.: "Loyalists and Slavery in New Brunswick," Transactions of the Royal Society of Canada, 2nd series, Vol. IV, 1898, pp. 137-185.

Landon, Fred: "The Anderson Fugitive Case," *Journal of Negro History*, July, 1922, Vol. VII, No. 3, pp. 233-242. A case that came into the Canadian courts on the eve of the American Civil War and which involved the question of surrendering a fugitive wanted in Missouri for murder committed while attempting to escape from slavery.

Landon, Fred: "The Anti-Slavery Society of Canada," *Journal of Negro History*, January, 1919, Vol. IV, No. 1, pp. 33-40.

Landon, Fred: "The Buxton Settlement in Canada," *Journal of Negro History*, October, 1918, Vol III, No. 4, pp. 360-367. This was the most successful of the distinctly Negro settlements in Upper Canada.

Landon, Fred: "Canada and the Underground Railroad," Proceedings of the Kingston Historical Society, 1923, pp. 17-31.

Landon, Fred: "The Canadian Anti-Slavery Group," *University Magazine* (Montreal), Dec., 1918, Vol. XVII, No. 4, pp. 540-547.

Landon, Fred: "Canadian Negroes and the John Brown raid," *Journal of Negro History*, April, 1921, Vol. VI, No. 2, pp. 174-182.

Landon, Fred: "Canadian Negroes and the Rebellion of 1837," *Journal of Negro History*, Oct., 1922, Vol. VII, No. 4, pp. 377-379.

Landon, Fred: "A Daring Canadian Abolitionist," *Michigan History Magazine*, July-Oct., 1921, Vol. V, Nos. 3-4, pp. 364-373. The career of Dr. Alexander Milton Ross, who assisted many Negroes to escape to Canada.

Landon, Fred: "Diary of Benjamin Lundy, written during his journey through Upper Canada, January, 1832," Ontario Historical Society, papers and records, 1922, Vol. XIX, pp. 110-133. Reprinted from the file of "The Genius of Universal Emancipation" in the New York Public Library, edited with notes. Lundy came to Canada primarily to investigate the condition of the Negro refugees.

Landon, Fred: "From Chatham to Harper's Ferry," *Canadian Magazine*, Oct., 1919, Vol. LIII, No. 6, pp. 441-448. John Brown's visit to Canada in May, 1858, and the part played by Canadian Negroes in his plans for striking at slavery.

Landon, Fred: "The Fugitive Slave in Canada," *University Magazine* (Montreal), April, 1919, Vol. XVIII, No. 2, pp. 270-279.

Landon, Fred: "Fugitive Slaves in London, Ont., before 1860." Transactions of the London and Middlesex Historical Society, part X (1919), pp. 25-38.

Landon, Fred: "Henry Bibb, colonizer," *Journal of Negro History*, Oct., 1920, Vol. V, No. 4, pp. 437-447. Bibb was active in promoting the settlement of Negroes on the land.

Landon, Fred: "History of the Wilberforce Refugee Colony in Middlesex county," Transactions of the London and Middlesex Historical Society, 1918, part IX, pp. 30-44.

Landon, Fred: "The Negro Migration to Canada after the Fugitive Slave Act of 1850," *Journal of Negro History*, Jan., 1920, Vol. V, No. 1, pp. 22-36.

Lapalice, O. M. H.: "Les esclaves noirs a Montreal sous le regime Francaise," *Canadian Antiquarian and Numismatic Journal*, 3rd series, Vol. XII, No. 3, July, 1915, pp. 136-158.

McDougall, M. G.: "Fugitive Slaves," Boston, 1891 (Fay House Monographs, No. 3).

Massicotte, E. Z.: "L'esclavage au Canada sous le regime Anglais," *Bulletin des Recherches Historiques*, Nov., 1918, Vol. XXIV, No. 11, pp. 344-346.

Mitchell, W. M.: "The Underground Railroad," London, 1860. Mitchell was for some years a missionary among his own people in Toronto and his book describes their condition.

Reade, John: "Slavery in Canada," *The Week*, April 21, 1887, pp. 333-4.

Riddell, Wm. Renwick: "Baptism of slaves in Prince Edward Island," *Journal of Negro History*, July, 1921, Vol. VI, No. 3, pp. 307-309.

Riddell, Wm. Renwick: "Notes on Slavery in Canada," *Journal of Negro History*, Oct., 1919, Vol. IV, No. 4, pp. 396-411.

Riddell, Wm. Renwick: "Notes on the Slave in Nouvelle France," *Journal of Negro History*, July, 1923, Vol. VIII, No. 3, pp. 316-330.

Riddell, Wm. Renwick: "The Slave in Upper Canada," *Journal of Negro History*, Oct., 1919, Vol. IV, No. 4, pp. 372-395. (Also printed in the Transactions of the Royal Society of Canada, May, 1919.)

Riddell, Wm. Renwick: "Slavery in Canada," *Journal of Negro History*, July, 1920, Vol V, No. 3, pp. 261-377.

Ross, Alex. Milton: "Memoirs of a Reformer (1832-1892)," Toronto, 1893. An earlier edition is somewhat different form and bears the title, "Recollections and experiences of an abolitionist, 1856-1865." This was published at Toronto in 1875.

Siebert, W. H.: "The Underground Railroad," New York, 1899. The most authoritative treatment of the subject. Has an extensive bibliography and contains much material on the Negro fugitives in Canada.

Smith, T. Watson: "Slavery in Canada," Nova Scotia Historical Society Collections, Vol. X, 1899.

Steward, Austin: "Twenty-two years a Slave and forty years a Freeman," Rochester, 1857. Steward was one of the founders of the Wilberforce Settlement in Middlesex county, Ontario.

Still, Wm.: "The Underground Railroad, a record, etc.," Philadelphia, 1872. A vast amount of material brought together in one volume but without much order or arrangement.

Ward, Samuel R.: "Autobiography of a Fugitive Negro," London, 1855. The author was for some time an agent of the Anti-Slavery Society of Canada.

Withrow, W. H.: "The Underground Railroad," Transactions of the Royal Society of Canada, 2nd Series, Vol. VIII, 1902, pp. 49-78.

Woodson, Carter G.: "Century of Negro Migration," Washington, 1916. Notes the movement of runaway slaves to Canada. Has a bibliography.

Woodson, Carter G.: "Education of the Negro prior to 1861," Washington, 1861. Some references to education of the Negro in Canada. Has a bibliography.

XI

ANTHONY BURNS IN CANADA

By Fred Landon, M.A.

The most dramatic fugitive slave case ever fought out in the courts of the United States was that of Anthony Burns. His fate interested millions, he was the cause of riots in Boston and he was returned to slavery in Virginia by the courts of the free state of Massachusetts under circumstances of a strikingly sensational character.

The body of Anthony Burns lies buried to-day in the cemetery at St. Catharines, Ontario, forgotten and neglected save for the attention that it gets from one humble coloured family in that city. In the summer of 1924 the tombstone lay in three pieces, as it had fallen over some time before. But the name of Anthony Burns is not forgotten, nor is it likely to be forgotten while men recall the great issue that divided the United States during the first six decades of the last century and that was settled at last by a long and costly civil war.

The career of Anthony Burns is one well known to students of American history, though probably few Canadians have heard of it. In the year 1850 there was legislation passed by Congress, known as the Fugitive Slave Act,[1] the purpose of which was to enable the owners of runaway slaves to secure their property, wherever it might be found within the bounds of the republic, and return it to the South. There had been other Fugitive Slave Laws before that of 1850, but none so drastic.[2]

President Filmore signed the bill on September 18, 1850, and at once consternation reigned among the coloured population in the Northern states. Those who were fugitives from the South knew that every effort would be made to track them down, while those who were legally free could not but fear that they might become entangled in the meshes of this new net and find themselves back in a condition of servitude. The consequence of this double fear

---

[1] James Ford Rhodes, the chief American historian of this period, describes the Act as "one of the most assailable laws ever passed by the Congress of the United States. . . . . Under this Act of ours, the negro had no chance: the meshes of the law were artfully contrived to aid the master and entrap the slave," History of the United States, Vol. I, pp. 185-6.

[2] No jury trial was allowed to the negro claimed as a fugitive. Master or agent had simply to present an affidavit before a United States judge or a commissioner, whose fee was doubled if he decided in favour of the claimant. The whole community was bound by the law to come to the aid of the commissioner as a "posse comitatus" to prevent the rescue or escape of the condemned fugitive, and the United States marshal was liable to a fine of $1,000 and a civil suit for the value of the slave in case the latter got away or was rescued. Finally, the law was *ex post facto* (and therefore unconstitutional) in that it applied to slaves who had fled from their masters at any time—even years before.

was that a movement of negroes into Canada began immediately, and it is estimated that within three months about 5,000 black people had entered the British Dominions.[1]

More than any other influence of the time, the Fugitive Slave Act stirred the conscience of the free North to a realization of what slavery actually meant. There was an intense, flaming opposition to the legislation. Men and women openly defied its provisions and some were subjected to imprisonment for so doing. Here and there a whole community would rise in protest against the law, and riots and bloody encounters between abolitionists and slave catchers mark the years after 1850. The sequel of many such an encounter is found in the brief statement that the escaped slave, the cause of the riot, has "gone to Canada."

Anthony Burns was a runaway slave living in Boston in 1854. He had formerly been the property of a Virginian and the latter eventually traced him to his place of refuge. The negro was arrested on the evening of the 24th of May, 1854, and next morning was taken, manacled, to the federal courtroom for examination. Proceedings there would have been of a brief character had not some Boston abolitionists happened to enter the court and there proceeded to set up a defence for the fugitive. The citizens of Boston soon learned by inflammatory handbills and through the newspapers of the court proceedings, and during the following days excitement ran high. A mass meeting of citizens for the purpose of protesting against the law was held in Faneuil Hall on the evening of May 26, and speeches of an inflammatory character were delivered by Wendell Phillips and Theodore Parker. These men raised a storm that they found themselves unable to control.[2] An immediate effect of the excitement raised was the rush of a mob to the jail where Burns was confined, two thousand men being determined to rescue him. The door was broken in and during the tumult one man was killed and several others injured. Two companies of artillery finally cleared the streets.

On the morning of May 29 the trial of Burns was resumed with soldiers on guard against any further violence. Counsel for the fugitive made a strong defence, but law was law and on the 2nd of June it was decreed by Commissioner Loring that the negro should be sent back to his former owner in Virginia.

Then came the most dramatic of all the incidents in connection with the case. The public officials were in fear of an attempt at rescue and a large military force was brought in to guard against any violence. The civic police force was reinforced by no less than twenty-two companies of state militia, the streets were patrolled by cavalry, artillery was in evidence and the city as a whole was practically under martial law.

At the appointed hour on the afternoon of June 2 the prisoner was taken from the jail and the parade started in the direction of the harbour, where the

---

[1] For a special study of this movement to Canada see Landon, "The Negro Migration to Canada after the Fugitive Slave Act of 1850," Journal of Negro History, Jan., 1920, Vol. V, No. 1, pp. 22-36.
[2] Phillips, says Rhodes, had the manner of Brutus, but his words were like those of Mark Antony, fitted to stir up mutiny. "See to it," he said, "that to-morrow, in the streets of Boston, you ratify the verdict of Faneuil Hall, that Anthony Burns has no master but his God . . . . Nebraska I call knocking a man down, and this is spitting in his face after he is down."

fugitive was to be taken aboard ship and returned to slavery. In the guard that marched that day through the streets of Boston surrounding Burns there was a regiment of artillery, a platoon of U.S. marines, the marshal's civic posse of 125 men close in about the prisoner, two further platoons of marines immediately behind with a field piece, and yet another platoon of marines to guard it.

Boston citizens showed quite emphatically what they thought of the whole business. Along the line of march both store and office windows were draped in black cloth. From a window opposite the old State House was suspended a black coffin on which were the words "The funeral of liberty." Here and there was to be seen the flag of the country reversed as a sign of mourning. It is estimated that 50,000 people stood on the sidewalks and saw the procession pass by. Thousands bared their heads. Hoots and hisses and cries of "Shame" were frequent. And all this military display was for one lone, friendless negro who passed along somewhat as Marie Antoinette had sat in a cart and passed through the crowded streets of Paris sixty odd years before. But this Boston crowd jeered at the guard while the Paris mob had jeered the royal prisoner. There was a grim spirit abroad in Boston that afternoon. A slight occasion might easily have precipitated a terrible riot. But there was no rioting, no violence, and towards evening the black man was put aboard a revenue cutter headed for slavery. As the boat passed out of the harbour it met another vessel coming in, a great passenger steamer carrying the Southern members of a commercial convention. They crowded the rail to witness the passing of the boat carrying Anthony Burns and their band struck up "The Star Spangled Banner." It was a great day for slavery. The New York *Times* said that it cost the federal government more than $40,000 to return Burns to slavery, but the Richmond *Whig* put the cost in another way when it said: "We rejoice at the recapture of Burns, but a few more such victories and the South is undone."

The later history of Anthony Burns has a more special interest for Canadians. Shortly after returning to Virginia he was sold to go to North Carolina. Within a few months, however, he was purchased with money that was raised by the Twelfth Baptist Church, of Boston, and its pastor, Rev. L. A. Grimes. Burns had been a member of this church. In 1855, through the kindness of a Boston woman, he secured a scholarship at Oberlin College and went there to study. Mr. Azariah S. Root, librarian of Oberlin College, says that the Oberlin College records show Anthony Burns first enrolled there as a student in 1855, that he continued there during the school year 1855-6, then seems to have been elsewhere for a year. In 1857 he returned and his name continues on the roll until 1862. Oberlin has no other record of his career. It is stated that he was at Fremont Institute for a time. This may have been during 1856-7. For a short time in 1860 he was in charge of the coloured Baptist church in Indianapolis, but was forced to leave by the threat of enforcement of the Black Laws of the state, which would have meant fine and imprisonment for him. It was shortly after this that he decided to come to Canada, where he located at St. Catharines and became pastor of Zion Baptist Church. Here he laboured with much zeal until his death on July 27, 1862.

A communication to a St. Catharines paper at the time of his death speaks in warm terms of his work while in that city. The article in part reads as follows:

"On Monday last, the mortal remains of the Rev. Anthony Burns, pastor of the colored Baptist church of this town, were conveyed to their last resting place, the St. Catharines cemetery. It is several months since the deceased was prostrated with disease, but it was not thought that the end was so near or that his labors were to have so abrupt a termination. The best medical aid was procured, but that most uncompromising and wasting disease, consumption, had taken a fast hold of him and all that human skill could do failed to wrest the sufferer from its grasp. . . . . He had been here only a short time. When he came he saw that there was much for him to do and he set himself to do it with all his heart, and he was prospering in his work, he was getting the affairs of the church into good shape. . . . Mr. Burns' memory will be cherished long by not a few in this town. His gentle, unassuming and yet manly bearing secured him many friends. His removal is felt to be a great loss and his place will not soon be filled."

Over his grave a simple stone was raised bearing this inscription:

In Memoriam
Rev. Anthony Burns
The fugitive slave of the Boston riots, 1854.
Pastor of Zion Baptist Church.
Born in Virginia, May 31, 1834.
Died in the Triumph of Faith in St. Catharines,
July 27th, A.D. 1862.

Rev. R. A. Ball, formerly pastor of the B.M.E. Church in St. Catharines, but now living in Toronto, has supplied some details of the personal appearance of Anthony Burns. Mr. Ball writes:

"He was a fine-looking man, tall and broad-shouldered, but with a slight stoop, indicating a weak chest. His colour was light brown. He was a fine speaker and was considered to be well educated. He was unmarried and very popular with both the white people and the people of his own race."

Mrs. Ball, wife of Rev. Mr. Ball, played the organ at the memorial service that was held in the church of which Anthony Burns had been pastor.

In November, 1918, a number of interesting letters and documents connected with the Burns case were sold by the Libbie Book Auction House of Boston. One of these was an offer of $500 from P. T. Barnum, the showman, if Burns would tell his story to the museum visitors for five weeks. The offer, however, was not accepted. A life of Anthony Burns, by Charles Emery Stevens, was printed in Boston in 1856, too early, of course, to have any details of the later years in Canada. Proceeds of this book appear to have aided Burns in securing his education at Oberlin, for there is a letter written in 1856 in which he says: "I have bought and sold nearly a hundred of these books in Oberlin."

In the same letter, referring to the presidential election of 1856, in which Buchanan was successful, he says: "I have been waiting to see which way the nation would turn, which seems to have turned together over the left. I suppose, sir, that the work of hell will go on in the south."

James Ford Rhodes, the historian, in summarizing the Anthony Burns case, says:

"To this complexion had it come at last. In a community celebrated all over the world for the respect it yielded to law, and for obedience to those clothed with authority; in a community where the readiness of all citizens to assist the authorities had struck intelligent Europeans with amazement,—it now required to execute a law a large body of deputy marshals, the whole force of the city police, 1,140 soldiers with muskets loaded, supplied with eleven rounds of powder and ball and furnished with a cannon loaded with grapeshot. If anything were needed to heighten the strangeness of the situation, it may be found in the fact that the marshal's deputies were taken from the dregs of society, for no reputable citizen would serve as a slave catcher.

"As the men of Boston and the men of New England reflected on what had taken place, they were persuaded, as they had never been before, that something was rotten in the United States, and that these events boded some strange eruption to our state. Nor was the significance of the transaction entirely lost upon the South."[1]

"The tables under the Fugitive Slave Law are beginning at last to turn against the law and in favor of humanity," Seward wrote to his wife under date of May 28, 1854. "There is deep and painful suspense here."[2]

Whittier, the poet, was moved to verse, and his poem, "The Rendition," commemorates the Anthony Burns affair. It may be found in his collected works:

> I heard the train's shrill whistle call,
> I saw an earnest look beseech,
> And rather by that look than speech
> My neighbour told me all.
>
> And as I thought of Liberty
> Marched handcuffed down that sworded street,
> The solid earth beneath my feet
> Reeled fluid as the sea.
>
> I felt a sense of bitter loss—
> Shame, tearless grief and stifling wrath,
> And loathing fear, as if my path
> A serpent stretched across.
>
> All love of home, all pride of place,
> All generous confidence and trust
> Sank smothering in that deep disgust
> And anguish of disgrace.
>
> Down on my native hills of June,
> And home's green quiet, hiding all,
> Fell sudden darkness like the fall
> Of midnight upon noon.
>
> And Law, an unloosed maniac, strong,
> Blood-drunken, through the blackness trod,
> Hoarse-shouting in the ear of God
> The blasphemy of wrong.
>
> "O Mother, from thy memories proud,
> Thy old renown, dear Commonwealth,
> Lend this dead air a breeze of health,
> And smite with tears this cloud.
>
> "Mother of Freedom, wise and brave,
> Rise awful in thy strength," I said;
> Ah me! I spake but to the dead;
> I stood upon her grave.

---

[1] Rhodes, History of the United States, Vol. I, pp. 505-6.
[2] Life of Seward, Vol. II, p. 230. Cited by Rhodes.

XII

COMMODORE ALEXANDER GRANT (1734-1813)

By George F. Macdonald

The subject of this sketch was born at Glenmoriston House, Inverness-shire, Scotland, on May 20, 1734. His father was Patrick Grant, Eighth of Glenmoriston, who with the members of his clan, was a strong supporter of "Bonnie Prince Charlie" and took an active part in the Jacobite uprisings. He was not with his clan at the memorable battle of Culloden in 1745, in which the Highlanders were disastrously defeated, and, it is possible for this reason, his estate was not forfeited to the Crown. He married Isobel Grant, daughter of John Grant of Craskie, their children being, John Roy, Patrick, Alexander, Allan, Alpine, Lewis and Helen. He died on March 30, 1776, and was succeeded by his second son, Patrick, whose elder brother, John Roy, had been killed fighting with his regiment in Flanders.

ALEXANDER GRANT AS A SOLDIER

After completing his education, Alexander joined the Navy, in which he served three years. The only portrait which we have of the Commodore belongs to this period of his life and represents him as a petty officer with a spy-glass under his arm. It was probably painted when he became of age, and is still to be seen at Glenmoriston House.

At the age of twenty-three he requested to be transferred to the 77th Regiment or Montgomerie's Highlanders, then being organized, and was given the rank of Ensign. He came to America with his regiment the next year, and took part in the war against France, which terminated in the Treaty of Paris and the conquest of Canada.

The 77th Regiment was called Montgomerie's Highlanders, from the name of its colonel, the Hon. Archibald Montgomerie, son of the Earl of Eglinton, to whom, when major, letters were issued for recruiting it. Being popular among the Highlanders he soon raised the requisite number of men, forming a regiment of thirteen companies, of 105 rank and file each, including sixty-five sergeants and thirty pipers and drummers. The colonel's commission was dated the 4th of January, 1757.

The regiment embarked at Greenock for America, and on the commencement of hostilities in 1758, was attached to the corps of Brigadier-General Forbes, who had command of the expedition against Fort du Quesne. The brigade reached Raystown, about ninety miles from the Fort, in September, having been delayed for some time in Philadelphia. Colonel Bouquet, with 2,000 men, was sent in advance to Loyal Henning, some forty miles nearer, where, on his arrival, he ordered Major Grant, with 400 Highlanders and 500 Provincials, to reconnoitre. When near the fort, Major Grant advanced with pipes playing and drums beating, as if he were entering a friendly town, whereupon the enemy instantly marched out and a warm contest took place. Major Grant ordered his men to throw off their coats and charge with sword in hand. The enemy fled on the first advance and dispersed among the woods; but being reinforced by a company of Indians, they rallied and surrounded the detachment. Major Grant then endeavoured to force his way out, but was taken in the attempt, on seeing which, his troops retreated. In this unfortunate affair the subject of this sketch is mentioned as having been wounded. The names of the officers killed were: Captains William Macdonald and George Munro, Lieutenants Alexander Mackenzie, Robert Mackenzie, Colin Campbell, and Alexander Macdonald; wounded, Captain Hugh Mackenzie, Lieutenants Alexander Macdonald, jr., Archibald Robertson, and Ensigns Alexander Grant and John Macdonald.

On the approach of the main army, the French retired from Fort du Quesne, leaving their ammunition, stores and provisions. General Forbes took possession on the 24th of November, and in honour of Mr. Pitt, named it Pittsburg.

The regiment spent the winter of 1758 in the fort, and in the following May joined the army of General Amherst in his operations at Ticonderoga, Crown Point and Lake Champlain.

After the signing of peace, an offer was given the soldiers either to settle in America or to return to their own country. Those who remained were to receive a grant of land in proportion to their rank in the army.

Alexander Grant as Commodore

We are fortunate in having a brief autobiography of the Commodore, from the year 1759 until 1784, which is entitled "The Memorial of Captain Alexander Grant."

To His Excellency Frederick Haldimand, Esq., General and Commander-in-Chief of the Province of Quebec, etc., etc., etc.

The memorial of Captain Alexander Grant sheweth:

That your memorialist having been in the very early part of his life bred to the sea was in the year 1759 appointed, by commission from Lord Amherst, to the command of a Sloop of 16 guns on Lake Champlain, where the 77th Regiment in which he was then a Lieutenant happened to be; that in the following year he was appointed by His Lordship to the command of a Brig of 20 guns, and the other vessels upon that Lake.

That when Captain Loring quitting the service upon the peace of 1763, your memorialist was continued by General Gage, then Commander-in-Chief, with the direction of all the vessels upon the several Lakes, until the commencement of the late rebellion when in 1777 he was commissioned, by His Excellency Sir Guy Carleton, to command all His Majesty's vessels upon the Lakes Ontario, Erie, Huron and Michigan.

That in 1778 Your Excellency thinking your memorialist's command too extensive for one and the same person, commissioned him to the command of Lakes Erie, Huron and Michigan, in which he has since remained.

That the reduction of the Marine Department and of the pay of the officers who do remain (upon an uncertain footing) which Your Excellency has necessarily made in consequence of the Peace, together with the loss of his half pay as Lieutenant in the Army since 1776 renders his income so very inconsiderable as to deprive him of the hope of maintaining his family and cannot, he flatters himself, be considered by Your Excellency as a reward for 30 years' faithful service, 25 of which have been spent on the lakes in a constant attention to his duty, which he is so happy as to have discharged to the satisfaction of his superiors.

Your Excellency's memorialist having thus past the best part of his life in the service of his King and Country and unable at this late period to seek bread by any other means, humbly implores Your Excellency's protection, in procuring for him such permanent subsistence as Your Excellency shall deem adequate to his long service, and in the meantime that you will be pleased to confirm to him a grant of land given to him by the Indians at Detroit at the entrance of the Huron River, whereon he may settle with such of the department as are desirous to join him therein, or such part thereof for himself as Your Excellency shall think proper.

Quebec, 8th Sept., 1784.

Endorsed: Capt. Alex. Grant's Memorial. (B. 216, p. 170.)

An interesting sidelight on this memorial is, that during the Spring and Summer of 1784, Captain William Caldwell of Butler's Rangers, having made a similar request for himself and other members of his regiment, was successful in securing a large grant of land which is now known as the townships of Malden, South Colchester and South Gosfield. The Commodore, seeing the success of Captain Caldwell, thought that he might be able to secure a similar concession. The Government, however, did not see fit to grant his request, probably for the reason that the land which he desired was in American territory and would ultimately have to be given over to them.

In order that we might appreciate the extent of the Commodore's duties, I submit the following letter:

Extract from a letter of Gen. Thomas Gage to Capt. Stephenson, dated New York, April 8th, 1768:

"Mr. Grant has engaged to build two vessels for the King, in which business you will please to assist him and give him such helps as your garrison affords, whenever he shall demand it, as for the merchants, they may build what vessels they please but you will not suffer either Mr. Grant's artificers or sailors to be taken from him, you have acted very properly in that respect already.

"I understand there is very good cedar to be had, which Mr. Grant will now use for the King's vessels, and if you find it necessary, you will reserve the cedar and suffer no person to cut it, but when it is used in the King's service.

"I hope that you have received the orders about fitting out the old vessels for this year's service."

(C. 249, p. 161.)

Letter of Lieutenant-Colonel Mason Bolton to Captain James Andrews, dated Niagara, May 25, 1778.

May 25th, 1778.

Sir,—His Excellency, the Commander in Chief, in his letter to me of the 23rd Oct., 1777, informed me that he has appointed Capt. Alex. Grant to be Commanding Officer of the Naval Department upon the Lakes, Erie, Ontario, Huron & Michigan, etc., etc.

MASON BOLTON,
Lt.-Colonel,
Commandant of Niagara.

To Capt. James Andrews.

Extract from a letter of Captain Grant to Brigadier-General Powell, dated at Detroit, January 24, 1782.

"By the last vessel I received a letter from the Commissioners enclosing me a plan and dimensions of a new vessel to be built here immediately, the timber for which we are collecting as fast as possible.

"Neither gold, silver or the orders that were framed last Summer at Quebec, for the payment, etc., of the Naval Department arriving, and it being time for the different parties to go to their wintering stations, it was necessary to pay the department. I accordingly gave orders to pay them off; the 30th of June last inclusive, and directed the Naval Storekeeper, he to appropriate the monies collected to that use, thinking it might be more agreeable to His Excellency than drawing bills.

"There is a master and eight men remaining at Michilimackinac in the sloop Welcome, that was condemned last year, who must come here otherwise I have it not in my power to man the vessels properly next Spring—I have requested Lt. Governor Sinclair of my ordering Mr. Ford and his crew to this place to mann the sloop Angelica allotted for that station."

Cap. Alexander Grant to Brig. Gen. H. Watson Powell.

Detroit, April 22nd, 1782.

Sir,—Notwithstanding the officers and seamen of the different wintering parties are not come in, Major De Peyster being very desirous of a vessel sailing for Fort Erie, I have fitted out the Hope which now sails. The Dunmore will be soon ready to ply with her between Fort Erie and here—the Wiandott will be ready to sail for Mackinac as soon as the navigation Northward will permit—the Angelica is preparing to go to Fort Erie to take a cargo for that post. The Gage & Faith with some gun-boats are in hand fitting for any actual service that may be necessary. The Felicity will then receive a repair, and soon be added to the Transports of this lake. I am sorry to inform you of the very great scarcity of grape-shot for four pounders, in magazine, as it is most destructive amongst boats or small craft.

The enclosed is the last of several applications from Francis Brown, a native of old France, for his discharge; who requests to be made a prisoner of war rather than serve. I therefore think it my duty to send him down to your disposal, in charge of Lieutenant Butler of the Rangers, but beg leave to observe that, from his knowledge of the lakes, he would be an improper person to remain in this country.

I have the honour to be, Sir, with great respect, your most obedient and humble servant,

ALEX'R GRANT.

To Brig. General Powell.

(B. 102, p. 30.)

The Commodore continued in office until January, 1812, when, upon the recommendation of General Isaac Brock he was superannuated and Captain George B. Hall was appointed to succeed him. Captain Hall held office until August, 1813, when on account of trouble with Commodore Barclay, he was transferred and given the appointment of Superintendent of Naval Stores at Amherstburg.

ALEXANDER GRANT AS A MEMBER OF THE LAND BOARD OF HESSE

After the conquest of Canada in 1759-1763, a great number of the French documents were either lost or destroyed, with the result that when the British came into possession of the country, they had comparatively no data for their land transfers.

On the 24th of July, 1788, Lord Dorchester, in order to assist settlers and also to establish titles for the lands already occupied, divided Upper Canada into four districts and in each he appointed a land board. Detroit was in the District of Hesse, which extended from Long Point on Lake Erie to Lake St. Clair and the River Thames. The first members of the board were Farnhem Close, major of the 65th Regiment of Foot, commanding officer at Detroit; William Dummer Powell; Duperon Baby; Alexander Grant; William Robertson; Alexander McKee and Lieutenant Adhemar St. Martin. On July 16, 1792, Lieutenant-

Governor Simcoe restricted the area of the Board to the counties of Essex and Kent and added three new members, George Leith, John Askin, and Martigny de Louvigny, the officer of the engineers at Detroit. During the five years of its existence, 1789-1794, the Land Board did some very valuable work in this neighbourhood. Their surveyor, Patrick McNiff, made an extensive report on the condition of the land from Long Point to Detroit. His plans are the first that we have of the counties of Essex and Kent. The French had surveyed on both sides of the river in the vicinity of Detroit but these plans were lost so the Board had to have this work done over again in order to settle the boundary disputes between the settlers. None of the Indian deeds were recognized by the Board and all claims had to be settled on their own merits.

ALEXANDER GRANT AS A MEMBER OF THE EXECUTIVE COUNCIL, AND ADMINISTRATOR OF UPPER CANADA

In 1791, Canada was divided into two separate provinces, known as Upper and Lower Canada, each having a separate government consisting of two houses, and an executive council, members of which were appointed for life by the governor. Lieutenant-Governor John Graves Simcoe in selecting the members of the Executive Council, chose the most representative men from each district. Those from Essex and Kent were Alexander Grant and James Baby, the other members being William Osgoode, Peter Russell and William Robertson.

In 1805, Lieutenant-Governor Peter Hunter died and in accordance with the instructions, Alexander Grant was made Administrator of the Province until another Governor was appointed. I have selected some of his addresses and correspondence during this period and trust that they may prove of interest.

The proclamation of George III to Lord Dorchester for the governing of Canada, dated September 12, 1791, provided that in case of the death of the Lieutenant-Governor, the oldest member of the Executive Council should take upon himself the administration of the government until the pleasure of the King should be known.[1] This was the authority for Mr. Grant occupying the position of Administrator of the Province. He issued a proclamation, dated September 17, 1805, notifying all Government officers that they should continue in their several offices.[2] On the same date he issued another proclamation convoking the Legislature of Upper Canada for October 15th, ensuing.[3] This session was later postponed three times and did not finally convene until February 4, 1806.

From the Askin Papers (Burton collection), Vol. 13, p. 236.

Upper Canada,
York, September 30, 1805.
My dear Sir,—

I wrote you a few days ago, by the Schooner, inclosed to Mr. Thos. Dickson———. A man, Mr. Allan tells, is going up with the horses by land and I take that opportunity. My other letter gives you full information of my being Established in the Presidency and Administration

---

[1]Ontario Archives, p. 168.
[2]Ibid., p. 230.
[3]Ibid., pp. 230, 231.

of this Province. Your suggestion, in your letter of the 16th of last month, was fairly right, a stout effort was made to avoid my administrating the Government. I also received your letter of the 10th ultimo. Your letters and Mr. Duff's with one from Capt. Gilkison, made me as happy as ever a man was, that my dear Mrs. Grant was on the recovery and our numerous connection well. I assure you I have got a troublesome place but I could not avoid it, agreeable to His Majesty's Instruction and I must carry it on in the best manner I can—the cursed blues —but business tumbles in so fast it will drive me out of the world—or the blues from me.

Remember me kindly to Dr. R. Richardson and Madeline and family, John and his lady, who, I am glad, by your letter, to find she is getting better, McKee and dear Therese. It must be Alice—that has roused our Nancy to join in such a row as they had at the Point. Offer my very best respects to Governor Hull and his lady, etc., my kind compliments to Mr. Brush and his two boys—with Charles, James and Nelly, and tell your Alick, I got a letter at last from my Alick.

Write to Mrs. Grant and tell her, thank God, I feel very hearty and well at present, and I lay an injunction upon you and Duff, not to let her stay at any time, long at the Point, keep her moving gently, for the sake of her health. I write now to Messrs. Burnett, Merideth & Co.

I am, Dear Askin,

Yours sincerely,

ALEX. GRANT.

To John Askin, Senior,
Near Sandwich, Western District.

Speech of His Honour Alexander Grant, Esquire, at the opening of the Parliament of Upper Canada, at York, February 4, 1806.

Honourable Gentlemen of the Legislative Council, and Gentlemen of the House of Assembly:

By the much lamented death of Lieutenant-Governor Hunter the administration of the Government of this Province hath devolved on me. I most sincerely condole with you on the melancholy event. His faithful and meritorious services to the Public in this part of His Majesty's Dominions will be long felt and remembered. It shall be my endeavour to imitate and follow his example.

Since the last Session of this Legislature, Commissioners have been appointed for carrying into effect the provisions of an Act for affording relief to those persons who may be entitled to claim land in this Province as Heirs or Devisees of the Nominees of the Crown to such lands. I make no doubt by the exertions and abilities of those Gentlemen to whom that important trust is delegated the Public will soon see the most important benefits from the operations of that Statutory Law.

I forbear on the present occasion to point out particular objects for your deliberations, being convinced that your knowledge of the respective situations of His Majesty's Subjects whom you here represent will be the surest guide to direct you in the enacting of such laws as may still be necessary for their security and comfort (as well as in the continuing of laws heretofore made but now about to expire) whose beneficial effects we have already felt and experienced.

Gentlemen of the House of Assembly, I have ordered the Public Accounts to be laid before you, not doubting but that you will pay that attention in the examination of them which the nature of the subject requires.

Honourable Gentlemen of the Legislative Council and Gentlemen of the House of Assembly, —It is with the highest satisfaction that I congratulate you on the great Naval Victory[1] which lately hath crowned the success of His Majesty's Arms, though our joy is not unmixed, as we have deeply to regret the loss of one of the bravest and most able defenders of his King and of his Country.

May Great Britain, Our Parent State, ever have such men to fight her battles, and may she by the blessing of Providence be enabled to defend herself and her widely extended Dominions from the assaults of her enemies, and transmit her Territories with her invaluable Constitution unimpaired to the latest posterity.

---

[1] Battle of Trafalgar, October 21, 1805, and the death of Vice-Admiral Lord Viscount Nelson.

The following address was engrossed and presented to Alexander Grant by the members of the Legislative Council, February 5, 1806:—

To His Honour Alexander Grant, Esquire, President administering the Government of Upper Canada, etc.

May it please Your Honour: We, His Majesty's most dutiful and loyal subjects, the Members of the Legislative Council of Upper Canada in Provincial Parliament assembled, beg leave to address your Honour with our respectful thanks for your speech.

The late Lieutenant-Governor Hunter's exertions to promote the welfare of this Province will long be remembered with gratitude, and his death sincerely lamented by its inhabitants We therefore fervently join your Honour in our condolence on that melancholy event, and highly approve your intentions to imitate and follow so good an example.

The Act affording relief to the persons entitled to claim lands in this Province as heirs or devisees of the nominees of the Crown to such lands has had our fullest approbation; and we are well assured that the commissioners appointed to carry it into effect will exert their ability to render the operation as beneficial to the public as possible.

We beg leave to assure Your Honour that the Legislative Council of this Province will not be wanting in zeal for its prosperity, and in giving its assistance to the enacting of such laws as may appear to be still necessary for the security and comfort of the King's subjects who dwell in it, and also to the continuing of these laws heretofore enacted and about to expire whose beneficial effects have been already felt and experienced by them.

With pleasure we reciprocate the congratulations of Your Honour on this great naval victory which has crowned with success His Majesty's arms; but while we thus exultingly join in expressing our joy, we equally lament that we have at the same time to regret the loss of that distinguished officer whose conspicuous abilities and great naval skill have closed a brilliant career of the most eminent services to his King and Country in adding this very splendid triumph to their number.

We also piously join Your Honour in praying that Great Britain, Our Parent State, may not only ever have such men to fight her battles, but that she may by the blessing of Providence which has hitherto protected her be enabled to defend her widely extended Dominions against the assaults of her enemies, and transmit them with her invaluable Constitution undiminished and unimpaired to the latest posterity.

By Order of the House.

RICHARD CARTWRIGHT,
Legislative Council Office, Speaker.
York, 5th February, 1806.

ALEXANDER GRANT AS LIEUTENANT OF THE COUNTY OF ESSEX

In the year 1799, Alexander Grant was appointed Lieutenant of the County of Essex by President Peter Russell, which is referred to in the following letter:—

York, July 22nd, 1799.

My Dear Sir:—The President has politely, in full Council, asked me to accept of the Lieutenancy of the County of Essex, which I have.

Your friend and well wisher,
To John Askin. ALEX. GRANT.

Governor Simcoe, after the custom in England, appointed County Lieutenants whose duty it was to represent the governor in each county, they having authority to appoint magistrates and officers of militia. In creating these lieutenants, the governor had chiefly in mind the organizing of the militia for the defence of the country. I have been successful in locating a copy of one of these appointments:—

Alexander Grant, Esquire, Lieutenant of and for the County of Essex, authorized and appointed by His Excellency Peter Hunter, Esquire, Lieutenant-Governor of His Majesty's Province of Upper Canada, by virtue of and conformably to the Powers and Provisions in a certain Act of the Legislature of this Province, contained and passed in the thirty-third year of the reign of His Present Majesty.

To Alexander Duff, Esquire:

Reposing especial trust and confidence in your loyalty, courage and conduct to do His Majesty's good and lawful service, by virtue of the said authority given unto me by said Peter Hunter, Esquire, Lieutenant-Governor of the Province aforesaid, and in pursuance of the said Act of the Legislature, I have nominated, constituted, appointed and given commission, and by these presents do nominate, constitute, appoint and give commission to you, the said Alexander Duff, Esquire, to be a Captain of a company in the North-East Regiment of the said county.

You are therefore to take the said company into your care and charge as captain thereof and duly train, exercise and discipline the inferior officers and other persons armed and arrayed or to be armed and arrayed in the same according to the Rules and Discipline of War, and the directions of the said Act of the Legislature. And I do hereby command them and every of them to obey you as their captain. And you are to observe and follow such orders and directions as you shall from time to time receive from the Governor, me, His Excellency's Lieutenant, or any other your superior officers pursuant to the trust hereby reposed in you and your duty to His Majesty.

Given under my hand and seal at Amherstburg, this 20th day of May, in the forty-second year of the reign of our Sovereign Lord, George the Third, by the grace of God, of the United Kingdom of Great Britain and Ireland, King, Defender of the Faith, etc., and in the year of our Lord one thousand eight hundred and two.

ALEX'R. GRANT,
L. of the County of Essex.

From the Askin papers (Burton collection), Vol. 13, p. 170.

Near Sandwich, June 15th, 1805.

Sir,—I have the Honour of transmitting to you the annual Returns of the North East Regiment of the Essex Militia for the 4th of June last. You should have had it on the 5th, had it not been for an officer who commanded a company, going away without giving me in the role of his company so that the general return was not then completed, nor did I receive it until last night. I am happy to say, I have very little fault to find with the conduct of either officers or men and very few were absent.

The quantity of powder I asked for and which His Excellency the Governor was pleased to grant, I found on the 4th of June last, not sufficient to furnish each man with three rounds. The regiment is daily increasing, so that in a short time there will be enough to make nine companies of from 25 to 30 men each, for a number of men have been left out, from a mistake, supposing them to belong to the Southern Battalion as formerly.

When I have formed the other company, I will, agreeable to your orders, let you know whom I think should be made officers, until then, there are sufficient.

I am with due respect, Sir, your most obedient very humble servant,

JOHN ASKIN.

To the Honourable Alexander Grant, Lieutenant of the County of Essex. (A.P. Vol. 13, p. 1.)

Annual returns of the North-East Regiment of the Militia of the County of Essex in the Western District, at Sandwich, this 4th day of June, 1804:

Colonel, John Askin; Major, Jacque Parent; Captains, Jno. Bapt'. Baby, Alexis LaBute, Jno. Bapt'. Barthe, Francis Drouillard, Alexander Duff.

ALEXANDER GRANT AS A CITIZEN

The private life of Commodore Grant was all that could be desired. He took an active part in everything that was for the betterment of his locality, and his home, "Castle Grant," at Grosse Point, always had a hearty welcome for the stranger or friend who happened to be in the neighbourhood. Whenever the officials from the east were at Detroit they usually accepted the hospitality of the Commodore.

On September 30, 1774, Alexander Grant was married to Theresa Barthe, daughter of Charles Barthe, and Theresa Campeau. Her sister, Archange, had been married in 1772 to Colonel John Askin, who was a lifelong friend, and to whose correspondence we owe much of the information concerning the Commodore. Theresa Barthe was born at Detroit in 1758 and died at Grosse Point on May 11, 1810. Their married life was very happy, he being a most kind and considerate husband. In his correspondence he usually instructed either Mr. Askin or Mr. Duff to see that Mrs. Grant was well cared for during his absence. They lived on a 200-acre farm at Grosse Point, which was considered one of the best and is now in the heart of the fashionable residential section of the lake shore.

We have a letter of the Commodore's which gives us an insight into his private life and was written to his brother Alpine in Scotland.

York, the Capital of Upper Canada.
July 15, 1811.

My dear Alpine:

The bearer of this letter is a son of Mr. McDonald that lived and enjoyed that property at Conlachy near Fort Augustus. I have written two or three letters but never recd. an answer, but now I hope to have one to this—by giving or conveying one to him Mr. McIntosh who is a merchant at Sandwich has a sister at Inverness with whom he constantly corresponds—She wrote him last year wherein she mentions that Mrs. Fraser a daughter of yours lives near her—who told her to mention to her brother that our brother Allan, was dead—and direct her brother to let her know about my family—Since then I very unluckily lost my dear wife—53 years of age, and on the 20th May last I was 77 years—She died the 11th of Nov. last as good a mother and as kind a wife as perhaps ever was—left me 8 daughters & one son. We had 11 daughters & only one son—he is a Lieutenant in the Canadian Fensibles and not two years yet since he got his commission—And, has £1000 left him by my friend Mr. McTavish Wh[ich] will purchase him a Company when he comes to his home—He is six feet three inches high now and will be only 21 years next March. The daughters are all married except one (Jane) Ive got here at School—now 11 years old. I am very anxious to hear from you respecting yourself & family and all the rest of our connections.

My son is in quarters at Quebec where [?] discipline is carried on—he is a good natured going man. Do write me all information about our family & connections.

I thank my Almighty, tho' old, I in general keep my health & strength, tho' losing my wife lay very heavy on me at this time of life—My duty where my naval command requires me is such a distance from here that I cannot travel it in the winter where the Legislature of this Province meets there, but I come down at my ease in the Summer and take some sittings of the "Council." A gentleman that has served his King & country upwards of 55 years requires indulgence and my superiors allow it me. I see by the Army list you are a Major of the Local Militia—For God's sake write me by hook or crook—

Thank your daughter Mrs. Fraser for her kind anxiety about my family—I have eight grandsons and 2 grand daughters—one of which is to be married this fall—I saw in a Scotch Magazine an account of one of our brother Peter's sons dieing in the East Indies & leaving a large sum of money to a certain sect of Religious people, so that he must have been rich—

My sincere affection to all your children—Being older by 24 years than my dear late wife I cultivated a very fine farm of excellent land with a good Mansion House & all other buildings—fine garden & a large orchard for my dear wife expecting according to the difference in our ages that I must die first but the Almighty has ordained it otherwise. My son is a good mannerly young man—Since my wifes death I had some serious thoughts of making a visit home to see you & family & the rest of our connections & relations—My wife and the precariousness of the voyage make me drop the thought of it now. I shd. like much to see the Caledonian Canal it must be very beneficial to the Glenmoriston estate & all other estates upon that communication. I am my dear Alpine, with every kind remembrance & affection

for you & yours, dear brother,

Major Alpine Grant Urquhart.   ALEX. GRANT.

(From typewritten copy, Burton Historical Collection Leaflet.)

The Commodore died at the age of seventy-nine on the 8th day of May, 1813, at his residence, "Castle Grant," from where his body was taken in a canoe to St. John's Church, Sandwich, for burial. On the wall of the church is a large memorial tablet with the following inscription:—

In Memory
of the late
HONOURABLE ALEXANDER GRANT,
Born in 1734. Died on May 13th, 1813
Commodore Grant was the fourth son of the
7th Laird of Glenmoriston, Inverness-shire, Scotland.

He was a member of the first Government of Upper Canada, an Executive and Legislative Councillor. County Lieutenant for Essex and Suffolk, and Administrator of the Province in 1805-1806

He was 53 years in command of the Lakes and 57 in his Sovereign's Service.

This Tablet is erected by his grandson, R. S. Woods.
Also of James Woods, Sr., Barrister. Born in Sandwich, 1806, Died 1832.
Alexander, Born 1810, Died 1826.
Mary, Born 1814, Died 1836.
All interred in the Churchyard of this Church.

Commodore Grant had the satisfaction of seeing the British capture Detroit and it was still in their possession at the time of his death. He was therefore saved the great disappointment and humiliation of Commodore Barclay's defeat at the Battle of Lake Erie, which took place in September, 1813.

In his will, the Commodore directed that his estate be divided evenly amongst his children.

In the family of the Commodore there were twelve children. A brief sketch of each follows:—

ALEXANDER, born at Detroit, March 19th, 1791. After completing his education he entered the Army and at the age of nineteen he received the rank of Lieutenant in the Canadian Fencibles, then stationed at Quebec. He later attained the rank of Major. After retiring from the Army he settled in Brockville, where he took an active part in the affairs of the town. He was much interested and assisted in organizing the Leeds Militia and was made Lieutenant-Colonel of the Regiment.

He never married and died at Brockville sometime in the sixties.

THERESA, born at Detroit, February 13th, 1776. Married Dr. Thomas Wright, an Army Surgeon stationed at Detroit; later they went to Kingston, Jamaica. Dr. and Mrs. Wright and three children died of yellow fever while returning from Jamaica to New York and were survived by a daughter of four years. She was brought up by her grandfather, Commodore Grant, and her aunt, Mrs. Dickson. She married, 1st, Colonel Robert Nichol of Port Dover and Queenston, member of the Provincial Parliament and friend of General Brock; he also took an active part in the War of 1812, and was present at the capture of Detroit; 2nd, Captain Boyd, an officer in the Navy; later he became an Admiral.

ISABELLA, born 28th September, 1777, died 19th October the same year.

NELLIE, born 25th September, 1778, died when a child, in 1788.

ARCHANGE, born 12th December, 1780, died at Dumfries, Scotland, April 20th, 1829. Married Lieutenant-Colonel Thomas Dickson of the 2nd Regiment, Lincoln Militia. They lived at Queenston; the Colonel figured prominently in the War of 1812 and was later a member of the Provincial Parliament. They had two daughters; one died young, the other married Mr. Lyon and settled in Scotland.

Commodore Alexander Grant, 1734-1813.

PHILLIS, born 29th August, 1782, died December, 1857. Married January 20th, 1801, Alexander Duff. They had three children, Alexander, William and Theresa, from whom are descended the Duffs of Amherstburg. One of the cherished possessions of Mr. Henry Duff, a great-grandson of Alexander Grant, is the Sword which belonged to the Commodore.

ISABELLA, born 20th December, 1783, died at Glasgow, Scotland in 1828. Married at Sandwich in 1803, Capt. William Gilkison. They had seven sons, one was Colonel Jasper, of Brantford; another, Archibald, County Judge, Picton.

ANN (Nancy), born 5th February, 1785. Married Simon Maillet of Detroit.

ELIZABETH, born 16th April, 1787. Married June 12th, 1804, James Woods of Sandwich. They had four sons and three daughters. The family later removed to Chatham.

ELEANOR (Nellie), born April 8th, 1789. Married October 31st, 1820, at Sandwich, George Jacob, of the River Thames.

MARIA JULIA, born in April, 1796. Married Wm. Robinson.

JEAN CAMERON, born August 29th, 1799, died at Ottawa in April, 1875. Married William Richardson of Brantford on February 11th, 1824. They had a family of two sons and two daughters.

JOHN GRANT, often spoken of as the adopted son of Commodore Grant. There are a great many stories concerning his advent into the Grant family. According to Judge Witherell, a friend and contemporary of the Commodore, Mrs. Grant and her husband were in Detroit when a band of Chippawa warriors returned with some captives, among them was a small boy of three years. She was at once touched at the sight of the boy and persuaded the Commodore to purchase his release.

They took him home and were surprised to find that he did not know his name or where he came from, so they called him John Grant.

His name is not mentioned in the Commodore's will and I have been unable to find any record of his having been adopted by the Commodore.

He was brought up and educated by the Grants, later he was married and many of his descendants still live in Detroit.

As an appendix to this sketch, I am adding copies of several documents. The one by James Woods is very interesting, inasmuch as it gives us an idea of what was considered the furnishing of a good home one hundred years ago.

WILL OF COMMODORE ALEXANDER GRANT

Summary of the will of Commodore Alexander Grant, Dated February 8th, 1811.

Real estate and personal effects to be sold and divided equally between his children:
    Alexander
    Phillis—Widow of Alexander Duff.
    Archange—Mrs. Thomas Dickson.
    Isabella—Mrs. William Gilkison.
    Elizabeth—Mrs. James Woods.
    Maria—Mrs. William Robison.
    Nellie.
    Jane Cameron.

"And that his daughter ANN has acted a most undutiful part towards him and in justice to his other children it is but proper that he should not place her on the same footing with them, but being desirous, in case she should have any children lawfully begotten, of making some provision towards their education, his will therefor is, that any such children should have their mother's portion, etc."

Executors—THOMAS DICKSON
    WILLIAM GILKISON
    JAMES WOODS

Codicil, dated May 18th, 1811.

That his daughter ANN shall receive the same as the other children and that the real estate, instead of being sold, is to be divided evenly amongst them.

Extract from the Records of St. John's Church, Sandwich.

"Alexander Grant, late Senior officer of His Majesty's Marine Department, departed this life on the eighth day of May, A.D. one thousand eight hundred & thirteen, and was buried at Sandwich on the 10th Inst."

RICHARD POLLARD,
Rector.

Account of the Estate of Commodore Alexander Grant with James Woods, one of the executors.

		£	s.	d.
1813	£3 15 9¾each			
May 11—By cash found in the Commodore's box, vis 2 doubloons		7	11	7½
1 Guinea, £1.3.4, and Commissariat bill, £1.10.0		2	13	4
Nett proceeds of Cattle sold at Auction including 1 cow missing on the day of the sale, and when found taken by estimation		62	12	6½
Mr. Innis—Box £2.9.4 Yk. Cy.		1	10	10
Aug. 30—1 Table sold Mr. Lang		1	10	0
Sept. 23—1 single stove, broke, sold Mr. Bent		7	10	0
Pay received from Mr. Gilmore		155	16	4¾
3 ox yokes, without boughs & without a ring 15/- each		2	5	0
1 ox chain, large		2	10	0
Nett proceeds of articles sold at Auction on the 19th. August, acc't sales rec'd 28th Sept. £44.8.10 Yk.		27	15	6
Nov. 29—Acc't of sales this day £47.8.0		29	12	6
1 double stove		15	0	0
1 Black horse		12	10	0
Dec. 6 —1 ox		7	10	0
2 barrels of salt rec'd by me in the Fall of 1809		5	0	0
		340	17	8¾

Dr. the Estate of the late Alexander Grant, deceased, with James Woods, one of the Executors.

		£	s.	d.
1813				
May 11—Paid for Coffin		2	10	0
Paid for digging and covering the grave			7	6
Paid three men for going to Grosse Point in a canoe for the corpse, etc., 5/- each			15	0
Carriages for self & men			5	0
2½ yds. superfine black cloth to cover the coffin 60/-		7	10	0
5½ yds. Irish linen 7/6		2	1	3
3 yds. fine white cotton 6/3			18	9
11 yds. white cotton 3/9		2	1	3
May 15—to man for taking Mr. Hands to make Inventory there		1	2	6
to Mrs. Duff for Mrs. Maillie to purchase mourning		2	0	0
to George and another, for bringing the cattle from Grosse Point, etc., 15/- Yk.			9	4½
to the ferry-man for crossing same			19	4½
Flour, butter, etc., to the baker to make cakes			7	6
2 quires best foolscap paper to write letters of invitation, 5/-			10	0
May 28—for going to Grosse Point for the furniture, etc., 2 men, 2 days each, 15/- and boat and provisions 12/6		1	7	6
June 6 —Paid Dr. Henry amt. of his acct. $15.75		3	18	9
13 days of pasturage of 17 head of cattle in my meadow, 1 square timber 35 ft. for posts to the paling about grave, 7½d		1	1	10½
5 scantling 63 feet in length			5	0
to Mr. Pollard for Church fees			12	6
to ferry-man going to the Lake for articles at Mrs. Duff's with his canoe, 15/- Provisions for him, 5/-		1	0	0

June 6	—Copies of Will and Codicil & copies of Lease and inventory sent to Mr. Dickson, the whole...	1	10
	to Drouillard, carpenter, for making paling about grave...............	2 10	0
	paid for repairing 2 prs. of Irons, which were broken, before putting up for sale..	5	0
	paid to Mr. Russell for a scabbard for the Sword.....................	6	3
Oct. 15	—Cash to Nancy Maillie...	3 0	0
	Drawing 3 certificates to be signed by Mr. Pollard—Amt. of my acct. less 2 barrels of salt rec'd in the Fall of 1809, credited on the opposite side, and for which the Commodore would make no charge, but I allow him the same price he sold Mr. Duff for, the same Fall—Besides £25.0.0 he agreed to allow me for the debt due by Robison's estate, provided it was recovered, for my trouble.......................	42 5	3½
1814			
Dec. 22	—Paid to Dr. Wm. Brown, balance of his draft on Thos. Dickson, Esq., £91.0.0 Yk. Cy...	56 17	6
1815			
Feb. 22	—Paid Mrs. Maillie on account of her share.........................	9 0	0
	Paid to Mrs. Duff...	10 3	1½
	1,000 brass tacks got from Mr. Davis, no account.		

(Copied by Miss A. Isabella Grant Gilkison, July 13, 1922, for Mr. G. F. Macdonald.)

Account Sales of the Property of the late Commodore Grant sold at public Auction on Wednesday, the 18th August, 1813, by desire of James Woods, one of the Executors of the Estate of the said Alexander Grant, Esquire—for cash.

Wm. Woods........................	3 tea kettles.......................	3	0
do	1 trunk of sundries....................	4	0
do	1 ox chain...........................	8	0
do	1 do	1 0	0
B. Geniac.........................	1 Scythe............................	1	0
R. Woods.........................	1 Leather trunk.......................	5 0	0
Mr. Gardner......................	5 Windsor arm chairs...................	3 16	0
Mr. McIntire.....................	5 do do	2 2	0
Mr. Woods........................	1 Mahogany liquor canister..............	7 4	0
Mr. McIntire.....................	1 Small Liquor Canister.................	2 10	0
Mr. Woods........................	1 Tin Canister........................	2	0
Serg't Bell.......................	1 Brass Candlestick....................	2	0
McIntire.........................	2 do do	18	0
C. Gronden.......................	15 Harrow Teeth } rec'd four dollars.......	1 15	0
do	15 do	1 16	0
Mr. Woods........................	11 Mahogany Chairs............... 12/4	6 12	0
Mr. Forsith......................	1 large Copper boiler...................	17	6
Serg't Bell.......................	1 do do do	1 4	0
Mrs. Duff & Mrs. Woods...........	1 Copper fish Kettle....................	1 16	0
Bapt. Gineac.....................	1 Iron Pot...........................	9	0
Serg't Bell.......................	1 Gridiron...........................	14	0
do	1 Tea Urn...........................	1 0	0
T. Lewis.........................	1 large Sauce pan......................	1 8	0
Wm. Forsith......................	1 large Iron Stand.....................	11	6
Mrs. Duff........................	1 Dutch Oven........................	1 5	0
Wm. Forsith......................	1 pr. Andirons, brass...................	1 19	0
I. Duseau........................	1 pr. do	2 8	0
T. Lewis.........................	1 Iron Pot...........................	16	0
Mr. Woods........................	1 Small Iron Pot......................	7	0
Mr. Forsith......................	1 do	7	0
Mr. Woods........................	1 Dutch Oven........................	1	6
		49 13	6

Received four pounds 13/6 on acc't of the above sale.

(signed) Js. Woods.

Hand's Papers—(G.F.M.)

List of officers of the 77th Regiment, 1757-1763

Lieutenant-Colonel Commanding.

> The Hon. Archibald Montgomerie, afterwards Earl of Eglinton, died a general in the army, and colonel of the Scots Greys, in 1796.

Majors.

> James Grant of Ballindalloch, died a general in the army in 1806.
> Alexander Campbell.

Captains.

> John Sinclair.
> Hugh Mackenzie.
> John Gordon.
> Alexander Mackenzie, killed at St. John's, 1761.
> William Macdonald, killed at Fort du Quesne, 1759.
> George Munro, killed at Fort du Quesne, 1759.
> Robert Mackenzie.
> Allan Maclean, from the Dutch brigade, colonel of the 84th Highland Emigrants; died Major-general, 1784.
> James Robertson.
> Allan Cameron.
> Captain-lieutenant Alexander Mackintosh.

Lieutenants.

> Charles Farquharson.
> Alexander Mackenzie, killed at Fort du Quesne.
> Nichol Sutherland, died Lieutenant-Colonel of the 47th Regiment, 1782.
> Donald Macdonald.
> William Mackenzie, killed at Fort du Quesne.
> Robert Mackenzie, killed at Fort du Quesne.
> Henry Munro.
> Archibald Robertson.
> Duncan Bayne.
> James Duff.
> Colin Campbell, killed at Fort du Quesne.
> James Grant.
> Robert Grant.
> Alexander Macdonald.
> Cosmo Martin.
> Joseph Grant.
> John Macnab.
> Hugh Gordon, killed in Martinique, 1762.
> Alexander Macdonald, killed at Fort du Quesne.
> Donald Campbell.
> Hugh Montgomerie, late Earl of Eglinton.
> James Maclean, killed in the West Indies, 1761.
> John Campbell of Melford.
> Alexander Campbell.
> James Macpherson.
> Archibald Macvicar, killed at Havannah, 1762.

Ensigns.

> Alexander Grant.
> Ronald Mackinnon.
> John Maclachlane.
> John Macdonald.
> Allan Stewart.
> William Haggart.
> George Munro.

Ensigns—*Con.*
William Maclean.
Archibald Crawford.
Lewis Houston.
Alexander Mackenzie.
James Grant.
James Bain.
Chaplain—Henry Munro.
Adjutant—Donald Stewart.
Quarter-master—Alexander Montgomerie.
Surgeon—Allan Stewart.

"Highland Clans," Keltie, Vol. II, p. 454.

XIII

ADDRESS OF THE PRESIDENT, WATERLOO COUNTY PIONEERS' MEMORIAL ASSOCIATION, TURNING-THE-SOD EXERCISES, JUNE 24, 1924

By D. N. Panabaker, Mayor of Hespeler

Officers of the Ontario Historical Society:

Ladies and Gentlemen,—On behalf of the Waterloo County Pioneers' Memorial Association, permit me to welcome you each and all to the exercises of this afternoon. We have gathered together to mark the beginning of a work which, we believe, will commend itself to every worthy Canadian, whether he or she may be a resident of the immediate locality or reside in the distant areas of our vast country. At such times as these we naturally wander in our thoughts to the great many fellow-citizens scattered throughout Canada, and many others also in other lands whose retrospective glances and thought no doubt focus upon the old Waterloo county settlement. To all of our kinsmen and friends throughout the world we should like at this time to extend sincere expressions of fraternity and good will. To those afar to whom our greetings may come we should explain that our exercises this afternoon are being held upon the site recently purchased by our Association from the present owner of one of the three farms first settled in the county in the year 1800; the location being upon the banks of the Grand River about midway between Preston and Freeport and about a mile west of the Wentworth and Waterloo highway. This farm was settled in the summer of 1800 by Samuel Betzner, Sr., whose son, Samuel Betzner, Jr., accompanied Mr. Joseph Schoerg earlier in the same year in locating their homes in the immediate neighbourhood. Mr. Schoerg, who was a son-in-law of Mr. Betzner, occupied the adjoining farm, while Mr. Betzner, Jr., took up what has later become known as the Bowman farm at Blair. These settlers came from Franklin County, Pennsylvania, arriving in Canada in the fall of 1799.

Mr. Schoerg spent the following winter at Niagara Falls and Mr. Betzner, Jr., came on to Ancaster for the winter. Within the memorial acre you have observed a small private cemetery of the Schoerg's and Betzner's, in which is found the grave of the pioneer, Joseph Schoerg, marked by a plain stone monument, upon which is noted in German script the dates of his birth and death and reference to his being among the first Mennonite settlers in Canada and giving the year of his arrival as 1799.

Here also are graves marked by rude pieces of limestone which are said to be the graves of Indians. That these Indians' graves should be here is not a matter of surprise when it is recalled that the early settlers and the local

Indians, probably not many in number, were invariably upon terms of sincere friendship. It is stated that it was a common thing for the kitchens of the early log houses of the settlement to be occupied at night by the Indians who sought the improved shelters of the newcomers when rough weather made their rude places of abode too uncomfortable.

The early settlers found many of the Indians so trustworthy that when going distances from home to trade or on visits to distant friends, they left their property and in many cases their children in charge of the Indians of the neighbourhood. In the fact that in this memorial cemetery there is evidence of this fraternal sentiment between the aborigines and the pioneer settlers, the unique fitness of the site for memorial purposes is unquestionably settled; I hope that this feature of its appropriateness for our purpose may not be lost sight of.

It is not my purpose to go into any detail of local history. Time will not admit of my doing so, and I am sure the papers to be presented this afternoon will serve to indicate that anything that I might be in a position to offer is preferably left to those better posted in these very interesting matters. A few words may be permissible regarding the probable reasons for the settlement of the Mennonites so far inland.

It has been stated that preference for British institutions prompted the Pennsylvanians to seek homes here; another explanation is that the districts in Pennsylvania from which they came were growing less productive agriculturally and thus less satisfactory to the younger element of this thrifty people. A third interpretation of the prompting motive is that the religious sentiments of the Mennonites being strongly pro-pacific had been to some extent violated by the Revolutionary War and that they sought homes more remote from these scenes of possible strife. I have reason to believe that it was probably a combination of the first and last-mentioned considerations that had most to do with their decision to brave all the hardships involved and accept the assurance of the British authorities that in locating in Canada their ideals of peace among men should not be violated. In the war of 1812 I believe that promise was implemented by the British Military authorities and while some of the younger men among the pioneers and their teams were pressed into transport service, it would appear that none were compelled to actually take up arms.

My principal duty this afternoon is to endeavour to express the pleasure of the Officers of the Waterloo County Pioneers' Memorial Association in having so many present including many distinguished members of the Ontario Historical Society. We are honoured and greatly delighted to have you present to participate in the exercises of the afternoon connected with the dedication of this memorial plot. The purpose to which we desire to dedicate this beautiful place, may I say, is to our mind of such outstanding importance as to impel us to carry forward the project with our utmost zeal and with the positive conviction that anything less than complete achievement of our object would be unworthy of the citizens of this prosperous county of Waterloo. The presence in the community of a memorial such as we aim to provide, we believe will foster a sentiment of reverence for the great and good men of our ancestry, which is, perhaps, the best safeguard against degeneration which any country can possess.

No community can boast of ancestry more virile and virtuous than those courageous and resolute pioneers who laid for us in what was at the time a country of stern and resisting aspect, the foundation for development in the pursuits of commercial and industrial as well as agricultural enterprise, unsurpassed in any country of the world.

Our most active imagination is enkindled when we permit ourselves to reflect on the wonderful inspiration to purposeful endeavour on the part of those generations who will succeed us, which will be the undoubted result of our present determination to show proper respect to the memory of our forefathers, whose traits of genuine manliness and inestimable stability of character we perhaps too dimly reflect in our own day and generation.

With reference to the proposed monument itself which it is our purpose to erect, let me say that we propose to get together the necessary funds to erect a fitting monumental shaft of a plain but somewhat massive type which will be in harmony with the traditions and sentiments of those quiet, unassuming, worthy types of men and women who formed the pioneer population of this greatly favoured community. Anything less than a stately enduring type of monument would not be appropriate as a memorial to the sturdy, honest, spiritually-minded and intelligent manhood and womanhood which was characteristic of those splendid progenitors of a thrifty, peace-loving and contented people. Anything less than such a monument established by this generation to which it is our privilege to belong would reflect discredit to ourselves and unworthiness which we should never outlive and which would indeed descend upon our children.

The progress which we have made up to the present moment of which you see evidences about you this afternoon, has been made possible by the subscriptions of only a comparatively few members of the Association, about six or seven in all, who have provided the funds for the purchase of the plot and the fencing materials, etc. Quite a goodly number of the descendants of the pioneers and interested friends, some thirty I think, have performed voluntarily the work necessary to set up the fence and put things in their present state of order. To all those who thus far have so kindly aided in this worthy work we cannot sufficiently express our appreciation. Also to the present owners of this pioneer farm, Mr. and Mrs. Isaac Furtney, for their co-operation and generous attitude in the transactions our Association has had with them, we are deeply indebted; and to the manufacturers of the artistic wire fencing, The Peerless Wire Fence Co. of Hamilton, who presented us with a considerable contribution to our funds, we are likewise indebted; also to Mr. Titus Shantz, who contributed a number of the fence posts for the enclosure; and to Messrs. E. B. and H. B. Betzner, who are largely to thank for the turning and painting of the posts.

But before we can hope to do justice to the project to which we have set our hands we must come for assistance to many, many more of the good citizens of this very greatly favoured community, and to those at a distance who may be interested in establishing a suitable monument to our worthy pioneers. For the bronze tablets which we expect to provide, upon which it is intended to inscribe the names of all settlers of the county who arrived here prior to the end of 1823—100 years ago—we will require a good round sum of money; and for the shaft itself, upon which these tablets will be fittingly placed, a further good sum will be required. I believe that even with proper economy and the utmost care in negotiating for these requisites to an enduring monument we cannot do with less than $10,000, and I believe this is not too great a sum to spend in so worthy a cause, as I have already said anything less would only reflect discredit upon ourselves.

We cannot occupy further time except to refer to a few of the living descendants of the two pioneer families. Mrs. Jacob Gengrich, who still resides upon the adjoining Sherk farm, and Mr. Benjamin Sherk, at Breslau, are the grandchildren of the first settler, Joseph Schoerg. Mrs. Joseph C. Snyder, now in her 85th year, residing at Natchez; Mr. Moses Betzner, aged 86, and his brother, Noah Betzner, in his 89th year, both residents of Kitchener,—these three venerable citizens of Waterloo County are the great-grandchildren of Samuel Betzner, Senior.

XIV

THE LEGISLATURE OF UPPER CANADA AND CONTEMPT

DRASTIC METHODS OF EARLY PROVINCIAL PARLIAMENTS WITH CRITICS

BY THE HONOURABLE WILLIAM RENWICK RIDDELL, LL.D., F.R.S.C., &c.

The two houses of the Legislature of the Province of Upper Canada provided for by the Canada or Constitutional Act of 1791, 31 George III, c. 31 (Imp.), were analogous to the House of Lords and the House of Commons in the Imperial Parliament.

In the Colony, the analogy was pressed so far that the Houses claimed the "privileges" of the Houses at Westminster in dealing with "contempt."

In England from the very beginning, the House of Lords has always enjoyed these privileges and others simply on the ground that the Lords "have place and voice in Parliament."[1] The privileges of the House of Commons may not go so far back, and may possibly derive from some other source, but they have for centuries been well established and wholly beyond question.[2]

One of these is the exemption from arrest on civil process during the sittings of Parliament and for a reasonable time before and after a sittings, generally, but apparently never authoritatively, fixed at forty days.[3]

That this privilege obtained in Upper Canada cannot be questioned[4]; and it was the basis of an incident in the second Session (1793) of the First Parliament.

On Monday, June 17, 1793, in the House of Assembly, "On motion made and seconded, Resolved, That the Speaker do inform W. B. Sheehan, Esquire, Sheriff of this District, that the House entertain a strong sense of the impropriety of his conduct towards a member of this House in having served a Writ of Capias upon the said Member contrary to his Privilege, and that the House has only dispensed with the necessity of bringing him to their Bar to be further dealt with, from a conviction that want of reflection and not contempt made him guilty of an infringement upon the privileges of the House."[5]

The self-restraint of the House was wise. A Capias ad Respondendum could be issued under the practice then in force, only when it was shewn that the debtor was about to leave the Province; and a Capias ad Satisfaciendum in certain cases after judgment if execution did not produce enough to pay the debt; in both cases, however, the defendant must be actually arrested. There is no pretence or suggestion that the Member was arrested; and it is as certain as the case permits, that it was not a "Writ of Capias" which was served. Such writs are not "served," but a Writ of Summons was directed to the Sheriff commanding the defendant to appear on a day fixed; a copy of the Writ was served by the Sheriff.[6]

If this be correct, the Sheriff had the right to serve the writ,[7] the old privileges of Members in that regard having been abolished in 1770; the Statute of that year allowed any suit to be brought at any time against a member, "Provided . . . that nothing in this Act shall extend to subject the person of the Members of the House of Commons to be arrested or imprisoned upon any such suit."[8]

There was one lawyer, a member of the House, John White, the Attorney-General, an English barrister, who should know the law, and it is not unlikely that he kept the House from making a false step.[9]

The next case of supposed contempt of Parliament was in 1803. The story is at least amusing; it cannot be fully appreciated unless the *mise en scene* be understood. The salary, £2,000 sterling, of the Governors was paid by the Home Government, but they had perquisites of great value. Every grant of land of 100-500 acres, for example, netted the Governor and his officers £3:5:2 Halfax currency, or £2:18:8 sterling.[10] General Peter Hunter who became Governor in 1799 was very diligent in making money in this way. By direct or indirect means he brought pressure to bear upon those entitled to patents of land who had from poverty omitted to take them out, hints not too obscure being thrown out that delay might be fatal. Mr. Justice Powell does not hesitate to say that Hunter was put up to discreditable, if not wholly illegal ways of increasing his income by Mr. Justice Allcock, who at Hunter's recommendation was made Chief Justice on Elmsley's removal to Lower Canada. However that may be, there were hundreds of patents issued in Hunter's time, unnecessarily as many thought. Another cause of irritation arose directly from what has been a reproach to this Province from the beginning, the policy of underpaying public servants, and compelling them to look to fees for an income. The Judges of the Court of King's Bench indeed had a fixed salary paid by the Home Government, £1,100 for the Chief Justice, and £750 for each Puisne; and therefore, the scandal of Judges in the Superior Court receiving fees, once a reproach to the English Courts, was avoided in that Court.[11]

But there was no provision for salary for the officers of the Court except that the Sheriff and the Clerk of the Crown and Pleas each received £100 per annum from the British appropriation. Consequently the Act establishing the Court provided fees to be paid to the Clerk of the Court, the Marshall, the Crier and the Sheriff.[12]

In the inferior Courts, i.e., the District Courts and Courts of Requests,[13] judges and officers alike were paid by fees from suitors. The people raised many and bitter cries against what they considered extortion; and their representatives in Parliament took action.

The Parliament had no control over the fees charged for patents of land and the like; the public land belonged to the Crown, represented by the Imperial Administration, and the fees for patents were fixed by the Executive Council in the Colony, subject to the approval of the authorities at Westminster.

But the fees in the Courts were wholly within the jurisdiction of the Legislature, and it was determined to attack them.

On Wednesday, February 2, 1803, on motion of Mr. Angus Macdonell, member for Durham, Simcoe and East York, a prominent lawyer, *persona non grata* with the Government, a committee was appointed by the Assembly "to report a revised and amended Table of Fees to be allowed and taken in the several Courts of Judicature within the Province." The committee examined William Weekes, a well-known barrister, along with the Clerk of the Peace and the Clerks of the inferior Courts, i.e., the District Court and the Court of Requests. The Clerk of the Crown and Pleas, David Burns, was Clerk of the only Superior Court in the Province, the Court of King's Bench; upon receiving notice to attend the committee at their meeting at 2 p.m., he wrote the chairman with a copy of the fees taken and received by him as Clerk of the Court of King's Bench and promising to attend at the hour mentioned. Burns, however, was also Master-in-Chancery and, therefore, an officer of the Legislative Council. It was quite well known that the attack upon the fees taken by the Clerks of the Courts,—who were of course all appointed by the Governor—was part of a general scheme of attack upon the fees taken by other officers, and to a certain extent an attack upon the Government itself. Burns was advised by the Law Officers, and at least informally instructed by the Governor, that he should not appear before the committee; and at 1 p.m., he wrote Alexander Macdonell (of Glengarry and Prescott) chairman of the committee, that he had been advised that he had done more than he was compelled to do and that his attendance on the committee would not be proper.[14] A letter from the chairman to Burns brought a similar reply. The committee reported to the House, and the House ordered the Sergeant-at-Arms, Thomas Ridout, to bring the body of Burns to the Bar of the House on the morrow "to answer for his contempt of the rights and privileges of this House by refusing to obey the orders of a committee thereof authorized to compel his attendance." The Speaker, Richard Beasley, of West York, First Lincoln and Haldimand, issued his warrant accordingly. The Sergeant-at-Arms went to Burns' house at 10 a.m. next morning and delivered to him a copy of the warrant; Burns gave his word of honour to surrender himself to the Sergeant-at-Arms at 12 noon,[15] (the hour fixed for his appearance at the Bar of the House) but failed to do so. The Speaker directed the Sergeant-at-Arms to bring Burns in as directed; he went to the door of the Legislative Council Chamber, where Burns was sitting as Master-in-Chancery, and was informed that that House was sitting, but would soon break up. He withdrew and waited outside for the House to adjourn. After waiting for about a quarter of an hour, the Gentleman Usher of the Black Rod, George Lawe, came to him and told him that the Speaker of the Council, Chief Justice Henry Allcock, had sent for him to come in. Ridout went in; the Chief Justice asked him his business; he answered that Burns being in his custody by virtue of a warrant from the Speaker of the Commons House of Assembly, he had attended to conduct him to the Bar of that House. Allcock then asked him if he had "the audaciousness, the effrontery to come here" to which Ridout replied that he was only obeying the orders he had received; the Chief Justice told him that he would do well to consider how he conducted himself. Ridout withdrew and reported to the House what had happened. The Speaker's casting vote (5 to 5) decided in the negative the motion of Angus Macdonell "that this House do proceed to no business until they have vindicated the rights and privileges of the Commons of this Province in respect of the contumacy of Mr. Burns," and the House adjourned.

The Council, as soon as Ridout withdrew, resolved itself into a Committee of the Whole to take "into consideration the extraordinary circumstances that had occurred, namely, the entrance of the Sergeant-at-Arms into the Lobby of the House for the purpose of taking into custody an officer of the House." The Speaker was directed to send a message to the Assembly complaining of "an insult offered to the Legislative Council by an officer of the Assembly, the Sergeant-at-Arms," and then the Council adjourned.

Next day, the Assembly adjourned for want of a quorum, only one of the malcontents attending; and the following day by a vote of eight to three it resolved itself into a Committee of Privileges. The committee reported progress. When the Speaker resumed the Chair, Hon. John McGill came down with the message of the Legislative Council. The Speaker in consequence of the message, "by the voice of the House, suspended the Sergeant-at-Arms . . . and appointed Charles Willcocks *pro tem* to do the duties of that office . . . until such time as the House do make enquiry into the conduct of the Sergeant-at-Arms." The committee resumed, and passed four resolutions: 1. "That the House of Assembly of the Province of Upper Canada is a Superior Court of Record and that every disobedience of the orders thereof is a high contempt and misdemeanour punishable at its own discretion; 2. That the arrest of Burns was proper and lawful; 3. That his offence was aggravated by his escape and breach of parole; and 4. That process should issue under the hand of the Speaker to bring him before the House at 10 a.m. on the morrow."

The House then went into committee on the Message from the Council; and determined to ask a conference for the better ascertainment of the facts.

By a vote of eight to two the Speaker was directed to sign a warrant to Willcocks, "Special Messenger to the Commons House of Assembly"; Willcocks arrested Burns, and on a vote of eight to three he was put to the Bar. On a vote of six to four he was asked if he had aught to say to extenuate or justify his contempt of the Orders of the House. He replied in writing that it was far from his intention to even appear to insult, "but as a servant of the Crown declines to answer any question except through the medium of the person who here represents the Sovereign." Now appeared for the first time the real contention, namely, that the Governor and his advisers contended that a servant of the Crown cannot give any information concerning his office without the leave of the Crown, and that such information must be sought from the Representative of the Crown, not the officer.

A motion to accept the statement and discharge Burns was voted down; and an amendment was adopted that if Burns should express contrition for his offence without assigning any reasons in justification he should be discharged. Burns refused. A proposed resolution that Burns be informed that if he had pleaded the privilege as an officer of the Legislative Council, it would have been allowed him, was voted down seven to four; Burns was asked what his offices under the Crown were, and whether he held any which required his necessary and daily attendance upon the Sovereign or His Representative in this Province; he answered that he was designated by His Majesty's Mandamus directed to him, Clerk of the Crown and Common Pleas of the Province; and the House decided by a vote of six to five that he was not as such "privileged from giving his attendance upon the Commons when they in their judgment for the public weal may demand it." He was then allowed to withdraw, but was to "remain in the custody of the Special Messenger at large" until further order.

The Council on the opening of the Sitting that day sent the Usher of the Black Rod to desire Burns to attend his duty on that House forthwith; Burns came in and stated "that he had been detained as a prisoner at the Bar of the House of Assembly, but that he was now considered a prisoner at large." Then came up the deputation from the House to ask for a conference; this was at once agreed to and the House was so informed.

The committees met at once; that of the House agreed that the conduct of the Sergeant-at-Arms deserved the severest censure, "even to the extent of addressing the Lieutenant-Governor to remove him from his office." This the Committee of the Council would not hear of. They thought that his offence proceeded rather from want of consideration than any design to offend, and they would be satisfied with his being reprimanded by the Speaker. They all agreed that when the attendance of an officer of either House was desired by the other, the House, whose officer he was, should be applied to to permit or order his attendance. The Committee from the Assembly added that if Burns had claimed his privilege as an officer of the Council he would have been immediately discharged.

Next day, Burns informed the Council that he was considered by the Messenger the prisoner of the Messenger of the House; the Speaker communicated this to the House and the House immediately ordered his release. Ridout was reprimanded and reinstated. In the message from the House announcing his discharge the House asked that Burns be "sent down to the Bar of the Commons to undergo examination touching a gross contempt of the privileges of the Commons of which as Clerk of the Crown and Pleas he stands charged." The Council replied that "however willing they may be to comply with the request . . . the latter part of the message is expressed in such terms as will not permit the Legislative Council to proceed thereon."

The House next day voted down (seven to five) a proposed resolution to receive no message of whatsoever nature from the Council until Burns should purge his contempt; an amendment was also negatived to send a message to the Council asking for Burns to attend to answer any questions which it might be thought expedient to ask him. Another resolution expressing regret at the determination of the Council to screen Burns and saying that the House would not receive any communication through him for the future, was lost by the Speaker's casting vote (six to six) and the House passed to the Order of the day.

The next day, a motion was voted down that the Council should be informed that before proceeding to extremities with Burns, the House desired a conference and also that "it would not be seemly in the Commons to receive any message or communication by or through the channel of . . . Burns" until after the conference. Thereafter the Session proceeded without any further reference to Burns or his contempt. This case is as good an example of "how not to do it," as our records show. Most of the trouble was due to Angus Macdonell, a somewhat hot-headed but thoroughly honest Highlandman who had lost his place as Clerk of the House through the Lieutenant-Governor, Peter Hunter, and never forgave him. On the other side there were the Solicitor-General, Robert Isaac Dey Gray[16] and the official class generally; but a little common sense would have avoided the difficulty.

That the advice, indeed orders, given to Burns not to attend the Committee without the leave of the Governor, cannot be supported by law, or reason, all will now admit. That Ridout was wholly justified in the first arrest is unquestionable; that Burns was guilty of an inexcusable breach of faith must be conceded; and no one would find fault with Ridout, his close friend, for taking his word. What put the House in the wrong and made possible the triumph of the placemen, was the first mistake made by Ridout in going to the lobby of the Legislative Council to take Burns into actual custody. All officers and indeed all others, including witnesses, in attendance at a sittings of either House or of a Committee, are privileged from all arrest; he should have waited for Burns away from the Chamber. That the real reason for Burns not attending was not his position of Master-in-Chancery in attendance upon the Council, has nothing to do with the matter. Even although nothing but a pretext, it was valid.

Ridout was properly rebuked; doubtless he would have been removed, but that he was one of the official class himself. There is no reason to accuse him, however, of bad faith notwithstanding rancorous contemporary gossip.

The proper *modus vivendi* was arrived at by the Conference, and there is no reason other than bad temper why an unexceptionable message should not have been sent to the Council. Perhaps the Council was somewhat finical in its objections to the terminology, but when the objection was taken, it could and should have been met by more temperate language. The Assembly showed sound sense in refusing to allow this tempest in a teapot to interfere with the regular work of the Session; but there was nothing done for the relief of the people during that session."[17]

The next instance of alleged violation of the "Rights and Privileges of the Commons House of Assembly" does not technically come under the head of Contempt; but it is worthy of consideration from a constitutional point of view.

The Committee on Public Accounts in the Assembly in 1806 reported, February 28th, "that it is the opinion of the Committee that the rights and privileges of the Commons House of Assembly in this Province have been violated by the application of several sums of money in the Provincial Treasury to various purposes without the assent of Parliament or a vote of the Commons House of Assembly, and that the Committee do therefore recommend to the Commons House of Assembly to address His Honour"[18] the President, praying that no money be used in future without the assent of Parliament or a vote of the House of Assembly, and that a sum of £617:13:7 be replaced in the Provincial Treasury to be at the disposal of Parliament." A schedule is attached showing how the amount is made up. It was quite obvious that the amounts had been properly expended, *i.e.*, that the payments were made to public officers entitled to receive them; the only objection was payment without the assent of Parliament.

There need have been no difficulty, as the irregularity was technical and might well have been overcome by an *ex post facto* vote. But there was in the country a mischievous, troublesome and disloyal faction; this was represented in the House by William Weekes of Durham, Simcoe and East York, an Irishman, the former student of Aaron Burr, and Benajah Mallory of Norfolk, Oxford and Middlesex. Weekes made this mistake on the part of the Administration a means of annoyance.

Weekes was a member of the Committee appointed to draw up the Address to the Administrator, and he made it as offensive as possible. The Address represented that "the first and most constitutional privilege of the Commons had been violated"; that "the comment on this departure from constituted authority and fiscal establishment must be more than painful to all who appreciate the advantages of our happy Constitution and who wish their continuance to the latest posterity"—"however studious we may be to abstain from stricture . . . we feel it as the representatives of a free people, we lament it as the subjects of a beneficent Sovereign and we hope that you in your relation to both will more than sympathize in so extraordinary an occurrence." All this over a mere slip—and that slip being in strict accordance with what had been often done before, as the House knew perfectly well. A schedule of the moneys misapplied was annexed to the Address, and the Address went on to express, "trust that you will not only order that sum to be replaced in the Provincial Treasury, but will also direct that no moneys be issued thereout in future without the assent of Parliament or a vote of the Commons House of Assembly."

The Administrator, Grant, consulted the Attorney-General, Thomas Scott, a timid man who avoided trouble whenever he could; Scott consulted Mr. Justice William Dummer Powell,[19] one of the most robust characters in our early Provincial life. Powell advised that the error should be frankly admitted, and a promise made to apply to the Secretary of State in England for a direction to replace the moneys out of the Imperial grant. The Attorney-General, however, preferred to retain his own form of answer. It set out, as the fact undoubtedly was, that the Administrator had followed the practice of the two preceding years, which had been acquiesced in by the Legislature; it concluded, "I am . . . desirous to give every reasonable satisfaction to the House of Assembly. I shall direct the matter to be immediately investigated and if there has been an error in stating the account, take measures to have it corrected and obviated for the time to come." A worse answer could hardly have been framed; and the enemies of the Administration did not fail to take advantage of it. Weekes moved, seconded by David McGregor Rogers, of Hastings and Northumberland, another malcontent (but not disloyal), that the House should go into Committee on the answer. Peter Howard, of Leeds, was in the chair. A report was preparing when the Gentleman Usher of the Black Rod, George Lawe, came to summon the House to attend His Honour in the Legislative Council for Prorogation. The doors were shut in the face of the Usher, and a Report was prepared. The House divided equally on the motion that the Report be received; the Speaker, Alexander Macdonell, gave the casting vote in the negative; the Gentleman Usher gave his Message and Parliament was prorogued with nothing further done.[20]

Grant sent a despatch to Lord Castlereagh, Secretary of State for War and the Colonies,[21] with a full account of the transaction and recommending a reimbursement of all sums paid without Legislative authority.

Francis Gore arrived as Lieutenant-Governor in August, 1806, and inherited the troubles of Grant; he received authority to replace the money; he was thus in a position when the House met in February, 1807, to state that he had given instructions to that effect.[22]

The troublesome Weekes was dead, killed in a duel by his friend William Dickson[23]; he had been succeeded in his seat by the more troublesome Mr. Justice Thorpe.[24] Thorpe was powerless to prevent the House giving a courteous reply: "We cheerfully embrace the present occasion to express our full satisfaction of Your Excellency's directions relative to certain moneys that have been taken from the Provincial Treasury without either the authority or concurrence of Parliament"; and when later on it was moved that the House would relinquish the money, £617:13:7, applied by General Hunter, Grant's predecessor, in the same way, Thorpe could get only one member to join him in opposition, Ebenezer Washburn, of Prince Edward;[25] and this episode came to an end.[26]

At a by-election in 1808, Joseph Willcocks was elected for West York, First Lincoln and Haldimand; if not yet, at least later, he was a traitor, as he showed in the war of 1812, in which he joined the American invaders and was found dead at Fort Erie in an American Colonel's uniform. Thorpe had gone to England, but his place was well filled by Willcocks. Willcocks was the proprietor and publisher of *The Upper Canada Guardian* or *Freeman's Journal;* in that paper he published an article which was considered by some a charge that the Members of the House of Assembly had been bribed by Hunter with land to vote against the interests of their constituents. Captain David Cowan, of Essex, gave notice of motion that the House should go into Committee to take into consideration that part of the article which referred to the House; for some reason or another, the motion was not made, but nearly three weeks afterwards Cowan informed the House that Willoccks had said that the members dared not proceed against him, and that he was sorry they did not as he could prove by a member of the House that they had been bribed by General Hunter. Cowan gave the names of those who were present and had heard Willcocks' statement. The House went into Committee and resolved that "the expressions said to be made use of by Mr. Joseph Willcocks are false, slanderous and highly derogatory to the dignity of the House."[17]

Willcocks was allowed the privilege of remaining in his place during his trial and also to cross-examine witnesses. Witnesses were examined for and against Willcocks, and at the close of the trial, on motion of Cowan, seconded by Samuel Sherwood, of Grenville (no friend of the Administration, be it said), the House unanimously resolved that Willcocks was guilty and ordered that he be committed to the common gaol at York. The Speaker issued his warrant and Willcocks went to gaol. After an imprisonment of twenty-five days, the House being about to be dissolved, Cowan moved, seconded by Allan McLean, of Frontenac, and the House resolved, that he should be discharged.

There is no extant record of the proceedings in the Assembly of 1809, the first Session of the Fifth Parliament in which Willcocks was member for First Lincoln and Haldimand. He was an exceedingly active member in this Parliament; and took part in the next Contempt proceeding now to be noticed.

John Mills Jackson, an Englishman who had been some years in the Province, returned to England, and in 1809 published in London a pamphlet, now very rare, called, "A View of the Political Situation of the Province of Upper Canada in North America."[28] He did not spare Lieutenant-Governor, officers of the Administration, the Courts, or Members of Parliament, and concluded with a call to the King, Lords and Commons to investigate. It does not appear that Jackson sent a single copy out to the Province; but one was sent out which came into the possession of a member of the Assembly. On March 9, 1810, Crowell Willson, of the Fourth Riding of Lincoln, moved, seconded by James McNabb, of Hastings and Ameliasburgh, that the House resolve that this pamphlet "contains a false, scandalous and seditious libel comprising expressions of . . . the grossest aspersions upon the House of Assembly" and others. The pamphlet was read; and next day, the House in Committee framed and presented a report along the lines of the motion—a motion to receive the Report was carried on a division of thirteen to four, Willcocks voting in the minority, and an Address drawn up in accordance with the Report was carried by a vote of twelve to four, Willcocks again with the minority.[29]

Nothing, however, could be done, Jackson was beyond the jurisdiction of the House.

In the Session of 1811, John Beikie, Sheriff of the Home District, summoned as Petit Jurors during the Sittings of the House, a Member, the Clerk, the Sergeant-at-Arms, and the Doorkeeper; he expressed his contrition, said it was by inadvertence and got off without even a rebuke.[30]

There can be no doubt that members of the House of Commons in England could not be compelled, during the Session, to attend Court as witnesses, jurors or in any other capacity without the leave of the House, and the officers of the House were in the same position. This rests on the paramount right of Parliament to the attendance and services of its Members and officers at all times during the Session, and the right has always been firmly maintained since early times.[31]

After the Session of 1811, Alexander Macdonell of Glengarry conceived that Dr. William Warren Baldwin, as Attorney at Law, had "grossly and flagrantly violated the privileges of that honourable body," the House of Assembly, by placing in the hands of the Sheriff of the Home District a writ for the purpose of arresting Macdonell's person; he considered "this violation of privilege . . . more unpardonable in Mr. Baldwin than it could possibly be in any other attorney," as he was also Master in Chancery. The Deputy Sheriff, Thomas Hamilton, refused to execute the writ notwithstanding Baldwin's insistence; and Macdonell informed the Speaker, Samuel Street, of the circumstances, "not doubting but that every individual Member will coincide . . . in opinion that Mr. Baldwin in his threefold capacity of Deputy Clerk of the Crown, Attorney and Master in Chancery has violated the privileges of the House of Assembly." The Speaker laid this letter before the House a few days after the opening of the Session of 1812. The House resolved that Baldwin had been guilty of a breach of the privileges of the House by suing out a *Capias* against a Member. Baldwin had got into trouble with the Assembly in another respect. His father, Robert Baldwin, of Darlington Township (Baldwin's

Creek, now Wilmot's Creek) a prominent Magistrate of the Newcastle District, was a Commissioner of Roads for the years 1808, 1809 and 1810. A Committee of the House in 1811 reported that he had in his hands unaccounted for £55:1:6. Dr. Baldwin complained openly and bitterly that the House was unjust to his father; and on motion of Thomas B. Gough, of East York and Simcoe, seconded by David McGregor Rogers, the House resolved, seventeen to three, that he thereby had been guilty of "a false, scandalous, audacious and contemptuous libel of this House."

Warned by past experience in the Burns matter, the House sent a message to the Legislative Council not doubting that "Honourable House will proceed towards the delinquent as to their wisdom may seem meet . . ." A copy of the Resolutions was sent up to the Council; the Council the next day read the Resolutions, and decided to dismiss Baldwin summarily. On this being reported to the House of Assembly, that body relented, thanked the Council for "so satisfactorily supporting the privileges of the Commons of Upper Canada," assured the Council that "though jealous of their privileges," they disclaimed "whatever might appear vindictive," and asked the Council "to extend their mercy and accede to the earnest and unanimous solicitations of the House that they will be pleased to restore William Warren Baldwin, Esquire, to his former situation in their Honourable House."

The Council, the next day, felt "great pleasure in complying with the wishes of the House," and sent a message to the House to that effect; and that episode closed, as John Small, the Clerk of the Crown who issued the writ of Capias against Macdonell, had already apologized to the House and had been graciously "allowed to retire"; and Thomas Hamilton, the Deputy Sheriff, into whose hands Baldwin had put the Capias for execution, had flatly refused to execute it, "because he conceived Mr. McDonell to be privileged from arrest."[32]

The privilege from arrest, as has been said, existed in England during the Session, and a convenient time (usually stated at forty days) before and after the Session; the Parliament had been called for September 18, 1811, and Baldwin's attempt to have Macdonell arrested earlier in the month was a clear contempt.

The next case is better known.[33] Robert Nichol, a prominent business man of the Village of Dover in Woodhouse Township in the London District, had been a Commissioner of Highways to apply in that District the moneys appropriated to help in building and repairing roads and bridges; he had received the moneys, but had not given an account of the expenditure. The House in 1811 received a Report from the Select Committee on Public Accounts—"they have received no account from Robert Nichol of the application by him of £300 appropriated for the year 1810"; and in Committee of the Whole, "Resolved that it is the opinion of the Committee that the Commissioners of Highways for the London District have abused their office by the misapplication of the moneys committed to their care, and that £300 rests in the hands of Mr. R. Nichol, a Commissioner, no part of which appears to have been applied to public uses." This came to Nichol's knowledge and he at once sent in his account of the application of the money; and with it a letter to the Secretary of the Governor explaining the circumstances. He concluded the letter by asserting his integrity, and adding,

"Experience has, however, convinced me that no integrity of heart nor rectitude of conduct are a defence against malevolence and detractions, and that actions the most upright and disinterested may be misrepresented when individual characters are to be sacrificed and party purposes are to be gained." This letter was read to the House on February 20, 1812, and Mr. Rogers, of Northumberland and Durham, moved, seconded by Thomas B. Gough, of East York and Simcoe, that "Robert Nichol has been guilty of a breach of the privileges of this House by making a false, malicious and scandalous representation to the person administering the Government relative to the proceedings of this House. . . ." This was carried on a division by a vote of twelve to six. It was ordered that a warrant should issue to the Sergeant-at-Arms to arrest Nichol; a warrant was issued and placed in the hands of Stephen Jarvis, Deputy Sergeant-at-Arms, who went to Nichol's house and brought him to York. He, Nichol, told Philip Sovereign, member for his constituency, Norfolk, and also Joseph Willcocks, of First Lincoln and Haldimand, that the House had no right to commit him for a breach of privilege. Sovereign and Willcocks so informed the House, and when Nichol was brought to the Bar, he had to defend the double contempt of written and oral statements. He was found guilty of both on a division of thirteen to nine; he was ordered to be committed to the common gaol at York on a vote of twelve to ten; and the Speaker issued his warrant to the Sheriff of the Home District, John Beikie, who placed him in gaol.

Nichol at once applied for a writ of Habeas Corpus, which was granted by Chief Justice Scott; on the return, the warrant was found to be fatally defective and Nichol was discharged by the Chief Justice; the House resolved, twelve to nine, that Scott had "been guilty of a violent breach of the privileges of the House," and sent a message to the Legislative Council where Scott sat as Speaker respecting his conduct and requesting them to proceed in the case as the nature of the offence required. The Council allowed Scott to give an explanation of his action which was entered in the Journals; and, disclaiming any right to interfere with the Chief Justice in his judicial capacity, they sent the explanation to the Assembly. The House refused, on a division of fourteen to eight, to give Nichol a copy of the proceedings relative to his being taken into custody, and determined to vindicate its rights and privileges. It decided, eleven to nine, to present an Address to the Prince Regent (King George was insane) representing the breach of its privileges by the unconstitutional interference by Scott in liberating Nichol. A Committee composed of Gough and Willcocks was appointed, twelve to nine, to draft the Address; the Address was received on a division, twelve to ten; and read the third time, twelve to ten; the Speaker was ordered to sign it, twelve to ten, the fifth Rule was dispensed with, twelve to six, to enable Willcocks to present the Address to the Administrator, General (afterward Sir) Isaac Brock with a request to transmit it to the Prince Regent. The address to Brock said *inter alia:* "We have the highest opinion of the integrity and good intentions of the Honourable the Chief Justice, and sincerely lament that he has been . . . so badly advised as to interfere with the privileges of the Commons; but a sense of our duty and a desire to preserve the Constitution unimpaired has compelled us to adopt the present method of obtaining redress." Brock promised to transmit the Address to the Prince Regent, and the Sheriff was given back his Writ of Habeas Corpus. Parliament was soon thereafter prorogued. Brock sent a dispatch to Lord Liverpool, the Secretary of State, with all the papers in the matter, but the fatricidal war of 1812 came on and the matter was forgotten.

That Nichol was guilty of a gross contempt of the House is certain; but it is equally certain that the Chief Justice was right in law, and the House was wrong in the contest between them.

NOTES.

[1]"Modus Tenendi Parliamentum," W. Hakewel, 1660, p. 82 (William Hakewel or Hakewill, M.P., Solicitor General to the Queen of James I. See D.N.B., Vol. XXIV, p. 10).

[2]The history is given in May's "Parliamentary Practice," 12th Ed., 1917, pp. 63 sqq. The discussion of the interesting question whether the House of Commons is a Court of Record or not is without the scope of this Paper. The House of Commons long most firmly maintained that it was; Lord Mansfield decided it was not; Jones v. Randall, (1774), 1 Cowp. 17; May, op. cit., p. 93; the House of Lords when exercising its judicial functions is undoubtedly a Court of Record, but Lord Kenyon said "when exercising a legislative capacity, it is not a Court of Record." Flower's Case, (1799), 8 Term Reports, 314; May, op. cit., p. 92.

[3]Blackstone's Commentaries, Bk. 1, p. 165 (p. 153 of Pitt Lewis' Ed. and notes). In Upper Canada, see Reg. v. Gamble and Boulton. (1832), 9 U.C.R., 546 and other cases down to Cox v. Prior, (1899), 18 P.R., 492; in England, 4 Coke Inst., 24, 25; Long Wellesley's Case, (1831), 2 Russell & Mylne, 639, esp. 665; In re Armstrong, (1892), 1 Q.B., 327.

[4]Rex v. Gamble and Boulton, (1832), 9 U.C.R., 546, a decision of the Full Court of the King's Bench, Robinson, C.J., Draper and Burns, JJ.

[5]Journals, House of Assembly, U.C., 1793; these are reprinted in 6 Ontario Archives Reports (1909), see at p. 31.

[6]See the Ordinance of April 21, 1785, 25 George III, C. 2 (the old Province of Quebec); (1792), 32 George III (U.C.), cc. 1.4; the practice was not changed till (1794), 34 George III, c. 2. (U.C.).

[7]Except perhaps in the Chamber when the House was in Session, which is not suggested here. See May, op. cit., p. 81.

[8](1770), 10 George III, c. 50, ss. 1,2; the earlier Acts cutting in on the privileges of the Members were (1700), 12,13, William III, c. 3; (1703), 2, 3 Anne, c. 18; (1738), 11 George, c. 24.

[9]There were in Upper Canada at this time only four persons regularly bred to the law: the Chief Justice, William Osgoode, who was Speaker of the Legislative Council, First Judge William Dunmer Powell at Detroit, John White, the Attorney General, and Walter Roe practising at Detroit. The first three were educated for the Bar in England (the first and third called there); Roe was educated and licensed in Montreal.

[10]This was in addition to 6d sterling per acre paid to the Government for surveying; for 1000 acres, there was paid £25 sterling, of which £5.11.0 went to the Officers and £19.9.0 into the Treasury. Can. Archives, Q. 294, p. 57, Hunter's Despatch to Lord Hobart, Secretary for State for War and Colonies, 1801-4 (the Colonies were transferred from the Home to the War Department in 1801) from York, May 15, 1805.

[11]When in 1802, Allcock drew up a scheme for a Court of Chancery for the Province, as the Home Administration declined to make an appropriation for the salary of the Chancellor, the table of fees for the proposed Court provided for fees for the Chancellor as well as the officers. See my Article "Early Proposals for a Court of Chancery in Upper Canada" 41 Canadian Law Times, December, 1921, p. 740; Hunter's Despatch to Hobart from York, November 8, 1802, Can. Arch. Q. 293, p. 105; the Table of Fees is at p. 111.

[12]The Statute was (1794), 34 George III, c. 2 (U.C.); the Table of Fees is in section 38.

[13]Corresponding to the present County Court and Division Court; the Courts of Requests were first organized in 1792 under the Act, 32 George III, c. 6 (U.C.), and became Division Courts under the Act (1841), 4, 5, Vict, c. 3 (Can): the District Courts were instituted in 1794, under the Act, 34 George III, c. 3 (U.C.), and became County Courts in 1849 under 12 Vict., c. 78, s. 2 (Can). The Court of King's Bench was instituted under the Act (1794), 34 George III,

c. 2 (U.C.), and continued until it was merged in the Supreme Court of Judicature in 1881, 44 Vict., c. 5 (Ont.), there having been in the meantime two other Superior Courts established which were both merged in the same way by the same Act of 1881—one a Court of Law, the Court of Common Pleas (1849), 12 Vict., c. 63 (Can.), and the other a Court of Equity, the Court of Chancery (1837), 7 Will. IV., c. 2 (U.C.), reorganized (1849), 12 Vict., c. 64 (Can.).

[14] The pretext for this was that as Clerk of the Crown he was a servant of the King and was paid by the King, that, therefore, it would be improper for him to say anything about his fees and that all such information should be sought from the King or his representative the Governor. This was a mere pretence; it was not the amount paid to him by the King in his office as Clerk of the Crown which was to be inquired into but the amount he received as Clerk of the Court of King's Bench which was controlled by the Legislature and paid by suitors. It is humiliating to learn that at least one Judge, the Chief Justice, Allcock, lent himself to this unworthy subterfuge.

[15] The Sergeant-at-Arms knew Burns well and he was so confident that Burns would keep his word that he reported to the Speaker that he had the body in his custody—this the Speaker informed the House at the opening Tuesday, February 8, 6 Ont. Archives, Rept. (1909), p. 339.

[16] Macdonell and Gray were, a little later, to meet together a watery grave in Lake Ontario when the Government Schooner *Speedy* foundered, and captain, crew and passengers were drowned, October, 1804. See my "Old Province Tales," Toronto, 1920, cap. VII, "The Tragedy of the Speedy," pp. 117, sqq.

[17] The inner history of this episode appears from the Powell and other contemporary MSS; the outward history will be found in the Journals, House of Assembly, U.C., 1803. Ont. Archives Rep. (1909), 332, 333, 337, 338, 339, 341-4, 346-8, 350, 351, 356-7, and the Journals, Leg. Col., U.C., 1803, 7 Ont. Archives Rep., (1910), 181, 183-6.

An analysis of the ten divisions shows that:
1. Angus Macdonell was uncompromising throughout and that he was supported by
2. David McGregor Rogers, Hastings and Northumberland,
3. Ralph Clench, Second, Third and Fourth Lincoln,
4. Timothy Thompson, Lennox and Addington, voted with him at all the divisions at which he was present except the two, one to tell Burns that if he had pleaded his position in the Council he would have been at once discharged, and the other affirming the right of the Assembly to command his attendance at any time. The same course was taken by,
5. John Ferguson, Frontenac.
And in all but his petulant motions to do no business until Burns had purged his contempt and to refuse to receive any message through Burns, Macdonell had the support of,
6. Ebenezer Washburn, Prince Edward.

Thorough-going supporters of the Government were:—
7. Robert Isaac Dey Gray, Stormont and Russell, the Solicitor-General.
8. Mathew Elliott, Essex (except an unimportant motion).
9. Richard Beasley, West York, First Lincoln and Haldimand (the Speaker).
10. Isaac Swayze, Second, Third and Fourth Lincoln.
11. Alexander Macdonell, Glengarry and Prescott, voted that the Assembly had the right to Burns' attendance and against proceeding with the Order of the Day; in all other divisions he voted against his kinsman.
12. Robert Nelles, West York, First Lincoln and Haldimand, voted for the right of the Assembly to Burns' attendance, for the Speaker to sign warrant for his attendance, to bring in the body and to interrogate; but on the merits, he was against Macdonell.
13. Thomas McCrae was erratic; he voted that Burns be put to the Bar, against the right claimed by the Assembly, for a warrant to compel attendance, to bring in the body, against interrogating Burns, against informing him that he would be released if he pleaded his office in the Council and against the proposition not to proceed, &c., &c.
14. David William Smith, Norfolk, Oxford & Middlesex, was in England; 15, Jacob Wenger, Dundas; 16, Samuel Sherwood, Grenville; 17, William Buell, Leeds; and 18, Thomas McKee, Essex, were not in attendance this Session or the preceding.

[18] In the Province of Upper Canada, the Lieutenant-Governor was styled "His Excellency"; the President of the Council, administering the Government in the absence of a Lieutenant-Governor, was styled "His Honour", as is the Lieutenant-Governor of Ontario. After the death of General Peter Hunter, the Hon'ble Alexander Grant, President of the Council, administered the Government from September, 1805, until the arrival of Francis Gore, in August, 1806.

In the Session of 1806, the Committee to draw up an Address to the President of thanks for his Speech from the Throne drew up a proposed Address to the Administrator and headed it

"To the Honourable Alexander Grant, Esquire, President administering the Government of the Province of Upper Canada, &c." This was adopted and ordered to be engrossed, whereupon the Speaker, the Honourable Alexander Macdonell, Member for Glengarry and Prescott, by permission of the House read a paper which was ordered to be inserted in the Journal. "The Speaker craves the indulgence of the House to have inserted on its Journals that he does not concur in opinion with the House in the new mode which it has adopted in Addressing the President; it has been the uniform and established practice in addressing Presidents administering a Government to say 'To His Honor' and not 'To the Honourable'. The former appellation the Speaker humbly conceives to be more respectful and more comprehensive than the latter. Mr. President Russell was invariably addressed by the former appellation during his administration of the Government by the Province; as Mr. President Dunn actually is in that of Lower Canada." Then we read that "at the hour appointed, Mr. Speaker, attended by the House, went up to His Honor the President with the Address of the House; and being returned, Mr. Speaker reported that the House had attended upon his Honor with its Address to which His Honor had been pleased to make the following answer . . . ." Journals, House of Assembly, U.C., 1806, 8 Ont. Archives Rep. (1911), p. 62: There is a misprint in this copy; the words are printed "went up to his Honourable President."

Thereafter the Addresses from the House read "To His Honor, Alexander Grant, President, administering the Government of the Province of Upper Canada." See do., do., pp. 69, 70, 112—"To His Honor Isaac Brock, President, &c." Journals, House of Assembly, U.C. (1812), 9 Ont. Archives Rep., (1912), pp. 7, 87, 89; in 1814, "To His Honor Gordon Drummond, Esquire, President, &c." do., do., pp. 106, 119,148, 151, 154, 156; in 1818, "To His Honor Samuel Smith, Esq., Administrator of the Government . . . ." do., do., pp. 434, 453, 459, 488, 513, 515, 519. There are no records extant of the proceedings in the House of Assembly during the Administration of Sir Roger Hale Sheaffe, October, 1812, to June, 1813. No Parliament met during the administration of Major General de Rottenburg (1813), Sir George Murray (1815), or Sir Frederick Phips Robinson (1815). The Addresses of the Legislative Council to the Administrators were punctiliously accurate.

See my article " 'His Honor' the Lieutenant Governor and 'His Lordship' the Justice, *infra*."

[19]The Chief Justice, Henry Allcock, was in England; he did not return to the Province, but was later in the same year, 1806, appointed Chief Justice of Quebec.

[20]For the proceedings in the Assembly, see Journals, House of Assembly, U.C., 1806, 8 Ont. Archives Rep. (1911), pp. 101, 107, 113, 114; see Powell's Statement and proposed Answer, Can. Archives, Q. 304, pp. 22, 26; Powell's advice was that the Executive should not descend to equivocate with the Commons but should frankly admit the mistake and promise to lay the matter before the Secretary of State.

[21]Castlereagh took office, July 10, 1805; he gave place to William Windham, February 14th, 1806, and replaced him again, March 25, 1807. Grant's despatch is dated at York, Upper Canada, March 14, 1806, Can. Archives, Q. 304, p. 10; his Answer to the House, Can. Archives, Q. 304, p. 20; the Address of the House, do., do., p. 15.

[22]Journals, Ho. Assy. U.C., 1807, 8 Ont. Archives Rep., (1911), p. 122.

[23]At Fort Niagara, New York State, October 10, 1806; see my Article "The Duel in Early Upper Canada," 35 Canadian Law Times (September, 1913), pp. 726. sqq.

[24]See my Article "Mr. Justice Thorpe" in 40 Canadian Law Times (November, 1920), p. 907; also in "Upper Canada Sketches," Toronto, 1922, p. 57.

It may be added that there is positive proof that Thorpe took part with Willcocks in founding his paper. An original letter from Thorpe, in his unmistakable handwriting, is in the possession of the County of York Bar Association, and reads as follows:—

York, July 1st, 1807.

Dr. Sir:

This is the first day I could receive my certificate and I now enclose it; there is a most horrid combination to oppress me that ever was formed, I never receive a Dollar here and the mode pursued is to prevent any one from cashing my bills, therefor my good Sir if you possibly can place me in some way to get cash for one hundred pd. bill on the Colony Agent every six months, these good people have unintentionally by the election put me to a thousand Dollars expense which oppresses me much at this time.

I dislike the Aurora paper very much there is nothing in it but party violence.

Dr. West lives on the American side I cannot account for the delay of letters, mine are mostly suppressed if not always opened, but the persons who have the management of our letters have thought fitt to suppress the whole March packet; in the midst of this despotism I am obliged to stand every attack and quite alone, except that I have the people with me from one end of the Province to the other. I hope you will not be deceived by Mr. Stewart (?) but they buy over every one. I will do all I can with him, however, if Mr. Powell should get the Court of Chancery I think you have no chance of succeeding as I fear he will be entirely under the Scotch party and the Montreal merchants.

I hope Col. Clause will prove your friend but I doubt it very much.

I had a letter from Mr. Wyatt at Halifax dated the 17th of April he was to sail that day for England.

Mr. Willcocks has got a press, Types, paper, Printer and everything for a Newspaper, he is expect this week at Niagara on his return from New York & will soon publish, the Types he has are not good, if you know of any good and cheap let him know and send all the News you can to him.

Ministry change so quickly & are so engrossed by the war that I fear making my impression about this Colony for by the time I have informed one Secretary perfectly I have a new one to begin with.

I enclose you an Advertisement of Mr. Willcocks the elder [i.e., William Willcocks]: all his property is in mortgage to a Mr. Gray of Montreal I think a bargain might be made with Mr. Gray and the Land and House in Town got cheap. I think if you could get a person with money to join with you who would keep a Store in York and you to attend to the settling of the land very much could be done, I could render you good service with the country people.

It will give me great pleasure if I can serve you in any way but unless there is a change in system I would not advise you to come here.

Yours most truly obliged & with great regards
ROBT. THORPE.

Endorsed with address (in Thorpe's hand):
"Mr. N. A. Farre,
Philadelphia."

Post Mark "A   Stamped "PAID" Marked "50 Paid"
——L 23"

A memo (in another hand)
"Robt. Thorpe, Esqr., 1st July, 1807
covering his life certificate of same date (?)
and a letter enclosed of 10 July
or 18
recd............... 26 Augt. 1807.
Sent the letter
of Judge Thorpe's that
came in this
to Mr. Sazalet (?)".

[25] Ebenezer Washburn was a Barrister and Attorney practising at Kingston. He was the preceptor of Marshall Spring Bidwell; he committed an infamous crime and left the country. He was No. 51 on the Roll of Members of the Law Society, No. 46 on the Law Society's Roll of Barristers; his name is erased and nothing appears in the Roll but a black bar.

[26] See Journ. House of Assy., U.C., 1807, 8 Ont. Archives Rep., (1911), pp. 121, 174, 175, 177. Gore's despatch (No. 19) to Windham, York, March 12, 1807, Can. Archives, Q. 306, pp. 48, 50, 52; that (No. 20) of March 13, 1807, do., do., Q. 306, pp. 59-115.

[27] 8 Ont. Archives Rep., (1911), pp. 199. 225 (where the name is wrongly given as W. Willcocks), 228, 274. Dent, "The Story of the Upper Canadian Rebellion," Toronto, 1885, Vol. 1, pp. 90-92, has a one-sided account of the episode; he relies wholly upon Gourlay's account in his "Statistical Account of Upper Canada," London, 1822, Vol. 2. pp. 655-662, and that is taken from Willcocks' own statements. Willcocks' defence is that while he did say that every Member did receive 1200 acres of land, he did not say "as a *bribe*."

[28] A fair account of this pamphlet is given in Gourlay's work mentioned in Note 27, Vol. 2, pp. 328, 329, 334, 335; its title is "A View of the Political Situation of the Province of Upper Canada in North America, in which her physical capacity is stated, the means of diminishing her burden, increasing her value, and securing her connection with Great Britain are considered. With notes and Appendix, London, Printed for W. Earle, No. 43 Albemarle Street, 1809."

[29] The four who voted in the minority were Joseph Willcocks, First Lincoln and Haldimand; Peter Howard, Leeds; John Willson, West York, and David McGregor Rogers, Northumberland and Durham. Dent makes the extraordinary statement, (*op. cit.*, Vol. 2, pp. 91, 192), "From some of his (Willcocks') votes in the Assembly, it would appear that he made tacit overtures towards reconciliation with his enemies"; he bases this upon Gourlay's partial account of the Proceedings of March 10. Gourlay gives the composition of the House in Committee, showing the presence of Willcocks, but does not give the division in the House. Dent thence concludes that Willcocks sided against Jackson. Journals, Ho. Assy., U.C., 1810, 8 Ont. Archives Rep., (1911), pp. 369, 370, 375.

[30] Journals, House of Assy., U. C., 1811, 8 do., do., do., p. 471.

[31] See May *op. cit.*, p. 111, and notes.

[32] For the Proceedings in the Assembly, see 9 Ont. Archives Rep., (1912), pp. 17, 19, 21, 23, 27, 28 (Small's apology is at p. 23); in the Council, 7 Ont. Archives Rep., (1910), pp. 410, 411, 412, 413; for the Report on Robert Baldwin as Highway Commissioner, see Journals Ho. Assy., U.C., (1811), 8 Ont. Archives Rep., (1911), p. 454.

[33] Accounts of this trouble may be found in Ont. Hist. Soc. "Papers and Records," XIX, 10-18 (Brig. Gen. E. A. Cruikshank), and in ditto, XX, 134-7 (Hon. W. R. Riddell).

XV.

WHEN A FEW CLAIMED MONOPOLY OF SPIRITUAL FUNCTIONS.

CANADIAN STATE TRIALS—THE KING AGAINST CLARK BENTOM.

BY THE HONOURABLE WILLIAM RENWICK RIDDELL, LL.D., F.R.S.C., &C.

Clark Bentom was an Englishman[1] connected with the London Missionary Society, which had been formed in the closing years of the eighteenth century for the conversion, if possible, of the heathen and heathen-like sinners. Its members consisted of ministers of various denominations and various views on Church Government; but Arians and Socinians were excluded. The Society was in great favour with the King, and its ships had privileges denied to others at London.

In 1799, certain of the inhabitants of the City of Quebec who were not satisfied with the means of grace afforded by the clergy of that city, petitioned the Directors of the Society to send them a minister of the gospel to minister to them in holy things; and the Directors endeavoured to procure such a minister from the several dissenting bodies in connection with the Society. The attempt was in vain; and though the design of the Society was to send out only ministers duly ordained by some church, the Directors thought fit in the difficulty, rather than not to send anyone at all, to send Bentom, who had two years before "been publicly and solemnly set apart to the work of the Gospel Ministry . . . by the Missionary Society" itself—(so Bentom himself says; but a certificate to be mentioned later seems to indicate that he was set apart by the ministers of the Independent body in England.)

Leaving London in March, 1800, he arrived at Quebec in June, but found most of the applicants gone from the place and the rest indifferent. Not discouraged, Bentom set about forming a congregation, and in January of the following year, a Church Communion was organized on the general principles of the Church of Scotland, both doctrinal and disciplinary, but without any connection with that church. There was a clergyman of the Church of Scotland in Quebec, with a church and congregation. Bentom and his flock, however, were entirely separate—the "people called themselves Presbyterian, because such they were in principle, and not Independents, which circumstances obliged them to be." The "circumstances" of course were their disinclination to unite with the officially formed and existing congregation of the Church of Scotland and their determination to lead an independent ecclesiastical life.

Bentom baptized, solemnized marriages, attended funerals, opened and kept the registers of baptisms, marriages and burials required by law. These were prescribed by the Provincial Act of 1795, 35 Geo. III, Cap. 4, (L.C.), which by section 1 provided that after the 1st day of January, 1796, "in each parish church of the Roman Catholic communion, and also in each of the Protestant churches or congregations" within the Province, there should be "kept by the Rector, Curate, Vicar or other priest or minister doing the parochial or clerical duty thereof, two registers of the same tenor" of baptisms, marriages and burials. These were made legal evidence in all Courts of Justice of the Province.

Doctor Jacob Mountain,[2] the Anglican Bishop of Quebec, demanded of Bentom by what authority he assumed the title of Protestant Minister, and informed him that no one but the Clergy of the Church of Rome, the Church of England and the Church of Scotland had the right to solemnize marriages, and that he might do mischief undesignedly in rendering illegitimate the offspring of marriages solemnized by him. Instead of thanking the Bishop for the information, Bentom stoutly maintained the validity of the marriages he had solemnized. The Bishop declined to discuss the matter, and said that the Chief Justice[3] and the Attorney-General[4] both had given the opinion that such marriages were invalid, and they knew better than either Bentom or himself.

This Bentom thought a strange idea, too gross and abominable to be true or to be entertained by the Government, and disregarded the assertion as too contemptible to deserve notice.[5] The Bishop then forbade him to attend funerals in the burial ground given by the Government to the Protestant inhabitants of Quebec. Bentom complained to the Lieutenant-Governor[6] who handed the matter over to the Attorney-General. The Attorney-General went to Bentom's house in person, interrogated him, told him he had no right to attend funerals or to perform the marriage ceremony. At first the lawyer admitted the right to baptize, but recanted that concession and denied Bentom's right even to baptize.

The following Sunday, a child of a member of his congregation was to be buried; Bentom wrote Mr. Salter Mountain, the bishop's nephew, asking him to produce the authority to exclude him from the burial ground, if there was any such. This was also referred to the Attorney-General, who again called at Bentom's house and threatened him with an Information in the Court of King's Bench if he attended the funeral of the infant. This threat Bentom regarded "as a mere *brutum fulmen*, thunder and lightning that kill nobody," and deliberately set the Attorney-General at defiance by officiating at the funeral.

This was in August, 1802, and nothing more of an official nature was heard of the matter till the following January, when Bentom applied for the signature of a Judge to his Annual Register.[7] The Judge, Jenkin Williams, refused, as the applicant was of neither of the three churches—of Rome, of England, or of Scotland. Bentom persisted in his course; to do otherwise "would have rendered me unworthy the name of an Englishman or of a Dissenting Minister of the Gospel"—although, indeed, he thought the solemnization of marriage might be dispensed with, as that was in itself a civil contract and not Divinely commanded as a part of the minister's duty; nevertheless, considering the marriages he had solemnized, slander would have fallen on those so married if he were now to cease. In the case of burials, too, they were not really Divinely enjoined on a minister to attend; but if he did not attend them, his congregation would be "marked by a persecuting distinction."

At length the Attorney-General filed an information *Quo Warranto* in the Court of King's Bench[8], March 23rd, 1803, and a warrant was issued to the Sheriff at Quebec as follows:—

"District of Quebec[9]

L.S.   George the Third, by the Grace of God of the United Kingdom of Great Britain and Ireland, King, Defender of the Faith; To the Sheriff of our District of Quebec, greeting:

"We do require and command you upon sight hereof to bring before our Justices of our Court of King's Bench now holden in and for the said District of Quebec for the cognizance of all Crimes and Criminal offences the body of Clark Bentom, to answer to us upon an Information fyled against him by our Attorney-General, for exercising without any Royal Grant, Legal Warrant, Right or Authority whatever the office of a Priest or Minister doing the Clerical Duty of a Protestant Church or Congregation within the Province (if the Court shall be then and there sitting) or if not, before any one of the Justices of our said Court of King's Bench, to find sufficient sureties for his personal appearance at this present Session to answer the same and all such matters as shall be objected against him, and if he cannot be taken during this present Session that then so soon after as he shall be taken you bring him or cause him to be brought before any one of the Justices of Our said Court of King's Bench to find sufficient securities for his personal attendance at the next Session of our said Court of King's Bench of and for the said District, to answer as aforesaid and further to be dealt with according to Justice." This writ was tested, March 23rd, 1803, and signed by E. Bowen, Deputy Clerk of the Crown.

Bentom heard of the warrant, avoided arrest by attending Court early, was produced by the Sheriff as his prisoner, gave bail, informing the Chief Justice that he meant to be his own advocate. "Then," said his Lordship, "you must proceed according to the forms of the Court." The puzzled prisoner, wholly ignorant of Court procedure, was obliged to retain an attorney. He employed Mr. Ker to file his plea and move the day of trial; instead of doing this, he says, Mr. Ker moved to put the business over till the next Session. Bentom, angered at this, tried to obtain other legal assistance, but could not get a lawyer in Quebec who would file a plea for him. He then petitioned the Court to appoint him an attorney to file his plea. The Court refused, saying that the course pursued was safest for the defendant and that Mr. Ker had acted perfectly rightly.

The Court of Oyer and Terminer sat in August, 1803; Bentom thought that, being on bail, he had a right to the benefit of the general gaol delivery[10] and employed Mr. Panet,[11] Speaker of the House of Assembly, to file a plea for him. Panet could not or would not understand what the accused wanted, and Bentom undertook the business himself. He learned the technical form from a plea of disclaimer which the Attorney General had, in vain, attempted to have him sign and, instead of signing "this diabolical paper," he drew up and filed the following plea:

"District of Quebec.   COURT OF KING'S BENCH.

March Criminal Term, 1803.

Dominus Rex.

versus   Upon an Information, &c.

Clark Bentom.   Quo Warranto.

"And now, that is to say, on the first day of July, in the year of our Lord, one thousand eight hundred and three, before the said Court of King's Bench for the district of Quebec, in the Province of Lower Canada, cometh the said Clark Bentom in his own proper person and saith, that he the said Clark Bentom was, in the month of January, in the year one thousand eight hundred and one, by a congregation of Protestant Dissenters from the form of worship used by the established church of England, assembling for worship of God in the parish de Notre Dame, commonly called the Parish of Quebec, in the City of Quebec, in the Province of Lower Canada, regularly and unanimously chosen and appointed their pastor to minister unto them in all holy things, that is to say, to preach the word, and to administer the sacraments of Jesus Christ, to solemnize marriages, and to give a word of exhortation at the grave of deceased persons, commonly called burying the dead. The defendant moreover saith that he the said Clark Bentom from the aforesaid month of January, in the aforesaid year one thousand eight hundred and one, has been and still continues to be at the date hereof the appointed, acknowledged pastor of the said congregation of Protestant Dissenters, in the parish aforesaid, in the city and Province aforesaid. Farther, that the said defendant then believed and still believes that neither he, nor the said congregation by these their actions, have transgressed or broken any law or ancient usage now in force or ever claimed to be in force in the said Province of Lower Canada, since the subjugation of the same to the Crown of Great Britain.

"That therefore the said Clark Bentom, minister of the gospel in the parish aforesaid, in the city and province aforesaid, conceives himself fully entitled to all the rights, liberties, privileges or franchises whatsoever, of Protestant Dissenting Ministers of religion in the Province of Lower Canada, and that he is bound by a penal statute, passed by the Provincial Legislature, in the year one thousand seven hundred and ninety-five, to have and keep two registers of baptisms, marriages and deaths of a certain description therein specified. The defendant therefore with confidence puts himself on his trial before the said honourable Court of King's Bench, pleading NOT GUILTY to the charge of His Majesty's Attorney-General, of having usurped without legal warrant, right, or authority whatsoever, the office of a priest, or minister of a Protestant church or congregation in the Province of Lower Canada; trusting for protection from oppression in his person, character or property to the excellent Constitution of the Canadian Provinces, the equity of the said Court of King's Bench, and the consciences of his jury.

"(Signed)   CLARK BENTOM."

He then drew up a petition that the Court of Oyer and Terminer should hear his cause. Of course this was necessarily refused, the matter being in the Court of King's Bench and the jurisdiction of the Commissioners of Oyer and Terminer being limited by their Commission.

Bentom then petitioned the Lieutenant-Governor, Sir Robert Shore Milnes, for relief; but equally of course he had no power to grant the prayer of the petition. A certificate that he had been set apart to preach the gospel was procured from four Independent ministers, John Townsend, John Towers, Charles Buck and Joseph Brooksbank, of Bermondsey, Barbican, Camomile Street and Haberdashers' Hall, respectively; but the only answer that was given or could be given was that His Excellency could not interfere with the matter, being "a question of right before the King's Bench."

The defendant, waiting for the next term of the Court, published at Troy, N.Y., 1804, a pamphlet (mentioned in note 1), setting out his grievances in considerable detail and arguing as to his rights.

At the next term of the Court of King's Bench, the Attorney-General demurred to the plea, and issue was joined. The case was fully argued, and judgment was given for the Crown on the demurrer, thus:

"That the plea of the said Clarke (sic) Benton, (sic) by him pleaded, is not sufficient in law, and it is thereupon adjudged that the said Clarke Benton do not, in any manner, intermeddle with, or concern himself, in the office of a priest or minister, doing the clerical duty of a Protestant church or congregation within this province, or the rights, liberties, privileges and franchises to the said office belonging and appertaining, nor any of them; but that he be from henceforth wholly prejudged from exercising and using the same, and every of them, and that the said Clarke Benton be taken to satisfy the King for the usurpation aforesaid."

This case was not regularly reported, but it is referred to and followed in *Ex parte* G. Spratt, Stuart's Rep. Cas., K.B., L.C., p. 90, and in Appeal, p. 149[12].

It may perhaps be noted that it was subsequently held that a minister of a Presbyterian Congregation in communion with the Church of Scotland was entitled to registers, although another congregation had been previously established in the same place in communion with the same church. *Ex parte* Reverend John Clugston, (1831), Stuart Rep. Cas., K.B., L.C., p. 448.

NOTES

[1]Most of the facts of this case are derived from a pamphlet published by Bentom in 1804:— "A Statement of facts and law relative to the prosecution of the Rev. Clark Bentom, Protestant Missionary from the London Missionary Society, for the assumption of the office of a dissenting minister of the gospel in Quebec by the King's Attorney-General of Lower Canada: "If thou seest the oppression of the poor, and violent perverting of judgment and justice in a Province, marvel not at the matter; for he that is higher than the highest regardeth, and there be higher

than they." Solomon. "Fear not thou worm Jacob, thou shalt thresh the Mountains, and beat them small." Isaiah. Troy: printed for the author, by O. Penniman & Co. 1804," 8vo, 32 pp. Some facts are also obtained from Stuart's Reports of Cases, K.B., L.C., mentioned at the end of the paper.

[2] Jacob Mountain, of Huguenot descent, (the name was originally "Montaigne"), was the first Anglican Bishop of Quebec,—born in 1749, educated at Caius College, Cambridge, he took holy orders. Through the friendship of William Pitt, he was made Bishop of Quebec, 1793. He was very active in promoting the interests, spiritual and temporal, of his church; during his episcopacy the church increased in numbers, wealth and influence. He died in 1825 at Quebec. His more famous son, George Jehoshaphat Mountain, became Bishop of Montreal and coadjutor to Bishop Stewart of Quebec, with very wide territorial jurisdiction extending over Upper Canada. He became Bishop of Quebec in 1837 and survived until 1863. Salter Mountain was a nephew of the elder Bishop.

The delightful story is told of the first Bishop—and *si non è vero, è ben trovato*—that conversing with Pitt (a variant has it, with King George III) about the See of Quebec and who should be sent thither, he combined Matt. xvii, 20, and Luke xvii, 6, and said: "If ye have faith as a grain of mustard seed, ye shall say unto this mountain, Be ye removed and planted in the Sea."

[3] The Chief Justice at this time was John Elmsley, who had been the second Chief Justice of Upper Canada and had been appointed Chief Justice of Lower Canada in 1802. A fairly full but not wholly accurate account of his life will be found in Read's Lives of the Judges.

[4] The Attorney-General was Jonathan Sewell, afterwards Chief Justice at Quebec. See an account of his life in note 13 to Rex v. David McLane, Transactions, Royal Society of Canada, Section II, 1916, pp. 321-337, at p. 331.

[5] It is a subject of remark that many ministers did not seem to appreciate the very great importance of the regular solemnization of marriage, the effect of invalid marriages in bastardizing the offspring, and the general misery and heart-breaking unhappiness which followed their acts in many instances. One can understand the view of priests of a Church which looks upon marriage as a sacrament that they, fulfilling the law of the church, need look no further—what the late Chief Justice Armour (O'Connor v. Kennedy, 1888, 20 O.R. at p. 23) called "the impudent assumption of an ecclesiastic" may have appalling results; but at least the sacrament has been duly solemnized. But in churches in which marriage is not a sacrament, one would expect the ecclesiastics scrupulously to obey the civil law and to avoid performing ceremonies of no legal validity. We find, however, ministers of several of such churches claiming the right, in the face of the law, to solemnize matrimony, and almost making it a matter of conscience. In the notes to an article in the Canadian Law Times for 1913, I have given instances of a Baptist Minister and several Methodist Ministers in Upper Canada violating the law in this regard, and have quoted the historian of early Methodism as boasting of their courage. See 33 Can. L.T., p. 103, note 4. Another instance will be found mentioned in Pringle v. Allen, (1859), 18 U.C.R. 575, where Dunham, an American (i.e., Episcopal) Methodist Minister, having no authority to solemnize marriage, nevertheless performed the ceremony illegally before the passing of the Act of 11 Geo. IV, Cap. 36. (U.C.).

Bentom's comment on the opinion of the Chief Justice and the Attorney General is "Aye, there, my Lord, you produce the strong argument of Bishops; men of power have frequently, alas, too frequently, proved superior in legal decisions to weak Christians, who wield no sword save the sword of the spirit." Such twaddle has passed muster for argument in some circles; but where the simple question is as to right in law, it is exasperating.

[6] It will be seen later that the Lieutenant Governor at the time was Sir Robert Shore Milnes.

[7] The whole difficulty in this case arose from the Provincial Statute of 1795, 35 Geo. III, Cap. 4, (L.C.), which was nothing more than a regulation as to evidence in the Courts of Law in the Province respecting births, marriages and sepultures. Before this Act, the law was laid down in an ordinance of 1667 entrusting to the Curés of the Roman Catholic Church only, the keeping of registers. The Act of 1795 extended this to "Protestant Churches or Congregations." At the time "there were no other protestant churches or congregations in the Province than those in communion with the Churches of England and Scotland." (Stuart, Rep. Cas., K.B., L.C., at p. 149). All churches or congregations were ordered to keep two registers of baptisms, marriages and sepultures, the registers to be signed on each leaf by a Judge of the Court of King's Bench, the one a bound volume to serve until filled, the other unbound, to be renewed annually. The Statute provided that these should be evidence in the Courts of the Province as "official declarations" (*actes authentiques*) and it was therefore a necessity that the keeper of the register should show that he was a public officer and entitled to make an official declaration.

On Bentom's applying for his annual register, the Judge had to determine whether he was such public officer; and in this case he rightly decided that Bentom was not.

Jenkin Williams was a gentleman bred at the English Bar; he had been Solicitor-General, and was a very sound lawyer.

[8] Bentom makes it a matter of complaint that he is styled "gentleman," as indicating that he was a layman; but all who were not priests of the Church of Rome, of England or of Scotland, were in law laymen. He writes "The Clergy of the Church of England are by the Church of Rome called a Pretended Clergy, and Dissenting Divines are by the Church of England called the same"—no doubt true enough at that time, and at least in part now; but he continues "who are in fact pretended Clergymen? Those who have not the love of God in their hearts nor the law of truth on their lips, whether Churchmen or Dissenters"; which may be very good theology but is very bad law.

[9] Before the Constitutional Act of 1791, 31 Geo. III, Cap. 31, (Imp.) the Province of Quebec was divided into two Districts, the District of Quebec and the District of Montreal. This division continued after the formation of the Province of Lower Canada.

[10] A Court of Oyer and Terminer was a Court held by Commissioners of Oyer and Terminer to try criminal cases on indictments found before the Commissioners: a Court of General Gaol Delivery was a Court of Commissioners to try the cases of all persons confined in the common gaol not under sentence. The Commissions generally issued concurrently. While generally Judges of the Court of King's Bench were appointed on such Commission, they had no relation to the Court of King's Bench. The Court of King's Bench was perpetual, these Courts ephemeral and for a particular purpose only.

A Court of Oyer and Terminer and General Gaol Delivery could not deal with an Information in the Court of King's Bench, as any lawyer would have told Bentom. Perhaps it was this on which the minds of Bentom and Panet could not meet—for Panet was a lawyer.

[11] Jean Antoine Panet was an advocate of great prominence at the bar of Quebec. He became Speaker of the first House of Assembly in 1792, and continued as such for some twenty years without remuneration. (In 1817, Governor Sherbrooke granted his widow a pension for life of £300 per annum). He was an ardent supporter of the rights of the French-Canadians, and was rightly considered a powerful champion of their cause. He was in conflict with Governor Craig, and lost his Commission as Colonel in 1809; but he did not lose his political significance.

He was for long a Judge of the Court of Common Pleas of Quebec. At least two other Judges of the same family name attained the Bench in early times in Quebec.

[12] The decision in this case (followed in *Exp*. Spratt, the King v. Spratt, 1816, Stuart, Rep. Cas., K.B., U.C., 90, 149) settled the law in Lower Canada that a "Dissenter" i.e., a minister not belonging to either of the three Churches, had no power to celebrate matrimony so as to create the legal relation of man and wife and render the issue legitimate. There was of course no interference with any ceremonial of a purely ecclesiastical significance; the question had no relation to the exercise of religious worship or ceremony. Without restraint, the Court neither could, nor did mean to touch or affect full religious toleration, nor was there any reflection on the education and moral character of the celebrant. The whole question was as to who under the existing law filled a civil office of great importance; and neither in Lower Canada nor in Upper Canada do those who violated the law deserve the slightest sympathy; they did not receive much outside of their own communion, and little more within. The course followed by the wiser was successful in both Provinces, that is, to have the law changed.

In Lower Canada, the following legislation was passed to enable ministers to perform the marriage ceremony validly:—

(1829) 9, 10 Geo. IV, Cap. 76 (L.C.), An Act to extend privileges therein mentioned to the religious classes of persons denominating themselves Wesleyan Methodists.

(1829) 9, 10 Geo. IV, Cap. 75, (L.C.), An Act to extend certain privileges, therein mentioned, to persons professing the Jewish Religion, and for the obviating certain inconveniences to which others of His Majesty's subjects might otherwise be exposed.

(1831) 1 Wm. IV, Cap. 56 (L.C.), An Act to afford relief to a certain religious congregation "at Montreal denominating themselves Presbyterians, although not regularly of the Established Church of Scotland nor in connection with same."

(1833) 3 Wm. IV, Cap. 27 (L.C.), An Act to enable the regularly ordained ministers of the United Associate Synod of the Secession Church of Scotland to keep authenticated registers according to law.

(1833) 3 Wm. IV, Cap. 28 (L.C.) gave John C. Nichols and his successors duly ordained and ministers of a religious congregation in the Township of Hull calling themselves Presbyterians the same rights.

(1833) 3 Wm. IV, Cap. 29 (L.C.), An Act to afford relief to a certain religious congregation at Montreal, denominated Baptists.

Other legislation followed, which it is unnecessary to trace. The present state of the law is thus declared in Article 42 and 7251 of the Civil Code of the Province of Quebec:

42—"Acts of civil status are inscribed in two registers of the same tenor, kept for each Roman Catholic parish church, church, private chapel or mission, and for each Protestant Church or congregation or other religious community, entitled by law to keep such registers, each of which is authentic, and has in law equal authority."

7251—"The Protestant churches or congregations referred to in article 42 of the Civil Code comprise all churches and congregations in communion with the Church of England or Scotland, and the several religious communities and denominations in the Province mentioned in the special acts concerning them, and the priests or ministers thereof, who may validly solemnize marriage, and may obtain and keep registers of civil status, subject to the provisions of the said acts with reference to each of them respectively."

In Upper Canada the course of legislation in this regard is traced in an article on "Some Early Legislation and Legislators in Upper Canada" in the Canadian Law Times for 1913, Vol. 33, at pp. 100, sqq. It will be sufficient here to refer to the following statutes: 1793, 33 Geo. III, Cap. 5; 1798, 38 Geo. III, Cap. 4; 1830, 11 Geo. IV, Cap. 36; 1857, 20 Vic., Cap. 66; 1896, 59 Vict., Cap. 39, and now R.S.O., 1914, Cap. 148, ss. 2, 3. The ministers duly ordained by any church may perform the ceremony; but the law does not justify anyone to get up a little denomination of his own of which he is Pope, Bishop, Synod and General Conference, and ordain himself as a minister thereof with power to perform the marriage ceremony. Rex v. Brown, 1908, 17 O.L.R., 197.

See my Articles, "The Law of Marriage in Upper Canada," *Canadian Historical Review*, September, 1921; "The Criminal Law in Reference to Marriage in Upper Canada," *21 Papers and Records, Ontario Historical Society*, 1924, "Some Marriages in Old Detroit," *Michigan History Magazine*, January, 1922: "Simon Girty's Marriage," *Canadian Magazine*, December, 1921.

XVI.

CRIMINAL COURTS AND LAW IN EARLY (UPPER) CANADA.

BY THE HONOURABLE WILLIAM RENWICK RIDDELL, LL.D., F.R.S.C., &c.

After the Conquest of Canada in 1759-60 and its formal Cession in 1763, a Province of Quebec was established as declared in the Royal Proclamation of October 7, 1763;[1] the western boundary of this Province was a line drawn from the point at which the present International line meets the River St. Lawrence to the south end of Lake Nipissing. The western boundary was in 1774 removed much further west by the Quebec Act;[2] the southern boundary ran along the Great Lakes, down the side of Pennsylvania and along the Ohio River to the Mississippi; and the western boundary ran "Northward"[3] from that point to the Hudson's Bay Company's territories. This brought into the Province of Quebec all the territory now the Province of Ontario and the States of Michigan, Wisconsin, etc.

By the Treaty of Paris, 1783, all territory to the right of the Great Lakes was allotted to the United States; but Britain retained for some years possession of much bordering on Lake Huron and the connecting Straits (including Detroit)[4] and did not surrender the possession of this to the United States till 1796. In 1788, Lord Dorchester formed four Districts—Luneburg, Mecklenburg, Nassau and Hesse—out of the western portion of the Province of Quebec.[5] Those Districts included most of what is now the Province of Ontario and also, *de facto* but not *de jure*, some of Michigan and Wisconsin, and that whole territory I call Upper Canada.[6]

The English law, criminal as well as civil, was introduced by the Royal Proclamation of 1763, above mentioned; and while, by the Quebec Act of 1774, the ancient French Canadian law was reintroduced in civil matters, the English criminal law remained in full force except as modified by Provincial legislation.

In each of the four Districts, there was erected a Court of Common Pleas with full civil jurisdiction; each District had also a Prerogative Court for probate of wills, etc., the judges of the one Court being also judges of the other. In criminal matters, the Courts were modelled on the English system, as in civil matters (except as to probate and administration) they were not.

In each District, there was a Commission of the Peace;[7] by the law of England the Justices of the Peace named in the Commission were empowered to sit as a Court of General Quarter Sessions of the Peace, a Criminal Court with extensive jurisdiction at which cases were tried by a jury; by both English and Canadian legislation, these Courts were to sit four times in each year.[8] While their Commission gave them power to enquire of all manner of felonies and trespasses they had, before the Conquest of Canada, ceased to try capital cases,[9] and the custom was to remit such cases for a more solemn trial at the Assizes, before the Commissioners of Oyer and Terminer and General Gaol Delivery.[10]

In England at this time, and for centuries before, a criminal case could be tried before the Court of King's Bench itself; but in the vast majority of cases, the trial was before Commissioners of Oyer and Terminer and General Gaol Delivery; and Commissions of this character were granted to the Judges of Assize, so that they might try Criminal cases on their circuits.[11]

In the Province of Quebec, there was erected in 1764 and continued by an Ordinance in 1777 a Court of Criminal Jurisdiction, the Court of King's Bench held before the Chief Justice of the Province (or Commissioners appointed for executing the office of Chief Justice) at Quebec and Montreal[12]; but the same Ordinance reserved to the Governor the power of granting Commissions of Oyer and Terminer and General Gaol Delivery. Such Commissions were not necessary so long as the Province of Quebec had its original boundaries; but when it was enlarged by the Quebec Act of 1774, it was obvious that the time would come when it would not be feasible to try all important criminal cases in Quebec or Montreal.

In Detroit, indeed, the Justice of Peace, Philip Dejean, was permitted by the commandant there to try capital cases with a jury; he had been commissioned in 1767, before Detroit became part of the Province, and was allowed to continue his office; but he went too far, for we find him trying capital cases and sentencing at least one convict to death.[13]

When the Independence of the United States was acknowledged in 1783, a large number of Loyalists—the Cavaliers of the 18th Century—came north, and it was to meet their requirements that the new Districts were formed. Commissions of Oyer and Terminer and General Gaol Delivery were issued for all these Districts.

Except Hesse, none of the new Districts had a gaol (the gaol at Detroit was of long standing and constantly in use); it was accordingly provided by the Ordinance of April 30, 1789, 29 George III, cap. 3, that where the Commissioners of Oyer and Terminer and General Gaol Delivery thought it unsafe to keep within their District any prisoner convicted of a capital offence, they should send him to a gaol in the old Districts. It was also provided that if the Chief Justice of the Province should not be one of the Commissioners, execution of the sentence, if extending to life or limb or any greater fine than £25 sterling, should be stayed until the pleasure of the Governor should be known; and that a full report of the evidence, the rulings, the charge to the jury, etc., should be sent to the Governor for his information.

The Quarter Sessions were also to send to the Governor, the substance of the evidence, etc., whenever they imposed a fine of £25 sterling or more.

The same deficiency in gaol accommodation induced the Council at Quebec to change the law as to larceny.[14] In England at this time petty (or petit) larceny was the stealing of goods not above the value of one shilling,[15] the punishment for which was at the Common Law, whipping, or by Statute[16] transportation for seven years; grand larceny, the stealing of goods above the value of one shilling, was punishable with death, although by the "benefit of clergy"[17] the thief would in most cases escape for the first offence.

The Ordinance of April 30, 1789, recites that "the detention of prisoners until the sitting of the Court of King's Bench, or the sitting of the Commissioners of Oyer and Terminer and General Gaol Delivery, has been very burthensome to the public and is likely to be increased by the insufficiency of the Gaols in the Old Districts, and the total want of them in the New Districts, and it often happens that persons committed for simple larcenies[18] are either acquitted or only found guilty of petty larceny." It was indeed notorious that the mercy of juries would often make them strain a point and bring in the article stolen to be under the value of twelve pence, when it was really of much greater value; but, as Blackstone says,[19] this was "a kind of pious perjury."

This Ordinance of April 30, 1789, made simple larceny of not more than twenty shillings sterling only petty larceny, thereby enormously reducing the number of capital offences, for twenty shillings, about $5.00, was a large sum in those days. Then to relieve the gaols, whenever anyone was committed to gaol for a breach of the peace or a simple larceny he must find bail within forty-eight hours to appear for trial at the Quarter Sessions; or three Justices of the Peace could call the prisoner before them and try him without a jury; in case of conviction they could sentence him to such corporal punishment (not extending to Life or Limb) as they thought fit. If the offender had not been a stated resident of the Province for twelve months preceding his commitment and was found in the District twenty days after his punishment and discharge, he could be further punished unless he gave sureties for good behaviour for seven years. Outside of this modification, the whole brutal English Common Law was in force; brutal as it was, it must, however, be acknowledged that it was not so cruel as the displaced French law which allowed torture, breaking on the wheel and arbitrary imprisonment.

The Courts of Oyer and Terminer and General Gaol Delivery were conducted in much the same way as those in England; it may be of interest to set out the proceedings in one of the records which are still extant.

At L'Assomption (the present Sandwich in Ontario) in September, 1792, the Court opened, presided over by William Dummer Powell, then First Judge of the Court of Common Pleas of the Western District and living in Detroit.[20]

After the formal proceedings, the Coroner filed an Inquisition held on the body of Alexander Clark: Verdict—Natural Death; on the body of Wawanipi, an Indian man at Michilimackinac: Verdict—Murder by persons unknown; on the body of Francis Lalonde, taken at Saguina: Verdict—Death caused by Louis Roy; on the body of Pierre Grocher, taken at Detroit: Verdict—Wilful murder by an Indian man called Guillet. At the Common Law, an accused can be tried on a Coroner's Inquisition,[21] but it was always allowable to have a Bill of indictment found by the Grand Jury and to proceed on that. The Court directed an Indictment to be presented in the cases of Lalonde and Grocher; in Grocher's case a True Bill was found, a warrant was issued for the Indian, Guillet,[22] but he was not arrested when the Court rose.

A true bill was also found against Louis Roy, who was tried by a jury half French and half English; it turned out that the deceased, the prisoner and one Antoine Prevost had been "diverting themselves by throwing sticks, stones and mud at each other" at "Saguinau," and the prisoner had hit Lalonde with a stone and killed him; the jury found excusable homicide by misfortune. Nowadays, the prisoner would at once receive his discharge, but not so at the end of the Eighteenth Century. The homicide was excusable and therefore not felonious, but it implied some fault; the delinquent had consequently to sue out a pardon. This he received as of course and of right, but he had to pay the fees for suing it out. If the judge was lenient, he might allow the jury, or even direct them, to acquit.[23] In the present case the unfortunate Louis Roy was remanded to the custody of the Sheriff until he should receive a pardon.

Josiah Cutan was not so fortunate; he, a negro labourer living in Detroit, was indicted for burglary, had broken into the store of Joseph Campau, "on the north side of the River Detroit, about half a league above the Fort in a house the property of M. Jacques Campau, leased by Mr. Joseph Campau," and stolen some smoked skins, a bundle of peltry and two kegs of rum. He admitted taking the goods when asked by the owner. As someone generally slept in the store, it was considered a "mansion house," and the negro was promptly convicted and sentenced to death.[24]

The Grand Jury complained that a True Bill had been found at the previous Sittings against Chabouguoy and Cawquochish, two Indians, for the murder of David Lynd alias Jacquo of the River La Tranche (now the Thames in Ontario); they were still at large, and a warrant was issued for their arrest.

The murder of Albert Graverot, of Michillimackinac, trader, was also inquired into,[25] but no Bill seems to have been found.

The Grand Jury sat at the house of "Madame Marantate,"[26] the Petit Jury and the Court at the Court House in L'Assomption.

The Quarter Sessions.

As has been said, the Quarter Sessions met four times a year and tried non-capital cases with a jury. The Justices had also certain duties to perform themselves, e.g., laying out roads and buildings, preventing cattle, horses, hogs, etc., running at large, appointing constables and many other duties of the same and different nature.

But the interesting features are found on the judicial side.

When serious charges were made against anyone at the Sessions, he was remanded to be tried at the Sittings of Oyer and Terminer and General Gaol Delivery, e.g., murder, grand larceny,[27] sodomy,[28] rape.[29]

By far the greatest number of cases tried at the old Quarter Sessions were cases of assault; whiskey was cheap and plentiful; generally a small fine was imposed.

In some cases of Petty Larceny, the prisoner on conviction was tied to a post and received thirty-nine or a smaller number of lashes[30] on the bare back; one unfortunate woman convicted with her husband escaped the lash—the Court considering her delicate situation, and thinking she might have been influenced by her husband. Whipping was also inflicted in cases of assault where a fine was not thought sufficient punishment; there was no gaol convenient.

Sometimes the petty larcenor was sentenced to the pillory; the stocks were the fate of those who threatened or abused a magistrate.[31] "Contemptible" or "contemptuous" words concerning a magistrate were punished by a fine or imprisonment.

Through all the latter part of the Eighteenth and the early part of the Nineteenth Century, there was an influx from the colonies to the south which had become the United States. Not all these immigrants were United Empire Loyalists, and not all were even loyal to the Crown. During all the years now under discussion there was considerable seditious talk, much of it only talk and whiskey talk at that, but a source of annoyance to the loyalist settlers who had seen what the like sentiments had brought about in their old home to the south. Prompt measures were taken with offenders in that regard—for example, at the first sitting of the "Court of General Quarter Sessions of the Peace" in and for the District of Luneburg, which sat at Osnabruck, June 15, 1789, the third case tried was that of John Clark, who was found guilty of seditious behaviour; the Court, finding that he was "not a Subject of this Province, as not having taken the oath of allegiance to His Majesty," ordered him to depart from the Province and to remain in custody till he could be conveyed from the Province.

In the following June (June 9, 1790), Powell Frederick Landerman was convicted of "Seditious Expressions and Riotous Behaviour"—righteously we must conclude, for he came naked into a room at Phillip Crysler's house and said "he was rebel and would stand by that." As he could "offer nothing in support of his character to recommend him as a settler" in that District, and "his conduct was disloyal and improper, he was ordered to be Immediately sent out of this District by conveying him from one Captain of Militia to another till he be out of the said District"; he was accordingly sent where being a rebel was a recommendation, although his Adamic conception of decorous attire would probably not be approved.

The Magistrates seem to have been more determined to stamp out sedition than even the juries or some of them. At the October Court, 1793, Leonard Hilmer was indicted "for speaking seditious words against the King and Country"; the jury returned with a verdict of "Not Guilty," but the Court ordered them "to reconsider of their verdict." They reconsidered and brought in the same verdict, whereupon the Court required Hilmer "to take the Oaths required by law and give sufficient security for his Peaceable and good behaviour for a year and a day or else leave the Country Immediately."

That such precautions were necessary was abundantly proved by the event. The opportunity of obtaining free grants of valuable land to the north of the International boundary induced many Americans to cross over and settle. In many instances these were loyalists, or at least had not been rebels; but in many the republican and anti-British sentiment was strong and it persisted. Generally this sentiment was quiescent, but *in vino veritas*, and not uncommonly in moments of weakness the truth came out. Perhaps the most dangerous were not detected. However that may be, many parts of Upper Canada were honeycombed with treason; and when the trying time came in 1812, many who should have defended their country were recreant, and either joined the American troops or neglected their duty to serve. The German-American of later times had his prototype in the American-Canadian. It is a matter of gratification that these were in the main thoroughly loyal as it is to be hoped are those.

Perhaps another function of the Quarter Sessions may be mentioned, i.e., the public reading of Proclamations and Statutes of general importance; for example, we find the Marriage Act read, "and thereby hangs a tale."

By the French Canadian law which was in force, 1774-1792, by virtue of the Quebec Act (1774), 14 Geo. III, c. 85, (Imp.), till abolished by the Statute of (1792) 32 Geo. III, c. 1, (U.C.), a marriage to be valid required the presence of a priest—by the English law the presence of a priest of the Church of England was required. But these in a new country were scarce and hard to find; and young couples were married by Commanders of Military Posts, and even by Chaplains or by Surgeons and others acting as Chaplains. The danger of such irregular unions was apparent to the Legislature of Upper Canada; and in 1793, the Act 33 Geo. III, c. 5 (U.C.), validated such marriages and provided for marriages being solemnized by Magistrates of any District until there should be "five parsons or ministers of the Church of England" in the District. The Act by Section 7, provided that it should be read in all the Districts of the Province at the opening of the first General Quarter Sessions of the Peace and then once a year for two years.

The celebrated Proclamation against Vice was also read, no doubt with the usual result or want of result.

NOTES

[1]This Proclamation will be found in the Fourth Report of the Ontario Archives (1906), pp. 2, sqq; also in Shortt & Doughty—Constitutional Documents, 1759-1791, Canadian Archives Reports, 1907 (Sessional Paper No. 18), pp. 119, sqq.
[2](1774), 14 George III, c. 85 (Imp.).
[3]The word "Northward" gave rise long after to a dispute between the Dominion of Canada and the Province of Ontario. The Dominion had (1876) created a Territory (Keewatin) with its eastern boundary, the western boundary of Ontario. Ontario had succeeded to all the territory of the Province of Quebec as constituted by the Act of 1774 north of the United States, and west of the present Province of Quebec; and claimed that "Northward" meant "Northward along the Mississippi." The Dominion claimed that "Northward" meant "due North." On the matter being referred to arbitration, the arbitrators (1878) found in favour of Ontario. The Judicial Committee of the Privy Council agreed with this finding; and on petition of the Parliament of Canada the question was placed beyond controversy by the Act (1889) 52, 53 Vic. c. 28, (Imp.).
[4]Without discussing the merits of the controversy, it will be sufficient here to state the facts. The Treaty of Paris, September 3, 1783, by Act IV, expressly provided that "creditors on either side shall meet no lawful impediment to the recovery of the full value in sterling money of all bona fide debts heretofore contracted." Some of the States passed legislation (declared valid by the local courts) which prevented British creditors from recovering from American debtors. The offending States refused to repeal these laws and the United States could not compel them to do so. To the many representations made by the United States concerning the retention by Britain of the border posts (Michillimackinac, Detroit, Miamis, Niagara, Oswego, Point au Fer and Dutchman's Point), the answer was returned that Britain should remain in possession of the territory until redress should be given to British subjects. At length, John Jay went to England and succeeded in obtaining a Treaty November 19, 1794, (commonly known as Jay's Treaty) by which the United States agreed to pay these debts and Britain to give up the retained territory. Britain carried out her part, August, 1796, and the United States in 1802 paid £600,000 in full.
[5]The Proclamation (or Patent) will be found in the Fourth Ont. Archives Report (1906), pp. 157, 158. Shortt & Doughty, *op. cit.*, p. 650. It may be added that these German names were changed to Eastern, Midland, Home and Western by the First Parliament of Upper Canada in 1792, 32 Geo. III, c. 8 (U.C.) They included the settlements around Cornwall, Kingston, Niagara and Detroit, and vast unsettled territory.
[6]In 1791, the former Province of Quebec was divided into the Provinces of Lower Canada and Upper Canada, the latter being the same territory as what I call "Upper Canada," but this appellation I employ to indicate the territory as well before as after Upper Canada came into existence.

⁷It may be interesting to give the Commission in full for the District of Hesse (including Detroit, Michillimackinac, etc.):—

General Commission: of the Peace for the District of Hesse.
(Signed)
Dorchester G:—

Fiat
Recorded in the
Office of Enrollment at Quebec
the 28th day
July, 1788, in
the third Reg.
of Letters patent and Commissions.
Folio 257.
G. Pownall.

GEORGE the third by the grace of God of Great Britain, France and Ireland, King, Defender of the faith, &ca. TO OUR trusty and Well-beloved Henry Hope, Lieut. Governor, William Smith, Chief Justice, Hugh Finlay, Thomas Dunn, Edward Harrison, John Collins, Adam Mabane, Joseph Gaspard Chaussegros Delery, George Pownall, Picotte de Bellestre, John Fraser, Henry Caldwell, William Grant, Paul Rock St. Ours, Francois Baby, Joseph de Longueuil, Samuel Holland, George Davison, Sir John Johnson, Bart., Charles de Lanaudiere, Rene Amable Boucherville and Le Comte Dupre, Members of Our Council for Our Province of Quebec, and to Our loving subjects, Alexander Grant, William Lamotte, St. Martin Adhemar, William Macomb of Detroit, Joncaire de Chabort, Alexander Maisonville of the opposite side of the River at Detroit, William Caldwell, Mathew Elliot of the new Settlement at the mouth of the River Detroit & Benac Porlier of River Raisin, Esquires.

GREETING. KNOW YE that WE have assigned you jointly and severally and every one of you Our Justices to keep Our Peace in Our District of Hesse in Our said Province of Quebec, and to keep and cause to be kept, all Ordinances Statutes and Laws for the good of the peace and for preservation of the same; and for the quiet rule and Government of Our People, made in all and singular their articles in Our said District of Hesse, (as well within liberties as without) according to the force form & effect of the same; And to chastise and punish all persons that offend against the form of those Ordinances Statutes and Laws, or any of them in the District aforesaid, as it ought to be done according to the form and purport of those Laws, Ordinances & Statutes; and to cause to come before you or any of you, all those who to anyone or more of Our People concerning their bodies or the Firing of their Houses have used threats to find sufficient security for the Peace or their good behaviour towards US and Our People and if they shall refuse to find such security then to cause them to be safely kept in Our Prisons until they shall find such security. We have also assigned you and every two or more of you, of whom any one of you the aforesaid Henry Hope, William Smith, Hugh Finlay, Thomas Dunn, Edward Harrison, John Collins, Adam Mabane, Joseph Gaspard Chaussegros Delery, George Pownall, Picotte de Bellestre, John Fraser, Henry Caldwell, William Grant, Paul Rock Saint Ours, Francois Baby, Joseph de Longueuil, Samuel Holland, George Davison, Sir John Johnson, Bart., Charles de Lanaudiere, Rene Amable Boucherville and Le Comte Dupre, Members of Our Council for Our said Province, Alexander Grant, Guillaume Lamotte and St. Martin Adhemar of Detroit—We will shall be one, Our Justices to enquire the truth more fully by the oath of good and lawful men of the District aforesaid by whom the truth of the matter may be the better known of all, and all manner of Felonies, poisonings, Enchantments, Sorceries, Art Magick, Trespasses, forestallings, regratings, engrossings, and extortions whatsoever and of all singular other crimes and offences, of which the Justices of Our Peace may or ought lawfully to enquire by whomsoever & after what manner soever in the said District done or perpetrated or which, or which shall happen to be there done or attempted; and also of all those who in the aforesaid district in Companies against Our Peace in disturbance of Our People with armed force have gone or rode or hereafter shall presume to go or ride. And also of all those who have there lain in wait, or hereafter shall presume to lie in wait to maim or cut or kill Our people, and also of all victuallers and all and singular other persons who in the abuse of weights or measures, or in selling victuals against the form of the Ordinances, Statutes and Laws, of Our said Province, or any one of them in that behalf made for the Common Benefit of Our said province, and Our people thereof, have offended or attempted, or hereafter shall presume in the said District to offend or attempt And also of all Sheriffs, Bailiffs, Stewards, Constables, Keepers of Gaols and other Officers who in the execution of their Offices, about the premises, or any of them have unduly behaved themselves or hereafter shall presume to behave themselves unduly or have been or shall happen hereafter to be careless, remiss or negligent, in Our District aforesaid, and of all and singular articles and circumstances and all other things whatsoever that concern the premises or any of them by whomsoever and after what manner soever in Our aforesaid District done or perpetrated, or which hereafter shall there happen to be done or attempted in what manner soever; And to inspect all Indictments, whatsoever, so before you, or any of you taken or to be taken or before others late Our Justices of the Peace in the aforesaid District made or taken and not yet determined, and to make and continue processes thereupon against all and singular the persons so indicted, or who before you hereafter shall happen to be indicted, until they can be taken, surrender themselves or be out-lawed, and to hear and determine all and singular the Felonies, Poisonings, Inchantments, Sorceries, Art Magick, Trespasses, Forestallings, Regratings, engrossings, extortions, unlawful assemblies, indictments aforesaid and all and singular other the premises according to the Laws and Statutes of England and the Laws of Our said Province, as in the like cases it has been accustomed or ought to be done:—

AND the same offenders and every of them for their Offences by Fines, Ransoms, Amerciaments, Forfeitures and other means, as according to the Law and Custom of England or form of the Ordinances and Statutes aforesaid and the laws of the said Province, it has been accustomed or ought to be done to Chastise and punish. PROVIDED Always that if a case of difficulty upon the determination of any the premises before you or any two or more of you shall happen to arise; then let Judgment in nowise be given thereon before you or any two or more of you unless in the presence of Our Chief Justice of Our Court of Kings Bench of Our Province aforesaid or of one, or more of Our Justices specially appointed to hold the assizes in the aforesaid District, and therefore WE command you & every of you that to keeping the Peace Ordinances, Statutes and all and singular other the premises you diligently apply yourselves, and at certain days & places which you or any such two or more of you as aforesaid, shall for these purposes appoint into the—Ye make enquiries and all and singular the Premises hear and determine and perform and fulfil them in the aforesaid form doing therein what to Justice appertains according to the Law and Customs of England and the Ordinances as above mentioned.

SAVING TO US the Amerciaments and other things to Us therefrom belonging; And WE Command by the tenor of these Presents OUR Sheriff of the said District of Hesse that at certain days and places which you or any such two or more of you as aforesaid shall make down to him, he cause to come before you, or such two or more of you as aforesaid, so many and such good and Lawful men of this District and Bailewick (as well within liberties as without) by whom the truth of the matter in the premises shall be the better known and enquired into; And lastly We Command the Keepers of the Rolls of Our Peace of the said District, that he bring before you and your said Fellows at the days and places aforesaid, the writs, precepts, processes, and Indictments aforesaid, that they may be inspected and by a due course determined as is aforesaid.

IN TESTIMONY whereof WE have caused these OUR Letters to be made patent and the Great Seal of Our said Province to be thereunto affixed, and the same to be recorded in one of the Books of Patents in Our Registers Office of Enrollments of Our said Province Remaining.

WITNESS OUR trusty and well beloved Guy Lord Dorchester Our Captain General and Governor in Chief of Our said Province At Our Castle of Saint Lewis in Our City of Quebec this Twenty-fourth day of July, in the year of Our Lord One Thousand seven hundred and eighty-eight and of Our Reign the Twenty-eighth.

(Signed) D.G.

(Signed) Geo. Pownall, Secy.

Dedimus potestatem
to Duperon Baby
Alexander McKee and
William Robertson Esquires
Justices of the Court
of Common Pleas for the
District of Hesse in Our
Province of Quebec to administer
Oaths. Tested at the Castle
of St. Lewis in Quebec 24th July
28 GEO III.

[8] 36 Edw. III, c. 12 ; 12 Ric. II, c. 10; 2 Hen. V, St. I, c. 4. The Quebec Ordinances are (1777) 17 Geo. III, c. 5; (1789) 29 Geo. III, c. 3.

[9] That previously, e.g., in the Tudor times, the Quarter Sessions had tried thousands of capital crimes and caused the hanging of thousands of thieves, etc., there can be no doubt. There is a tradition that the Quarter Sessions of the District of Mecklenburg (at Kingston) tried and sentenced to death a supposed thief, which sentence was duly carried out and the very tree where the innocent man was hanged was long pointed out. But this is certainly a myth.

[10] See Blackstone's Commentaries, Book IV, pp. 268, 269.

[11] A Commission of Oyer and Terminer authorized the Commissioner to try criminal cases on which the True Bill was found in his own Court: that of General Gaol Delivery to try all persons in the Gaol by whomsoever the True Bill was found. In practice they were united. An actual Commission is here copied. (The Commission of Special Gaol Delivery to try special cases only was very rare in either England or Canada and needs no comment.) The history of these Commissions is touched on in my Article, "New Trial at the Common Law", *Yale Law Journal*, Nov. 1916, pp. 57, 58.

(Sig'd)
Dorchester Gov:
Fiat
Recorded in the
Office of Enrollments
at Quebec the 20th
Day of January, 1791,
in the third Register
of Letters Patent &
Commissions, folio 472.
Geo. Pownall.

  GEORGE THE THIRD, by the Grace of God, of Great Britain, France and Ireland, KING, Defender of the Faith and so forth. TO OUR Trusty and Well beloved William Dummer Powell OUR first Justice of OUR Court of Common Pleas of and in OUR District of Hesse in OUR Province of Quebec, and to William Lamothe, St. Martin Adhemar, William McComb, John Askin and George Meldrum, Esquires, Justices of the Peace for the said District, GREETING: KNOW YE that WE have assigned you and any three of you (of whom WE will that you the said William Dummer Powell be one) to inquire by the Oath of Good and Lawful Men of the District aforesaid by whom the truth of the matter may be the better known, and by other ways, methods and means whereby you can or may the better know, as well within liberties as without, more fully the truth of all Treasons, Misprisions of Treason, Insurrections, Rebellions, Murders, Felonies, Manslaughters, Killings, Burglaries, Rapes of Women, unlawful meetings and Conventicles, unlawful uttering of words, unlawful assemblies, misprisons, Confederacies, false allegations, Trespasses, Riots, Routs, Retentions, Escapes, Contempts, Falseties, negligencies, Concealments, Maintenances, Oppressions, Champarties, Deceits, and all other Misdeeds, Offences and injuries whatsoever, and also the accessories of the same within the District aforesaid, as well within Liberties as without, by whomsoever and howsoever, done, perpetrated and Committed, and by whom and to whom, when, how and in what manner, and of all other Articles and Circumstances whatsoever, the premises and every or any of them howsoever concerning, and the said Treasons and other the premises according to the Law and Custom of England and the Laws of this Province for this time to hear and determine. And therefore WE command you that at certain days and places which you or any three of you (whereof WE will that you the said William Dummer Powell be one) shall for this purpose appoint within and for the space of six Calendar Months from the day of the Date of these Presents, you do concerning the Premises make diligent inquiry, and all and Singular the Premises hear and determine and those things to do and fulfil in form aforesaid which are and ought to be done and to Justice doth appertain according to the Law and Custom of England and the Laws of OUR said Province, SAVING to us OUR Amerciaments and other things to us thereupon belonging. For WE have Commanded OUR Sheriff of the said District that at certain Days and places which you or any three of you (of whom WE will that you the said William Dummer Powell be one) shall make known within and for the space of Six Calendar Months from the day of the Date of these Presents he cause to come before you or any three of you (of whom WE will that you the said Wm. Dummer Powell be one) such and so many Good and Lawful Men of his Bailiwick (as well within liberties as without) by whom the truth of the Premises may be the better inquired of and known

  AND KNOW YE further that WE have also Constituted and assigned you or any three of you (of whom WE will that you the said William Dummer Powell be one) OUR Justices the Goal of OUR said District of the Prisoners in the same being for this time to deliver. AND therefore WE command you that at a certain Day which you or any three of you (of whom WE will that you the said William Dummer Powell be one) shall appoint you do meet at Detroit, OUR GOAL of OUR said District to deliver, and to do thereupon what to Justice may appertain, according to the Law and Custom of England and the Laws of OUR said Province, SAVING TO US OUR Amerciaments and other things to us thereupon belonging. For WE have Commanded and hereby command OUR Sheriff of OUR District of Hesse that at a certain Day which you or any three of you (of whom WE will that you the said William Dummer Powell be one) to him shall make known, all the Prisoners of the said Goal and their attachments before you or any three of you (of whom WE will that you the said William Dummer Powell be one) there he cause to come. IN TESTIMONY whereof WE have caused these OUR Letters to be made Patent and the Great Seal of Our said Province of Quebec to be hereunto affixed. WITNESS OUR Trusty and Wellbeloved GUY LORD DORCHESTER OUR Captain General and Governor in Chief of OUR said Province. AT OUR CASTLE of Saint Lewis in OUR City of Quebec this Twentieth Day of January, in the year of OUR LORD One thousand seven hundred and ninety-one and of OUR REIGN the Thirty-first.

(Signed) D.G.
(Signed) Geo: Pownall. Sec'y.

[12]Ordinance of March 17, 1777: 17 Geo. III, c. 5. There had been a Court of King's Bench of both civil and criminal jurisdiction erected by Governor Murray in 1764, September 17; but this was abolished by the Quebec Act of 1774.

[13]As to Detroit and this Justice of the Peace, I have said in "The First Judge at Detroit and his Court," an address before the Michigan Bar Association:

"Turning now to the state of affairs at Detroit—from the surrender of Detroit by the French for a few years, the occupation by the British was by force of arms and conquest; but the Treaty of 1763 made legal what had previously been by force.

"During this period of two or three years, there does not seem to have been anything in the way of civil courts, the British commandants following the example of their French predecessors.

"They took it upon themselves after the formal cession to commission Justices of the Peace—it is said that Gabriel Le Grand acted under some commission of the kind as early as 1763.

"In the 'Pontiac Manuscript,' under date May 20th, 1763, mention is made of 'Mr. Le Grand who has been substituted as judge in the place of Mr. St. Cosme'; and he seems to have been acting as judge in 1765.

"Two years later, Philip Dejean received a similar commission. In the same year, 1767, the Commandant, Major Bayard, gave Dejean another commission as 'Second Judge' to hold a 'Tempery Court of Justice to be held twice in every month at Detroit, to Decide on all actions of Debt, Bond, Bills, Contracts and Trespasses above the value of £5 New York Currency.' (In the New York currency, a shilling was 12½ cents—a York shilling or 'Yorker,' still in vogue on the north shore of Lake Ontario in my boyhood, fifty years ago; £1 = 20s. = $2.50.

"When Henry Hamilton was sent as Lieutenant-Governor in 1775, he allowed Dejean to continue in his Court as Justice of the Peace, and Dejean went far beyond the limits of the authority of a Justice of the Peace. We are told that a man and woman were tried in 1776 by Dejean with a jury, six English and six French, on a charge of arson and larceny, but the jury 'doubted of the arson.' The man was executed, it is said, by the hands of the woman, who thus bought her freedom. The attention of the authorities at Quebec was drawn to the state of matters in Detroit, by the extraordinary proceedings, and warrants were issued for Governor and Justice. The Grand Jury at the Court of King's Bench at Montreal on Monday, September 7th, 1778, presented Dejean for divers unjust & illegal Terranical & felonious Acts' during 1775, 1776 and 1777 at Detroit; and Henry Hamilton, the Governor, for that he 'tolerated, suffered and permitted the same under the Government, guidance and direction'—hence the warrant.

"The stirring times following the American invasion of Quebec were on, and the offenders escaped immediate punishment.

"By letter of April 16th, 1779, Lord George Germain, Secretary of State for the Colonies (afterwards Viscount Sackville), wrote: 'The presentments of the Grand Jury at Montreal against Lieut.-Gov. Hamilton and Mr. Dejean are expressive of a greater degree of jealousy than the transaction complained of in the then circumstances of the Province appeared to warrant. Such stretches of authority are, however, only to be excused by unavoidable necessity and the justness and fitness of the occasion.' He therefore ordered that the Chief Justice should examine the evidence of 'The Criminal's Guilt, and if he be of opinion that he merited the Punishment . . . tho' irregularly inflicted . . . a 'nolle prosequi' should be entered.' This was done."

[14]All these provisions are to be found in the Ordinance of April 30, 1789, 29 George III, c. 3.
[15]Blackstone's Commentaries, Bk. IV, p. 229.
[16](1717) 4 George I, c. 11. See Blackstone's Commentaries, Bk. IV, p. 238.
[17]A second conviction for grand larceny meant felony "without benefit of clergy." No lawyer is at all likely to think with some popular writers that this means "without the benefit of

clerical attention and advice." Of course it originally was the privilege allowed to a Clerk in Holy Orders, when prosecuted in the temporal Courts, of being discharged from such Court and turned over to the ecclesiastical Courts—in other words to get clear almost altogether. This privilege was gradually extended to all who could read, and many a notorious rascal escaped well-merited punishment by reading his "neck verse" possibly by a recently learned accomplishment. Ultimately, in 1706, by 6 Anne, ch. 9, the privilege was extended to all convicted persons whether they could read or not.

This privilege did not extend to all felonies, but only to capital felonies, and even of these some were "without benefit of clergy"; moreover, by an early Statute, (1488) 4 Henry VII, ch. 13, laymen allowed their clergy were burned in the hand, and could not claim it the second time; and the practice grew up of imprisoning for life, clergymen where the offence was heinous and notorious.

"Benefit of Clergy" was abolished in England by sec. 6 of the Criminal Law Act of 1827, and in Upper Canada in 1833 by 3 William IV, ch. 3, sec. 25 (U.C.). This Act provided that all crimes made by the Act itself punishable with death—murder and accessory before the fact to murder, rape, carnal knowledge of a girl under ten, sodomy, robbery of the mail, burglary, arson, riot after the reading of the Riot Act, destruction of His Majesty's dockyards, etc. (a sufficiently long list indeed) should be so punished; but that all other felonies should be punishable by banishment or imprisonment for any term not exceeding fourteen years. Thus the thief escaped the punishment of death, to the great grief of many very good and very intelligent people who thought that a death sentence for the offender was the only safeguard for society.

[18]"Simple larceny" is the felonious taking and carrying away of the personal goods of another, "plain theft unaccompanied by any other atrocious circumstance"; it may be grand or petty larceny; while "mixed or compound larceny includes in it the aggravation of a taking from one's house or person." Blackstone's Commentaries, Bk. IV, pp. 229, 230.

[19]Blackstone's Commentaries, Bk. IV, p. 239.

[20]He was born in Boston, Mass.; educated there, in England and on the Continent, practised law at Montreal, became First Judge in 1789 and afterwards (1794) Justice and (1816) Chief Justice in Upper Canada. An admirable lawyer and a man of much force of character, he played no inconsiderable part in the public and private life of Upper Canada for many years; he died in 1834. See my "Life of William Dummer Powell," Lansing, Mich., 1924.

[21]Blackstone's Commentaries, Bk. IV, p. 299. This practice was abolished in Canada by the Criminal Code of 1892.

[22]A Canadian called Guillet is spoken of by Vaudreuil in 1717 as having influence over the Indians (Mich. Pioneer & Hist. Coll., vol. 33, p. 591), and a family of that name lived at Detroit.

[23]The absurdity of compelling the unfortunate man to sue out a pardon was introduced by the Statute in 1278 of Gloucester, 6 Edw. 1, c. 7: "the King shall make him his Grace if it please him" ("face le Rei sa grace si lui plest," as the delightful Norman French has it). This was abolished in England in 1828 by the Statute 9 Geo. IV, c. 31, s. 10 (Imp.); in Canada in 1841 by 4, 5, Vic., c. 27, s. 8 (Can.).

[24]The death penalty was prescribed for all kinds of burglary in Canada until 1841, although for many years before 1841 there was almost (if not quite) always a commutation. The Act (1841) 4, 5, Vic., c. 25, s. 14 (Can.), restricted the death penalty to breaking and entering a dwelling house and assaulting some person therein, while the ordinary burglary was punishable with imprisonment for life, s. 15. The death penalty was removed altogether in 1869 by 32, 33 Vic., c. 21, s. 51 (Can.).

The address to the convicted person by the Judge, William Dummer Powell, may be quoted. After speaking of the crime the Judge says: "This crime is so much more atrocious and alarming to society as it is committed by night when the world is at repose and that it cannot be guarded against without the same precautions which are used against the wild beasts of the forest, who like you go prowling about by night for their prey. A member so hurtful to the peace of society, no good laws will permit to continue in it, and the Court in obedience to the Law has imposed on it the painful duty of pronouncing its sentence, which is that you be taken from hence, etc., etc."

[25]Graverat & Viger were a well-known trading firm in Detroit, trading to Michillimackinac; possibly the murdered man was connected with them. The name is spelled "Graverod," "Graverad," "Graverat," and "Graverot."

[26]Marantate, Marantete, Marantette, was a well-known name in Detroit and L'Assomption. "Francois Marantete a Frenchman" is spoken of by Lieut.-Governor Henry Hamilton in his report to Governor-in-Chief Haldimand, Sept. 22, 1778 (Mich. Pion. Coll., vol. 9, p. 479). This Francois Marantete was probably a merchant from Montreal, the father of Dominique Marantete.

Dominique married Archange Marie Louise Navarre, the daughter of Col. Robert Navarre of the French army. They had a large family of whom there are still a number of descendants in Michigan and Ontario. The house of "Madame Marantate" (the above-named wife of Dominique Marantete) was on the banks of the Detroit River about a quarter of a mile above the old French church near Sandwich, Ontario. (Mich. Pion. Coll., vol. 6, p. 497.)

[27] I intend to quote from the records of the District of Luneburg only, and from 1789 to 1794. In Canada at this time larceny of more than twenty shillings sterling was grand larceny and punishable with death; in 1833, by the Act, 3 Wm. IV, c. 3 (U.C.), the penalty of death was removed and banishment or transportation for not less than seven years or imprisonment for not more than fourteen years was substituted in grand larceny; petty larceny was not affected.

In 1837, by the Statute, 7 Wm. IV, c. 4 (U.C.), the distinction between grand and petty larceny was abolished, and the Quarter Sessions given power to try all simple larceny, grand as well as petty. Banishment, which had been substituted for the English transportation in 1800 by 40 Geo. III, c. 1 (U.C.), could be awarded by the Quarter Sessions for seven years or imprisonment for two years. The Quarter Sessions was allowed by Sec. 5 of the Act of 1837 to leave difficult or important cases for the Courts of Oyer and Terminer and General Gaol Delivery. These Courts could banish or imprison as before. Transportation might be substituted for banishment, (1837) 7 Wm. IV, c. 7 (U.C.). In 1841, by the Act, 4, 5, Vic., c. 25, an imprisonment alone was the punishment, banishment and transportation being abolished; and so it stands to-day. The English Acts 7, 8 Geo. IV, c. 29; 7 Wm. IV, c. 90, may be compared.

[28] Punishable with death till 1870, 32, 33 Vic., c. 20 (Dom.).

[29] Punishable with death until 1873, 36 Vic., c. 50 (Dom.), which allowed the Court to substitute imprisonment for not less than seven years; the English Statutes are 9 Geo. IV, c. 31, and 4, 5 Vic., c. 31.

[30] The lash for petty larceny did not absolutely disappear from the law of Upper Canada until 1837.

[31] The pillory was abolished in 1841 by 4, 5 Vic., c. 24, s. 31 (Can.); the stocks disappeared at the same time. Neither had been in use for several years before. In England, the use of the pillory was in 1816 limited by 56 Geo. III, c. 138 and abolished by 7 Wm. IV, c. 23 (1837).

XVII

THE "ORDINARY" COURT OF CHANCERY IN UPPER CANADA

An Attempt by the Lieutenant-Governor to Act as Chancellor

By the Honourable William Renwick Riddell, LL.D., F.R.S.C., &c.

Until the Legislature of Upper Canada made other provisions, the law in the Province in civil matters was the French Canadian law, practically the *Coutume de Paris*. In this law, based as it was on the Civil Law, there was not the distinction of Law and Equity, which is an English conception. The Courts of Common Pleas in the four Districts in Upper Canada (being the only courts of civil jurisdiction) decided accordingly, not being hampered by the technical rules of English law and procedure; these courts had, and frequently exercised, equitable jurisdiction and gave relief quite unknown to the English Common Law.[1]

The first Act of the Legislature of the new Province (in 1792) enacted "that in all matters of controversy relative to property and civil rights, resort shall be had to the laws of England as the rule for the decision of the same."[2]

When by the Royal Proclamation of October 7, 1763, the English law had been substituted for the previously existing French Canadian law in the original Province of Quebec, it was recognised that there might be necessity for something in the way of a Court of Equity. The Governor-General, James Murray, (as afterwards Sir Guy Carleton and others), being entrusted with the Great Seal of the Province of Quebec, was considered to be *ipso facto* Chancellor of the Province; and he sat as such in a Court of Chancery at Quebec.[3]

Nothing of the kind was done in Upper Canada; while the Lieutenant-Governor, as Keeper of the Great Seal of the Province, was considered in law to be Chancellor of the Province, he did not assume to sit as such for thirty years.

There was nothing in the Act of 1792 which expressly deprived the existing Courts of Common Pleas of Equitable Jurisdiction; but it was interpreted, and rightly so, to leave to these Courts, the powers of an English Court of Common Law only.[4]

When in 1794 these Courts were abolished and the Court of King's Bench erected for the whole Province, there could be no semblance of doubt that there was no Court of Equitable Jurisdiction. The Judicature Act of 1794 gave to the Court of King's Bench thereby created the powers of "His Majesty's Courts of King's Bench, Common Bench or in matters which regard the King's revenue . . . the Court of Exchequer in England."[5]

There were in the following two decades several propositions looking to the establishment of a Court of Chancery, but none came to fruition.[6] In the official correspondence, indeed, it was suggested that the Lieutenant-Governor might have the power under his Commission and Instructions to erect a Court of Chancery; but it was not considered wise for him to attempt to do so without the concurrence of the Legislature. It came to be considered the better opinion that since the Bill of Rights, the Crown could not "by the exercise of its prerogative merely, erect any jurisdiction with power to judge otherwise than according to the course of the Common Law,"[7] and notwithstanding the precedent of the Old Province of Quebec, Nova Scotia and several of the West India Islands, the Governor did not erect a Court of Chancery by the exercise of a supposed prerogative. The Legislature did not see fit to erect such a Court until 1837.[8]

But the fact that there was no statutory Court of Chancery did not prevent the Lieutenant-Governor acting as a Chancellor; and the object of this paper is to give an account of two curious incidents of this kind in our legal history.

The word "Chancery," "Cancellaria," has a wide connotation in English law including as it does all the agencies whereby the functions of the Chancellor were performed (except such as selecting judges, presiding in the House of Lords, etc., etc.). The Chancellor was recognised as one of the representatives of the King—as Chief Justice William de Shareshull said in 1354, a command of the King to appear *coram nobis* may be *Coram nobis* which means before the King in person in his own hall, *Coram nobis ubicunque, etc.*, which means in the Court of the King's Bench or *Coram nobis in cancellaria nostra* which means before the Chancellor.[9]

The Cancellaria in England it has been usual to divide into the Ordinary Court and the Extraordinary Court (or Court of Equity). The former was always open; and from it issued all original writs, Commissions of Lieutenants of Counties, of Justices of Assize, of Oyer and Terminer and General Gaol Delivery, of Justices of the Peace, etc., etc. So, too, when elections for Parliament came into existence, the Writs of Election were issued therefrom, and were returnable thereto into the custody of an officer called the Clerk of the Crown in Chancery. The latter Court, the Extraordinary Court, was the Court of Chancery proper, a Court of Equity. In this paper, it will not be further spoken of except incidentally.

Upper Canada began her Provincial career in December, 1791, with provision for a Parliament, one of the Houses of which was composed of elected members; the Constitution was intended to be "the very image and transcript of that of Great Britain";[10] it was accordingly necessary for that, if for no other reason, that there should be at least theoretically an "Ordinary Court" of Chancery. Whatever may have been the law in England before 1562—and that may not be quite certain—in that year, Parliament gave to a Keeper of the Great Seal the same power and authority for the time being as a Chancellor.[11] In the nature of things and *ex necessitate*, he was the Keeper of the Great Seal to whom the Great Seal was entrusted as such. As we have seen, from the earlier times in British Canada, as in other British Provinces, the Governor, who was entrusted with the Great Seal of the Province[12] was, as such Keeper, considered to be the Chancellor of the Province. The Lieutenant-Governor, or Administrator for the time being, from the first year of the separate life of the Province until 1841,[13] was considered Chancellor of Upper Canada. The duties of Clerk of the Crown in Chancery were performed by the Provincial

Secretary (who was not yet a Member of Parliament); he used the title of "Clerk of the Crown in Chancery," however, only in matters relating to Parliament, elections, etc.[14]

It was not routine or administrative business alone which came under the cognizance of the "Ordinary" Court of Chancery; in England, it had, amongst other things, jurisdiction in Writs of *Scire Facias* for the repeal of Letters Patent when issued improvidently or in error, through fraud or the like. This was part of the Common Law jurisdiction of the Chancellor; and in such cases, as in the "Ordinary" Court generally, the proceedings were carried on judicially and in accordance with the rules and maxims of the Common Law of England.

One instance has been found of the exercise, or attempted exercise, of this power judicially by the Lieutenant Governor of the Province of Upper Canada.[15]

First Incident

A "Military Settlement" was projected in the County of Carleton, as then bounded, in the second decade of the 19th Century; and members of several of the Corps who had borne arms in the War of 1812-15 were settled upon land in the Township of Bathurst. Before they could obtain their patents, it was necessary for them to make certain specified improvements. Abraham Parsall was placed on the east half (sometimes called the northeast half) of Lot 20 in the 2nd Concession of the Township of Bathurst; on this lot was a valuable waterpower, and Parsall not only made large improvements, but he also built a mill which was a great convenience to the settlement.[16]

Samuel Swan, who had been in the field train department during the war, was settled on the east half of Lot No. 20 in the 4th Concession; he also, in expectation of receiving a grant of the land, made the improvements on this lot, required to entitle him to his patent from the Crown. When these two men and others were settled in the first instance on their lots, their names were written across their lots on the map in the Landgranting Department. Both seem to have been of United Empire Loyalist extraction. The Superintendent of the Military Settlements in Upper Canada reported that both Parsall and Swan were entitled to their Patent; a clerk in the Department of Lands, copying the return, by a slip of the pen made Swan entitled to the lot upon which Parsall had been placed and upon which he had made his improvements. Thereupon, on April 15, 1820, a Patent issued to Swan of the 100 acres to which Parsall had become entitled. Parsall, indeed, was dead, but he had left a will whereby he devised this land to Joshua Adams; Adams succeeded to the rights of Parsall and should have received a Patent for the land. The Letters Patent were sealed and recorded in the office of the Registrar General and actually delivered to Swan without the error being discovered. At once, complaint was made by the devisee, Adams, to Lieutenant Colonel J. H. Powell, Land Commissioner at Perth, and he brought the matter before the Surveyor General, Thomas Ridout; enquiry was instituted and the mistake and its cause were speedily discovered. Swan was seen and at first he professed readiness to surrender the grant on having his title confirmed to the lot to which he was actually entitled, i.e., the east half of Lot No. 20, in the 4th Concession. A Patent dated April 12, 1820, had been issued to him for the east half of Lot No. 19 in the

2nd Concession but not of the east half of Lot No. 20 in the 4th Concession; this latter was withheld. Swan seems to have sought legal advice and to have been advised that there was no machinery for cancelling the erroneous grant; at all events he changed his mind about surrendering his patent and determined to take and hold the land upon which his neighbour had expended much money and had made valuable improvements. He set the Government at defiance and brought an action in ejectment to gain possession.

There had been cases in the Province in which Patents of land had been issued improvidently or had been obtained by fraud and misrepresentation of some person to the prejudice of others or of the Crown; but no steps had been taken to set them aside or to correct the error. This case, however, was so grave an outrage that the Attorney General, John Beverley Robinson, brought the matter before the Executive Council. On Wednesday, February 7, 1821, the Council directed that steps should be taken to cancel Swan's Patent.[17]

After another and abortive attempt to move the stubborn Swan, a Writ of *Scire Facias* was issued, August 2 (registered August 4), 1821, ordering the Sheriff of the District of Johnstown that "by good and faithful men of your Bailiwick, you give notice to the said Samuel Swan that he be before us in our Chancery on the first day of Michaelmas Term next wheresoever it shall be, to show if he hath or can say anything for himself why the said Letters Patent . . . . . ought not to be cancelled, vacated, disallowed."[18]

This writ was of course based upon the record of the Letters Patent in the Registrar General's office; and it comes under the second of Coke's three cases in which the writ lies: "Secondly, when the King granteth anything that is grantable, upon a false suggestion, the King by his prerogative *jure regio*, may have a *scire facias* to repeal his own grant."[19]

The Sheriff served Swan with a copy of the writ and a summons to appear. Swan through his attorney (there were as yet no solicitors)[20] entered his appearance in the office of the Clerk of the Crown in Chancery. A "Declaration," *i.e.* Statement of Claim, was delivered on the part of the Crown and the defendant Swan pleaded "in abatement" and denied that there was any such Court or jurisdiction in the Province as that in which the proceeding by *Scire Facias* purported to be instituted. To this the Attorney General demurred, which definitely brought up the question of the constitution of the Court and its jurisdiction.

Sir Peregrine Maitland, the Lieutenant Governor of Upper Canada, sat at his house in Court as Chancellor; and with him sat William Dummer Powell, Chief Justice of the Province. The question of the existence of the Court was argued at length[21] and judgment reserved.

There is no report of the argument—the first Court Reporter was not appointed until 1823[22]—but there are two letters and an opinion of Chief Justice Powell from which we can reconstitute the position taken on either side.[23] The argument was two-fold—first as to the existence of the Court itself, and second as to the jurisdiction of the Court, if it did exist, over the particular Letters Patent under attack. Upon the first point, the legal existence of the Court, defendant's counsel based his case upon the familiar principle that while the King by his Royal Prerogative may prescribe for territory acquired by

15 H.P.

conquest or cession such laws, courts, etc., as he sees fit,[24] he may derogate from that power, e.g., by assenting to an Act granting the power to others. The Royal Proclamation of October 7, 1763,[25] issued after the cession of Canada by the Treaty of Paris of February 10 of the same year, declared that His Majesty had erected the "Government" of Quebec with its western boundary, a straight line from the south end of Lake Nipissing to the point at which the parallel of 45 degrees, N.L., crosses the St. Lawrence. The Proclamation further declared that the King had given to the Governor with the consent of the Council, power to make laws and erect and constitute "Courts of Judicature and public Justice." When the limits of the Province were extended by the Quebec Act (1774), 14 George III, c. 83 (Imp.),[26] so as to cover all the territory afterwards the Province of Upper Canada, the Act, to which the King had assented, provided for the appointment of a Council with power to make Ordinances for the good government of the Province with the consent of the Governor for the time being; while the Canada or Constitutional Act (1791), 31 George III, c. 31 (Imp.), under which Upper Canada was constituted provided that His Majesty should have power by and with the advice and consent of the Legislative Council and Legislative Assembly to make laws for the good government of the Province.[27] It was argued that neither the old Province of Quebec nor the Province of Upper Canada had erected a Court of Chancery, and that it was not competent for the King by his Commission and Instructions to empower his representative, the Lieutenant Governor, to constitute such a Court without the authority of the Provincial Legislature. It is obvious from the Chief Justice's opinion that the main dependence of the defendant was upon the Proclamation of 1763. It is singular that no one, Counsel or Court, noticed that the Township of Bathurst, in which the land in question was situated, was not within the old Province but was within the territory reserved for Indians and the fur traders in 1763.

On the question of the Jurisdiction of the Court, assuming that it did exist in law, it was argued that *Scire Facias* can be based only on a record in the Court of Chancery; and the Letters Patent proposed to be cancelled were admittedly records only in the office of the Registrar General of the Province.[28]

The argument of the Attorney General[29] pointed out the assignment of the Great Seal of the Province to the Lieutenant Governor by the express words of his Commission, thereby making him Chancellor of the Province, and his oath "to administer justice" and "to execute all the powers of the Governor." It was argued that by the Common Law of England—which had been introduced into the Province by the Act of (1792), 32 George III, c. 1 (U.C.)—the Chancellor had the power and duty to sit as a Common Law Court for the purpose of hearing and deciding actions of *Scire Facias* in England; that consequently the Lieutenant-Governor had the same power and duty in his Province, and there was no need of Provincial or other legislation. On the question of Jurisdiction the Attorney General argued that the Patent being recorded in the usual office for the registration of such grants in the Province, it must be considered a Record of Chancery for the purposes of a *Sci. Fa.*

Once it was granted that the Common Law of England was in force in the Province and that the Lieutenant Governor was the Chancellor, the conclusion seemed inevitable that the Court actually existed; and there would remain only the technical difficulty as to the Record of the Letters Patent. The Chief Justice, while modestly disclaiming acquaintance with the technical words and forms of Chancery practice, advised that it would be sufficient for the Governor to declare that the Court existed and had jurisdiction over the subject matter; and he drew, or at least assisted in drawing, the formal judgment allowing the demurrer.[30] From the documents extant, it cannot be found that the technical difficulty as to the Record of the Letters Patent was given any thought— it was probably considered too trivial.

But as this was the first case of the kind in the Province, and as the question of jurisdiction was most important, it was agreed that no further proceedings should be had in the matter until the opinion of the Law Officers of the Crown in England could be taken.

The Attorney General was going to England to represent the Upper Province in its claims against Lower Canada in connection with the duties collected by the latter Province on goods coming to the former, etc., and it was accordingly arranged that he should draw up the Case for the Law Officers at Westminster, and submit it on his arrival in England. He drew up the Case and handed it to the Secretary of State for War and the Colonies,[31] Lord Bathurst, October 23, 1822;[32] and Lord Bathurst submitted it to the Law Officers of the Crown, November 2, 1822.

The Attorney General in the Case sets out the constitution of the Province under the Constitutional Act (1791), 31 George III, c. 31 (Imp.); the Legislation of (1792), 32 George III, c. 1 (U.C.), whereby the Province introduced the laws of England as the rule of decision as to property and civil rights; the establishment by the Province of the Court of King's Bench and its jurisdiction; the method of granting land by Letters Patent under the Great Seal of Upper Canada registered in the office of the Provincial Registrar; and also the facts of the Swan case in outline. He points out that there is no Court of Chancery in ordinary operation in the Province or any words in the Governor's Commission expressly conferring on him the power of exercising jurisdiction as a Chancellor; and that there is no Record Office in Chancery for the registry of Letters Patent, etc. He argues, however, that the Great Seal being formally assigned to the Governor by express words, he became Chancellor, *ipso facto;* that the jurisdiction being Common Law, no legislation was required, and that the enrolment of the Letters Patent in the office of the Registry of the Province should be considered a record in the Chancery of Upper Canada on which the *Scire facias* might be grounded.

The Lieutenant Governor asked the opinion of the Law Officers "whether it was competent to him as Chancellor to repeal Letters Patent for sufficient cause upon such proceedings as that instituted in Swan's case, and whether the same end could not be more properly attained by proceeding in any other Court now existing in the Province."[33]

The Attorney General of England was Sir Robert Gifford (afterward Baron Gifford, Chief Justice of the Common Pleas and Master of the Rolls) a sound but not a brilliant lawyer, whose practice at that time lay almost entirely in the Court of Chancery and House of Lords; he apparently did not consider the matter of sufficient importance to be taken up immediately. Robinson had a long conference with him, December 17, upon this and other matters of greater importance.[34] Gifford naturally was reluctant to give an opinion in a matter which had been judicially considered and suggested an appeal by the defendant; Robinson, however, was encouraged to think that he would give an opinion ultimately, and it was arranged for Robinson to meet him again.[35] Robinson on this first interview was convinced that Gifford wholly agreed with him that the Court was properly constituted; the opinion of the Solicitor General, Sir John Singleton Copley (afterward Lord Lyndhurst, Lord Chancellor), a much greater lawyer, does not seem to have been sought by Robinson. Robinson returned home in 1823 without an answer. At length, April 19, 1824, the Lieutenant-Governor, Sir Peregrine Maitland, wrote Bathurst asking for the opinion of the Law Officers on both this and the Bidwell matter. Bathurst, being then at Cirencester, wrote at once to London urging a speedy answer.[36] Gifford had become Lord Gifford and Chief Justice of the Common Pleas in January of that year, and had been succeeded by Copley as Attorney General, while Sir Charles Wetherell (afterward Attorney General) had succeeded Copley as Solicitor General. These two, Copley and Wetherell, gave an opinion, Serjeants' Inn, November 13, 1824, as to the Bidwells,[37] but said nothing of the Court of Chancery.

Six months passed and, April 22, 1825, Maitland again wrote Bathurst for an opinion as to his power to act as Chancellor to repeal Letters Patent;[38] no answer is extant and no opinion was ever given.[39] Copley became Master of the Rolls as Lord Lyndhurst in 1826, being succeeded by Wetherell, who was himself succeeded by Sir Nicholas Conyngham Tindal (afterwards Chief Justice of the Common Pleas). In 1827 Wetherell gave place to Sir James Scarlett (afterward Lord Abinger, Chief Baron of the Exchequer).

There was not quite the same unrest in the Solicitor General's office: Tindal held office until he became Chief Justice in 1829.

The question as to the right of the Lieutenant-Governor to sit as a Common Law Court to repeal Letters Patent does not seem to have been considered by the Law Officers at Westminster; at all events, there is no record of any opinion having been given on the subject.

But there was a proposition to constitute a Court of Equity by creating the office of Master of the Rolls for the Province, and giving him a Patent conferring Equity powers, not unlike those possessed by the Master of the Rolls in England.

Lord Goderich became Secretary of State for War and the Colonies; in 1827 he submitted to the Law Officers of the Crown the question whether His Majesty could by Letters Patent under the Great Seal, or in any other lawful manner, lawfully create the office of Master of the Rolls in Upper Canada.

Scarlett and Tindal gave a written opinion (The Temple, September 25, 1827), that they were in doubt as to the power of the King, without the intervention of Parliament or the Local Legislature, to create any new Judge in Equity by whatever name he might be called, in Upper Canada. They recommended that any Judge to receive Equity powers should be called Vice Chancellor, and not Master of the Rolls; and advised an Act of Parliament or of the Local Legislature.⁴⁰ The advice was followed; a Court of Equity was formed by the Local Legislature in 1837, and the Judge was called Vice Chancellor. That Court when formed was given the power: "To institute proceedings for the repeal of Letters Patent erroneously or improvidently issued."⁴¹ We hear no more of an "Ordinary" Court of Chancery with such powers.

All the trouble might have been avoided had Swan kept his promise to give a surrender of the land, receiving a Patent of the land to which he was honestly entitled. But he persisted in his refusal for years; and as he would not surrender this lot, he was not given a Patent for the east half of Lot No. 20 in the 4th Concession. Adams remained in possession of the mill and lot undisturbed; finally Swan agreed to quit claim the lot to Adams, and he received a grant of his own land. He gave a Quit Claim to "Joshua Adams, legatee under the Will of Abraham Parsall," August 9, 1833, and received a Patent of the east half of Lot No. 20 in the 4th Concession of the Township of Bathurst, February 24, 1834.⁴²

The Writ of Ejectment, issued by Swan against Adams does not seem to have been proceeded with; no record of it is to be found in the Term Books.⁴³

Second Incident

The other incident may be related more succinctly as the supposed power was not in fact exercised or attempted.

In 1823, Alexander Wood,⁴⁴ a Justice of the Peace in York (Toronto) brought an action in the Court of King's Bench against William Dummer Powell, Chief Justice of the Province and head of the Court, for refusing to administer the proper oath to Wood as Commissioner for the investigation of Claims of Loss suffered during the War of 1812.

At the trial before Mr. Justice Campbell (afterward Chief Justice Sir William Campbell), the defendant decided on a Bill of Exceptions,⁴⁵ a most unusual course even in England and without precedent in Upper Canada. The Bill was drawn up at the close of the trial, and tendered to Mr. Justice Campbell⁴⁶ for his seal; he asked time to read it at his leisure as he was then exhausted by the eight hour trial of the case. He subsequently, after consideration, returned the Bill, declining to seal it. If the facts alleged in the Bill were true— and no one pretends that they were not—the Judge should have sealed it under the provisions of the Statute of Westminster the Second, 13 Edw. I, c. 31, and upon refusal, the party tendering the Bill might, according to the English practice, obtain a compulsory writ from Chancery against the Judge commanding him to seal it. Powell, upon the refusal, lodged a petition to Sir Peregrine Maitland as "Lieutenant Governor of the Province of Upper Canada and Chancellor therein," praying that "Your Excellency will address the said William Campbell, as Justice of Assize as aforesaid, commanding him forthwith to put his seal to such Bill of Exceptions." His Excellency referred the matter to the Attorney General, John Beverley Robinson. That able lawyer desired first to see the Bill of Exceptions tendered, before giving an opinion. "The application being unprecedented here and of extremely rare occurrence in England, I am unwilling to hazard an opinion hastily; but when I learn the nature of the Bill of Exceptions tendered, I shall give the matter immediate consideration." This was notified to Powell, the Bill as proposed was handed in, and the following day the Governor's Secretary, Major Hillier, wrote Powell that it was not for the purpose of preparing the Writ prayed for that the papers were handed to the Attorney General, but "that His Excellency might be satisfied (if he should be advised that he can in any case legally issue the required writ) that the case in question is one in which such a writ ought to be awarded . . . as His Excellency is advised that there are some cases in which a Bill of Exceptions will not lie." The letter went on to say that if desired, His Excellency would sit as Chancellor in the Council Chamber on Thursday, November 13; but added, significantly enough, "the question which has been made of his jurisdiction as Chancellor being at present, as you are aware, under the consideration of His Majesty's Law Officers in England, he has necessarily forborne, until a decision is received, to make those arrangements which would have afforded a more known and regular access for the purposes of justice; and His Excellency hoped that in the meantime it might have been found possible to avoid a resort to a jurisdiction, the existence of which has been called in question." Powell at once answered saying that he did not know that any doubt existed as to the power to issue the writ, otherwise he would not have solicited it. He knew the proceeding was novel, but thought it a proceeding of course. After saying that the "writ was to be prepared by the officer (the Attorney General) which induced me to inform you of the probable application by anticipation"—not the only suggestion against the good faith of the Attorney General—he continues, "I cannot for a moment continue any application for the exercise of a questionable jurisdiction." It is plain he had no hope of success and made a virtue of necessity.[47]

NOTES

[1] For example, in the Court of Common Pleas in and for the District of Hesse, held at L'Assomption (now Sandwich), September 1, 1792, in the case of Askin, Sr., v. Sanscrainte, the plaintiff saying that by the conduct of the defendant he was "utterly deprived of any legal testimony . . . but by referring his said demand to the decisive oath of the defendant agreeable to the law and usage of the Customs of Paris," prayed "that a writ be made on the defendant to appear in his proper person before this Court on Tuesday, the 4th inst. . . . to purge himself by his decisive oath from the demand of the plaintiff, failing which the said account filed shall be taken and held to be confessed and acknowledged." This meant that the plaintiff agreed to be bound by the oath of the defendant. The Court (William Dummer Powell) granted the motion, the writ was issued and served; on the 4th, the defendant did not appear and the case was adjourned until the 5th. On the 5th, the defendant did not appear and judgment went against him.

A perfectly similar proceeding was taken against the same defendant on the same days with the same result, at the suit of Shieffeling & Askin. See 14th Ont. Archives Rept. (1918), pp. 152-155.

[2] (1792) 32 Geo. III, c. 1, s. 3 (U.C.).

³The first entry is as follows:

"PROVINCE }
OF QUEBEC } In Chancery:

Before His Excellency the Honble James Murray, Esqr., Keeper of the Broad Seal of the Province aforesaid, &c., &c., &c., on Fryday, the 25th January, 1765,

JOHN HAY } The Atty. Genl. opened the Court by reading this
agst. } Bill.
Gilbt. Barkly } And then moved that a *ne exeat Provinciam* might be granted against the defendant.
The solicitor for the defendant opposed it.
Ct. Denyed this motion as thinking it oppressive but ordered on consent of defendant that he should enter into a Recognizance of £1,000, sterlg., to stand to and abide such order and decree on the hearing of this cause as this Honble Court shall direct."

This Court of Chancery is so little known that its very existence has been denied. The records, still extant and in the Archives at Ottawa, show that Murray sat in Chancery thirteen times from January 25th to August 2nd, 1765; Carleton sat at least nine times from February 4th, 1768, to April 10th, 1770, and there were at least five cases from 1771 to 1774. See my Articles, "The First Court of Chancery in Canada," *Boston University Law Review*, October, 1922, and January, 1923.

⁴In the Court of Common Pleas of the District of Hesse, September 10th, 1792, in the case of William Macomb v. William Groesbeck, a "Commission in the nature of a commission rogatoire" was issued to Daniel Campbell, John Robertson and John Stevenson of Schenectady in the United States, Esquires, to take the answers of Mathew Lound of said Schenectady to certain interrogatories." Letters Rogatory had anciently been in use in the Common Law Courts, 1 Rolle Abr., 530, pl. 13; but at this time the practice had entirely ceased. The Commission was returned and at the "Court of Common Pleas holden at the house of Alexis Maisonville, Esq., in the Parish of L'Assomption in the Western District and Province of Upper Canada, September 12, 1793, Walter Roe, "Attorney for the plaintiff, moved that the said answers be filed among the records and taken as legal testimony in this cause"; but the judge, William Dummer Powell, afterwards Chief Justice of Upper Canada, held that the Ordinance of Quebec under which the Commission was issued was "virtually repealed" by (1792) 32 Geo. III, c. 1, s. 5, and that this Statute now directed the proceedings of the Court; consequently "Mr. Roe can take nothing by his motion." 11 Ont. Archives Rept. (1917), p. 156.

⁵(1794) 34 Geo. III, c. 2, s. 1 (U.C.); it will be noticed that the Equity powers of the English Court of Exchequer are not included.

⁶The most promising was in the time of Governor Peter Hunter, when it looked as though Allcock would be vested with equity powers; but Hunter's sudden and mysterious death in 1805, aided perhaps by Allcock's previous elevation to the Chief Justiceship, seems to have put an end to the project.

⁷See judgment of Sir John Beverley Robinson, C.J., in Simpson v. Smyth (1846), 1 U.C. E. & A. 9, at p. 66.

⁸By the Act (1837), 7 Will. IV, c. 2 (U.C.), the Lieutenant Governor was to be the Chancellor with a Vice-Chancellor; Robert Sympson Jameson, the Attorney General, became our first Equity Judge as Vice-Chancellor in this Court.

I do not go into the general history of Law and Equity in Upper Canada. The interested may advantageously consult an article under the title "Law and Equity in Upper Canada," by Mr. John Delatre Falconbridge of the Ontario Bar, in *63 Univ. of Pennsylvania Review and American Law Register* (54 N.S. 1915), pp. 1 sqq.; *34 Canadian Law Times* (1914), pp. 1130, sqq.

⁹See "Select Bills in Eyre," Selden Society, London, 1914, Introduction, xv, xvi. Shareshull, whom Foss thinks "more a political and parliamentary judge than a man of law" (Foss, Biog. Dict., Judges of England, Murray, London, 1870, 610, col. 2), was right in this: "Il y ad iii distinctions de *Coram nobis;* scilicet *Coram nobis* suppose devant le Roy mesme en sa chambre; *Coram nobis ubicunque,* etc., en ceste place, et *Coram nobis cancellaria nostra* devant le Chanceler," Liber Assisarum, anno 28 (Edw. III), p. 155, pl. 52.

[10]The words of the first Lieutenant Governor, John Graves Simcoe, on proroguing the first Legislature at Newark (Niagara-on-the-Lake), October 15, 1792, 6 Rept. Ont. Archives (for (1909, p. 18. See his opening address, September 17, 1792. Simcoe said that the Act of Parliament (1791), 31 George III, c. 31 (Imp.), the Canada or Constitutional Act, had "established the British Constitution and all its forms which secure and maintain it io this distant country," 6 Rept. Ont. Archives (for 1909), p. 1.

[11]See Coke, Inst., IV, 87; Statute (1562), 4 Eliz., c. 18, s. 2.

[12]In the old Province of Quebec from 1764 till 1774 the Governor was in the proceedings in the Court of Chancery called indifferently Keeper of the Great Seal, of the Broad Seal, and of the Public Seal of the Province. See the Proceedings in Chancery in the Province of Quebec, 1764-1774, now preserved in the Public Archives at Ottawa. This differing terminology was not new. In the "Nicholas Papers" printed by the Royal Historical Society, 1920, we find in 1659, "Olivers Great Seale is Brooke to peeces"; and a few months later, Commissioners of the "Broad Seal" are appointed, pp. 139, 156.

[13]The Union Act of (1840), 3, 4, Vic., c. 35 (Imp.), coming into force, February, 1841, united Upper and Lower Canada into one Province, Canada. Thereafter until the Chancery Act of 1849, 12 Vic., c. 64 (Can.) created a Court with a Chancellor and two Vice-Chancellors, the Governor General was Chancellor. The original Chancery Act of 1837, 7 Will. 4, c. 2 (U.C.), left the Lieutenant Governor, Chancellor of the Province with a Vice-Chancellor to be appointed.

[14]For example, when a petition came in against an election to the House, the "Clerk of the Crown in Chancery" was ordered to produce the writ of Election and Return. See, for example, in the Bidwell cases in 1822 and 1823.

[15]So far as I know, there is no reference to this curious incident in our legal history by any other writer; it first came to my knowledge when searching through the Sundries, Upper Canada Series, Public Archives, Ottawa; and I have made diligent enquiry in every quarter in which information concerning it could be expected to be found. We can confidently rely upon the accuracy of the story here told; it is taken from the original contemporary records.

[16]H. A. O'Donnell, Esq., barrister, of Perth, has been kind enough to give me information concerning this lot, the registrations, etc. My thanks are due to Mr. O'Donnell and his partner, Hon. J. A. Stewart, K.C. (now, alas, no more—*valde deflendus*), for their courteous attention and answer to my request for such information. Mr. O'Donnell writes me, September 30, 1921:—

"In the early days, as far back as anyone in this locality can remember, there were a grist mill and sawmill situated on the east half of lot 20, in the second concession of Bathurst; and about sixty or seventy years ago a large woollen mill, known as Hargraves and Dodds' Mill, was in operation on the site of the old woollen mill. This mill has not been operated for over thirty years; and as a matter of fact the old building was one of the picturesque ruins at Glen Tay until the last year or two when the old walls were torn down.

"In 1896, the water-power on the mill site was sold to the Perth Waterworks Company, and this has now passed to the Corporation of the Town of Perth; but the water-power is not used at the present time."

[17]Can. Archives, Land Book L., Upper Canada, pp. 20, 21:

"At the Council Chamber at York, on Wednesday, 7th February, 1821.
Present:
        His Excellency Sir Peregrine Maitland, K.C.B.,
        The Honourable Wm. Dummer Powell, Chief Justice,
        The Honourable James Baby,
        The Honourable Samuel Smith,
        The Honourable & Reverend Doctor Strachan.

Report of a Committee of the Executive Council in Your Excellency's reference of the subject of a Lot of Land in Kitley by Captain Livingston.

Perth, No. 27—On the certificate of Major Powell and others respecting an Error in a Patent granted to Samuel Swan—the North East half of Lot No. 20 in the 2nd Concession of Bathurst instead of North East half of No. 20 in the 4th Concession of Bathurst.

Reconsidered, and it appearing that the Grantee Swan will not voluntary surrender the patent, it is recommended to direct steps to be taken to cancel the Patent."

At that time Chief Justice and Robinson had not had their historic quarrel; both Powell and the Lieutenant-Governor were much under Robinson's influence, the Rev. John Strachan more so, while Baby and Smith were nonentities on the Council Board. It is not too much to say that the action was really Robinson's own.

THE "ORDINARY" COURT OF CHANCERY IN UPPER CANADA   233

[18]As few have seen a Writ of Scire Facias, I here copy this one; a copy has been supplied me by the kindness of Mr. Thomas Mulvey, Under Secretary of State at Ottawa, from "H" Coms. in the office of the Registrar General of Canada, folio 217:

[SEAL]

UPPER CANADA

MAITLAND. GEORGE THE FOURTH, by the Grace of God of the United Kingdom of Great Britain and Ireland, King, Defender of the Faith, to the Sheriff of the District of Johnstown,

GREETING:

Whereas the Lord George the third, late king of the United Kingdom of Great Britain and Ireland by his Letters Patent made under the Great Seal of our Province of Upper Canada, bearing date the fifteenth day of April in the year of our Lord one thousand eight hundred and twenty, in the sixtieth year of his reign, of his special grace, certain knowledge and mere motion did give and grant unto Samuel Swan of the township of Bathurst in the county of Carleton, in the District of Johnstown, Yeoman, late of the Field Train Department, his heirs and assigns forever, all that parcel or tract of land situate in the township of Bathurst in the county of Carleton in the District of Johnstown in our said Province, containing by measurement one hundred acres be the same more or less, reserving to the crown the waters of the river Tay which pass through the said lot, being the east half of lot twenty in the second concession of the said Township, together with all the woods and waters thereon lying, and being, under the reservations, limitacions and restrictions in the said Letters Patent expressed, which said one hundred acres of land are described in the said Letters Patent as follows, that is to say: Commencing in front of the said concession at the south East angle of the said lot, then North thirty-six degrees West, Sixty-six chains seventy links more or less to the allowance for road in the rear of the said Concession, then South fifty-four degrees, West fifteen chains more or less to the centre of the said lot. Then South thirty-six degrees East, sixty-six chains seventy links more or less to the allowance for road in front of the said concession. Then North fifty-four degrees East, fifteen chains more or less to the place of beginning. To have and to hold the parcel or tract of land thereby given and granted to him the said Samuel Swan his heirs and assigns forever, saving nevertheless to the said Lord the late King, his heirs and Successors, all mines of gold and silver that should or might be thereafter found on any part of the said parcel or tract of land thereby given and granted as aforesaid, and saving and reserving to our said Lord the late King, his heirs and Successors, all white pine trees that should or might then or thereafter grow or be growing on any part of the said Parcel or tract of land thereby granted as aforesaid as by the said Letters Patent enrolled in our Chancery is more fully manifest and appears; and whereas we are given to understand that the said Letters Patent issued improvidently and by error to the said Samuel Swan by reason that it was falsely and erroneously suggested to our said Lord the late King that the said Samuel Swan had before the sending of the said Letters Patent been located upon the said lot under the authority of the said Lord the late King, and had settled and made improvements thereupon, whereas in truth and in fact the said Samuel Swan had not before the sealing of the letters patent been located upon the said lot under any authority derived from our said Lord the late King or settled or made improvements thereon, but on the contrary thereof one Abraham Parsall had by the authority of our said Lord the late King been located upon the said lot before the making of the said Letters Patent and had under the assurance of receiving a grant from our said Lord the late King or his Successors made divers erections and improvements thereon and resided upon and cultivated the same, and now by reason of the issuing of the said Letters Patent under such false and erroneous suggestion as aforesaid, the said Abraham Parsall is subject and liable to be dispossessed of the said tract or parcel of land and to be deprived of his interest therein, contrary to right and justice and to his great damage by reason of which said premises and in as much as our said Lord the late King hath been deceived in making the said Grant, the Letters Patent aforesaid to the said Samuel Swan are and ought to be void and of no force and effect in law and we being willing that what is just should be done in the premises command you that by good and lawful men of your Bailiwick you give notice to the said Samuel Swan that he be before us in our chancery on the first day of Michaelmas Term next wheresoever it shall be to show if he hath or can say anything for himself why the said Letters Patent to him in form aforesaid granted and the enrollment of the same for the reasons aforesaid ought not to be cancelled, vacated, disallowed, and those Letters Patent restored into our said chancery there to be cancelled, and further to do and receive those things which our said chancery shall consider in this behalf, and have the name of those by whom you shall give notice, and this Writ.

Witness ourself at York, the second day of August in the second year of our Reign.

JNO. B. ROBINSON.   By Command, D. CAMERON, S.J., P.M.

[19]Coke, Inst. iv, 88. In England, the Writ would be issued out of the Petty Bag Office: 2 Tidd's Practice, 8th Ed., 1139; 2 Wm. Saund, 72n; Foster on Scire Facias (1851) 12, 228.

[20]While the original Law Society's Act of (1797), 37 George III, c. 13 (U.C.), contemplated the Solicitor, i.e. the Practitioner in Chancery, there was no Court of Equity until 1837, and consequently no Solicitor properly so called till that time. See (1837) 7 Will. 4, c. 2, s. 12 (U.C.), and my "Legal Profession in Upper Canada," pp. 33 (n), 36, 147.

[21]The Attorney General, John Beverley Robinson, appeared for the Crown; I could for long find no record of the counsel for the defendant, and could only conjecture that it was Dr. William Warren Baldwin; now, I have ascertained that it was Henry John Boulton, afterwards Chief Justice of Newfoundland.

[22]Thomas Taylor, under the provisions of the Act (1823), 4 George IV, c. 3 (U.C.). See my "Legal Profession, etc.," 107, 108.

[23]Letter from Chief Justice Powell to Major Hillier, Secretary to the Lieutenant Governor, York, January 19, 1822, and letter from Powell to the Lieutenant Governor, January 21, 1822, with opinion enclosed. Can. Archives, Sundries, U.C. (1822); the opinion is elaborate and able.

[24]See Blackstone's Commentaries, Bk. 1, pp. 106-107.

[25]This Proclamation has often been reprinted; it will be found in Shortt and Doughty's "Constitutional Documents, 1759-1791," 2nd Edit., pp. 163, sqq.; the Treaty of Paris at pp. 97, sqq.

[26]The Quebec Act, Shortt and Doughty, *op. cit.*, pp. 570-576.

[27]The Canada or Constitutional Act, Shortt and Doughty, *op cit.*, 1031-1051.

[28]That a *Scire Facias* out of Chancery to repeal Letters Patent must be based upon a Record in Chancery, see R. v Sir O. Butler, 3 Lev. 233; Foster on Scire Facias, 12.

[29]This can be determined without difficulty from the Case stated for the opinion of the Law Officers of the Crown in England, mentioned later in the text.
The "Ordinary" Court of Chancery being a Court administering the Common Law, the troublesome question of the right of the King to erect Courts administering any but the Common Law after the Bill of Rights did not actually arise in this case.

[30]Writing to Major Hillier, the Governor's Secretary, York, January 19, 1822, Powell says:
"Not having practised in Chancery, I am not much conversant in the technical words and forms, but I have in the enclosed stated my ideas on the matter which, compared with those of the Attorney General, may lead to a good result. It is to be regretted that some step had not been taken before the sitting to put things in order, but I had no information on the subject before I attended at the Governor's house as I understood by your advice.

"As to the decision on the demurrer, it seems to me that it is quite sufficient for His Excellency to say that the Court exists and has jurisdiction over the subject which, not being possessed by any other Court having jurisdiction, the Demurrer is sustained and that the Defendant must answer over to the Sci. Fa., or that its contents shall be taken as admitted and the Letters Patent vacated." Can. Archives, Sundries, U.C., 1822, also in the Powell MSS.
In his letter to the Lieutenant Governor, York, January 21, 1822, Powell encloses his opinion and says: "If His Excellency conceives no impropriety in calling upon the Attorney Genl. to insert the opinion in his entry, and whatever be the proper course in this first act., if the Court had time afforded it might have been proper to settle these forms before the cause was heard in which case Yr Excellency would undoubtedly have called upon that advice and assistance to organize the Court." Can. Archives, Sundries, U.C., 1822, and Powell MSS. (a draft only).
The implied rebuke to the Attorney General may have been due to the bitter quarrel between the Chief Justice and him (bitter on the side of the Chief Justice at least and almost contemptuous on the other) arising from the fact that on the request of both Houses of Parliament, Robinson accepted the duty of representing in England to the Home Authorities the case of Upper Canada against Lower Canada concerning its share of certain duties, etc. This broke up a long friendship which never was renewed. The conduct of the Chief Justice was petulant and childishly unreasonable; it can be pardoned only when it is remembered that he was now a man of sixty-seven, who was in great financial straits, and whom a long and strenuous life had broken down in body and probably a little in mind. He had become a querulous valetudinarian. However, the opinion enclosed is long and convincing. It is in the Can. Archives, Sundries, U.C., 1822, and a draft in the Powell MSS. The Chief Justice, by a *lapsus calami*, calls the defendant "Adams" instead of "Swan," Adams being the person entitled to the land. The form of judgment he proposed was also enclosed in this letter.

THE "ORDINARY" COURT OF CHANCERY IN UPPER CANADA   235

³¹Henry, the third Lord Bathurst, became Secretary of State for War and the Colonies in Lord Liverpool's Administration, 1812, and held that office until 1827, when he was succeeded by Frederick John, Lord Goderich, Bathurst becoming next year President of the Council in the Duke of Wellington's Ministry. He died in 1834, having been out of office about four years.

³²The formal letter from Robinson to Bathurst is dated London, 76 Gower Street, October 30, 1822. It refers to a minute by Maitland, laid before Bathurst by Robinson, and adds: "His Excellency is, I know, extremely desirous that I should be enabled to communicate with him on my return the opinion of His Majesty's Law Officers upon it," Can. Archives, Sundries, U.C., 1822. A copy of both letter and case are in the same series in the Archives at Ottawa; a copy also in Q 337, p. 386. The indexing as of 1824, in the Report Can. Archives for 1898, p. 215, is an error.

³³The question as to other Courts having this jurisdiction arose from the fact that it was considered that a Writ of Scire Facias to repeal Letters Patent might be brought before the Court of King's Bench. Coke, Inst. IV, 72, says specifically: "A Scire fac' to repeal a patent of the King may be brought in this Court."
Chitty's Archbold, 9th Edit., 1076: "A *Scire facias* . . . when brought to repeal letters patent may in fact be an original writ returnable in Chancery or a judicial writ returnable in a Superior Court," citing 3, H. 4, 6, 29 (which I cannot find). Coke cites 3 H. 4, 7, which also escapes me. See also Foster, Scire Facias, 12; Tomlins' Law Dict., Vol. 2, 3, Z, 2, *sub voc*. "Scire Facias."

³⁴One of these was as to the qualification for election to membership of the Legislative Assembly of Upper Canada of Barnabas Bidwell, who had been Attorney General of Massachusetts, 1807-1810, and his son, Marshall Spring Bidwell, born in the United States, neither of whom had been naturalized.

³⁵Robinson's letter to Maitland from 76 Gower Street, London, December 18, 1822, Can. Archives, Sundries, U.C., 1822: "I had yesterday a long conference with the Attorney General . . . . . upon Swan's case, I had a long conversation with the Attorney General; he hesitated to give an opinion in a matter which had been judicially considered, and seems inclined to recommend that the party be left to his appeal if he contests the jurisdiction. However, I think he will express an opinion when he has duly considered it. I am to see him again." January 6, 1823, Robinson, writing from 76 Gower Street, London, to Henry John Boulton, Solicitor General, informs him as to the practice in the Province as to Writs of Error and advises that it be followed "until it shall be publicly announced that His Majesty's representative in the Province will sit as a Chancellor and determine such business as may be brought before him." Can. Archives, Sundries, U.C., 1823.

³⁶Writing from Circencester, October 29, 1824, to Maitland, Bathurst says: "I have received your letter of August 19. I readily understand the desire you must have to have an answer to the Question respecting your power of repealing Patents in the Province." He wrote at once to London and found: "It stands still; the reference I made to the Law Officers in the year 1822 remains locked up in their box," but he had written strongly urging a speedy answer. Can. Archives, Q. 337 A, p. 191.

³⁷Can. Archives, Q. 337, 1, 45.

³⁸Can. Archives, Q. 338, 1, 167. The question does not seem to have been submitted to Sir James Stephen, permanent Counsel to the Colonial Office (1825), who about this time passed upon a number of questions of law for that office; for example, Can. Archives, Q. 342, pp. 52, 55, 90, 106, 109, etc.

³⁹The question soon broadened out into the more important one whether a Court of Equity could be erected in the Province without an Act of Parliament of Great Britain or of the Legislature of Upper Canada.

⁴⁰Can. Archives, Q. 345, pp. 46 sqq.; the following is the official opinion:—
To the Right Honble. William Huskisson, &c., &c., &c.
Sir,—We have had the honour of receiving from Lord Goderich, a Copy of the Commission under the Great Seal appointing the Earl of Dalhousie Governor of the Provinces of Upper and Lower Canada, the draft of a proposed Patent for the appointment of a Master of the Rolls in the Province of Upper Canada, and a copy of the Patent of Master of the Rolls in England,—accompanied by a Letter from his Lordship in which after pointing out to our attention that the law of England has been generally adopted in Upper Canada, that the custody of the Seal intrusted to a Colonial Governor has already been considered to invest him with the office of Chancellor, but that the Governors of Upper Canada have always declined assuming the judicial functions

of Chancellor, that the want of a Court authorized to enforce the execution of trusts and to protect the property of Infants has been productive of great inconvenience of which representations have been made to His Majesty's Government although no attempt has been made to institute a Court of Equitable Jurisdiction by any Statute of the Governor in Council and Assembly, for supplying which defect it has been suggested, that the most appropriate remedy would be the erection of the Office of Master of the Rolls, his Lordship desires us to take the proposed draft of a Patent into our Consideration, and to Report for His Majesty's information, whether His Majesty can by Letters Patent under the Great Seal or in any other manner lawfully create the Office of Master of the Rolls in Upper Canada, and whether such Letters Patent could properly be passed in the form suggested and to make such alterations in the draft as may appear to us to be necessary.

In compliance with his Lordship's desire we have duly considered the several matters referred to us and have now the honour to report for His Majesty's information, that the result of our investigation leaves us in considerable doubt, whether His Majesty lawfully can, by Letters Patent under the Great Seal, or in any other manner, without the intervention of Parliament, or of the local legislature, create any new Judge in Equity by whatsoever name he may be called in Upper Canada; that the Office of Master of the Rolls in England is a very ancient office, deriving its authority and jurisdiction from usage, and the various relations by which that Office is connected with the general establishment of the Courts both of Equity and Common Law; that the same office, and the same relations, much less the same Fees and Emoluments, could not be transferred to Canada, by the mere Creation of an Office of that name, which would nevertheless be there a new Office, the functions of which ought to be specified in the law which authorized, or in the Patent which created it. And we therefore humbly submit, that in order to prevent any misconception of the authority and jurisdiction of the office by reason of analogies drawn from the name, it would be more expedient, if consistent with His Majesty's Pleasure, that the intended Equity Judge should be called Vice-Chancellor to the Governor, and made his Deputy for the desired purposes to which it is supposed the Governor's authority may be usefully employed in a Court of Equity. But in order to prevent doubts on the subject we would recommend this to be done by the aid of Parliament or of the local legislature.

We therefore beg permission to return the Draft of the proposed patent, and to defer any alterations it may require, until His Majesty's Pleasure be further known to us.

We take the liberty of submitting further to your consideration as connected with this subject, whether with a view to avoid the clashing of jurisdictions and the dissensions which may possibly arise upon the new Establishment of distinct Courts of equal power, but proceeding by different rules, it might not be expedient instead of creating a distinct Court of Equity, to add to the Judges who constitute the present Common Law Court in that Province, the proposed Equity Lawyer in the Character of a Puisne Judge, and to give to the Court so constituted, by the authority of Parliament or of the local legislature, so much of an Equitable Jurisdiction as upon due consideration may be thought necessary or useful to the Province, to be exercised as in the Court of Exchequer, in England, in the same tribunal, and by the same Judges, who administer the Common Law.

We have the honour to be, Sir,

Your most obedient humble servants,

(Sgd.) J. SCARLETT,
N. C. TINDAL.

Temple, 25th September, 1827.

[41](1837) 7 Will. IV, c. 2, s. 1 (U.C.).

[42]The deeds are registered in the Registry Office at Perth, Ontario. The information I have obtained from Mr. O'Donnell (see Note 16), and the Registrar generously refused to charge any fees for searches in this historical enquiry, for which I thank him.

[43]I have searched the records in the Term Books of the Court of King's Bench now in the Ontario Archives, Toronto, and find no mention of this action. It is quite certain that the case never came to trial or we should find a Term Motion upon the verdict; and it is almost certain that no proceedings were taken afterwards or there would be a record of a motion to stay. That the Court of King's Bench would under the circumstances stay proceedings in ejectment there can be no doubt.

"In Ejectment, where the lessor of the plaintiff has two actions depending at the same time for the same premises in different Courts, the proceedings in one of them may be stayed until the other be determined." Tidd's Practice, Vol. I, p. 572: Thrustout *ex dem.* Park v. Troublesome (1738), Andrews' Reports, K.B., 297; 2 Selwyn's Practice, 144; Adams on Ejectment, 2 Ed., 321.

But very great care was always exercised to see that the very same point was involved in the proceedings in Chancery, Murphy v. Cadell (1800), 2 Bos. & Pul. 137.

There is no record of any proceedings in Lunacy, or Ad Quod Damnum, in the Ordinary Court of Chancery in Upper Canada, although both were taken in the old Province of Quebec before the Quebec Act of 1774.

[44]Alexander Wood was a well-known personage in York (Toronto) at the time. His brother came from Aberdeen very early in the history of Upper Canada; he went into partnership with William Allan in York and later carried on business on his own account. He died, leaving considerable property which Alexander came to York to attend to. Alexander was a close friend of Dr. John Strachan who had himself come from Aberdeen. Some of the correspondence between them is still in existence. He seems to have become a close friend of the Powell family also; during Mr. Justice Powell's absence in Europe in 1806 seeking the release of his son Jeremiah from a Spanish-American prison, Mrs. Powell had successfully applied to Wood for money for the support of herself and family.

He became, in 1812, Secretary of the Loyal and Patriotic Society. Not long after this lawsuit, Wood v. Powell, he returned to Scotland, where at Stonehaven, not far from Aberdeen, he had a family estate; he was never married. Alexander and Wood Streets in Toronto are named after him.

[45]It may interest members of the legal profession to know that the costs taxed to the plaintiff which the defendant was ordered to pay, were £39.10.0 ($158.00), the costs of his own attorney, Dr. William Warren Baldwin, were £17.10.2 ($70.04), and counsel fees amounting to £25 ($100).

A "Bill of Exceptions" is in the nature of an appeal examinable not in the Court out of which the Record issues for the trial at *Nisi Prius*, but in the next immediate Superior Court upon a writ of error after judgment given in the Court below. Blackstone, Comm. III, 372.

The Bill of Exceptions in this case would have come on for decision in the Court of Appeals, not in the Court of King's Bench.

The curious may find all the learning as to this obsolete proceeding in the pages of Tidd and Buller; Tidd's Practice, p. 913; Buller's Nisi Prius, pp. 316, 317. Maddox's Chancery, Vol. I, pp. 15, 16, also discusses the matter from the Chancery side.

[46]Mr. Justice D'Arcy Boulton, the other Puisne Justice, was also on the Bench.

[47]Powell was already looking towards retirement on a pension. The granting and the amount of such a pension depended largely upon the Lieutenant Governor; and Powell did not want to displease him.

See my "Life of William Dummer Powell," *Michigan Historical Commission*, 1924.

The verdict was for less than five hundred pounds, so that Powell could not appeal to the King in Council.

The plaintiff, Wood, offered later to discharge the judgment if the costs were paid to his attorney, who had then become a Justice of the King's Bench, but this offer Powell "rejected as a tacit admission of the justice which it would be dishonourable to acknowledge." He shows no gratitude to Wood for his offer, which certainly does not seem ungenerous, but, childishly enough for a lawyer, complains that the judgment "hangs over him and his posterity as a charge on his real property."

In 1833, some years after retiring from the Bench, Powell wrote the following letter to Wood:—

"Toronto, 5th July, 1833.

Sir,—When you obtained a judgment against me by the concurrence of my brother judges on a charge of refusing to administer an oath to you from base and unworthy motives, I was Chief Justice of this Province, and esteemed the judgment so iniquitous that I declined to cancel it at the expense of paying the costs to your Attorney, the present Judge Macaulay.

I did not appeal because the amount of the judgment would not carry it to the King in Council; and for nearly ten years, have expected execution to consummate the injustice.

It hangs a cloud on my real property, to no part of which can I give a title whilst that judgment remains unsatisfied on the Record. This delay of that entry on the Record is becoming an additional injury as the value of my real estate (is) now at its summit and probably really diminishing.

If therefore such entry on the record as will free my land from the judgment (be not made), I shall be constrained to petition the Legislature for that purpose at its first meeting."

We find among his MSS. a draft Bill to meet the case. It provided that "Hereafter any judgment of the Superior Court from which no appeal has been made within twelve months from the date of entry of the judgment and for which no writ of execution shall have been sued out within fifteen months of the said entry, shall be no longer binding upon the moveable or real estate of the judgment (Debtor), but shall be esteemed to have (been) satisfied." This bill does not seem to have been brought up in the Legislature; certainly it was not passed.

At this time and till after Powell's death, it was considered by many that a judgment bound the land even without a Writ of Execution; and it required express decisions of the Court of King's Bench to establish the doctrine that not the judgment but the Writ of Execution bound the land, and that not before its delivery to the Sheriff. Doc. dem, McIntosh v. McDonell (1835), 4 U.C.R., O.S. 195. Powell seems to have been of opinion to the contrary.

XVIII

PIERRE DU CALVET: A HUGUENOT REFUGEE IN EARLY MONTREAL; HIS TREASON AND FATE

BY THE HONOURABLE WILLIAM RENWICK RIDDELL, LL.D., F.R.S.C., &c.

Du Calvet was a French Protestant[1] born in Quercy, Province of Guienne, near Toulouse, of a good and fairly wealthy family, his father having a considerable estate in land in that district. He received a good education as education was then understood; his writings (in French, he did not understand English) are in good literary form, his classical quotations apt, and his reasoning logical.

Canada still being French, in 1758 he resolved to emigrate to that Province, New France, and settle in it as a merchant. He accordingly loaded a vessel with goods suited to the trade of Canada and set sail for Quebec early in April, 1758. He was shipwrecked in the St. Lawrence about a hundred miles below Quebec and lost his merchandise; but this did not prevent him pursuing his voyage to Quebec where he arrived in June. The following month he was sent[2] by the authorities in Quebec to Miramichi, in what was then Acadia, as Commissary[3] of the Royal Stores at that port; some three or four thousand French settlers, "Acadians," who had been forced to leave their homes through their antagonism to British rule, had settled in that neighbourhood and were being supported by the French King out of his stores at Miramichi. About one hundred British soldiers were prisoners at this port at the time; these received the greatest kindness from Du Calvet, both at Miramichi and at Restigouche, about two hundred miles away, to which Du Calvet removed the stores and the remaining prisoners in May of the following year. Some of these were released at Miramichi; but Lieutenant Caesar Cormick of Rogers' Rangers and about thirty men were taken to Restigouche. In August, 1759, it was determined to release these also and to send them by sea to Fort Cumberland near Halifax. The Indians of the neighbourhood, fearing that the result of this would be to make known to the English the conditions of the post of Restigouche and invite attack, resolved to destroy the British detachment on its way. Du Calvet learning of the plot, took steps to prevent its success. He selected about sixty Acadians, well armed, and went with them on another vessel to attend the vessel upon which the released prisoners were being carried, and to guard it until it was wholly out of danger.

Shortly after this, Du Calvet returned to Canada, but Quebec had capitulated to the British and he went on to Montreal, arriving there January, 1760.—Montreal was still French. Du Calvet was at once commissioned to return to the same parts of Acadia, and investigate the number and condition of the "Acadians." He left on that mission, January 18th, accompanied by some sixty Acadians and three or four Indian guides. He returned in April to Montreal and remained there until the surrender of that City (and of Canada) in the following September to General Amherst. Fortunately Lieutenant Cormick was amongst Amherst's troops, and he spoke of Du Calvet in high terms to Amherst and the British authorities. He does not seem at first to have intended to become a British subject, as he obtained a passport in 1761 to go to Quebec to take passage thence to Europe. Arriving at Quebec, Governor Murray asked him to delay his voyage that he might perform an important and delicate service for the British Crown.

The Acadians, driven from their settlements in Nova Scotia in 1757, taking refuge on the coast of the Gulf at Miramichi, Restigouche, Nipissiquit and other places as far as Gaspé Bay, had refused to consider themselves British subjects; they had made attacks on British ships (they took fifteen or sixteen during Wolfe's expedition); Amherst had refused to include them in the favourable terms granted to Canadians by the 39th article of the Capitulation of Montreal in September, 1760, and they continued attacks on British vessels in the Gulf of St. Lawrence through the winter of 1760 and the spring of 1761. This piracy was a serious detriment to the St. Lawrence navigation, and Murray resolved to put a stop to it. He sent out a brave and active Canadian, Grandmaison, to placate the pirates, promising them indemnity and rewards in the way of land in place of that in Nova Scotia which they had lost. Grandmaison was also instructed to capture one Sergeant Car, a deserter from the British Army, who had become a leader amongst these Acadians and their Indian friends. Car heard of what was intended, collected a small force, attacked and wounded Grandmaison; and that enterprise failed. This was in the spring of 1761.

Murray then, July, 1761, sent Du Calvet on the same mission; he set sail for the "Baye Des Chaleurs" in a large sloop, evaded a party commanded by Car and one Roussi lying in wait at Percé, and landed at Bonaventure, about nine miles from Paspébiac. He was received by the Canadians with open arms as well as by the Indians, Car and Roussi alone standing aloof. This Roussi was a French captain of a merchantman, which had been taken by the British. Being placed on an English vessel he with the other French prisoners rose against the English crew and seized the vessel. Taking it to the Bay of Gaspé, he joined the Indians and lived with them their lawless life.

Du Calvet took a survey of the Acadian settlements and was reasonably successful in his mission. He got back to Montreal, January, 1762, with the thanks of Murray, who ever after retained a very strong and grateful sense of the value of his services.

He began trade as a merchant in Montreal and continued this business till 1764.

Toward the end of 1763 his father died in France, leaving him considerable landed and other estates; but Du Calvet made up his mind to remain in Canada, a British subject. In the spring of 1764 he sailed for England, where in consequence of recommendations given him by Murray, he was received with great consideration. He then passed over to France, and through the influence of the English Ambassador and other English friends in high places, he obtained a license from the King of France to sell his estates; this was necessary, as at that time Protestants were prohibited by the laws of France from selling their estates without a Royal license. Certain restrictions in the license made the sale less remunerative; but Du Calvet was determined to live under the British flag and in Canada; and he sold even with this disadvantage. This business kept him in France until the end of 1765. In January, 1766, he went to London, and embarked in April for Quebec. Arriving there in June, he remained till November, when he crossed the Atlantic again; he returned, however, in April, 1767, and did not leave Canada again till August, 1783.

In June, 1766, Murray had given Du Calvet a Commission as Justice of the Peace for the Province of Quebec. At that time, the Ordinance of September 17, 1764, was in force, which gave Justices of the Peace certain civil jurisdiction, any one Justice of the Peace having jurisdiction up to £5 currency ($20); any two up to £10 ($40); and three or more sitting in Quarter Sessions from £10 up to £30 ($120); and two Justices of the Peace were to sit weekly in rotation at Quebec and Montreal for these purposes.

Du Calvet had settled in Montreal as a merchant and while he had not desired the Commission, he says that, once he received it, he entered upon the duties of the office with ardour, rather with a view to compose difficulties between neighbours than to administer rigid law. He declined to accept any fees, he paid his own clerk, and even went so far as often to pay the expenses of those appearing before him. It does not therefore astonish us to learn that in the three months from September to December, 1769, he heard 3,700 of these little causes.

Other magistrates[4] were not so thoughtful. The financial condition of most of them was such as to make the receipt of fees a matter of great importance, and many of them did not hesitate to increase their income by means, fair perhaps in some instances, but improper in more. For example, when a fact had been well established by the testimony of two or more witnesses it was a common thing for the Magistrate to ask if there was nobody else who could bear testimony to it. Generally a number of those present would say "Yes, I saw it," etc.; whereupon the Justice would order them all to be sworn, charging a shilling for each oath. Some of the Justices of the Peace kept runners to stir up strife and bring grist to their mill. They were a nuisance and a menace to the community, and many complaints reached the Government in respect of their noxious activities.

At length, February 1, 1770,[5] an Ordinance was passed abolishing the civil jurisdiction of Justices of the Peace in and out of Sessions. Both the Governor, Carleton, and Chief Justice Hey speak in high terms of Du Calvet; and it is reasonably clear that his conduct had nothing to do with this abolition. He continued to act as J.P. in criminal matters, till, by reason of the provisions of the Act of 1774[6] his Commission, with that of all others in Quebec, came to an end, May 1, 1775.

In 1770, he complained to the Chief Justice, Hey, of a decision of ex-Captain John Fraser, Judge of the Court of Common Pleas at Montreal. Du Calvet had obtained judgment against one Moses Hazen (whom we shall meet again) in that Court for about £50 Sterling for some goods sold him. Judge Fraser refused to allow a writ of execution to issue until after the issue of a writ of execution at the instance of another creditor whose judgment was later than that of Du Calvet. The consequence was that Du Calvet was not able to obtain payment of his debt; and in fact, he never did obtain payment. The Chief Justice was of opinion that Du Calvet had had great injustice done him by these proceedings, but that it was not a matter upon which an appeal lay to his Court, the Court of King's Bench;[7] and Du Calvet had nothing for it but to submit to the injustice.

This action by Du Calvet was probably the ultimate cause of a bitter quarrel which broke out between him and the Judge in the following year. At all events, such a quarrel did break out in June, 1771, ostensibly on most trivial grounds; and it was never abated. Du Calvet claims the enmity of Fraser[8] as the real cause of all his subsequent troubles, and it is not unlikely that there is some truth in the claim. Fraser a few days after the open rupture took place attempted the physical chastisement of Du Calvet, but he came off second best. The Frenchman says, triumphantly: "Mr. Fraser . . . being five feet, eleven inches or six feet, English measure, high, and Mr. Du Calvet only about five feet, five inches." Fraser's antagonism continued and Du Calvet complains that thereafter he could receive no justice in the Court of Common Pleas. Fraser's colleague, M. de Rouville, was also antagonistic to Du Calvet, as he thinks, at Fraser's instigation. Nor was the unfortunate man better off in Quebec. Mabane, one of the Common Pleas Judges there, took up Fraser's quarrel and had a verbal altercation with Du Calvet.

There were several acts of gross violence to his property both in Montreal and at the Seigniory of the River David which he had bought near Sorel. The Judges, Fraser and de Rouville in Montreal, and Mabane in Quebec (the great favourite and adviser of Haldimand the Governor) were, he says, his enemies. He could not even get an advertisement offering a reward for the apprehension of the trespassers inserted in the *Gazette*, and he despaired of justice.

In the issue of the *Gazette Litteraire* of Montreal of May 26, 1799,[9] he had a letter published complaining of his treatment, mentioning some of the proceedings of the judges which he conceived to have been most unjust to him, and generally making an attack upon the Court of Common Pleas and its Judges.

An information was laid against him for criminal libel by the Attorney General, and it came on for trial at the ensuing sittings of the Court of King's Bench at Montreal.

Peter Livius,[10] the Chief Justice of the Province, was across the Atlantic, and the office of Chief Justice was in commission; Mabane, already mentioned, Thomas Dunn, a Member of the Legislative Council, and Jenkins Williams, Register of the Council (a lawyer of capacity and the only lawyer of the three) being the Commissioners.

A young lawyer, William Dummer Powell,[11] afterwards Chief Justice of Upper Canada, had just arrived in Montreal. He had been warned by the Attorney General, James Monk,[12] afterwards Chief Justice, to whom he had brought letters of introduction, that the whole force of the Government was levelled against Du Calvet, and that he would probably desire to retain Powell. A "friendly hint" was given the young lawyer "that the advocate of Du Calvet would be marked for the resentment not only of the Judges but the Governor, on which account no English barrister could be retained by" him. To the credit of the profession and of Powell, Du Calvet was received by Powell with courtesy and treated with respect; and when he admitted the writing of the letter, and stated that he had sent it to the Judges openly by his own liveried servant, and that his sole and only defence was the truth of what was alleged, Powell accepted his retainer and entered heartily into his defence. Du Calvet told Powell that no gentleman at the Bar would accept a fee from him for fear of the consequences; and Powell's action in taking up the case is but characteristic of the perfect courage exhibited by him on many an occasion afterwards both before and after his elevation to the Bench.

A Special Jury was sworn of the principal English inhabitants of the city; and they had no difficulty in finding a verdict of "Not Guilty." Both barrister and client say that the jury were clearly of the opinion that the charges were well founded, "not false and injurious but true and notorious"—and it is plain that that must have been the case.

Du Calvet's troubles were by no means over. The following year, September, 1780, he required to go to Quebec to attend the Court of Appeals in order to enter into a bond on an appeal taken by him to the King in Council against a judgment of the Court of Appeal in a case brought against him by Messrs. Watson and Rashleigh of Montreal. He called upon the Governor, Haldimand, was received with great politeness, and had a conversation on indifferent subjects for about a quarter of an hour. He told the Governor he was returning to Montreal the following day and intended to go to England in October. They parted with great civility on both sides, and Du Calvet had no suspicion that any trouble was brewing. On the way home, having passed Three Rivers about four and a half miles, he was arrested by Captain George Laws of the 84th Regiment (Royal Emigrants), without warrant or written order but simply on the oral order of Brigadier General MacLeane. Du Calvet was searched and his letter case taken away, and he was taken back to Three Rivers, the next day to Des Chambaud, and the next to Quebec. He might easily have escaped, but declined to avail himself of the opportunities. He was brought before Governor Haldimand and forthwith consigned to H.M.S. *Canceaux*, Captain Shanks, Commander, of about 400 tons burden and carrying 28 guns, then anchored in the river, and was held a close prisoner.

The charge against him never seems to have been precisely formulated. It rested largely on the belief and, much more, on the suspicion that during the occupation of Montreal by the American troops he had had dealings with the enemy, and that he had kept up correspondence with the Americans after their retreat.[13] There was a rumour, too, that he was gathering at his Seigniory at the River David, grain, cattle, hogs, etc., for the supply of an army which was expected to invade Quebec from the Colonies to the south: his Seigniory was searched but nothing suspicious was found. His house at Montreal was also searched without result; but the unfortunate prisoner did not obtain his freedom. His affairs going to wreck, bail was offered by his friends and he was about to be released on bail when he wrote an injudicious letter, at which the Governor took offence, and the direction for his release was countermanded.[14]

From the *Canceaux*, he was taken to the military prison at Quebec, and a few months later to the Convent of the Récollet Monks at Quebec, where he remained till May 2, 1783. His treatment was, according to his account, inhumane: he was not allowed to supplement his meagre fare and imperfect bed clothes at his own expense, while his room at the Convent was insanitary and filthy, not to say noisome and disgusting.

Several attempts were made to find evidence that he had been in communication with the revolted rebels, but without much avail; very little of what can rightly be called legal evidence was produced. The main dealings, so far as known, he had had with the Americans were before their evacuation of Montreal, but the American troops when evacuating that city upon their retreat under Benedict Arnold when Burgoyne arrived in Quebec in May, 1776, took by force out of his warehouse at Montreal a quantity of goods of the value of about $5,000 giving a receipt therefor.

It was during the imprisonment at the Récollet Convent that an application was made by Du Calvet to the Court which is the direct occasion of this article.

One Charles Hay, "a person in trade" in Quebec, had been arrested in the spring of 1780 as arbitrarily as Du Calvet was later on in the same year. In November, 1780, he applied to the Court of King's Bench (in which were sitting the Commissioners already named) for a writ of Habeas Corpus. The Court would hardly hear Hay's Counsel, and told him, truly enough, that the English law of Habeas Corpus was not in force in the Province. Haldimand let it be known that he would not permit any of his prisoners to be brought to their trials or set at liberty by orders of the Courts of Justice, even if the laws of England might so direct.

But in November, 1782, a conversation between Haldimand and "a gentleman of distinction" in the Province was reported to Du Calvet, which seemed to indicate that Haldimand would no longer impede or be displeased at an application for discharge by the prisoner to the Court of King's Bench on Habeas Corpus. This conversation took place at the Governor's house, "Saint Lewis's Castle," with Major Henry Caldwell[15] an Irish gentleman of good family who had bought Murray's Seigniory of Point Levis opposite Quebec, and was a member of the Legislative Council of the Province. Haldimand expressed on that occasion an inclination that Du Calvet should be set at liberty after his long confinement if some decent method could be found to bring it about without injury to the Governor's honour or reputation. Caldwell told this to L'Evecque, a known and tried friend of Du Calvet, and also informed him that Charles Hay had made another application to the Court for Habeas Corpus, that the Court had taken the application into consideration, and it was hoped the result would be favourable.

Mr. Russell,[16] Du Calvet's Quebec lawyer, as Powell was his Montreal lawyer, was sent for and instructed to make an application accordingly. It gives one a painful impression of the state of Bench and Bar at that time in Quebec to know that due regard for the consequences to himself impelled Russell to take precautions and not to move directly for a writ. He had Du Calvet draw up a short petition himself, desiring the Court to allow him to bring before them the hard case of his long imprisonment and to employ Mr. Russell, his lawyer, to address them in support of his application. The petition further asked the Court to require Mr. Russell, before he entered in the business, to take an oath before them that he would discharge his duty toward his client on this occasion faithfully and uprightly and to the best of his ability.

The Court complied. Russell was sworn, and, November 21, 1782, he presented a formal memorial to the Court on behalf of Du Calvet, praying a writ of Habeas Corpus to bring him into Court to be there dealt with according to law. In the presence of a large audience, Mr. Russell argued upon the laws of England, it is said, with great ability and eloquence. The Court reserved judgment for six days, and, November 27, 1782, gave judgment dismissing the application. The judgment was given orally by Mr. Jenkins Williams, in the name of all the three Commissioners, "that since the establishment of the French laws in the Province in all matters of property and civil rights, by the Act of Parliament passed in the year 1774 for regulating the government of Quebeck, the English laws concerning the writ of Habeas Corpus were not in force in the Province with respect to such persons as were imprisoned by the order of the Governor."

The formal Record is as follows:—

"In the Court of King's Bench: Province of Quebeck. To the Honourable Adam Mabane, Thomas Dunn and Jenkins Williams, Esquires, His Majesty's Commissioners for executing the office of Chief Justice in and for the Province of Quebeck.

The Memorial of Pierre Du Calvet, late of Montreal, Esquire,
Humbly Sheweth

That your Memorialist, on the 27th day of September in the year one thousand seven hundred and eighty, was arrested upon the publick highway between Three Rivers and Pointe du Lac by Captain George Laws of the eighty-fourth Regiment accompanied by another officer.

That he was brought to Quebeck, under a guard, and put on board His Majesty's ship the Canceaux then in the river Saint Lawrence; afterwards was put amongst a number of other prisoners and finally shut up in an apartment at the Récollets, where he remains in close confinement in the greatest distress in the custody of a Mr. Miles Prenties (who styles himself Keeper of the prévôt), without being able to procure a copy of the warrant of his commitment, or to know the causes of his capture and detention, though he has made frequent application for that purpose.

That yesterday the 20th instant, your Memorialist made two other applications to the said Miles Prenties for a copy of the warrant of his capture and detention, but was absolutely refused; as in and by the annexed affidavit may fully and at large appear.

That your Memorialist is informed that the capture and detention aforesaid and the refusal of a copy of the warrant of commitment are altogether illegal.

And therefore he humbly prays that your Honours may be pleased to award His Majesty's remedial writ of Habeas Corpus *ad subjiciendum* returnable *immediate*, directed to the said Miles Prenties commanding him to produce to this Honourable Court your Memorialist's body with the day and cause of his capture and detention *ad faciendum, subjiciendum et recipiendum*, to do, submit to and receive whatever this Honourable Court shall consider in that behalf.

And that your Honours will thereupon be pleased to discharge your Memorialist or, in case that his accusers appear against him, that he may be tried, or admitted to bail, or that he may be otherwise dealt with according to law.

(Signed) ROBERT RUSSELL,
Barrister-at-Law.

Nov. the 21st, 1782.
Quebeck.

Court of King's Bench, Province of Quebeck.

Personally appeared Mr. Jacques Le Moine and Mr. Thomas Davidson of Quebeck, gentlemen, and made oath on the Holy Evangelists that yesterday the twentieth instant between the hours of two and three of the clock in the afternoon these deponents in company with each other waited upon Miles Prenties of Quebeck, Keeper of the Prévôt, at his dwelling house in Palace Street, and then and there demanded of him a copy of the warrant of the commitment and detention of Pierre Du Calvet, Esquire, now a prisoner at the Récollets, which he, the said Miles Prenties, absolutely refused to deliver.

That afterwards to wit on the same day and between the hours of eight and nine of the clock at night, these deponents repeated the same demand on the said Miles Prenties but to no purpose; being refused as above.

And the said deponent Jacques Le Moine for himself further saith, that the said Pierre Du Calvet, Esquire, has been for a long time past and is now shut up in an apartment at the Récollets under the guard of a centinel at the door (which opens to the said apartment) with a screwed bayonet. And further the deponents say not.

(Signed) JACQUES LE MOINE.
(Signed) THOMAS DAVIDSON.

Sworn in Court
this 21st day of Nov. 1782.
(Signed) THOMAS DUNN.

Court of King's Bench, Wednesday, Nov. the 27th, 1782.

THE KING AGAINST PETER DU CALVET, ESQ.

The Court, having maturely deliberated upon the Memorial of Peter Du Calvet, and the arguments offered by his Counsel in support of the motion, made upon that Memorial for a writ of *Habeas Corpus* are of opinion 'that nothing be taken by the said motion and that the Memorial be dismissed.'

By the Court.

(Signed) DAVID LYND,
Acting Clerk for the Crown.'"[17]

Du Calvet says that the very next day, Haldimand, who was exceedingly pleased with the judgment, created a new office for Williams, and made him Solicitor General for the Province with a salary of £200 sterling per annum.

Du Calvet remained in prison till May 2, 1783, when Prenties, the Provost-Martial, came to him and informed him that he was no longer a prisoner and could leave when he pleased, at the same time removing the sentinel. But he refused Du Calvet's request for a copy of the warrant or order under the authority of which he had kept him so long in prison.

The prisoner, after resting a time in Quebec, made his way to Montreal, where he found his property stolen, his business ruined. He determined to go to England to endeavour to obtain redress for his ill-treatment and to be safe from its repetition. He was refused a passport which would enable him to go to Philadelphia to obtain from the United States payment for the goods taken from him, May, 1776, but was granted a passport for England. Even this, it would seem, Haldimand endeavoured to rescind, but too late—the bird had flown; Du Calvet had taken a small sloop and caught up with the brigantine *Tarleton*, which had sailed for England.

Arriving in England in September, he applied to Lord North and Charles James Fox, Secretaries of State, for an order that Haldimand should return to England so that he might be sued for damages in the English Courts, or that he might be judged by a Commission sent out to Canada for that purpose, as had been done with Murray in 1762. Of course, Haldimand could not be sued in the Canadian Courts even if they offered any chance of relief.

These requests were not acceded to; but at length, in 1784, Haldimand obtained leave to return to England, receiving at the same time the assurance that his conduct had received the approbation of the King in the fullest manner.

Du Calvet sued him in the Court of King's Bench at Westminster, for damages, but the action never came to trial. Du Calvet came to this continent to obtain evidence on a Commission for use in the English Court. Returning, March 15, 1786, he sailed from New York for London on the *Sherburne*, an old Spanish prize, renamed. A terrible storm sprang up,· more violent than any within human recollection. Ship, crew and passengers were lost and never heard of again.[18]

NOTES

[1] The facts in this paper are derived from two publications by Du Calvet, the title pages of which are set out below, the Haldimand Papers in the Canadian Archives, Manuscripts of Chief Justice Powell in my hands, the property of Æmilius Jarvis, Esquire, Toronto (unpublished), and other reliable sources. Some account of Du Calvet will be found in the Reports of the Canadian Archives (Douglas Brymner, Archivist), 1888, pp. XV, sqq., and Report for 1885.

The two works of Du Calvet are not very uncommon and are to be found in many reference ₁ibraries. They are as follows:

1. "The | Case | of | Peter DuCalvet, Esq., | of Montreal in the Province of Quebeck | Containing | (Amongst other Things worth Notice) | An Account of the long and severe imprison- | ment he suffered in the said Province by the | Order of General Haldimand the present | Gouvernour of the Same, without the least | offence or other lawful Cause whatever | To which is prefixed | A Dedication of it in the French Language | (Mr. DuCalvet not understanding English) | To the

King's Most Excellent Majesty | Humbly imploring the Protection and Countenance | of His Majesty's Royal Justice in his Endeavours | to procure some Compensation for the Injuries he | has received | London | Printed in the year M.DCC.LXXXIV"
8vo, xi, 284 pp.
(This will be cited as "Case.")

2. "Appel à la Justice de l'Etat; | ou | Recueil de Lettres | au Roi | Au Prince de Galles | et aux Ministres | avec | une Lettre | à Messieurs les Canadiens | où sont fidèlement exposés les actes horribles de la violence arbitraire | qui a régné dans la Colonie, durant les derniers troubles, & les vrais | sentiments du Canada sur le Bill de Quebec, & sur la forme de Gouvernement la plus propre à y faire renâitre la paix & le bonheur | public | Une Lettre | au Général Haldimand lui-même | en fin | Une Dernier Lettre | à Milord Sidney's | où on lit un précis des nouvelles du 4 & 10 de Mais dernier, sur ce | qui s'est passé en Avril dans le Conseil Législatif de Quebec, avec les | Protêts de six Conseillers, le Lieutenant-Gouverneur Henri Hamilton | à leur tête, contre la nouvelle Inquisition d'Etat établie par le Gou- | verneur & son parti | Par Pierre DuCalvet, Ecuyer | Ancien Juge à Paix | de la Ville de Montreal | Avec une Table, & un Errata à la fin. | Imprimé à Londres | Dans les mois de Juin & Juillet de l'année 1784 | "
8vo, xiv, 320; viii.

The Archivist's report is of course quite common; it exhibits much scepticism of some of DuCalvet's statements.

²The Archivist doubts this for two reasons: first, the long established rule that no Huguenot was employed in such a capacity in the French Colonies, and, second, that his name cannot be found in any of the lists of officers and others in the French service in Acadia. What is thought by the Archivist (p. xvii) to be "a somewhat different statement" is not so in reality. He says: "il arracha à la cruauté des sauvages plusieurs officiers anglois prisonniers, il leur rendit avec la liberté d'autres services importans et sa satisfaction fut complete. Lorsque par la conquête il partagea avec les conquerans la liberté de penser et d'agir suivant les mouvements de sa conscience il s'attacha au commerce . . . M. Murray, alors Gouverneur ayant été informé que le S. DuCalvet s'étoit prêté avec distinction à ce qui pouvoit obliger la nation chercha à le connoitre et à luy prouver qu'il y étoit sensible; il se chargea de vaincre la repugnance de quelques accadiens pour le Gouvernement anglois: C. S. Ducalvet partit les alla trouver, et les eut bientôt persuadé, alors la méfiance disparut et le gouverneur fut satisfait de la soumission de ces accadiens:" i. e.:

"He rescued from the cruelty of the savages certain English officers, prisoners; in addition to setting them free he rendered them other valuable services and his satisfaction was complete. When by the Conquest he shared with the conquerors freedom of thought and action according to the dictates of his conscience, he devoted himself to trade . . . Murray, the Governor at the time, having been informed that Du Calvet had won distinction in his labours for the nation, desired to know him and to prove to him that he was sensible of his services. He entrusted to him the task of overcoming the repugnance to the British Government on the part of some Acadians. DuCalvet went and sought them and soon persuaded tnem; their distrust disappeared and the Governor had the satisfaction to receive the submission of these Acadians."

The task committed to him by Murray was in 1761, and will be found mentioned in the text. Du Calvet's services under Murray were wholly distinct in point of time and otherwise from those rendered to the English prisoners.

That Du Calvet was favourably regarded by Murray is undoubted; and it is difficult to believe that Du Calvet would detail with such circumstantiality, with names, dates and places, what was wholly untrue. Many persons were living in 1784 who knew the facts, and no contradiction was ever made. It is to be remembered that Du Calvet for a long time was pressing his claims upon the British Government, and it is not likely that he would venture on misstatement of such facts. Haldimand in London and Mabane in Quebec had considerable correspondence about Du Calvet, but they do not charge him with misrepresentation in the matters now under consideration.

The omission of Du Calvet's name from the list of officers, etc., may be susceptible of several explanations; and it is not without precedent that one has been employed by a Government when the law says he shall not.

³The Archivist seems to have misunderstood Du Calvet as to his position as Commissary. What he says is that "he was appointed *Garde-magazin en chef*, a principal commissary of the French King's provisions and stores at that port (Miramichi) at which many of the poor French settlers . . . who are generally known by the name of the Acadians . . . had taken refuge." "Case" p. 2. It is to this that he refers in his petition to the King of January 30th, 1767, (Can. Arch. xviii). "Envoyé en 1758 dans l'accadie par le gouvernement français en qualité de commissaire j'ay guaranty la liberté et la vie d'une foule de soldats anglois que la fortune avoit rendus prisonniers de guerre, etc." The Archivist takes this as meaning that he was a Commissary,

part of the garrison at Louisbourg, but there is no statement of the kind and Du Calvet never suggests that he was at Louisbourg. Possibly had he used the term "Garde-magazin" instead of "Commissaire" the error would not have arisen.

⁴The magnanimity of Du Calvet rests upon his own testimony; the improper conduct of the Magistrates in general was a matter of notoriety, at least in Montreal. We had within a very few years a similar scandal in our own metropolitan County of York—that was, however, in quasi-criminal cases.

⁵The Ordinance of February 1st, 1770, is to be found in the Const. Docs. printed as Vol. 3 to the Archives Report, 1905, p. 280, sqq., of the English Edition (now out of print and difficult to procure). A second and much improved edition has been published by The Historical Documents Publications Board, "Documents relating to the Constitutional History of Canada, 1759-1791 . . . Selected and Edited with Notes by Adam Shortt and Arthur G. Doughty . . ." Ottawa, The King's Printer, 1918—often quoted thus: S. & D.

The Ordinance of February 1, 1770, appears in this edition at pp. 401-416. It recites "Whereas it has been found by experience that the several Provisions contained in an Ordinance bearing Date the Seventeenth Day of September One thousand seven hundred and sixty-four . . . by virtue of which certain Powers and Authorities are given to the Justices of the Peace for this Province . . . to hear and determine in matters of private Property between Party and Party, instead of answering the good purposes for which they were ordained have become an intolerable Burthen to the Subject and proved the means of great Disgust, Vexation and Oppression."

The Report of the Committee of Council to take into Consideration the State of the Administration of Justice in Quebec, made September 11th, 1769, gives a vivid view of the scandals of the Magistrates' Court; for example, it is said that suing for a debt of eleven livres cost in one instance eighty-four livres. The Committee also found "the Magistrates to have assumed . . . high and dangerous Authority in the exercise of which the Gaols are constantly filled with numbers of unhappy Objects and whole families reduced to beggary and ruin. It being a Common practice and the usual Method of their process to take Lands in Execution and order them to be sold for the payment of ever so small a debt or in case there are no Lands to satisfy the debt to commit the party to prison. The sad Consequences whereof and wretched Servitude to which a people are reduced whose persons and property are thus exposed," the Committee does not need to enlarge upon.

For this illuminating Report see S. & D., pp. 396, sqq.

[Since the above note was written I have received by the courtesy of the Archivist a volume published by his Department in 1917: "Ordinances | made and passed | by the | Governor and Council | of the | Province of Quebec | 1763-1791 | Ottawa | . . . . | 1917"

The Ordinance of February 1, 1770, will be found printed on pp. 26-38 of the second part of this volume; also in Appendix C of the Archivist's Report of 1914-15, of which the second part is a reprint.

⁶The Imperial Act, 1774, 14 Geo. III, c. 83,—the well-known "Quebec Act" (S. & D., pp. 570, sqq.),—annulled "all commissions to Judges and other officers . . . from and after the First day of May, 1775." See p. 403.

⁷The Ordinance of September 17th, 1764, gave the right of appeal to the Court of King's Bench from the Court of Common Pleas "where the Matter in Contest is of the Value of Twenty Pounds and upwards"; but the matter of complaint in Du Calvet's case was not the decision between the parties but the question of mere practice as to which of two creditors should have the prior writ of *fieri facias;* and this would be non-appealable.

⁸Du Calvet's powers of description, which were by no means contemptible, are shown in his delineation of the Judges of whose enmity he complains.

In "Case" at pp. 46, sqq., he thus speaks of Judge Fraser:

"Mr. John Fraser, a scotch Gentleman who had been a Captain in His Majesty's 60th regiment of Foot called the North American (which consisted of four batallions) in the war which ended in the year 1763, in which regiment he became acquainted with General Haldimand, who was then a Field officer in the same regiment . . . After the peace (he was) put on half pay. After serving in Canada during the war, he settled there after the peace and married a Roman Catholick Lady of the name of Des Chambaud with whom he lived in Montreal. As he was well acquainted with the French language, General Murray when Gouvernour of the Province in 1764, made him one of the Judges of the Court of Common Pleas . . . at Montreal . . . In this office he conducted himself with considerable ability and great gravity, though not without some complaints . . . of . . . partiality in his decisions upon some occasions."

In the French work "Appel" at pp. 72, sqq., he is even more vigorous:

"C'étoit l'Excapitaine Frazer (du sang du dernier Lord Lovat) qui dans la guerre de 1756 rangé sous les étendards Royaux dans le 66e Regiment avoit essayé d'effecer par des services de marque ses disgraces domestiques de 1745 & 1746. Il dépouilla en 1756 la casque et la cuirasse pour endosser la robe longue . . . le Juge Frazer est un homme d'assez bon esprit, quand il lui plâit d'en faire usage, doué d'assez belles connoissances, supérieures à ce que sembleroit indiquer une jeunesse passée dans les camps et dans les armées; il annonce par ses manières, l'homme d'éducation; d'ailleurs, naturellement juste quand la haine ou l'amitié ne dictent point ses Arrêts. Mais c'est un homme à tics, à caprices, à petitesses; d'une délicatesse qui souvent s'offusque de son ombre; mais sur tout si impérieux, si haut, que s'il monte sur ses échaffes (elevation d'accès convulsifs & d'habitude chez lui) du sommet de sa hauteur, il n'appercevroit plus le clocher de S. Paul, que dans le fond d'une vallée . . . si enflé de sa grandeur personelle & entaché encore du levain de la fierté & du despotisme militaire . . ."

I translate with a reasonable regard to literalness:—

"This was ex-Captain Frazer (of the family of the last Lord Lovat) who having in the war of 1756 served under the Royal flag in the 66th Regiment endeavoured thus to efface by services of note the disgrace of his family in 1745-6. In 1756 he exchanged the helmet and cuirass for the long robe of the lawyer . . . Judge Frazer is a man of considerable talent when he cares to make use of it; is possessed of respectable learning, superior indeed to what might be expected from a youth passed under arms in the camps. His bearing shows a man of education and he is, moreover, just by nature where hate or friendship does not dictate his decrees.

"But he is a man of fads, caprices, littlenesses, of an overrefinement which often eclipses itself; but above all so imperious, so arbitrary, that when his pride is at its height, which habitually happens with him, he looks on the dome of Saint Paul only as in a valley . . . so blown with personal grandeur and infected with the leaven of pride and military despotism . . ."

Of Frazer's colleague on the Bench of the Court of Common Pleas at Montreal, Du Calvet writes thus in "Case," pp. 66, sqq.:—

"A French or Canadian Gentleman named Monsieur de Rouville who was employed in a judicial office at Trois Rivieres, or Three Rivers, in the time of the French government . . . in the month of May in the year 1775, Mr. de Rouville was advanced to be one of the Conservators of the Peace for the District of Montreal . . . and upon the restablishment of the two Courts of Common Pleas . . . Mr. de Rouville has been appointed one of the Judges of that Court at Montreal . . . This appointment . . . to so great a judicial office was by no means agreeable to the French (or Canadian) inhabitants of Montreal and its neighborhood, as the violence and haughtiness of his temper was well known to them, and some of them remembered how ill the people of Trois Rivieres had been satisfied with his conduct as a Judge . . . in the time of the French government."

In "Appel," pp. 90, sqq., we find the following:—

"M. de Rouville est un Gentilhomme Canadien, mincement initié dans les mystères de la Jurisprudence Française & a ce titre personnage peu competent pour la judicature mais d'un genie si impérieux, d'un caractère si superbe, d'une humeur si identifiée avec le despotisme, qu'elle se trahit surtout, non seulement sur les Tribuneaux de Justice où elle peut dogmatiser & trancher de la souverain sans contrôle, mais dans le commerce même de la vie civile & jusque dans le sein de sa famille. Aureste, homme tout paîtri et boursoufflé des prétentions de l'amour propre, preoccupé de ses prétendues lumières entier dans ses jugemens, intolérant de la plus juste & de la plus humble opposition, grand formaliste, partial non-seulement de système réfléchi, mais d'instinct, assez chaud pour ses amis, que j'appellerois plus pertinemment, ses cliens & ses protégés, mais tout de flammes & de volcans contre ses ennemis, que son ame, naturellement vindicative, ne juge jamais assez punis. Tel avoit éclaté M. de Rouville sous le Gouvernement François où assis sur les fleurs de lis des Trois Rivières, il se concilia l'estime de bien peu de ses concitoyens, le confiance & l'amitié de personne, aussi son elevation à la dignité de Conservateur de paix, en 1775 et depuis de Juge des Plaidoyers Communs a Montreal, fut-elle reçue comme un coup de foudre en Canada pour qui elle étoit l'annonce & le précurseur du despotisme qui alloit desormais présider aux oracles de la justice & y dicter les arrêts de sa partialité & de sa faveur. Les appréhensions publiques n'ont été, helas! que trop justifiées par l'évènement.

Voilà ce Monsieur de Rouville que la nature avoit si fort rapproché de M. Frazer, dans la fabrique de leurs ames, toutes paîtries du levain du despotism . . ."

I translate:—

"M. de Rouville is a Canadian Gentleman but slightly initiated into the mysteries of French jurisprudence and in that respect little qualified for the Bench; but of a nature so imperious, a character so proud, a humour so identified with despotism, that it betrays itself on all occasions, not only on the Bench, where it can dogmatise and play the sovereign without control but also in the relations of ordinary life and even in the bosom of his family. Moreover, a man all filled and inflated by his affectation, taken up with his pretended sagacity, obstinate in his judgments, intolerant of the most trifling opposition, however just, a stickler for formality, partial not only on system but by instinct, cold towards his friends (whom I should rather call his clients and protégés) but all fire and volcano towards his enemies, so that his soul, naturally vindictive, never thinks them sufficiently punished.

"Such a man notoriously was M. de Rouville under the French rule when, seated under the fleur-de-lis at Three Rivers, he obtained the respect of very few of his fellow citizens, the confidence and friendship of none; and so his elevation to the dignity of Conservator of the Peace in 1775 and afterwards of Judge of the Common Pleas at Montreal, was like a thunderclap to Canada, for which it was the declaration and the forerunner of the despotism which was thereafter to preside over the oracles of justice and there dictate the decrees of its partiality.

"These apprehensions of the people were unfortunately only too well justified by the event. Such is M. de Rouville, whom nature has made so like Mr. Frazer in their very souls, all filled with the leaven of despotism."

Mabane, one of the Judges of the Court of Common Pleas at Quebec, is thus described, "Case," pp. 56, sqq.:—

"Mr. Mabane, another Scotch Gentleman, who lived at Quebeck where he was Surgeon of the Garrison and one of the Judges of the Court of Common Pleas for that district and who was a great friend of Mr. Frazer . . ."

In "Appel," pp. 92, sqq., we find the following description of Mabane:—

"Le Juge Mabane est un original si singulier, si unique, qu'il conte bien peu de copies: C'est un homme que n'est jamais lui-même, dans ce qu'il paroît au dehors; il ne s'offre par-tout qu'en masque: Magistrat à Quebec & Sagefemme à Edinburgh, c'est là qu'il a pris ses grades de Docteur en jurisprudence Françoise, dans les écoles de Chirurgie. Chez lui ce n'est point communément le coeur qui decide de son amitié ou de sa haine: c'est l'esprit national & cette nationalité va d'autant plus loin dans ses vengeances qu'il imagine avoir toujours tort le corps de ses compatriotes à venger avec lui : si des interêts de passion personelle viennent encore s'allier & renforcer le ressentiment de nation, le dénouement de la scène vindicative ne peut se développer, que par la ruine de la victime ou par le désespoir eclatant du venger. Un tel personnage étoit le dernier homme que la sage politique auroit dû montrer sur-tout en place, dans une conquête. Son tempérament semble s'incliner vers la méditation, la contemplation; ou le prendroit pour un philosophe un être pensant; point du tout; ce n'est qu'un esprit inquiet qui se démène & qui s'agite; & son humeur bourrue & brusque jointe à une mine naturellement grimaçante, annonce qu'il n'est pas toujours d'accord avec lui-même; comment le fervit-il avec les autres? Ses inclinations pancheroient assez vers l'économie; mais il rassemble sur sa tête cinq à six places, la plupart de judicature; la vanité fait les honneurs de chez lui, il ne thésaurise point: en fait de hauteur naturelle & d'arrogance impérieuse, il pourroit bien aller de pair avec ses deux collègues mais l'intérêt le dénature encore ici & le rend souple, flexible, rampant, sur-tout auprès des grands; il étoit né sans fortune; les places y suppléent & la lui donnent; voilà ce qui en fait tout à la fois un des plus lâches & des plus adroits flatteurs, qui aient jamais obsédé les palais de la grandeur; c'est à la faveur de cette flatterie habile, qu'il s'étoit concilié les bonnes graces des deux premiers Gouverneurs; mais comme rien n'est naturel chez lui & qui tout n'est que de circonstance, il trahit a leur départ la cause de ses deux protecteurs; sans doute qu'il prépare la même marche de tergiversation au Gouverneur d'aujourd'hui ce sera le comble d'ingratitude; car M. Mabane est le conseil, le confident & la règle du Général Haldimand qui n'est que la dupe de son subalterne & ne gouverne qu'en second sous la tutèle & la dictée de ce favori . . ." p. 167 "le chirurgien Juge, l'imperieux M. Mabane."

. . . .

I translate:—

"Judge Mabane is so singular, so almost unique a creature that he has very few copies. He is a man who is never himself in his external manifestations; he never appears except with a mask. At Quebec a magistrate, at Edinburgh a midwife, it was at Edinburgh that he took his degree in French jurisprudence, in the medical schools. With him it is generally not the heart which decides by hate or friendship, it is national feeling; and that feeling of nationality enters so much the deeper into his revenge that he is always under the impression that he has to avenge the whole body of his fellow countrymen with himself. If personal resentment adds its force to national feeling the scene is not complete except with the ruin of the victim or despair of revenge. Such a person was the last man whom wise policy should have placed in office, especially after a conquest. His temperament seems to lean towards meditation, contemplation; one would take him for a philosopher, a being given to deep thought—not at all—he is but an unquiet soul, restless and uneasy, and his humour, surly and abrupt, joined to a manner naturally grotesque, shows that he is not always at peace with himself; how, then, can he be expected to be so with others? His inclination leans towards economy, but although he has accumulated for himself five or six places (chiefly connected with the courts), he does not lay anything by, as vanity is the master in his establishment. In the matter of natural hauteur and imperious arrogance he is a fit mate for his two colleagues; but even there, self-interest denatures him and makes him pliant, flexible, servile, especially towards those in high station. Receiving no means by descent, places supply the defect and give him means. One of the most cowardly and at the same time most adroit of flatterers who have ever beset the palaces of the great, it was by virtue of that skilful flattery that he obtained the favour of the two first governors; but as he is never his natural self and is always guided by circumstances, upon their departure, he betrayed the cause of his two protectors. Beyond question he is now preparing to take the same devious course with the present Governor. This would be the very height of ingratitude, for Mr. Mabane is the councillor, the confidant and the guide of General Haldimand, who is only the dupe of his subordinate and governs only as second in command under the tutelage and dictation of this favourite" . . . (p. 167)—"The Surgeon-Judge, the imperious Mabane." General James Murray in his official Report of the State of the Government of Quebec in Canada, June 5, 1762, gives "Mr. Mabane" as one of the Surgeon's Mates of His Majesty's Hospital there. S. & D., p. 48. It is well known that he became the confidential adviser of Governor Frederick Haldimand and a man of great consequence in the old Province. Some account of him is given in my "Life of William Dummer Powell...", Lansing, Michigan, 1924. See Index, *sub nom*.

The Archivist doubts Du Calvet in his statement of facts by reason of his vicious attacks upon all in authority in Quebec; this is not a sound reason in my view. In Upper Canada some years later we find Robert Fleming Gourlay, whose attacks upon the authorities in this Province were quite as savage and quite as extensive, but there is no reason to believe that he was capable of misstating a fact. See my life of Robert Fleming Gourlay, Ontario Hist. Socy. 1916.

⁹See Haldimand papers in the Canadian Archives, B. 205; Can. Archives, Rep. for 1889, p. 41 ad fin.

¹⁰Peter Livius was born about 1727 (it is said) at Lisbon, Portugal, of a German father, an employee in an English establishment there. Certainly he was not of British ancestry and even his right to be called a British subject was in controversy. He was a man of some means and of liberal education; we find him receiving an honorary degree from Harvard in 1767. At what time he came to America is uncertain; but, taking up his residence in Portsmouth, New Hampshire, he before 1770 had served some years as Judge of the Court of Common Pleas and was also a member of the Governor's Council. He fell out with the Governor, the second Wentworth, and, being deprived of his seat upon the Bench by the legislation of 1773, he went to England and pressed his own grievances and those of others upon the Home authorities. He was appointed Chief Justice of New Hampshire but never acted as such; it was thought that such a proceeding would increase the discord, already too great, and Livius was sent out to Quebec in 1775 as a Judge of the Court of Common Pleas. In Canada he had a dispute with the Governor, Carleton, partly over his emolument and partly over appointments of Notaries, etc. Appointed Chief Justice of Quebec in 1777, he continued his strife with the Governor, till at length Carleton suspended him in May, 1778. He appealed to the Privy Council and was reinstated in his Office; he, however, never re-entered his Province but remained in England and Ireland till his death in 1786. (For an account of his quarrel with Carleton see an article, "The Tragedy of Chief Justice Livius" by A. L. Burt, *Canadian Historical Review*, Sept., 1924.)

His absence from the Province was the cause of much bitter complaint as it was thought to conduce to the arbitrary character of Haldimand's government. Du Calvet's English work has many references to it; and he again and again attempted to get an order passed for the return to Canada of the Chief Justice, without avail as we have seen.

During his absence his office was in Commission, as in olden days was often the case with the office of Lord Chancellor and is always now with that of Lord Admiral and Lord Treasurer.

¹¹The story of the connection of Powell with Du Calvet is taken from Powell's manuscripts (unpublished) in my possession. It is satisfactory to know that Powell's defence of Du Calvet, instead of injuring him, was the beginning of a very flourishing practice, especially, as Powell says, among the official classes. (See my "Life of William Dummer Powell." Michigan Historical Commission, Lansing, 1924).

¹²James Monk and Powell were afterwards in close business and personal relations. They fell out over money matters, and Monk sued Powell in the Montreal Court, and afterwards (on the Lower Canadian judgment) in our Upper Canada Court of King's Bench. An account of this action, extraordinary in many features, will be found in full in Powell's MSS. See also my "Life, etc.," Appendix E.

Monk became Chief Justice of the King's Bench at Montreal in 1794. He had considerable trouble with Parliament, and was impeached: At length he resigned with a pension in 1783.

¹³The truth of this charge is not quite clear. It does appear that Du Calvet, having changed his allegiance once, was not averse from changing it again. He acted as agent in 1776 for the invading American General Montgomery in spreading his proclamation amongst the French-Canadian Habitants, and he seems even to have accepted a commission as ensign in the Canadian Regiment commanded by his debtor, Moses Hazen. He had considerable correspondence with

Lafayette, also indicating if not proving treason; and his desire, upon being released, to go to Philadelphia was not based alone on his claim against the Continental Congress (or the United States).

His imprisonment was amply justified as a measure of State, in the uncertain state of the Colony, however it may have been as a strict matter of law. The late Dr. Benjamin Sulte, F.R.S.C., some years ago gave an informal address in Section II of the Royal Society of Canada, in which he spoke of Du Calvet—he was wholly convinced of his guilt.

[14] This letter is just such as a hot-headed man would write (Powell calls Du Calvet a "hot-headed Huguenot") but not offensive except to an arbitrary governor. It is set out on pp. 116 to 124 of "Case."

[15] Afterwards Sir Henry Caldwell, Receiver General.

[16] Powell in some of his MSS. speaks as though he conducted the motion on Du Calvet's behalf, but this is clearly an error. In the MSS. of Powell during the latter part of his life, mistakes are occasionally to be found in matters of detail. It is probable Powell was consulted, and that he advised in the matter; but it is too plain for doubt that it was Russell who appeared in person in court on Du Calvet's behalf.

[17] The accuracy of this decision depends upon the effect of the wording of the Quebec Act, 1774, 14 Geo. III, cap. 83, that "in all matters of controversy relative to Property and Civil Rights Resort shall be had to the Laws of Canada as the Rule for the Decision of the same," but that "the Criminal Law of England . . . shall continue to be administered and shall be observed as Law in the Province of Quebec as well in the Description and Quality of the offence as in the Method of Prosecution and Trial and the Punishments and Forfeitures thereby inflicted to the Exclusion of every other Rule of Criminal Law . . ."

It is generally said, somewhat loosely, that the English Criminal Law was introduced by the Royal Proclamation of 1763 and continued by the Quebec Act of 1774. This is not strictly correct. The English Criminal Law was continued by the Quebec Act only as to (1) the Description and Quality of the offence, (2) the Method of Prosecution and Trial, and (3) the Punishment and Forfeitures. It is obvious that release by writ of Habeas Corpus does not come under any of these heads. In the troublous time of 1838, a writ of Habeas Corpus was obtained for one Teed, charged with participating in the Rebellion, from Justices Panet and Bedard of the Queen's Bench at Quebec, in the absence of the Chief Justice in Montreal. These two Judges held that the Quebec Act introduced the Criminal Law of England, including the Habeas Corpus Act, 31 Car. II; but their action did not receive approval; they were suspended, as was Judge Vallières de St. Real, Three Rivers, who admitted a prisoner to bail on Habeas Corpus. The matter was settled, the Judges reinstated, and the last named afterwards advanced to be Chief Justice at Montreal. It is probable, however, that this was done in pursuance of the policy of conciliation followed after the Rebellion.

That Haldimand did not believe the Habeas Corpus Act to be in force in Quebec is certain. Chief Justice Livius seems to have been of the same opinion, and it was one of the demands of the agitators of the Province who in 1784 sent three commissioners—William Dummer Powell, Adhemar, and De Lisle—to England to present their grievances.

Briefly stated, they demanded:
1. French law with English constitution.
2. Restoration of Habeas Corpus.
3. The Governor justiciable by the Laws of the Province.
4. Institution of an Assembly.
5. Six members to represent Canada in the Imperial Parliament, three from Quebec, three from Montreal.
6. Religious equality.
7. Reform of judicature by re-establishment of the Conseil Supérieur of Quebec as in the French System.
8. Formation of a Canadian Regiment with two battalions.
9. Liberty of the Press.
10. Institution of Colleges for the education of youth.
11. Naturalization of Canadians throughout the British Empire, opposed by "la faction bruyante & courroucée des Mabane, des Frazer, des de Rouville & de quelques mercenaires flatteurs en place." i. e., "the noisy, angry faction of the Mabanes, Frazers, de Rouvilles and some mercenary place-holding flatterers." (Appel, p. 237.)

When the treaty of peace and amity was signed, 1783, acknowledging the independence of the United States, there was no longer in Haldimand's view any reason for preventing the Courts investigating the case of a prisoner, and an Ordinance was passed, April 29th, 1784, which in effect introduced the provisions of the English Habeas Corpus Act into Quebec. This was amended from time to time: 34 Geo. III, c. 6, s. 37; 52 Geo. III, c. 8, ss. 1 to 7; 1 Geo IV, c. 8, ss. 1, 2; 2 Geo IV, s. 5, s. 10; and temporarily suspended in the times of the Rebellion, 1 Vic., c. 2; 2 Vic., St. 2, c. 4; 2 Vic., St., 3, c. 31; 3 & 4 Vic., c. 2.

A Bill was introduced into the House of Commons at Westminster in 1786 by Mr. Powys (or Powis), a prominent member of the Opposition, to make the English Habeas Corpus Act applicable to Quebec, but this failed to pass; it was not then necessary.

[18] The perils of the seas were very real in those days; e.g., two of Chief Justice Powell's children were drowned at sea at different times and thousands of miles apart.

XIX

"HIS HONOUR," THE LIEUTENANT GOVERNOR, AND "HIS LORDSHIP," THE JUSTICE

By The Honourable William Renwick Riddell,
Justice of the Supreme Court of Ontario

The official and "courtesy" titles of functionaries in this Province have had a varied history, some account of which may be of interest.

When Upper Canada began her separate Provincial career in 1791-2, she was given a Lieutenant Governor, Colonel John Graves Simcoe. He was a real *Lieutenant* Governor, the Lieutenant of the Governor-in-Chief of Upper Canada and Lower Canada. Simcoe's powers were, according to his Commission, to be exercised only in case of the death or absence from the Province of the Governor-in-Chief, Guy, Lord Dorchester, the well-known Sir Guy Carleton.

Simcoe, though but a Lieutenant Governor, acted as Governor during his whole residence in Upper Canada, 1792-1796; Dorchester never came within the Province. Simcoe had the official title, "His Excellency," and was invariably so addressed by the Houses of Parliament, by the Judges in their official Reports and, when occasion required, by the Home authorities.

When Simcoe went to England in the summer of 1796 (intending to return later), the administration of the Government was taken over by the Honourable Peter Russell, President of the Executive Council; he was never addressed as "Your Excellency," but always as "Your Honor."

General Peter Hunter became Lieutenant Governor in 1799; he had the title, "His Excellency," as had all his successors as Lieutenant Governors of Upper Canada down to the Union in 1841. At his death in 1805, the Honourable Alexander Grant, President of the Executive Council, became Administrator, September, 1805. Parliament was called for February, 1806; and before the Session, Grant was always called "His Honor."

On the second day of the Session, February 5th, a Committee was appointed by the Legislative Assembly to draft an address to "His Honor, the President, in answer to his Speech," of which Committee Captain Mathew Elliott, of Essex, was chairman. He and Grant were old acquaintances; and whether for personal reasons or otherwise, he framed the Address reading "To the Honorable Alexander Grant, Esquire, President, administering the Government of the Province of Upper Canada, &c." This was read in the Assembly first by Elliott in his place and then by the Clerk of the House; then it was engrossed, and read, passed and signed by the Speaker, Alexander Macdonell, of Glengarry.

After the Administrator had set a day and hour for receiving the Address, the Speaker, by permission of the House, read a paper which was ordered to be inserted in the Journal.

"The Speaker begs the indulgence of the House to have inserted on its Journals that he does not concur in opinion with the House in the new mode which it has adopted in Addressing the President; it has been the uniform and established practice in addressing Presidents administering a Government to say, 'To His Honor,' not 'To the Honorable.' The former appellation the Speaker humbly conceives to be more respectful and more comprehensive than the latter. Mr. President Russell was invariably addressed by the former appellation, during his administration of the Government of this Province, as Mr. President Dunn actually is in that of Lower Canada." The Address was not changed; but "at the hour appointed, Mr. Speaker attended by the House went up to His Honor the President, with the Address of this House; and being returned, Mr. Speaker reported that the House had attended upon His Honor with its Address, to which His Honor had been pleased to make the following answer, &c."

The Legislative Council always spoke to and of Grant in the proper style, "Your Honor," "His Honor"; and after the remarks of Speaker Macdonell, the House of Assembly did not again fail to give the Administrator his proper title. Brock, Drummond, Samuel Smith, were all so styled; there was no Sittings during the administration of de Rottenburg, Murray or Robinson; and there are no records extant of the Sittings in Sheaffe's time.

Until the Union of the two Canadas, in 1841, the Lieutenant-Governor continued to be "His Excellency," the Administrator "His Honor" (or "His Honour"—the earlier spelling being usually "His Honor").

After the Union of 1841 and before the Confederation in 1867, there was no Lieutenant Governor of this Province by any name.

On Confederation, there was a change: the Canadian statesmen who framed the British North America Act, which is in form and legal effect an Imperial Statute, but in fact a compact between the Provinces, agreed that "for each Province there shall be an officer styled the Lieutenant Governor appointed by the Governor General in Council."

This was to be a Canadian and not an Imperial appointment, like the Lieutenant Governorship of the old Province of Upper Canada; the Governor General was to be an Imperial appointment, and he remained "His Excellency," but the Lieutenant Governor is no longer such.

Regulations were made by Her Majesty that from and after July 1, 1867 —the natal day of the Dominion—Lieutenant Governors should be addressed as "His Honour." Notwithstanding this express regulation, these officials were for more than five years addressed in official correspondence from Ottawa as "His Excellency."

The conduct of the Imperial Commander at Halifax in discontinuing salutes, guards of honour and all other military honours to Sir Hastings Doyle, the Lieutenant Governor of Nova Scotia, was complained of by Sir Hastings to Sir John A. Macdonald early in 1869; and Sir John expressed great surprise; he said that this was without reference to or consultation with the Canadian Government. He thought that the practice complained of was due to the assumption by the Commander that since the Union, the Lieutenant Governors were civilians, holding no direct commission from Her Majesty and in no way connected with the military force; but he expressed the opinion that this sort of thing might be carried too far and cause a feeling of irritation in the Province. (Private Letter from Sir John A. Macdonald to Sir Hastings Doyle, February 1, 1869.)

The irregularity of styling Lieutenant Governors, "His Excellency," continued until Lord Dufferin's time. Dufferin was not satisfied with the slender household assigned to him as Governor General; he wanted a Steamer for his own use, and generally magnified his office. In February, 1873, he took up the matter of the official style of the Lieutenant Governors—there were new ones about to be appointed. He suggested to Sir John that it would be well to get rid of the irregular practice of giving them the title of "Excellency." Dufferin's reasons are interesting: "It seems to me that the true policy of the Dominion will be to subordinate the prestige and jurisdiction, both of the local legislatures and their chief executive officer to the supreme authority of the Canadian Parliament and the Governor General. Their proper legal title is that of 'Their Honours,' which might very well content them. The Lieutenant Governors of Bengal, Madras and Bombay have no higher." (Private letter, February 11, 1873.) Six days thereafter, Sir John wrote Hon. Joseph Howe that His Excellency desired the Royal Regulation to be adhered to in all official correspondence; and this has ever since been faithfully followed.

Accordingly the Lieutenant Governor, the first personage in the Province who, to Sir John's great amusement, takes precedence even of the Prime Minister who appointed him, must be content to share the title "His Honour" with Judges of the County Courts, which is certainly an anomaly.

The highest Courts in the Province were originally the four Courts of Common Pleas; the Judges of which, all laymen but one, were "Your Honor," "His Honor." When, in 1794, these Courts were abolished and the Court of King's Bench was created, the Judges permanently appointed were all lawyers; but they succeeded to the title "Your Honor." They were, from the beginning, described as at present, "The Honourable Mr. Justice Powell," &c. I find the appellation "Judge" only once in the Term Books—when at the first Sittings of the Court, November 5, 1804, after the appalling tragedy of the shipwreck of the *Speedy*, in October, 1804, all causes except such as were merely of course were ordered to stand over, "the late disasterous loss of the *Speedy* on her voyage to Newcastle with Judge Cochran and suit having occasioned this vacancy of the Bench."

The style "His Honor" followed the example of the British Colonies generally; the title "Your Lordship," "My Lord," was not given to the Judges of the Colonial Courts.

In olden times in England the Judges were often called "The Reverend"; but by the time of Coke, i.e., in the reigns of Queen Elizabeth and King James I, Judges even if not Peers had come to be called "My Lord"; while there was no "Lord Coke" or "Lord Hale," it was quite proper and common to say "My Lord Coke," "My Lord Hale." But this style of address was never introduced into the Colonies in America.

And, indeed, the courtesy title "My Lord" was not given to the Vice-Chancellors in England when the Vice-Chancellor's Court was erected in 1813.

The title "Your Honour" has for centuries been given to persons of rank and station; and still is commonly so used by all but the legal classes.

The appellation "Your Honour," "His Honour," was applied to the King's Bench Judges in this Province, Chief Justice and Puisnes, not only out of Court, but in Court for several decades. It was not until the Chief Justiceship of Sir John Beverley Robinson, beginning 1829, that the English custom was introduced—"His Lordship," "My Lord," "Your Lordship." When the Court of Chancery was established in 1837, Robert Sympson Jameson, the Vice-Chancellor, was styled "His Honour," like the Vice-Chancellors of England.

When the Court of Common Pleas and the reorganized Court of Chancery were established in 1849, the appellation given to Judges of the King's Bench, "My Lord," &c., was practically universal; the Judges of these two new Courts received the same honour, and since that time all Judges of the Superior Courts have been so styled.

County Court Judges have for more than half a century been "Your Honour." It is a curious circumstance that Judges of the Inferior Courts share with the highest functionary in the Province, the title "Your Honour"; while Judges of the Supreme Court have the higher title "My Lord."

Not that we always get it—I have been called "Your Lordship," "The Lord," "Your Honour," "Your Worship," once even "Your Reverence"—my friend, Col. Denison, when Police Magistrate, was once called "Your Holiness" by an anxious defendant.

It is but the other day that the Judges in the Province of Quebec ceased to be "Your Honour" and became "Your Lordship."

Although the conventional style is retained by the bar, and properly so, I have often said to an embarrassed witness that "Sir" is a perfectly proper and perfectly respectful mode of address to a Judge upon the Bench.

[This Paper has also been published in the "Canadian Magazine" of March, 1925.]

XX.

THE PLACE AND STREAM NAMES OF OXFORD COUNTY, ONTARIO

By W. J. Wintemberg

Introduction

Several of the places in this county are called after the township in which they are situated. Others are named either after their founders, British statesmen, prominent men, well known local families, or places in England, Scotland, Ireland, Europe, Asia and the United States. A few seem to have reference to their geographical or topographical position. The Crimean War is responsible for one of the existing and several of the lapsed names. Some of the names were given by the Post Office Department, but, unfortunately, no record was kept as to why a name was chosen. It appears to have been the practice of the Department to adopt any suitable names, avoiding, of course, as far as possible, the duplication of names; but the question of the local origin or the local application of a name was not considered. This is to be regretted. If local topographical conditions did not suggest names, we have had public men—wardens, reeves, councillors, and members of Parliament—in our county who could have been honoured by having a place named after them. Then, too, we might have had more Indian names.

Some of the creeks and rivers were named after streams in England and Scotland. Others were named after the owners of the farms on which they had their source, or through which they flowed.

I am including some of the lapsed place and stream names, especially those indicated on maps of 1852, 1857 and 1876.

The date of the establishment of the post office is given below each place name. The lines and verses, containing a reference to the topical name, were selected to show either some variation in spelling, the original or some archaic form of the name, or its place in prose and poetical literature. The etymology of most of the names is given.

I will discuss the origin of the names in the following order:—(I) the name of the county; (II) the names of the townships; (III) the names of the cities, towns and villages; and (IV) the names of the rivers, creeks and lakes.

My thanks are here gratefully tendered to all those who kindly contributed information.

List of Books and Maps Consulted[1]

Anderson, William.
 Genealogy and Surnames, Edinburgh, 1865.
Arthur, William
 The Derivation of Family Names, New York, 1857.

---

[1] As the books on place and personal names either have the names arranged alphabetically, or are indexed, I have not thought it necessary to give references to pages.

BARDSLEY, C. W.
  (1) English Surnames, their Sources and Significations, Second edition, London, 1875.
  (2) Dictionary of English and Welsh Surnames, Oxford, 1901.
BARBER, H.
  British Family Names, London, 1894.
BLACKIE, C.
  Dictionary of Place-Names, London, 1887.
BOWDITCH, N. I.
  Suffolk Surnames, Second edition, Boston, 1858.
BROWN, E. B.
  Short Sketch of the Life of Brinton Paine Brown of Brownsville, Ontario; Brownsville, 1904.
DIXON, B. HOMER.
  Surnames, Boston, 1857.
DOMINION ANNUAL REGISTER, THE, 1880-81.
DUDGEON, PATRICK.
  A Short Introduction to the Origin of Surnames, Edinburgh, 1890.
DUN, CHARLES O'CONOR.
  The O'Connors of Connaught, Dublin, 1891.
FARMER, AUSTIN.
  Place-Name Synonyms Classified, London, 1904.
FERGUSON, ROBERT.
  English Surnames, London, 1858.
GARDINER, HERBERT F.
  Nothing but Names, Toronto, 1899.
GUPPY, H. B.
  The Homes of Family Names in Great Britain, London, 1890.
HAWTREY, FLORENCE M.
  The History of the Hawtrey Family, London, 1903.
HEINTZE, ALBERT.
  Die deutschen Familiennamen, Halle, 1903.
HUNTER, J. HOWARD.
  From Toronto Westward, Picturesque Canada, Toronto, n.d.
JAMESON, Mrs.
  Winter Studies and Summer Rambles, Vol. I, New York, 1839.
JOHNSTON, JAMES B.
  Place-Names of Scotland, Edinburgh, 1892.
JONES, REV. PETER.
  History of the Ojebway Indians, London, 1861.
JOYCE, P. W.
  The Origin and History of Irish Names of Places, Vol. I, Dublin, 1883.
KNOX, ALEXANDER.
  Glossary of Geographical and Topographical Terms, Supplementary Volume to Stamford's Compendium of Geography and Travel, London, 1904.
LOWER, MARK ANTHONY.
  (1) English Surnames, London, 1875.
  (2) Patronymica Britannica, London, 1860.
MAXWELL, SIR HERBERT.
  Scottish Land Names, Edinburgh and London, 1894.
McIAN, R. R.
  Costumes of the Clans of Scotland, Glasgow, 1899.
Militia and Defence, Department of: Maps—Brantford, Woodstock and London sheets, 1914.
Names of Persons to Whom Marriage Licenses were issued by the Secretary of the Province of New York, Previous to 1784. Printed by order of Gideon J. Tucker, Secretary of State, Albany, 1860.
Norman People, The, London, 1874.
ROSS, W. A.
  History of Zorra and Embro, Embro, 1909.
SHENSTONE, THOMAS S.
  The Oxford Gazeteer, Hamilton, 1852. Also Map.
SIMS, CLIFFORD STANLEY.
  The Origin and Significations of Scottish Surnames, Albany, N.Y., 1862.
SULLIVAN, ROBERT.
  A Dictionary of Derivations, Dublin, 1851.

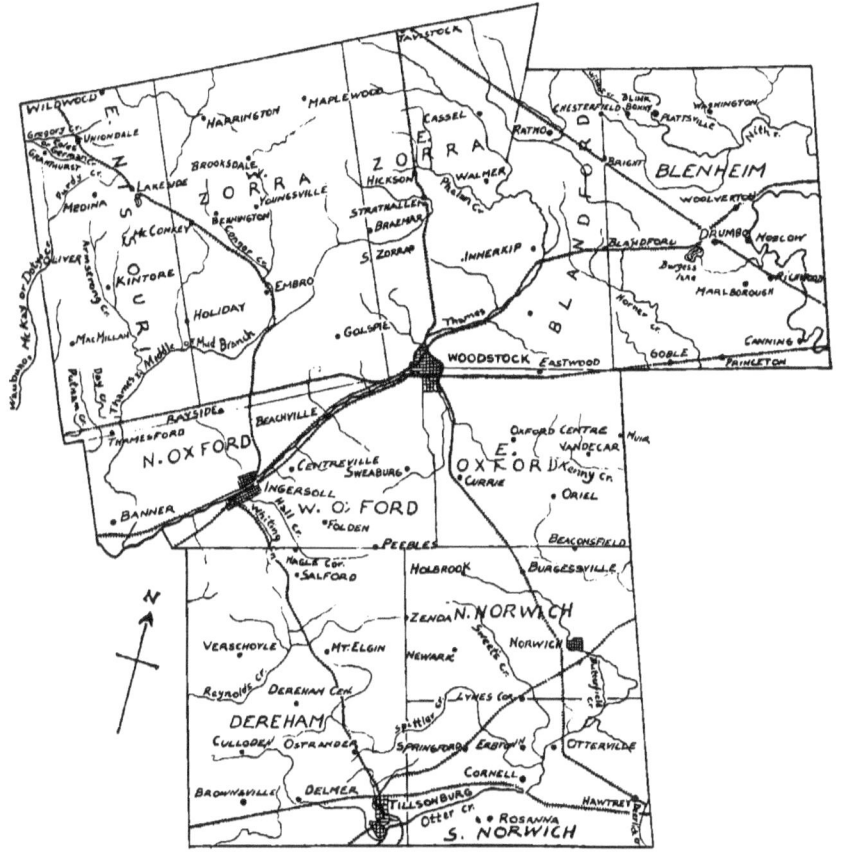

MAP OF OXFORD COUNTY, ONTARIO,
SHOWING LOCATIONS OF PLACES AND STREAMS.

SUTHERLAND, JAMES.
   County of Oxford Gazeteer and General Business Directory for 1862-3, Ingersoll, 1862.
TAYLOR, ISAAC.
   (1) Words and Places, London, 1873.
   (2) Names and their Histories, London, 1896.
Topographical and Historical Atlas of the County of Oxford, by Wadsworth, Unwin and Brown, P.L.S., Toronto, 1876, Maps.
TREMAINE, GEORGE C.
   Map of Oxford County, Canada West, Kingston, 1857.
TRIMBLE, W. C.
   Historical Sketch of the County of Brant, Illustrated; Historical Atlas of the County of Brant, Ontario. Page and Smith, Toronto, 1875.
WAGNER, LEOPOLD.
   Names and their Meanings, New York and London, 1892.
WEEKLEY, ERNEST.
   (1) The Romance of Names, London, 1914.
   (2) Surnames, Second edition, Toronto, 1917.
YONGE, CHARLOTTE M.
   History of Christian Names, London, 1884.

I.

THE NAME OF THE COUNTY.

Although most of the townships now composing it had been named, Oxford county did not come into existence until 1798, when it was enacted by the Act 28 George III, chap. 5, "That the Townships of Burford, Norwich, Dereham, Oxford upon the Thames, Blandford and Blenheim, do constitute the County of Oxford." Later, by the Act 7 William IV, chap. 30 (1837), it was called the District of Brock, which included the following townships: Zorra, Nissouri, Blandford, Blenheim, North, East and West Oxford, Burford, Oakland, Norwich and Dereham. By the Act 12 Victoria, chap. 78 (1849), "districts" were abolished and counties substituted therefor; and so, in the Acts 14 and 15 Victoria, chap. 5 (1851), it is again referred to by its present name. By this enactment the following townships constituted the county: East and West Zorra; North, East and West Oxford; Dereham, Blenheim, Blandford, Norwich, and Nissouri. These constitute the present County of Oxford, except that Norwich and Nissouri have both been divided into two townships, and that the west half of the latter township now forms a part of Middlesex county.

The county, according to Gardiner, "Takes its name from Oxford city, the capital of Oxfordshire, an inland county of England. . . . The name is derived from a ford of the river Ouse—Ouse-no-ford, altered to Oxnaford, and Oxford, hence the city arms show an ox crossing a river." No one, however, can be certain if it is derived from Oxen- or Ousen-ford, although the former is regarded as the most probable derivation.

Oxford was called Oxnaford by the Saxons, and, in *Domesday Book*, it is Oxeneford. The forms Oxanaford and Oxoneford occur in other early Anglo-Saxon charters; and "in the ninth century," according to Taylor (2), "on coins of Alfred, we have *Oksnaforda* and *Orsnaforda*." In the time of Chaucer the name appeared as Oxenford, which in the course of time was sharpened and shrilled into Oxford. Oxenford survives to this day as a surname, and it is also the name of a castle near Edinburgh, Scotland.

II.

BLANDFORD TOWNSHIP.

> To Lambeth Lords Blandford and Shaftesbury hurried,
> Declaring that Exeter Hall was in arms.
> —*Punch.*

According to Gardiner this township "is named from the second title of the Duke of Marlborough, 'Marquis of Blandford,' conferred in 1792, and borne by the heir apparent to the dukedom."

There is a town of the same name in Dorsetshire, England, which is mentioned in *Domesday Book*. It is near the ford called Trajectus Belaniensis by the Romans, and, perhaps, the latter name, in the course of time, was abbreviated to Blan.

BLENHEIM TOWNSHIP.

> Yes, Agincourt may be forgot,
> And Cressy be an unknown spot,
> And Blenheim's name be new.
> —Sir W. Scott: *The Field of Waterloo.*

According to Gardiner this township is named after Blenheim House, which is situated near Oxford, England. This beautiful palace was bestowed by the British nation on John Churchill, Duke of Marlborough, for his victory over the French and Bavarians at the village of Blindheim-Hochstädt, in Bavaria, August 13, 1704.

Blenheim is a corruption of Blindheim (i.e., "dull home"). According to Voltaire the Germans called it Plentheim. Another spelling is Plintheim.[1]

Blenheim, the capital of Marlborough County, New Zealand, has been most appropriately named. A street in London, England, is named Blenheim. There is a village of the same name in Kent county, Ontario.

DEREHAM TOWNSHIP.

> Dereham's old church our grave attention calls;
> The gentle Cowper sleeps within its walls.
> —*Manson.*

> Saint Withburg, who herself to contemplation gave,
> At Deerham in her cell, where her due hours she kept.
> —M. Drayton: *Polyolbion.*

This township was called after the ancient town of Dereham, in Norfolkshire, England. The name was applied to the township before the counties of Oxford and Norfolk were separated.

The name is said to mean "the home of wild beasts," just as Derby (anciently Deorby) signifies "the village of wild beasts, deer, or perhaps wild animals generally." Taylor (2) thinks Dereham is derived from a personal name.

---

[1]*Quarterly Review*, 1870.

East Nissouri Township.

When the first territorial division of the Province was made on July 16, 1792, the township of Nissouri was not known. It was first alluded to by the Act 2 George IV, chap. 3 (1821).

According to Gardiner, Nissouri "is probably Indian, akin to Missouri, which means 'mud river,' or river of the big canoe tribe."

Others, as Gardiner states, think the name is a corruption of "nigh Zorra," i.e., near Zorra, a term used by settlers from the United States in referring to the township. It has also been suggested that the name probably means "gurgling or struggling waters, as there is, or was, a place in the river which would warrant such a name."

North and South Norwich Townships.

> To stout Saint George of Norwich merry,
> Saint Thomas, too, of Canterbury.
> —Sir. W. Scott: *Marmion.*

Norwich township, now divided into North and South Norwich, until 1798, formed part of the county of Norfolk, hence it received the name of a Norfolkshire city.

The name is derived from the Anglo-Saxon *nord,* the "north," and *wic,* "town." The root of the latter word is the Latin *vicus.* Gardiner gives the Latin derivation Nordo-Vicus, and he may be right.

East, West, and North Oxford Townships.

> Away rode the abbot, all sad at that word,
> And he rode to Cambridge and Oxenford.
> —*English Ballad.*

What are now East, West, and North Oxford, in all the early Acts of Parliament, were collectively referred to as "Oxford upon the Thames,"[1] and at the first territorial formation of the county they were thus described. East Oxford became detached from West Oxford between the years 1820 and 1822, and North Oxford became a separate township on January 1, 1842.

East and West Zorra Townships.

> We come thy friends and neighbors not unknown,
> From Eshtaol and Zora's fruitful vale.
> —J. Milton: *Samson Agonistes.*

When the first territorial division of the Province was made, July, 1792, the township of Zorra was unsurveyed and unknown. The first allusion made to it by an Act of Parliament was in 1821, by which Act it was with Nissouri added to the county of Oxford. East Zorra was detached from West Zorra in 1845.

---

[1]Gardiner says that Oxford township, Grenville county, "was called Oxford on the Rideau to distinguish it from Oxford on the Thames."

Gardiner says, "Some prefer to derive this name from Zorah,[1] the birthplace of Samson, mentioned in Judges xiii, 2." The derivation suggested is interesting, but cannot be accepted as correct. Zorra, the Spanish word for a female fox, as he points out, is the most probable derivation.

Governor Maitland, or whoever named the older townships, must certainly have had a *penchant* for Spanish names. Thus, besides Zorra, we have Oro (gold), Lobo (wolf), Rama (branch), Mariposa (butterfly), Mono (monkey), Oso (bear), and Sombra (shadow or shade), as township names in Ontario.

III.

Banner.
(1893.)

This place was so named by E. N. Minkler, because he considered Oxford to be the "Banner County" of Western Ontario. Banner, in the sense of foremost, has come into extensive use lately.

Beachville.
(1836.)

> Of Beachville, village of the plain,
> We now will sing a short refrain.
> —James McIntyre: *Beachville.*

Beachville, which was at one time the post-town for the entire neighbourhood, including Woodstock, was named after a man named Beach, who established the first grist mill and store in the settlement.

According to Bardsley (2) the name Beach means "at the Beach tree." The suffix *ville* enters into the composition of many place-names. Taylor (1) says, "This suffix is not, as is commonly supposed, due to the Roman word *villa*, but is identical with the German *weiler* (Old High Ger. *wilari* or *wilre*) an abode, a single house, which is so common in the Rhinegau and other parts of Germany, as Breitwil."

Beaconsfield.
(1877.)

> Leaving his brightest Beacon's wider field,
> That House of Commons, where for forty years,
> His ready tongue hath been both sword and shield,
> In battle with the worthiest of his peers.
> —*Punch's Essence of Parliament.*

This place was named by the Post Office Department, probably in honour of the statesman Benjamin Disraeli, who was made a peer, with the title of Earl of Beaconsfield, in 1876, the year before the post office was established.

---

[1] In an "Abstract from the Auditor's Docket Books of Grants of Land," etc., of 1821, *Canadian Archives Report* (1897), p. 125, Zorra is spelt with a single *r*, which fact might lend colour to the "birth-place of Samson" theory, the biblical Zorah, as in *Samson Agonistes*, being also spelt with a single *r*.

It will perhaps be unnecessary to say that the name means "the field of the beacon," where signals were given. "The numerous Beacon Hills throughout the island," says Taylor (1), "call to mind the rude though efficient means by which, before the days of the electric telegraph, the tidings of great events would be communicated from one end of the island to the other." Lower (1) says, "Nearly every spot of unusual height in the county of Sussex is called a beacon and was until a comparatively recent date crowned with its stack of fuel."

BENNINGTON.
(1874.)

> To Bennington they went,
> To plunder and to murder,
> Was fully their intent.
> —*The Fate of John Burgoyne.*

From information given by Mrs. A. M. Thorne, Princeton, Ontario, it appears that when they wanted a name for the new post office, they were trying to think of an uncommon one, and the neighbours knowing that Captain Turner (Mrs. Thorne's grandfather) and others there came from the same place, they named it after the town of Bennington, in Bennington county, Vermont. This town was probably named after a place in Lincoln or Herts, England.[1]

The name Bennington may be derived from the Bennings, an Anglo-Saxon clan, which apparently has given its name to other places in England—namely, Benningworth, in Lincoln; Benningbrough, in York; and Bonnington, in Kent, Essex and Notts. In Germany we find Benningen, Benninghausen and Bönningheim. Then, too, there is the German patronymic Benninger.

BLANDFORD.
(1883.)

Was named after the township.

BLINK BONNY.

> And health, o' happiness the queen,
> Blinks bonny, wi' her smile serene.
> —*Robert Ferguson: Auld Reekie.*

Some son of Auld Scotia is probably responsible for this local name. It occurs as a place name in Falkirk and Gladsmuir, Scotland. The designation appears to be the equivalent of the French *Belle Vue*.

This place is now called Chesterfield, owing to the removal of the post office here some years ago.

---

[1]Henry Gannet (The Origin of Certain Place-Names in the United States, U.S. Geol. Survey, 1902, p. 40) is probably in error when he says that the town and county of Bennington, in Hillsboro county, N.H., and the county, township and town in Vermont, were named for Governor Benning Wentworth, of New Hampshire.

Braemar.
(1862.)

> Gladly he breathed the breeze that blew from lofty Loch-na-gar
> And his eyes roamed freely o'er the purple braes of broad Braemar.
> —J. S. Blackie: *The Highlander's Lament.*

This place was probably named after Braemar, in Aberdeenshire, Scotland. According to Johnston the name is derived from *brae*, "a slope" or "bank" and Mar—that is, "the banks of the Marr." The Gaelic form is *braigh*, "the upper part." Mar, according to the same authority, is "Possibly Gaelic *mear* or *meur*, a bough, branch, branch of a river." In 1560 Braemar was known as the Bray of Marr. On a map of 1654 it is the Brae of Mar.

Bright.
(1863.)

> Our Gladstones, Brights and Disraelis.
> —A. H. Wingfield.

Bright was for many years known as "Platt's" or "Plattsville Station." In 1863, or some years previous, the late George Baird had the site of the present village surveyed and laid out in lots. Mr. Baird then decided to give the place a more suitable name, and being an admirer of the Hon. John Bright, the great British orator and statesman, he is said to have called it after him.

According to a local tradition, also, Mr. Baird had two oxen named Buck and Bright,[1] the latter being his favourite, and when the place secured mail accommodation, he gave it this name.[2]

Bardsley (2) tells us that Bright means "the son of Bricht," and gives the following different spellings of the name: Brite, Brith, Briht, Bricht, Bryte, and Bryght.

Brooksdale.
(1859.)

This place was named Brooksdale at the suggestion of Dr. McLeod.[3]

Brownsville.
(1854.)

> The next is all the Browns
> With their little town.
> —B. P. Brown.

This place was named after its founder Brinton Paine Brown. He was the son of Captain Benajah Brown, who settled a few miles west of what is now the town of Ingersoll in 1797. After Captain Brown's death, about eight

---

[1]"Buck and Bright, the names of three-fourths of all the working oxen in Canada."—Mrs. Moodie, *Backwoods of Canada*, p. 194.
[2] I have heard, too, that the oxen were owned by another resident of the place and that the southern part of the village was called "Bright" and the northern part "Buck."
[3] Ross, p. 85.

years later, his widow moved to Walsingham township, Norfolk county. Brinton Paine Brown was born at Genesee, N.Y., August 1, 1797. After serving in the War of 1812, he received an honourable discharge and was granted a pension for life by the Canadian government. In 1817 he married Elizabeth Hoy. Seven years later they settled in Southwold township, Elgin county, and in 1841 removed to lots 22 and 23, in the ninth concession, Dereham township. Mr. Brown for many years was a local preacher, and, about the year 1830, was ordained a minister of the Methodist church. He was a Liberal in politics and a personal friend of the Hon. Francis Hincks, through whose efforts the Brownsville post office was established. Mr. Brown had eleven children, most of whom are still residents of Brownsville. Mrs. Brown died in 1882 aged eighty-three years, and Mr. Brown died the following year at the advanced age of eighty-six years.

It will hardly be necessary to say that, as Anderson tells us, "The English surname Brown, Broun, or Browne, the German Braun, and the French Brune, mean simply brown-haired or brown-complexioned."

BURGESSVILLE.
(1853.)

A Meyer, and Alde-mann, Burgess, and Ward,
A Wiseman, a Trueman, a Freeman, a Guard.
—A Rhymer: *Wesleyan Worthies or Ministerial Misnomers.*

This place was known as Snyder's Corners[1] until the post office was established, when it was named after Edward Burgess. He was born in 1821 and died October 19, 1896, aged seventy-five years. He was for some years reeve of the township of North Norwich and also a local magistrate. Mr. Burgess' father came from the state of Massachusetts in 1818 and settled two miles east of the village.

The ancestor of the Burgess family was a *burgess*, that is, an inhabitant of a borough or walled town. Magistrates of certain towns were also called burgesses. According to Blackstone a burgess was "a representative of a borough in parliament." Bardsley (1) says: "A sobriquet like 'Richard le Burgess' or 'John le Burges' reminds us of the freemen of the borough town."

CANNING.
(1842.)

Remember Canning's name.
—O. W. Holmes: *Poetry, A Metrical Essay.*
Then Mr. Canynge sought the king.
—T. Chatterton: *Bristow Tragedy.*

This place was first settled in 1812 and was known as Mudge Hollow (after Richard Mudge) until 1842, when it received its present name. It may have been named after the Hon. George Canning, the British statesman and orator.

Lower (2) thinks the name is "Probably from Cannings, co. Wilts (Bishop's Cannings). The two viscounts, Canning and Stratford de Redcliffe, are descended

---

[1]After Elias Snyder, an early settler.

from W. Cannynges, the pious founder of St. Mary Redcliffe, Bristol, in the XV. cent." According to Guppy "The Cannings bear the name of an Anglo-Saxon clan, that originally had its home in Wilts and Somersetshire."

CASSEL.
(1874.)

Cassel was so called because several residents of the locality were natives of or came from near Cassel, the capital of Lower Hesse, Germany.

According to some etymologists this name was originally *Castellum*, the Latin name for a "fort." Thus *Castellum Menapiorum*, a town of Belgium on the Maese, became Kessel; *Castellum Marinorum* became Mount Cassel, in Flanders; and *Castellum Cattorum* became Hesse Cassel. The name appears as Chaselle in 913 and Cassela in 1008. Cassel is also a common German and English patronymic.

CENTREVILLE.

This place is indicated on Shenstone's and Tremaine's maps in the centre of lot 14, broken front, West Oxford township, hence the name. There is a post office of the same name in Addington county, Ontario.

CHESTERFIELD.
(1851.)

> When Leachfield was a market town,
> Chesterfield was gorse and broom;
> Now Chesterfield's a market town,
> Leach-field a marsh is grown.
> —*Old Rhyme.*

Nothing is known as to who is responsible for the name of this place. It may have been named at the suggestion of the Post Office Department.

Chesterfield, in Derbyshire, England, after which it was probably named, is said to derive its name from Chester, a corruption of the Latin *castra*, "a camp," and field—i.e., "field of the camp."

CORNELL.
(1875.)

Cornell was formerly called Farmersville, and it appears on a township map of 1876 as Cornellville. It was named after John H. and Samuel P. Cornell, early merchants, who came from New Jersey. John Cornell was one of the councillors of the Brock district for the years 1847 to 1849. He was also the first postmaster.

Various origins have been given for the surname itself. Lower (2) thinks it is "a local pronunciation of Cornwall." According to Bardsley (2) it may either be derived from Cornhill, a part of London ("Cornhell, Cornhile, Cornhull, Cornel . . . 1273"), or may mean "of Cornwall."

CULLODEN.
(1855.)

> My Donald and his country fell
> Upon Culloden-field.
> —R. Burns: *The Highland Widow's Lament.*

No one in the place or neighbourhood seems to know why or at whose suggestion this place was so named. It was probably called after Culloden Moor, in Nairn, Scotland, a place celebrated for the total defeat of Charles Edward Stuart, by the English under the Duke of Cumberland, in 1745.

According to Maxwell the name is derived from the Gaelic *cul lodain*, "back of the swamp." Johnston says the name means "at the back of the little pool" (Gaelic *lodan*).

CURRIE.
(1878.)

> "I came a piece frae west o' Currie."
> —Sir W. Scott: *Epilogue.*

> There's a Bodkin, a Patten, a Rose, and a Currie,
> And a man that's still Hastie, though ne'er in a hurry,
> —*Punch.*

This place was long known as Currie's Crossing. It was named after George Currie, a native of Berwick, England, where he was born in 1818. The family came to Canada in 1832, settling first in Toronto township, Peel county. In 1840 Mr. Currie came to East Oxford township, where for thirty years he was one of the prominent men of the township, holding the office of councillor for some years and then that of reeve. He died June 10, 1901, aged eighty-three years.

The personal name may be derived from the Scottish place-name Currie, which, Johnston thinks, is from the Gaelic *coire*, "a cauldron," "a ravine." Maxwell thinks it is probably from Old Gaelic *currach*, "a marsh."

DELMER.
(1881.)

> Good people, give attention, a story you shall hear,
> It is of the king and my lord Delamere.
> Old Ballad: *Lord Delamere.*

This place was named at the suggestion of the Post Office Department, but why so called, or after whom, is not known.

The name seems a variant either of Delamare, Delamere, or Delmar, which, Bardsley (2) thinks, are from " 'de la mere,' at the lake, from residence beside a lake; M.E. *mere*, a pool." Lower (2) derives it from the French *de la mer*, "of the sea." The author of *The Norman People* makes Delmer an abbreviation of De la Mare. De-la-Mare, he says further, is "from La Mare, near Pont-Audemar, a castle built on piles in a lake." According to this authority, "Norman de la Mare lived *c.* 1030," and the name of "Hugo de la Mare (1070) occurs in a Breton Charter (Morice, 'Hist. Bret. Preauves,' I, 434)". According to Bardsley (2) the name of John De la Mere occurs in the *Hundred Rolls* (1273), and there was a Henricus del Mere in 1379 (Poll Tax). Arthur derives Delmar from the Spanish *Del Mare.*

There are places called Delmar in the states of Delaware, Iowa, New York, Pennsylvania, and South Carolina.

DEREHAM CENTRE.
(1882.)

Was called after the township.

DRUMBO.
(1852.)

> There's Dromara, Drumcondra, Drumquin,
> Rathdrum, Drumconrath, and Drumcree,
> And many more Drums in Ireland,
> But only one Drumbo this side of the sea.
> —Anon.

Drumbo was named by the late Henry Muma, former Dominion arbitrator. Mr. Muma claimed that it was called after a place in Germany, but the name bears clear impress of its Celtic origin. According to Sullivan the initial portion of the name—Drum—is derived from the Irish *Druim* which means a ridge or a hill. It is a word which enters into the composition of many other place-names, some of which are contained in the lines above. The termination *bo* means a cow. Joyce says, "The Parish of Drumbo in Down is called *Druimbo* by the Four Masters, that is, the Cow's Ridge."

There is a place called Drumbow in Lanarkshire, Scotland.

EASTWOOD.

> All this is o'er—but still, unseen,
> Wilfrid may lurk in Eastwood green.
> —Sir W. Scott: *Rokeby.*

Eastwood owes its name and existence to the eccentric Admiral Vansittart. In the year 1834 he sent out as his agent "the daredevil Captain Drew of *Caroline* enterprise" to oversee his estate in Canada. The Captain took up his lot where Old Saint Paul's Church, Woodstock, now stands. He also built a residence for Vansittart, but when the latter came to the country he refused to live there, and located five miles farther east, where he built his "forest Chateau," of which Mrs. Jameson gives us such a lively description. The Admiral named his residence Eastwood in honour of his sister, Mrs. East, who, Mrs. Jameson says, was "an accomplished woman of independent fortune." The name naturally was retained by the settlement after its crystallization into the village.

Eastwood is also an English surname.

Embro.
(1836.)

> For Em'brugh wells are grutten dry.
> —R. Burns: *Elegy on the Year 1788.*

> As on to Embro' town we cam,
>   My guid father welcomed me;
> He caused his minstrels meet to sound,—
>   It was no music at a' to me.
> —Old Ballad: *Jamie Douglas.*

Embro is the old Scottish name of Edinburgh, which city is supposed to derive its name from Edwin, a Northumbrian king, during the time of the Heptarchy, by whom it was founded. Simon of Durham, who mentions it as existing in the eighth century, calls it Edwinesburch. In the charter of the foundation of the Abbey of Holyrood by David I (1128), it is called Edwinesburg. The Celtic name of the place is Dun-Edin, or fort on the hill slope, a designation which occurs for the first time in the Register of the Priory of St. Andrews, dated 1107, in recording the death of Edgar.

Erbtown.

This is one of the lapsed names and occurs on a map of 1876. It was probably called after Abram Erb, who lived on lot 14, concession IX, one mile west of Otterville.

Folden.
(1896.)

Was first called Folden's Corners, after Franklin Folden, who came from Ireland to Oxford county in 1834, and settled on lot 18, concession IV, West Oxford township. He died October 19, 1898.

Folden is probably derived from the Anglo-Saxon *fald*, "a fold," and *den*, "a valley, an enclosure for deer, etc." There are places called Foulden in England and Scotland, which, Johnston thinks, are probably derived from "O. E. *ful* (Icel. *full*) *denu*, 'fould valley' or 'Dean.' " The name also occurs as a place-name in Norway.

Goble.
(1855.)

This place, also known as Goble's Corners, was named after the late William L. Goble. He was the son of the Rev. Jacob Goble, who came from New York state and settled near the site of the present village in 1823. He bought his father's property and later started a general store. After the post office was established, he was made postmaster. When the Great Western Railway was completed, the station here was also called Gobles, but for some reason was changed to Arnold,[1] by which name it was known for a number of years. Mr. Goble died in 1895, aged eighty-four years.

---

[1] Named after T. H. Arnold, the owner of a steam sawmill.

Goble appears to be of German origin, as the German patronymic Gœbel is frequently changed to Gable and Goble. Bowditch thinks Goble is akin to Gobble. According to Weekley (2) the name is probably a survival of Godbeald. There is a place called Goble in the state of Washington, U.S.A.

GOLSPIE.
(1896.)

This place was called Elmsdale when the post office was established here in 1895. The name was changed to Golspie the following year, because there was another Elmsdale (now Emsdale) in Parry Sound district. The present name was chosen because there are several families living in the neighbourhood who came from Golspie, in Sutherlandshire, Scotland.

According to Johnston the name is derived "Either from some Norseman *Gold* or *Goa*, or from G. *gall*, a stranger," and "Dan. *by, bi, bae,* town." Maxwell thinks it may be derived from the Gaelic *cill espuig*, "bishop's chapel."

GRANTHURST.
(1890.)

This place is said to have been named after John Grant, merchant and postmaster. Hurst (A.S. "a wood") seems to have been added for the sake of euphony.

The name Grant is supposed to be derived from Granda, meaning "handsome," an epithet applied to Gregor, second son of Malcolm, chief of the MacGregors, the founder of the clan, who flourished in 1160. According to Sims, Grant means "swarthy" and "grey-headed."

HAGLE'S CORNERS.

This place, which was indicated on a township map of 1876, was probably named after Peter and Samuel Hagle, who lived on lot 16, concession I, Dereham township.

HARRINGTON.

> The later Sydney, Marvel, Harrington.
> —W. Wordsworth: *Great Men Have Been Among us.*

> Luxurious, there, rove through the pendant woods
> That nodding hang o'er Harrington's retreat.
> —James Thomson: *The Seasons.*

This place was formerly called Springville.[1] Its present name was given by Sir Francis Hincks, when he was Postmaster General, in honour of his friend, the late John Harrington. Mr. Harrington settled near the site of the present village early in the forties. He was born in Shaftesbury, Vermont, on February 6, 1789. After removing to Rome, N.Y., and living there a short time, he eventually, in 1820, emigrated to Canada, locating in what is now West Oxford, near the Old Stage Road. He removed later to the Zorras. During the years 1842 and 1849 Mr. Harrington was county councillor, Oxford being then still known as

---

[1] Ross says it was called Springfield (p. 74).

the Brock district. He was reeve of East Zorra from 1850 to 1852, and again in 1856. He became warden of the county in 1860. Mr. Harrington was also a police magistrate, having received the appointment in 1849, and held the office up to the time of his death, which occurred December 6, 1880.

The Harrington family originally got its name from a place in Cumberland, England, which, in turn, as some claim, obtained its name from the Harrings, an Anglo-Saxon clan, the name signifying "the town of the Harrings." (Harring is even yet a German patronymic.) Anderson, however, thinks the name "is either herring town, or a contraction of Haverington, heifer's meadow town, most likely the former." Arthur erroneously believes it to be a corruption of "Haverington, so called from *Haver*, Dutch, *Haber*, Teut., oats, *ing*, a field, and *ton*. The town in or surrounded by wild oats."

This name has been borne by some eminent men, Sir John Harrington, being, perhaps the best known. The one referred to by Wordsworth, in the line above, was a well-known poet. We read that James I granted a patent to Lord Harrington for making farthings out of brass, and so these coins were afterwards called Harringtons. It is to this that *Drunken Barnaby's Journal* has reference in the lines

> Thence to Harrington be it spoken,
> For namesake I gave a token,
> To a beggar that did crave it.

Ben Jonson, also, in his *The Devil is an Ass*, says, "I will not bate a Harrington of the sum."

HAWTREY.
(1866.)

According to the late C. J. Treffry, who was the oldest resident of the place and the postmaster for nineteen years, the name was given by the Post Office Department. He believed it was the name of a poetess.

The etymology of this name is interesting. Lower (2) says the Hawtrey "family were in Sussex in Norman times, and founded Heringham Priory, temp. Henry II. Their name was derived from their residence on a high bank or shore—Norman-French *haulte-rive*—and hence the latinization De alta Ripa, often modified to Dealtry and Dawtrey, while Hawtrey and Haultrey are closer adhesions to the primitive form." Daughtrey, Daltry and Daltree are variations of the names given by Lower. The Hawtreys, also, according to Miss Hawtrey, seem to have brought their name from "Dauterive" in Switzerland, from Brabant, and from Normandy.

HICKSON.
(1883.)

> Over the bright blue sea
> Comes Sir Joseph Hickson, K.C.B.,
> Tho' 'twould be better far
> To say, Sir Joseph Hickson, G.T.R.
> —*Grip*.

This place did not come into existence until after the advent of the railroad. The post office was established in 1883, and the station having been named after Sir Joseph Hickson, the name was retained. Hickson was born at Otterburn, Northumberland, England, in 1830, and died in Montreal on January 4, 1897. He came to Canada in 1862 and steadily worked his way from the post of accountant to general manager of the Grand Trunk Railway, the latter office being assumed in 1874 and retained until 1890, when he retired. He was knighted in the year of his retirement. It was Hickson who suggested the construction of the St. Clair tunnel.

Bardsley (1) suggests that the name is derived from a corruption of the name Isaac, but in a later work (2) he gives an entirely different origin—namely, that Hick, Hicks, Hickson, etc., are baptismal names, "the son of Richard, from the nickname Hick or Higg."

HOLBROOK.
(1867.)

This place may have been called either after a person, or after Holbrook in Derbyshire and Suffolk, England. Bardsley (1) says, "Both places seem to have given rise to surnames." He says, further, "Holbrook has ramified very strongly in the Puritan settlements of America." He (2) gives the following different spellings of the name: Holbrook, Holebrook, and Hullbrook. The name seems to be derived from *Holl* (Sax. *hol*), meaning "hollow" or "deep"—opposed to shallow; and should this surmise be correct, it would mean "deep brook" or "the brook in the hollow," just as Holborn (Holeburn) is believed to be "the *burne* or stream in the hole or hollow." This interpretation seems to be borne out by the spelling Holan-brōc, given in an Anglo-Saxon charter. Anderson thinks the name is derived from "holytree brook," and Dixon also derives it from *"Wood* or *Holly-tree brook."*

HOLIDAY.
(1897.)

> Then messengers he called forth,
> And bade them hie them speedelye—
> "Ane of ye gae to Halliday,
> The Laird of the Corehead is he."
> —*Song of the Outlaw Murray.*

This place was long known as Nissouri, receiving the name in 1853. I have not succeeded in ascertaining why it was afterwards named Holiday. It was no doubt named after a person, possibly at the suggestion of the Post Office Department.

Halliday, Holiday, and Holliday, Bardsley (2) informs us, are baptismal names—"the son of Holiday—a name given to a child born on a holy day." Anderson says: "The old border cry of Halliday originated in the family slogan or war cry of 'a holy day, a holy day!'—the border clan known by this name probably viewing their marauding expeditions and contests with their 'auld enemies' of England, in the light of a holy war."

INGERSOLL.
(1821.)

> Throughout the world they do extoll
> The fame of our town Ingersoll.
> —James McIntyre: *Ingersoll*.

This place, long known as Ingersollville, was named by Charles Ingersoll in memory of his father Major Thomas Ingersoll, who came to this country from Great Barrington, Massachusetts, in 1793. The Ingersolls originally came from Bedfordshire, England, two brothers, John and Richard, settling in Massachusetts, in 1627.

Major Ingersoll died in 1812. He was married three times and had eleven children. Laura, his firstborn, was the well known Canadian heroine Laura Secord. Charles, of the third wife, to whom the town owes its existence, served through the War of 1812. In 1817 he bought his father's farm on the Thames, and removed his family there in 1821. When the post office was established, the same year,[1] he was made postmaster. He was also Commissioner in the Court of Requests, Lieutenant-Colonel of the Oxford Militia, and was twice returned as member of Parliament. He died of the cholera during the plague which visited the town in 1832. James, the youngest son of Major Ingersoll, was the first white child born in the county. In 1834, on the death of Thomas Horner, he was appointed registrar of the county, and held the office until his death in 1886.

The name is sometimes spelt Ingersole in some of the early records. In 1433 the name occurs as Hynkersell. According to Barber this name is derived from Inkersale, a locality in Derbyshire, England. Bardsley (2) says that Ingersoll, Ingersaul, Inkersoll, and Inkersole mean "the saule or sale[2] of Inger." And Inger means " 'The son of Ingvar,' (a Scandinavian personal name, founded on the root Ing)."

INNERKIP.
(1851.)

> Amang the shaws of Inverkip.
> —Alex Rodger: *The Lovely Lass of Inverkip*.

> In Innerkip the witches ride thick,
> And in Dunrod they dwell;
> The grittest loon amang them a'
> Is auld Dunrod himsel'!
> —*Old Rhyme*.

This place was first called Melrose, but when it was discovered that there was another place named thus, Mrs. Barwick (widow of Major Hugh Barwick) suggested that the place be called after Innerkip, her old home in Renfrewshire, Scotland.

Innerkip means the mouth (Inver) of the Kip, a little stream which flows through the shire. "Inver," says Johnston, "always tends to slide into Inner, as both old charters and modern pronunciation amply testify, e.g., Inver- or

---

[1] It was the first one in the county and was known for many years as the "Oxford Post Office."

[2] "Sale, a hall (Fr. *salle*) is commonly found in the 12th, 13th, and 14th century registers." Bardsley (2).

Inner-arity, Inver- or *Inner-kip*, etc." Kip, according to the same authority is Gaelic and Irish *ceap*, a block; trunk of a tree; in Gaelic a shoelast.

This place is locally known as Kip.

KINTORE.
(1862.)

> Lord Rollo, no fear'd,
> Kintore and his beard.
> —Scottish Ballad: *We Ran and they Ran.*

This place was named by the late Hon. George Alexander after a town on the river Don, in Aberdeenshire, Scotland. The name means "head of the hill." It is derived from *Kin*, the Gaelic *cinn* "at the head of," and *torr*, a "hill" or "mound." According to Johnston the name was spelt Kyntor in 1273.

LAKESIDE.
(1856.)

This place was so named because it is at the side of a small lake.

There is a place called Lakeside, in Jacques Cartier county, Quebec.

LYNES CORNERS.

This place was indicated on Tremaine's map and on a map of the township of 1876. It was probably named after Thomas Lynes (spelt Lines by Tremaine) who occupied lot 15, concession IV, North Norwich township. This is now a station on the Canadian National Railway and is known as Middletown line.

According to Lower (2) the name may be derived either from Lynes, "a parish in Peebleshire; an estate near Newdigate, county Surrey; and rivers in counties Peebles, Devon, and Fife."

McCONKEY.
(1909.)

This is the name of a station on the Ingersoll-St. Mary's division of the Canadian Pacific Railway. It was probably named after members of the McConkey family, who occupied lot 20, concession I, West Zorra township. Thomas McConkey probably was the earliest occupant of this lot as his name appears on Tremaine's map, which gives the name as McCunkey.

According to Lower (2) McConkey is a corruption of MacConnochie—the son of Duncan.

MACMILLAN.
(1901.)

> To witch away fowk's minds frae doing well,
> As saith Rab Kerr, M'Millan, and M'Neil.
> —A. Ramsay.

> He ne'er could look straught on Macmillan's cup:
> They watch'd—but nane saw him his brose ever sup.
> —W. Nicholson: *The Brownie of Blednoch.*

This place was named after the MacMillan family, early settlers in the neighbourhood.

According to an old historian the patronymic is derived from Methlan, an ancestor of the clan, who flourished in the time of King Alexander II (1214 to 1249), "but the Gaelic appelation," according to McIan (page 275), "pronounced Gille-Vaolain, although much resembling the aspirated sound of the other, indicates the religious character of the individual, who was bald-headed, i.e., was distinguished by the clerical tonsure." Anderson says "MacMillan is from the Gaelic, Mac Mhaoil-avin, and means 'the son of the bald man'."

MAPLEWOOD.
(1874.)

The derivation of this name is quite obvious. It was probably so called at the suggestion of the Post Office Department.
There is another Maplewood in New Brunswick.

MARLBOROUGH.

> It was the Duke of Marlborough who put the French to rout,
> But what they fought each other for, I never could make out.
> —R. Southey: *The Battle of Blenheim.*

A little settlement west of Richwood, was formerly called Marlborough, obviously after the Duke of Marlborough.
According to Taylor (2) this name appears in the Saxon Chronicle as *Mærle-beorh*, apparently from *mærlic*, "noble," "glorious," or "lofty," and *beorh*, a "hill."

MEDINA.
(1862).

> There was the Countess of Medina Celi.
> —Longfellow: *The Spanish Student.*

> Half mistress and half saint thou hangs't as even
> As doth Medina's tomb, 'twixt hell and heaven.
> —T. Moore: *Lalla Rookh.*

Joseph H. Beck, the postmaster, named this place when the post office was established.
Next to Mecca, Medina, or, as it is known to the Mohammedans, *Medinet el Nabi* ("City of the Prophet"), is the most sacred city of the Moslems, its mosque containing Mohammed's tomb. It was known as Yethreb before the flight of the Prophet. The name was introduced into Spain by the Moors, and it now even occurs as a Spanish surname. Medina-de-las-torres (the "city of the towers"), Medina-del-campo ("city of the plain"), Medina-del-pomar ("city of the apple orchard"), Medina-del-rio-seco ("city of the dry river-bed"), Medina-Sidonia ("city of the Sidonians"), and Medina-Celi, show how generally the name has been adopted. It is also the name of one of our geological subdivisions, and of several localities in the United States.

Moscow.

> . . . And Moscow was no more.
> —Lord Byron: *The Age of Bronze.*

This name appeared on Shenstone's map of the county. The place was also called Howell's Mills, because the local flour mill was owned by Wesley Howell. Enjoying many natural advantages, the place seemed destined to become a flourishing hive of industry; but after the founding of Drumbo, which afterward also became the railway station, Moscow's prosperity gradually began to wane. The high, steep hill, east of Drumbo, is still called "Moscow Hill," but in time even that name may be forgotten.

It is scarcely necessary to say that it was called after the Russian city of Moscow, which was so named because it is built on the river Moscowa. And those who are curious to know what Moscowa means, will find that Taylor (2) thinks "The name of the river is probably Finnic, signifying a place of washing. . . . The name has also been referred to the Slavonic *mokschow*, 'wet'."

Mount Elgin.
(1851.)

> Oh, Elgin toon is brawly kenn'd.
> —David Grant.

This place was probably called after Lord Elgin, who was Governor-General of Canada in 1851. The "Mount" was added because the village is situated on a high hill.

Johnston says the name Elgin is "Said to be from Helgy, a Norse general, victor near here *c.* 927. But Rhys thinks it pre-Celtic or Ivernian. Elga is a character in Irish mythic history, and also poetic name for Ireland, perhaps meaning 'noble'." He says the name is spelt Helgyn on old corporation seal.

The word "Mount" is very frequently used in the composition of place-names in Canada, there being no less than sixty names of which it is a compound.

Muir.
(1901.)

> Muir, Murray, and McLean's coming;
> Buchanan, Binny, Baine's coming.
> —A. H. Wingfield: *The Gathering of the Clans.*

The name of this post office perpetuates the name of a well known Scottish family living in the neighbourhood.

Anderson says: "The English name Moor and Moore, and the Scottish Muir, are from a Saxon word meaning heathy ground."

Newark.
(1851.)

> He passed where Newark's stately tower
> Looks out from Yarrow's birchen bower,
> —Sir W. Scott: *The Lay of the Last Minstrel.*

Newark was formerly called Unionville. It may have been named after Newark in England, or after a place near Glasgow.

The Scottish Newark, according to Johnston, means " 'New work,' i.e., 'new castle.' There was a castle here." Blackie says it means the "new fortress."

NORWICH.
(1830.)

This place was named after the township and was long known as Norwichville. It was the second post office established in the county.

OLIVER.
(1878.)

> Castles, Oliver, and such.
> —T. Moore: *The Fudge Family in Paris.*

This place was named after Thomas Oliver, through whose efforts the place secured the post office in 1878. Mr. Oliver was Member of Parliament for North Oxford in the Canadian Assembly from 1866 to the Union of 1867, and in the House of Commons from 1867 to 1880. He was born in Kildonan, Sutherlandshire, Scotland, in 1821, and died at Woodstock, Ontario, November 8, 1880. "Educated in Scotland, Mr. Oliver followed for two years the office of a teacher, and in 1842, along with his parents, emigrated to Canada, and settled in West Zorra . . . where for some years he had charge of the Rosehill school at Braemar. Subsequently he followed mercantile pursuits at Woodstock and was in the wool trade. He entered the town council in 1859, from which he passed as reeve to the county council, and became warden of Oxford in 1866, in which year he also entered Parliament."[1]

The name Oliver is derived from the baptismal or Christian name. It is of Roman origin and means "an olive tree," which is the symbol of peace.

ORIEL.
(1876.)

> All Souls' and Abingdon look quite grand;
> And Woodstock and Worcester are hand-in-hand;
> While Iffley and Oriel take their stand
> Next door to Sandford and Merton.
> —*Punch: Oxford Commemoration, 1870.*

This place was probably named by the Post Office Department. It may have been named after Oriel College, Oxford, England, which was founded by Adam de Brome, Archdeacon of Stow and almoner to King Edward II, in 1626. It is said to derive its name from a tenement called l'Oriole, on the site of which the building stands. It is also the name of "a fairy, whose empire lay along the banks of the Thames, when King Oberon held his court in Kensington Gardens," and the name of a river in Russia. Taylor (2) says: "Oriel was an Irish kingdom comprising the modern counties of Armagh, Monaghan, and Louth. A legend explains the name as the 'golden hostages,' *Oir-ghilla,* because of the stipulation that hostages should be fettered with chains of gold."

---

[1] *The Dominion Annual Register,* 1880-1881.

Ostrander.
(1876.)

This place was named after Henry B. Ostrander. Born at Chippewa, Ontario, May 29, 1816, he first settled on Talbot street, in Norfolk county, where he remained until 1854, when he removed to the north half of lot 7, concession IX, Dereham township. Mr. Ostrander was postmaster, school trustee and a township councillor for a number of years. He died February 2, 1892. The Ostrander family was of U. E. Loyalist stock.

The name seems to be of Dutch origin. Arthur gives the following derivation of the name: "Ostrander (Dutch). The Lord of the east shore, from *oste*, east, *strand*, the shore and *heer*, lord or master; he that must have his due of a stranded ship." This derivation, however, seems far-fetched. *Oste*, east, for instance, is not the true orthography, it should be *Oost*. This is borne out by the spelling Oostrander in marriage records of 1761, 1764 and 1772. According to Taylor (2) the somewhat similar name of Ostmanton, means "the town of the man from the east."

There is a place called Ostrander in Waupoos county, Wisconsin.

Otterville.
(1836.)

This place was called Otterville after Otter creek which flows through the village.

Oxford Centre.
(1853.)

Being nearly in the centre of the township this place quite naturally received this designation. It was known until 1853 as the "Town Hall," for here the township council met for many years.

Peebles.
(1876.)

> At Beltane quhen ilk bodie bownis
> To Peblis to the Play.
> —King James V: *Peblis to the Play.*

> Wes nevir in Scotland hard nor sene,
> Sic dansing nor deray,
> Nouther at Falkland on the grene,
> Nor Pebillis at the play.
> —*Idem: Christ's Kirk on the Green.*

The late James Lawson named this place after the town in Scotland.

The Scottish Peebles is a town of great antiquity and must from a very early period have been a seat of population, as seems to be indicated by the name, which is said to mean shielings or dwelling places. Johnston derives the name from Welsh *pabell*, plural *pebyll*, a tent. The *s* is the English plural. This name has undergone some change in spelling; thus in 1116 we have Pobles, in

1126 Pebles, and in the following centuries it has been variously spelt Peiblis, Peblis and Pebillis. The corresponding Spanish form is Pueblo. All the forms are related to the Latin *populus*.

Peebles is also a common surname.

PLATTSVILLE.
(1855.)

> Oh Plattsville thou art a beautiful town,
> In a pleasant valley.
> —*The Echo.*

Plattsville was named after its founder, Samuel Platt, who came to Canada in the summer of 1844. After working for a few years as a millwright in New Dundee, he settled in Blenheim, locating on the east bank of the Nith, and embarked in the milling business long known as the "Blenheim mills." Some years later he went to Goderich and conducted a milling business there. He was also the founder of the first salt works in Goderich, and for many years carried on an extensive business in that commodity. He was Plattsville's first postmaster and also held the office of Justice of the Peace for many years. Mr. Platt was born in Berkshire, England, April 19, 1822, and died October 3, 1885.

Bardsley (2) says Platt and Platts mean "of the platt." In an earlier work (1) he says: "Our 'Platts' found in such an entry as 'Robert del Plat,' but in the 'plat' there was less thought of general surroundings." According to Lower (1) Platt is "a little piece of ground; a field or even surface."

PRINCETON.
(1793.)

Princeton was known as the Governor's Road Settlement until Thomas Watson, who came out with his cousin, Thomas Horner, in 1793, named it after Prince Town—now Princeton—his native city in New Jersey, which place, no doubt, obtained its name from Princetown, in Devonshire, England. A town in Massachusetts still preserves the original form of the name.

RATHO.
(1855.)

> To the ship of Haco came his stanchest men—
> Holder, Sweno, Ratho, Hingst, and Innisfen.
> —Charles Mackay: *The Invasion of Scotland by the Norsemen.*

When the post office was established, Mrs. Barwick (who also named Innerkip), was asked to name the place, and she called it after the village of Ratho, in Midlothian, Scotland, the home of her childhood. The name is given as Rathoville on Tremaine's map.

According to Johnston the name is derived from *rath*, a Gaelic word meaning a "fort." The second syllable he regards as doubtful. He gives the following different spellings of the name: Ratheu (1250), Radchou (1292), Rathou (1293), and Rathoe (1316).

Ratho also occurs as a surname in *Domesday Book*.

RAYSIDE.
(1897.)

This name was a local suggestion. It is said that when the post office was established someone remarked, "It is by the wayside, let's name it Rayside," and as no one, including the Post Office Department, objected, the name was adopted. It may also have been named after James Rayside, who was a member of the Ontario Legislature (1882-1898).

There is a township of the same name in Algoma.

RICHWOOD.
(1851.)

An old resident informed me that the name is supposed to be derived from *rich* and *wood*, in allusion to the spot selected for the site of the village. I have also been informed, and it seems the more probable story, that it was so called by a man named Rockwood, one of the pioneer storekeepers, who gave his own name to the place, but, owing to the fact that the name had already been appropriated by another village, it was changed to Richwood.

The name Richwoods occurs as a place-name in Union county, Ohio, and Miller county, Missouri. Richwood is a common surname.

ROSANNA.
(1895.)

When the post office was established the Post Office Department sent a list of names to the postmaster and he selected Rosehill. The Department, however, named it Rosanna, but why, or after whom, can not be ascertained.

Rosanna is a girl's name, a variant of Rose or Rosa.

SALFORD.
(1855.)

This place was known as Manchester until 1855, when the name was changed to Salford, which is the name of a suburb of the city of Manchester. There are five places called Salford in England. The name is said to mean "the ford at the sallow or willow tree" (Anglo-Saxon *sealh*, "a willow").

SOUTH ZORRA.
(1852.)

Was named after the township. It was long known as Huntingford, having been so named after H. Huntingford, who owned lots 12, 13, and 14, concession XI, of East Zorra.

SPRINGFORD.
(1852.)

This place derives its name from a fording of Spring brook, a small stream which flows through the village.

The name is given as Springfield on Shenstone's map.

STRATHALLEN.
(1865.)

> Glen-Ogle! Strath-Allan! fly swift as the roe.
> —James Hogg: *The Queen's Wake.*
>
> Macdonald's men, Clanranald's men;
> Mackenzie's men, Macgilvray's men;
> Strathallan's men, the Lowland men,
> O' Callander and Airley.
> —A. Laing: *The Standard on the Braes of Mar.*

This place was known as Alma until 1865, when the name was changed to Strathallen, which had been the name of the school-section for many years, having been given by three of the trustees, who came from Perthshire, Scotland.

Strath is a Celtic word meaning a long and broad valley through which a river or stream flows. Strathallen, therefore, is the valley of "Allen Stream" or "Allen Water." Allen is probably derived from Gaelic *aileen*, "a green plain."

SWEABURG.
(1857.)

> . . . Sebastopol gone; Kertch and Kinburn too!
> Sveaborg in ruins; Bomarsund destroyed!
> Our troops repulsed at Kars.
> —*Punch: Constantine's Dream.*

This place was formerly called Floodtown, after H. Flood; but when mail accommodation was secured the name was changed to Sweaburg, or, as it should be, Sviaborg. This is the name of a port on the Gulf of Finland, its fortifications protecting the city of Helsingfors. In 1855, during the Crimean war, Sviaborg was bombarded with no great result for two days and nights by the allied fleet.

Taylor (2) says the name is composed of two Sclavonian words: *Svia* meaning "holy," and *borg*, "town." Viborg, the name of another Russian place, has the same meaning. There are also *Svia*toinos ("Holy cape") and *Svia*ga ("Holy river") in Russia.

TAVISTOCK.
(1857.)

> Tavy's voiceful stream, to whom I owe
> More strains than from my pipe can flow.
> —W. Browne: *Britannia's Pastorals.*

Est in Domnonia cænobium monachorum juxta Tau fluvium, quod Tavistok vocatur.—Malmesbury *de gest. Pontific.*

According to the late Valentine Stock there were originally several little settlements in the neighbourhood, named respectively Sebastopol, Balaclava, Inkerman, Eckstein, and Bell's Corners, the first three being called after battles fought during the Crimean war. From another source we learn that Henry Eckstein had called the place Freiburg and that during the Crimean war it was changed to Inkerman.[1] When the post office was established the Department

---
[1] This is the name given on Tremaine's map.

called it Tavistock, after a place in Devonshire, England. This town is on the bank of the Tavy, whence its name. "Tavistock," says Taylor (2), "is the *stoc* or 'place on the Tavy.' The name appears in a charter of 1042 as *Tæfingstoc*, and in a forged charter of later date as Tavistoc." *Taefig-stoc* is another early spelling of the name. A. J. Kempe, in his "Historical Notices of the Abbey," in the *Gentleman's Magazine*, says there can be little doubt "that the Tavy is an abbreviation of the British words *Tau vechan*, or the little Tau, thus distinguishing the tributary branch from the *Tau mawr* (afterwards Tamar), the great Tau. When the Saxons established this town and monastery on the banks of the *Tau vechan*, they were content to affix a short adjunct from their own language to the original British words, and the abbreviated form, so much sought by common parlance, easily moulded *Tau vechanstoke* into Tavistock."

THAMESFORD.
(1851.)

Was first called St. Andrews. The origin of the present name is obvious.[1] Thamesville, Ontario, was also named after the Thames.

TILLSONBURG.
(1869.)

After him who did the mills own,
This place was called in honor Tillson.
—James McIntyre: *Tillsonburg.*

This place was originally called Dereham Forge on account of bog iron ore from the neighbourhood having been smelted and manufactured here. It was afterwards called Dereham. The name appears as Tillsonburg on Tremaine's map, and the northern part of the town was called Campbellton. The town was incorporated as Tilsonburg in 1869. The name was given at the suggestion of the Private Bills Committee. Through a clerical error in preparing the bill for incorporation one of the *l*'s was dropped, and the name had to struggle along with a single *l* until 1902, when several public-spirited citizens of the town, in consideration of the "many valuable and enduring services" rendered by the late E. D. Tillson, asked the Ontario Legislature to have the name changed from Tilsonburg to Tillsonburg. The Act was given assent to March 24, 1902. We doubt if the historic annals of our Province can furnish a similar instance where the name of a municipality had its spelling changed by Act of Parliament.

George Tillson, the founder of the place, was born in Massachusetts in 1782, and settled in the township in 1825. He died March 15, 1864.

The etymology of the name Tillson is interesting. Bardsley (1) says: "Mr. Lower, who does not quote any authority for the statement, alleges that there was an old provincial nickname for 'William'—viz., 'Till'; whence 'Tilson,' 'Tillot,' 'Tillotson,' and 'Tilly.' That these are sprung from 'Till' is evident, but there can be no reasonable doubt that this still existing curtailment of 'Matilda,' which, as the most familiar name of the period, would originate many a family so entitled." In a later work (2), the same author says that the name is "Chiefly found in Yorkshire where Matilda was extremely popular."

---

[1]See under Thames river.

UNIONDALE.
(1909.)

The origin of this name is obvious. It is a station on the Ingersoll-St. Mary's division of the Canadian Pacific Railway.

VANDECAR.
(1863.)

This place was called Sageville[1] on Tremaine's map. It was later called Vandecar's Mills, which name it retained until 1863, when it received its present name. Israel D. Vandecar, or Van Decar as it is given on Tremaine's map, after whom it was named, built the first saw and grist mill about 1854. He was one of the Justices of the Peace of the county. He is said to have been the inventor of the first steam dredge.

This surname seems originally to have been Van de Carr. The name occurs as Van Decker in a list of marriage licenses issued in 1771. Dixon says Decker is Dutch for "the thatcher."

There is a place called Van Decar in Isabella county, Michigan.

VERSCHOYLE.
(1870.)

It is said that when the post office was established, the post office inspector of the London District named it after a family then living in London, Ontario, who were, no doubt, descendants of the well-known Dublin family, which migrated from Utrecht to Ireland, to escape the persecutions of Phillip II. The *Irish Builder* (December 15, 1887) gives an almost unbroken history of the Verschoyles. The name "belongs to the same class as the names Verbeeck, Verbrugge, Verhoef, Vermeulen, Verplanck, Verschure, and others, having as prefix the syllable *ver*, contracted from *van der*, 'of the.' Sometimes the fuller form occurs, as Vanderbeeck, Vandermeulen. The French equivalent would be *de la*, as in De la Planche. *Schuyle* in old Dutch and Flemish is a feminine substantive, meaning a hiding-place, nook, or corner, whence comes also another well-known surname Schuyler. The personal name Verschoyle corresponds to such English surnames as Corner, Hearne, and Wray, all three of which have much the same sense. The spelling Verschoyle, instead of Verschuyle, is either corrupt or a Flemish provincialism, as in some dialects (for instance, in that of Antwerp) the difficult diphthong uy changes to oy."[2]

WALMER.
(1866.)

A guard of honor kept its watch in Walmer's ancient hall.
And sad and silent was the ward beside the Marshal's pall.
—Samuel Lover: *The Flag is Half-Mast High.*

This place was named by the Post Office Department, probably after Walmer, a parish near Deal, in Kent, England. The name means "the embank-

---

[1] After Ceymour Sage who owned one of the farms near the village.
[2] James Platt, jun., in *Notes and Queries* (10 S. III, p. 115-116).

ment by the sea," (*Wal*, which, according to Knox, is derived from Anglo-Saxon *weall* = "wall," and *mer*, "the sea"); or, in other words, as Blackie thinks, "the sea-wall."

WASHINGTON.
(1852.)

> Yes—one . . . .
> . . . .
> Bequeath'd the name of Washington.
> —Byron: *Ode to Napoleon Bonaparte.*

Washington was long known as "The Corners," but when the post office was established the residents decided to give the place a more suitable name. Some former residents of the United States having suggested the name of Washington, it was named after that great American. This is on the authority of one old resident. Another told me an entirely different story. According to his account one of the early tavern-keepers built his own tavern. When it was nearly completed he stood on the roof and, while flourishing a bottle of whiskey above his head, he named the village. This occurred several years before the place received mail accommodation. I have also been informed that the name was given by Levi Sherk, the first postmaster.[1]

We are informed by one of the many biographies of George Washington that the family originally came to England with William the Conqueror, and that the original name was de Hertburn, which was taken from a village in the Palatinate. The family is first mentioned in the *Bolden Book*, which was a record of all land belonging to the diocese at that time. Herein it is stated that William de Hertburn[2] had exchanged his village of Hertburn for the manor and village of Wessyngton. The family naturally changed its name with its estate and assumed de Wessyngton. We again find the name, but slightly altered, in the list of loyal knights who fought for Henry III in the Battle of Lewes (1264). The name in this instance is "William Weshington of Weshington." A still later record has "Sir William de Weschington." In course of time the *de* was dropped and the name underwent a gradual change from Weshynton, Wassington, Wasshington, and finally to its present form.

John Washington, the progenitor of the American branch of the family, was a loyal cavalier, and stood staunchly by his king, Charles I. He emigrated to Virginia in 1657, when Cromwell and his party came into power.

Taylor (1) says "Washington (A. S. Hwessingatùn and Wassingatùn) signifies the tun of the Hwessings or Wassings." According to Dixon the name signifies *"Town of Wasa's sons."* The suffix *ing* means "son"; in the plural, "a family" or "tribe." Wasa, or Vasa, he says further, is the early English for faun or satyr. Ferguson claims that the first element in this name is derived from Wass, a personal name. "The etymon of the name," he says, "is probably Ang.-Sax. *hwaes*, Old Norse *hvass*, sharp, keen, bold. And it may

---

[1] The residents of the neighbouring village of Plattsville facetiously claim that Washington was so called because one of Plattsville's estimable ladies used to send her *washing* there!
[2] Dixon says that "the descendant of Wm. de Hertburn, John Washington of Whitfield, is believed to have been the first who assumed the name of Washington."—P. 79.

perhaps be identical with that of the illustrious Gustavus Wasa, King of Sweden."

The name occurs as a place name in Derby, Durham, and Sussex, England. There are nearly one hundred and seventy places bearing this name in the United States.

WILDWOOD.
(1896.)

L. W. Lang, having a friend in Wildwood, Florida, suggested this as the name of the post office when it was established.

WOODSTOCK.
(1835.)

> But Woodstock 's the place of all places, d'ye see,
> Of all the towns in Canady—Woodstock for me.
> William Hargrave in the *Woodstock Gazeteer* (1853).

Woodstock was long known as the "Town Plot." Governor Simcoe in one of his early letters to Dundas, Secretary of State, among other matters, tells how he has marked out Oxford (Woodstock) for a town site.

Woodstock was named after the place in Oxfordshire, England. The name probably means "the dwelling in the wood."

That part of Woodstock lying north of Ingersoll Avenue and bounded by Tecumseh and Riddell streets was called Brighton in the early thirties. It was named after Brighton, England, Henry Perrin one of the settlers in the village and possibly others, having come from there.[1]

WOLVERTON.
(1851.)

In 1848 Enos Wolverton called this place Warsaw, but as another place had already appropriated the name, the post office authorities named it Wolverton, in honour of its founder. It was for many years still known as Warsaw, however, notably on Shenstone's map of the county. Mr. Wolverton was the founder of the milling industry in the village, which is still being carried on by his son. He was born in New York State, April 18, 1810, came to Canada about 1816, and died in 1894.

The Wolvertons seem to have taken their name from a town in Bucks county, England. Parishes in Norfolk, Hants, and Warwick are also so named. The name is said to mean the stead or dwelling of Wolf, the first settler.

---

[1] "Blunderbus: The History of Brighton, being the Story of Woodstock's Settlement from the early thirties," Woodstock *Daily Express*, Dec. 20, 1900, and Jan. 12, 1901.

Youngsville.
(1874.)

> Brown, Hardy, and Ironsides, Manly and Strong,
> Lowe, Little, and Talboys, Frank, Pretty and Young.
> —A Rhymer: *Wesleyan Worthies, or Ministerial Misnomers.*

This place is said to have been named after Gabriel Youngs, who purchased a thousand acres on the site of the village.[1] The fact that E. Youngs was one of the early postmasters may also have had something to do with the selection of the name.

Bardsley (2) says Young and Youngs are nicknames—"the Young," probably in the sense of junior.

Zenda.
(1895.)

The names Bowell and Willard were both suggested by the Post Office Department when the post office was established, but as there was already a place called Bowell and Willard being similar to other place-names, Zenda was finally chosen. This name seems to have been suggested by Anthony Hope's novel *The Prisoner of Zenda*, which appeared in 1894.

Zenda is an imaginary place and is supposed to be a castle in Ruritania, a mythical principality in Germany.

IV.

Armstrong Creek.

> Ye need not go to Liddesdale;
> For when they see the blazing bale,
> Elliots and Armstrongs never fail.
> —Scott: *Lay of the Last Minstrel.*

This creek was called Silver Creek on Tremaine's map. It owes its present name to the fact that it flows through the farm of William Armstrong, lot 14, concession X, East Nissouri township.

Bardsley (2) thinks the name is from the nickname "armstrong." Lower (2) says it is "Doubtless from strength of limb, as displayed in war and athletic sports."

Burgess Lake.

This lake was called after the Burgess family, early settlers in Drumbo and vicinity.

Butterfield Creek.

This creek is marked on Shenstone's map as flowing in a southerly direction and joining the Otter in lot 4, concession VII, South Norwich township. It

---

[1] See Ross, p. 16.

was probably named after David S. Butterfield, J.P., who was an early settler in the township He was born at Rodman, New York, April 4, 1823, and died March 26, 1907. Mr. Butterfield was township councillor for many years and also held the office of reeve for four years.

Bardsley (2) says the name is "Local 'of Butterfield,' some small spot, seemingly in W. Rid. Yorks. The surname has crossed the border into co. Lanc., where it is to-day familiar." It also occurs as Botterfield, *circa* 1379. Barber derives it from Butterfell, a locality in Cumberland. Weekley (1) seems to derive the name from a dialect name for the bittern and field.

COLES CREEK.

Havell, and Harvey Hafter,
Jack Travell, and Cole Crafter.
—J. G. Skelton: *Why Come ye Not to Courte.*

This creek was called German creek on Tremaine's map, and on a map of 1876 the name is given as Coles creek, its source being on the farm of Samuel A. Coles, lot 29, concession XII, East Nissouri township.

According to Bardsley (2) Cole is "Bapt. 'The son of Nicholas, from nickname Cole."

CONNOR CREEK.

And Conchobar
Moaned in his troubled dreams.
—J. B. Dollard: *March of the Ultonians.*

The Clans of Conn and Conor round you stand.
—Teig Dall O'Higgin: *Address of Brian O'Rourke*, etc.

A small creek emptying into the Thames at Embro is so named on Tremaine's map and on a township map of 1876. It flowed through the farm of George Connor, lot 17, concession III, West Zorra township, which probably accounts for the name.

Connor and Conor, according to Arthur, are derived "from *Conchobar*, the chief of men, powerful among men, a leader. O'Donovan," he says, "derives this name from *Conn*, 'strength' and *eobhair*, aid, assistance, *Con-a-fir*, 'the head of men,' " Dun says, "The Irish Conchobar means a hero or champion." Barber derives the name from the Irish O'Conchobair, "endowed with strength."

DAY CREEK.

Thomas Black and Mary White,
Peter Day and Ellen Knight.
—*Couplets about Couples.*

A creek so named on Tremaine's map was probably called after Elmer Day, because it flowed through his farm, on lot 4, concession IX, East Nissouri township.

Bardsley (2) thinks this surname is derived from the occupation " 'the deye' or 'day,' a maid, a dairy maid."

DEERLICK CREEK.

The woods are full of deer-paths which run to the streams and licks.
   J. F. Cooper: *Last of the Mohicans.*

This stream which flows through the southeast corner of South Norwich township, was indicated and named on Shenstone's map. It does not appear on any later map, although the name is still in use. There must have been a "lick" in the neighbourhood to warrant such a name, but the late Charles Treffrey, of Hawtrey, one of the oldest residents, did not know where it was located.

DOTY CREEK.

This creek, which has its source in East Nissouri township, is called Doty creek on Shenstone's map. It is not known after whom this creek was named, but it may have been called either after William Doty, who in 1857 lived on lot 34, concession IX, East Nissouri township, or Darius Doty, who owned part of lot 17, concession X, of the same township. Darius Doty was town clerk of Ingersoll in 1849, census enumerator for West Oxford and Ingersoll in 1852, and Deputy reeve of the town council in 1862.

Doty may be a variant of the surname Doughty. Arthur derives the name from "Welsh Diotty, an ale-house." It is also known as McKay and Waubuno creek (*q. v.*).

GERMAN CREEK.

*St. German who for Christ his bishopric forsook,
and in the Netherlands most humbly him betook.*
   —M. Drayton: *Polyolbion.*

A branch of Gregory creek is called German creek on Tremaine's map. It flowed through the farm of James German, west half of lot 29, concession XI, East Nissouri township, hence, probably, the name.

According to Lower (2) German is from the "Latin *Germanus*, of the same stock; a near kinsman. . . . As a personal name it is of great antiquity in Britain, dating from St. German, the successful opponent of the Pelasgian heresy in the fifth century. Possibly in some instances derived from the country, like French, Irish, etc."

It is also known as Coles creek (*q.v.*).

GREGORY CREEK.

Ac Gregory was a goodman.
   —*Piers Ploughman.*

This creek is shown on Tremaine's map, but is not named on any later map. It was probably named after R. Gregory, on whose farm, lot 30, concession XI, East Nissouri township, it had its source.

According to Miss Yonge, Gregory is from the Greek Gregorius, which means a "Watchman."

HALL CREEK.

> With Garrets and Chambers, Halls, Temples and Flowers.
> —A Rhymer: *Wesleyan Worthies, or Ministerial Misnomers.*

This creek, shown on Tremaine's map, was probably so named because it flowed through the farm of Elisha Hall, who lived on lot 19, concession I, West Oxford township. Mr. Hall, familiarly known as "Rebel" Hall, was one of the pioneers of Ingersoll. A street in the town is also named after him.

Bardsley (2) says of this name: "Hall.—Local, 'at the hall.' This has, of course, produced separate stocks all over the country. . . . The *hall* was almost as familiar as the *green*. It seems to have been a kind of superior or more pretentious dwelling, but not 'the Hall,' as understood in the present day."

HORNER CREEK.

> When Dunkrey's top cannot be seen,
> Horner will have a flooded stream.
> —*Somersetshire Rhyme.*

Horner creek has its source in Perth county, and flows diagonally through the townships of East Zorra, Blandford and Blenheim.

Nothing definite is known as to when the name was first applied to this stream, but it is so named on Shenstone's map.

Thomas Horner, after whom it appears to have been named, was the first white settler in Oxford county. His uncle, a man named Watson, had served under Colonel Simcoe, who took a great liking to him, and, when appointed Lieutenant-Governor of Upper Canada, promised him a township of land, with the understanding that he was to build saw and grist mills and bring in settlers. It was for the purpose of spying out this promised land that Watson sent out his two nephews,[1] and they selected the township of Blenheim, where they both subsequently settled—Watson on lot 13 and Horner on lot 15, in the first concession. This was in 1793, soon after Augustus Jones completed the survey of the first three concessions of the township. Mr. Horner located on the north half of the lot. He soon cleared a small field on the west bank of the creek, built a home, a dam, and had his sawmill running about two years later. This mill and also a grist mill, which he had erected, were destroyed by fire in 1809, and were never rebuilt. Governor Simcoe's successor refused to recognize the claims of these two settlers and they were both cheated out of their rights and years of hard labour. This resulted in Watson returning to New Jersey, but Horner remained and afterwards became the first member of Parliament for Oxford county. His feelings, owing to this unjust treatment, had become very bitter against the ruling faction and this brought him into active political life. He was elected and served in four parliaments between the years 1820 and 1834, and during his entire parliamentary career he fought against the "Family Compact." Besides serving the country in this way, he took part in the war of 1812-1814; was Captain of the Norfolk Militia; Deputy-Lieutenant of Oxford

---

[1]Sutherland's *Gazetteer* says one of them was a son of Watson.

county; a Justice of the Peace; and Registrar of the London District up to the time of his death, which occurred on August 4, 1834. He was born at Bordentown, New Jersey, March 17, 1767.

It is unfortunate that we have not had preserved for us in a more permanent form the name of a man who was so closely connected with the early history of our county. However, Horner creek may well perpetuate his name for some time to come.

Horner, according to Dudgeon, means a worker in horn. Bardsley (1) likewise thinks the name is derived from the occupation horn-making. A horner, also, was one who blew the hunting horn, a huntsman or master of the hounds. The name is frequently spelt Hornor.

Kenny Creek.

> One cheer on Carrick's rocky Hill,
> And Donal Kenny's gone forever.
> —John K. Casey: *Donal Kenny.*

> While Kenney's "World"—ah! where is Kenney's wit?
> —Byron: *English Bards and Scotch Reviewers.*

This creek is so named on Tremaine's map and on the Militia map. Trimble calls it Kinny's creek. It was probably named after some person of that name in Burford township. Israel Kenny lived on lot 1, concession V, of that township in 1900.

According to Lower (2) "The Kenneys, who settled in Ireland, temp. Edward IV, A.D. 1472, were of high antiquity in Somersetshire, deriving their name from Kenne in that county. So early as 12 Henry II, John de Kenne held two knight's fees in Kenne. The name has been variously spelt Kenne, Kenei, Kenny and Kenney."

McKay Creek.

> The Browns and Hopes,
> McKays, Dunlops,
> And a' their wives and weans coming.
> —A. H. Wingfield: *Gathering of the Clans.*

This stream, formerly called Doty creek (q.v.), is locally known as McKay creek, because it flows through two of the McKay farms. The McKays were early settlers in East Nissouri township.

"The old form of the name," according to Lower (2) "is Mac Aaiodh (Aoi) 'the son of Hugh,' or, as others say, 'the son of the Guest'."

Also known as Waubuno creek (*q.v.*).

Nith River.

> The Irish Rian, Ken, the silver Ayr,
> The snaky Doon, the Orr with rushy hair,
> The crystal-streaming Nith, loud bellowing Clyde;
> Tweed, which no more our kingdoms shall divide.
> —W. Drummond: *The River of Forth Feasting.*

This river is more commonly known by the less classical name of "Smith's creek." John Smith, to whom it owes this name, was a squatter on the site of the present village of Wellesley, in Waterloo county, which is even yet called Smithsville by German residents. It probably owes its present name to the fact that, like its Scottish namesake, it flows through the township of Dumfries.

Otter Creek.

> I'll strive to draw
> The nymphs of Tamar, Tavy, Exe and Taw,
> By Turridge, Otter, Ock, by Dart and Plym.
> —W. Brown: *Britannia's Pastorals*.

Otter creek was so called either after the river Otter, which flows through the eastern part of Devonshire, England, or because otters were once numerous in the neighbourhood. If the former, it may have been named by Governor Simcoe, who was a native of Devonshire. It was known by its present name as early as 1821.[1]

Phelan Creek.

O'Faelans, or Phelans, of the Desies, whose son, Mothla, commanded the Desie of Munster in the same memorable battle.—Lower (2) II.

This creek is indicated on Tremaine's map but is not named on later maps. It may have been named either after Daniel and T. Phelan, who were residents of Eastwood in 1857, or after Valentine Phelan, who was a lawyer in Woodstock at the same period. Daniel Phelan was a Justice of the Peace and postmaster at Oxford (Centre?) in 1850.

Purdy Creek.

> Then Henry Purdie proved his cost,
> And very narrowly had mischief'd him,
> And there we had our warden lost,
> Wert not the grit God he relieved him.
> —*The Raid of the Reidswire*.

This creek is so named on Tremaine's map, but the name does not appear on any later map. It is still known as Purdy creek.

While the names of H., L., and W. H. Purdy appear on Tremaine's map, their farms are not traversed by the creek. It does flow, however, through the farms of Alfred and William Purdy, whose names are given in a later record as occupying lot 26, concession IX, East Nissouri township.

According to Bardsley (2) Purdy is a nickname, probably a corruption of Pardew.

Putnam Creek.

The name of this creek also appears on Tremaine's map, but it does not occur on any later map. There were no Putnams in this part of Oxford county when Tremaine's map appeared. The creek flows into North Dorchester township, Middlesex county, and may have received its name from either Joshua or Thomas Putnam, who were early settlers in that township.

Bardsley (2) says the name is "local, 'of Puttenham', parishes in cos. Hertford and Surrey."

---

[1]Observations made in the year 1821 by Lieutenant-Colonel Cockburn, Deputy Quartermaster General to the Forces when in attendance on His Excellency Lieut.-General the Earl of Dalhousie, G.C.B., on a tour of inspection made by His Lordship to the Western Frontier of this Command." *Canadian Archives* report, 1897, p. 71.

REYNOLDS CREEK.

> Here Reynolds is laid and to tell you my mind,
> He has not left a wiser or better behind.
> —O. Goldsmith: *Retaliation.*

This creek was first named on Shenstone's map and appears on several later maps. I have not succeeded in ascertaining from whom it obtained its name. The name of M. Reynolds appears on Tremaine's map as owner of the east half of lot 4, concession X, Dereham township, and the creek may have been named after him.

According to Bardsley (2) Reynolds is "Bapt. 'The son of Reynold', *i.e.*, Reginald, Fr. Regnaud and Reynard. One of the most popular font names of the surname period." Barber says it means God's wielder or ruler. Guppy thinks it "takes its origin from Rainhold, a Teutonic name of great antiquity."

SPITTLER CREEK.

The name first appears on Shenstone's map and occurs on most later maps of the county. The creek was probably named after Joseph Spittler who settled along its banks, between concessions VI and VIII, in 1808.

Spittler is a German patronymic and means "one out of the hospital."[1]

SWEETS CREEK.

This creek name also first appears on Shenstone's map. The creek was probably named after Robert Sweet who located near Otterville in 1808.

Lower (2) thinks the name Sweet was probably a Saxon personal name having reference to character. Bardsley (2) says it may have reference to disposition.

THAMES RIVER.

> Sweet Themmes! run softly, till I end my song.
> —E. Spenser: *Prothalmion.*

> Wanton Thamysis that hastes to greet
> The brackish court of old oceanus.
> —Chapman: *The Thames.*

Besides the Bacheler's Barge spouting flamys of fire in Temmys ther wer meny other gentilmanly pajants wel and curiouslie devised.—Britton: *History of the Tower.*

Some time after 1744 the still water of this river "seems to have suggested the name of 'The Moat'—*La Tranchee*, which presently became *La Tranche*, under the same process that converted *Sainte Claire* into 'Saint Clair,' and *Lac Erie* into 'Lake Erie'. Governor Simcoe's Proclamation of July 16, 1792, which would fain have converted *Le Grand Riviere* into "The Ouse,' permanently transformed *La Tranche* into 'The Thames'."[2]

Thames, the Tamesis of Caesar, according to Taylor (1) is a Celtic word meaning "the tranquil" or "smooth" river. In Saxon charters the name appears as Taemese, Tamese, and Temis. In another work on place names (2) he says: "The word tam, spreading, quiet, still . . . appears in the names of the *Tem-ese*, or Thames."

---

[1] "Spittler, 'einer aus dem Spittal.' In vollerer Form Spitaler."—Heinte, p. 239.
[2] Hunter, "From Toronto Westward," p. 502.

WAUBUNO CREEK.

This is the name of a creek flowing into the Thames. It has its source in East Nissouri township.

Waubuno, according to the Rev. Peter Jones, means "the morning light," and was the name of his grandfather, a celebrated chief.[1]

Also known as Doty and McKay creek (*q.v.*).

WHITING CREEK.

> Budding, Browning, Bedding, Baring,
> Watering, Wedding, Whiting, Waring.
> —T. Clark: *Surnames Metrically Arranged*, etc.

This creek was so called on Tremaine's map. It does not appear on any later maps. It may have been named after Whiting street, Ingersoll, which, apparently, was named after General John Whiting, of Great Barrington, Mass., father-in-law of Major Thomas Ingersoll.

Bardsley (2) regards this surname as probably local, and in this connection cites the hamlets called Whittington and Whittingham. Anderson thinks the name means "son of White."

WILMOT CREEK.

> With doubtful strife Humanity and Art
> For conquest vie in Wilmot's head and heart.
> —*William Duncombe.*

This stream was doubtless so called because it rises in Wilmot township, Waterloo county, which was most likely named after Major Samuel Street Wilmot, one of the early surveyors. He was born in 1774 and died in 1856. Gardiner mentions several other Wilmots after whom the township may have been named.

There are various origins given for this surname. Bardsley (2) thinks it is a baptismal name, " 'the son of William,' from dim. William-ot, used for both sexes." He says, further: "It existed in Cornwall as a girl's name till the close of the last century." Barber derives it from "Old G. Wilmod; Fl. Wilmart; Fr. Wilmotte; p.n. (resolute courage)." In *The Norman People* it is deduced from Villa Mota.

There is also a Wilmot creek in Durham county, Ontario.

---

[1] P. 163.

XXI.

THE REVD. JOHN OGILVIE, D.D., AN ARMY CHAPLAIN AT FORT NIAGARA AND MONTREAL, 1759-1760

By Professor A. H. Young, M.A., D.C.L. (Trinity College, Toronto)

What the Seven Years' War meant to the British colonists in America becomes clear on a perusal of the letters of the "servants" of the Society for the Propagation of the Gospel in Foreign Parts, written home to the Secretary between 1755 and 1763. From Newfoundland to Georgia and Jamaica they felt the pressure of high prices; anxiety lest the Empire should come out second best in the struggle, unduly prolonged by the incompetence of successive commanding officers; and fear that their religious liberty would be seriously infringed, if not taken away altogether, in the event of the French winning the war. Therefore it is the easier to understand the exultation and the high hopes for the future engendered in the people by the success of the plan of campaign devised by Pitt and carried out by Sir Jeffrey Amherst and the officers fighting under him in 1759 and 1760—Wolfe, Monckton, Murray, Haviland, Haldimand, Gage, Prideaux, and Johnson.

Preparatory to the siege of Quebec, Cape Breton had to be secured. When Quebec had fallen, Montreal, which, in 1759, was looked upon as the key to Canada, had yet to be taken. In order to do that, the upper posts of the French had also to be reduced. Hence the operations directed against Fort Duquesne, Fort Niagara, and Fort Frontenac; and the expeditions from Oswego and Lake Champlain, which, with that from Quebec, were to converge upon Montreal.

With his base at Oswego, which had been captured and burned by Montcalm in August, 1756, but which had been rebuilt and held by Colonel Haldimand in 1759, General Prideaux laid siege to Fort Niagara. With him, in command of the Indian auxiliaries, went Sir William Johnson, chief superintendent of Indians for the northern division of the American continent. Prideaux being killed by misadventure by one of his own gunners, July 19, 1759, the command was taken over by Sir William without regard to the fact that Haldimand, who was at Oswego, thought that he ought to have had it.

The presence of the Indians being deemed to be again necessary when the expedition which was to sail in 1760 from Oswego against Montreal was being organized, it was arranged that Sir William Johnson should once more accompany the commanding officer, who this time was Sir Jeffrey Amherst himself. But, lest the details of the plan of campaign should be divulged to the French by the Indians, Sir Jeffrey took care not to let Sir William know too many of the details.

The Rev. John Ogilvie.
1722-1774.

With Sir William on both of these expeditions went the Revd John Ogilvie, in whose discretion and ability to influence the Indians Sir William had full confidence as the result of his observation of him during the ten years preceding as missionary to the Mohawks at Fort Hunter and to the Whites at the important military post and trading town of Albany.

The mission had fallen vacant in 1746, on the withdrawal of the Revd Henry Barclay to the rectory of Trinity Church, New York. The Indians, who had, through the effectiveness of the work done by the French agents, held aloof from the English in the war which was then in progress, had become so distrustful of their missionary that he felt it to be impossible to do anything with or for them until peace should be re-established.

Being deeply solicitous for their welfare, occupying in his new cure an almost Episcopal position, and enjoying peculiar advantages in the matter of keeping himself in touch with different colleges, Barclay was presently able to report to the Society that he had found in John Ogilvie a candidate for Holy Orders who would make a suitable missionary. Not only was the young man filled with a desire to be serviceable to the Indians, but, on account of his proficiency in the use of the Dutch language, he would be able to minister to the large numbers of Dutch people, who, notwithstanding the fact that it was some seventy-five years since the province had been transferred to Great Britain, were still unable to speak anything but their mother tongue.

The writer of the Society's Report for the year 1749, which bears date 1750, tells of the Dutch language being "very like the Indian one in its rumbling Sound." The implication was, of course, that the young ordinand would accordingly have little difficulty in acquiring a competent knowledge of the latter. This, as a matter of fact, he did, as letters from the publishers of a Mohawk version of the Book of Common Prayer prove. (*See O'Callaghan's Documentary History of New York, Vol. IV, pp. 386, 396 and 405.*)[1]

Though born in New York, as his sponsors wrote to the Society (*See letters of March, Michaelmas, and November, 1747, following*), Ogilvie, as many a New Yorker of social standing does to-day, went to Yale for his college course. There he came under the notice and influence of the Revd Samuel Johnson, D.D., who was, in 1754, to become, for nine years, President of King's College, New York, as Columbia University was called down to the establishment of the United States of America.

Ogilvie, at the age of twenty-six, took his degree of Bachelor of Arts from Yale in 1748 and his Master of Arts in 1751. Three years after his return to live in New York, King's College conferred upon him, in 1767, an honorary M.A., which it followed up in 1770 with an honorary D.D. In 1769 he had received the honorary D.D. from Aberdeen, though from which of the two universities which were then giving degrees in that ancient city, does not appear in the note courteously furnished by the Secretary of Columbia University.

The Secretary is unable to find in the University's records anything to justify the statement in O'Callaghan's very valuable *Documentary History* that Ogilvie was at any time a member of the teaching staff or of the governing

---

[1]All page references to O'Callaghan are to the octavo edition.

body of King's. But he was, as his own letters show, very anxious to find suitable young men for missions in his own province and in others.

In connection with his certificates to candidates going over to London for ordination it is interesting to find him vouching for the character of John Doty, who was to be probably the very first Loyalist clergyman to make his way to Canada in 1777. The letters about Doty and Fredericksburgh touch upon persons and places connected with the Robinson family, well known in the history of New Brunswick and Upper Canada.

Colonel Beverley Robinson, Colonel Roger Morris and Dr. Ogilvie himself were, it would appear, all made wealthy by their matrimonial alliances with members of the Philipse family. It had been founded in the Dutch period by Frederick Philipse, a young Dutchman of good birth, who enriched himself in trade, became a member of the Provincial Council, allied himself in marriage first with the De Vries and secondly with the Van Cortland family, and founded the two manors of Philipseburgh, now Yonkers, and Fredericksburgh.

For Ogilvie at any rate it was fortunate that he had private means, for the records of Trinity Church show that the Corporation had at times difficulty in discharging its obligations to him and to his fellow assistant, Dr. Inglis. They received an interest-bearing bond each to secure their claims. Embarrassment on the part of the Corporation is, quite frankly, referred to by the rector, Dr. Auchmuty, in his letter of April 13, 1765, when speaking of the additional salary of which he wished to procure the continuance for Ogilvie as a catechist to the negro slaves of the city.

Although the Society thought that the masters of the slaves, if not the Corporation of the Church, were sufficiently opulent to bear this expense, they continued down to the close of the revolutionary war to pay the salary of the master of the charity school attached to the Church. These two items show how willing the well-to-do New Yorkers, like many another congregation in the "old Colonies," as well as in Nova Scotia and Canada, were to let the Society shoulder burdens which they themselves ought to have carried.

Generous above most of the men with whom Ogilvie came in contact either at New York or at Albany was Sir William Johnson, the wealthy, scrupulously honest trader, the owner of vast acres on the Mohawk river, the protector of the Indians, the builder of churches, the patron of the clergy, the ardent advocate of the extension of missions and education among the Indians, a willing, generous contributor to the fund for the endowment of a bishopric, or bishoprics, for America, a member of the Provincial Council, the successful manager of matters diplomatic in which the Indians were concerned, and their victorious leader at Lake George, Fort Niagara, and the expedition from Oswego to Montreal.

That there was no provision for a chaplain to accompany the Indians or the other soldiers to Lake George, was apparently a keen disappointment to their zealous missionary, who had manifestly been of material assistance to Sir William in inducing the former to volunteer their services. However, he takes comfort from the fact that "Good Old Abraham" had performed Divine Service for them every morning and evening. *Letter of December 25, 1755.*

Of the quarrel between Sir William and Governor Shirley in regard to the proposed expedition to Niagara at this same date and of the disaster which attended it, the discreet missionary utters not a word. Concerning the death of General Prideaux, in 1759, and of his second in command, Colonel Johnstone, also he is silent, although he buried them both; nor does he give any account of the siege of the Fort or the cutting off the relieving troops, who were hastening from the south and west to the succour of the besieged.

Greater interest for him lay in the exemplary behaviour of his Indians and in the praise meted out to him by Sir William for the moderation which they displayed. As a matter of course, he told of the services which he held in the Roman Catholic Chapel within the Fort—the first, probably, which any Anglican clergyman ever held so far to the westward of Albany.

When he speaks of the "Parade" of the Roman service, he is not to be understood as sneering at what he witnessed. If he had been writing at the present day, he would, unless he were very bigoted and prejudiced, have likely used some such word as complexity or impressiveness of the ritual, as compared with the simplicity of that of his own Church.

For the Jesuits, as missionaries and as relators, he evidently had great respect, as witness his letter of August 9, 1760. It was their propagation of what he regarded as wrong views of the Christian religion and their influencing the Indians from the Mohawk river westward in favour of the French to which he objected. Yet in his own eyes he himself was doing nothing but right in exerting whatever influence over the Indians he possessed in order to induce them to take up arms on the side of Great Britain. In this particular it was simply another case of the ownership of the ox that was at the moment being gored.

He was wide awake to the advantages accruing to the Mother Land and to the American Provinces from the reduction of Niagara: "it gives us the happy opportunity of commencing & cultivating a friendship with those numerous tribes of Indians who inhabit the Borders of *Lake Erie, Huron, Michigan,* & even *Lake Superiour;* And the Fur trade which is carried on by these tribes, which all centers at Niagara, is so very considerable, that I am told by very able judges that the French look upon Canada [as] of very little importance without the possession of this important Pass [i.e., portage, as we should now say]; it certainly is so and must appear obvious to any one who understands the geography of this country. It cuts off & renders their Communication with their Settlements [Canada and Louisiana] almost impracticable." After a brief digression, he recurs to the same theme in this letter of February 1, 1760:— "We have now, by the Blessing of Heaven, obtained the whole object of the war upon this Continent, and upon the Conclusion of a Peace, if we may only keep those places to which we have an undoubted right, by grants from the natives, & confirmed by solemn Treaties, particularly by that of *Utrecht,** and Niagara is certainly one of those places; I think we shall have it in our power to frustrate the extensive & ambitious views of the Court of France upon this Continent of America, by effectually securing the alliance of all the Indian nations."

---

*See the note on the letter.

But, although Quebec had fallen, Montreal had yet to be reckoned with; and there was apparently the fear, as there was in the minds of the men who fought in France from 1914 to 1918, that they might not obtain "an honourable Peace." Strange to say, in spite of the views of later generations in regard to the Treaty of Paris of 1763, contemporary opinion was not by any means unanimously favourable. The Revd Charles Inglis, from 1787 to 1816 Bishop of Nova Scotia, suggested that the Convention of Clergy in his Province should send to the King an humble address of congratulation; and at that date the Reverend gentleman had not yet obtained his promotion even to the position of second assistant to the Rector of Trinity Church, New York.

The success of Wolfe at Quebec had made Ogilvie's hopes run high, notwithstanding the fact that Murray was shut up in the city during the ensuing winter in none too pleasant circumstances. Nor had the additional fact that he had been defeated by Levis at Ste. Foy in April been sufficient to put a damper on those hopes, if indeed the news of that defeat had, as was probable, reached Albany by May 20. "The issue of this Campaign, I trust in God," he writes, "will be the Compleat Conquest of Canada. We have a very promising Prospect before us, of bringing the affairs of America to a safe & honourable Issue."

"We are now all preparing to take the field, which we shall do in a few days," he says in an earlier paragraph, "As the Mohawks all go, I imagine the Genl. will expect my attendance, which I hope will be agreeable to the Venl. Society, as I shall still be in the way of my Duty as their Missionary."

Not the least interesting parts of the letters herewith printed are those which relate to the mission at Fort Hunter. Not only were his Indian parishioners the ancestors of the Indians now resident near Brantford and Deseronto; but they presented to their spiritual guide some, if not all, of the difficulties which his predecessors and his successors alike had to meet in prosecuting their laudable work. The war, naturally, made his task a very hard one.

It is easy to understand that he had to show hospitality to the Indians when they were passing through or simply visiting Albany. As there was no official provision for this extra expense, except in seasons such as that of 1755, when he appears to have been compensated by Sir William Johnson, he might well wish that he had an allowance such as he records as having been allowed by the French to the Franciscan father at Fort Niagara. He can hardly be blamed for mentioning to the Society as Christmas was drawing near in 1756, that "he finds it hard to support his Family, as every thing is as dear again as it was, tho' he is King's Chaplain at Albany with £50 Sterling p. annum upon which there are considerable deductions; if by any means he could get his Salary increased to the same Value with that at Boston, Viz- £100 p. annum it would enable him in a great measure to support the unavoidable expences he is at in this important Mission: it is mere necessity (he says) compels him to mention this, for he had no Assistance from his Parishioners, who are not indeed able to help him."

As "King's Chaplain," he was under obligation, apparently, to minister to the troops quartered in the fort in the city in time of peace. This chaplaincy, it was subsequently claimed, was necessarily conjoined with the rectory.

Certainly it was held both by Dr. Barclay and by his father before him; and just as certainly it was obtained for Ogilvie in his turn by the Society.

Whether the emolument came out of Queen Anne's Bounty, does not appear. Mention of that source of income was made by Ogilvie's successor, Mr. Munro, after Ogilvie had removed to New York; and the latter was reported by the new rector to be willing to resign it.

One of Ogilvie's reasons for withdrawing from Albany (*See the letters of September 29, 1764, and April 23, 1765*.) was that, as a retired Army Chaplain, he could draw in New York his half pay, which would have been incompatible with his pay as Chaplain at Albany. In the light of what has just been said about Queen Anne's Bounty, it would seem therefore that the grant from that fund was quite distinct from the salary for the chaplaincy.

Like all other missionaries, Ogilvie was subject to the income tax levied in Great Britain. Hence the "deductions," of which he speaks.

What he says about receiving nothing from his parishioners is corroborated by the author of the "History of St. Peter's Church in the City of Albany," at page 103. Their whole contribution appears to have consisted of twelve pounds for firewood. But besides its being war time, the regular inhabitants who could do so had withdrawn to a safer distance from the seat of war; and naturally their subscriptions must have lapsed.

The "surplice fees," according to the authority already cited, all went for charity, any surplus from that source of revenue being paid over to the Church Wardens. That these fees were numerous, may be concluded from the statement made on pages 92 and 93 of the same book,—"Mr. Ogilvie's work was largely increased by the presence of the troops in the city. He ministered to the soldiers, gave them good food, good advice, and often supplied them with uxuries and necessities. There are many marriages of soldiers recorded in the church register, and before each campaign of the war a large number of children of the soldiers were baptised. He was also the consoler of the widow and orphan, for many of the troops died in battle and in the weary journey through the woods to the seat of war."

Letters such as many a chaplain has had to write to mothers and brothers of the fallen Ogilvie had also to write. Specimens of them given in Dr. Severance's book, "An Old Frontier of France," (pages 296-298 of Vol. II) show him to have been possessed of deep feeling and great delicacy.

Over and above all this was the heavy duty connected with the military General Hospital, which was set up in Albany.

In Montreal he had fresh opportunities for displaying the same gifts, the same generosity, and the same devotion to duty that he had displayed at Albany and Fort Niagara. "After the Reduction of the Regiment, I had the Honor to serve in [the 60th Royal American], on the 24th of August, 1763, I should have immediately left Canada, & have devoted some time to a Review of my private estate, which had suffered considerably during my absence. But the deplorable state in which I must have left the protestant congregation at Montreal, affected my Mind so much, that I came to a Resolution to devote, without Fee or Reward, another year to the service of that infant congregation;

And indeed for four years service in that City I have never received the least gratification from the Government."

The influx of civilians, traders and curiosity-mongers, after the capitulation, and, more especially, after the Peace, must have been very great. By their probable manner of life and their equally probable indifference to religion, they, most likely, added not a little to the Chaplain's duty and to his anxieties, amid which he found comfort in General Gage's example and countenance.

Having been pleased to say that "he could by no means dispence with my absence, as the Honor of the protestant Religion must be kept up, in a Town where all the inhabitants were of a contrary persuasion," etc. (*See letter of October 14, 1760.*), General Amherst ought surely to have seen to it that something more than the chaplain's army pay, and, after the reduction, a good deal more than his half pay, was secured to him. But Amherst does not seem to have been afflicted with a superabundance of generosity or to have had much consideration for anybody but himself. His desire to acquire a goodly share of the Jesuits' estates for himself is a matter of history. So too is his unwillingness to recompense people from whom he took property or supplies under the pretext of military necessity.

The missionary on Staten Island, for instance, complained to the Society of "the desolate state to which the Church on Staten Island is reduced by the encampment of General Amherst's Army upon Ducksbury Glebe, & some Fields adjacent, that the fences round the Glebe were entirely destroyed by the Soldiers for Fewel, & then the Woodland became the subject of their Ravage. Besides this, the pits they sunk, & the Huts of turf they raised, have rendered the whole farm unfit for tillage, or even pasture. . . . . He had presented a Petition to the General upon the occasion (a Copy of which he has enclosed) but says, that the General is deaf, & the Assembly obdurate, so that all his resource must be in the Society's Support. Three hundred pounds currency will scarce make the Farm tenantable." *Journal XV, pp. 214-215.*

Sundry entries in the Society's Journals refer to this matter; but the last one, which was printed in the annual report in 1764, suffices to show the issue of it and the influence which the Society could upon occasion exert. "And in his Letter dated *May* 27, 1763, he [Mr. Charlton] acquaints the Society that in Consequence of a Letter from the Secretary at War to Sir *Jeffrey Amherst*, he has received of the General the Sum of £271, 2s, 7d. upon an Estimate made: For which seasonable Relief he expresses his highest Gratitude. And the Society take this Opportunity to return their Thanks to the Secretary at War for his kind Offices on this Occasion."

From a letter received from Mr. Dibblee of Stamford "in New England" it can be learned that the Government of New York proclaimed a fast on account of the war in the earlier part of 1762. The letters of other missionaries recount the hardships which they were then enduring. The Revd. Mr. Langman of St. John's, Newfoundland, for example, describes his hard case on the 14th of July, one week after the date on which Mr. Dibblee wrote, and again on the 2nd November: "giving a melancholy Account of the Siege, Surrender and plundering of St. John's Town, together with the Interception of all Provisions, which arrived from New England and other Places, not knowing the Town was taken; by which the Protestant Inhabitants were reduced to great Distress. It was soon after determined by the French General, with the consent of the French Commander, to send all the Protestant Families out of the Place, which was almost done before the Place was retaken by the English Sept. 18 last; so that there are but few Protestant Families now in St. John's, even reckoning about 70 Souls sent back at the Expence of the Government since it was retaken. The sudden death of his Wife in Child-bed, and his own being confined to his Bed and Chamber by a dangerous flux till some time after the Place was retaken, prevented his being sent away with the rest of the protestant English Families. His Losses by plunder he computes at £130 at least, besides being deprived this Year of all Profits arising from the Fishery." *Journal XV, pp. 319-320.*

Meanwhile Ogilvie at Montreal was taking note of the conditions which obtained there and of the prospects for the establishment of the Protestant Religion. On the 29th of July, 1763, he gives the Society details as to the clergy, the Religious Orders, the charitable institutions, and the material resources at their command, all of which it is interesting to compare with the inventories furnished by General Gage in his capacity of Lieutenant-Governor of Montreal and printed by Doctors Shortt and Doughty in their admirable edition of the *Constitutional Documents of Canada.*

He notes that the Jesuits are disestablished in France and consequently in Canada; and he suggests that out of their estates a handsome provision might be made for the Established Church of England. But on this subject, as set out in the notes on this letter of his, the Government, General Amherst, and Sir Guy Carleton (Lord Dorchester) had conflicting views.

Withal he has some very interesting remarks to make upon the priests of St. Sulpice and upon their Head, Mgr. Montgolfier, further notice of whom will be found in the notes to the letter. Only this part of the letter, apparently, and that referring to the possibility of an endowment for the Church made any impression upon the Committee and the Society, who relegated to the future consideration of Ogilvie's application to be appointed Rector of Montreal at that time.

Montreal, according to Ogilvie's temporary successor, the Revd. Samuel Bennet, was "inhabited by near 100 British Families, besides many French Protestants." "It is," he continues, "also a Garrison containing two Regiments of Soldiers who frequently marry with French Women, & for want of Protestant Clergymen are obliged to have recourse to Romish Priests to baptise their Children." *Journal XVI, pp. 284-285.*

Prophecy is notoriously not a safe thing to indulge in; but, by anybody who may live to see it, no surprise need be felt if some day the women of Quebec and their clergy reconquer Canada for their race and for their Church. The women and their husbands, unlike those of English speech, are not ashamed to have large families; and they do not draw back from the burden of rearing them. And the clergy, like their predecessors who saw to the protection of the religious interests of their people when the capitulations of Quebec and Montreal were being drawn up in 1759 and 1760, are ever zealous for the extension of their form of the Christian faith.

In this connection, as much as for its appreciation of Ogilvie's work between 1760 and 1764, the letter written to the Society by Colonel Daniel Claus in 1782, eight years after the chaplain's death, makes very interesting reading. One cannot help making the observation that then, as now, it was counted a meritorious thing to bring over to one's own communion a convert from another, and a most reprehensible thing to allow a member to be lost to one's own church.

"How ought we to blush at our coldness, & shameful indifference in ye propagation of our most excellent Religion," Ogilvie had written after the reduction of Fort Niagara. *"The Harvest is great but the Labourers are few.* The Indians themselves are not wanting in making very pertinent Reflections upon our inattention to these points! . . . . . And as the situation we shall be in, in all probability, if we obtain an honourable Peace, will give us the happy opportunity of sending Missionaries not only to the six Nations, but to ye other tribes, in their Alliance, I pray God the Government may think it an object worthy of their attention."

On the way to Montreal, in August of the same year, he wrote from Oswego: "I would to God, we had Labourers in this Part of the Vineyard to keep alive the spark that is kindled among some of these Tribes, & spread the glad tidings of the Gospel among the numerous Tribes with whom we have now a free communication;" and again: "I hope soon to congratulate the Venr. Society upon the intire Conquest of Canada, and I pray God that by that means, there may be a more effectual door open'd for the Propagation of the blessed Gospel among the Heathen."

Having returned to Albany for a short space after the capitulation of Montreal, he wrote exultingly to the Society on October 14: "It is with the highest pleasure I congratulate the Venr. Society upon the success of his Majesty's arms both by sea & land, and more especially upon the glorious Conclusion of this Campaign in America, by the intire reduction of Canada to the obedience of our most gracious Sovereign; An event so deeply impressed with such obvious characters of its own importance, that every Lover of his Country must feel his mind transported with admiration, Gratitude & Joy upon this happy occasion. May these remarkable smiles of divine Providence upon our national Interest make such a lasting impression upon the minds of all the subjects of the British Government, that a universal Reformation of Manners may be the Tribute of our gratitude to the supreme Regent of the Universe! . . . . . I am unable to express the universal Joy & Triumph that prevails among us at this period of public success. How remarkably has God in his Providence sustained the Cause, & restored the honour of our country, By the successes of the last & the glorious conclusion of this year. The Inhabitants of this northern Region of America are now happy in the quiet possession of their estates. *No more leading into* captivity, a Captivity big with danger & Horror, *no more complaining in our streets.*"

During the twelve years that he had been responsible for Albany and Fort Hunter, which were then on the frontier of the British settlements, Ogilvie had known all of the horrors of war and of Indian raids planned by the enemy, not forgetting the reprisals. Although he was not to return to that mission on

St. Peter's Church, Albany, N.Y.
1716–1802.

his departure from Montreal, he continued to take a deep interest in its welfare, as several of his letters prove.

In New York he rendered faithful service from 1764 to 1774, dying, at the comparatively early age of fifty-two, on November 26 of the latter year, four months and two weeks after his great patron, Sir William Johnson. It was the year also in which, by virtue of the extension of the boundaries provided for in the Quebec Act, Fort Niagara, at the capture of which they had both been present in 1759, became a part of Canada.—Of Canada it remained an integral part down to 1796, when it was handed over to the United States in pursuance of the Treaty of Versailles of 1783 and of Jay's Treaty of 1794.

Reading these old letters emphazies the facts that down to 1783 the history of the United States is British history and that from 1759 to 1783 practically all of North America east of the Mississippi and of the Great Lakes was one and was British—facts which, to our own loss, we are too apt to forget, even though we do not wish to make any breach in the Unity of the Empire, for the preservation of which the real pioneers of Ontario, New Brunswick, and parts of Nova Scotia, Prince Edward Island, and Quebec exiled themselves from the "Old Colonies." Among those "Old Colonies" none, so far as Ontario is concerned, contributed so large a proportion of the exiles as did the Province of New York and, in particular, that portion of it which lies contiguous to its present capital, Albany.*   Albany with Schenectady, continued for many a year after the recognition of the independence of the United States to have intimate trade relations with Montreal and, later, with "muddy little York."

BIBLIOGRAPHY.

Society for the Propagation of the Gospel in Foreign Parts: Original Letters; Manuscript Journals (or Minutes); Annual Reports; and Digest of Records.

Canniff: Settlement of Upper Canada. 1 Vol.

Champlain Society (A. G. Doughty, Editor): Knox, Historical Journal of the Campaigns in North America. 3 Vols.

Diocese of Connecticut; The Records of Convention, A.D. 1790-A.D. 1848. 1 Vol.

General Convention of the Protestant Episcopal Church of the United States: The Hobart papers, 6 Vols.

General Collection of Treaties, 1732; (Toronto Reference Library).

Gosselin, L'Abbé Auguste: Histoire de l'Eglise du Canada. Several Vols.

Hooper: A History of Saint Peter's Church in the City of Albany. 1 Vol.

O'Callaghan: Documentary History of New York. 4 Vols.

Parkman: A Half Century of Conflict; Montcalm and Wolfe. Each 2 Vols.

Severance: An Old Frontier of France. 2 Vols.

Shortt and Doughty: Documents of the Canadian Constitution. 2 Vols.

Stone, W. L., Jr.: Life of Sir William Johnson, 2 Vols.

University of the State of New York (James Sullivan, Editor): Sir William Johnson Papers, 3 Vols.

---

*A note from Mr. George P. Hoff, of the office of St. Peter's Church, Albany, to whom the writer is indebted for the loan of the History and the picture of that old foundation, contains the interesting information that in Volume I of the Register of the Parish occurs, on March 16, 1759, the original entry of the baptism of the Hon. Richard Cartwright, M.L.C., of Kingston, who died in Montreal in 1815.

Letter: 1—From the Secretary of the Corporation of St. Peter's Church, Albany.
        2—From the Secretary of the Genealogical and Biographical Society of New York—quoting from the "Biographical Sketches of the Graduates of Yale College with Annals of the College History." Vol. II. May 1745-May 1763. By Franklin Bowditch Dexter, M.A.
        3—From the Secretary of Columbia University in the City of New York, quoting from the records of the University.
        4—From George H. Wyeley Birch, Esq., Montreal West.

Dictionary of National Biography.

Appleton's Cyclopædia of American Biography.

The National Cyclopædia of American Biography.

Illustrations.

Portrait of Dr. Ogilvie, after Copley; by the kindness of the Corporation of Trinity Church, New York.

Plan of Fort Niagara, 1759, from O'Callaghan's *Documentary History of New York*, Vol. II, facing page 868.

View of St. Peter's Church, Albany, opened November 25, 1716, rebuilt and provided with a steeple in 1751, made way for a new Church, 1802; by the kindness of the Corporation of St. Peter's Church.

Views of the Chapel of the Hôtel-Dieu, and of the Récollet Church, Montreal, from *Hochelaga Depicta*; by the kindness of George H. Wyeley Birch, Esq., Montreal West.

View of old Trinity Church, as it was in Dr. Ogilvie's time; by the kindness of the Corporation of Trinity Church.

A Perspective View of the Town and Fortifications of Montreal in 1759 can also be seen in Vol. II, p. 566, of the Champlain's Society's edition of Knox's Journals.

LETTERS FROM AND CONCERNING THE REVEREND JOHN OGILVIE, M.A., D.D., WRITTEN TO THE SOCIETY FOR THE PROPAGATION OF THE GOSPEL IN FOREIGN PARTS, 1747-1774

From the Revd Dr Johnson,   Journal, XI, pp. 1-2.
Stratford (Conn.), Michaelmas, 1747.

. . . . . "but there being then many vacant Churches in those Parts he had been obliged to be very frequently absent from his own Church, when one Mr Ogilvie, a worthy young Gentleman of the College of Newhaven, who is a Candidate for Holy Orders, and an Excellent Reader, and a very serious Person, read Prayers and Sermons there in his Absence, ... and all the Candidates, who have been recommended to the Society, await patiently for Calls to Missions."

From the Churchwardens at Norwalk,   Ibid., p. 43.
    April 26, 1748, and
Petition, dated March 5, 1747,

"in Favour of Mr. Ogilvie who reads to them in a Lay Capacity, that he may be allow'd to come to England for Holy Orders, and be appointed Missionary to their Church and they promise, besides the Glebe, with the House therein already provided, to give Bond to the Society for the Payment to him of £30 Sterling p. Annum, as long as he shall officiate to them.

"The Committee also read a Letter Sign'd Saml Johnson,[1] Joseph Lamson,[2] John Beach,[3] three of the Society's Missionaries in New England, recommending the said Petition in Favour of Mr. Ogilvie, whom they represent to be a young Gentleman of good Abilities, bred up in the Church of New York from his Infancy, and educated at Yale College in Newhaven, and of much Piety and Zeal, and of a virtuous Life, and that he reads the Liturgy with great Decency, and they are fully Satisfied it would much contribute to the Advancement of true Religion if Mr. Ogilvie should be appointed Missionary to the Churches of Norwalk and Ridgefield."

From the Revd Henry Barclay, D.D.,[4] Ibid., pp. 89-90.
Rector of Trinity Church, New York,
November 7, 1748.

"acquainting that he had been looking for a proper Person to be sent to the Indians, and had his Eye upon Mr. Ogilvie, a young Gentleman of that City, who understands the Dutch Language, which is a very necessary Qualification, and hath been educated at Newhaven, and Mr Ogilvie gave him Hopes of accepting that Mission, but having some Time read Prayers and Sermons at Norwalk in Connecticut, that People are very unwilling to part with him; he hath wrote to him on this Subject, and if he should not prevail on him will endeavour to get some Gentleman from New-England for this Service:"

---

[1] The Revd Samuel Johnson, D.D., first President of King's College, New York (now Columbia University), 1754-1763, was from 1723 to 1754 and from 1763 to 1772 Rector of Stratford, Conn. He was born at Guilford, Conn., November 14, 1696; graduated from Yale, 1714; appointed Tutor there; ordained a Congregationalist minister, 1720, and an Anglican clergyman, 1723; given the degree of M.A. by Oxford and Cambridge, 1723, and D.D. by Oxford, 1743. He declined the presidency of the College of Philadelphia. He engaged in controversies over Episcopacy with the Revd Messrs. Dickenson, Foxcroft, and Graham. He was zealous in his search for candidates for Holy Orders and was a trusted adviser of the Society. His son, William Samuel Johnson, became the first President of Columbia University.

[2] The Revd Joseph Lamson was at the date of the letter of recommendation of young Ogilvie in charge of the mission of Fairfield and Ridgefield, Conn. He had been appointed to it in 1747, after spending a year or rather more at Rye, in the Province of New York. On his voyage to England, with a fellow ordinand, Miner, who died, apparently as a result of his experiences, he was taken prisoner by an enemy ship. After a sojourn of five months in Spain and France, he was allowed to proceed to England; and there he had an attack of fever at Salisbury, a place with which our first Canadian contingent became well acquainted in the winter of 1914-1915. He served at Ridgefield and Fairfield till 1773.

[3] The Revd John Beach, rector of Newtown, Conn., served there for a period of fifty years —1732-1782—and visited other places also, among them being Reading, New Milford, and Ridgefield. Although he was a staunch Loyalist, he did not close his Church at the time of the Rebellion, as a great many of the missionaries in other provinces did, when the order not to pray for the King was promulgated. Instead, he and several of his brother clergy of Connecticut used a form of service, which was deemed innocuous and which was formally adopted by them in Convention. He died in Newtown, March 19, 1782, in his 82nd year.

Two items in an address which, as noted by the Editor of the *Diocese of Connecticut; The Records of Convocation*, was sent to the Society by the Convention in 1739, are interesting;—the eviction of one of their number from his glebe by a "dissenting" mob and the inability of another to obtain, without a suit at law, the share of the public taxes which was due to him. In Connecticut the "dissenters" were established; and the "Churchmen," like our Separate School supporters in Ontario, had to declare themselves as such in order that their clergyman might receive his portion of the taxes. Even so, as the Editor states, recourse to the courts was not infrequently necessary; and, as the records of the Society show, the same could be truthfully said in the matter of quiet possession of glebes and church sites and buildings.

[4] The Revd. Henry Barclay, D.D., son of the Revd. Thomas Barclay, a former Rector of Albany, who had built St. Peter's Church in 1715-1716, and Missionary to the Mohawks, acted as catechist to the Mohawks as early as 1734. On January 20, 1737, he was ordained and, immediately upon his return to America, he took charge of his father's old parish and mission, in succession to the Revd John Miln (or Milne). His work was highly successful down to 1744, when the machinations of the French stirred up the Indians against him to such a degree that he deemed it advisable to accept the rectorship of Trinity Church, New York, vacant in 1746, because of the death of Dr. Vesey. This very influential position he held till his death, in 1764.

From the Honble George Clinton, Esqre,[1] Ibid., pp. 101-102.
Governor of New York.
Fort George,[2] January 3, 1748.
"recommending the Bearer, Mr Ogilvie as the most proper Person to be appointed Missionary to Albany and the Mohock Indians.
"Whereupon it was agreed to recommend to the Society that Mr John Ogilvie be appointed Missionary to Albany, and the Mohock Indians, upon his obtaining Deacons and Priests Orders from the Lord Bishop of London, with the usual Salary of £50 per Annum to commence from Christmas last, and to recommend him to the Lord Bishop of London to be appointed Chaplain to the Garrison at Albany.
"Resolved to agree with the Committee."

General Meeting of the Society, Ibid., p. 136.
May 19, 1749.
"Dr Brackenridge acquainted the Committee that he had heard the Revd Mr Ogilvie Preach on the 8th Verse of the 5th Chapter of St Matthews Gospel, and that he had performed very much to his Satisfaction."

From the Revd John Ogilvie, Ibid., p. 200.
New York, November 30, 1749.
"giving an account of his safe Arrival there after a tedious Passage of ten Weeks, but in so bad a State of Health, that he was not able to proceed immediately to Albany, and by the Advice of Mr Barclay, he should stay a few Weeks at New York, and employ his Time in the Study of the Mohock Language under him."

From the same, Ibid., pp. 200-201.
New York, December 26, 1749,
"acquainting that he was yet at New York, thro' the Inclemency of the Weather, but had officiated on Sunday, Decr 3 at Elizabeth Town, in New Jersey to a numerous Congregation, and that he must say in Justness to the Congregation, that he never saw our Liturgy perform'd with greater Propriety and Decency; and Mr Chandler[3] the Society's Catechist has merited the Esteem both of the Church People, and the Dissenters; He likewise reads Prayers and Sermons at Ranway, a Village about 5 Miles distant, where there seems to be a universal Disposition to conform to our Church; and at the Request of the People, Mr Ogilvie Preached there on the Thursday the 14th of Decemr in the Dissenting meeting House, which was kindly offer'd him by the Dissenting Teacher, who attended with his Congregation, and Mr Ogilvie Baptiz'd there 4 Children; and all the Dissenters express'd the strongest Desire that Mr. Chandler might be appointed Missionary, and the good People of Elizabeth Town were purchasing a Glebe, and entering into Measures to contribute generously to the Support of their Minister; Mr Ogilvie adds that he waited then only for a favourable Opportunity to proceed to Albany, and he hoped to get there by the Time the Indians return from Hunting."

From the same, Ibid., pp. 296-299, and
Albany, July 27, 1750. S.P.G. Letters,
  B. 18, New England, p. 102.
Revd. Sir,
I should have been earlier in acquainting the Venr. Society with my arrival & reception at Albany, but did not know the time of the ship's sailing before it was too late.
As soon as the season of the year would admit it, I left New York & arrived at Albany the last of March. I was recommended by his Excell: our Governour to the countenance and favour of the commanding officer of Fort Frederick in this City, & was received by him & many of the principle (sic) gentlemen with the strongest expressions & respect.
The Congregation in Albany is very much decreased occasioned by the removal of many of the principle (sic) English families to New York on account of the late war. The number of

---

[1]The Hon. George Clinton is referred to in the letter of June 29, 1752, as his Excellency Govr. Clinton. The footnote on page 314 gives further information concerning him.
[2]Fort George had been built on the shore of Lake George for defence against the French. The Lake, which was formerly called St. Sacrement, was renamed in 1755 by Sir William Johnson.
[3]The Revd. Thomas Bradbury Chandler (1726-1790), for many years Rector of Elizabeth Town, N.J., was distinguished as the author (1767) of an "Appeal to the Publick" in the matter of the desire for the appointment of Bishops for America. This he followed up by a "Defence of the Appeal" and "A Farther Defence of the Appeal." Writing to the Society on February 22, 1775, he tells of publishing "The American Querist," a "Friendly Address," and "What think Ye of the Congress now?" Continuing, he says: "And the consequence of these publications by himself & friend was, that thousands were proselyted to the side of Government, and

people that attend divine service in the Church on Sundays (besides the Garrison) far exceeds my expectations. I administred (sic) the holy Communion on Easter Sunday to 15 persons, & have admitted two since, Persons of an unblemished character. Besides preaching twice on Sundays I have prayers & catechize on Wednesdays, many of the inhabitants send their children so that I've near 50 that attend catechetical instruction constantly.

Many of the Negroes are very desirous of Instruction, to encourage this good disposition I constantly catechize them on Sundays after divine service in the afternoon. Since my arrival here I have baptized eight children two of which were negroes.

The Indians being at this time from home I did not immediately proceed to Fort Hunter, but waited for their Return. In the mean time many of the Indian women visited me at Albany, expressing the greatest pleasure at my arrival. In Easter Week I went to the Mohawks & was kindly received by Col. Johnson[1] a gentleman of the greatest influence & interests in these parts. I visited the few who were at home & promised to declare my intentions when the rest returned. I preached to a very large congregation on Sunday the 22nd. of Apr: & baptized three children one of which was an Indian Child. I waited at Albany till the 5th of June & then went up with the Interpreter of the Province; we were met by two of the principle (sic) Sachems, who in the name of the rest, congratulated me upon my arrival, expressed great thankfulness to the Society for sending them a Minister upon the conclusion of the Peace, promising they would use their endeavours to influence the Indians to be attentive to my instructions, & do all in their power to make my life agreeable.

---

that the N. York Assembly rejected the Proceedings of the Congress, by which the American Confederacy is broken, and the people of N. England will be left to act for themselves. But in serving the great Cause, he hath considerably injured his own private Interest. The suspicion that he wrote the *Address* has shorten'd the Supplies from his Parishioners, and 4 or 5 of the Wealthiest of them have scarcely shewn themselves at Church during the winter." Retiring in 1775 to England, he is said to have been offered the bishopric of Nova Scotia, but to have declined it because of the poor state of health in which he then was, 1787. He was ordained in 1751 and was given the honorary degree of D.D. by the University of Oxford in 1766. He returned to Elizabeth Town in 1785 and died there.

[1]Col. Johnson here mentioned was Sir William Johnson, the great man of the country lying between Albany and Oswego. Originally a sort of factor to his uncle, Admiral Warren, he became a merchant and trader on his own account. By his fair dealing, truthfulness, and honesty he commended himself to the Indians and obtained great influence over them. This influence led to his being made Chief Superintendent of Indian Affairs for the North. It also was the reason for his being placed in command of the expedition which resulted in the victory of Lake George in 1755 and in his being made a baronet. It likewise explains the position which he held on the expedition against Fort Niagara in 1759 and against Montreal in 1760. He acquired large possessions in the Mohawk valley, some idea of which may be obtained from O'Callaghan's *Documentary History of New York* and from the inventory of his son, Sir John Johnson's, claims as a Loyalist, which can be seen at the Public Archives of Canada in Ottawa. A considerable number of his letters and State Papers appears in O'Callaghan and many more were recently published in three volumes by the Division of Archives and History of the State of New York. The standard Life was written by W. L. Stone, jr., a son of the author of the Life of Joseph Brant.

Francis Parkman hardly does him justice. Certainly he does not leave the impression that he was in any sense a religious man. Yet a study of the documents shows that he had a very real interest in religion, which was not due simply to considerations of statecraft or of private advantage to be derived from the enhancement of the value of his holdings of real estate by having churches, schools, parsons, and schoolmasters upon or near them. He offered large tracts of land as an endowment for a bishopric or bishoprics in America; he built stone churches in and near Johnstown, his place of residence; and he contributed handsomely toward the salaries of the clergymen and schoolmasters of the district. He was firmly of opinion that members of the Church of England were "the surest Support of the Constitution, & the most faithful Subjects of the Crown"; and he preferred Anglican to "Dissenting" missionaries and schoolmasters for the Indians because of the "Gloom" of the Indians trained by the latter.

On the nomination of the Revd. Thomas Barton, of Lancaster, Pa., and the Revd. Dr. Auchmuty, of Trinity Church, New York, he became a member of the Society for the Propagation of the Gospel in Foreign Parts, the members of which looked to him as a trusted adviser on matters connected with the Indians and with the other missions in and around Albany.

Born at Smithtown, County Meath, Ireland, in 1715, he died at Johnstown, N.Y., July 11, 1774, the summer in which the rebellion began to wear a serious aspect. He divided his estate impartially among his white and his half-breed children, all of whom adhered to the Royal cause and came to Canada. The present Baronet lives in Montreal. See pp. XXXIV-XLIV, Vol. 1, *Sir William Johnson Papers.*

These congratulatory expressions were very pleasing to me, & things seemed to appear with a promising aspect. But alas! I am sorry I'm obliged to say I find them universally degenerated. Since the war they are intirely given up to Drunkenness. Many seem to have lost all sense of religion, and the best are in a state of indifference. However I find a good foundation laid by my worthy predecessor [Dr. Barclay]. I hope God will succeed my endeavours to build thereon. My hopes are intirely (sic) fixed on the rising generation, the children are universally disposed to learn, & if we can lay a good foundation by the education of the youth, the conversion of the heathen will be very much facilitated to succeeding missionaries.

The inclosed (sic) is a copy of a letter sent clandestinely to our Indians by an Independent Schoolmaster in New England. I am informed one Mr. Hollis has given a sum of money for the maintenance & instruction of a number of Indian children at Stockbridge. He, the Schoolmaster, has for some time been soliciting the Indians without my knowledge.

I can truly say I rejoice that there are any measures taken to instruct the Indians in our language, but can by no means approve of their making themselves popular by entering into the Society's labours. Therefore in justice, to the Ven: Society (who have always done their utmost to promote the conversion of these nations, & being satisfied that they would encourage this disposition in the indians to learn English) I refused my consent to send the children, promising the Indians that I would acquaint the Society with their desire of having a schoolmaster. I am persuaded a Schoolmaster in these parts may do extensive good not only to the Indians but other of the inhabitants. The children here have no education, but the little they receive from their parents, & even many of them not able to read & very few who understand the English language. I would wish there was proper encouragement given for a young gentleman from Yale College to act in the capacity of a Schoolmaster, it would be very acceptable to the Indians, & as I'm obliged to be half my time at Albany in my absence he may still be carrying on the good work, & by learning their language & customs may hereafter be an instrument of promoting the Society's pious intention to the Indian Nations. In the mean time to encourage this good disposition in the Indians I act as Schoolmaster myself and every day I have near twenty Indian children to teach reading besides some of the young men who learn to write.

I preach to the Indians twice every Sunday by the help of an Interpreter whom I hire for that Purpose, & read most of our Liturgy to them myself in their own language. On Sunday the 24th of June I administred (sic) the holy Sacrament to 13 of the Indians, who seem to have preserved some sense of religion on their minds, & have behaved very soberly since.

Beside care of the Indians I have divine service and preach twice to the Garrison & other of the inhabitants who attend in the Indian Chapel. On Sunday the 8th of July I visited the upper Castle [Canajoharie] about 38 miles above Fort Hunter.

Here things have a better appearance, & I find some who are not so much addicted to drunkenness, which has been greatly prevented by a very pious Indian whose name is *Abraham;* this Indian has for some time past intirely (sic) neglected his hunting in order to instruct his Brethren in the principles of Religion, & to keep up divine service among the aged people & children whilst the others are in the woods. He has likewise visited some of the upper Nations to instruct them; & seems intirely (sic) devoted to the interest of Religion. I mention this Indian because I apprehend some notice taken of his services, may have good effects.

While I was at this place the Indians received a belt of money from a popish priest settled at a place call'd *Cadraghque* (Cataraqui).¹ The substance of the message was to invite them to embrace the true religion, expressing a most tender concern at their being Hereticks, promising kind entertainment at his Habitation &c. The Mohawks refused compliance with the strongest intimation of resentment; I was quite pleased with their behaviour upon this occasion. I am informed by some of our Indians that he has made considerable impressions upon the *Onandagas* & many others in our alliance. I very much fear (if some measures are not taken to prevent it) that the French priests by their craft & policy will lead away most of the Indians into the French interest. Since the 5th of June I've baptized in ye Branch of ye Mission 9 children, 3 of which are Indian Children. The number of the Mohawks is very much decreased within these few years, as will appear by the accounts transmitted by my Predecessors. The castle at Fort Hunter consists at present of 204, & the upper Castle of 214. This from the best information is chiefly owing to the Numbers who have gone over to the French Interest & settled in their territories.

I wish I could be more sanguine in my hopes of success, but the want of Missionaries & Schoolmaster; the opposition of the Romish priests; the ill examples of Christian professors; the Indians strong propensions to strong liquors, are such impediments to this glorious work, as fills me with very dark apprehensions; but I'm somewhat relieved when I consider whose Cause I have in Hand, even His, who is exalted at God's Right Hand to be a Prince & Saviour, who is Lord of all; who has promised to be with his Ministers to support & assist them in accomplishing the purposes of his grace.

---

¹Cataraqui and Fort Frontenac were respectively the Indian and French names of Kingston, Ontario.

May our good & gracious God (who hath not left this noble design altogether without a Blessing) please to prosper it more & more & open an effectual door for the conversion of the Gentiles; may he by his Providence remove every obstacle, & by the influence of divine grace engage y^r attention to the truths of the Gospel & lessen their prejudices against them.

May God in His Providence ever smile upon the Venr. Society to raise them generous benefactors to support them in this noble design is the fervent prayer of

Revd. Sir their
& your most obedient
& humbe. Servt.
JOHN OGILVIE.

The Society's action on this letter is thus set down on pages 299 and 300 of Journal XI.:—
"It appeared to the Committee that the Sachem Abraham had lately a Gratuity Granted him of Five Pounds, and that his Son Petrus Paulus is appointed Schoolmaster to the Mohock Indians under Mr. Ogilvie, with a Salary of £7/10 p. Annum."

From the same,   S.P.G. Letters,
Albany, April 14, 1751.   B. 19, New England, etc., p. 71, and Journal XII, p. 114.

Revd. Sir,

I hope my letter of July 1750 is come safe to hand, wherein I've given the Venerable Society the best account I could obtain of the state of the Mohawk Indians. I should have wrote punctually at the time specified in the Society's instructions but by the severity of the weather I had no opportunity of conveyance at the season of the ship's sailing.

I still continue my method of instructing the children as far as the other duties of my office will admit. I am verily persuaded 'till some scheme be concerted for the education of the children, this generous work will proceed very slowly; I mean such a scheme as will, by the Blessing of God, change their whole Habit of thinking & acting & tend to form them into the condition of a Civil Industrious people so that the principles of Virtue & Piety may be instilled into their minds in such a way, as will be most likely to make the most lasting impression upon them, and withal introduce the English language among them instead of their own barbarous dialect.

I have been among them the whole winter past, & preached every Lord's Day twice, by the Interpreter (who I am obliged to pay for that purpose) & am now able to read the Liturgy to them in their own tongue. While I am with them they seem to have some regard to their Conduct; but no sooner am I gone to Albany but they fall to drinking to such excess, as to erase any good impressions they have received.

However they attend divine service on Sunday & at eight every evening, I administer the Holy Communion the first Sunday in every other month to the few that have some serious sense of Religion to the number of 14 at the lower Castle & as many at Canijohare (sic).

I have baptized in this part of my Mission (since my last) 22 white & 10 Indian children, exclusive of the upper Castle of which I've desired Mr. Oel[1] to transmit a faithful account. I preach to the Garrison constantly while I'm here on Sundays, & have prayers on Wednesdays & Frydays & all the Holy Days.

The obstacles to my Ministry among the Indians seem almost insuperable, & very much depress my spirits; I shall do my utmost by the divine assistance & ever pray, that Providence that superintends the affairs of Mankind, may remove every discouraging circumstances, and by the gracious influence of his Grace incline their hearts to the Reception of divine truth.

At Albany the Church is much the same, only that my Catechumens of the Dutch Children are increased to near 150; this I hope will tend in some measure to introduce the English Language more universally and lessen their prejudices to our excellent Liturgy.

I have dispers'd the small tracts the Society gave me I hope to good purpose, & should be extremely grateful if the Venr. Society would favour this Mission with a few of Lewises Catechism, as there are some who are arrived to riper years, would be glad to be instructed therein.

---

[1] The Revd. John Jacob Oel, one of the German immigrants from the Palatinate, who, according to a letter in Latin, which language he commonly used in his communications to the Society, appears to have been born in the year 1689. He seems to have been originally a Lutheran pastor, but in 1722 he was given Anglican Orders by Dr. Robinson, Bishop of London. Living with a wife and four small children on a small plantation about 18 miles from Fort Hunter, he was, early in Ogilvie's career, made his assistant for Indian work. As late as November 1, 1761, he tells of speaking to his congregations by an interpreter.

May God hasten the accomplishment of the Promises to the Mediator, in bringing in the Gentiles as his Heritage, and to this end may the Divine Providence succeed the labours of the Society to this glorious purpose, is the prayer of, Revd. Sir,

Their & your
most obedient & humble Servt.

JOHN OGILVIE,

From the same,
Albany, August 7, 1751

S.P.G. Letters,
B. 19, New England, &c. p. 72,
and Journal XII, pp. 115-116.

Revd. Sir,

I received your favour of the 27th of Octbr. with the greatest pleasure, & most lively sentiments of gratitude to the Venerable Society for their kind notice of this Mission.

I have informed Mr. Oel and given him directions for drawing & put him into a method of instructing the Indians at Canijohare as far as his age & infirmities will admit.

I have directed Abraham to draw for his money & hope this benefaction to him will have a good effect. As to Petrus Paulus, I never heard of such an Indian unless it be a son of Abraham's that has been dead some years since. I have not recommended any other Indian as Schoolmaster upon account of the strong inclination there seems at present in most of them to have their children instructed in the English language. There might be a great deal of good done among them, if there was proper encouragement given for something of that nature.

The Government of Boston are sensible of this & are concerting a scheme for educating the Indian children upon their frontiers, & are lik'wise soliciting the Mohawks to relinquish their own habitations & settle in their Government. Our province in general dislike the Indians Removal as it would lead to divert the trade from us & leave our frontiers naked & defenceless in case of another War; but I sincerely wish they would express their dislike, by contributing generously to a scheme of the like nature in this Province. For my own part I am against the Indians going from hence upon no other reason than an apprehension that their coming to the knowledge of the unhappy divisions subsisting among Protestants may so prejudice their minds as to render them a more easy prey to the craft of Popish Missionaries.

I am informed that Sr. Peter Warren[1] has something under his direction for the education of some Mohawk children. I make no doubt Sr. Peter would chuse to have any thing of that kind under the direction of the Venr. Society & that the Indians would be instructed in their own country upon the frontiers of this Province. I can truly say I rejoice in any Measur's that have the least probability of promoting the conversion of the Gentiles tho concerted & executed by the Dissenters but I must say I always desire to see the five nations under the patronage & direction of the Venr. Society.

I hope my letter of the 14th of Apr. is safe come to hand since which nothing of moment has occurred. I am Revd. Sir with fervent prayers for the Venr. Society & sentiments of the most perfect regard to you,

Your very affectionate Servant & Brother,

JOHN OGILVIE.

---

[1]Admiral Sir Peter Warren (1703-1752), uncle of Sir William Johnson, was the youngest son of Michael Warren of Warrenstown, County Meath, Ireland. Entering the Navy as an ordinary seaman, he served off the coast of Africa, in the Baltic, and in the western parts of the Atlantic. In 1744 and 1745 he took very valuable prizes, which greatly increased his wealth. In the former year he was Commodore in Command and in the latter he blockaded the harbour of Louisbourg, forcing the capitulation of the town. This brought him the promotion to be Rear-Admiral of the Blue and Second in Command of the Western Squadron. Two years later, after the defeat of the French Squadron off Cape Finisterre, he was promoted to the Chief Command, being made a Grand Cross of the Order of the Bath, a freeman of the City of London, and Vice-Admiral. From the City of New York, of which his wife, Susannah de Lancy, was a native, he received a gift of land. The year 1748 saw the last of his service at sea. After the Peace he settled down in London, having been elected Member of Parliament for Westminster, July 1, 1747. Declining twice to serve as Alderman for Billingsgate ward, he paid a fine of £500. On July 29, 1752, he died, leaving 3 daughters—Lady Abingdon, Lady Southampton, and Mrs. W. Skinner.—*Dictionary of National Biography.*

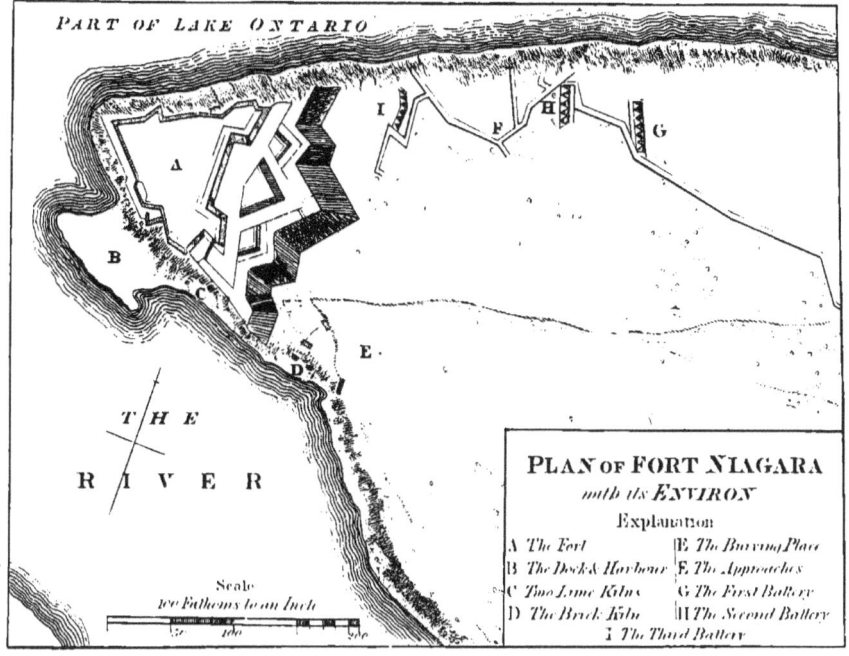

From Dr. E. B. O'Callaghan's "Documentary History of the State of New York," Vol. 2.

THE REVEREND JOHN OGILVIE, D.D. 313

Albany, July 6th, 1751.
Reverend Sir,
 I have this day taken the liberty to draw a sett of Bills of exchange at thirty days sight for £5 Ster. in favour of Mr. Thomas Benson being for a gratuity that the Venerable Society hath been pleased to bestow on me of which the Reverend Mr. Ogilvie gave me notice. I hope the Venerable Society will honour the Bill which ever shall be gratefully acknowledged by
Reverend Sir,
Your most obedient and most humble Servant,
Abr. Pietress's Mark.

To the Reverend Dr. Philip Bearcroft,
 Secretary to the Venerable Society for the
  Propagation of the Gospel in foreign parts
   At the Charter House,
    London.

From the Revd. John Ogilvie,   S.P.G. Letters,
Albany, June 29, 1752.   B. 20. New England &c., p. 55,
                                         and Journal XII, pp. 232-233.

Revd. Sir,
 It is with the most tender concern that I am obliged to inform the Venerable Society that my Prospects among the Mohawks still continue to be very unpromising, & rather more so than when I wrote in August 1751.
 Their strong & stil growing propension for spirituous liquors, proves the most fatal obstruction to the Progress of the glorious Gospel of Christ, among that unhappy people. The disolute lives of the greatest part of those, who converse with them upon account of trade, seem to have a very ill-effect upon y^r Minds, & I fear in a great measure influences them to think that Christianity is not of that importance that the Missionaries represent it of.
 The generality of the Professors of Christianity, who have any considerable dealings with the Indians by y^r conduct give the most convincing proof that they regard them only as meer *Machines* to promote y^r secular interest; & not as y^r fellow creatures, rational & immortal agents, equally dear to the Father of spirits, capable of the same Improv'ments in Virtue, & the purchase of the same precious Blood; in short, *the salt of the earth hath* (in these parts) *lost its savour;* & not one thing that I can mention, as a circumstance of encouragement, in this momentous undertaking. I have made use of everything that had the least probability of being serviceable to the main end. I've only been (as it were) rowing against stream, & have not been able to stem the torrent by reason of the extravagant quantities of rum, that is daily sold to those poor creatures.
 It is impossible for me to express, in a proper manner the shocking effects of strong drink upon these people; they commit the most barbarous actions; they grow quite mad, they attempt to burn y^r own little hutts, threaten the lives of y^r wives & children, abuse y^r neighbours & cast off all signs of regard to every body. Upon these occasions I shun them, & as soon as they are sober, I severely reprove them, & set before them, the fatal consequences of this detestable vice; they seem penitent and promise amendment but upon the first opportunity fall to the same extravagancies.
 As I am now entred (sic) into the married state,[1] my removal from Albany to Fort Hunter is attended with more trouble & expence but notwithstanding I go punctual as usual. I stayed with them throughout the last winter, & proceed regularly with the same method of instruction, that I informed the Society of before.
 Since my letter of the 7th of August, I've baptized at the Mohawks, 17 white, 18 Indians, & 2 negroe Children.
 Mr. Oel by letter informs me, that from Jany. ye 1rst. 1751 to June ye 25th he had baptized 50 children white & Indians, and that on the 20th of May, he administred (sic) the holy Communion to 29 persons; 5 Indian men, 20 Indian women & 4 white persons. I returned to Albany about Easter & no sooner had I left them, but they fell to drinking in ye excess, barbarously murdered a worthy woman, the wife of a Sachem, who officiates as reader in Church, during my

---

[1]Mrs. Ogilvie, his first wife, was Susanna Catharine, daughter of Lancaster Symes, Junior, of New York, and sister of Mrs. Theodorus Frelinghuysen, of Albany. "He had one son, George, who graduated at King's College in the year of his father's death and became a clergyman of the Episcopal Church; his only daughter survived him, as well as his second wife," for whom see note 3 to page 336.—*Copied, through the courtesy of the Secretary of the Genealogical and Biographical Society of New York, from the "Biographical Sketches of the Graduates of Yale College, etc."* Vol. II.

absence. I tremble for the consequences of this fact because it was committed by an Indian of a considerable large family, & no doubt, agreeable to ye constant custom in such cases, the life of the murderer will be pursued, & so we shall be constantly perplexed with the broils of these families. I have encouraged them to attention by little gratuities, which with the charge of paying the Interpreter & other contingent expenses, obliges me to be very frugal in my family, or I should soon run behind in my interest.

I had almost forgot the death of a great Sachem known by the name of *Seth* a Communicant of ye Church, which was likewise the effect of a drunken frolick; for in his intemperance he fell into the fire, & was burnt to that degree, as in a short time proved the cause of his death. I cannot well express the Sentiments I feel, while I am writing these unpromising facts; & my only relief is the promise of God that the Kingdom of this world, shall once become the Kingdom of God and Christ; & tho so many benevolent attempts to this purpose have failed, yet we have sufficient reason to expect that the purposes of divine grace shall be accomplished in the bringing in the heathen world [to] the fellowship of the Gospel.

As to the Church of Albany, no great alteration only that I've received five persons to the Communion & baptized 22 white & 4 black children & two adult negro women, who had passed thro' a regular course of catechetical instruction, & brought a Certificate of y^r good behaviour from y^r masters.

The good people of ye Church in this place, have in the last year rebuilt the Church which was very much fallen to decay; & by the generous contribution of his Excellency Govr. Clinton,[1] & the Honle. Council & most of the principle (sic) inhabitants of Albany, have erected a handsome steeple, & purchased a very good Bell & other ornaments of the Church, so that the publick offices of Religion are attended with circumstances of Dignity & Solemnity.

I fear I shall exceed the bounds of a letter, & trespass too much upon your patience, & therefore I conclude with my most fervent prayers for blessing upon the Society's generous & pious endeavours for the propagation of the Redeemer's Kingdom & am Revd. Sir,

With the most dutiful &
perfect regard Y^r & ye Society's
most obedient humble Servt.
JOHN OGILVIE.

From the same, Journal XII, pp. 307-309.
New York, July 19, 1753.

"acquainting that he had lately Baptized in his Mission 28 Children, 7 of them Indians, also 2 Adult Indians, and receiv'd 3 new Communicants, and he had for some Time read Catechetical Lectures in the Dutch language at Albany, on Sundays in the Afternoon, which were highly agreeable, and he hoped usefull to those, who do not understand English; the Indians, Mr. Ogilvie says, are at present very poor, occasion'd by a Worm, which has devour'd almost all their Corn; and notwithstanding they have had it in their power, to procure all the Necessarys of Life by a Root known by the Name of Chinsang, which was in great Demand, most of them spent all the Profits arising from it, in strong Drink, and were continually intoxicated, while they had a Penny left, and as they have been always expensive to Mr. Ogilvie, they were more so then; when they come to Albany, they expect he should find them in Victuals and Drink, which proves so chargeable, that he is hardly able to Bear it, besides many other contingent Expences, that arise among so mercenary a People: He thinks it may be of some Service to employ an Indian, to instruct the Indian Children in their own Language, and there is one Paulus qualified for that Service, setled (sic) at Fort Hunter, whom he recommends to the Society for that Purpose, instead of Petrus Paulus, who has been some Time dead; and Paulus may at the same Time officiate as Clerk, and read Prayers to the Indians in his Absence, and Mr. Ogilvie promises to do all he can, to preserve the Children from the Corruption among their Parents, and to endeavour by all Means, to dispose them to a cordial Reception of the Gospel of Christ; When at Albany, Mr. Ogilvie preach'd twice every Lord's Day, besides a Catechetical Lecture on Frydays and he had within the Year Baptiz'd of his Catechumens 14 White, and 10 Negro Children, and 4 Adult Slaves."

---

[1]This Governor Clinton is not to be confused with Governor George Clinton, of Irish extraction, who became the first Governor of New York State in 1777. The former was the Royal Governor from May 21, 1741, to October, 1753, having been appointed Commander and Governor of Newfoundland as early as 1732. During his tenure of the New York appointment he had a good deal of trouble with the Assembly, which was due, it is said, to the instigation of the Chief Justice, the Hon. James DeLancy. His son, Lieutenant-General Sir Henry Clinton, played an important part in the effort to suppress the American rebellion, 1776-1779. His father was Francis, 6th Earl of Lincoln. After leaving New York, Clinton himself became Governor of Greenwich Hospital and Admiral of the Fleet, in 1757. He had been made Vice-Admiral of the Red in 1745.

From the same,   Journal XIII, pp. 2-3.
May 1, 1754.

"acknowledging the receipt of the Secretary's Letter of August preceding & expressing his great pleasure in hearing of the Society's Approbation of his Endeavours. He had not yet had an Interview with Mr. Barclay & Colonel Johnson has been so much from home that it has prevented their proposing any thing with respect to the Education of the Indian Children. Mr Ogilvie writes that on his first coming among them he chose a boy of the most promising capacity, & cloath'd & maintain'd him at a considerable expence & had brought him to speak English tolerably well, as also to read in a Psalter; but after all his Parents took him from Mr Ogilvie, & gave no other reason, but that they were afraid he would learn to despise his own nation. Mr Ogilvie's Labours at Albany are not unsuccessfull, the number of Communicants is encreas'd to 28; he has prevail'd upon the young People to attend catechizings on Sunday Evenings to the number of 40: he has also begun a Montnly Lecture on Sunday Evening to instruct the youth in the nature of the Lord's Supper, and a great many of them attend upon these occasions."

From the Revd Mr Barclay   Ibid., p. 3.
Minister of Trinity Church
in the City of New York,
June 5, 1754.

"acknowledging the receipt of the Secretary's Letter of February, & acquainting that he delivered the Paragraph relating to the Indians to the Lieutenant-Governor, which he promised to lay before the next Assembly, but nothing has yet been done, as the dispute occasioned by the 39th Article of the Instructions [to secure from the Assembly "a permanent revenue solid, indefinite, and without limitation"] given the late Governor, Sr Danvers Osborne,[1] obstructed all business, but what was immediately necessary. But Mr. Barclay promises to remind the Governor [De Lancy] of his promise next Spring."

From the Revd John Ogilvie,   Ibid., pp. 181-182.
December 25, 1755.

"acknowledging the receipt of ye Secretary's Letter of May ye 2, & acquainting, that his best Endeavours have not been altogether unsuccessfull; many of the Indians of both Castles seem to have a serious & habitual sense of Religion; they regularly attend Divine Worship & participate regularly of the Lord's Supper, and tho' at this season they are all out upon ye Hunt several of ye principals came near 60 miles to communicate at Christmas; there are now between both castles about 50 Communicants. Mr Ogilvie wrote to ye Society the 25th of June 1755, acquainting them that Genl Johnson was then holding a treaty preparatory to ye intended Expeditions,[2]

---

[1]Sir Danvers Osborne succeeded Admiral the Hon. George Clinton as Governor of New York in 1753 and committed suicide, through grief over the death of his wife, on the 12th of October.
—O'Callaghan's *Documentary History of New York*, Vol. IV., pp. 1048 ff.

[2]These "intended Expeditions" were the movements of the British forces against the French in the Lake George and the Lake Champlain country. They resulted in the victory of the battle of Lake George, mentioned a few lines lower on the page. It was for this victory that Sir William was made a Baronet. Of the engagement, which took place September 9, 1755, an account, which is reproduced from the "London Magazine," XXIV, is to be found in O'Callaghan's *Documentary History of New York*, Vol. II, p. 691 ff. Sir William himself was wounded in the thigh, but on the 24th of the month he had the satisfaction of writing to the Lords of Trade from his Camp at Lake George as follows: "Since my last Said Letter, the Enemy paid us a visit at this Camp. We were so happy as to give them a pretty Severe repulse & took their General, The Baron De Dieskau who commands all the French Kings Troops in Canada, Prisoner."—*Op. cit.*, II, p. 698.

Writing to Governor Delancy, on the 27th of June, Sir William had said in reference to the "Treaty" which Ogilvie mentions above:—"I have now 1100 and odd Indians with me, men, Women, and Children, and the Interpreters tell me there are more men than ever they knew at any meeting before.

"I have made them an Introductory Speech, to which I have received a very respectful answer. The 24 Inst I made them another Speech, a very long one, in which I gave them a general view of the present state of affairs, & prepared them by various arguments to comply with the Contents of General Braddock which I delivered to them the next day. In both speeches I gave the War Belt wch they took, ever since they have been in seperate & joint Council & have not yet given me their answer. If it should not be equal to all we wish, it will I hope be more than we had reason to expect.

"I am in private working with the Sachems & leading men from morning to night. The fatigue I have undergone has been too much for me. It still continues & I am scarce able to support it. I am distressed where to get victuals for such numbers, they have destroyed every green that he was like to engage a considerable number of Warriors in our favour, that Mr Ogilvie himself was giving all ye assistance he could for ye publick good; & in the same Letter gave an account of ye success of the School, & the diligence of Paulus in his Office, but is extreamly sorry to find that this Letter was never sent from New York, thro' the negligence of ye person to whose care it was committed. Mr Ogilvie referrs to the Minutes of Indian Affairs transmitted to Lord Halifax,[1] a Worthy Member of the Society to prove that he has not been remiss in his Duty. Of 12 principal men of our Mohawks, which fell in the Action at Lake George 6 were constant Communicants of ye Church. The Indians when they took the field were very desirous Mr Ogilvie should go out with them as their Chaplain, but as there was no provision for that purpose he was obliged to decline it; but Genl Johnson says that Good Old Abraham performed Divine Service every morning & evening. From ye 28th of August 1754 to ye date of his letter, Mr Ogilvie had baptized in Albany 49 White & 20 black Children, & received 4 new Communicants: at ye Mohawks he had baptized 30 White, & 18 Indian Children, & admitted 4 Indians to the Communion, who gave a very good Account of the Christian Faith. The Church at Albany is very crouded (sic), occasioned by Col^l Dunbar's Regiment[2] posted there, so that there is a great deal of occasional Duty to do. Mr Ogilvie intends for ye Mohawks very soon, where he punctually performs his usual Duty, which consists of 4 different Services every Lord's Day. Paulus is diligent in his Office as Schoolmaster; he teaches above 40 Children every day, several begin to read, & some to write; they have ye Church Catechism, & have made a considerable Progress in Psalmody—The Indians of ye lower castle have signified their desire to have a Schoolmaster, as they formerly had; & Mr. Ogilvie thinks it would be of considerable service, as there are a large number of promising Children; if this is agreeable to the Society, he would be glad to have no particular Indian named to that Office, only ye same Salary that is granted to ye upper Castle, to be paid by Mr. Ogilvie (or any one ye Society shall think proper) to ye person who duly executes that Service; Mr. Ogilvie's reason for this is, that he knows an Indian well qualified

thing upon my Estate & destroyed all my meadows. I must humour them at this critical juncture." *Op. cit.,* Vol. II, pp. 665-666.

Dr. Frank H. Severance, in Vol. II of his valuable book, *"An Old Frontier of France,"* says at page 109, that Ogilvie was present at this Council, "at which Johnson announced his appointment as Indian Superintendent and asked for volunteers for Crown Point and Niagara," against the latter of which Governor Shirley of Massachusetts designed to send an expedition. The volunteers were forthcoming for Crown Point but not for Niagara.

Dr. Severance also notes that Ogilvie stood high in the favour of the Baronet, who suggested to the Lords of Trade that his emoluments at Albany ought to be increased. On this head the distinguished author had in mind possibly the letter to their Lordships of March 6, 1756, which is given on pages 712-715 of Volume II of Dr. O'Callaghan's *Documentary History* already quoted from.—"I beg the liberty to mention to your Lordships the Reverend Mr Ogilvie Missionary to the Mohawk Indians who has upon all occasions done everything in his power for the promotion of true Religion, this Gentlemans Sallary both for this place [Fort Johnson], and the City of Albany is verry inconsiderable, some further Encouragement to him by some Addition to his Sallary, would be of Service to the common Interest as it would enable him to proceed in his Mission with greater Spirit, and to support the Expences that must attend the keeping up of common Hospitality among so mercenary a people."

[1]George Montagu Dunk, 2nd Earl of Halifax, 1716-1771, succeeded his father in 1739 and was also Ranger of Bushey Park. In 1742 he was in opposition to the Government and became Lord of the Bedchamber to the Prince of Wales. Having made his peace with the Pelham ministry, he was made, in 1744, Master of the Buckhounds. To help quell the Rebellion of 1745, he volunteered to raise a regiment. In 1748 he became President of the Board of Trade, which office he filled with satisfaction to the mercantile interest till 1756, Halifax, Nova Scotia, taking its name from him, in 1749. In 1757 he was back again at the Board of Trade and there he remained till March 21, 1761, when he was appointed Lord Lieutenant of Ireland. In 1762 he became Secretary of State under Lord Bute and in 1763 under Grenville, he, Grenville, and Lord Egremont being known as the Triumvirate. He was involved in the controversy with Wilkes and went out of office in 1765, remaining out till January, 1770, when he was appointed Lord Privy Seal under his nephew, Lord North. In 1771 he was again Secretary of State; and in June of the same year he died. He was styled the "Father of the Colonies."—*Dictionary of National Biography.*

[2]Col. Thomas Dunbar, who died a Lieutenant-General, in 1767, was at the date of this letter Colonel of the 48th Regiment of Foot. He joined General Braddock in the advance against Fort Duquesne. While the General pressed forward with 1,200 chosen men, Dunbar was left with the residue of the army to follow at more leisure. After the defeat Dunbar "destroyed his remaining artillery, burned stores and baggage worth £100,000, pretending that it was done by Braddock's orders, and ignominiously retreated." In 1756 he was made Lieutenant-Governor of Gibraltar and in 1760 Lieutenant-General.—*Appleton's Dictionary of American Biography.*

for this Service; but he is much addicted to strong drink, & therefore should be employed only upon condition he keeps himself sober. The six-United-Nations seem at present to be in good temper notwithstanding the Craft & Intrigue of ye French, who by their Priests are extreamly industrious at this critical conjuncture of Affairs. Genl Johnson is indefatigable, & no doubt will prevail on numbers of them to join us next Season; Mr. Ogilvie is much obliged to ye General for ye countenance he gives him, & ye particular marks of affection he has shewn him. Last summer [1755] Mr. Ogilvie had a great deal of fatigue & Charge, as ye Indians were constantly passing thro' Albany; he had the care of providing for all ye War-parties of Indians that went thro' that place, by order & at ye Expence of Genl Johnson, which he performed to ye Gen^{ls} entire satisfaction. Mr. Ogilvie adds that he pleases himself with the hopes of seeing (after these disputes are ended) an effectual Door opened to introduce Missionaries into most of ye Castles of ye six Nations, for nothing will contribute more to make them firm friends, than uniting them to us by ye sacred ties of Christianity."

The Society allowed him to appoint a schoolmaster, as requested, at a salary of £7.10.0. per annum.

From the same, without a date. Ibid., pp. 202-203.
Read at the meeting of
December 17, 1756.

"in which he writes, that immediately after Christmas [1755], he went to the Mohawks & continued there till the Sunday before Easter, proceeding in his usual Method of Instruction, & in the last half year preceding he had baptized 10 White & 9 Indian Children, two of which were the Chi|dren of the famous Indian half King,[1] who distinguished himself so much in the fatal Expedition under Genl Braddock[2]—he is now settled with his Relations & family at the Mohawks to the number of 40 Persons, some of them Christians & most of them well disposed to the Christian Religion. Early in the Spring about 140 of those persons inhabiting the frontiers of New Jersey came up to ye Mohawks—these poor Creatures were intirely uninstructed in Religion, though many of them speak the English Language, & Mr. Ogilvie will endeavour to instruct them. Mr. Ogilvie says he has almost more Duty at Albany than he is able to do, by reason of the great number of Strangers & Soldiers quartered there, he performs three Services on Sundays, as the Church will not contain every body at one time. he has baptized 16 White & 6 Negro Children, & 2 Adult Negroes at Albany, since Christmas last [1755]. At this time (Mr. Ogilvie adds) he finds it hard to support his Family, as every thing is as dear again as it was, tho' he is King's Chaplain at Albany with £50 Sterling p. annum upon which there are considerable deductions; if by any means he could get his Salary increased to the same Value with that at Boston, Vizt—£100 p. annum it would enable him in a great measure to support the unavoidable expences he is at in this important Mission: it is mere necessity (he says) compels him to mention this, for he had no Assistance from his Parishioners, who are not indeed able to help him. There is at present a great Call for Common prayer books, & Mr. Ogilvie would be glad of some Copies of the Soldiers Monitor, & some practical Tract for the use of the Hospital, as the General Hospital of the Army is fixed at Albany, & he constantly attends it & he adds that the School Master is diligent in his Office."

The Society granted him a gratuity of £30 "in consideration of his great Labours & long Services, & to encourage him to persevere in them"; also £5 worth of Common Prayer Books and tracts for distribution.

---

[1] The Half King was with Washington on his mission to Fort Le Boeuf, at the instance of Governor Dinwiddie, in 1754, and subsequently also at the brush with the French, in the same year, near Great Meadows, which was the real beginning of hostilities. At the battle of Great Meadows and the siege of Fort Necessity he held aloof, according to Parkman's *Montcalm and Wolfe*, Vol. I, pp. 157-161.

[2] Edward Braddock, whose name is ever memorable in the annals of British American history in connection with the disaster of Fort Duquesne in the summer of 1755, was born in 1695. He entered the Coldstream Guards August 29, 1710, and rose to be 1st Major and a Lieutenant Colonel of it November 21, 1745. He saw service in Holland under the Prince of Orange between 1746 and 1748. In 1753 he received a commission as Colonel of the 14th Foot at Gibraltar and in 1754 he was promoted to be Major-General. On the 20th day of February, 1755, he arrived in Hampton Roads, Virginia, and shortly afterwards he held a council of Colonial Governors to form a plan of campaign. Four expeditions were decided upon—against Fort Niagara, Crown Point, Nova Scotia, and Fort Duquesne—Braddock becoming responsible for the last mentioned.—*Dictionary of National Biography*.

From the same,   Ibid., p. 277.
Albany, January 8, 1757,

"giving notice y^t he has drawn a set of Bills for two years Salary due to Paulus, ye Societies Indian Schoolmaster."

From the Same,   Journal XIV, pp. 6-7.
June 25, 1757,

"in which he writes, that ye Indian Affairs in General have taken a most unfavourable turn, but notwithstanding ye danger he has still visited the Mohawks; he was there ye whole Month of Augst & returned in Sepr to officiate to ye Garrison at Albany, which was very numerous & had no Chaplain: he went up again in Jany & staid till March, but bad Example, frequent use of Strong Drink & the excursions at this time, take off their attention to Religion; in ye last year Mr. Ogilvie baptized in this part of his Mission 25 White & 16 Indian Children, & 2 Adult Indians. The Congregation at Albany is numerous, occasioned by ye great number of Merchants & others who follow ye Army; he continues to have 3 Services on Sundays, that all Ranks of people may have ye benefit of Divine Worship; he administered ye Communion on Christmas Day to 70 Persons, & on Easter Day to 60, & had baptized in this City of Albany last year 89 White & 10 Negro Children. And ye Earl of Loudon[1] observing Mr. Ogilvie's daily calls to officiate to ye Army was pleased to give him a Commission as one of the Chaplains of ye Royal American Regiment;[2] Mr. Ogilvie hopes this will be agreeable to ye Society, & that they will indulge him in holding it, so long as it interferes not with ye Duty of his Mission."

"Agreed as ye Opinion of ye Committee that there is no objection to Mr. Ogilvie's keeping the Chaplainship to ye Royal American Regiment, so long as it is not inconsistent with his Duty to ye Society."

"Resolved to agree with ye Comittee."

From the same,   Ibid., pp. 106-107.
May 25, 1758,

"acknowledging the receipt of the Secretary's Letter of July 2d 1757, but acquainting that he had not received a Letter impowering him to Appoint a Schoolmaster at the lower Mohawk Castle, nor the Common Prayer Books and other pious tracts granted him by the Society. He returns his thanks for the Society's Bounty of £30 and wishes he could give a better Account of his success among the Indians, but at present the Mohawk's River is a scene of all the Horrors of War, and continued circumstances of the most horrid cruelty; notwithstanding which he has visitted (sic) his Mission, and stayed there two Months in the Winter; in which time he Preached to the Garrison at the German Flats and Preached and administered the Sacrament at Canajohare (sic); while he was there the French and Indians came down upon the Settlement, burnt three Houses, and Captivated the Families: While things are in such a Melancholy State Mr. Ogilvie does not think it proper to appoint a Schoolmaster, and has done that Duty himself during his stay among them; in that part of his Mission since the 25th of June 1757 he has Baptized Twenty White and Sixteen Indian Children. As the Troops were taking the field and there was no Chaplain to attend Six Regiments of Regulars (Except a Deputy Chaplain[3] to the Highland Regiment) and as the Mohawk Indians are to take the field Mr. Ogilvie was resolved to go with

---

[1]John Campbell, fourth Earl of Loudon, 1705-1782, succeeded his father in 1731 and from 1734 to 1782 he was a representative peer for Scotland. He entered the army in 1727 and became successively Governor of Stirling Castle and A.D.C. to the King. His best work was done in the suppression of the Rebellion of 1745, for which he raised the 54th Regiment. (It was, however, almost wiped out at the battle of Preston.) He became Colonel of the 30th Foot, Colonel in Chief of the 60th Foot, Captain General and Governor in Chief of Virginia, and, on March 20, 1756, Commander in Chief in America, landing in New York, July 23, and proceeding immediately to Albany, because the French had taken possession of Oswego and thus had control of Lake Ontario. He was recalled on account of his inaction at Halifax when it was a question of attacking the French at Louisbourg.

[2]The Royal American Regiment, which had Amherst as its Colonel for many years from 1758, consisted of four battalions, of which Haldimand and Monckton were Lieutenants-Colonel. One or another of these battalions was in every important engagement of the Seven Years War in America, the 2nd and 3rd being at the Plains of Abraham and the 4th at the reduction of Montreal.

[3]It was very common for the Chaplains of Regiments to regard their commissions as sinecures and to draw the pay, leaving the duty to be performed by deputies while they themselves remained in comfort and safety in the Old Country.

them, and he hopes the Society will approve of it. At Albany (Mr. Ogilvie says) his Duty is Extensive, and he trusts not without good effect; he administered the Holy Sacrament to Ninety Persons at Christmas, to Sixty at Easter, and has Baptized Seventy Six White and Seven Negro Children; he has likewise Baptized an Adult Negro and his Wife, after previous instruction, and admitted them to the Holy Sacrament. Mr. Ogilvie adds that Mr Oel has in the last year Baptized 30 Children."

From the Revd J. J. Oel,   Ibid., p. 107.
February 8, 1758.

"A Latin Letter from the Revd Mr. Oel, Assistant to Mr. Ogilvie among the Mohawk Indians dated February 8th, 1758, in which he writes that he lives in continual fear of the Cruelty of the Indians, which prevents him doing as much good as he could wish. He was along with Mr. Ogilvie when he Catechized the Indian Children in the Church at the Mohawk; and administered the Holy Sacrament in the Indian Tongue: He referrs to Mr. Ogilvie for the Account of his Service this year."

From the Revd John Ogilvie,   Ibid., pp. 186-187.
February 25, 1759.

"acknowledging the receipt of the Secretary's Letter of the 3d of May 1758, and returning thanks to the Society for their approbation of his acceptance of the Chaplainship to the American Regiment, which has hitherto been compatible with his Duty as Missionary. Mr. Ogilvie was at the date of his Letter employed as usual in his Indian Mission. He had agreed with a very worthy Indian to teach School there upon the Society's Salary, but was disappointed by his sudden Death a few Days after. Mr. Ogilvie has not drawn for the Salary of Paulus, Schoolmaster at Canajohare (sic), because of several Complaints that he was so taken up with War-parties, that he had greatly neglected the Instruction of the Children.

"The People of those parts are so immoderately given to the use of strong Liquors, that the banefull Effects of it are very conspicuous, for since September there have died in the Mohawk Castle 55 Persons, and more are dying daily; and against this Mr. Ogilvie has in vain given them the most earnest Exhortations. By the late Mortality the Church is much diminished, however Mr. Ogilvie, on the Day he wrote this Letter had administered the Sacrament of the Lord's Supper to 36 Persons, 15 of them Indians. He catechises the Children daily, and frequently calls their Parents together for Divine Worship; since the 25th of May he has Baptized 20 White and 10 Indian Children. The Church at Albany is much in the same state as when he wrote last; he continues to catechise the Young People, and administred (sic) the Sacrament of the Lord's Supper to 60 Persons on Christmas Day: since the 25th of May there have been Baptized by the Dutch Minister[1] and Mr. Ogilvie 94 White and 10 Negro Children, and 3 Adult Negroes."

From the same,   S.P.G. Letters, B. New York,
Albany, February 1, 1760.   Part I, p. 105, and
                                                    Journal XIV, pp. 296-297.
Revd. Sir,

I beg leave to congratulate the Venble. Society upon the great Successes with which it hath pleased the Supreme Disposer of all events, to crown the arms of our most gracious Sovereign by sea & Land, both in *Europe & America*. May the issue of all these important events tend to the Glory of God, the Honour of our King, the Security of the protestant Religion and the Peace & Happiness of our Nation & its Colonies.

I have the Pleasure to acquaint the Society that my duty as their Missionary has hitherto been intirely compatible with my Chaplaincy in ye Army & particularly so the last summer. I attended the royal American Regiment upon ye Expedition to Niagara; And indeed there was no other Chaplain upon that Department, tho' there were three regular Regts. & ye provincial Regt. of New York. The Mohawks were all upon this Service, and almost all the six Nations, they amounted to 940, at ye time of ye Siege. I officiated constantly to ye Mohawks & Oneidoes [Oneidas] who regularly attended divine service. I gave them Exhortations suitable to the Emergency & I flatter myself my Presence with them contributed in some Measure to keep up Decency & Order amongst them; the Oneidoes met us at the Lake near their Castle, & as they were acquainted with my coming, they brought ten children to receive Baptism; and young women, who had been previously instructed in ye Principles of Christianity, came likewise to receive that Holy ordinance. I baptized them in the presence of a numerous Crowd of spec-

---

[1] This "Dutch Minister" was, according to the historian of St. Peter's Church, the Revd. Theodorus Frelinghuysen; and, according to the historian of Yale College, Mrs. Frelinghuysen was a sister of Ogilvie's first wife, who was apparently still living at the date of this letter.

tators, who all seemed pleased with the attention & serious behaviour of the Indians upon that solemn occasion; and indeed, bad as they are, I must do them the justice to say, that whenever they attend the offices of religion it is with great appearance of solemnity & Decency.

During this campaign I have had an opportunity of conversing with some of every one of ye Six Nation Confederacy & their Dependants and of every nation I find some who have been instructed by ye priests of Canada, & appear zealous roman Catholicks, extremely tenacious of ye Ceremonies & Peculiarities of that Church; and from very good authority I am informed, that there is not a Nation bordering upon ye five great lakes, or the Banks of ye Ohio, the Mississipi, all the way to Louisania (sic), but what are supplied with priests & Schoolmasters, & have very decent Places of Worship, with every splendid utensil of their Religion. How ought we to blush at our coldness & shameful indifference in ye propagation of our most excellent Religion. *The Harvest is great but the Labourers are few.* The Indians themselves are not wanting in making very pertinent Reflections upon our inattention to these points!

The possession of the important Fortification of Niagara, is of the utmost consequence to the English, as it gives us the happy opportunity of commencing & cultivating a friendship with those numerous tribes of Indians who inhabit the Borders of *Lake Erie, Huron, Michigan* & even *Lake Superiour;* And the Fur trade which is carried on by these tribes, which all centers at Niagara, is so very considerable, that I am told by very able judges that the French look upon Canada [as] of very little importance without the possession of this important Pass; it certainly is so and must appear obvious to any one who understands the geography of this country. It cuts off & renders their Communication with their Southern Settlements almost impracticable. In this Fort, there is a very handsom (sic) Chapel, & the Priest who was of the Order of St. Francis, had a Commission as the King's Chaplain to this Garrison. He had particular instructions to use the Indians who came to trade, with great Hospitality, (for which he had a particular allowance) and to instruct them in ye Principles of the Faith; the service of the Ch^h here was performed with great ceremony & parade. I performed divine service in this Church every day, during my stay there, but I am afraid it has never been used for that Purpose since, as there is no Minister of the Gospel there; this neglect will not give the Indians the most favourable Impressions of us.

We have now, by the Blessing of Heaven, obtained the whole object of the war upon this Continent, and upon the Conclusion of a Peace, if we may only keep those places, to which we have an undoubted right, by grants from the natives, & confirmed by solemn Treaties, particularly by that of *Utrecht*[1], and Niagara is certainly one of those places; I think we shall have it in our power to frustrate the extensive & ambitious views of the Court of France upon this Continent of America, by effectually securing the alliance of all the Indian nations.

And as the situation we shall be in, in all probability, if we obtain an honourable Peace, will give us the happy opportunity of sending Missionaries not only to the six Nations, but to ye other tribes, in their Alliance, I pray God the Government may think it an object worthy of their attention.

My Mission is in much the same Circumstances, as when I wrote last Febr; only that my Indian Congregation is very much decreased by the late Mortality that prevailed amongst the Mohawks. I shall soon transmit an account of the Numbers baptized in both branches of my Mission. In the mean time with prayers to almighty God for a Blessing upon the pious endeavours of the Venl. Society for the Promotion of true Religion & Virtue,

I am, Revd. Sir,
with the most dutiful sentiments
their & your most devoted
Humble Servt.

JOHN OGILVIE.

---

[1]How Ogilvie could have given this interpretation to the Treaty of Utrecht (1713), concerning which there was a good deal of dissatisfaction and of consequent discussion in Parliament for two years subsequently, it is difficult to understand. Article X provides for the cession of all French claims to the Hudson Bay and Straits, reserving the trading rights of the Quebec Company; Article XII cedes absolutely Nova Scotia, or Acadia; and Article XIII withdraws all territorial claim to Newfoundland. Further mention of territory there is none, so far as America is concerned. Article XIV guarantees to the Acadians their religious rights so far as they are compatible with the British order of things; and they were scrupulously regarded. Article XV provides that the Americans (that is, the Indians), especially the Five Nations, were not to be molested by the French and that they were to have freedom of trade. In view of recent developments on the Reserve near Brantford, it is interesting to note that the Five Nations are called *subjects* of Great Britain, not *allies*. The chief negotiator for Great Britain was the Right Revd. John Robinson, Bishop of Bristol, an ancestor of Sir John Beverley Robinson, of Toronto.

Chapel of the Hôtel Dieu, Montreal, as in 1760–1764.

Récollet Church, Montreal, with façade of 1830.

From the same,
Albany, May the 20th, 1760.

Ibid., p. 106, and
Journal XIV, pp. 306-307.

Revd. & Dear Sir,

I did myself the Honour to write to the Venr. Society, the 1rst. of Febr. last which I hope is come safe to hand.

Since the above Letter, I have spent two Months upon my Indian Mission, going on in the same method of instruction, that I have always made use of since my first arrival in this Province; I could wish that I could say, consistent with the truth, that the Propagation of the blessed Gospel among the Natives of this Continent, was attended to by the leading men of this country, with that zeal & application, the importance of the subject demands. They do nothing to oppose it, but I really can't say, that I ever met with any actual countenance in this service from any of them, excepting Sir *William Johnson* who, I must do him the justice to say, has been very much my Patron & Friend, which has been of no small consequence to me among the Indians.

I have baptized in this Branch of my Mission, from the 25th of Febr. 1759 to the 25th of Febr. 1760, 20 white children, & 13 Indian Children & two adults, & admitted four young Indian women to the Holy Communion, after a careful instruction of them in ye Principles of ye Christian Faith. I can't yet procure proper persons to teach school as they are all taken up with the affairs of the war, preparing for the approaching Campaign.

My Church at Albany is in the same way as when I wrote last only that I have admitted six of my young Catechumens to the Holy Sacrement, who upon examination gave me very satisfactory account of their faith. I have baptized in this City & the Township of Schonectady (sic), from the 25th of Febr. 1759 to the 25th of Febr. 1760 one hundred & four white children, & fifteen black. I administered (sic) the Sacrament on Christmas Day to sixty Persons, & on Easter Sunday to fifty seven.

We are now all preparing to take the field, which we shall do in a few days; As the Mohawks all go, I imagine the Gen[1] will expect my attendance, which I hope will be agreeable to the Venl. Society, as I shall still be in the Way of my Duty as their Missionary.

The issue of this Campaign, I trust in God, will be the compleat Conquest of Canada. We have a very promising Prospect, before us, of bringing the affairs of America to a safe & honourable issue.

Every thing is kept a profound secret by the Gen[1] but from very good circumstances, we conjecture that the Grand Expedition will be by the way of Oswego, & so down the river St. Lawrence to the Town of Montreal; whilst Brigadier Gage[2] will operate with a considerable Army by the way of Crown Point, & so down the Lake Champlain. We have lately had some accounts by some Deserters from Canada, that the Govr. of that country with all his force were just going

---

[1] The General himself is responsible for the statement that it was inadvisable to divulge all of his plans to Sir William Johnson, lest, through his Indians, they should be given to the French—without Sir William's knowledge or intention, of course.

[2] Thomas Gage, second son of Thomas, Viscount Gage, in the Peerage of Ireland, was born in 1721 and died in 1787. At the age of twenty years he was given a Lieutenant's commission in Col. Cholmondeley's new regiment, which was later known as the 48th Foot. He served with various regiments on the Continent of Europe in the "Old French," or "King George's," War, becoming A.D.C. to Lord Albemarle in Flanders, 1747-1748. As Lieut. Col. of the 44th Regiment he was under Braddock in America, commanding the advanced column on the march to Fort Duquesne and receiving a wound, 1755. Subsequently he was with the 44th at Oswego, where he was stationed in 1759, when Sir William Johnson was securing his victory at Niagara. In the preceding year he had been commissioned to raise a provincial regiment, which was known as the 80th. He commanded the Light Infantry, under General Abercromby, against Ticonderoga. Promoted to be Brigadier-General, in July, 1758, he had command of the rear guard, under General Amherst, in the advance upon Montreal from Oswego, the command spoken of in the letter being entrusted to Haviland. After the capitulation of Montreal, Gage was made Military Governor of it and of the surrounding district, as such making a return of the inhabitants, resources, and public and religious institutions. An appreciative reference to him will be found in Ogilvie's letter to the Society, written from Montreal, July 29, 1763. In 1761 he had been promoted to be Major-General; in 1763 to be Acting Commander in Chief of North America; and in 1764 Commander in Chief. As Amherst's reputation had suffered from the war consequent upon the conspiracy of Pontiac, so did that of Gage, by that time a Lieutenant-General, from that of the American Rebellion. He left America finally in 1775 and lived thenceforth in England, being made a full General in April, 1782. *Dictionary of National Biography*.

to make a grand effort for the retaking Quebec.¹ If the Intelligence be true, & the scheme should prove abortive, 'tis generally thought we shall meet with little Resistance, for, from the deplorable situation they must be in, one would imagine they would make the best Terms for themselves they can. I pray God, the supreme Disposer of all events, to direct & bless the public Counsels at ye important Conjuncture, that he would be both with our Fleets & Armies, & smile upon our Nation's interests & bring this war to a speedy & honourable issue. That the peaceable Kingdom of the Blessed Jesus may flourish from the rising, to the setting sun, & that the labours of ye Venbl. Society may be prosper'd to this blessed Purpose.

This is the prayer of him who has the Honour to subscribe himself, Revd. Sir, with the most dutiful respect,

Their & your most obedient
Humble Servt.

JOHN OGILVIE.

From the same,   S.P.G. Letters, B. New York,
Oswego, August 9, 1760.   Part I., p. 107. and
                                   Journal XV, pp. 19-20.

Rev. Sir,

I did myself the Honour to write to the Venr. Society the 20th of June, in which I gave a full account of the state of my Mission at that time.

I have the honour to acknowledge your favour of the 12th of Aug. 1759 which I received at this Place but four days since; I am pleased to think my services are acceptable to the Society, and shall always endeavour to merit their esteem, by a punctual & conscientious regard to the duties of my sacred function.

By this I beg Leave to inform the Society that I left Albany the 24th of June in order to join the Army, who were proceeding under Genl Amherst² to Oswego. I tarried at Fort Hunter three days, I preached twice during that time, and administred (sic) the Sacrament of Baptism to several white and indian children. The Mohawks were preparing for the Field, & told me they should overtake me near the Oneida Lake, at which place a considerable number of Indians join'd us. Genl Amherst being at the *Oneda* (sic) Lake on the preceeding (sic) Sunday went up as far

---

[1]After the Capitulation of Quebec, September 18, 1759, General Murray shut himself up in the city for the winter, during which great hardships were endured, apparently with not a little of the good humour which was characteristic of the troops in France and Flanders during the recent war. From October on rumours, which are referred to in succession in Knox's Journal, reached the Officer Commanding to the effect that the French intended, from month to month, to lay siege to the place; but it was not till April that they did so. They were repulsed, but Murray suffered defeat at Ste. Foy in the same month. The arrival of the British fleet as soon as navigation opened decided the fate of the town—and of Montreal—in favour of the British.

[2]Sir Jeffrey, later Baron, Amherst was born January 29, 1717, the second son of Jeffrey Amherst of Riverhead, Kent. After serving as page to the Duke of Dorset, he became Ensign in the Guards, 1731, and later A.D.C. to General Ligonier, with whom he was at Roucroux, Dettingen, and Fontenoy. He served on the Staff of the Duke of Cumberland at Lauffeld and Hastenbeck, and in 1756 he was made Lieut. Col. of the 15th Regiment. Promoted to be Major-General, at the instance of Pitt, in 1758, he sailed for Louisbourg, Cape Breton, in May, Admiral Boscawen having command of the Naval Forces. Appointed to be Colonel of the 60th (Royal American) Regiment and Commander in Chief in North America, in succession to General Abercromby, Amherst proceeded to Albany and thence to Fort Duquesne, which he took and then waited for instructions from home. Following out these, he took Ticonderoga in July, 1759, and Crown Point in August. Setting out from Oswego, as Ogilvie chronicles, he advanced upon Montreal, which surrendered, in the face of his force and of Haviland's from Crown Point and Murray's from Quebec, September 8, 1760. For this distinguished service he received the thanks of Parliament, the honour of K.C.B., and the appointment to the Governor-Generalship of all the British Colonies in North America. Failing to suppress the war caused by Pontiac's Conspiracy, he returned to England in 1763, when he was made Governor of Virginia. This and all his offices and commands he resigned in 1768, as the result of a quarrel with the King. A reconciliation taking place, he again became Colonel of the 60th Regiment and of the 3rd. He became successively Governor of Guernsey, a Member of the Privy Council, Lieut. General, officiating Commander in Chief of the Forces, Baron Amherst (ultimately with remainder to his nephew), Colonel of the 2nd Horse Guards, adviser in quelling the Gordon Riots, Commander in Chief, and Field Marshal, refusing an earldom. He died at Montreal, his seat in Kent, August 3, 1797.—*Dictionary of National Biography* and A. G. Doughty's edition of *Captain Knox's Journals* (publications of the Champlain Society).

as the Oneida town, upon his arrival there he found them at their worship and expressed a vast pleasure at the Decency which the Service of our Church was performed with by a grave Indian Sachem. They applied to the Gen[l] to leave directions for me to come to the Castle upon my arrival at the Lake.

Agreeable to the General's directions, I went to the Oneida Town the 19th day of July; I had sent a Mohawk Indian before, so that upon my coming into their town I found a large congregation met for divine service, which was performed with great solemnity. Six adults presented themselves to be examined for Baptism, who all of them gave a very satisfactory account of the Christian faith & appeared to have a serious sense of Religion, I baptized them & immediately after join'd them in Marriage, they were three principle (sic) Men, & their wives who had lived many years together according to the Indian Custom. I baptized 14 Children, & in all I join'd nine couple in the holy Bands of Marriage.

I was much pleased with this days solemnity, it would have been a noble subject for the pen of one of the Jesuites of Canada. I would to God, we had Labourers in this Part of the Vineyard to keep alive the spark that is kindled among some of these Tribes, & spread the glad tidings of the Gospel among the numerous Tribes with whom we have now a free communication.

Beside my duty in the Army, I attend the Indians, & give them prayers, as often on Week days, as the public service of the Camp will admit, and on Sunday, the Gen[l] always gives public orders for divine service among the Indians.

I hope soon to congratulate the Venr. Society upon the intire Conquest of Canada, and I pray God that by that means, there may be a more effectual door open'd for the Propagation of the blessed Gospel amongst the Heathen.

I beg your candour in excusing the Inaccuracies of this letter, for I am now embarking for the River St. Lawrence.

> I am, Revd. Sir, with the most respectful
> & Dutiful Sentiments the Venr. Society's
> and your most obedient
> Humble servant,
> JOHN OGILVIE.

From the Revd Henry Barclay, D.D.,
New York, December 10, 1760. Journal XV, p. 74.

"Dr Barclay also at the request of Mr. Ogilvie, whom General Amherst hath detained for the Winter to officiate to the Garrison at Montreal in Canada sollicits the Society for some French Bibles, & Common Prayer Books, which will be of great service among them."

From the Revd. John Ogilvie, S.P.G. Letters, B. New York
Albany, October 14, 1760. Part I, p. 108, and Journal
XV, pp. 74-75.

It is with the highest pleasure I congratulate the Venr. Society upon the success of his Majesty's arms both by sea & land, and more especially upon the glorious Conclusion of this Campaign in America, by the intire reduction of Canada to the obedience of our most gracious Sovereign; An event so deeply impressed with such obvious characters of its own importance, that every sincere Lover of his Country must feel his mind transported with admiration, Gratitude & Joy upon this happy occasion. May these remarkable smiles of divine Providence upon our national Interest make such a lasting impression upon the minds of all the subjects of the British Government, that a universal Reformation of Manners may be the Tribute of our gratitude to the supreme Regent of the Universe!

I left Albany the beginning of June, & returned (after a very fatiguing campaign) the 30th of September. I did myself the Honor of writing to the Venr. Society the 20th of June from Oswego, giving them an account of the good disposition I found the Oneidoes in, & of my services among them. Would to God there might be a due encourag'ment given to proper persons to undertake the Propagation of the blessed Gospel among the natives of this Country! There seems now to be a fair Prospect for this generous work, from our great successes upon this Continent. During this campaign, I have been particularly attentive to perform the offices of Religion among the Indians, great Numbers attended constantly, regularly, & decently. During our stay at Oswego I baptized six Indian & four white children.

It is with real concern I am obliged to inform the Venr. Society that by express Order from Gen[l] Amherst, I am preparing to return to Montreal for the Winter Season. The Gen[l] seemed extremely sensible of the Inconveniency of removing me from my Mission for so long time. But was pleased to say that "he could by no means dispense with my absence, as the Honor of the protestant Religion must be kept up, in a Town where all the inhabitants were of a contrary persuasion, by the regular & decent performance of the public offices of our Church, & that he had fix'd upon me for that Purpose. He was extremely sensible of the necessity of a Minister in this City, & therefore directed me to endeavour to procure some Clergyman to do the Duty here. I have therefore partly engaged the Revd. Mr. Jacob Townshend,[1] formerly resident upon the Frontiers of Virginia, to do my duty this winter. He is now gone to New York in order to settle his affairs for his return to this place. Upon his punctual performance of the Duty I have promised him the Society's allowance during his stay, upon condition of the Society's approbation. He is likewise to visit the Mohawks as often as possible. As I hope to return early in the Spring, I flatter myself the Society will still consider me as their Missionary, and should I be obliged to quit their service, (in which I should be glad to have the honour to spend my life) I shall give the earliest Notice, & consult with my worthy Predecessor the Revd. Mr. Barclay & the Rev. Dr. Johnson, to procure a proper Person to succeed me in this important Mission. By the terms of Capitulation, the Society will observe, that the Priests are all left in their respective Parishes amongst the Indians as well as the French Inhabitants.[2] I shall do all in my power to recommend our excellent religion by the public & constant performance of the duties of divine worship, & by keeping up a friendly correspondence both with clergy & Laity, to answer which good purpose I could wish for a number of French Bibles & common prayers and some plain Accts. of the protestant religion, wherein the points in dispute between us is treated of, with a spirit of Moderation & Christian charity. Surely these might be distributed to very good purpose. The french Mohawks & other Tribes of Indians in this Neighbourhood are all zealous roman Catholicks, however I shall endeavour to contract an Acquaintance with them, & gain an Interest among them, & do all I can to promote the generous designs of the Society.

I observe all the Lands upon the Island of *Montreal & Isle Jesu* are vested in the Church, the soil is good the country well cleared & cultivated & should our Stock of consequence be so great, that at the settlement of a general peace we may be able to retain this most valuable acquisition, I make no doubt but a proper attention will be paid to the establishmt of Religion, & a sufficient provision made for the support of a regular & orthodox Clergy; and if I might be indulged the thought I could wish to see part of these valuable lands vested in the venr. Society in order to enable them to propagate true Christianity among those numerous tribes of Indians who inhabit this extensive country.

Upon my arrival at Montreal, I shall do myself the honour of writing to the Society, & give all the Intelligence I can collect of the state of Religion in this country. I am unable to express the universal Joy & Triumph that prevails among us at this period of public success. How remarkably has God in His Providence sustained the Cause, & restored the honour of our country, By the successes of the last & the glorious conclusion of this year. The Inhabitants of this northern Region of America are now happy in the quiet possession of their estates. *No more leading into captivity*, a Captivity big with danger & Horror, *no more complaining in our streets.*

May all these happy events conspire to bring about a speedy, safe & honourable peace! May the peaceable Kingdom of the Redeemer universally prevail among Mankind, and all the World know the *only true God & Jesus Christ whom he hath sent!* And that the pious labours of the Venr. Society may be instrumental in bringing about this Happy event is the prayer of their

Most dutiful Missionary,
& humble Servt.

JOHN OGILVIE.

---

[1]The Revd Jacob Townshend, whatever was the reason, did not undertake the duties of the mission of Albany and Fort Hunter, which were entrusted, as the subsequent letters prove, to the Revd. Thomas Browne.

[2]Of the Articles of Capitulation of Montreal ten (numbers 27 to 35 inclusive and 40) deal with the Roman Catholic religion, the clergy, missionaries, Grand Vicars, the Bishop, religious communities, and the rights of members to return to France, if they so desired. Only three articles were granted outright, the others being either refused or reserved in whole or in part for the King's pleasure. Articles 27, 28, and 40 are those which refer in any sense to the point mentioned in this letter.

27. "The free exercise of the Catholic, Apostolic, and Roman Religion, shall subsist intire, in such manner that all the states and the people of the towns and countries, places and distant posts, shall continue to assemble in the churches, and to frequent the sacraments as heretofore, without being molested in any manner, directly, or indirectly. . . . . . 'Granted, as to the free exercise of their religion; the obligation of paying the tithes to the Priests will depend on the King's pleasure.'

28. "The Chapter, Priests, Curates, and Missionaries, shall continue, with an intire liberty, their exercise and functions of cures, in the parishes of the towns and countries.—'Granted.'

40. "The savages, or Indian allies of his Most Christian Majesty, shall be maintained in the lands they inhabit; if they chuse to remain there, they shall not be molested on any pretence

"Agreed to recommend to the Society to send Mr. Ogilvie 50 French Bibles & Common Prayer Books & 40 shillings worth of Tracts in French on the chief points in dispute between the Protestants & Papists, wrote with the most Christian Temper.
"Resolved to agree with the Committee."

From the Revd. Henry Barclay, D.D.,   Journal XV, pp. 133-134.
New York, June 3, 1761.

"and that Mr. Ogilvie and Mr. Houdin[1] are still detained by General Amherst in Canada, and he should much lament, should Mr. Ogilvie be removed from the Care of the Mohocks & other neighbouring Indians, but if he should, Dr. Barclay begs his place may not be supplied by any person now in America without Testimonials from the Clergy that are acquainted with his Character & Conduct; that he gives this Caution by no means with an Eye to any of the Missionaries, for he has the pleasure of saying that those of them whom he is acquainted with behave in Character almost to a Man, not one of them is chargeable with gross immorality whatever the Enemies of Religion & of the Society may insinuate."
"Agreed that the Caution given by Dr. Barclay be observed upon the appointment of a Missionary to succeed Mr. Ogilvie, should that be found necessary."

---

whatsoever, for having carried arms, and served his Most Christian Majesty; they shall have, as well as the French, liberty of religion, and shall keep their Missionaries. The actual Vicars General, and the Bishop, when the Episcopal See shall be filled, shall have leave to send them new Missionaries, when they shall judge it necessary.—'Granted,' except the last article, which has been already refused." A. G. Doughty: *Op. cit.*, Vol. II, pp. 579-583; and Shortt and Doughty: *Documents relating to the Constitutional History of Canada.*
It is interesting to compare these articles with those of similar import in the Capitulations of Quebec and with the clauses in the Treaties of Utrecht and Paris which relate to the subject of religion.

[1]The Revd. Michael Houdin, according to the Annual Report of the Society for the year 1760, "is of French extraction, and formerly Superior of a Convent in *Canada*, but some Years ago became a Convert to the Church of *England*, and after some Years of Probation was appointed the Society's Itinerant Missionary in *New Jersey*, where he hath acquitted himself well in that Station, and is esteemed a worthy Missionary of considerable Learning, and irreproachable Morals." As early as May 24, 1757, Dr. Barclay had notified the Society that Lord Loudoun had bought out the Chaplain to the 18th Regiment and had presented the commission to Houdin. From the latter's own letters it appears that he had been ordered to Cape Breton by General Abercromby, going thence with General Wolfe to Quebec, where he was detained by General Murray and General Amherst, as "there was no other person to be depended upon for intelligence of the French Proceedings." The Journal continues (XV, p. 235): "Mr. Houdin adds, that he is deprived of his expectations by the Death of the brave General Wolfe, who promised to remember his Labours and Services, which being unknown to General Murray, he keeps him there without any Advantage; and Mr. Houdin hopes the Society will take these circumstances into consideration and continue their kindness to him; and he will return to his Mission next Spring." In February of the same year, 1759, his brethren of New Jersey and New York, in Convention assembled, had written to the Society: "They hope it will not be taken as a want of Brotherly Love to Mr. Houdin, if they observe, that as he is now a Chaplain to one of his Majesty's Marching Regiments, and his pronunciation of the English Language continues to be bad, and an unhappy breach subsists between him and his Parishioners, they are humbly of opinion there is little Prospect of his being usefull in that Mission [Trenton, N.J.]: at the same time in Justice to him they are obliged to say, that he is a Gentleman of considerable Learning and irreproachable Morals; and they conceive, that in Nova Scotia or at Louisbourgh, he might be employed as a Missionary to good purpose." The Society not being in a position to open missions in either of those quarters, Houdin was appointed in 1761 to New Rochelle, N.Y., a French Settlement, where he laboured till his death, in 1766. He left "a distressed Widow & several Children," as Dr. Auchmuty, the then Rector of Trinity Church, New York, informed the Society, who voted Mrs. Houdin a gratuity of half a year's salary.
Among the signal services performed by Houdin, it has been said, was that of informing Wolfe of the possibility of scaling the bank of the St. Lawrence above Quebec. Dr. Doughty states, on page 28 of Volume II of Knox's Journal, that Houdin was chaplain to the 48th Regiment and that he received his appointment on the 29th of April, 1757.

From the Church Wardens and Vestry,   Ibid., pp. 295-296.
Albany, June 17, 1762.

"begging leave to inform the Society that by Mr. Ogilvie's absence on his Majesty's service, two Years, their Church & Congregation have been almost destitute of the benefit of hearing the word of God, except the time that Mr. Browne,[1] Chaplain to the 27th Regiment officiated in Mr. Ogilvie's place, till he was himself obliged to embark with the Troops for Martinico; That Mr. Browne is now returned and performs divine Service to the Satisfaction of the whole Congregation and as he is willing to stay with them, they beg he may be appointed their Missionary."

From the Revd. Thomas Browne,   Ibid., p. 296.
Albany, September 2, 1762.

acquainting that he "at the Mohock Castle baptized 9 Children, and married 4 Couple, besides what Children were baptized by Mr. Oel. He finds the Duty at the Mohock Castle very difficult, for want of a proper knowledge of their language; but hopes by the Blessing of God and a particular application to surmount that difficulty."

"Agreed as the Opinion of the Committee, that Mr. Browne be continued at Albany for the present, but not appointed Missy till the Society receive farther accounts of his Usefulness in that Mission, and till it be certainly known, whether Mr. Ogilvie may not have some thoughts of returning."

From the Revd. Henry Barclay, D.D.,   Ibid., pp. 343-344.
New York, December 3, 1762.

"Mr. Ogilvie cannot yet determine any thing as to his return to Albany; but Dr. Barclay could wish the Mission might be kept open for him." . . . .

"Agreed to recommend to the Society to give leave to Mr. Browne to draw for six Months Salary, allowed to the Missry at Albany during which time he has officiated at that place, & that he be permitted to continue there on the same footing, till it be certainly known, whether Mr. Ogilvie intends to return."

"Resolved to agree with the Committee."

From the Revd. Thomas Browne,   Ibid., pp. 395-396.
Albany, April 29, 1763.

"representing that the Society's Church in Albany has been several Years without a Minister, except the time he has officiated there, that he should have returned to his Regiment under General Amherst, had not the Congregation laid before him the bad consequence of the Church being left without a Minister, and informed him of their having sent a Petition to the Society on his behalf; that by his continuance here, he has been obliged to give up his Salary in the Army of 5 Shillings p. day in order to take care of the Church at Albany, which he hopes the Society will take into their Consideration and if they think him worthy of their Service, assures them, nothing can be more agreeable to the Congregation in general and to himself."

Annual Report,
1764.

"In the mean Time, as they learn that Mr. *Ogilvie* cannot return to *Albany*, they will supply that Mission in the best Manner they are able."

---

[1]The Rev. Thomas Browne (or Brown, as the name is sometimes spelled) was, according to the *Documentary History of New York*—Vol. III, p. 1153—the only child of the Revd. G. Brown, of Oxford, England. He was a member of St. Alban's Hall, Oxford, of which university he was a Bachelor of Arts. He was ordered deacon by the Bishop of London, September 23, 1754, and, after serving as a military chaplain in America, priest, July 8, 1764. Succeeding to the rectorship of St. Peter's, Albany, and to the post of missionary to the Indians at Fort Hunter, in 1764, he discharged the functions till 1767, when he resigned and removed to Maryland. Appointed to the rectory of Dorchester in that Province, May 30, 1772, he died May 2, 1784, leaving a wife (formerly Martina Hogan, of Albany) and seven children. From his letter of April 29, 1763, it would almost seem that Dr. O'Callaghan's statement, on page 304, Volume IV, of his *Documentary History*, to the effect that Brown was at some time a deputy chaplain in the Royal American Regiment was correct; but he certainly was chaplain to the 27th when he first appeared upon the scene in Albany.

From the Revd. John Ogilvie, Journal XVI, pp. 45-48.
Montreal in Canada,
July 29, 1763.

"In which he writes, that since he left Albany he has been officiating in this City, where the British Merchants with the Garrison make a considerable Congregation, who assemble regularly for divine Worship on Sunday and other Festivals. He has baptized since ye 1st of Novr 1760 to the date of this Letter 100 Children, and administred (sic) the holy Communion to 30 or 40 Persons at a time. As by the Capitulation there is no Provision made for a place of Worship for the Established Church, they are under a Necessity of making use of one of the Chapels, which is the cause of much discontent; but hopes this will soon be remedied by the Government. The Jesuits, he says, have a small College and a Church adjoining, as yet unfinished: could this be procured, it would be extreemly convenient, and could be put in order at a small Expence. At present it only serves as an Habitation for one Jesuit Priest, and two or three Lay Brothers: In the Government of Montreal there are 36 Parishes, 10 of which are upon the Island. The Property of the Soil of the Island and two other Parishes in the Government, is vested in the Seminary of St. Sulpice in Paris, whose Affairs are negotiated by a Branch of said Seminary, consisting of about 20 Priests, whose Mansion House is in this City, from whom they supply the Parishes upon their Estates as Curate Miss^ies. The annual Income of their Estates is computed at near 3000£ sterling. They have a vast Influence upon the People, are exemplary in their Lives, and extreemly attached to the Ritual and external Parade of their Church. In every point of view this is a Body of Priests, whose Influence ought, by every means consistent with Truth and Virtue, to be lessened as much as may be: for they and the Jesuits (who have a large Estate likewise) will ever keep up a Spirit inconsistent with the genius of a British Government. The Superior of this Community and grand Vicar of this Government, Monsr Montgolfier,[1] comes over by this Conveyance. He is a Gentleman of considerable knowledge & polite Address: his design is to sollicit the affairs of their Church in general, and their own Estate in particular: in either case it is interesting and must have a great Influence upon the state of religion in this Country, should he succeed in his Views. Mr. Ogilvie thought it his Duty to give the Society this Notice, that this Gentleman may be observed in his Application to the Government by some Persons of Interest and Influence. In the City they have one Convent of Recollects, consisting of four Priests and as many Lay Brothers. There are three religious Houses for Women, one of which is a kind of Boarding School for Girls, the other for the Accommodation of the Sick, and for Lunaticks and Foundlings. Within 9 Miles of this there is an Indian Mission[2] supplied by two Jesuits, and at the distance of 40 Miles, there is another[3] supplied by two Priests of the House of St Sulpice: these Savages are extremely attached to the Ceremonies of the Church, & have been Taught to believe the English have no Knowledge of the Mystery of Man's Redemption by Jesus Christ. As these Indians speak the Mohawk Language, Mr. Ogilvie has endeavoured to remove their Prejudices, and by shewing them the Liturgy of our Church in their Mother Tongue, has convinced many of them that we are their fellow Christians.

Having winked at the departure from their own programme, the Government in London wanted to have the nomination of the Bishops, leaving the consecrations to Rome. At Sydney's instance therefore, it is said, Montgolfier was offered the post of Coadjutor to Bishop Desglis, Briand's successor; but he was wise enough to decline it, thus presenting an instructive contrast to Bailly de Messein, a protégé of Dorchester, to whose sons he was tutor.

Of Montgolfier's trial of strength with General Sir Frederic Haldimand, who, differently from Dorchester, took his instructions quite literally, the Abbé Gosselin writes thus: "L'affreuse et inintelligible politique anglaise avait toujours refusé à M. Montgolfier la permission de faire

---

[1]Montgolfier, in addition to being Superior of the Seminary of Saint-Sulpice, was Grand Vicar of Montreal and the Upper Country. He was appointed by the last Bishop of the French period, Pontbriand, to be his executor; and he attended him in his last illness, which took place at Montreal on Sunday, June 8, 1760.

In the novel circumstances which confronted them, the members of the Cathedral Chapter still remaining in Canada met together, as they said, in accordance with primitive Christian practice, to elect a new Bishop. The lot fell upon Montgolfier, who presently resigned in favour of Briand, whether, as is sometimes said, because of his inacceptability to General Murray or because of the Pope's unwillingness to recognize the mode of procedure which had been followed. When finally the new Bishop had obtained consecration in France, after a good deal of temporizing on the part of the British Government, who could not be brought to consent formally to the recognition of any functionary but a "Superintendent of the Romish Church," Montgolfier went to Quebec for the *prise de possession* of the See; and he was rewarded by again being appointed Vicar-General.

[2]Caughnawaga.
[3]St. Regis.

venir quelques prêtres du Seminaire de Paris pour soutenir sa maison. Le vénérable Supérieur avait voulu faire ce que les Anglais appellent un *test case*, en faire venir deux à ses risques et périls; et l'on sait la manière brutale avec laquelle Haldimand les avait chassés du Canada." The documents on file at the Archives in Ottawa would fairly absolve the dauntless Swiss Governor of *brutalité*, especially when it is remembered that till after the *émigration* there was a possibility, if not the danger, that any French priest might tend to spread disaffection among the people. Besides, there was no objection to bringing in priests from Savoy, but Montgolfier, and, apparently, Briand and his coadjutor and successors, would not have them.

"A School and an Exemplary Clergyman for this Town is absolutely Necessary; and should the Society have the supplying this Country, Mr. Ogilvie humbly begs their particular remembrance for the City & Island of Montreal, where he has already formed a decent Congregation. He is apprehensive his half-pay will be incompatible with the Chaplaincy at Albany, and the Mission without it would not be a sufficient Support. His Services are at the Society's Command, if they may be of any Consequence to the Protestant Cause in this Colony. Upon this occasion he begs leave to give a hint relative to the raising a Support for the Protestant Clergy here. The Jesuits are dissolved as a Body in France,[1] and consequently so here, and their Estates here of course devolve to the Crown. If this be the case, surely an application from the Society for a Provision from hence would have its due weight, and merit consideration from the Government. While inattention to the weighty concerns of religion prevails but too much among them, he is bound in Justice to mention the exemplary conduct of Genl Gage, who is a constant Attendant upon the Offices of religion; & endeavours to support its Influence in its present low Estate, the Church having no Provision for any of the decent Appendages of divine Worship.[2] He hopes the Society will excuse this Liberty in one who is not, properly speaking, in their immediate Service."

"Agreed in the Opinion of the Committee, that it may be proper to take Mr. Ogilvie's application into Consideration, when the business of appointing Miss^{ries} to Canada shall come before them."

"Resolved to agree with the Committee, and that their Graces the Archbishops of Canterbury and York be desired to make Application to his Majesty's Ministers on the Subject of this Letter."

---

[1] Owing to the influence over Sir Guy Carleton exercised by that accomplished diplomat and devoted Bishop, Briand, no difference was made in the treatment of the Jesuits even after the suppression of their Order by the Pope. Carleton expressly intimated to the Home Government that he wished to have liberty of action in matters ecclesiastical and religious; but his liberty certainly did not lead him to see that those articles of his instructions which enjoined upon him to have the services of the Church of England properly and decently held were carried out, either before or after his quarrel with the Government over the conduct of the war against the Rebels of 1776. In most things he wished to be a law unto himself during both periods of his tenure of the Governorship-in-Chief, some twenty years in all.

Besides the (very proper) objection urged by Carleton to the devotion of Roman Catholic Church property to the uses of the Church of England, an obstacle to the carrying out of the suggestion contained in Ogilvie's letter was presented by the fact that Amherst wished to have at least a considerable portion of the Jesuits' estates vested in himself as a reward for his services in the final acts in the drama of the war. Again and again his agent is found in the records at the Archives pressing for a settlement of his principal's claims.

Regarding the estates as a trust, the Government from time to time ordered payments to be made in the form of salaries to Roman Catholic missionaries to the westward of Montreal, especially to those who worked among the Indians. It is even probable that the same ground was taken in the matter of providing a salary for the First Roman Catholic Bishop of Kingston, who was thus favoured many years before the Anglican Bishopric of Toronto was erected. At the date of the latter event, 1839, no salary was provided by Government; and it was necessary for the Bishop to continue to hold with his bishopric the rectory of Toronto and the archdeaconry of York down to 1847, in order that he might have the means of subsistence.

The persistence of the Jesuits' Estates question down to the closing years of Sir John Macdonald's last administration, the split over it in the ranks of the Conservative party, and the defection also of certain prominent Liberals to the Equal Rights party, whose chief organ was the *Mail*, are matters well known to many men still living who take an interest in politics.

[2] The following note has been very kindly furnished by George E. Wyeley Birch, Esq., of Montreal: "The Revd. Mr. Ogilvie officiated at the services for the Royal American Regiment and for the Indians, at Fort Ontario, in July and August, 1760. He was appointed to officiate as chaplain to Murray's Regiment on Sept. 20th, 1760. An order of Saturday, Nov. 15th, 1760, at Montreal, states that Divine service was to be performed by him at the Chapel of the Hôtel-Dieu. In a deed dated Sept. 21st, 1762, he is described as 'The Revd. Mr. John Ogilvie, Chaplain to the 60th Regt.'"

Trinity Church, New York.
Burned 1776.

From the Revd. Thomas Browne, Ibid., pp. 130-131.
Albany, November 19, 1763.

"Mr. Browne writes, that he has long expected to hear from the Society, and to be regularly appointed to this Mission, as the various Petitions signed by the Congregation and Vestry sufficiently show how desirous they are of his Continuance with them."
"Agreed, as the Opinion of the Committee, that Dr. Barclay be consulted, whether it may be proper to appoint Mr. Browne Miss^{ry} at Albany and to the Mohawk Indians: if the D^r has any objections to his appointment, he be desired to acquaint the Society with them, that if he has none, he may give Mr. Brown encouragement to hope for the Society's favour."
"Resolved to agree with the Committee."

From the Congregation of Ibid., pp. 166-167.
St. Peter's Church, Albany,
March 3, 1764.

"setting forth the many Inconveniences they laboured under by Mr. Ogilvie's leaving them to attend the Army, and afterwards by Mr. Browne's being Ordered to join his Regiment and go to the West Indies, that when Martinico was taken, Mr. Browne returned to Albany sick, but soon recovered so well as to do the Duties of the Church, which he has constantly attended ever since, and Resigned his Regiment for the Service of the Church. The Congregation therefore humbly hope the Society will indulge them with a Miss^{ry} to their Satisfaction, and as such recommend the Revd. Mr. Browne to the Society's favour. Inclosed is a Certificate from the Church Wardens and Vestry, importing that Mr. Brown has diligently and punctually performed the Duty of the Mission from Novr 15th, 1763 to May 15th, 1764."
"Agreed to recommend to the Society to order Mr. Brown's Salary for the last half Year due on the 15th of May to be paid, and to give Mr. Brown leave to return to Albany."
"Resolved to agree with the Committee."

From the Honble John Bradstreet,[1] Ibid., p. 187.
Albany, May 5, 1764.

"He wishes a Clergyman of Exemplary Life may be fixed here, & recommends Mr. Brown for ye purpose."

From the Revd. John Ogilvie, S.P.G. Letters, B. Part I,
New York, September 29, 1764. p. 109, and
  Journal XVI, pp. 244-245.

Revd. & Dear Sir,

I am extremely unable to express the grateful Resentments I feel when I reflect upon the many Favours conferred upon me, by the Venbl. Society whilst I had the Honor of being in their Service, in the Mission of Albany. And I have great Reason to be deeply humbled upon the consideration of the little success my endeavours have had, in that important Mission.
After the Reduction of the Regiment, I had the Honor to serve in, on the 24th of August 1763, I should have immediately left Canada, & have devoted some time to a Review of my private estate, which had suffered considerably during my absence. But the deplorable state in which I must have left the protestant congregation at Montreal, affected my Mind so much, that I came to a Resolution to devote, without Fee or Reward, another year to the service of that infant congregation; And indeed for four years service in that City, I have never received the least gratification from the Government.
In this uncertain & unsettled situation, I received the melancholy tidings of the death of the late & worthy Dr. Barclay with letters from many of my friends, signifying the unanimous

---

[1]This was apparently the officer who reduced Fort Frontenac (Kingston), August 27, 1758, and captured a large quantity of vessels, guns, stores, and goods, thus crippling the enemy's ability to carry out his designs upon the Mohawk River and at his own forts, Niagara and others to the southwestward. He was, according to the biographical note on page 264, Vol. I, Knox's Journal, born in Horbling, Lincolnshire, England, in 1711; Lieutenant-Governor of St. John's, Newfoundland, 1746; Lieut. Col., 1757; D.Q.M.G. in America, under Abercromby and Amherst; commandant of the expedition to relieve Detroit, 1764; Major-General, May 25, 1772, and died, in New York, September 25, 1772. He wrote to the Society at different times in reference to Church matters and made proposals concerning investments in wild lands for endowment purposes.

desire of the People to have me called as one of the assistant Preachers[1] to that large & populous Parish. In answer to these pressing Solicitations, I resolved upon a visit to New York, where I arrived the 3rd inst. & was unanimously elected as one of the Assistants, by the Rector, Church Wardens & Vestry of Trinity Church the 24th, which I accepted; & in two or three days shall proceed to remove my family, if the Inclemency of the Season will permit.

I flatter myself this step will meet with the Society's approbation & should there be any Services, in which I could contribute to promote their pious Designs, in this important & extensive Parish, I hope for an Interest in their Remembrance.

I am unable to express the great Concern I feel for the Protestant interest in Canada, & shall do every thing in my power to promote it, & should be glad to be honor'd with the Society's Commands relative to that Province, so far as my other duties will permit; I have already at my own expence, distributed a number of useful French books, which have had this good effect, at least, that they have removed some of their prejudices; two ladies, in particular, who were married to British Officers, have already become conformists to the protestant Church.

My stay at Montreal has been a considerable damage to my private estate, & no establishment obtaining in favour of the protestant church there, my family & friends unanimously thought I should be imprudent in refusing the offer of N. York; especially as it would be compatible with my Half-pay.

I beg leave, by your hands, to present my most dutiful & affectionate respects to the Venbl. Society, assuring them that I am always at their Devotion, notwithstanding any personal Inconveniences. May God succeed their pious endeavours in the propagation of the glorious Gospel in these remote Regions & particularly bless their endeavour to reform it where it is essentially corrupted.

I am dr. Sir, with sentiments of Duty & affection,

Their & your most devoted
most obedient humble Servt.

JOHN OGILVIE.

From the Revd. Samuel Auchmuty,[2]   Journal XVI, pp. 297-298.
Rector of Trinity Church,
New York; without a date.
Read February 15, 1765.

"Mr. Auchmuty further writes, that on Mr. Browne's return to Albany [apparently from being priested in England] a part of the Congregation of St. Peter's refused to admit him into the Church, not that they had any thing to object against him, but because he did not produce proper Credentials from the Society. Mr. Auchmuty hopes he has settled these Differences till the Society's Pleasure can be known. He adds, that Mr. Ogilvie is settled here as one of his Assistants, to whom he has for the present delivered up the Charge of the Negroes."

---

[1] It has been frequently said by authors depending upon O'Callaghan that Ogilvie succeeded Barclay as Rector, which is incorrect. He was only assistant to Dr. Auchmuty, Barclay's successor as Rector.

[2] The Revd. Samuel Auchmuty, second son of Judge Robert Auchmuty, was born in Boston, Mass., January 16, 1722, and died in New York, March 6, 1777, amid the turmoil of the Rebellion and after the destruction by fire of his church, charity school, and dwelling-house. He was a graduate of Harvard, 1742, studied divinity in England, became Assistant at Trinity Church, New York, 1763, and Rector, 1764. He is said by the author of the note on him in the *National Cyclopædia of American Biography*, though on what authority does not appear, to have intended to return to England to be consecrated Bishop of New York; "but the breaking out of the revolution compelled him to remain at home in order to keep his flock together." At various dates in the eighteenth century the question of appointing bishops for America was agitated, especially after the successes in Canada; but the opposition in America itself was so strong, particularly at the time of the Stamp Act, that no action was taken till 1787. Then two Bishops were, under a special Act of the Imperial Parliament, consecrated for work in the new United States. Only after that had been done was Dr. Inglis, Dr. Auchmuty's successor at Trinity Church, New York, consecrated as first Bishop of Nova Scotia.

Dr. Auchmuty's son, Sir Samuel Auchmuty, K.C.B., was, like his father, loyal to the Unity of the British Empire. For it he fought through three campaigns, from 1776 on. Leaving his native land on the conclusion of peace, he served with great distinction in India, Egypt, South America, and Java. In the year of his death, 1822, he was appointed Commander in Chief in Ireland.

Report for 1765.
p. 70.
"The Revd. Mr. *Thomas Brown*, who has for some Years past had the Care of *Albany*, and of the *Mohawk Indians*, in the Absence of the Revd. Mr. Ogilvie, is now appointed to that Mission, upon the Petition and Recommendation of the Congregation of St. Peter's Church in Albany, who have already had some Years' Experience of his Diligence in the Discharge of his Duty."

From the Revd. Samuel Auchmuty,   Journal XVI, pp. 384-386.
New York, April 13, 1765.

"He wishes Mr. Ogilvie, who is settled as his assistant, and has from his first coming, faithfully attended the Negroes, might be appointed the Society's Catechist, with a Salary of £30 instead of £50, as he is persuaded the Masters of the Slaves will not, and the Church cannot at present contribute to their Instruction, having already contracted a debt of £10,000 Currency. There are now near 30 Black Communicants, and almost double the Number of Adult Catechumens. The Congregation at Albany, he says, still persist in opposing Mr. Brown; and will not consent to his officiating in the Church, supposing him to have no appointment from the Society to the Mission. Mr. Brown has therefore been sometime at Schenectady, officiating to a small Congregation, who have entered into a Subscription, & intend to appoint Mr. Brown, or any other worthy Clergyman their Missy. If the Society should not choose to appoint Mr. Brown for Albany, he begs leave, if the Mission be continued, to concur with Dr. Johnson in the recommendation of Mr. Giles[1] as a fit Person for that purpose."

"In another Letter dated May 3 he incloses the Petition of the People of Schenectady; acquaints the Society with the death of Mr. Watkins,[2] again recommends Mr. Giles & Mr. Ogilvie, & writes that the Missions of Hempstead & Rye are still unsupplied."

"Agreed to refer the request of giving Mr. Ogilvie a Salary as a Catechist to the Negroes to the Consideration of the Society, ...

"Resolved . . . . that the People of New York be acquainted, that it is expected they should support the Catechist to the Negroes themselves, without any assistance from the Society, they being well able to do it."

From the Revd. John Ogilvie,   S.P.G. Letters, B. New York,
New York, April 23, 1765.   Part I, p. 116, and
             Journal XVI, p. 387.

Revd. Sir,

At the desire of several of the Clergy in the Neighbourhood of this City, I take the liberty to write to the venerable Society in behalf of one Mr. Giles a Person of a worthy character, and (as Dr. Johnson assures me) every way well qualified to promote the pious designs of the Society in the Character of a Missionary; especially at Albany, as he is acquainted with the dutch language, which much prevails there. I entirely agree with them and upon conversing with that gentleman I find he answers the character given of him by the good Doctor. I am therefore persuaded he will prove a faithful and useful Missionary; and, if the Society will admit of it, as Albany stands in need of a very speedy supply, I beg he may have leave to go for Orders as soon as may be; and if possible by next Fall.

I did myself the Honor to acquaint the Society of my discouraging situation at Montreal the Inconveniency attending my return to Albany on account of my Half-pay & my removal to New York in September last, where I am going on in the duties of my Function with some pleasing appearances of success; especially in the Instruction of the Negroes, who in all appearance discover a sincere desire for divine knowledge.

I am extremely anxious to hear what establishment there will be for the protestant Church in Canada; I have a most affectionate regard for that Province & could wish our pure religion may be effectually propagated there. I am always, with the most entire Duty, at the Society's Command,

             And am, with real esteem
             Your most affectionate, &
             most obedient humble Servant,
                       JOHN OGILVIE.

---

[1] The Revd. Samuel Giles and the Revd. Hugh Wilson, who accompanied him to London for the purpose of being ordained by the Bishop of London, which was necessary in those days, were, like several other ordinands, shipwrecked and drowned on the voyage home to America.

[2] This was apparently the Revd. Hezekiah Watkins, a graduate of Yale, who, according to the *Digest of the Records of the S.P.G.*, was a servant of the Society from 1744 to 1764 at New Windsor or Newburgh.

From the Revd. Samuel Auchmuty,
New York, September 25, 1765.

Journal XVI, p. 488.

"acquainting that the People of Albany are not yet reconciled to the thought of accepting Mr. Browne for their missionary, tho' his Behaviour of late has been discreet & unexceptionable. There is a heavy Charge brought against him, which, if true, will certainly render him unworthy of the Society's Continuance. Mr. Auchmuty has written to him, & insisted upon his clearing this Point. Mr. Inglis,[1] he says, has determined to settle at New York in Nov: & Mr. Auchmuty recommends Mr. Giles to succeed Mr. Inglis at Dover."

From the Revd. John Ogilvie,
New York, September 29, 1765.

S.P.G. Letters, B. New York, Part I, p. 116, and Journal XVI, p. 481.

New York, Sept. 29th, 1765.

Revd. Sir,

The Bearer hereof is that Mr. Giles I took the liberty to recommend to the Venble. Society sometime in April last, as a very proper Person to succeed to the Mission of Albany. Dr. Johnson gives very ample testimony as to his Literature, and it is with pleasure I can assure the Society, his Loyalty, Orthodoxy & Morality are unsuspected.

I am extremely disappointed, (as well as many more) in not being so happy as to effect his settlement at Albany, which I find is not now to be hoped, as the Society have fixed Mr. Brown in that Mission: God grant it may be to the Honor of our most holy Religion!

Mr. Inglis is lately chosen an Assistant Minister here, and will move hither very soon, and is desirous Mr. Giles may suceed him at Dover, where, I have great reason to believe, he will prove a diligent, faithful Missionary, if the Society shall think proper to employ him. I have the pleasure to inform the Society that Mr. Avery[2] is generally acceptable at Rye; and, excepting an instance or two, our Ch'hes flourish, *have Peace & are edified.*

I can, with Truth, assure the Society, that the catechetical Lecture established here, for the Instruction of the Negroes, is very punctually attended, by great Numbers; who really appear to be unfeignedly desirous to be instructed in the important Principles of Christianity. I give them constant attendance on Sundays, and have baptized, since the 28th of Sept. last, five Adults, a very considerable number of their children, & admitted five to the Communion upon a very rational account of their Faith, & full Testimonials from their Masters of their pious and moral Deportment.

I am, Revd Sir, with real regard & esteem,
Your most humble,
& most obedient Servant,
JOHN OGILVIE.

---

[1]The Right Revd. Charles Inglis, first Bishop of Nova Scotia (1787-1816) and the first Colonial Bishop in the British Empire, was a schoolmaster at Lancaster, Pa., and missionary at Dover, Delaware, before becoming second assistant to Dr. Auchmuty at Trinity Church, New York. On the latter's death, in 1777, Dr. Inglis succeeded to the rectorship. In spite of threats, he continued to say the prayers for the King; and he did not a little in the way of succouring the refugee clergymen, who crowded into New York in the later years of the Rebellion. He was deeply interested in the mission to the Mohawks, drawing up a memorial on the subject, which was presented to the Lords of Trade through Sir William Johnson. He wrote several pamphlets, among them being one against Tom Paine's "Common Sense." Withdrawing to England after the Peace of 1783, he spent some four years there before finally being consecrated. He had Episcopal jurisdiction also over Canada from 1787 to 1793, and over Newfoundland and Bermuda till the date of his death. He held only one visitation of the Clergy in Canada—at Quebec, in 1789.

[2]This was the Revd. Ephraim Avery, of Rye, N.Y., a Yale man, who served the Society from 1765 to 1776. Writing on January 1, 1777, Mr. James Wetmore, Schoolmaster at Rye, informed the Society "that Mr. Avery was found dead near his own house the beginning of Novr last." (*S.P.G. Journal XXI, pp. 157.*) "By a private letter since received from Mr. Inglis," the Journal states, on pages 132-133, "it appears that Mr. Avery was murdered by the Rebels on the third of Nov^{br} last, for not praying for the Congress, in a most barbarous manner, his body having been shot thro', his throat cut and his Corpse thrown into the public highway." There was, however, the suspicion of suicide, as hinted by the Revd. Samuel Seabury, himself a "suffering Loyalist," albeit he decided, after the Peace, to remain in the United States and became, in 1784, the first Bishop of Connecticut and of the Protestant Episcopal Church. If it was a case of suicide, the very great hardships which Mr. Avery, in common with his fellow-missionaries, had undergone, had probably undermined his health and unhinged his mind.

Convention of the Journal XVIII, p. 186.
Clergy of New York
and New Jersey,
May, 1769.

The Revd. John Ogilvie was President.

From the Revd. Samuel Auchmuty, Ibid, pp. 300-301.
New York, May 24, 1769.

He, Dr. Cooper,[1] Mr. Ogilvie, and Mr. Inglis join in recommending for ordination by the Bishop of London Mr. Gideon Bostwick,[2] whom the Clergy of Connecticut, in Convention assembled, desired the Society to appoint Missionary upon the Eastern Frontiers of Albany and at Great Barrington, Lanesbury, and places adjacent.

From the Revd. John Ogilvie, S.P.G. Letters, B. New York,
New York, October 23, 1770. Part I, p. 117, and
  Journal XVIII, p. 471.

Dear Sir,

Though I have not the Honor of being a Member of the venerable Society I flatter myself there will be no Impropriety in giving my Testimonial in Favor of any gentleman who may offer himself as a Candidate for their Patronage & Favor.

Permit me therefore to introduce to your friendly notice the bearer of this Mr. John Doty,[3] a young gentleman born & educated in this City; in whose Favor I can, with the strictest truth testify, that I have the highest reason to believe him orthodox in the Faith, loyal to the King & well affected to our excellent constitution in Church & State. His moral character is unimpeached, & he appears to me to be influenced by pious Motives to offer himself as a Candidate for Holy Orders, & I sincerely believe (should the Society admit him into their Service) that he will zealously exert himself to promote the Interest of true Religion & the Good of Mankind.

I have most cordially joined with my Brethren in recommending the good people who have called Mr. Doty to the favourable regards of the venerable Board: I can only add, that every Circumstance concurs to recommend them as objects of the Society's charitable attention. They are most ardently desirous of the regular & decent administration of the Ordinances of the Gospel, have exerted themselves to the utmost of their abilities in building a Church, & are now fixing

---

[1]The Revd. Myles Cooper, second President of King's College, New York, in succession to the Rev. Dr. Johnson, was born in England in 1735 and was educated at Oxford, becoming a Fellow of Queen's College and, in 1762, Professor of Mental and Moral Philosophy in King's College, New York. On the 12th of April, 1763, he was appointed to the presidency. Adhering to the cause of the King, he was mobbed and, on the 5th of May, 1775, he escaped to a British sloop and went to England. He held two livings, one in Berkshire and the other in Edinburgh, in the latter of which he lived till his death, in May, 1785. He wrote poetry for the "Gentleman's Magazine" and, in 1776, he delivered at Oxford, an address "On the Causes of the Present Rebellion in America." He was the author also of an "Address to the Episcopalians of Virginia"; and he is said to have been a contributor to the "American Querier."—*National Cyclopædia of American Biography.*

[2]The Revd. Gideon Bostwick, fifth son and eighth child of Captain Nathaniel and Esther (Hitchcock) Bostwick, was born in New Milford, Conn., September 21, 1742. Graduating from Yale in 1762, he was for some seven years lay reader and schoolmaster at Great Barrington, Mass., of which he was the ordained missionary and rector from June 4, 1770, to June 13, 1793, the date of his decease. Some time before his decease, the Bishop of Nova Scotia and Dr. John Stuart, of Kingston, the Bishop's Commissary, or Official, for Upper Canada, had tried, unsuccessfully, to induce Mr. Bostwick to remove to Elizabethtown, as Brockville was then called.— The Revd. Joseph Hooper, M.A.: *Diocese of Connecticut; The Records of Convention, A.D. 1790- A.D. 1848. New Haven, MCMIV.;* and *Correspondence of the Bishop of Nova Scotia and of Dr. John Stuart with the S.P.G.*

[3]The Revd. John Doty (or, as the name is sometimes spelled, Doughty) is of interest, though not exactly of importance, to Canadians because he was the first Loyalist clergyman to make his escape from the Province of New York to Montreal. He settled presently at Schenectady and ultimately at Sorel, but, after a few years of ministering there, he ceased to exercise clerical functions. He was followed to Canada by Dr. John Stuart, of the Mohawk Mission, who settled in 1785 at Kingston, and by Mr. Munro of Albany, who, after a few months of work as a military chaplain, returned to England, where he remained. Doty wrote a very lengthy and interesting account of the Church in Canada, which exists in manuscript in the Archives of the S.P.G.

a very good Glebe. The neighbourhood is extensive, & very rarely any public worship in any form whatever, 'till the Measures were taken which are set forth in their Petition to the Society. I most earnestly solicit your Interest in favor of these poor people. I am convinced you are ever ready to serve the Interest of Christianity in general, & to promote the Discipline & Liturgy of our most excellent church in particular; I am therefore fully persuaded you will excuse the liberty I have now taken, in addressing you in particular upon this Occasion.

May God ever smile upon the pious Labours of the Society in advancing the Kingdom of the blessed Jesus; & give you everything that may any way contribute to your Happiness. This is the fervent Prayer of him who esteems it an honor to subscribe himself,

Their & your most obedient
Humble Servant,
JOHN OGILVIE.

The Revd. Dr. Burton.

From the Clergy of New York,   Journal XVIII, pp. 471-472.
October 22, 1770,

"representing to the Society that . . . . . Mr. Doty is a well disposed youg man, and if he be appointed Missy to that place [Peek's Hill], they are confident he will promote the interest of religion."

From the Church Wardens & Vestry of   Ibid., pp. 472-473.
St. Peter's Church, in the Manor of
Cortland near Peak's Hill, West Chester
County, N.Y., October 15, 1770.

"That about 4 years ago they began to build a church, which has since been consecrated by Mr. Ogilvie of New York, by the Name of St. Peter's, and made decent (tho' not finished) for the performance of divine service. That a charter has been obtained from Lt. Governor Colden.[1] That Mr. John Doty, educated at King's College in New York—has performed divine service in it the most part of last summer to their general satisfaction, so that they have unanimously agreed to give him a call as soon as he shall be properly ordained. . . . . ."

From the Revd. Samuel Auchmuty,   Ibid., p. 508.
Dr. Myles Cooper, and Mr. Charles
Inglis, New York, December 10, 1770.

They recommend for membership in the Society the Revd. John Ogilvie and 7 clergymen in Maryland, among whom was the Revd. John Claggett, D.D., who later became the first Bishop of the Protestant Episcopal Church in that State.

General Meeting of   Journal XIX, p. 25.
the Society,
April 19, 1771.

Record of the election of the aforementioned gentlemen to membership in the Society.

From the Revd. Uzzal Ogden,   Ibid., p. 137.
Sussex County, N.J.,
Newton, N.J., July 8, 1771.

"In January last, he published a pamphlet, recommending union & brotherly love among different sects, wch was favorably received, and has been singularly useful. Dr. Ogilvie defrayed the cost for 500 copies of it."

---

[1]Cadwallader Colden (1688-1776) was the son of the Revd. Alexander Colden, of Dunsie, Scotland. Graduating in Arts from the University of Edinburgh, he studied Medicine in London and emigrated to Philadelphia in 1710. Visiting New York in 1718, he became the protégé of Governor Hunter, who appointed him Surveyor-General of the Province. Called to the Provincial Council by Governor Burnet, in 1722, he, as Senior Councillor, was called upon to administer the Government on the death of Lieutenant-Governor De Lancy, in 1760. For three years or more between 1761 and 1765, in 1769-1770, and 1774-1775 he was Lieutenant-Governor of the Province. He is credited with having been the first to suggest the formation of the American Philosophical Society, of Philadelphia. His work of special interest to Canadians is the "History of the Five Nations depending on the Province of New York," which was published in 1722. A second edition appeared in 1747 under the title of the "Five Nations of Canada, with an account of several Nations of Indians in North & South America." O'Callaghan: *Documentary History of New York*, Vol. III, pp. 829-832.

THE REVEREND JOHN OGILVIE, D.D.

From the Revd. John Ogilvie,
New York, July 16, 1774.

S.P.G. Letters, B. 3, New York.
Part II, and
Journal XX, p. 221.

Revd. Sir,

The inclosed Petition from the Inhabitants of Fredericksburgh was put into my hands, accompanied with an earnest request, that I would transmit it to you as Secretary of the venerable Society, in order to be presented to their Board for their charitable Consideration. I am fully convinced (from personal knowledge of the subscribers) that it speaks the hearty disposition of most of the inhabitants of that District, that it is not the result of a sudden Heat, or start of zeal, but the genuine effect of a serious regard to Christianity, and a well-grounded sense of the superior excellency of the worship and Discipline of the Church of England, and its natural tendency to propagate the pure Doctrines and impress the mind with a practical sense of the precepts of that most holy Religion.

I beg leave to give testimony to the truth of the facts set forth in that Petition, and to assure the Society that the Petitioners have had, for some years past, the establishment of an episcopal Church in contemplation. The Precinct of Fredericksburgh comprehends a considerable tract of country, is very populous and has no regular or stated Provision for divine worship of any denomination; and (excepting the Members of the episcopal Church) are so divided among themselves in religious sentiments, that it is not probable, that the Dissenters of any Sect, will be able to make any permanent establishment for that very important Purpose. This being the deplorable state of that country, with regard to the instituted means of promoting Religion and Virtue, I most earnestly beg the compassionate attention of the venerable Society to their humble Petitioners; and if the state of their funds will any ways admit it, a small annual allowance for a few years, will, I am perfectly persuaded, be most seasonably applied to this infant Church, and, at the same time, be productive of the most salutary influence upon the moral and religious state of the adjacent Country. The Members of our Church in this Precinct are cordially disposed to do their best, but, at present, their circumstances will not permit them to do great things.

This will be delivered by Mr. James Sayre[1] (brother to the Society's worthy missionary of that name), who comes over as a Candidate for Holy Orders, upon a Title given to the Lord

---

[1]These two brothers suffered for their loyalty to the King on the outbreak of the rebellion, James then being stationed at Col. Beverley Robinson's Manor in the Province of New York and John at Fairfield, Connecticut. The former, according to a letter from his brother to the Society, bearing date, New York, July 20, 1780, "was, he thinks, the first Clergyman in the Province of New-York who was noticed by Congress, as a person inimical to their views. For this he was banished to Massachusetts-Bay; there he remained some considerable time; and at last, was ordered to remove himself within, what they called, the Enemy's Lines, by a certain short-set day, for refusing to abjure the King's authority, and to acknowledge theirs. In consequence of this Mandate, he removed to Huntington on Long-Island; where he officiated about half a year; and from thence he removed to Brooklyn, where he now continues zealously to preach &c. in a Church belonging to the Dutch Congregation, on such Sundays as they do not occupy it themselves. Excepting the Rations, allowed by Government, he now subsists on the scanty Subscriptions of the few Church-people there. This is a very different situation from that which he enjoyed some years ago, when he was in the possession of a handsome estate, which he chearfully forsook, rather than do violence to his conscience: it is such a one, indeed, as he hopes the Society will think loudly calls for their kind interposition." After a sojourn in Nova Scotia, he returned to the States and died, in 1798, at Fairfield, Conn.

John himself lost all his property in the burning of Fairfield by the Royal troops in 1779, as he says in writing to the Society from Flushing, Long Island, in November of that year. He had previously been placed under surveillance, then banished and banned, and, after seven months of absence, allowed to return to his home, under condition of keeping within strictly defined bounds. In May, 1780, he removed to New York, and took up afresh the practice of his original profession, Medicine; but, his patients being for the most part distressed Loyalists, the practice was not highly remunerative. He notes having acted as pallbearer to the Revd. Thomas Barton and to the Revd. Matthew Graves, sometime of New London, Connecticut, who had been sponsor to the Society for the Revd. Samuel Peters at his ordination. (Dr. Peters was recommended, unsuccessfully, to the Home Government by Lieutenant-Governor Simcoe for the Bishopric of Upper Canada, which was not established at that time.) Mr. Sayre also speaks gratefully of the services rendered to himself and to other clergymen by Major-General William Tryon. He settled in New Brunswick, where he died in 1874. His daughter Esther married Christopher Robinson, to whom she bore, among other children, John Beverley, who at his death, in 1863, was Chancellor of Trinity College, Toronto, a Baronet, and Chief Justice of Canada West, as Ontario was then called. A few years subsequent to her first husband's death Mrs. Robinson became Mrs. Beeman. Sayre Street, Toronto, was called after her.

Bishop of London, by the subscribers of the inclosed Petition, and recommended to his Lordship by the Clergy here.

I have only further to observe, that a Glebe will, as soon as possible be provided; to consist of, atleast, an hundred acres of the best improved land; nothing more is wanting to effect this necessary provision, than merely the location. The Right of soil is vested in Col. Roger Morris,[1] one of his Majesty's Council for this Province, Col. Beverly Robinson,[2] one of the Judges for Dutchess County, and myself in right of my wife;[3] I can therefore assure the Society for myself and the other gentlemen concerned, that this condition shall be fully complied with.

I conclude with my most fervent prayers for success to the truly Christian designs and undertakings of the venerable Society, and am, with sentiments of the most affectionate respect,

Their and your most obedient humble Servt.

JOHN OGILVIE.

From the Revd. Samuel Auchmuty,   Ibid., p. 284.
New York, December 7, 1774.

"but had not then the time [to write at length], being greatly hurried, and fully imployed, since the death of his worthy Assistant Dr. Ogilvie lately departed."

---

[1] Col. Roger Morris, who was born in England, January 28, 1717, and who died at York, September 13, 1794, came to America as a Captain in the 48th Foot and was at Fort Duquesne as A.D.C. to General Braddock and in 1757 he was with the Earl of Loudoun. Having exchanged into the 35th Regiment, he was at Fort Frederick in 1758-1759, whence he took part in Indian expeditions against Nova Scotia. He was with Wolfe in his attack upon Quebec and at the Plains of Abraham; he was also at Sillery, April 28, 1760, and at Montreal with Murray. He retired from the army in 1764 and settled in New York, having married, in 1758, Mary, daughter of Frederick Philipse, second Lord of Philipse Manor. Thus it was that he, with Col. Beverley Robinson and Dr. Ogilvie, had the right of soil in the Manor. In 1776 he returned to England with his wife, who, it is said, had had Washington as one of her suitors. Their plate and other belongings were sold and their estates confiscated, for which the British Government allowed £17,000 by way of compensation. The writer in Appleton's *Dictionary of American Biography* states that John Jacob Astor bought for £20,000 their children's reversionary rights in Col. and Mrs. Morris's holdings, as it was held that they were not included in, or affected by, their parents' attainder. Mrs. Morris, who was thirteen years younger than her husband, survived him by thirty-one years. A monument in St. Saviour's Gate Church, York, commemorates her.

[2] Col. Beverley Robinson belonged to the same family as Christopher Robinson, mentioned in the note on page 00, being the son of John Robinson, who was the President of the Council of Virginia in 1734 and, later, Speaker of the House of Burgesses. He was born in Virginia in 1723; took part in the attack upon Quebec, under Wolfe; married Susanna Philipse, sister of Mrs. Morris; raised, and became Colonel of, the Loyal American Regiment at the time of the American Rebellion; had knowledge of Benedict Arnold's treason; pleaded with Washington for Major André's life; went to New Brunswick and was appointed to the Council of the Province, but did not take his seat; retired to Thornbury, near Bath, England, where he died, in 1792, his wife surviving him till 1822. Like Col. and Mrs. Morris, they received from the British Government £17,000 as compensation for the losses which they had sustained through their loyalty. Their fourth son, Sir Frederick Philipse Robinson, G.C.B., had a distinguished military career in the West Indies, the Peninsula, and Canada. In 1815-1816 he administered the Government of Upper Canada, in succession to Sir Isaac Brock and other Commanders in Chief, during the absence of Lieutenant-Governor Francis Gore. Appleton's *Dictionary of American Biography*.

[3] This was Dr. Ogilvie's second wife, Margaret Philipse, daughter of Nathaniel Marston, Junior, a merchant of New York, and widow of Philip Philipse, also of New York, who had died in May, 1768. Mrs. Ogilvie herself died February 4, 1807, aged 79 years and 10 months. It was evidently through her first husband that she had community of interest with Mrs. Morris, Mrs. Robinson, and their husbands in the lands at Fredericksburgh, or Sleepy Hollow, a name applied by the late Lieutenant-Governor Robinson to his place in College Street, Toronto, where the old Technical School and the Board of Education's Administration building stand.

From Col. Daniel Claus,[1] 		Journal 23, 1782.
Montreal, October 9, 1782.

"The National Church has been and is under many disadvantages in Quebec. It was not, though it certainly should have been regarded at the conquest of the Country. A Dissenting Governor was appointed over the Province; who represented the number of French Protestants in Canada as consisting of some hundreds of Families, when, in fact, there were hardly a dozen. Hence French Clergymen, usually strangers to the language and the religion of England, were sent over, and Doctor Ogilvie, a Servant of the Society's, superseded, who resided there four years as Chaplain to the 60th Regiment, and was an ornament and a blessing to the Church he belonged to. This has been a fatal measure. His Congregations were numerous, and flourishing; but now many Converts, who under him had renounced the errors of Popery, again return to the bosom of their former church, and carry with them also sometimes some members of our's."

---

[1]Col. Claus was a son-in-law of Sir William Johnson, under whom he served in the Indian Department and whom he ultimately succeeded. He also was elevated to the rank of an Executive Councillor in Canada. He was much interested in the education of the Mohawks, for whom he prepared primers and translations of the Prayer Book and of the Bible.

The "dissenting Governor" to whom he refers was General Sir James Murray, who nevertheless was elected to membership in the S.P.G. The French clergymen who were appointed as the result of the Governor's suggestion were de Montmollin at Quebec, de Veyssière at Three Rivers, and de Lisle at Montreal, the first being a Swiss, the second a convert from a monastery in Quebec itself, and the third a Frenchman, apparently. They held office till 1789 when they were superannuated by the Bishop of Nova Scotia (Inglis) on the occasion of the first, and only, visitation of the clergy which he held in Canada. Canada, it is important to remember, did not at that time include Nova Scotia.

As these French-speaking clergymen were appointed only in 1766, after General Murray's departure from Canada and after his place had been taken by Sir Guy Carleton, it cannot be exactly said that Dr. Ogilvie, who went to New York in 1764, was "superseded." On the 19th of November, 1764, according to the record of Journal XVI, pp. 284-285, the Revd. Samuel Bennet had written to the Archbishop of Canterbury from Montreal, where he was "accidentally stationed by General Gage's Orders." "As Mr. Bennet's Circumstances," the Journal continues, "will not permit him to stay here gratis, he proposes in the Spring to return to England with his Regiment, unless the Society should please to appoint him a Salary: in which case he would decline his Chaplainship, and defer all thoughts of returning to England at least for some Years."

Writing from Lancaster, Pa., on January 23, 1766, the Revd. Thomas Barton, the heroic Travelling Missionary in that district, notified the Society: "In the month of July last I had the honour to receive a letter from General Gage, of which the following is an extract—'There is not at present any Chaplain nominated for the Garrison of Montreal; if you should think it for your advantage to accept of that in preference to the livings you now enjoy, you will please to acquaint me. Should you be of that opinion, & willing to make trial of Canada, you may in the mean time till an answer can arrive to my Recommendation of you to the Chaplainship of the Garrison, be appointed Deputy to two Regiments. The Chaplain of Montreal will have the same pay as those in other Regiments, &c.'" On this the Committee's comment, with which the Society agreed, was: "As to the Offer which Genl Gage has made him at Montreal, Mr. Barton must judge for himself in that affair. The Soc^{ty} will have no Objection, if it will be for his Advantage." Mr. Barton finally declining, the appointment went to the Revd. Chadbrand de Lisle, who was also made the first Anglican Rector of Montreal, as already noted.

www.ingramcontent.com/pod-product-compliance
Lightning Source LLC
Chambersburg PA
CBHW020319240426
43673CB00039B/859